C000264120

The
Yorkshire County
Cricket Club Limited

Registered Number 28929R

YEARBOOK
2019

121st EDITION

Editor:
DAVID WARNER

Production Editor:
JAMES M. GREENFIELD

Records and Statistics
Yorkshire First Eleven:
JOHN T POTTER

Yorkshire Second Eleven:
HOWARD CLAYTON

Official Photographers:
SIMON WILKINSON, ALEX WHITEHEAD
and ALLAN MCKENZIE. *SWpix.com*

Published by
THE YORKSHIRE COUNTY CRICKET CLUB LTD
EMERALD HEADINGLEY CRICKET GROUND
LEEDS LS6 3BU
Tel: 0843 504 3099   Fax: 0113 278 4099
Internet: http://www.yorkshireccc.com
e-mail: cricket@yorkshireccc.com

Solicitors:	*Auditors:*
DLA PIPER UK LLP	KPMG Audit plc

Medical Officer: Dr NIGEL MAYERS, MBChB, MRCGP
Burley Park Medical Centre, 273 Burley Road, Leeds LS4 2EL

The opinions expressed by contributors are not necessarily those of the Board.

TELEPHONE AND FAX NUMBERS

EMERALD HEADINGLEY CRICKET GROUND

Tel: 0843 504 3099
Fax: 0113 278 4099

NORTH MARINE ROAD, SCARBOROUGH **Tel: 01723 365625**
Fax: 01723 364287

SHIPTON ROAD, YORK **Tel: 01904 623602**

ST GEORGE'S ROAD, HARROGATE **Tel: 01423-525000**

© The Yorkshire County Cricket Club Ltd 2019

Produced by:

Great Northern Books
PO Box 1380, Bradford, BD5 5FB
www.greatnorthernbooks.co.uk

ISBN: 978-1-912101-13-9

CONTENTS

Colour Plates — Facing Pages 32 and 256

Officers for 2019

4

EMERALD HEADINGLEY READY TO SPARKLE THIS SUMMER

By David Warner

Yorkshire suffered disappointments and misfortunes both on an off the field in 2018, but in the end nothing was quite so bad as it might have been, and they can look forward with energy and enthusiasm to one of the most momentous summers in the Club's history.

Had they been relegated to the Second Division of the Specsavers County Championship, as looked quite likely at the end of August, it would certainly have taken some of the sparkle away from Emerald Headingley in the current year.

Not only did they survive, but they finished in a respectable fourth place, which is as it should be for a Club about to host World Cup matches and an *Ashes* Test on a ground now complete with a magnificent new grandstand.

Facilities are now better than they have ever been at the venue, and how the fans should relish the international and top county cricket which will be on offer over the coming months.

Of course, performances overall should have been better last year, particularly in the Vitality T20 Blast, in which Yorkshire failed to reach the knockout stages, despite being urged on by record crowds.

But all sorts of unforeseen mishaps conspired against the team, including player unavailability for various reasons, untimely injuries, constant unsettling changes in the captaincy and Adil Rashid's decision not to play red-ball cricket for his county, a situation now happily resolved, plus bad weather wiping out all four days of the opening Championship fixture against Champions Essex.

Following Gary Ballance's withdrawal from the captaincy because the stresses of it all were badly affecting his game, Steve Patterson eventually took on the role on a permanent basis, and did a splendid job — which I confidently predict he will continue doing this summer. There is nothing flash about Patto, but his good, honest, dour Yorkshire qualities have already earned him the respect of team-mates and management,

Two to watch: Skipper Steven Patterson, right, hands fast-bowler Ben Coad his County cap on September 18, 2018

and he is bound to have had a strong input into how he wants the game to be played and who he wants in his side.

Also unsettling for the Club as a whole last year was the departure from the Board of its Chairman, Steve Denison, who felt forced to resign following his involvement as a PwC partner in the BHS saga.

Appointed Yorkshire Chairman in 2015, Steve tackled the job with unbridled enthusiasm and vigour, and he chaired the Club's annual general meeting with a combination of skill and humour that made him extremely popular with the members.

Fortunately for Yorkshire CCC, the void left by his absence was quickly filled by his Board colleague, Robin Smith, who is no newcomer to the role and who was able to apply a steadying hand to the tiller. No doubt Robin privately wished that his days of hard graft were over but, as ever, his major concern for was the wellbeing of the Club.

As you will read elsewhere in this *Yearbook*, Yorkshire have a squad bursting with talent. Success will not come easily, it rarely does, but if Steve Patterson and his team do go on to collect some trophies in 2019 their successes will not have come at a more appropriate time.

Officials of the Yorkshire County Cricket Club

President	President (Continued)	Chairman (Continued)	Captain (Contd)
T R Barker 1863	Harold 'Dickie' Bird OBE 2014-15	R A Smith TD, LLB, DL 2002-5	A B Sellers 1933-1947
M J Ellison 1864-97	John H Hampshire 2016-17	C J Graves 2005-15	N W D Yardley 1948-1955
Lord Hawke 1898-1938	Richard A Hutton 2017-18	S J Denison 2015-18	W H H Sutcliffe 1956-1957
Rt Hon Sir F S Jackson 1939-1947	*Treasurer*	R A Smith TD, LLB, DL 2018-	J R Burnet 1958-1959
T L Taylor 1948-1960	M J Ellison 1863-1893		J V Wilson 1960-1962
Sir W A Worsley Bart 1961-1973	M Ellison, jun 1894-1898	*Captain*	D B Close 1963-1970
		R Iddison 1863-1872	
Sir K Parkinson 1974-1981	Chas Stokes 1899-1912	J Rowbotham 1873	G Boycott 1971-1978
N W D Yardley 1981-1983	R T Heselton 1913-1931	L Greenwood 1874	J H Hampshire 1979-1980
The Viscount Mountgarret 1984-1989	A Wyndham Heselton 1932-1962	J Rowbotham 1875	C M Old 1981-1982
Sir Leonard Hutton 1989-1990	M G Crawford 1963-1979	E Lockwood 1876-1877	R Illingworth 1982-1983
Sir Lawrence Byford QPM, LLD, DL 1991-1999	J D Welch 1980-1984	T Emmett 1878-1882	D L Bairstow 1984-1986
	P W Townend 1984-2002	Hon M B (Lord) Hawke 1883-1910	P Carrick 1987-1989
R A Smith TD, LLB, DL 1999-2004	*Chairman*	E J R H Radcliffe 1911	M D Moxon 1990-1995
David Jones CBE 2004-6	A H Connell, DL 1971-1979	Sir A W White 1912-1918	D Byas 1996-2001
Robert Appleyard 2006-8	M G Crawford 1980-1984	D C F Burton 1919-1921	D S Lehmann 2002
Brian Close CBE 2008-10	H R Kirk 1984-1985	Geoff Wilson 1922-1924	A McGrath 2003
	B Walsh, QC 1986-1991	A W Lupton 1925-1927	C White 2004-6
Raymond Illingworth CBE 2010-12	Sir Lawrence Byford CBE, QPM, LLD, DL 1991-1998	W A Worsley 1928-1929	D Gough 2007-8
	K H Moss MBE 1998-2002	A T Barber 1930	A McGrath 2009
Geoffrey Boycott OBE 2012-13	G A Cope 2002	F E Greenwood 1931-1932	A W Gale 2010-16

Officials of the Yorkshire County Cricket Club

Captain (Continud)	Secretary (Continued)	Company Secretary	Chief Executive (Cont)
G S Ballance 2017-18	**F C (Sir Fredk.) Toone** 1903-1930	**B Bouttell** 2002-5	**Colin J Graves** 2002-5
S A Patterson 2018-	**J H Nash** 1931-1971	**C Hartwell** 2011-14	**Stewart Regan** 2006-10
Secretary	**J Lister** 1972-1991	**P Hudson** 2014-	**Colin J Graves** 2012-13
Geo Padley 1863	**D M Ryder** 1991-2002	*Chief Executive*	**Mark Arthur** 2013-
J B Wostinholm 1864-1902		**C D Hassell** 1991-2002	

Will is welcomed back

Yorkshire have regained the services of Huddersfield-born opening batsman Will Fraine on a three-year deal.

Fraine, 22, signed for Nottinghamshire last May, having played for their Second XI and featuring for Durham MCCU. After agreeing terms with Yorkshire during the summer he joined his *White Rose* teammates for pre-season training in November.

"I never thought I would play for Yorkshire," he said, "but I've always had the dream to do it. There's always that pull of being a Yorkie lad. All my friends speak of one day playing for Yorkshire. I never thought it would happen because I made my own way elsewhere. It was a difficult decision, but the opportunities and the place where the Club is going was too much of a pull. Settling back in with the lads I've known growing up makes me very happy with the decision I've made."

Fraine is a product of the long-standing MCCU system, and has enjoyed considerable and consistent success for Durham MCCU: "I first played for Yorkshire when I was 14," he said, "and I have played age-group and Academy cricket since I was 16-17. Then I went to boarding school in Worcester, and played for Worcestershire for three years."

COUNTY FIXTURES — 2019

SPECSAVERS COUNTY CHAMPIONSHIP — Division 1
(All four-day matches)

Date			Opponents	Venue
Fri	5-8	April	Nottinghamshire	Trent Bridge
Thu	11-14	April	Hampshire	Southampton
Tue	14-17	May	Kent	Canterbury
MON	**27-30**	**MAY**	**HAMPSHIRE**	**HEADINGLEY**
MON	**3-6**	**JUNE**	**ESSEX**	**HEADINGLEY**
Mon	10-13	June	Surrey	Guildford
MON	**17-20**	**JUNE**	**WARWICKSHIRE**	**YORK**
SUN	**30-3**	**JUNE/JULY**	**SURREY**	**SCARBOROUGH**
Sun	7-10	July	Essex	Chelmsford
SAT	**13-16**	**JULY**	**SOMERSET**	**HEADINGLEY**
SUN	**18-21**	**AUGUST**	**NOTTINGHAMSHIRE**	**SCARBOROUGH**
Tue	10-13	September	Somerset	Taunton
MON	**16-19**	**SEPTEMBER**	**KENT**	**HEADINGLEY**
Mon	23-26	September	Warwickshire	Edgbaston

ROYAL LONDON ONE-DAY CUP

WED	**17**	**APRIL**	**LEICESTERSHIRE**	**HEADINGLEY**
Fri	19	April	Warwickshire	Edgbaston
SUN	**21**	**APRIL**	**LANCASHIRE**	**HEADINGLEY**
FRI	**26**	**APRIL**	**DERBYSHIRE**	**HEADINGLEY**
Sun	28	April	Nottinghamshire	Trent Bridge
Wed	1	May	Northamptonshire	Northampton
Sat	4	May	Worcestershire	Worcester
MON	**6**	**MAY**	**DURHAM**	**HEADINGLEY**
Fri	10	May	Quarter-Finala	TBC
Sun	12	May	Semi-Finals	TBC
Sat	25	May	Final	Lord's

VITALITY BLAST

FRI	**19**	**JULY**	**NOTTINGHAMSHIRE**	**HEADINGLEY**
Sat	20	July	Derbyshire	Chesterfield
Tue	23	July	Leicestershire	Leicester
THU	**25**	**JULY**	**LANCASHIRE**	**HEADINGLEY**
Sun	28	July	Northamptonshire	Northampton
FRI	**2**	**AUGUST**	**WORCESTERSHIRE**	**HEADINGLEY**
SUN	**4**	**AUGUST**	**BIRMINGHAM BEARS**	**HEADINGLEY**
Fri	9	August	Lancashire	Old Trafford
SUN	**11**	**AUGUST**	**DERBYSHIRE**	**HEADINGLEY**
FRI	**16**	**AUGUST**	**DURHAM**	**HEADINGLEY**
Fri	23	August	Durham	Chester-le-Street
Sun	25	August	Nottinghamshire	Trent Bridge
THU	**29**	**AUGUST**	**NORTHAMPTONSHIRE**	**HEADINGLEY**
Fri	30	August	Birmingham Bears	Edgbaston
Wed	4-7	September	Quarter-Finals	TBC
Sat	21	September	Semi-Finals and Final	Edgbaston

OTHER MATCHES

SUN	**31-2**	**MARCH/APRIL**	**LEEDS BRADFORD MCCU**	
			(FIRST-CLASS)	**WEETWOOD**

INTERNATIONAL MATCHES PLAYED AT HEADINGLEY

SUN 19 MAY   FIFTH ONE-DAY INTERNATIONAL
                                              ENGLAND V. PAKISTAN

THU 22 AUGUST THIRD TEST ....ENGLAND V. AUSTRALIA

WORLD CUP MATCHES PLAYED AT HEADINGLEY

FRIDAY	21 JUNE ....ENGLAND	v. SRI LANKA
SATURDAY	29 JUNE ....PAKISTAN	v. AFGHANISTAN
THURSDAY	4 JULY ....AFGHANISTAN	v. WEST INDIES
SATURDAY	6 JULY ....SRI LANKA	v. INDIA

SECOND ELEVEN CHAMPIONSHIP

WED	24-26	APRIL	NOTTINGHAMSHIRE ....HARROGATE
Tue	14-16	May	Worcestershire ....Away
Tue	21-23	May	Leicestershire ....Away
TUE	28-30	MAY	DERBYSHIRE ....YORK
MON	17-19	JUNE	DURHAM ....HARROGATE
Wed	10-12	July	Lancashire ....Away
Tue	16-18	July	Warwickshire ....Stamford Bridge
Tue	30-1	July/August	Northamptonshire ....Away
Tue	3-6	September	Final ....TBC

SECOND ELEVEN TROPHY

THU	18	APRIL	LANCASHIRE ....SCARBOROUGH
TUE	23	APRIL	NOTTINGHAMSHIRE ....YORK
Fri	10	May	Durham ....Away
Mon	13	May	Worcestershire ....Away
Mon	20	May	Leicestershire ....Away
Fri	31	May	Derbyshire ....TBC
Fri	21	June	Semi-Finals ....TBC
Thu	27	June	Final ....TBC

SECOND ELEVEN TWENTY20 (TWO MATCHES IN THE SAME DAY)

MON	8	JULY	WORCESTERSHIRE ....WEETWOOD
MON	15	JULY	WARWICKSHIRE ....WEETWOOD
Wed	24	July	Derbyshire ....Away
Thu	25	July	Lancashire ....Away
Mon	29	July	Northamptonshire ....Away
Mon	5	August	Durham ....Marske-By-Sea
Thu	15	August	Semi-Finals and Final ....TBC

SECOND ELEVEN FRIENDLIES

TUE	16-17	APRIL	LANCASHIRE ....SCARBOROUGH
Tue	7-9	May	Durham ....Away
Wed	7	August	Leicestershire ....TBC
Tue	27-29	August	Surrey ....York
Tue	10-12	September	Sussex ....Away
Mon	16-18	September	Durham ....Scarborough

YORKSHIRE ACADEMY IN THE YORKSHIRE LEAGUE

Sat	27	April	Harrogate	Harrogate
Sat	4	May	Stamford Bridge	Stamford Bridge
MON	**6**	**MAY**	**STAMFORD BRIDGE**	**WEETWOOD**
SAT	**11**	**MAY**	**CLIFTON ALLIANCE**	**WEETWOOD**
Sat	18	May	Sheriff Hutton Bridge	Sheriff Hutton Bridge
SAT	**25**	**MAY**	**SESSAY**	**WEETWOOD**
MON	**27**	**MAY**	**BEVERLEY TOWN**	**WEETWOOD**
SAT	**1**	**JUNE**	**SCARBOROUGH**	**WEETWOOD**
Sat	8	June	Dunnington	Dunnington
SAT	**15**	**JUNE**	**WOODHOUSE GRANGE**	**WEETWOOD**
Sat	22	June	Castleford	Castleford
SAT	**29**	**JUNE**	**YORK**	**WEETWOOD**
Sat	13	July	Clifton Alliance	Clifton Alliance
SAT	**20**	**JULY**	**SHERIFF HUTTON BRIDGE**	**WEETWOOD**
Sat	27	July	Sessay	Away
Sat	3	August	Scarborough	Scarborough
SAT	**10**	**AUGUST**	**DUNNINGTON**	**WEETWOOD**
Sat	17	August	Woodhouse Grange	Woodhouse Grange
SAT	**24**	**AUGUST**	**CASTLEFORD**	**WEETWOOD**
Mon	26	August	Beverley Town	Beverley Town
Sat	31	August	York	York
SAT	**7**	**SEPTEMBER**	**HARROGATE**	**WEETWOOD**

YORKSHIRE ACADEMY FRIENDLIES

Sun	14	April	Worcestershire Academy	Kidderminster
Sat	20	April	Woodhouse Grange	Away
Tue	16-17	July	Scotland Development	TBC
Thu	18	July	Scotland Development	TBC

YORKSHIRE UNDER-17s in THREE-DAY CHAMPIONSHIP

TUE	**9-11**	**JULY**	**DURHAM**	**HOME TBC**
Tue	23-25	July	Derbyshire	Away
TUE	**30- 1**	**JULY/AUG**	**CHESHIRE**	**WEETWOOD**
Tue	6- 8	August	Lancashire	Away
Tue	13-15	August	Semi-Final	Home Tie
Tue	27-29	August	Final	TBC

YORKSHIRE UNDER-17s in ONE-DAY CHAMPIONSHIP

TUE	**28**	**MAY**	**CHESHIRE**	**WEETWOOD**
THU	**30**	**MAY**	**DURHAM**	**WEETWOOD**
Sun	9	June	Lancashire	Ormskirk
Sun	16	June	Derbyshire CB	Away
Sun	30	June	Semi-Final	Home Tie
Sun	7	July	Final	TBC

YORKSHIRE DIAMONDS IN THE KIA SUPER LEAGUE

TUE	**6**	**AUGUST**	**SURREY STARS**	**HEADINGLEY**
SUN	**11**	**AUGUST**	**LOUGHBOROUGH LIGHTNING**	**HEADINGLEY**
Tue	13	August	Lancashire Thunder	TBC
THU	**15**	**AUGUST**	**WESTERN STORM**	**YORK**
Sun	18	August	Loughborough Lightning	TBC
Tue	20	August	Surrey Stars	Guildford
Wed	21	August	Southern Vipers	Southampton
FRI	**23**	**AUGUST**	**LANCASHIRE THUNDER**	**SCARBOROUGH**
SUN	**25**	**AUGUST**	**SOUTHERN VIPERS**	**YORK**
Wed	28	August	Western Storm	Taunton
Sun	9	July	Final	TBC

13

GEOFF COPE NOMINATED
FOR THE PRESIDENCY

By David Warner

After two years of loyal service Richard Hutton's term of office as Yorkshire CCC President drew to a close at the County Club's annual general meeting in March when former Yorkshire and England off-spinner Geoff Cope, right, was nominated by The Board to succeed him.

Richard clearly enjoyed his time in office, and rarely missed a home match in addition to willingly carrying out all the duties which came his way. He retains many fond memories of the past two years, and although the first team were unable to win any trophies during this time they at least preserved their Division One status in the Specsavers County Championship, which gave him considerable satisfaction.

Like Richard, Geoff was a Yorkshire player during the 1960s, when the team enjoyed a golden period under the captaincy of Brian Close, and by the time he hung up his boots in 1980 he had earned his place in the County's Hall of Fame with 630 first-class wickets at 24.80 runs apiece. Geoff's close association with Yorkshire did not end upon his retirement, however, and as well as giving valuable service on the Committee he was one of the Gang of Four who formed the Board in 2002 and helped to save the Club from financial disaster.

He was instrumental in bringing in Colin Graves as Chief Executive, with Robin Smith serving as Chairman and Brian Bouttell as Director of Finance while Geoff himself was Chairman at the start before serving as Director of Cricket in 2003.

In more recent years Geoff has hosted visiting committee members and guests at Emerald Headingley on match days, and his witty observations and fine sense of humour have become a feature of the Club's official lunches. "When I was approached by the Club to be their recommendation to succeed Richard Hutton as President I was taken aback somewhat, and could only think of people like Philip Sharpe and Freddie Trueman who would have been in a similar position of being invited but were never able to fill the role," Geoff said.

"During my term of office I will remember these great stalwarts of Yorkshire cricket, and reflect on how much they would have enjoyed the Presidency.

"I will also look back to the very beginning, and to my mum and dad. Although I lost my mum when I was only 16 they had by then set out for me the basics in life which have seen me through in times both of joy and sadness.

"Had they been with me now I know how proud they would have been at this invitation. I am extremely fortunate that my wife, June, and our family are very supportive, and they will share with me this ultimate

Tweaker Geoff: The concentration and determination that brought 630 first-class wickets.
(Photo: Mick Pope Archive)

position in the game of cricket. It is the pinnacle of a career which so many have shared with me. It is for them and for all the friends, members and supporters of the Club who have been with me for so long that I take special pride in this role.

"The 2019 season promises to be one of the most important in the Club's history. The ground redevelopment is virtually complete, and the office staff have worked very hard in planning for Emerald Headingley the one-day international, the four World Cup matches and the ultimate — the Test match against Australia. I hope that all their hard work is appreciated and that the Club have a very successful season, both financially and from a playing perspective.

"When you go back to 2002 and the threat of administration, and then fast forward to where we are today, the prospect for 2019 must give every Yorkshireman great joy and a deep pride in their Club."

15

LATE SEASON RECOVERY HELPS AVOID THE DROP

By Graham Hardcastle

A season which spelt danger for Yorkshire in the County Championship ended on a high as they won two of the last three matches to finish fourth in Division One for the second year running.

Call-ups and injuries — more so than usual — left coach Andrew Gale and the rest of the management scratching their heads, and had a significant impact on the *White Rose* heading into September second bottom in Division One.

Some may view the following paragraphs as just a list of excuses for a middling campaign, but Gale would be the first to stress that the players at his disposal could have been better. He knows that improvements in batting consistency have to be made if his side are to be challenging for the title as they were between 2013 and 2016 when he was captain.

Adil Rashid's decision to step back from red-ball cricket and prioritise white in February — he later reversed it to play in England's summer programme of Test Matches — was the catalyst for a number of unexpected issues, continuing when David Willey and Liam Plunkett opted to accept IPL contracts days before the start of the season in April.

Plunkett's lack of availability for Yorkshire ended up proving a key factor in the Club's decision midway through the summer not to offer him a new contract, hence a move to Surrey.

There were problems with overseas players. Che Pujara struggled for form in the Championship, although he was exceptional in the Royal London One-day Cup, while Kane Williamson's availability as Pujara's replacement midway through the season was reduced by his New Zealand bosses. Towering Australia fast bowler Billy Stanlake had also been signed for T20 cricket, but that move was cancelled by Cricket Australia in a bid to manage his workload.

Injuries? There were plenty, highlighted by Steven Patterson suffering two broken fingers during the summer. He had not previously suffered one in his entire career.

That brings us to the captaincy. Gary Ballance started his second campaign in charge, but suffered from anxiety and opted to resign after briefly stepping away from the game altogether. Patterson would take

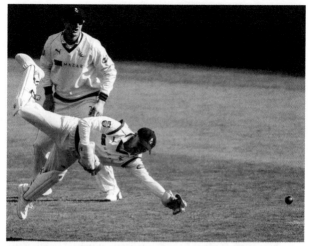

High diver: Yorkshire wicket-keeper Jonathan Tattersall takes to the air in the *Roses* match at Emerald Headingley

over, impressively steering the ship. Weather-wise, an unusually dry and hot summer started in bizarre manner with Yorkshire's first seven days of first-class cricket at Emerald Headingley all washed out.

The three-day friendly against Leeds/Bradford MCC Universities was cancelled with the outfield in no fit state after a particularly wet start to the year. Then, the opening Championship match against Champions Essex was abandoned without a ball bowled as the area of the outfield at the old Football Stand End had not shown significant improvement. Both sides came away from the "draw" with only five points.

Yorkshire won two of their first four matches against Nottinghamshire at Headingley and then Essex at Chelmsford — after being bowled out for 50 in the first innings in one of the more remarkable matches you will see. Harry Brook's brilliant second-innings century will live long in the memory, and was the highlight of an encouraging breakthrough campaign for the teenager.

Unfortunately, Yorkshire were unable to build on that start as they struggled for runs and did not live up to the standard Gale and co. would have wanted. They were beaten twice by runaway champions Surrey, and later suffered a damaging innings defeat against bottom side Worcestershire at Scarborough when England all-rounder Moeen Ali struck a double-century and took eight wickets — including a second-

17

innings six-for. Another loss to Somerset at Headingley followed in the final week of August, and at that stage the *White Rose* were second-bottom in Division One.

That is when things picked up markedly, with departing seamer Jack Brooks to the fore to secure a fourth-placed finish.

Just before that Somerset game Brooks had revealed that he would be leaving Headingley at the end of the season to move to, ironically, Taunton. He claimed five wickets in a defeat as part of a 25-wicket haul in the last five rounds, including a career-best nine-wicket match tally in a crucial home win over Lancashire at Headingley to all but secure safety and send the *Red Rose* down.

England Lions batsman Tom Kohler-Cadmore also impressed with scores of 81, 106, 105 not out and 63 in three successive matches against Somerset, Nottinghamshire and Lancashire.

Ballance ended a difficult campaign on a high with a century at Trent Bridge and then scores of 194 and 60 in the final-week win over Worcestershire at New Road. He finished with 906 runs, the sixth-best haul in Division One, while 51 wickets for Brooks earned him the Yorkshire Members' Player of the Year award.

A special mention must go to Ben Coad, who battled against injury to claim 48 wickets in nine matches, securing the Players' Player Award. Jonny Tattersall impressed greatly in his first campaign behind the stumps, having replaced the retiring Andrew Hodd in June.

Yorkshire's five wins were an improvement on 2017's four, leaving them with plenty to build on ahead of the new season.

Royal London One-Day Cup

Vince ends Final bid

Yorkshire's campaign threw up more positives than negatives as they won five of their eight group games, including their last four in a row, to secure third place in the North and reach the knockouts.

Some late hitting from Matthew Fisher crucially won a rain-shortened game at Derby, when the Vikings were behind the eight ball. They then impressively beat Essex at Chelmsford in a semi-final eliminator clash, by this stage without their six international players. Then a brilliant James Vince century in a high-scoring semi-final against eventual champions Hampshire at the Ageas Bowl proved too much.

Openers Kohler-Cadmore and Lyth were formidable at the top of the order, both passing 400 runs, while Pujara was not far behind and Willey impressed upon his return from the IPL, most notably hitting a breathtaking *Roses* century against Lancashire at Emirates Old Trafford.

Having reached the knockouts regularly over the last few years,

Yorkshire have failed to secure a one-day final berth since beating Somerset to win the C&G Trophy in 2002.

Now Gale, Patterson, Martyn Moxon et al must work out how to change that.

Season extended

Yorkshire's season was extended by a week into early October when they accepted an invitation to play in the inaugural six-team Abu Dhabi T20 competition.

They were alongside Hobart Hurricanes, eventual winners Lahore Qalandars, the Titans from South Africa, Auckland Aces and Afghanistan side Boost Defenders.

The teams were split into two groups, the top team in

DAVID WILLEY: Breathtaking

each advancing to the final at the end of the three days.

Yorkshire were beaten in their opening match by Lahore as opener and captain Sohail Akhtar struck a superb century in pursuit of 186, but it was a controversial knock as, on 51, he was caught at long-off by Adam Lyth, who straddled the boundary rope as he juggled. The match-turning decision was referred to the third umpire before being ruled not out, much to Yorkshire's surprise, as there did not seem sufficient evidence to overturn the original out decision.

In the second and final group game, a dead rubber, Yorkshire hammered a weakened Hobart side by nine wickets as Kohler-Cadmore's blistering 72 not out helped to chase down 141 with 43 balls remaining. Across the two matches, leg-spinner Josh Poysden impressed with three cheap wickets.

Graham Hardcastle is a cricket journalist who writes extensively on Yorkshire CCC

THREE DOUBLE DISASTERS
FOIL LAST EIGHT BID

By Paul E Dyson

For the second consecutive season Yorkshire finished fifth in the North Group, and just failed to qualify for the quarter-final stage. The team fell at the last hurdle when it lost a home game against Nottinghamshire by the wide margin of eight wickets. That county, who went through at Yorkshire's expense, did the double over the *White Rose*, as did Lancashire, who finished third, but it was the two losses to Derbyshire, coming in consecutive games in the space of three days, which caused most psychological damage.

Worcestershire, who finished top of the North Group and were the competition's eventual winners, were defeated, and Durham, who finished the group stage in second place, were beaten twice. Yorkshire used the same team for these first three games, but that sequence was never repeated, although the same top five in the batting order played in all of the final nine matches.

A total of 17 players were used in the 14 games, and although injuries played a part in this a severe loss of form from some key players led to defeats in three of the last four matches after the county had been nicely placed in third position.

Gary Ballance, Adam Lyth and Jonny Tattersall were the only players to appear in all 14 games, but skipper Steven Patterson, had he not broken a finger with three games to go, would undoubtedly have done so. David Willey, who had not led any team for three years, took over the reins, but came up twice against Nottinghamshire who were then the in-form team.

Patterson was badly missed. Aside from his captaincy he was easily the leading wicket-taker, and he was one of only three main bowlers to concede fewer than eight runs an over, the others being Jack Brooks and Liam Plunkett, who played in only five matches. Brooks, who made 10 appearances, was playing in his first games in this format for three years and usually led the attack effectively.

Tim Bresnan was a huge disappointment. He played in 11 games, but conceded over 10 runs per over and lost form so badly that he played in the final match only as a batsman. It was a similar case with Azeem Rafiq: he conceded only 7.33 runs an over in the first three games, but

ADAM LYTH: Biggest and fastest run-scorer

when joined by Adil Rashid, with whom he had previously formed a very effective partnership, for the next three matches it rose to 9.57.

Rafiq did not appear in the two final games, and Yorkshire had no specialist spinner in either team.

As in 2017 Lyth was the leading batsman. He not only scored most runs, but scored them faster than anyone else who played regularly in the top order. He often gave the start of the innings real momentum, and he became the second Yorkshire batsman to pass a career-total of 2,000 runs.

Willey usually batted at No. 3, and when he and Lyth made 150 for the second wicket in 80 balls at Northampton they broke Yorkshire's record for all wickets.

Lyth's opening partner was normally Tom Kohler-Cadmore, but he epitomised the team's inconsistency in that he was dismissed for single figures in seven of his 13 innings.

That the lower order often did not capitalise on good starts was best illustrated by Yorkshire scoring 130 in the first 12 overs — Kohler-Cadmore and Willey 129 from 70 balls — in the Headingley *Roses* match, but making only 51 in the last eight.

The most exciting match took place at Old Trafford, where Lancashire triumphed by one run. After rain the hosts posted a colossal 176-2 from only 14 overs, but after rapid half-centuries from Lyth and Joe Root the visitors fell tantalisingly short of the target. In complete contrast the worst defeat was at Headingley against Derbyshire, when an all-out total of 102 saw a painful loss by 77 runs.

Bresnan created a new record with 109 career appearances as well as equalling Richard Pyrah's record of 108 wickets. At the other end of the spectrum were two debutants: Tattersall usually kept wicket tidily, but after an undefeated half-century in the first game he batted too low in the order and five times did not even get to the wicket; Jordan Thompson started his career promisingly, and played in all of the final seven games.

Some players could hold their heads high, but more needed to have done so to have got through the group stage.

TROPHY DEFENCE HIT FOR SIX BY UNLAWFUL BAT

By John Virr

As this is my first report as Second Eleven scorer I would like to start by thanking my predecessor, Howard Clayton, for his continued help with his record-keeping.

The season started with a four-day friendly at Bristol, which saw the playing kit never leave a bag due to persistent rain. It ended in similar fashion at Scarborough, when the friendly against Durham was curtailed by gale-force winds and then rain. The vision of the North Marine Road covers being lifted into the air will live long with all who witnessed it.

Despite record breaking temperatures there were several days where no play was possible, predominantly because of rain, but play was also lost in the Championship game against Lancashire at Southport which was abandoned on the second morning due to an "unfit pitch". It was, apparently, too dry and deemed dangerous.

The downs — aside of road closures, motorway diversions and speed restrictions — saw Yorkshire unable to replicate the previous year when they won the Second Eleven Trophy and reached the *T20* Finals Day. The ups saw the introduction of several promising young players, who produced some outstanding performances. Due to various circumstances 34 players were used across all formats. Nine of these were teenagers, and six were 17 or younger.

The Trophy defence was on course despite Yorkshire being well beaten by Leicestershire in the first game as this was followed by three victories, two of which saw Lancashire and Derbyshire dismissed for 51 and 67. However, a hearing followed an "indiscretion" in the game against Durham at Headingley, where a bat was deemed too large to fit the new gauges. The outcome was a two-point deduction, one suspended, which was enough to ensure that qualification for the semi-final was no longer possible. Yorkshire finished third, winning four and losing two of their six games.

The *T20* campaign never really took off, as the first five games of the season were lost, and despite a slight upturn only five of 12 games were won, Yorkshire finishing sixth.

The Championship saw a mid-table finish – fifth out of 10, winning three, losing one and drawing five. The team had the second-highest batting-bonus points but the second-lowest bowling-bonus points.

Jordan Thompson was the highest run-scorer with 515 at an average of 73.57, and there were centuries from Tom Loten, James Wainman, Harry Brook, Jonny Tattersall and Tom Kohler-Cadmore.

Loten was the only other batsman to reach 500 runs. As for the bowling Karl Carver led the way with 22 wickets at 28.55, but only he and Ben Coad took five wickets in an innings.

Several three-day friendlies and one-four day friendly were played. No further five-wicket hauls occurred but Josh Shaw,

JAMES WHARTON: Second Eleven Performance of Season

Ben Birkhead and Jack Leaning (twice) posted centuries. Perhaps, the most impressive innings of the summer came from 17-year-old James Wharton, who made 162 against Leicestershire at Kibworth a week after captaining the Under-17s to the Championship title. This innings was enough for him to be awarded the Second Eleven Scorers Performance of the Season.

I am aware of only James Wainman leaving the county, and best wishes and thanks are sent his way.

John Virr is the Yorkshire Second Eleven Scorer

SULLIVAN BROTHERS PUT
FINE SPIN ON SEASON

By Ben Birkhead

After a tough but enjoyable indoor winter the lads were all keenly looking forward to an exciting pre-season trip to Cape Town that set us up nicely for the 2018 season.

The season began with a couple of tough games against York and Harrogate, where the lads stuck together well, playing some good cricket but lacking that final push to get over the line. Throughout the early games it was clear we had a special set of young lads with large amounts of talent who were ambitious to win and get the results we wanted.

Finishing fifth in the Yorkshire League North gave a good indication of how our season went. There were several outstanding individual and team performances, followed by moments that were used to develop and take into the rest of the season. Eddie Barnes and Mathew Taylor regularly set the tone up top with the ball, followed magnificently by the Sullivan brothers, Harry and Josh, with their spin bowling.

Academy all-rounder and Player of the Year award winner Tom Loten also contributed to the successful Academy season by being their leading run-scorer. He was involved in several match-winning innings in which he was supported by George Hill who, along with fast bowler Dom Leech, was invited to be part of the England Under-19s training squad in the first half of the winter, the programme including a 20-day training camp in Bangalore, India.

After struggling to raise a side for the *T20* Hunters competition we looked forward to the pink-ball 40-over competition in which the Academy has had a good record. We progressed through the Cup, beating Driffield and Appleby Frodingham, before facing Barnsley in an entertaining semi-final. Knocking up 194-3 with contributions from Harry Brook, 52, and Ben Birkhead, 88, we made it through, but unfortunately got no further due to confusion over the eligibility of a couple of players. This was a shame, but the team had done themselves proud and played some good competitive cricket by adapting their skills to the limited-overs format.

Overall, the 2018 Academy season was successful and a learning curve for each member who participated both on and off the field. This was shown through a very talented and successful two days in Scotland

and an Under-17 team that became national winners of the three-day competition that included several Academy players. On behalf of the Academy side we would like to say a massive thanks to the members, coaches, club and ground staff who have contributed and supported us throughout the season.

Ben Birkhead was Academy captain and wicket-keeper

YORKSHIRE ACADEMY BATTING IN YORKSHIRE LEAGUE NORTH AND LEAGUE KNOCKOUT CUP MATCHES

Player	I.	N.O.	Runs	H.S.	Avge	100s	50s	Balls Faced	Strike Rate	4s	6s	Ct/St
H G Duke	4	2	125	51*	62.50	0	1	177	70.62	12	0	7
T W Loten	23	5	873	127*	48.50	1	7	1141	76.51	65	5	1
G C H Hill	16	2	584	122	41.71	2	3	686	85.13	56	7	12
B D Birkhead	20	1	756	116	39.79	1	4	898	84.19	82	1	31/8
H C Brook	7	0	271	90	38.71	0	4	232	116.81	41	7	3
Vikram Sharma ..	3	1	55	24	27.50	0	0	61	90.16	4	0	1
J Wharton	15	1	337	69	24.07	0	2	601	56.07	39	0	5
Bilal Anjam	22	1	484	78	23.05	4	0	772	62.69	57	3	8
M L Revis	17	0	380	82	22.35	0	2	669	56.80	37	0	5
E Barnes	16	5	227	51*	20.64	0	1	251	90.44	26	2	12
M A Taylor	20	4	243	57	15.18	0	1	275	88.36	14	8	13
W Whitford	11	2	136	77*	15.11	0	1	184	73.91	9	0	6
D Leech	8	3	75	16*	15.00	0	0	89	84.26	11	1	2
H Harding	3	0	28	17	9.33	0	0	48	58.33	3	0	0
J Sullivan	13	8	40	12*	8.00	0	0	78	51.28	1	0	2
J Mukerjee	2	0	11	7	5.50	0	0	25	44.00	0	0	1
Arjun Ramkumar .	2	0	9	7	4.50	0	0	29	31.03	0	0	0
H Sullivan	6	2	13	8	3.25	0	0	37	35.14	0	0	2
H Quarmby	1	0	0	0	0.00	0	0	2	0.00	0	0	0
S Wisniewski	2	2	1	1*	—	0	0	11	9.09	0	0	1

YORKSHIRE ACADEMY BOWLING IN LEAGUE AND CUP MATCHES

Player	Overs	Mdns	Runs	Wkts	Avge	Best	5wI	Econ.	Strike Rate
H Sullivan	145	19	500	30	16.67	5-29	1	3.45	29.00
T W Loten	55.3	6	202	12	16.83	4-45	0	3.64	27.75
G C H Hill	68.3	7	249	14	17.79	3-32	0	3.64	29.36
H C Brook	50.4	8	172	9	19.11	3-32	0	3.39	33.78
Bilal Anjam	56.1	4	269	14	19.21	5-70	0	4.79	24.07
E Barnes	116.2	17	431	22	19.59	4-20	0	3.70	31.73
M A Taylor	162	20	617	31	19.90	5-23	1	3.81	31.35
J Sullivan	188.1	19	889	37	24.02	4-46	0	4.72	30.51
H Harding	15	0	81	3	27.00	2-30	0	5.40	30.00
Vikram Sharma	13	2	58	2	29.00	1-6	0	4.46	39.00
H Quarmby	24	0	121	4	30.25	2-22	0	5.04	36.00
S Wisniewski	13	1	62	2	31.00	1-23	0	4.77	39.00
J Mukerjee	11	0	65	2	32.50	1-16	0	5.91	33.00
D Leech	49	8	251	6	41.83	2-33	0	5.12	49.00
W Whitford	20	3	98	1	98.00	1-12	0	4.90	120.00

Yorkshire Academy Statistician: Andrew Hinchliffe

CATCHES WIN MATCHES
FOR THE YOUNG ONES

By Richard Damms

In a summer of fantastic weather Yorkshire's Under-17s enjoyed a challenging and ultimately successful season. Although they failed to progress in the one-day competition the squad made the final of the three-day County Championships, having won the North group and destroyed an excellent Nottinghamshire team in the semi-final. Showing no little skill and character, James Wharton led his side to a well deserved victory over a strong Surrey at Arundel Castle.

2016 had seen the introduction of a new structure. One-day cricket is now played with white balls and in coloured clothing, and the multi-day competition has been extended to three-day games. 2017 saw the additional change, whereby teams could play up to three Under-18 players. I made the conscious decision not to do this, but circumstance dictated that I would bring in Josh Sullivan as our "over age" player.

Josh was outstanding, and contributed in all of our three-day games. He finished as national leading wicket-taker in the County Championship with 29 victims, a fitting reward as he had been cruelly ruled out in 2017 with a broken finger.

In the one-day national tournament Yorkshire failed to qualify for the semi-finals. Despite impressive victories over Cheshire and Durham, a poor performance in the *Roses* match prevented any progress. Having addressed the lack of white-ball experience the previous summer and during the winter, we hit the ground running and were far too good for our first two opponents. Against Lancashire the wheels came off, and we were dismissed for 132. Lessons were learned, and the lads responded well, chasing down 252 with ease to beat Derbyshire in their final game.

There were encouraging white-ball efforts from Matthew Revis, Harry Sullivan, James Wharton and Sam Wisniewski, but one poor innings against the old enemy proved our undoing. Lancashire went on to play in the final, but lost out to Middlesex.

The three-day competition was a different show. Played in excellent weather, it provided the lads with all the challenge and examination that only multi-day cricket can. Our first opponents were Derbyshire, who had played confidently in our 50-over game the week before, but the three-day game was completely different. We won by an innings and 222 runs. Yorkshire dismissed the visitors for 189, and replied with 560-8 declared, Finlay Bean top-scoring with a record 213, assisted by Harry Duke's unbeaten 138. Captain Wharton chipped in with 75, his second notable score of a season to remember. Declaring with 40 minutes to play on the second day, Yorkshire reduced Derbyshire to 15-6 overnight. A remarkable performance, including several amazing slip catches. We won next morning, and we were on our way...or so we thought.

Our second fixture, away to Cheshire, saw us beaten inside two days, having made disappointing scores of 138 and 125. The hosts played good cricket and adapted to the conditions far better than Yorkshire. Next came the *Roses* clash, and in a terrific advertisement for Under-17 cricket Yorkshire defeated a tough Lancashire unit in the final session by three wickets. Wharton with 146 and 36 and the attack led by Dom Leech and Harrison Quarmby saw us home. An innings victory was sealed against Durham by Wharton, 152, George Hill, 122, and Harry and Josh Sullivan, who claimed 15 of the 20 wickets.

This ensured our passage to the semi-final, where we met Nottinghamshire at Caythorpe Cricket Club. Despite being dismissed for a below-par 184 Yorkshire showed genuine spirit and quality, bowling Nottinghamshire out for 141 before amassing 377 in our second innings. We rolled them over for 130 in a dramatic final session to win a place in the three-day final for the first time.

Yorkshire's build-up was beset with injuries to Matthew Revis (broken finger) and Harry Sullivan (hamstring) suffered while playing for the Academy's Saturday team. It cost Matthew a place at the Super 4s tournament at Loughborough. We had also lost James Mukherjee and Sam Wisniewski earlier in the summer — although Sam returned for the semi-final. Vikram Sharma played as a batter, while recovering from a side strain, and Harry Harding returned, having last played in April. Both were to play significant roles.

Being sent in was not part of our plans, but a fine opening partnership from Wharton and Bean, along with decent contributions from Hill and Harding, got us to a respectable 353. Yorkshire's bowling and fielding had been outstanding all summer, and it was no different now. Josh Sullivan broke the back of the Surrey first innings before Archie Greaves produced an inspired spell of swing bowling, grabbing 4-13 to dismiss the opposition for 216. With time lost to rain and being ahead on first innings our final challenge was to bat out the remaining three sessions to secure the championship.

Despite an early wobble at 79-4, calm heads and a 125-run unbroken partnership from Harry Duke, 60, and Vikram Sharma, 67, saw Yorkshire home. It was a fantastic victory, and perhaps the main reason Yorkshire won the Championship was the catching, primarily at slip.

Richard Damms is YCCC Academy Coach

FIVE-YEAR PLAN AIMING TO PRODUCE BEST BOWLERS

By Jim Love

The Yorkshire County Age Group Cricket 2018 season consisted of 155 matches, the fixtures being a mixture of two-day, 50 overs, 40 overs and *T20*. The 190 players who took part were introduced to quality match preparation and game scenarios.

The Under-17s won the National Competition with a convincing final win. The Under-15As won the National ECB Trophy for the second year in succession, being undefeated in the Trophy matches, and the Under-14As won their Northern Championship, they

TONY PICKERSGILL

too being undefeated. Each of the 12 CAG teams had the option of two training days, which were used in a variety of ways to develop the players. Once the match programmes had begun the days were used to improve fielding, bowling and batting skills, plus general match awareness and tactics.

This season we introduced two equal teams at Under-10s, Tykes and Phoenix. Under-10s have been described as elite; they are now seen as development. This will continue with Under-11s in 2019.

There were many fine individual performances, too many to mention, with some Development Team players playing their way into A Teams. There are some very exciting players within the system who have been identified for further skill sets during the winter.

Thanks to the YCCC coaching staff who provided the support and expertise to help us to achieve this. We say goodbye with our best wishes to Tony Pickersgill, who has retired, and wish Alex Morris well — he steps up to become County Age Group Bowling Coach as he and Richard Pyrah look to develop a bowling programme over the next five years that will give Yorkshire the best young bowlers in the country.

It would be remiss not to mention our managers, coaches, scorers and umpires who help to make the programme, and we thank them for all the effort and time that they put in. Mention should be made of all the clubs who give up their grounds and facilities for us. It is much appreciated.

2018	Played	Won	Lost	Drawn	Tied	No Result
U15A	21	19	0	1	0	1
U15 Dev	10	3	6	1	0	0
U14A	14	10	2	1	0	1
U14 Dev	11	7	3	0	1	0
U13A	19	9	9	0	0	1
U13 Dev	13	10	3	0	0	0
U12A	14	10	2	0	0	2
U12 Dev	11	9	2	0	0	0
U11A	10	7	2	1	0	0
U11 Dev	10	8	0	0	0	2
U10 Tykes	13	8	5	0	0	0
U10 Phoenix	9	7	2	0	0	0
	155	107	36	4	1	7

Jim Love is Yorkshire County Age Group Coordinator

Grayson is new batting coach

Paul Grayson, the former Yorkshire right-hand bat and left-arm spin bowler who went on to have an outstanding career as a player and then coach with Essex, began his new role as Yorkshire's batting coach on March 1.

Born in Bedale on March 31, 1971, Paul had a career record of 181 first-class matches, in which he scored 8,655 runs at an average of 31.70 with 16 centuries. He claimed 136 first-class wickets at 44.39 runs apiece. Paul played in 246 List A matches, scoring 3,426 runs and taking 206 wickets.

For Yorkshire he played in 52 first-class matches between 1990 and 1995, scoring 1,958 runs and claiming 13 wickets. In List A matches for his native county he scored 587 runs, and took 39 wickets, turning out in 66 games.

Upon being appointed Yorkshire's batting coach Paul relinquished his duties as head coach with Yorkshire Diamonds and as coach of Durham University MCCU. His new job also sees him become batting coach of the Academy and Second Eleven.

His appointment followed a robust recruitment process, which saw seven candidates interviewed by a panel comprised of Director of Cricket Martyn Moxon, First Eleven coach Andrew Gale, Club captain Steven Patterson and Second Eleven coach and Academy director Ian Dews.

MISSED OPPORTUNITIES SO COSTLY FOR DIAMONDS

By Kevin Hutchinson

The success and growing popularity of the Kia Super League over its first two seasons went some way towards the England and Wales Cricket Board's decision to expand the competition in 2018, resulting in the Yorkshire Diamonds, under the watchful eye of head coach Paul Grayson and assistant Gareth Breese, playing each of the other competing sides on a home and away basis, thus doubling the number matches from five to 10 in the initial group stage.

Two key partnerships were formed prior to the start of the season with the news that St Peter's School, York, would host the team for the duration of their time together, while in addition providing excellent on-site practice and recreational facilities. A further boost came with the announcement that the club had linked up with jewellers Odendaal Diamonds, a move which would see the company's brand on the front of the team's shirts from 2018. Yorkshire Diamonds general manager Jane Hildreth said: "We are thrilled to partner Odendaal Diamonds for the 2018 and 2019 seasons. The brands align perfectly, and we are very grateful for the support they are offering women's cricket in Yorkshire."

There were a number of on-field changes, with only six players from 2017 retained in a largely new-look squad. Lauren Winfield remained as captain alongside Katherine Brunt, while the third of the previous season's England trio, Jenny Gunn, moved to Loughborough Lightning with Beth Langston coming in the opposite direction. Sri Lankan Chamari Athapaththu returned for a second season, and the other overseas slots were taken by Australian duo Beth Mooney and Delissa Kimmince. Beth was a member of the squad in 2016 before being ruled out through injury last year.

Kimmince made an immediate impact with an unbeaten half-century in the first match at Taunton against Western Storm. Another making her debut, Helen Fenby, made a dream start, the young leg-spinner trapping New Zealand international Rachel Priest with her first delivery. The game finished in defeat, but the Diamonds went away in good heart having competed well against the reigning champions. Defeats to

YORKSHIRE *ROSES*: Katherine Brunt, left, and skipper Lauren Whinfield in action against Lancashire Thunder

Lancashire Thunder and Loughborough Lightning, when on both occasions the side struggled to reach 100, came either side of a washed-out game at Guildford against Surrey Stars, leaving the side only two points from their opening four matches. This was having their *Roses* rivals in deep trouble at 25-4, and fighting back to restrict the Lightning to what should have been a manageable total.

The first of two games played at Clifton Park produced a change in fortunes, Winfield with 64 and Athapaththu, 43, putting Southern Vipers to the sword as the hosts registered a record total of 175-5 before Katherine Brunt, 5-26, produced a devastating spell to become the first bowler in the competition's history to take five wickets in an innings.

The second half of the season began with a trip to Scarborough's North Marine Road, which was the setting for a second defeat at the hands of Western Storm. Despite a century opening stand between skipper Winfield, 48, and Mooney, 69, once again the bowlers were unable to contain the reigning champions' powerful top order. The team headed

KATIE LEVICK   **BETH MOONEY**   **HELEN FENBY**

to Southampton's Ageas Bowl to take on Southern Vipers, and were dealt a blow when their in-form captain was ruled out through illness. Strong performances from Katie Levick, 3-35, and Thea Brookes, 45, could not prevent another defeat, so Diamonds needed to win all three remaining games for a top-three finish and a place in Finals Day.

For most, the highlight of the season came against Surrey Stars at Clifton Park, when an outstanding performance in the field saw the eventual champions bowled out for 66, the resulting nine-wicket win keeping the season alive as the team headed to Blackpool for a *Roses* re-match. In a must-win game for both sides the visitors were set 154, almost half the total coming from Indian Harmanpreet Kaur, who made 74 after being dropped on 11. In a gripping climax it looked as though Brunt might just see the Diamonds over the line, but in the end they fell nine runs short, effectively ending their hopes of a semi-final place.

The final game of the campaign, played under lights at Emerald Headingley, provided a thrilling three-run victory over table-topping Loughborough Lightning with notable performances from Bess Heath and Katie Thompson. Bess was having only her second outing, and Thompson appeared for the first time in 2018.

A third successive fifth-place finish and a record of three wins and six defeats may not appear to represent progress, but victories over both the season's finalists show if nothing else the unpredictable nature of the game's shortest form. On a number of occasions the Diamonds worked themselves into a strong position, only to fail to take full advantage. In many ways it was a season of missed opportunities. Looking to next season, the current flush of Diamonds if kept together has shown enough glimpses of its potential to sparkle, particularly as the young players gain more exposure at this level.

**Kevin Hutchinson is the Yorkshire Diamonds scorer
and Competitions and Records Secretary,
Hunters ECB Yorkshire Premier League North**

PLAYERS' PLAYER OF THE YEAR

CAPPING DISPLAY: Paceman Ben Coad, who was awarded his County cap in 2018 and was to named as Yorkshire Players' Player of the Year at the end-of-season Gala Dinner, leads his side home after taking 5-53 v. Surrey at Scarborough. Ben topped the Yorkshire first-class averages with 48 wickets at 16.33.

MAN OF THE SERIES: England Test captain Joe Root on the way to his 100 not out and *Man of the Series* Award in the Third Royal London One-Day International against India at Headingley.

LIKE FATHER: Alfie Root, the son of Joe and his wife, Carrie, is only two years old, but he still expects his net at the end of a hard day out there...

MAN OF THE MATCH: Yorkshire's leg-spinning all-rounder Adil Rashid, whose three prized wickets blunted India's ambitions and earned him the *Man of the Match* award in the Third Royal London One-Day International at Emerald Headingley. Adil was also to regain his England Test place in 2018.

TEST ALL-ROUNDER:
Yorkshire's Jonathan
Bairstow drives during the
only innings England needed
to defeat Pakistan in the
Second NatWest Test Match
at Emerald Headingley.
Wicket-keeper Bairstow,
right, who was to pouch
three catches, worries about
an appeal against opening
batsman Azhar Ali.

CHRISTMAS CHEER FROM THE CRICKET

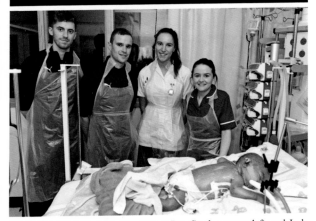

IN GOOD HEART: Yorkshire players Ben Coad, extreme left, and Josh Poysden don hospital garb for their Christmas visit to the Children's Congenital Heart Unit at Leeds General Infirmary. BELOW, left to right: Andy McNally, Marketing and Communications Manager for the Children's Heart Surgery Fund, Tim Bresnan, Ellie Brown, Fundraising Manager; "Dickie" Bird OBE, Children's Heart Surgery Fund Ambassador; Coad, Poysden and Fay Richardson, Corporate Partnerships Manager. The team handed out cards and toys, including Junior Vikings goodie bags.

EMERALD JEWEL IN HEADINGLEY CROWN

THIS BIG... Yorkshire County Cricket Club Chief Executive Mark Arthur welcomes guests to Headingley's iconic north-south Emerald Stand as building work enters its final phase. The stand, which will seat 4,300 and has cost £39m including the rugby side, will be opened for the Fifth Royal London One Day International between England and Pakistan on Sunday, May 19, 2019.

THE WAY WE WERE: It is August 2017...and the stand which had stood at Headingley since 1932 is witnessing its final countdown.

EMERALD JEWEL IN HEADINGLEY CROWN

LENGTHENING SHADOWS: September 2018, and the season is dying away, but already can be seen the bright new dawn.

ALMOST THERE: It is late January 2019, and the builders have entered their end game. Bookings have flooded in for Yorkshire's showpiece international matches of the summer to come. *(Photos: Allan McKenzie, Bob Dale and John Heald.)*

YORKSHIRE 2018: Back Row, left to right: Ian Fisher, Lead Strength and Conditioning Coach; Jonathan Read, Ed Barnes, Jack Shutt, Jared Warner, James Logan, Jordan Thompson, Harry Brook, Matthew Waite, Jonny Tattersall and Tony Pickersgill, Age Group Bowling Coach. Middle Row: Richard Damms, Academy Coach; Peter Sim, Strength and Conditioning Coach; Richard Pyrah, Bowling Coach, Josh Shaw, James Wainman, Jack Leaning, Ben Coad, Tom Kohler-Cadmore, David Willey, Alex Lees, Karl Carver, Azeem Rafiq, Ian Dews, Second Eleven Coach and Academy Director; Kunwar Bansil, First Eleven Physiotherapist; and Jim Love, Yorkshire County Age Group Cricket Co-ordinator. Front Row: Liam Plunkett, Adam Lyth, Tim Bresnan, Andrew Gale, First Eleven Coach; Gary Ballance, Martyn Moxon, Director of Cricket; Steven Patterson, who was to succeed Ballance as Club Captain during the season; Jack Brooks and Andrew Hodd.

CRICKET REMINISCENCES ON AND OFF THE FIELD

I was born in 1938, but not from an immediate cricketing family, although there were some in the wider family.

One of my grandfathers, Charles Raper, played with and was captain of Girlington for 25 years or so in the early 20th Century, and then my uncle, J R Stanley Raper, was captain of YCCC Second Eleven and later served on the Club's committee.

It was he who took me to my first match at Bradford Park Avenue in 1948 versus Worcestershire.

By J C David Allan

We lived in Heaton, Bradford, in my younger days, and I remember spending hours levelling a width of lawn and rolling it into a flat strip upon which my friends and I played cricket.

My first recollection of formal matches was when I played for my school colts side, probably 1953, when I was brought on to bowl. I managed to take a wicket or two. I can recall our opponents' umpire saying to their batsman: "You had better watch this bowler, he is bowling off-spin." I don't recall knowing that this was the case then, and do not recall ever bowling again other than for a total joke in the next 30 years.

I played in my school, Bootham York First Eleven, in 1955-56, initially under the captaincy of Nigel M Pullan, known to many of you as a stalwart Yorkshire member. He left in 1955, but returned to watch us play in a fixture the following season. I scored over 50, and am told that Nigel asked who had hit that six straight back over the bowler? He was told it was Allan, to which he apparently replied: "I didn't know that the lad had it in him to play a shot like that."

At the end of that season I earned my First Eleven colours. After leaving Bootham I returned each year to play for the Old Boys' XI versus The School for the next 18 years, and was captain/convenor of the side for the last nine of them.

In the late summer of 1956 I joined Bradford CC, and was selected to play in their Sunday Eleven with such distinguished players as J D H Blackburn, R K Platt, A M King and H J McIlvenny. In 1957 I joined the club nearest to home, Salem Athletic, and stayed there for four seasons. I won the First Eleven batting prize in 1958, and we were Group A Champions in 1960.

Having obtained my HND Building Certificate, I started full-time employment with William Irwin's. I came into contact with fellow employees and clients, some of whom played cricket, and as a result I joined Leeds Springfield, a nomadic club, in about 1961 and played the rest of my career with them.

I started as a youth member of YCCC in 1954, and in 1965 I spent one of my annual bonuses on a life-membership subscription. It cost me £60 and was much treasured, but it was later commercialised and carried fewer benefits. I joined the Northern Cricket Society when it was run by Len Horton and Ron Yeomans. We used to meet in the Griffin Hotel in Boar Lane, Leeds. How many can remember that? I am still an active member. In the early 1960s I qualified as a quantity surveyor.

Old boys of the Quaker Schools had in 1902 found the Falcons Touring Club, which organised a week's tour of cricket matches in the Shropshire, Hereford and Monmouth region, and I very much enjoyed being part of the squad.

I married in 1964 Carol, who previously hadn't been near cricket, but we spent one day of our honeymoon at Park Avenue watching Yorkshire v. Australia. Ever since, and increasingly so, she has taught herself about the game and is now as enthusiastic as I am. We moved from Horsforth to Calverley in 1970. Not long after, a neighbour discovered my cricket interests and I was asked to join the Calverley CC committee. This I did, and over the next 40 years became chairman and then president, after which they made me an honorary life member.

Around 1990 Bob Appleyard and Bruce Moss invited me to join the Friends of Park Avenue because of my experience when working as a quantity surveyor in the construction industry, and I played my part in bringing first-class cricket back to the famous ground. It came as a bitter blow when Yorkshire decided that their use of most outgrounds would cease after 1996.

I was invited to join the YCCC Charitable Youth Trust in the early 1990s and the Yorkshire Cricket Taverners' Club in the early 2000s. I have continued to enjoy the facilities and camaraderie that this affords their members. I joined the Taverners' committee, and shortly afterwards Robin Smith asked Harold North to become founder chairman of the YCCC Archives Committee. In 2010 I succeeded David Hall to become that committee's third chairman, and I served in that role until retiring from the committee at the end of 2017.

More recently, Carol and I joined the Yorkshire CC Supporters' Association's fund-raising group with the Academy and younger professionals very much in mind when Yorkshire come calling.

The Club's annual meeting in 2018 awarded me a President's medal in recognition of my endeavours with the Archives Committee. I am truly honoured to have retired with this recognition.

WHY I WAS REBUKED
BY PERCY HOLMES

By David S Hall

An early interest in cricket was inspired by my father on his return from war service in 1945. I watched Yorkshire for the first time in 1946, led by Brian Sellers at The Circle, the home then of Hull CC.

My schooling took place at Scarborough College, where the cricket coach was Percy Holmes, who did his best to develop my playing abilities. This included a telling-off for taking golf lessons, which he inferred would inhibit my ability to play straight.

In 1948, while on holiday, I was taken to see the Australians play Sussex at Hove. This was the side led by Don Bradman, which was full of very talented cricketers, including Keith Miller. The Sussex side included three "blues" in David Sheppard, John Dews and Hubert Doggart just down from University.

After leaving school my call-up for national service was delayed, and I had a season playing club cricket. On joining the Army my first posting after basic and officer training put me under the command of one Colonel Alan Martin-Jenkins, the uncle of Christopher Martin-Jenkins. As a consequence I spent the summers playing a considerable amount of Army cricket while serving.

On leaving the Army it was a requirement then that you transferred to the Territorial Army for two years which, in my case, became 35 years. My civilian career was to take me into retailing, and both would limit my availability to play cricket, but my interest continued and I was encouraged to qualify for MCC, resulting in my election in 1966. My retailing career brought me back to Yorkshire in 1972 and opportunities to renew my close observations of Yorkshire cricket. In 1982 we moved to Barwick-in-Elmet, and I became involved with the village cricket club — as President for 20 years. During this period we made a successful application for a Lottery Grant to build a new pavilion.

In 2005, shortly after I had finally retired from business, I received a phone call from Robin Smith, whom I had known for many years through cricket, business and T A service, asking me if I would take on the chairmanship of the recently formed YCCC Archives Committee. Harold North, who had formed the committee, was not well and a replacement was being sought.

Robin had realised the need for the memorabilia of YCCC to be properly cared for. Since the death of Tony Woodhouse the many items of memorabilia had drifted around Headingley, spread among cupboards, drawers, under the stands and in garages with little understanding of what we had and, even less, where it might be. Tony, being concerned, had removed some valuable items for safekeeping to his home, a situation he had talked to Robin about before his death.

I don't think I had comprehended initially the size of the task when I agreed to become chairman. Efforts had been started to make an inventory of items, pack them securely and transfer them to West Yorkshire Archives, where there were safe and appropriate storage conditions.

It became clear to me that we had too many items which were of genuine cricket interest but not specific to Yorkshire. We needed to concentrate on a Yorkshire archive. With the agreement of the committee it was decided to sell non-Yorkshire memorabilia, and use the monies to acquire Yorkshire items as they became available at auctions and from other sources.

At the same time it was decided to display items from the collection in the Long Room. We purchased four cabinets for this purpose and arranged for the exhibits to be changed regularly. I was keen, too, to enhance the appearance of the Long Room, and we decided to install the Test Honours Boards which would be updated as performances arose.

The *Wisden* Board was added in 2013 on *Wisden* and Yorkshire's 150th anniversaries. A war memorial was installed adjacent to the Hutton Gates and unveiled by Field Marshal P Inge, who had served in the same Green Howards Battalion as Hedley Verity.

It had been an aspiration of the Club for many years to have a museum with the Club's rich heritage. That opportunity came in 2010 with the move of the Club's offices from the East Stand to the new Headingley Carnegie Pavilion building. Through the immense generosity of Dr Keith Howard and the Emerald Foundation we had the funds, too. Work began designing and selecting the items and themes for the museum, a task which took several months. It included sourcing material from the BBC, among others, who loaned us interesting exhibits. The museum opened in 2011, and I continued to operate it until I retired at the end of the 2016 season.

My life-long interest in cricket has provided me with many friends, and I would particularly like to thank the numerous people who have assisted me during my work with the Archives and Museum and given generously of their time. It has been a pleasure to be involved and help to contribute to the maintenance of the rich heritage of Yorkshire Cricket.

THE PRESIDENT'S MEDAL WINNERS

2008	Geoff Holmes, Vivien Stone and Mollie Staines
2009	Veronica Denby and Clifford Gregg
2013	Ron Deaton and Joan Pickering
2014	Bob Stott
2016	Nigel Pullan
2017	Stephen Mann
2018	J C David Allan and David S Hall

Adil signs new deal

Leg-spinning all-rounder Adil Rashid agreed a new one-year all-format deal with Yorkshire. The new contract will see him make himself available for all forms of the game, continuing his 12-year affiliation with the *White Rose* county.

Adil, capped in 2008, renegotiated his Club contract at the start of last season so that he was only involved in one-day formats. But he was selected for England's summer Test series against India, playing all five Tests in a 4-1 victory. He was then an integral part of England's successful tour of India.

FAREWELL TO DOUBLE -WINNING QUARTET

By David Warner

Four Yorkshire players who each made significant contributions in the 2014 and 2015 Championship-winning seasons left the county at the end of last summer.

Perhaps the one who will be missed the most is fast bowler and self-styled headband warrior Jack Brooks, who went out in a blaze of glory before moving to Somerset on a three-year contract.

Brooks made no secret of the fact that he would have stayed at Yorkshire

BLAZE OF GLORY: Jack Brooks

had the terms been right, but in end he felt he had to accept Somerset's offer. Ironically, Somerset were at Emerald Headingley soon after his transfer had been announced, and he gave them ample evidence of his ability with a five-wicket haul.

It was the start of spell which brought him 25 wickets from the last five matches, including career-best match figures of 9-113 against Lancashire and 6-94 in the first innings of the final game against Worcestershire at New Road, which Yorkshire won by seven wickets to finish fourth in the table. He ended the season with 51 Championship wickets, three more than his nearest rival, Ben Coad, and he went on to scoop the Members' Player of the Year award at the Club's gala dinner.

Brooks moved to Yorkshire from Northamptonshire ahead of the 2013 season, and although he never quite achieved his stated ambition of going on to play for England he gave his everything for his adopted county, and he became a firm favourite with his frenzied gallops around the field whenever he took a wicket.

A major part of Jason Gillespie's great team, Brooks easily led the field with 68 wickets in 2014 when Yorkshire snatched their first title win since 2001, and the following year he topped the list again with 65 dismissals to help to retain the Trophy. In all he claimed 316 first-class wickets for Yorkshire at 26.39 out of his career tally of 434. He also bagged five wickets or more on 15 occasions.

At the same time that Brooks joined Yorkshire so did **Liam Plunkett** from Durham in a successful bid to resurrect his England career, and at times he showed himself to be the fastest bowler on Yorkshire's books. He took 24 wickets in seven matches in 2014 as well as knocking up 209 valuable runs in his usual aggressive style, and the following season he had 14 wickets in five matches.

Plunkett, who has moved to Surrey on a three-year contract, became one of England's most dependable one-day bowlers, and he focussed entirely on limited-overs cricket last season. From 2013 to 2017 he took 98 first-class wickets for Yorkshire, 33 in List A matches and 44 in Twenty20 cricket.

Nobody did more to help Yorkshire to win their two titles than **Alex Lees**, whose star at that time was in the ascendancy. Not only did he seem a small step away from becoming an England batsman, but it also appeared as if he and Adam Lyth would be opening Yorkshire's batting together for years to come.

In July 2013 Lees plundered an unbeaten 275 against Derbyshire at Chesterfield to become Yorkshire's youngest double centurion, and in the 2014 title win he was his side's second top-scorer with two centuries and five half-centuries in his 971 runs. The following year he made 795 runs with one century and a further five half-centuries.

Lees was appointed Yorkshire's one day captain in 2016, Gillespie's last season in charge, and he also enjoyed his best first-class season with 1,165 Championship runs at 40.17.

His form deserted him in more recent times, and after a generally disappointing 2017 he could muster only 50 runs in eight Championship innings last season before agreeing a move on loan to Durham until the end of the summer and then taking up a three-year contract. Everyone hopes that Lees will rediscover his best form in his new surroundings.

Acknowledged by all to be one of the best wicket-keepers in the game, **Andrew Hodd** announced that he would be retiring from active service at the end of 2018. Signed from Sussex in 2012, he was a loyal and worthy stand-in behind the stumps for Jonny Bairstow until Jonny Tattersall took on the role early last season, although Hodd did reappear in "emergency" circumstances against Somerset at Headingley in late August. Typically, he was to the fore, top-scoring with 85 in the first innings and holding on to four catches.

Hodd managed five matches in helping Yorkshire to win the Championship in 2014, scoring 144 runs and, more importantly, holding 18 catches and pulling off a stumping.

He appeared in half the matches in 2015, scoring 180 runs and claiming 21 catches and two stumpings. One of the dressing room's most popular

DOUBLE-CENTURION: Alex Lees

characters, he leaves with everyone's best wishes.

Yorkshire, as part of their rebuilding process, said farewell at the end of 2018 to off-spinner **Azeem Rafiq**, who was in his second spell with the Club, having returned in 2016. Rafiq and his wife had a terrible time last year when their son, Alyaan, was stillborn in May after a difficult pregnancy. Despite these tragic circumstances Rafiq still turned out in 12 consecutive *T20 Vitality Blast* matches for the Vikings, doing the bulk of the spin bowling and taking eight wickets, one of them against Leicestershire Foxes being his 100th in the competition. He dedicated it to Alyaan. A resolute cricketer, Rafiq was determined to rebuild his career, and the hope is that he will succeed in so doing.

Also leaving Headingley at the end of 2018 was Harrogate-born left-arm seamer, **James Wainman**, who played in six limited-overs matches for the first team between 2014 and 2018. He was part of the Second Eleven Trophy winning team of 2017.

JACK ALEXANDER BROOKS

FIRST-CLASS MATCHES FOR YORKSHIRE

BATTING AND FIELDING

Seasons	M	I	NO	Runs	HS	Avge	100s	50s	Ct
2013-18	81	102	34	1229	109*	18.07	1	2	21

BOWLING

Seasons	Matches	Overs	Mdns	Runs	Wkts	Avge	Best	5wI	10wM
2013-18	81	2278.2	452	8341	316	26.39	6-65	15	0

LIST A CRICKET FOR YORKSHIRE

BATTING AND FIELDING

Seasons	M	I	NO	Runs	HS	Avge	100s	50s	Ct
2014-16	12	4	1	7	6	2.33	0	0	3

Seasons	Matches	Overs	Mdns	Runs	Wkts	Avge	Best	4wI
2014-16	12	101	7	461	15	30.73	2-22	0

TWENTY20 CRICKET FOR YORKSHIRE
BATTING AND FIELDING

Seasons	M	I	NO	Runs	HS	Avge	100s	50s	Ct
2013-18	23	0	0	0	0	—	0	0	11

BOWLING

Seasons	Matches	Overs	Mdns	Runs	Wkts	Avge	Best	4wI
2013-18	23	72.3	1	582	22	26.45	5-21	2

ALEXANDER ZAK LEES

FIRST-CLASS MATCHES FOR YORKSHIRE
BATTING AND FIELDING

Seasons	M	I	NO	Runs	HS	Avge	100s	50s	Ct
2010-18	82	140	11	4528	275*	35.10	11	22	56

BOWLING

Seasons	Matches	Overs	Mdns	Runs	Wkts	Avge	Best	5wI	10wM
2010-18	82	9	1	77	2	38.50	2-51	0	0

LIST A CRICKET FOR YORKSHIRE
BATTING AND FIELDING

Seasons	M	I	NO	Runs	HS	Avge	100s	50s	Ct
2011-17	42	39	2	1109	102	29.97	1	8	15

TWENTY20 CRICKET FOR YORKSHIRE
BATTING AND FIELDING

Seasons	M	I	NO	Runs	HS	Avge	100s	50s	Ct
2013-17	37	36	2	857	67*	25.20	0	4	12

LIAM EDWARD PLUNKETT

FIRST-CLASS MATCHES FOR YORKSHIRE
BATTING AND FIELDING

Seasons	M	I	NO	Runs	HS	Avge	100s	50s	Ct
2013-17	36	51	7	1241	126	28.20	1	7	20

BOWLING

Seasons	Matches	Overs	Mdns	Runs	Wkts	Avge	Best	5wI	10wM
2013-17	36	795	128	2925	98	29.84	6-33	2	0

LIST A CRICKET FOR YORKSHIRE
BATTING AND FIELDING

Seasons	M	I	NO	Runs	HS	Avge	100s	50s	Ct
2013-18	28	21	10	327	53	29.72	0	1	17

BOWLING

Seasons	Matches	Overs	Mdns	Runs	Wkts	Avge	Best	4wI
2013-18	28	202.4	9	1060	33	32.12	4-52	1

BATTING AND FIELDING

Seasons	M	I	NO	Runs	HS	Avge	100s	50s	Ct
2013-18	42	31	10	353	36	16.80	0	0	13

BOWLING

Seasons	Matches	Overs	Mdns	Runs	Wkts	Avge	Best	4wI
2013-18	42	139.1	1	1146	44	26.04	3-42	0

AZEEM RAFIQ

FIRST-CLASS MATCHES FOR YORKSHIRE

BATTING AND FIELDING

Seasons	M	I	NO	Runs	HS	Avge	100s	50s	Ct
2009-17	35	41	4	814	100	22.00	1	4	14

BOWLING

Seasons	Matches	Overs	Mdns	Runs	Wkts	Avge	Best	5wI	10wM
2009-17	35	784.3	148	2511	63	39.85	5-50	1	0

LIST A CRICKET FOR YORKSHIRE

BATTING AND FIELDING

Seasons	M	I	NO	Runs	HS	Avge	100s	50s	Ct
2009-18	30	21	8	222	52*	17.07	0	1	12

BOWLING

Seasons	Matches	Overs	Mdns	Runs	Wkts	Avge	Best	4wI
2009-18	30	200.2	4	1160	41	28.29	5-30	2

TWENTY20 CRICKET FOR YORKSHIRE

BATTING AND FIELDING

Seasons	M	I	NO	Runs	HS	Avge	100s	50s	Ct
2008-18	95	37	24	153	21*	11.76	0	0	36

BOWLING

Seasons	Matches	Overs	Mdns	Runs	Wkts	Avge	Best	4wI
2008-18	95	322.5	0	2489	102	24.40	5-19	1

ANDREW JOHN HODD

FIRST-CLASS MATCHES FOR YORKSHIRE

BATTING AND FIELDING

Seasons	M	I	NO	Runs	HS	Avge	100s	50s	Ct/St
2012-18	57	79	10	1803	96*	26.13	0	14	165/11

BOWLING

Seasons	Matches	Overs	Mdns	Runs	Wkts	Avge	Best	5wI	10wM
2012-18	57	1	0	14	0	—	0-14	0	0

LIST A CRICKET FOR YORKSHIRE

BATTING AND FIELDING

Seasons	M	I	NO	Runs	HS	Avge	100s	50s	Ct/St
2013-18	32	23	5	368	69*	20.44	0	1	39/1

TWENTY20 CRICKET FOR YORKSHIRE

BATTING AND FIELDING

Seasons	M	I	NO	Runs	HS	Avge	100s	50s	Ct/St
2013-16	26	17	4	147	70	11.30	0	1	9/6

CRICKET'S BACK— AND YORKSHIRE ARE TOPS

By Anthony Bradbury

As the Great War started in August 1914 Yorkshire played on with a few more Championship matches. When they finally left the field at Brighton on September 1 the 11 men who began the long journey home were, in batting order, Ben Wilson, Major Booth, David Denton, Roy Kilner, Wilfred Rhodes, Edgar Oldroyd, George Hirst, Percy Holmes, Alonzo Drake, Tommy Birtles and Arthur Dolphin. The county captain, Sir Archibald White, had already left the side to take on military responsibilities, and on their own way back to Yorkshire Major Booth and Roy Kilner determined to join the armed forces immediately.

It is now well known that Lieutenant Major Booth died on the Somme on July 1,1916, and that Alonzo Drake, broken by ill health, died in February 1919. James Rothery, who had last played for the county in 1910, died of his war wounds in June 1919. Sadly, the Club Committee failed to mention his loss in the 1919 annual report. Ben Wilson, considered too slow a scorer of runs, would not be selected to play for his county again, but nearly five years later all other members of that final 1914 side would again wear the *White Rose* cap with pride. Even so, George Hirst in early 1919 was aged 47, Denton was 44, and Rhodes 41.

That any first-class cricket took place at all in 1919 was due to the determination of the Advisory County Cricket Committee, chaired by the President of MCC, who agreed a fixture list in February 1919 that enabled Yorkshire to play 26 matches, and numerous other counties, concerned about the availability of players, as few as 12 or 14 matches. The controversial decision, never to be repeated, was that all of these games, two innings a side, were to finish in two days with close of play at 7.30pm. There was even a proposal, never taken up, to abandon the tea interval following an experiment by Surrey in Edwardian times when refreshments were brought out to players on the field at appropriate intervals. This scenario led to lots of drawn games and tired players, who sometimes were playing three games at three different venues in six-day periods, Sunday being the rest day.

Yorkshire started 1919 with an annual general meeting in January, with the powerful President, Lord Hawke, using his military title of Colonel The Lord Hawke in the chair — and he was also still then

43

All-round legend: George Hirst batting v. MCC at Lord's. The wicket-keeper is Francis Brooke. *(Photo: Mick Pope Archive)*

Journey's start: Debutant Herbert Sutcliffe on march

President of MCC — allocating fixtures in the County to Bradford, Sheffield, Leeds, Dewsbury, Hull, Huddersfield, Harrogate and a non-championship match v. MCC at Scarborough. A century later we can reflect that for some years Scarborough has been the only Yorkshire ground away from Headingley to host Championship cricket, although the County will take a game to York in 2019.

At the AGM Sir Archibald White was reappointed captain, but he also was aged 41, and he had a change of mind before the season started in late May. A new captain had to be found, and Lord Hawke, with those he may have consulted, made a good choice in appointing Mr D C F Burton.

Cecil Burton, an amateur, had played occasionally for Yorkshire in pre-war years, and was outstanding in the outfield. His skills there would sharpen up the whole side. When he was badly hurt in a keenly contested match that was lost to the Australian Imperial Forces it was George Hirst,

YORKSHIRE 2019: The team that played Kent at Dover in August. Standing, left to right: Arthur Dolphin, Roy Kilner, Abe Waddington, A C (Billy) Williams and Herbert Sutcliffe. Seated: George Hirst, Wilfred Rhodes, Cecil Burton (captain), Rockley Wilson and David Denton. Kneeling: Percy Holmes and Emmott Robinson. *(Photo: Ron Deaton Archive)*

with whom Burton often happily consulted, who took over mid-season as captain for a number of Championship games.

Yorkshire started their season with an easy match against Gloucestershire. The opening batsmen were Rhodes and Holmes, in contrast to that last match of 1914 when they had been Wilson and Booth. A 24-year-old made his first-team debut at No. 6. The *Wisden* writer did not know his initial. He was simply named Sutcliffe, and he scored 11 runs. In his next game he batted behind the captain at No. 7. At least he was now called H Sutcliffe, and he scored 38 and three.

Thereafter Sutcliffe made steady progress, and when Rhodes in late June made nought and one, opening against Nottinghamshire, Burton after, he says, consulting Hirst pushed Sutcliffe up to open with Holmes. Rhodes went down the order to concentrate on bowling. In his first game as a Yorkshire opener, alongside Percy Holmes, Sutcliffe made 20 against Kent — not many, but then Yorkshire as a team made only 64, and Sutcliffe had been top scorer. Rhodes may not have minded, for he took 5-35 in 26.4 overs in Kent's only innings in this rain-spoilt game.

Sutcliffe's career then continued its upward march as five centuries followed, starting with 145 against Northamptonshire and finishing with

174 in the return Kent fixture. By the end of the season Sutcliffe had scored 1,839 runs at 44.85. Only Jack Hobbs and Holmes had scored more.

So Holmes too, had done rather well. He had played a little for Yorkshire before the war, but not with much success. In 1919 he reached 99 v. MCC at Lord's, and then, with an impetuous swing, was out.

How crestfallen he must have felt. But then he got going with a maiden 100 (exactly) against Nottinghamshire at Trent Bridge, and for good measure four more centuries. He edged Sutcliffe in scoring 1,887 at an average just below Sutcliffe of 43.88.

How these two men must have thrived upon each other's company, and their highlight would have been a partnership of 253 in the *Roses* match against Lancashire at Sheffield — 15,000 people saw them on each day of this special game. When the *Wisden Almanack* 1920 was published each of them

Partnership forged: Percy Holmes, whose run tally just edged Sutcliffe's in 1919

appeared in the feature article and photographs of the Five Batsmen of the Year.

On the results front, despite the limitation of matches to two days, Yorkshire had much success, especially in mid-season. Some of the poorer county sides, without settled teams, were hammered by bat and ball. In one seven-match sequence against Essex, Hampshire, Northamptonshire, Leicestershire, Surrey, Northamptonshire (again) and Gloucestershire the *White Rose* won four games by an innings, one by 10 wickets, one by 74 runs and drew the other fixture with Leicestershire. Old hands made big contributions — David Denton (4), George Hirst (3) and Wilfred Rhodes (1) scored centuries to be joined thrice by Roy Kilner and once by the captain. Rhodes took an astonishing 164 wickets — more than anyone in England — and at an average of 14.42. No one else took more than 20 wickets at a lower average.

Two newcomers made notable starts to their first-class careers. The first was Abe Waddington, who although he did not join the side until July still took 100 wickets. A left-arm fast bowler, he was to trouble many batsmen, though he was already 25 years old. The second was Emmott Robinson, a very late arrival aged 34 on debut. He provided good variety with Waddington as a pair of opening bowlers, and Robinson was also a good batsman and a brilliant fielder. In time he became a Yorkshire legend for his tenacity and hard work.

Another player passed through the team like a comet with one astonishing performance. A C Williams had played sporadically for Yorkshire over some years before he was picked at Dewsbury to play against Hampshire. He replaced Mr R C Chichester-Constable, who had been given a trial of one match and who was later to be captain of the Second Eleven. In the Dewsbury game Hampshire were bowled out for 82, and Williams took nine of those wickets for 29 runs. It was, and remains, one of the very best Yorkshire bowling performances. Eight of the nine wickets were bowled to make it an even more remarkable feat, but in a few subsequent matches he was unable to obtain much success, and he left the Yorkshire first team at the end of the 1919 season.

The Championship table formation was based on a percentage of the number of wins obtained against matches played. So, any team who played 10 games and won five would have a percentage average of 50. No points were allocated for draws or any form of bonus for runs or wickets. By mid-August Yorkshire had a percentage of 54.5, having won 12 out of 22 games. Kent were chasing them, having opted to play only 14 matches, of which they were to win six. In a late match between Kent and Yorkshire at Dover the hosts were forced to follow on, but came out with a draw, and when the final matches started on August 30 Kent knew that if they could beat Middlesex at Lord's and if Yorkshire could not beat Sussex at Brighton they would be champions.

The first day of the Sussex-Yorkshire match was rained off, and a draw became inevitable. When such play as there was ended early on the second day Yorkshire had to travel by train to London Victoria, not knowing whether Kent were about to beat Middlesex. Middlesex had to follow on (then a 100-run deficit) and had only just got into a runs credit with nine wickets down when time ran out on Kent and the match was drawn. At Victoria station the Yorkshire Secretary was on the telephone to enquire whether his team were Champions or not. To the relief of all those travelling to the North he came back with a beaming smile. Yorkshire were County Champions for the 10th time in their history.

A fortnight later Yorkshire returned to the South to play The Rest of England at The Oval. That match was lost by 10 wickets, with both Jack Hobbs and Frank Woolley scoring centuries for The Rest. In contrast to the Championship games it was played over four days, and the two games against MCC and the one against the Australian Imperial Force were played over three days.

The match against the AIF at Bramall Lane, Sheffield, was a thriller with Jack Gregory, the great Australian fast bowler, taking 13 wickets and then being in a second-innings last-wicket undefeated partnership of 56 to take his side to victory by one wicket. Gregory's bowling remains the best match performance by an Australian in the 55 games played by Australian teams against Yorkshire.

On membership and financial matters some comparison with 2019 may be of interest. The Yorkshire Committee were determined to build up a strong membership base after the Great War, and were satisfied with the initial 1919 membership of approaching 3,000 and that 112,000 people paid for admission to the home matches. Lady and youth members were not entitled to vote at meetings.

JAMES ROTHERY
Died of war wounds

The Club balance sheet showed net assets of over £11,000 (about £550,000 in 2019) with no repayable loans at all to banks, building societies, councils or private trusts. Indeed, before the Great War the Club was lending money to councils rather than borrowing from them. By 1919 these councils including Sheffield and Bradford had repaid their debt, and the Club was investing its money in a variety of stocks including the Madras and Southern Mahratta Railway at four per cent and the Assam-Bengal Railway at three per cent. These must have been seen as safe investments at a time when railway mania was rife in India.

The Committee thanked those who had won the Championship by reporting: "Your Committee decided to commemorate the winning of the Championship by gifts to each player, feeling confident that Members would cordially endorse this action." A sting in the tail followed. At the end of the season a proposal by Yorkshire was passed by the Advisory County Committee — "In all representative matches at home, on tours abroad, and in festival and other fixtures organised by county clubs no player who does not pledge himself to assist his county when required shall be invited to take part in such matches."

Will something similar to this proposal be applicable in 2019?

YORKSHIRE'S FIRST CLASS
HIGHLIGHTS OF 1919

Wins by an innings (8)

Yorkshire (380-3 dec) defeated Northamptonshire (72 and 112) by an innings and 196 runs at Northampton

Yorkshire (401-8 dec) defeated Hampshire (82 and 176) by an innings and 143 runs at Dewsbury

Leicestershire (161 and 136) lost to Yorkshire (423) by an innings and 126 runs at Leicester

Yorkshire (448-4 dec) defeated Gloucestershire (121 and 202) by an innings and 125 runs at Leeds

Warwickshire (183 and 107) lost to Yorkshire (381) by an innings and 91 runs at Bradford

Yorkshire (277) defeated Gloucestershire (125 and 89) by an innings and 63 runs at Gloucester

Yorkshire (371-8 dec) defeated Warwickshire (115 and 193) by an innings and 63 runs at Birmingham

Yorkshire (241) defeated Essex (106 and 77) by an innings and 58 runs at Hull

Wins by 10 wickets (2)

Derbyshire (74 and 172) lost to Yorkshire (221 and 26-0) at Bradford

Yorkshire (264 and 25-0) defeated Surrey (143 and 145) at Bradford

Totals of 400 and over (4)

528-8 dec v. MCC at Lord's
448-4 dec v. Gloucestershire at Leeds
423   v. Leicestershire at Leicester
401-8 dec v. Hampshire at Dewsbury

Opponents dismissed for under 100 (6)

72 v. Northamptonshire at Northampton   82 v. Hampshire at Dewsbury
74 v. Derbyshire at Bradford   87 v. Derbyshire at Chesterfield
77 v. Essex at Hull   89 v. Gloucestershire at Gloucester

Century Partnerships (17)

For the 1st wicket (6)

279	H Sutcliffe and P Holmes	v. Northamptonshire at Northampton
253	P Holmes and H Sutcliffe	v. Lancashire at Sheffield
197	P Holmes and H Sutcliffe	v. Leicestershire at Leicester
159	P Holmes and H Sutcliffe	v. Middlesex at Lord's
150	W Rhodes and P Holmes	v. Australian Imperial Force at Sheffield
106	P Holmes and H Sutcliffe	v. Warwickshire at Bradford

For the 2nd wicket (2)

237	H Sutcliffe and D Denton	v. Gloucestershire at Leeds
222	H Sutcliffe and D Denton	v. Kent at Dover

For the 3rd wicket (2)

165	W Rhodes and R Kilner	v. Gloucestershire at Gloucester
100	P Holmes and R Kilner	v. MCC at Lord's

Century Partnerships *(Continued)*

For the 4th wicket (1)

169	R Kilner and G H Hirst	v MCC at Lord's

For the 5th wicket (3)

196*	R Kilner and G H Hirst	v. Gloucestershire at Leeds
118	D Denton and G H Hirst	v. Middlesex at Leeds
106	H Sutcliffe and G H Hirst	v. Kent at Dover

For the 6th wicket (1)

156	W Rhodes and E Robinson	v. Derbyshire at Chesterfield

For the 7th wicket (1)

254	W Rhodes and D C F Burton	v. Hampshire at Dewsbury

For the 10th wicket (1)

103	A Dolphin and E Smith	v. Essex at Leyton

Centuries (22)

P Holmes (5)

140	v. Leicestershire at Leicester
133	v. Northamptonshire at Northampton
133	v. Middlesex at Lord's
123	v. Lancashire at Sheffield
100	v. Nottinghamshire at Nottingham

H Sutcliffe (5)

174	v. Kent at Dover
145	v. Northamptonshire at Northampton
132	v. Lancashire at Sheffield
118	v. Gloucestershire at Leeds
108	v. Middlesex at Lord's

D Denton (4)

122	v. Gloucestershire at Leeds
120	v. Middlesex at Leeds
114	v. Kent at Dover
110	v. Leicestershire at Huddersfield

G H Hirst (3)

180	v. MCC at Lord's
120	v. Essex at Leyton
120	v. Warwickshire at Birmingham

R Kilner (3)

120	v. MCC at Lord's
115	v. Gloucestershire at Leeds
112	v. Gloucestershire at Gloucester

D C F Burton (1)

142	v. Hampshire at Dewsbury

W Rhodes (1)

135	v. Hampshire at Dewsbury

5 wickets in an innings (30)

W Rhodes (11)

- 8 -44 v. Warwickshire at Bradford
- 7 -47 v. Gloucestershire at Gloucester
- 7 -74 v. Nottinghamshire at Sheffield
- 6 -33 v. Northamptonshire at Northampton
- 6 -66 v. Hampshire at Dewsbury
- 5 -16 v. Warwickshire at Birmingham
- 5 -35 v. Kent at Leeds
- 5 -42 v. Middlesex at Lord's 2nd innings
- 5 -46 v. Sussex at Harrogate
- 5 -74 v. Lancashire at Manchester
- 5 -80 v. Middlesex at Lor''s 1st innings

A Waddington (8)

- 6 -58 v. Gloucestershire at Leeds 1st innings
- 6 -66 v. Leicestershire at Huddersfield
- 6 -68 v. Gloucestershire at Leeds 2nd innings
- 5 -30 v. Essex at Hull
- 5 -42 v. Leicestershire at Leicester
- 5 -57 v. Kent at Dover
- 5 -61 v. Surrey at Bradford
- 5 -75 v. Middlesex at Leeds

W E Blackburn (4)

- 5 - 17 v. Derbyshire at Bradford
- 5 - 39 v. Gloucestershire at Gloucester
- 5 - 60 v. Australian Imperial Forces at Sheffield
- 5 -113 v. Cambridge University at Cambridge

E Robinson (2)

- 5 -42 v. Warwickshire at Bradford
- 5 -64 v. Leicestershire at Leicester

A C Williams (2)

- 9 -29 v. Hampshire at Dewsbury
- 5 -67 v. Lancashire at Sheffield

E R Wilson (2)

- 7 -46 v. MCC at Scarborough
- 6 -28 v. Middlesex at Lord's

E Smith (1)

- 5 -138 v. MCC at Lord's

10 wickets in a match (6)

W Rhodes (4)

- 10 -52 (7-47 and 4- 5) v. Gloucestershire at Gloucester
- 10 -67 (4-34 and 6-33) v. Northamptonshire at Northampton
- 10 -122 (5-80 and 5-42) v. Middlesex at Leeds
- 10 - 75 (2-31 and 8-44) v. Warwickshire at Bradford

A Waddington (1)

- 12 -126 (6-58 and 6-68) v. Gloucestershire at Leeds

A C Williams (1)

- 10 -66 (9-29 and 1-37) v. Hampshire at Dewsbury

3 catches in an innings (10)

A Dolphin (5)

4	v. Derbyshire at Bradford 1st innings
4	v. Derbyshire at Bradford 2nd innings
3	v. Australia Imperial Force at Sheffield
3	v. Lancashire at Sheffield
3	v. Kent at Dover

P Holmes (2)

3	v. Leicestershire at Leicester
3	v. MCC at Scarborough

W Rhodes (2)

3	v. Nottinghamshire at Sheffield
3	v. Northamptonshire at Northampton

W E Blackburn (1)

3	v. Lancashire at Manchester

3 dismissals in an innings (7)

A Dolphin (7))

5 (4ct, 1st)	v. Derbyshire at Bradford
4 (2ct, 2st)	v. Nottinghamshire at Nottingham
4 (2ct, 2st)	v. Rest of England at The Oval
3 (1ct, 2st)	v. Warwickshire at Birmingham 1st innings
3 (1ct, 2st)	v. Warwickshire at Birmingham 2nd innings
3 (2ct, 1st)	v. Kent at Leeds
3 (2ct, 1st)	v. Warwickshire at Bradford

5 catches in a match (1)

A Dolphin (1)

8 (4 + 4)	v. Derbyshire at Bradford

Debut (10)

In First Class cricket (9): W E Blackburn, H Sutcliffe, T J Wright, E Robinson, G W A Render, N Kilner, A Waddington, R C J Chichester-Constable and T H Hoyle
Yorkshire (1): G Wilson

Caps (3): P Holmes, H Sutcliffe and A Waddington

100 YEARS AGO

YORKSHIRE AVERAGES 1919

ALL FIRST-CLASS MATCHES

Played 31   Won 12   Lost 5   Drawn 14

County Championship: Played 26   Won 12   Lost 3   Drawn 11

BATTING AND FIELDING *(Qualification 10 completed innings)*

Player	M.	I.	N.O.	Runs	H.S.	100s	50s	Avge	ct/st
H Sutcliffe	31	45	4	1839	174	5	8	44.85	22
P Holmes	31	47	5	1876	140	5	6	44.66	35
G H Hirst	30	37	3	1312	180*	3	5	38.58	21
D Denton	28	39	3	1213	122	4	6	33.69	10
W Rhodes	31	43	9	1138	135	1	8	33.47	28
R Kilner	31	42	4	1135	120	3	6	29.86	24
D C F Burton	27	31	4	685	142*	1	1	25.37	10
A Dolphin	30	30	9	361	62*	0	2	17.19	52/30
E Robinson	20	19	0	283	94	0	1	14.89	14
E Smith	11	14	3	119	49	0	0	10.81	5
A Waddington	20	16	6	65	15*	0	0	6.50	12
Also played									
A C Williams	9	9	7	73	48*	0	0	36.50	4
G Wilson	7	7	0	182	70	0	2	26.00	2
E R Wilson	10	10	2	129	51	0	1	16.12	5
N Kilner	3	4	1	40	29	0	0	13.33	2
T J D Birtles	6	9	0	113	40	0	0	12.55	1
T J Wright	1	1	0	12	12	0	0	12.00	0
H M Claughton	3	4	0	32	15	0	0	8.00	1
G W A Render	1	1	0	5	5	0	0	5.00	0
W E Blackburn	9	11	4	25	6	0	0	3.57	8
T H Hoyle	1	2	0	7	7	0	0	3.50	0
R C J Chichester-Constable	1	1	0	0	0	0	0	0.00	0

BOWLING

(Qualification 10 wickets)

Player	Overs	Mdns	Runs	Wkts	Avge	Best	5wI	10wM
W Rhodes	979.5	279	2233	155	14.40	8 -44	11	4
E R Wilson	279.5	98	597	36	16.58	7 -46	2	0
R Kilner	350.3	117	766	45	17.02	4 -12	0	0
A Waddington	718.1	186	1874	100	18.74	6 -58	8	1
A C Williams	160.2	32	472	25	18.88	9 -29	2	1
W E Blackburn	315.1	45	1058	45	23.51	5 -17	4	0
E Robinson	351.1	106	900	38	23.68	5 -42	2	0
E Smith	398.3	105	885	31	28.54	5-138	1	0
G H Hirst	149	29	441	13	33.92	3 -40	0	0
Also bowled								
H M Claughton	43.4	6	144	2	72.00	1 -27	0	0
R C J Chichester-Constable	4	1	6	0	—	0 - 6	0	0

BLUNT IN CHAMPIONSHIP
BUT SHARP IN GILLETTE

By Anthony Bradbury

Until 1969 Yorkshire had had a splendid run of success in the County Championship throughout the 1960s, winning the title six times in that decade and achieving a hat-trick of being Champion County from 1966 to 68. At the close of the 1968 season Fred Trueman and Ken Taylor had announced their retirements, and Ray Illingworth, having been refused a three-year contract by Brian Sellers, the powerful Cricket Committee chairman, had moved to Leicestershire. The loss of Trueman and Taylor was significant, but understandable. The loss of Illingworth, then aged 36, became a grievous blow, not just because of his skills as an all-rounder, but also because in times of change his great tactical skills were still much needed. In 1969, while a Leicestershire and not a Yorkshire player, he was to be appointed captain of England.

Yet at the start of the 1969 season Yorkshire retained reasonable hopes of another successful Championship season. An early team photograph of the 1969 squad shows 13 players, of whom 11 had or would play for England — those 13 being Leadbeater, Balderstone, Hampshire, Old, Hutton, Nicholson, Boycott, Cope, Sharpe, Binks, Close, Padgett and Wilson. Close, no longer captaining England, remained the powerful inspiring leader, but injury led to his missing nine of the 24 Championship games. Though Jimmy Binks was an experienced substitute captain, the flair and energy of Close were to be much missed.

To win just three of those 24 games was a severe and unexpected blow. The ultimate Champions, Glamorgan, won 11 games, and the runners-up, Gloucestershire, were victorious 10 times. Yorkshire were well behind, and their final position of 13th in a table of 17 teams was to be the worst (at the time) in their long history. There were to be some close calls in the pursuit of victories: by way of example Glamorgan had at Swansea in early May lost nine wickets in their second innings, but hung on for a draw, and immediately afterwards Warwickshire won by Bradford by five runs. Then there was an extraordinary draw against Lancashire at Bramall Lane in August when Yorkshire, having been in charge throughout much of the match, were left to score 65 runs in 19 overs to be winners. At the start of the last over they had three wickets down and needed one to win. Higgs was the Lancashire bowler.

Leadbeater was lbw to the third ball; Wilson was stumped two balls later, and Hutton was caught off the last ball of the game.

There must have been much angst in the dressing room a few minutes later. At the other end had been that year's beneficiary, Doug Padgett, a fine player who with 983 Championship runs did better than any of his colleagues.

But even if Yorkshire had won those three close games they would still have finished in the bottom half of the table.

It was not an easy summer in which to be a batsman. Too much rain, and too many bowlers taking advantage of good conditions saw to that, but on truer wickets

Experienced stand-in: Jimmy Binks, who was soon to retire, captained Yorkshire in the absence of Brian Close.
(Photo: Mick Pope Archive)

Boycott, Hampshire and Sharpe (and Illingworth) all scored Test centuries. Hampshire, to the delight of all, became the first Englishman to score a century in his maiden Test innings at Lord's.

Only Boycott from all those who played for his county that year managed a single century for Yorkshire – 105 not out in a drawn game against Somerset. Two Somerset players, Galley and Roy Palmer, played out the last 15 overs without a run being scored, each coming in on 0 not out.

English Test calls and injuries to others, including not just Close but Nicholson also, did give opportunities to others. Chris Old made rapid progress, taking 57 wickets in all Yorkshire matches at an average of 18.61. He was given his county cap in August, and in 1970 he was playing for England.

Barrie Leadbeater, of whom more below, made some steady progress and was given his cap in the unlikely month of November. Among Colts chosen for the Yorkshire side for the first time were Rodney Smith, a solid league batsman, Andrew Dalton, an attractive batsman and left-arm bowler Mike Bore. Bore played first-class matches for Yorkshire

YORKSHIRE 1969. Back row, left to right: Barrie Leadbeater, Chris Balderstone, John Hampshire, Chris Old, Richard Hutton, Tony Nicholson, Geoffrey Boycott and Geoff Cope. Front row: Philip Sharpe, Jimmy Binks, Brian Close (captain), Doug Padgett and Don Wilson.
(Photo: Sport and General Press Agency)

LOST LEADER: All-rounder Raymond Illingworth, who left Yorkshire to captain Leicestershire...and England

and Nottinghamshire on a somewhat sporadic basis for the best part of 20 years.

The innovation of the season was the introduction of the 40-over-per-side John Player League, games that took place on Sunday afternoons and which became hugely popular.

By way of comparison when Yorkshire played Essex in the Championship at Sheffield the attendance was 2,744. That was on June 21, 23 and 24. On the intervening Sunday, June 22, when those two teams played the 40-overs fixture at Hull, the attendance was 4,135.

The gate receipts for the three days at Sheffield were £482, and for one day at Hull £940. No wonder the county treasurers were rubbing their hands in glee. Gate receipts for the seven home Sunday fixtures totalled £5,158 against £6,492 for 15 Championship and Tourist games, or potentially 45 days.

Within the John Player League Yorkshire performed satisfactorily. They finished in eighth position, winning and losing seven games with two no-results. Asserting its editorial priority the *Yorkshire Yearbook* in 1970 (dealing with the 1969 season) gave the scorecards for these League matches after the scorecards for the 1969 Yorkshire Second Eleven. No batsman scored a century, and Philip Sharpe topped those League averages with 292 runs at 36.33.

Richard Hutton took most wickets, 22 at 18.86, and as he also scored useful runs he illustrated the value of all-rounders in this competition. Not all commentators were impressed. That tremendous Yorkshire enthusiast Anthony (Tony) Woodhouse wrote about the 1969 season in his subsequent (1989) *History of Yorkshire County Cricket Club*: "There are many who claim that county cricket was saved by the advent of the 40-overs Sunday League. That is true if one accepts that the ills that had smitten county cricket since the war were to be shoved under the carpet instead of an effort being made to cure them. Another school of thought would claim that limited-overs cricket has ruined county cricket and that all grades of English cricket have fallen to astonishingly low levels..."

Thirty years on from that writing the argument continues to rage.

There was one area of limited-overs cricket in which Yorkshire did thrive. The Gillette Cup, started in 1963 and now played over 60 overs a side, had become another winner with the public, and Yorkshire, having won that competition in 1965 on the back of an astonishing Boycott century, were to win again in 1969. Though they started by being bowled out by Minor County Norfolk for 167, they bowled out their opponents for 78. That banana skin having been averted, they then had confident and easy victories against Lancashire, Surrey and Nottinghamshire. What might Brian Close have muttered when lbw for 96 to Intikhab Alam at The Oval?

The final was to be against underdogs Derbyshire in front of a full house at Lord's. Geoffrey Boycott had broken a finger, so an unlikely opening partnership of Barrie Leadbeater and John Woodford, sent in to bat, took Yorkshire to a quiet start. Leadbeater, batting with a fractured finger and making 76, was the rock around which Close, Padgett and Hutton provided impetus. A score of 219-8 in 60 overs might not seem much of a target in 2019 — some might consider it achievable in 20 overs — but it was too much for Derbyshire, particularly when Close asked Nicholson to bowl his 12 overs in one spell, and just 14 runs resulted. Yorkshire won comfortably by 69 runs and Leadbeater was man-of-the-match. No one could possibly have imagined that Yorkshire

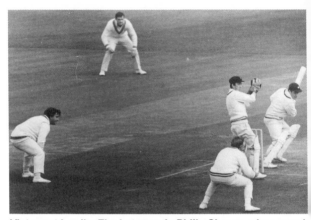

**Victory at Lord's: The batsman is Philip Sharpe, who scored
101 and 37 as Yorkshire beat MCC by seven wickets late on
the third day at headquarters in 1969. Bob Taylor, of
Derbyshire and England, is behind the stumps, and Colin
Milburn, of Northamptonshire and England is at leg-slip.**
(Photo: Mick Pope Archive)

would win this form of one-day competition only once more in the following 49 years.

Yorkshire finished their season on a high, but still well down on their
aspirations for that 1969 summer. The admirable Jimmy Binks was soon
to announce his retirement. He was aged only 34, but 491 matches for
Yorkshire, 412 of them in consecutive Championship games, had been a
remarkable achievement for him, and he had also played Test cricket.
His stability and acumen would be missed in 1970, but Close was to
remain captain, and hopes for the future of Yorkshire cricket remained
strong. The writer in *Wisden* 1970, reviewing the Yorkshire season, concluded: "Few doubt that Yorkshire, who played 10 Colts during the season, will soon be among the sides in the Championship race once more."

Yorkshire did do better in 1970 Championship cricket, but there was
to be a thunderbolt at the end of that season which would affect the
county for years to come. This article next year will have the details.

RICHARD IS STILL BETTER
THAN ALL OF THE REST

By John Potter

A new One–Day competition began in 1969 with every county playing each other once in a match of 40 overs per side. Yorkshire finished eighth with seven wins and seven losses and two matches abandoned without a ball bowled. *Roses* rivals Lancashire were the League's first winners.

The highlight for Yorkshire was Richard Hutton's 7-15 off 7.4 overs against Worcestershire at Leeds on June 29, giving Yorkshire a win by 97 runs. This is still Yorkshire's best List A bowling 50 years on. The only other bowler to take seven wickets in a List A match is Darren Gough with 7-27 against Ireland at Leeds in 1997.

Yorkshire faired much better in the Gillette Cup, which they won for the second time. They started with a rain-hit match at Lakenham against Norfolk. Play did not begin until 4.30pm, Yorkshire batting first and posting a total of 167, T I Moore taking 4-16. This score never looked like being passed by Norfolk on the second day, as they were all out for 78, the last six wickets falling for 23 runs.

The next round took Yorkshire to Manchester in front of a crowd of nearly 10,000. The *Red Rose* found runs hard to come, their openers managing only 16 off 17 overs, and they closed their innings at 173-8 off 60 overs. Geoff Boycott and Philip Sharpe put on 137 in an opening stand, and with 11.1 overs and seven wickets to spare the *White Rose* had inflicted a humiliating defeat. Surrey were seen off at The Oval as Boycott and Brian Close added 159 for the second wicket, both departing in the nineties as Yorkshire were all out for 272. Surrey never looked like reaching their target, and were all out for 134 as Don Wilson took four wickets and Tony Nicholson three.

Nottinghamshire provided the opposition in the semi-final at Scarborough. The gates were closed with 15,242 people paying £5,230, which was believed to be the ground record. Yorkshire quickly lost Boycott and Barrie Leadbeater, but a third-wicket stand of 101 by Sharpe and Doug Padgett helped them to 191 all out. Nottinghamshire's openers put on 40, but at a slow rate, and when Garry Sobers fell to a catch behind Yorkshire took control as they bowled Nottinghamshire out for 123. Chris Old and Stringer each took three wickets.

Last hurrah for Close: Yorkshire celebrate their Gillette Cup triumph of 1969, but the sacking of skipper Brian Close was little more than a year away. Left to right: Tony Nicholson, Richard Hutton, Close, Jimmy Binks, Philip Sharpe, Don Wilson and John Hampshire. *(Photo: Mick Pope Archive)*

BARRIE LEADBEATER
The rock around which Yorkshire's Gillette Cup triumph was built

Yorkshire travelled to Lord's without Boycott, out with a broken finger, to play Derbyshire in the final. Yorkshire were asked to bat first, and Leadbeater held them together with 76 as Yorkshire took their total to 219-8 off their 60 overs.

Yorkshire kept a tight rein on Derbyshire as Old and Nicholson opened the attack, Nicholson bowling his 12 overs in a single spell for 14 runs. Close and Wilson had three wickets each.

Leadbeater took the man-of-the-match award. He, too, had a broken finger, but he had it strapped in order to play.

The match was a sell out with 21,000 in attendance.

John Potter is Yorkshire CCC Scorer

YORKSHIRE'S FIRST CLASS HIGHLIGHTS OF 1969

Win by an innings (1)

Yorkshire (202) defeated Gloucestershire (42 and 108) by an innings and 53 runs at Leeds

Win by 10 wickets (1)

Oxford University (90 and 152) lost to Yorkshire (227 and 16-0) at Oxford

Totals of 400 and over (none)

Opponents dismissed for under 100 (3)

41	v. Gloucestershire at Middlesbrough	90	v. Oxford University at Oxford
72	v. Warwickshire at Bradford		

Century Partnerships (12)

For the 1st wicket (5)

125	R A Hutton and J D Woodford	v. New Zealand at Bradford
119	D E V Padgett and B Leadbeater	v. Derbyshire at Leeds
115	B Leadbeater and J D Woodford	v. Worcestershire at Sheffield
103	G Boycott and B Leadbeater	v. Oxford University at Oxford
101	P J Sharpe and J D Woodford	v. Middlesex at Harrogate

For the 2nd wicket (2)

148	PJ Sharpe and D B Close	v. Leicestershire at Leeds
101	B Leadbeater and D E V Padgett	v. Kent at Folkstone

For the 3rd wicket (2)

135	P J Sharpe and J H Hampshire	v. MCC at Lord's
121	P J Sharpe and D E V Padgett	v. Sussex at Hove

For the 4th wicket (2)

142	D B Close and C Johnson	v. New Zealand at Bradford
109	C Johnson and J H Hampshire	v. Somerset at Weston-Super-Mare

For the 7th wicket (1)

111	J G Binks and C M Old	v. Derbyshire at Leeds

Centuries (3)

G Boycott (1)

   105*   v. Somerset at Leeds

D B Close (1)

   146   v. New Zealanders at Bradford

P J Sharpe (1)

   101   v. MCC at Lord's

5 wickets in an innings (9)

D Wilson (4)

    7- 19 v. MCC at Scarborough
    6- 36 v. Leicestershire at Leicester
    5- 66 v. Kent at Folkstone
    5- 114 v. Derbyshire at Chesterfield

R A Hutton (2)

    7-39 v. Somerset at Leeds
    5-55 v. Hampshire at Bournemouth

C M Old (2)

    7-20 v. Gloucestershire at Middlesbrough
    5-34 v. Lancashire at Sheffield

G A Cope (1)

    5-49 v. Somerset at Weston-Super-Mare

10 wickets in a match (1)

CM Old (1)

    11-46 (7-20 and 4-26)   v. Gloucestershire at Middlesbrough

3 catches in an innings (12)

J G Binks (5)

    5   v. Essex at Sheffield
    4   v. Oxford University at Oxford
    3   v. Middlesex at Lord's
    3   v. Gloucestershire at Gloucester
    3   v. Somerset at Weston-Supe-Mare

R A Hutton (2)

    3   v. Worcestershire at Sheffield
    3   v. Lancashire at Sheffield

P J Sharpe (2)

    3   v. Derbyshire at Chesterfield
    3   v. Somerset at Leeds

J H Hampshire (1)

    3   v. Somerset at Weston-Super-Mare

C M Old (1)

    3   v. Lancashire at Manchester

D Wilson (1)

    5   v. Surrey at The Oval

3 dismissals in an innings (1)

J G Binks (1)

    5 (4ct, 1st) v. Oxford University at Oxford

5 catches in a match (3)

J G Binks (2)

    5 (5)   v. Essex at Sheffield
    5 (2 + 3) v. Somerset at Weston-Super-Mare

D Wilson (1)

    5 (5)   v. Surrey at The Oval

Debut (4)

In First Class cricket: C Johnson, R Smith, M K Bore and A J Dalton
Caps awarded: C M Old and B Leadbeater

50 YEARS AGO

YORKSHIRE AVERAGES 1969

ALL FIRST-CLASS MATCHES

Played 29   Won 4   Lost 7   Drawn 18

County Championship: Played 24   Won 3   Lost 6   Drawn 15

BATTING AND FIELDING *(Qualification 10 completed innings)*

Player	M.	I.	N.O.	Runs	H.S.	100s	50s	Avge	ct/st
G Boycott	16	26	4	843	105*	1	6	38.31	9
P J Sharpe	18	29	2	1,012	101	1	4	37.48	20
D B Close	20	27	4	812	146	1	4	35.30	10
J H Hampshire	21	32	3	863	93	0	7	29.75	12
D E V Padgett	27	45	8	1078	83	0	7	29.13	12
J D Woodford	11	16	1	422	56	0	1	28.13	4
B Leadbeater	17	31	1	771	77	0	6	25.70	9
C Johnson	8	13	1	255	61*	0	1	21.25	6
R A Hutton	29	42	7	734	75	0	4	20.97	24
J G Binks	29	37	8	497	76	0	1	17.13	57
D Wilson	27	36	3	474	54	0	1	14.36	16
C M Old	22	26	7	195	40	0	0	10.26	10
A G Nicholson	26	22	9	106	22*	0	0	8.15	5
G A Cope	23	26	9	113	24*	0	0	6.64	9

Also batted

Player	M.	I.	N.O.	Runs	H.S.	100s	50s	Avge	ct/st
R Smith	4	7	3	97	37*	0	0	24.25	0
J C Balderstone	8	7	1	109	44	0	0	18.16	3
M K Bore	4	4	2	35	20*	0	0	17.50	2
P M Stringer	7	6	0	40	13	0	0	6.66	1
A J Dalton	2	3	0	19	12	0	0	6.33	1

BOWLING *(Qualification 10 wickets)*

Player	Overs	Mdns	Runs	Wkts	Avge	Best	5wI	10wM
D Wilson	931.1	374	1705	101	16.88	7 -19	4	0
C M Old	433	97	1061	57	18.61	7 -20	2	1
P M Stringer	113.2	19	268	12	22.33	2 - 9	0	0
R A Hutton	598.2	137	1530	66	23.18	7 -39	2	0
A G Nicholson	620.4	185	1380	56	24.64	4 -22	0	0
G A Cope	484.3	174	1171	43	27.23	5 -49	1	0

Also bowled

Player	Overs	Mdns	Runs	Wkts	Avge	Best	5wI	10wM
M K Bore	95.1	34	185	8	23.12	3 -26	0	0
J C Balderstone	41.5	16	95	3	31.66	3 -29	0	0
D B Close	115	47	282	7	40.28	1 - 4	0	0
C Johnson	28	6	84	1	84.00	1 -53	0	0
G Boycott	4.3	2	13	0	—	0 - 1	0	0
P J Sharpe	2.4	0	10	0	—	0 -10	0	0
D E V Padgett	1	0	4	0	—	0 - 4	0	0
J D Woodford	1	0	14	0	—	0 -14	0	0

50 YEARS AGO

YORKSHIRE AVERAGES 1969

LIST A

Played 19   Won 12   Lost 7   Abandoned 2

BATTING AND FIELDING

BATTING AND FIELDING (Qualification 4 completed innings)

Player	M.	I.	N.O.	Runs	H.S.	100s	50s	Avge	ct/st
P J Sharpe	13	13	0	452	81	0	5	34.76	7
B Leadbeater	11	11	1	342	76	0	3	34.20	6
G Boycott	11	11	1	335	92	0	3	33.50	6
D B Close	12	12	0	263	96	0	2	21.91	8
J D Woodford	9	9	0	175	56	0	1	19.44	3
R A Hutton	19	15	4	197	65	0	1	17.90	7
J C Balderstone	9	8	2	104	46	0	0	17.33	2
D Wilson	18	17	3	220	46	0	0	15.71	8
D E V Padgett	17	17	1	227	46	0	0	14.18	4
J G Binks	19	15	2	175	34	0	0	13.46	17/4
C M Old	16	12	4	99	22	0	0	12.37	7
J H Hampshire	15	15	1	148	55	0	1	10.57	4
A G Nicholson	16	9	5	8	2*	0	0	2.00	3

Also batted

Player	M.	I.	N.O.	Runs	H.S.	100s	50s	Avge	ct/st
A J Dalton	1	1	0	27	27	0	0	27.00	0
P M Stringer	11	8	6	29	13*	0	0	14.50	0
R Smith	2	2	0	17	17	0	0	8.50	1
C Johnson	4	4	1	18	11	0	0	6.00	1
R G Lumb	1	1	0	0	0	0	0	0.00	0
M K Bore	4	1	1	0	0*	0	0	—	2
G A Cope	1	0	0	0	—	0	0	—	1

BOWLING

BOWLING (Qualification 4 wickets)

Player	Overs	Mdns	Runs	Wkts	Avge	Best	4wI	RPO
D Wilson	147.3	34	435	29	15.00	6-18	3	2.94
C M Old	120.2	18	404	26	15.53	3-14	0	3.35
A G Nicholson	133	24	390	25	15.60	3-15	0	2.93
P M Stringer	70.2	10	256	15	17.06	4-35	1	3.63
J D Woodford	12	0	69	4	17.25	3-42	0	5.75
R A Hutton	153.4	20	529	29	18.24	7-15	1	3.44
D B Close	48	11	162	7	23.14	3-16	0	3.37

Also bowled

Player	Overs	Mdns	Runs	Wkts	Avge	Best	4wI	RPO
G A Cope	8	2	24	3	8.00	3-24	0	3.00
J C Balderstone	9	9	28	1	28.00	1-10	0	3.11
M K Bore	32	11	71	0	—	0-11	0	2.21

REMEMBERING NEIL LLOYD — A SPECIAL CRICKETER

By Andrew Bosi

People of a certain age remember where they were when they heard of the assassination of President Kennedy. I recall the same sense of shock when I learned of the death of Neil Lloyd. I was at Beckenham Cricket Club, and overheard a conversation between two people who, as far as I know, had no connection with Yorkshire.

Neil Lloyd was 17 years and 114 days old — five years younger than Martyn Moxon. He had already played two seasons with the Yorkshire Second Eleven and represented England in Under-19 Tests. In the first season, 1981, his top score was the highest of a match against Middlesex Seconds at Uxbridge, 65; in the second he made two centuries, both against Lancashire. He died that September, following the contraction of a rare virus.

The young Lloyd lived for cricket, and he regarded playing for Yorkshire as a far greater honour than representing England Under-19s. Shortly before his second-team debut he carried out 12th man duties for the first team at Edgbaston. I can still recall the sheer joy on his face as he left the field in company with the Yorkshire team, eight of whom had or would gain international recognition. His bedroom was a shrine to Geoffrey Boycott, whom he followed into the Ackworth side.

The Yorkshire Southern Group had been formed only recently, and it was decided that an annual award should be made each year to a young player uncapped at the start of the season. The Award was dedicated to the memory of Neil Lloyd, and is made at the start of the following season based on the votes of Southern Group members.

Understandably with the passage of time winners of the Award — Matthew Fisher in the 2017 season —are no longer aware of Neil Lloyd or the significance of the dedication. The Group has considered whether it remains appropriate to remember Neil in this way, and has agreed that it is. Neil is the only entry in Tony Woodhouse's *Who's Who of Yorkshire County Cricket Club* (1992) not to have played first-class cricket for Yorkshire. He really was that special.

Star-struck: Neil Lloyd, right, and a young Martyn Moxon welcome Graham Gooch to a meeting of the Wombwell Cricket Lovers' Society in 1980. Gooch was to captain Essex and England and become the most prolific batsmen across all formats of the game; Moxon, a future international, was to captain Yorkshire and is now the Club's Director of Professional Cricket. *(Photo: Mick Pope Archive)*

WINNERS OF THE NEIL LLOYD YOUNG CRICKETER AWARD

1982	M D Moxon	1983	M D Moxon	1984	P E Robinson
1985	P Jarvis	1986	A A Metcalfe	1987	R J Blakey
1988	S D Fletcher	1989	R J Blakey	1990	R J Blakey
1991	J D Batty	1992	S A Kellett	1993	D Gough
1994	D Gough	1995	A McGrath	1996	C W Silverwood
1997	P M Hutchison	1998	M J Wood	1999	R J Sidebottom
2000	R J Sidebottom	2001	R J Dawson	2002	R J Dawson
2003	T T Bresnan	2004	T T Bresnan	2005	J J Sayers
2006	A U Rashid	2007	A U Rashid	2008	A U Rashid
2009	J M Bairstow	2010	A Lyth	2011	J M Bairstow
2012	J E Root	2013	A Z Lees	2014	J A Leaning
2015	W M H Rhodes	2016	no award	2017	M D Fisher

HOW HIRST AND BRADMAN
LIT UP AYLESTONE ROAD

By Nigel Pullan

I left Grace Road early so that I could go down to Aylestone Road. This ground is nearer to the centre of Leicester. Electricity Sports Second Eleven were playing. I wandered around the ground, and then sat in the old pavilion among the players. Then I realised that everyone was looking at me and wondering why I was there.

So I explained that I had come to see the ground where George Hirst made 341 against Leicestershire in 1905. It is still the highest score for Yorkshire after all these years. In 2006 Darren Lehmann made 339 against Durham at Headingley, and possibly got out to preserve Hirst's record.

This Aylestone Road ground was opened in 1901, and looking at illustrations I would guess that it is the same pavilion as was used in 1905. It even survived occupation of the ground in the Second World War by the American Pioneer Corps. So we could well be climbing up the same steps as George Hirst used in 1905.

The players were welcoming, and showed me some mementos kept in the pavilion, including a framed copy of the local paper's report on the Leicestershire v. Australians match in 1930. It was the tradition for tourists to start at Worcester, and then move on to Leicester.

As this was Don Bradman's first tour of England this would be his second appearance in this country. On his English debut at Worcester he had made 236. There was, of course, no TV, newsreels perhaps, but for most of the crowd it would have been their first sight of Bradman. It would probably be a half-day's holiday. Large crowds would come in from the hosiery factories and local businesses, mostly men, mostly standing around the ground. They would see Bradman coming down these steps, maybe comment on how small he was. His first 50 actually took two hours, and then he moved on to 185 not out before rain ended the match.

I was discussing cricket with a friend, as one does. He said the best innings he had ever seen was when Len Hutton made 269 not out in 1949. You might expect great innings to be played in great arenas, Lord's perhaps or The Oval or on a home ground like Bramall Lane or

Headingley. But this innings was at Wellingborough School against Northamptonshire. Hutton made his runs out of 523-8, and this is what *Wisden* says:

"A great not-out 269 by Hutton reduced almost everything else to insignificance. After playing himself in he exploited nearly all the strokes with astonishing ease and assurance, and during a stay of 6½ hours scarcely made a mistake. His chief hits were 32 fours."

And no sixes!

The most memorable feature of the Wellingborough School ground, where Yorkshire played in 1981, is a small thatched pavilion in one corner. Just outside its white gate is a stone slab in the grass. I enquired about this, and was told it was W G Grace's doorstep. There was a master at the school devoted to cricket and its history. He heard that there was to be a sale of the effects of Grace, so off he went and returned with his doorstep. So Len Hutton would walk on it in 1949, as would small boys making their debut for Wellingborough School Under-14s.

Some outstanding performances are achieved on important grounds. Hedley Verity took his 10-10 at Headingley while building works were being carried out on the stand just demolished. But the record Verity beat was 10-18, a world record at the time, by George Geary, and this was achieved at Pontypridd. I went to Ynysangharad Park on a wet week in September. It is a small, modest ground in a splendid park built as a war memorial by the town and opened by Field Marshal Lord Allenby in 1923. Glamorgan had first played there in 1926, so Geary's record in 1929 was set on a new outground in South Wales.

In my match in 1989 we had a rain-interrupted first day and perhaps a record short second day when 13 balls were bowled. There was some consolation for two Yorkshiremen sheltering in a dripping tent: if Glamorgan had taken seven points from the game Yorkshire, who had completed their fixtures, would have finished bottom of the Championship table.

A final ground wander in the footsteps of George Geary, who took that 10-18. He was born at Barwell in Leicestershire, where the county played three first-class matches in 1946 and 1947. I visited Barwell recently when a league match was being played. They had information about Geary's career but, better than that I was shown the house just outside the ground where he was born. He came from a family of 16 living in a terraced house and went on to play 14 Tests for England. His first was at Headingley in 1926, when he and George Macaulay added 108 for the ninth wicket against Australia. And he took 4-85 in 35 overs in that match at Aylestone Road where our wanderings began.

AN INTREPID TRAVELLER
AND CRICKET SUPREMO

By Jeremy Lonsdale

TOM EMMETT: Gruelling life in Victorian England

Today's top-class cricketers travel the world to appear in different competitions and forms of the game, and they must get used to long journeys and varied climates.

As demanding as this may be modern players at least have the benefit of travelling in comfort and safety, and with their needs usually taken care of by others.

Looking back 150 years, the top players could rely on none of this, and for men like the great Yorkshire all-rounder, Tom Emmett (1841-1904), making a good living from the different formats of the Victorian game involved a gruelling life on the road.

Emmett was one of the most significant figures in English cricket in the 19th Century. In the 1860s he once took 16 first-class wickets in an afternoon for Yorkshire, remarkable regardless of the weakness of the opposition. In the 1870s only one other player scored over 4,000 runs and also took over 400 wickets in English first-class cricket: W G Grace. In the 1880s Emmett had the most successful season of his career as a bowler at the age of nearly 45 before retiring in 1888 with a total of 1,572 first-class wickets at 13.55 and over 9,000 runs to his name. For Yorkshire, he provided stability and quality to a county side which experienced many highs and lows during this period.

Emmett's ability to earn a living as a professional cricketer was dependent on his willingness to make endless journeys on the expanding Victorian rail network or in horse-drawn vehicles. Such travel was no fun, and as one writer has put it, for cricketers like Emmett...journeys were arduous, trains were slow...sometimes their journeys began in long-distance trains, and the victims finished their ordeal, aching with cramp and sheer fatigue, in wagonettes or, in times of emergency, even farm carts. In May or September journeys that went on through the night and into the sharp early morning could leave the wanderers hungry and bitterly cold.

Emmett was renowned for his cheerful nature and good humour. Yet, for all that, he took the game very seriously because it was his livelihood, and he had to provide for a large family. This helps to explain why he pieced together his gruelling schedule of fixtures — some in local cricket, some for and against the famous touring XIs, and others in the growing number of county matches. To take one season — 1869 — he travelled an estimated minimum of 4,000 miles between May and September. This included two trips to London and an overnight journey from Chesterfield to Glasgow. He was away from home for long periods, and frequently played back-to-back matches. Between June 14 and July 7 he played cricket on 20 days out of 24 — in one Yorkshire game, a Players v. Gentlemen match, and in five All-England Eleven and United South of England Eleven fixtures.

If the travel was tiring it could also be dangerous. In 1868 Tom appeared at Somercotes in Derbyshire. The match was less remarkable for the play than for an accident involving Yorkshire players Luke Greenwood, George Freeman and Emmett as they were travelling to their lodgings in an omnibus. The vehicle came apart and overturned, with the result that Greenwood suffered such serious injuries that initially he was not expected to live. Freeman, Emmett and several others were badly cut and bruised. Readers of one paper, the *Huddersfield Chronicle*, might reasonably have feared for Greenwood's life, but a later addition to the story stated that earlier reports had been "slightly exaggerated", and he lived. To make matters worse for Emmett, having escaped from the accident he was handed a telegram notifying him of the sudden terrible death of one of his young children. Despite his injuries and this tragic news he seems to have recovered, and a week later he was with the United All-England Eleven in Northampton, where he took 17 wickets and top-scored in the second innings. Life went on.

A common feature of Emmett's existence was overnight travel. Frequently, he would take off immediately after a day's play — often after some of his greatest performances — to travel hundreds of miles through the night to start again on a new ground before midday. In 1868 he took 9-34 against Nottinghamshire at Dewsbury, one of his best-ever bowling figures for Yorkshire, but then travelled overnight to play for the United All-England Eleven in Bristol. Luckily, his side batted first and Emmett was not needed until the end of the innings. The same summer he appeared in Chesterfield, where he took 22 wickets against the local Twenty-Two, bowling for much of the game. The reward for this performance was an overnight trip from Derbyshire to Glasgow to start the next morning. The onerous travelling appeared to have little impact on Emmett, who had figures of 48-27-48-11 and 45-27-21-3. But it could take its toll. In 1873 Emmett and the Yorkshire side caught a 10 o'clock evening train from London to Bristol, arriving at 6.30am. After getting little sleep they conceded over 400 to Gloucestershire on the first day, and Emmett bowled over 50 overs without taking a wicket.

The 1860s and 1870s saw the growth of overseas tours for English cricketers, which were great opportunities to popularise the game and, for professionals, to earn more money over the winter. Emmett made three long journeys to Australia in 1876-77, 1878-79 and 1881-82, and to North America in 1879. For Emmett they were chances not to be missed, but also a challenge, since he suffered terribly from sea-sickness. His dislike of sailing was so bad that in the summer of 1881 he took short boat trips while playing at Scarborough and Brighton so that the shock might be lessened when he came to cross the Atlantic.

Descriptions of these overseas tours emphasise what great experiences they must have been for a man who grew up in industrial Halifax. Emmett enjoyed his visits to Australia, particularly loving the climate in Tasmania. The tours were also full of incident and adventure. While in New Zealand during the 1876-77 tour he was involved in a terrible 80-hour journey to Christchurch, when one of the party's coaches broke down in the middle of the Otira Gorge as the river rose. Their horses had to be pulled out of the raging water, while fellow Yorkshireman Tom Armitage carried a female passenger to safety. The group found shelter, and the players slept on the floor in front of an open fire, eventually getting to their destination in time for a match with the local side for which they were very badly prepared.

In 1881-82 Emmett went with Alfred Shaw's team to Australia via the United States. The journey across the Atlantic was very rough, and Emmett was so frightened by the rolling of the ship that he was unable to eat. The team played matches on the east coast, and then set off on a 3,000-mile train journey through the "wild west" to San Francisco to catch the boat for Australia. They stopped off to play in St Louis, where the local side had to be made up with baseball players because cricket was not sufficiently popular to generate a full team. Emmett and his fellow players afterwards crossed the Mississippi River and the plains of Nebraska, then Wyoming, through the Black Mountains and across the Laramie Plains, and into the Rocky Mountains. At times the train was so slow that the players and a regiment of soldiers who accompanied them got out and ran alongside it. Later they changed for Salt Lake City, passed snow-topped mountains, and crossed deserts, where the dust continually filled their carriages. They travelled through the Sierra Nevada at night and arrived in San Francisco after five and a half days of travelling. The journey across America by train had been possible for only just over a decade when Emmett made it, and was not without risk.

Playing at a time when many people in England stayed fairly close to home throughout their lives, cricket gave Tom Emmett great opportunities to travel at home and abroad. It was a tiring existence, and he probably covered over 200,000 miles in his lifetime, but it was a life full of excitement and interest. Without the willingness and ability of men like Emmett to spend long periods away from home and to travel to all parts to popularise cricket among people eager for new forms of entertainment the game's development as a major national sport might well have been significantly different.

Jeremy Lonsdale is the author of *Tom Emmett: The Spirit of Yorkshire Cricket*, published by ACS Publications in 2018 (available at www.acscricket.com). He is also the author of *A Game Taken Seriously: The Foundations of Yorkshire's Cricketing Power*, also published by ACS Publications in 2017, which covers the development of cricket in Yorkshire in the 19th Century.

Hard work rewarded

Wicket-keeper batsman Jonny Tattersall in December signed a new three-year contract with Yorkshire. He penned a provisional one-year extension for 2019 mid-way though the 2018 season, but will now stay at Emerald Headingley until the end of 2021.

The Harrogate-born, former England Under-19s player made one first-team appearance in 2013, scoring a duck against Glamorgan in a one-day fixture, before being released at the end of 2015. He impressed after being invited back to play in the second team towards the end of 2016, and likewise the following season, earning himself a one-year deal for 2018.

CLERGYMAN CRICKETER WHO 'DISCOVERED' LORD HAWKE

By Nigel Pullan

REVEREND E S CARTER — A Yorkshire Cricketing Cleric **By Tony Bradbury** *(ACS Publications £15, available at www.acscricket.com)*

REV. E S CARTER
(Photo: Mick Pope Archive)

The Rev. Edmund Sardinson Carter was the man who first invited Lord Hawke to play for Yorkshire.

In a match at Harewood House on August 28, 1878, between Harewood and Yorkshire Gentlemen, the Hon Martin Hawke, a lanky schoolboy on holiday at Wighill, came in to bat for Harewood and was bowled by Carter for only two runs.

It began a close friendship, an association with Yorkshire Gentlemen and a place in the Yorkshire side at the Scarborough Festival in 1881. "It was the best day's work I ever did," Carter recalled.

This excellent book, assiduously researched by Tony Bradbury, tells the story of a conscientious Victorian churchman, an accomplished musician, a father of eight children and an active all-round sportsman who played 15 games for Yorkshire.

Edmund's father was Perpetual Curate at Malton, Rector of Burythorpe and then of Slingsby. Edmund went to Durham School and Worcester College, Oxford. There he achieved something that would be impossible today — he won both cricket and rowing blues. After five years in Ealing he came back north in 1875 to be Vicar Choral at York Minster. He was made curate of St Martin-cum-Gregory Church on Micklegate, and then Perpetual Curate, effectively Vicar, of St Michael-le-Belfrey, next to the Minster. Tony Bradbury's account of life in 19th Century York is an important feature of this biography.

Apparently the Dean of York did not approve of Edmund Carter playing in cricket matches. But he had appointed a man dedicated to the game. He had played at Oxford and at Ealing, but Yorkshire Gentlemen was his team. He was an all-rounder, a hard-hitting batsman and fast bowler, but he also bowled lobs or what he called twisters, and occasionally kept wicket. He well understood the value of a parson being an active sportsman.

Carter's appearances for Yorkshire are covered in detail. His debut was at Prince's Ground v. Middlesex in May 1876 in Roger Iddison's last match for Yorkshire. Although most of his matches were at Scarborough he captained Yorkshire at Cheltenham where "Mr Carter, after rattling up 15 in four hits, returned one to Mr Grace." He was also much involved in the Scarborough Festival as player and official and talent-spotted Edmund Peate.

Edmund Carter retired from York in 1908 and became Vicar of Thwing until his death in 1923, aged 78. This fine account of "muscular Christianity" at its best in Victorian Yorkshire is strongly recommended.

Waite's new deal

Leeds-born all-rounder Matthew Waite has penned a new one-year contract extension, keeping him at Emerald Headingley until the end of next season. He had ankle surgery after missing the second half of 2017, and spent nearly two months on the sidelines in the early stages of 2018. However, Yorkshire's Young Player of the Year in 2016 returned impressively, and ended last season strongly in the Specsavers County Championship team, playing three out of the last four matches and returning some useful contributions with bat and ball.

DAVE CALLAGHAN

By David Warner

DAVE CALLAGHAN
Batting for Yorkshire

The Yorkshire cricket media and players, officials and supporters of Yorkshire County Cricket Club were all shocked by the sudden death on March 12 last year of Dave Callaghan at the age of 63.

Dave had justifiably earned the tag *The Voice of Yorkshire Cricket* for his reporting of Yorkshire matches for Radio Leeds and his on-line ball-by-ball commentaries. Perhaps more than anyone else in his profession he was held in the highest esteem by his media colleagues and players alike.

He gave tirelessly of his time in fronting a wide variety of events for Yorkshire CCC, and was closely involved with the Dickie Bird Foundation, for which he helped to raise thousands of pounds.

Three days before his death Dave had lunched with Dickie Bird before returning to his Wetherby home, where he collapsed with a heart attack and never regained consciousness.

A former sports editor of Radio Leeds, Dave also worked for the Rugby League in between his two spells of reporting on Yorkshire cricket for the BBC. His popularity was such that a darts tournament he was due to host last June was renamed The Dave Callaghan Memorial Darts Knockout Competition. It had been organised by The Otley Tavern in association with the Dickie Bird Foundation.

In all, Dave commentated on 415 Championship matches, and presided over many great moments, such as promotion from Division Two in 2012, Ryan Sidebottom's Championship wicket in 2014 that clinched the title, and their successful defence of the crown a year later.

A full member of The Cricket Writers' Club, he was a much valued member of their dinner subcommittee, and at Yorkshire CCC's 150th anniversary and awards lunch in 2016 he fronted a question-and-answer session with Australian Jason Gillespie, who was about to end a five-year association with the county which saw them win the Championship in two consecutive seasons. Almost immediately that Jason joined Yorkshire he and Dave became the best of friends. Tributes to Dave poured in, and they included the following from the media and the Club:

David Warner, *Yorkshire Yearbook* Editor: His sudden and untimely death came as a terrible shock to me, and my heart went out to his wife, Pat, and their family. In all of my 44 seasons of covering Yorkshire cricket I have not come across a more likable or friendly colleague, who was a larger-than-life figure, and who was a consummate professional.

"It was when he began covering Yorkshire CCC home and away that he found his perfect niche in life. When the BBC local radio stations began their ball-by-ball coverage of county cricket I wondered if the long hours and total commitment which was necessary would prove too arduous for Dave, but I couldn't have been more wrong.

"He relished the challenge and was absolutely brilliant, not only giving day-long live commentary, but also cutting in several times each hour to serve the local radio stations throughout Yorkshire.

"Dave led the way, and his expertise was admired by colleagues doing a similar job with other counties around the country. Both the media and YCCC have lost a dear friend, whom it will be virtually impossible to replace, but it must be of some comfort to all who knew him that he went out at the very top of his game."

Kevin Howells, BBC Radio 5 Live cricket commentator: Deep sadness and awareness that what will follow for myself and others will be acute moments of hollowness when we walk into a room or reach a moment when we might have picked up a phone to chat with DC and realise the lovely man is no longer with us.

Chris Waters, Yorkshire Post Cricket Correspondent: How one wishes that DC could see the torrent of tributes that have poured in for him. Were that possible, he could have been in no doubt as to the unanimous esteem in which he was held, with everyone ranging from international cricketers to the humblest spectator uniting in profound grief at the loss of one of the game's greatest supporters and, most importantly, one of life's greatest gentlemen.

"Indeed, it is difficult to think of anyone connected with the vast institution of Yorkshire County Cricket Club — including its most celebrated players, past and present — who was more well-liked and respected than the *Voice of Yorkshire Cricket*, a voice now stilled but not forgotten by those for whom it was the soundtrack to more than 30 summers."

John Potter, Yorkshire First Eleven Scorer: He was the life and soul of any gathering, and was respected by all of the players he was so closely connected with. I will miss this great gentleman and friend. We travelled many miles together in England, Wales and Scotland. We had two trips to Holland, and I shared a cabin on the return from Rotterdam.

"Abu Dhabi was a new venture for us. Endless miles covered with him driving and myself as navigator, getting lost a rarity. Cricket was discussed, but many other subjects as well as we put the world to rights.

"His working conditions varied. Inside or outside, cold or hot, DC just got on with it. I remember a hot Guildford in 2002, when the Press Corps and I had a tent to work in, but DC was in the full glare of the sun for four days. He was red-faced after that, but that did not bother him.

"Sadly, no more night caps with him. The *Voice of Yorkshire Cricket* is now silent, but my wonderful memories will always remain."

Martyn Moxon, Yorkshire's Director of Cricket: He was a brilliant broadcaster and journalist, but at the same time he understood the pressures and challenges sports people have, so there was always that sympathetic ear or slant to his reporting. He didn't make it easy, but he always understood.

Steve Denison, former YCCC Chairman: Cally was one of the finest, most generous men I've had the privilege to meet. His radio commentary was peerless, full of his passion for Yorkshire while always respecting the opposition.

"Seeing DC squeezed into a variety of commentary boxes is a lasting memory...the shoebox at Scarborough and the cell on the cricket side of the old rugby stand at Headingley are particular favourites. His love of cricket was matched only by the affection for him of his thousands of listeners. Every county cricket fan has lost a treasured friend."

Mark Arthur, Yorkshire Chief Executive: Dave was a very special person, who loved Yorkshire County Cricket Club. He will be missed by everyone associated with Yorkshire Cricket."

Graham Hardcastle, Yorkshire cricket journalist: DC made such an impression on me. A massive help professionally, and he made covering the county all that more enjoyable as a friend. I've had numerous thoughts, particularly about very early mornings at Headingley and how we used to have 10-15 minutes chat about all manner of things before the day became hectic.

James Greenfield, *Yorkshire Yearbook* Production Editor: Dave reached his biggest audiences through his radio commentaries on the professional game, but he was a tireless encourager of the grassroots and the cricket societies of God's own cricket county. He would come along on dark, cold winter nights, sometimes to deliver a pithy summary of the season just past, sometimes with a Yorkshire player, with whom he would lead a question-and-answer session rich in content and analysis.

Tony Loffill, former YCCC announcer: A man made of the stuff of Yorkshire. Full of cheerfulness and bonhomie, who always saw the best in people; passionate in the pursuit of excellence in his trade, proud of his roots and a doughty companion. Our fellowship is much diminished.

ROY BOOTH

Marsden-born wicketkeeper, Roy Booth, right, who began a distinguished career with Yorkshire before moving on to Worcestershire where he became the Club's president, died on Sunday, September 23, just days short of his 92nd birthday.

Roy, a product of Golcar Cricket Club, played for Yorkshire from 1951 to 1955 and was a fringe player in the side until Don Brennan retired at the end of 1953. He then became their regular wicketkeeper until the middle of the 1955 season, when he lost his place to Jimmy Binks. Roy moved to Worcestershire in 1956 after playing in 65 first-class matches for Yorkshire, in which he scored 730 runs and claimed 79 catches and 29 stumpings.

Roy was a part of the Worcestershire side which won the County Championship for the first time in 1964 and retained the title the following year. When he retired in 1970 he had taken 948 first-class catches and pulled off 178 stumpings. He continued to play an active part in Worcestershire cricket, and his late wife, Joyce, was well known for serving the renowned teas in the Ladies Pavilion at New Road.

Roy Booth
Born: October 1, 1926
Died: September 23, 2018

PETER TOWNEND

Peter Townend, left, who gave 18 years of outstanding service as Yorkshire County Cricket Club's Treasurer, died last September in retirement at Lewes, Sussex, aged 89.

He and his wife, Joan, moved from Elland 10 years ago, and his funeral service took place at Lewes on September 13. A thanksgiving service was held at Blackley Baptist Church, Elland, on November 4, when Yorkshire Chairman Robin Smith was among those to pay tribute.

Peter followed David Welch as Treasurer in 1984 and stayed in the post until the Board replaced the 12-strong General Committee in 2002. He was then elected a vice-president of the Club. Former Yorkshire cricket chairman Tony Vann said: "He played an

78

important role in the financial debate which led to the indoor cricket school being built in St Michael's Lane, opposite the main entrance to the cricket ground, rather than at Bradford Park Avenue, which was some 11 miles away.

"Peter enjoyed the annual general meeting, when his engaging smile and sense of humour allowed him to explain in clear terms the Club's financial situation, irrespective of whether there had been a profit or a loss. He was a gentleman to his finger tips.

"He was still playing tennis up to his 80th birthday, and it was his wife, Joan, who was the bigger cricket fan in the family."

CHRIS ALLINSON

Chris Allinson, a former Yorkshire Academy player who marked his Second Eleven Championship debut by scoring 127 and 72 not out against Somerset Seconds at Taunton in August 2006, died suddenly on November 8 at his home in Guisborough, aged only 28.

Chris was with the Yorkshire Academy from 2006 to 2008, during which time he and his close friend, Jonny Bairstow, were members of the England Under-17 development squad, the pair also representing the North in the regional Under-17 competition at Loughborough.

As well as Jonny, several of his teammates went on to become top players, including Joe Root, Andrew Gale, Steven Patterson, Adil Rashid and Adam Lyth.

At the time of his death Chris was attached to Marton Cricket Club, but he had also enjoyed spells with Guisborough, Marske, Stokesley and Great Ayrton, scoring over 6,500 runs and taking 277 wickets in the North Yorkshire and South Durham ECB Premier League.

Chris played in 10 Yorkshire Second XI Championship matches, and in May 2009 he turned out for Nottinghamshire Seconds against Leicestershire Seconds. A hugely talented squash player, he was a local champion, and at one stage he was considered one of the best prospects in the country.

The cause of death was sudden and unexpected death epilepsy syndrome (Sudep).

The Players

Steven Andrew PATTERSON

Right-hand batsman, right-arm medium-fast bowler
Born: Beverley, October 3, 1983

First-Class Cricket:
Debut: v. Bangladesh A at Leeds, 2005
Highest score: 63* v. Warwickshire at Leeds, 2016
Best bowling: 6-40 v. Essex at Chelmsford, 2018

One-Day:
Highest score: 25* v. Worcestershire at Leeds,
2006
Best bowling: 6-32 v. Derbyshire at Leeds, 2010

t20:
Highest score: 3* v. Derbyshire at Leeds, 2010
Best bowling: 4-30 v. Lancashire at Leeds, 2010

Joe Edward ROOT

Right-hand batsman, right-arm off-spin bowler
Born: Sheffield, December 30, 1990

First-Class cricket:
Debut: v. Loughborough MCCU at Leeds, 2010
Highest score: 254 for England v. Pakistan
at Manchester, 2016
Highest for Yorkshire: 236 v. Derbyshire
at Leeds, 2013
Best bowling: 4- 5 v. Lancashire at Manchester,
2018

One-Day:
Highest Score: 133* for England v. Bangladesh
at The Oval, 2017
Highest for Yorkshire: 83 v. Warwickshire
at Birmingham, 2017
Best bowling: 2-10 for England Lions v.
Bangladesh A at Sylhet, 2011/12

Best bowling for Yorkshire: 2-14 v. Kent at Leeds, 2012

t20:
Highest score: 92* v. Lancashire at Manchester, 2016
Best bowling for England: 2-9 v West Indies at Kolkata, 2016-17
For Yorkshire: 1-12 v. Warwickshire at Leeds, 2011

Gary Simon BALLANCE

Left-hand batsman, leg-break bowler
Born: Harare, Zimbabwe, November 22, 1989
First-Class Cricket:
Debut: v Kent at Canterbury, 2008
Highest score: 210 for Mid-West Rhinos v.
Southern Rocks at Masvingo, Zimbabwe, 2011-12
For Yorkshire: 203* v. Hampshire at West End,
Southampton, 2017

One-Day:
Highest score: 152* v. Northamptonshire
at Northampton, 2017

t20:
Highest score: 79 v. Birmingham at Birmingham,
2018

Jonathan Marc BAIRSTOW

Right-hand batsman, wicket-keeper
Born: Bradford, September 26, 1989
First-Class Cricket:
Debut: v Somerset at Leeds, 2009
Highest score: 246 v. Hampshire at Leeds, 2016
One-Day:
Highest score: 174 v, Durham at Leeds, 2017
t20:
Highest score: 102* v. Durham
at Chester-le-Street, 2014

Timothy Thomas BRESNAN

Right-hand batsman, right-arm medium-fast bowler
Born: Pontefract, February 28, 1985
First-Class cricket:
Debut: v. Northamptonshire at Northampton, 2003
Highest score: 169* v. Durham
at Chester-le-Street, 2015
Best bowling: 5-28 v. Hampshire at Leeds, 2018
One-Day:
Highest score: 95* v. Nottinghamshire
at Scarborough, 2016
Best bowling: 5-48 for England v. India
at Bangalore, 2011
Best bowling for Yorkshire: 4-25 v. Somerset
at Leeds, 2005
t20:
Highest score: 51 v. Lancashire
at Manchester, 2015
Best bowling: 6-19 v. Lancashire at Leeds, 2017

Adam LYTH
Left-hand batsman, right-arm medium bowler
Born: Whitby, September 25, 1987
First-Class cricket:
Debut: v. Loughborough UCCE at Leeds, 2007
Highest score: 251 v. Lancashire
at Manchester, 2014
Best bowling: 2-9 v. Middlesex at Scarborough,
2016

One-Day:
Highest score: 144 v. Lancashire at Manchester,
2018
Best bowling: 1-6 v Middlesex at Leeds, 2013
t20:
Highest score: 161 v. Northamptonshire
at Leeds, 2017
Best bowling: 2-5 v. Derbyshire
at Chesterfield, 2014

Adil Usman RASHID
Right-hand batsman, leg-break bowler
Born: Bradford, February 17, 1988
First-Class cricket:
Debut: v. Warwickshire at Scarborough, 2006
Highest score: 180 v Somerset at Leeds, 2013
Best bowling: 7-107 v. Hampshire
at Southampton, 2008
One-Day:
Highest score: 71 v. Gloucestershire at Leeds, 2014
Best bowling: 5-27 for England v.Ireland
at Bristol, 2017
Best bowling for Yorkshire: 5-33 v. Hampshire
at Southampton 2014
t20:
Highest score: 36* v Uva Next
at Johannesburg, 2012/13
Best bowling: 4-19 v. Durham at Leeds, 2017

Jack Andrew LEANING
Right-hand batsman, right-arm medium
and off-break bowler
Born: Bristol, October 18, 1993
First-Class cricket:
Debut: v. Surrey at Leeds, 2013
Highest score: 123 v. Somerset at Taunton, 2015
Best bowling: 2-30 v. MCC at Abu Dhabi, 2016
One-Day:
Highest score: 131* v. Leicestershire
at Leicester, 2016
Best bowling: 5-22 v Unicorns at Leeds, 2013
t20:
Highest score: 64 v. Northamptonshire
at Northampton, 2016
Best bowling: 0-12 v. Derbyshire at Leeds, 2014

David Jonathan WILLEY

Left-hand batsman, left-arm fast-medium
Born: Northampton, February 28, 1990

First-Class cricket:
Debut: for Northamptonshire v. Leicestershire
at Leicester, 2009
Debut for Yorkshire: v. Nottinghamshire
at Nottingham, 2016
Highest score: 104* for Northamptonshire
v. Gloucestershire at Northampton, 2015
Highest for Yorkshire: 22 v Middlesex
at Lord's, 2016
Best bowling: 5-29 for Northamptonshire
v. Gloucestershire at Northampton, 2011
For Yorkshire: 3-55 v. Surrey at Leeds, 2016

One-Day:
Highest score: 167 for Northamptonshire v. Warwickshire at Birmingham, 2013
Highest for Yorkshire: 131 v. Lancashire at Manchester, 2018
Best bowling: 5-62 for England Lions v. New Zealand A at Bristol, 2014
For Yorkshire: 4-47 v. Derbyshire at Derby, 2018

t20:
Highest score: 118 for Yorkshire v. Worcestershire at Leeds, 2017
Best bowling: 4-9 for Northamptonshire v. Surrey at Cardiff, 2013
For Yorkshire: 3-30 v. Northamptonshire at Northampton, 2018

Tom KOHLER-CADMORE

Right-hand batsman, right-arm off-break bowler
Born: Chatham, August 19, 1994

First-Class Cricket:
Debut: For Worcestershire v. Hampshire
at West End, Southampton, 2014
Debut for Yorkshire: v. Somerset
at Scarborough, 2017
Highest score: 169 for Worcestershire
v. Gloucestershire at Worcester, 2016
Highest score for Yorkshire: 106 v. Nottinghamshire
at Nottingham, 2018

One-Day:
Highest score: 164 v. Durham at Chester-le-Street,
2018

t20:
Highest score: 127 for Worcestershire v. Durham at Worcester, 2016
For Yorkshire: 75 v. Leicestershire at Leicester, 2017

Benjamin Oliver COAD

Right-hand batsman, right-arm fast-medium bowler
Born: Harrogate, January 10, 1994
First-Class Cricket:
Debut: v. Durham at Chester-le-Street, 2016
Highest score: 33 v. Nottinghamshire at Leeds, 2018
Best bowling: 6-25 v. Lancashire at Leeds, 2017

One-Day:
Highest score: 9 v. Hampshire at West End, 2018
Best bowling: 4-63 v. Derbyshire at Leeds, 2017

t20:
Highest score: 2* v. Northamptonshire
at Northampton, 2015
Best bowling: 2-24 v. Northamptonshire
at Northampton, 2015

Harry Charrington BROOK

Right-hand batsman, medium-pace bowler
Born: Keighley, February 22, 1999
First-Class Cricket:
Debut: v. Pakistan A at Leeds, 2016
Highest score: 124 v. Essex at Chelmsford, 2018
Best bowling: 1-54 v. Somerset
at Scarborough, 2017

One-Day:
Highest score: 24 v. Lancashire at Manchester, 2018

t20:
Highest score: 44 v. Durham at Leeds, 2018

Karl CARVER

Left-hand batsman, slow left-arm orthodox bowler
Born: Northallerton, March 26, 1996
First-Class Cricket:
Debut for Yorkshire: v. Warwickshire
at Birmingham, 2014
Highest score: 20 v. Somerset at Taunton, 2017
Best bowling: 4-106 v. MCC at Abu Dhabi, 2016

One-Day:
Highest score: 35* v. Somerset
at Scarborough, 2015
Best bowling: 3-5 v. Lancashire
at Manchester, 2016

t20:
Highest score: 2 v. Worcestershire at Leeds, 2015
Best bowling: 3-40 v. Durham at Leeds, 2016

Matthew David FISHER

Right-hand batsman, right-arm fast-medium bowler
Born: York, November 9, 1997
First-Class Cricket:
Debut: v. Nottinghamshire at Nottingham, 2015
Highest score: 37 v. Warwickshire at Leeds, 2017
Best bowling: 5-54 v. Warwickshire at Leeds, 2017
One-Day:
Highest score: 36* v. Worcestershire
at Worcester, 2017
Best bowling: 3-32 v, Leicestershire at Leeds, 2015
t20:
Highest score: 17* v. Birmingham at Birmingham,
2018
Best bowling: 5-22 v. Derbyshire at Leeds, 2015

Matthew James WAITE

Right-hand batsman, right-arm fast medium bowler
Born: Leeds, December 24, 1995
First-Class Cricket:
Debut: v. Somerset at Taunton, 2017
Highest score: 42 v. Nottinghamshire at
Nottingham, 2018
Best bowling: 3-91 v. Nottinghamshire at
Nottingham, 2018
One-Day:
Highest score: 71 v. Warwickshire
at Birmingham, 2017
Best bowling: 4-65 v. Worcestershire
at Worcester, 2017
t20:
Highest score: 19* v. Glamorgan at Cardiff, 2016
Best bowling: 1-6 v. Glamorgan at Cardiff, 2016

James Edwin Graham LOGAN

Left-hand batsman, slow left-arm orthodox bowler
Born: Wakefield, October 12, 1997
First-Class Cricket:
Debut: v. Worcestershire at Worcester, 2018
Highest score: 6 v. Worcestershire at Worcester,
2018
Best bowling: 0-4 v. Worcestershire at Worcester,
2018
Best bowling: 3-55 v. Surrey at Leeds, 2016
One-Day:
Awaits debut
t20:
Awaits debut

Joshua SHAW

Right-hand batsmen, right-arm medium-fast bowler
Born: Wakefield, January 3, 1996
First-Class Cricket:
Debut: For Gloucestershire v. Durham MCCU
at Bristol, 2016
Debut for Yorkshire: v. Durham
at Chester-le-Street, 2016
Highest score: 42 v. Somerset at Leeds, 2018
Best bowling: 5-79 for Gloucestershire
v. Sussex at Bristol, 2016
Best bowling for Yorkshire: 3-58 v. Pakistan A
at Leeds, 2016
One-Day:
Awaits debut

t20:
Highest score: 1 v. Durham at Chester-le-Street, 2016
Best bowling: 2-39 v. Hobart Hurricanes, at Abu Dhabi, 2018

Joshua Edward POYSDEN

Left-hand batsman, leg-break bowlerr
Born: Shoreham-by-Sea, August 8, 1991
First-Class Cricket:
Debut: for Cambridge MCCU v Essex at
Cambridge, 2011
Debut for Yorkshire: v. Lancashire at Manchester,
2018
Highest score: 47 for Cambridge MCCU v. Surrey
at Cambridge, 2011
Highest score for Yorkshire: 20 v. Lancashire
at Manchester, 2018
Best bowling: 5-29 for Warwickshire v. Glamorgan
at Birmingham, 2018
Best bowling for Yorkshire: 3-128 v. Worcestershire
at Scarborough, 2018

One-Day:
Highest score: 10* for Unicorns v. Gloucestershire at Wormsley, 2013
Best bowling: 3-33 for Unicorns v. Middlesex at Lord's 2013
Awaiting Yorkshire debut

t20:
Highest score: 9* for Warwickshire v. Northamptonshire at Northampton, 2016
Has not batted for Yorkshire
Best bowling: 4-51 for Warwickshire v. Derbyshire at Birmingham, 2015
Best bowling for Yorkshire: 2-26 v. Lahore Qalandars at Abu Dhabi 2018

Matthew William PILLANS

Right-hand batsman, right-arm fast bowler
Born: Westville, South Africa, July 4, 1991

First-Class Cricket:
Debut: for Northerns v North West at Pretoria, 2012
Debut for Yorkshire: v. Nottinghamshire
at Nottingham, 2018
Highest score: 56 for Leicestershire v.
Northamptonshire at Northampton, 2017
Highest score for Yorkshire: 8 v. Nottinghamshire
at Nottingham, 2018

One-Day:
Highest Score: 20* for KwaZulu-Natal Inland
v. North West at Pietermaritzburg, 2013
Best bowling: 3-14 for KwaZulu-Natal Inland
v. Namibia at Pietermaritzburg, 2016
Awaits Yorkshire debut

t20:
Highest score: 34* for Leicestershire v. Warwickshire at Leicester, 2017
Best bowling: 3-15 for KwaZulu-Natal Inland v. Northerns at Bloemfontein, 2015
Awaits Yorkshire debut

William Alan Richard FRAINE

Right-hand batsman, right-arm medium pace bowler
Born: Huddersfield, June 13, 1996

First-Class Cricket:
Debut: For Durham MCCU v. Gloucestershire at
Bristol, 2017
Highest score: 30 for Nottinghamshire v. Surrey
at Nottingham, 2018

One-Day:
Highest score: 13 for Nottinghamshire v.
Lancashire at Manchester, 2018

t20:
Highest score: 14 for Nottinghamshire v.
Derbyshire at Derby, 2018

Awaits debut for Yorkshire in all forms

YORKSHIRE'S FIRST-CLASS HIGHLIGHTS OF 2018

Wins by an innings or by 10 wickets (None)

Totals of 400 and over (2)

498	v. Nottinghamshire at Nottingham
439	v. Worcestershire at Worcester

Century Partnerships (11)

For 4th wicket (3)

148	G S Ballance and T Kohler-Cadmore	
		v. Hampshire at West End, Southampton
143	G S Ballance and H C Brook	v. Lancashire at Manchester
133	H C Brook and J M Bairstow	v. Lancashire at Leeds

For the 5th wicket (5)

133	A Lyth and J A Tattersall	v. Nottinghamshire at Leeds
108	H C Brook and J A Leaning	v. Hampshire at West End, Southampton
105	T Kohler-Cadmore and J A Tattersall	
		v. Lancashire at Leeds
103	G S Ballance and J A Leaning	v. Nottinghamshire at Nottingham
102	T Kohler-Cadmore and J A Tattersall	
		v. Hampshire at Leeds

For the 6th wicket (1)

| 173 | T Kohler-Cadmore and A J Hodd | v. Somerset at Leeds |

For the 7th wicket (1)

| 100 | J A Tattersall and T T Bresnan | v. Surrey at Scarborough |

For the 9th wicket (1)

| 171 | G S Ballance and J A Brooks | v. Worcestershire at Worcester |

Centuries (7)

G S Ballance (3)

194	v. Worcestershire at Worcester
109	v. Hampshire at West End, Southampton
104	v. Nottinghamshire at Nottingham

T Kohler-Cadmore (2)

| 106 | v Nottinghamshire at Nottingham |
| 105* | v Lancashire at Leeds |

H C Brook (1)

| 124 | v Essex at Chelmsford |

A Lyth (1)

| 134* | v. Hampshire at Leeds |

5 wickets in an innings (10)

J A Brooks (5)

    6- 94   v. Worcestershire at Worcester
    5- 57   v. Somerset at Taunton
    5- 66   v. Lancashire at Leeds
    5- 116   v. Somerset at Leeds
    5- 124   v. Hampshire at West End, Southampton

B O Coad (3)

    6- 81   v Nottinghamshire at Leeds
    5- 24   v Lancashire at Leeds
    5- 53   v Surrey at Scarborough

T T Bresnan (1)

    5- 28   v. Hampshire at Leeds

S A Patterson (1)

    6- 40   v. Essex at Chelmsford

10 wickets in a match (1)

B O Coad (1)

    10-130 (4-49 and 6-81)   v Nottinghamshire at Leeds

3 catches in an innings (9)

J A Tattersall (4)

    4   v. Hampshire at West End, Southampton
    4   v. Surrey at Scarborough
    3   v. Nottinghamshire at Nottingham
    3   v. Lancashire at Leeds

A J Hodd (3)

    3   v. Nottinghamshire at Leeds
    3   v. Somerset at Taunton
    3   v. Somerset at Leeds

J M Bairstow (1)

    3   v. Lancashire at Manchester

J A Leaning (1)

    3   v. Nottinghamshire at Leeds

5 catches in a match (1)

J M Bairstow (1)

    5 (2 + 3)   v. Lancashire at Manchester

5 dismissals in a match (None)

Debuts (5)
In First Class cricket (2): J A Tattersall and J E G Logan
In First Class cricket for Yorkshire (3): J E Poysden, J A Raval and M W Pillans

Caps: B O Coad

SPECSAVERS COUNTY CHAMPIONSHIP FACTFILE

Compiled by John T Potter

Versus Leeds/Bradford MCCU at Leeds

1. This was Yorkshire 39th First Class match without a ball bowled, 36 because of the weather and three due to war
2. It was Yorkshire's first abandoned match since the fixture at against Oxford University at The Parks in 1992
3. This was Yorkshire's third First Class match to abandoned without a ball bowled at Leeds. The other two were against Nottinghamshire in 1926 and Leicestershire in 1967

Versus ESSEX at Leeds

1. This abandoned match was Yorkshire's first four-day fixture to have no play. Yorkshire's last abandoned Championship match had been at Hastings against Sussex in 1987
2. It was the second match against Essex to be abandoned, the previo- one being at Abbeydale Park, Sheffield, in 1985 when Essex came as the Champion County

Versus NOTTINGHAMSHIRE at Leeds

1. Yorkshire's 2018 season finally began after seven blank days
2. G S Ballance passed 6,000 First Class runs for Yorkshire
3. J Shaw's dismissal in Yorkshire's first innings was H F Gurney's 250th Championship wicket. The same batsman's dismissal in Yorkshire's second innings gave L J Fletcher his 250th Championship wicket

Versus SOMERSET at Taunton

1. The opening day washout was Yorkshire's eighth day lost in four matches
2. M J Waite made his second First Class appearance, both having been at Taunton
3. M T Renshaw's 112 was his highest Championship score
4. T T Bresnan passed 5,000 Championship runs for Yorkshire
5. Somerset had last won at Taunton against Yorkshire in 2012

SPECSAVERS CHAMPIONSHIP FACTFILE *(Continued)*

Versus ESSEX at Chelmsford

1. Yorkshire's first inning total of 50 was their lowest against Essex in Essex, the previous lowest being 74 in 2017.
2. Yorkshire have had 29 innings totals lower than 50. Yorkshire's last five innings against Essex have been 113, 150, 111, 74 and 50
3. H C Brook's 124 was his maiden First Class century
4. Only L Hutton in 1934, C W J Athey in 1976 and Azeem Rafiq in 2009 have scored Championship hundreds before turning 19. H C Brook's age was 19 years and 72 days
5. R A Kettleborough, an umpire in the match, also scored his maiden First Class century against Essex. It was at Leeds in 1996, and again was a match Yorkshire looked destined to lose, but they won
6. S A Patterson's 6-40 was his First Class career-best
7. The last time Yorkshire won a County Championship match after being all out for 50 or fewer in the first innings was in 1922 against Sussex at Hove
8. This win was the sixth in all Championship cricket by a team who had scored 50 or fewer in their first innings

Versus SURREY at The Oval

1. O J D Pope's 158* was his highest First Class score
2. J M Bairstow passed 6,000 Championship runs for Yorkshire
3. R Clarke passed 10,000 First Class career runs
4. J A Brooks reached 400 First Class wickets when he dismissed R J Burns
5. This was Surrey's 20th win by an innings against Yorkshire and the first since 2002 at Leeds. The last one at The Oval was in 2001

Versus HAMPSHIRE at Southampton

1. This was Yorkshire's second day/night Championship match and their third First Class day/night game
2. J A Tattersall made his First Class debut
3. O P Rayner made his First Class debut for Hampshire
4. G S Ballance's 109 in Yorkshire's first innings was his third century in consecutive innings at West End in two seasons

SPECSAVERS CHAMPIONSHIP FACTFILE *(Continued)*

Versus SURREY at Scarborough

1. C A Pujara took 70 minutes to get off the mark in Yorkshire's first innings, but he passed 13,500 First Class career runs
2. B O Coad's dismissal was J W Dernbach's 300th First Class career wicket
3. Yorkshire's first-innings total was increased by five penalty runs given during Surrey's first innings
4. Surrey last chased over 200 runs to win in their second innings in 2015 against Leicestershire at The Oval and Essex at Colchester
5. This win gave Surrey a season double over Yorkshire, which they last achieved in 2002
6. Surrey's win at Scarborough made them the sixth county in six years to win at this venue and go on to win the Championship. The others were Essex in 2017, Middlesex 2016, Yorkshire 2015 and 2014, and Durham in 2013

Versus LANCASHIRE at Manchester

1. J E Poysden made his First Class debut for Yorkshire
2. J Clark's 5-58 was his first five-wicket haul in an innings in First Class cricket, and during Yorkshire's first innings he took a hat-trick — Root, Williamson and Bairstow
3. K Higgs in 1968 at Leeds was the last Lancashire player to take a hat-trick in a Roses match, but Yorkshire won that match also
4. S A Patterson passed 2,000 First Class career runs
5. J E Root's 4-5 was his First Class career best

SPECSAVERS CHAMPIONSHIP FACTFILE *(Continued)*

Versus WORCESTERSHIRE at Scarborough

1. Worcestershire's 572-7 dec was their highest total against Yorkshire, surpassing their 456-8 dec at Worcester in 1904

2. M M Ali's 219 was only the second score of over 200 in a match against Worcestershire at Scarborough, the other being D Byas's 213 in 1995

3. The visitors' second-wicket partnership of 294 was their highest against Yorkshire

4. M M Ali, with 219 and 6-49, was the first player for 72 years to score 200 and take five wickets in an innings in the same match. The last man to do it was W J Edrich (222* and 7-69) for Middlesex against Northamptonshire at Northampton in August 1946

5. The only other player to do this for Worcestershire was E G Arnold (200* and 7-44) against Warwickshire at Birmingham in August 1909

6. It was the first time a player had scored a double-century and taken five wickets in an innings in a match involving Yorkshire

7. This was Worcestershire's fifth innings win against Yorkshire and only their second in Yorkshire, the previous one being at Hull in 1974, the last First Class match played there

8. It was Yorkshire's fifth defeat in their last six matches at Scarborough

Versus SOMERSET at Leeds

1. J H Davey's 5-65 was his first five-wicket haul in an innings in First Class cricket

2. A Lyth passed 9,000 First Class runs for Yorkshire

3. Somerset did the season double over Yorkshire. The last time they did this was in 2009

4. This was Somerset's third win in three years in Yorkshire

Versus NOTTINGHAMSHIRE at Nottingham

1. M W Pillans and J A Raval made their First Class debuts for Yorkshire.
2. B M Duckett made his First Class debut for Nottinghamshire
3. T Kohler-Cadmore's 106 was his maiden First Class century for Yorkshire
4. Yorkshire took maximum batting points for the first time since they played Surrey at The Oval on July 11-14, 2016
5. A Lyth became Yorkshire's fifth captain of the season. The last time this happened was in 1956
6. Yorkshire captains 2018: G S Ballance, J E Root, S A Patterson, D J Willey and A Lyth — 13 matches played
   Yorkshire captains 1956 — W H H Sutcliffe, F A Lowson, J H Wardle, W Watson and J V Wilson — 35 matches played

Versus LANCASHIRE at Leeds

1. G S Ballance passed 6,000 Championship runs
2. T Kohler-Cadmore's 105* was his second century for Yorkshire in consecutive innings
3. Yorkshire did the season double over Lancashire for the first time since 2001 — but this time no Championship Trophy

Versus HAMPSHIRE at Leeds

1. G S Ballance passed 10,000 First Class career runs
2. T T Bresnan's 5-28 was a career best
3. J A Brooks passed 400 Championship wickets
4. No play was possible in the last five sessions of the match, as Yorkshire ended their season at Emerald Headingley as it began. There was no play on the opening day, and none on the final day

Versus WORCESTERSHIRE at Worcester

1. J E G Logan made his First Class debut for Yorkshire
2. J A Brooks's dismissal of D Y Pennington gave him 50 wickets for the season
3. B O Coad took his 100th First Class wicket
4. Yorkshire's ninth wicket partnership of 171 between G S Ballance and J A Brooks was their highest against Worcestershire, surpassing Azeem Rafiq and M J Hoggard (150) at Worcester in 2009
5. The last time Yorkshire gained maximum points in a match was also against Worcestershire — at Scarborough on July 19-22, 2015

Specsavers Championship
Division 1, 2018

Captains: G S Ballance and S A Patterson

*Captain

§ Wicket-Keeper

Figures in brackets ( ) indicate position in 2nd Innings batting order,
where different from 1st Innings

DETAILS OF PLAYERS WHO APPEARED FOR YORKSHIRE IN 2018
(ALL FIRST-CLASS MATCHES)

Player	Date of Birth	Birthplace	First-Class debut for Yorkshire	Date Capped
G S Ballance	November 22, 1989	Harare, Zim	July 11, 2008	Sept 4, 2012
S A Patterson	October 3, 1983	Beverley	August 3, 2005	May 16, 2012
T T Bresnan	February 28, 1985	Pontefract	May 14, 2003	July 19, 2006
A Lyth	September 25, 1987	Whitby	May 16, 2007	Aug 22, 2010
J M Bairstow	September 26, 1989	Bradford	June 11, 2009	Aug 17, 2011
J E Root	December 30, 1990	Sheffield	May 10, 2010	Sept 4, 2012
J A Brooks	June 4, 1984	Oxford	April 5, 2013	Aug 2, 2013
K S Williamson	August 8, 1990	Tauranga, New Zealand	August 21, 2013	Aug 21, 2013
A Z Lees	April 14, 1993	Halifax	June 5, 2010	Sept 23, 2014
C A Pujara	January 25, 1988	Rajkot, India	April 12, 2015	April 12, 2015
A J Hodd	January 12, 1984	Chichester	August 15, 2012	May 29, 2016
J A Leaning	October 18, 1993	Bristol	June 21, 2013	Aug 13, 2016
D J Willey	February 28, 1990	Northampton	May 1, 2016	Aug 13, 2016
J A Raval	May 22, 1988	Ahmedabad, India	September 4, 2018	Sept 4, 2018
B O Coad	January 10, 1994	Harrogate	June 20, 2016	Sept 18, 2018
K Carver	March 26, 1996	Northallerton	June 22, 2014	
M D Fisher	November 9, 1997	York	April 19, 2015	
J Shaw	January 3, 1996	Wakefield	June 20, 2016	
H C Brook	February 22, 1999	Keighley	June 26, 2016	
M J Waite	December 24, 1995	Leeds	June 9, 2017	
T Kohler-Cadmore	April 19, 1994	Chatham	July 3, 2017	
J A Tattersall	December 15, 1994	Harrogate	June 20, 2018	
J E Poysden	August 8, 1991	Shoreham-by-Sea	July 20, 2018	
M W Pillans	July 4, 1991	Westville, South Africa	September 4, 2018	
J E G Logan	October 12, 1997	Wakefield	September 24, 2018	

Match-By-Match Reports ANDREW BOSI and NIGEL PULLAN

Yorkshire v. Essex

At Emerald Headingley, Leeds, on April 13, 14, 15 and 16, 2018
Match abandoned without a ball bowled

Toss: None

Umpires: I J Gould and R K Illingworth

Yorkshire 5 points, Essex 5 points

Scorers: J T Potter and A E Choat

Specsavers County Championship Division 1
Yorkshire v. Nottinghamshire

Played at Emerald Headingley, Leeds, on April 20, 21, 22 and 23, 2018
Yorkshire won by 164 runs at 11.47am on the Fourth Day

Toss: None. Nottinghamshire opted to field   Yorkshire 21 points, Nottinghamshire 3 points
Close of play: First Day, Nottinghamshire 53-4 (Taylor 34*, Wessels 8*); Second Day, Yorkshire 189-4 (Balance 76*, Leaning 37*); Third Day, Nottinghamshire 181-8 (Moores 10*, Ball 8*

	First Innings	YORKSHIRE	Second Innings	
A Lyth, lbw b Wood	45		c Moores b Wood	12
A Z Lees, c Taylor b Ball	6		lbw b Ball	0
C A Pujara, lbw b Fletcher	2		run out (Libby/Gurney)	18
* G S Ballance, c Patel b Ball	0		b Gurney	82
H C Brook, b Wood	22		b Ball	36
J A Leaning, b Wood b Fletcher	12		lbw b Gurney	37
§ A J Hodd, b Gurney	62		lbw b Gurney	3
T T Bresnan, b Fletcher	10		not out	68
J Shaw, c Moores b Gurney	17		c Moores b Fletcher	6
J A Brooks, not out	30		c Moores b Ball	13
B O Coad, c Patel b Fletcher	18		c Mullaney b Fletcher	33
Extras b 3, lb 18, w 5, nb 6	32		Extras b 5, lb 17, nb 4	26
Total	256		Total	334

FoW: 1-25 (Lees), 2-36 (Pujara), 3-37 (Ballance), 4-87 (Lyth), 5-93 (Brook),
1st   6-137 (Leaning), 7-155 (Bresnan), 8-191 (Shaw), 9-212 (Hodd), 10-256 (Coad)
FoW: 1-5 (Lees), 2-28 (Pujara), 3-37 (Lyth), 4-95 (Brook), 5-198 (Leaning),
2nd   6-199 (Ballance), 7-204 (Hodd), 8-228 (Shaw), 9-257 (Brooks), 10-334 (Coad)

	O	M	R	W		O	M	R	W
Ball	17	2	51	2	Ball	22	4	69	3
Fletcher	18.1	8	47	4	Fletcher	23.2	10	45	2
Gurney	20	4	46	3	Gurney	27	4	86	3
Wood	13	0	70	1	Wood	19	1	63	1
Patel	6	1	21	0	Patel	15	4	45	0
					Nash	2	0	4	0

	First Innings	NOTTINGAMSHIRE	Second innings	
* S J Mullaney, b Brooks	0		lbw b Coad	13
J D Libby, lbw b Coad	6		b Coad	38
C D Nash, c Hodd b Brooks	0		c Hood b Bresnan	23
L R P L Taylor, c Leaning b Coad	57		c Hodd b Brooks	30
S R Patel, b Brooks	4		b Coad	7
M H Wessels, c Leaning b Bresnan	40		c Hodd b Shaw	33
§ T J Moores, c Leaning b Coad	1		(8) not out	40
L Wood, c Lyth b Bresnan	17		(9) c Leaning b Coad	10
L J Fletcher, run out (Brooks)	8		(7) b Brooks	2
J T Ball, not out	44		b Coad	30
H F Gurney, c Bresnan b Coad	2		c Lyth b Coad	0
Extras b 5, lb 2, nb 2	9		Extras b 1, lb 10, w 1	12
Total	188		Total	238

Bonus points — Yorkshire 3

FoW: 1-0 (Mullaney), 2-6 (Nash), 3-6 (Libby), 4-39 (Patel), 5-100 (Taylor),
1st   6-102 (Moores), 7-127 (Wood), 8-130 (Wessels), 9-179 (Fletcher), 10-188 (Gurney)
FoW: 1-21 (Mullaney), 2-59 (Nash), 3-81 (Libby), 4-101 (Patel), 5-135 (Taylor),
2nd   6-143 (Fletcher), 7-151 (Wessels), 8-172 (Wood), 9-238 (Ball), 10-238 (Gurney)

	O	M	R	W		O	M	R	W
Brooks	14	3	58	3	Brooks	18	2	77	2
Coad	13.2	4	49	4	Coad	19.4	6	81	6
Bresnan	13	3	45	2	Shaw	10	0	46	1
Shaw	6	0	29	0	Bresnan	8	2	19	1
					Lyth	3	2	4	0

Umpires: N G B Cook and M A Gough   Scorers: J T Potter and R Marshall

Yorkshire v. Nottinghamshire

Coad conquers again

Yorkshire's first Championship match at Headingley against Essex was abandoned without a ball bowled over four days.

For the start of the second there was bright sunshine as Nottinghamshire exercised the visitors' right to bowl

BEN COAD: Leads Yorkshire off with 10

first. By lunchtime Yorkshire were 107-5 as Ball led an eager four-man seam attack with Fletcher, Gurney and Wood. Lyth batted well, but Hodd played the best innings, and while batting was never comfortable on a competitive pitch 256 would be a good score. Fletcher, making a welcome return after serious injury, had four wickets.

By the close on Friday Nottinghamshire had lost four wickets, three to Brooks during an inspired spell of 3-11, including Mullaney second ball. The best batting came during the partnership of Taylor and Wessels, but without some muscular hitting by Ball the Nottinghamshire total would have been very low. Coad and Bresnan bowled well, so Yorkshire had a lead of 68. Lyth's diving sprawling catch to dismiss Wood was remarkable – how does he do it?

After another good start by the visiting bowlers and the self-destructive run-out of Pujara, Ballance stayed at the crease to collect 82 runs, supported by Brook who played some well-timed strokes, and an obdurate Leaning. Then Bresnan batted responsibly after Gurney had taken three wickets in 10 balls, and he put on 77 for the last wicket with Coad.

Nottinghamshire found 402 beyond them, so Yorkshire won easily despite some late resistance from Moores, a promising young wicket-keeper who had made two spectacular high catches, and Ball. An extra half hour had been claimed on Sunday evening at 7.05, but only one wicket fell and play extended to a fourth day.

Coad had a very good opening match, taking 10 for 130 and making 51 runs. He bowls straight, reasonably fast, gets disconcerting bounce and has developed his out-swinger over the last two years.

Specsavers County Championship Division 1
Somerset v. Yorkshire

Played at The Cooper Associates County Ground, Taunton, on April 27, 28, 29 and 30, 2018
Somerset won by 118 runs at 3.47pm on the Fourth Day

Toss: None. Yorkshire opted to field   Somerset 20 points, Yorkshire 3 points

Close of play: First Day, no play; Second Day, Somerset 6-0 (Trescothick 2*, Renshaw 4*);
Third Day, Yorkshire 49-1 (Lyth 25*, Pujara 6*)

SOMERSET	First Innings		Second innings	
M E Trescothick, c Brook b Brooks	4	c Lyth b Coad		2
M T Renshaw, c Hodd b Brooks	112	b Brooks		8
G A Bartlett, lbw b Coad	39	c Hodd b Coad		4
J C Hildreth, c Brook b Coad	0	b Brooks		10
* T B Abell, b Brooks	4	b Coad		82
§ S M Davies, c Hodd b Coad	6	c Pujara b Coad		33
L Gregory, lbw b Brooks	8	lbw b Waite		14
C Overton, not out	19	b Brooks		18
D M Bess, c Hodd b Brooks	0	c Lyth b Waite		14
J H Davey, c sub (A Z Lees) b Bresnan	11	c Ballance b Bresnan		11
T D Groenewald, lbw b Bresnan	5	not out		0
Extras b 4, lb 1, w 1, nb 2	8	Extras lb 4		4
Total	216	Total		200

Bonus points — Somerset 1, Yorkshire 3

FoW: 1-5 (Trescothick), 2-145 (Bartlett), 3-153 (Hildreth), 4-166 (Abell), 5-171 (Renshaw),
1st   6-179 (Gregory), 7-181 (Davies), 8-182 (Bess), 9-206 (Davey), 10-216 (Groenewald)
FoW: 1-6 (Trescothick), 2-10 (Renshaw), 3-20 (Hildreth), 4-24 (Bartlett), 5-90 (Davies),
2nd   6-107 (Gregory), 7-129 (Overton), 8-171 (Bess), 9-200 (Davey), 10-200 (Abell)

	O	M	R	W		O	M	R	W
Coad	16	2	67	3	Coad	20.3	6	61	4
Brooks	15	3	57	5	Brooks	15	4	44	3
Bresnan	6.1	0	36	2	Bresnan	13	2	43	1
Waite	8	0	41	0	Waite	9	1	48	2
Lyth	2	0	10	0					

YORKSHIRE	First Innings		Second Innings	
A Lyth, run out (Bartlett/Overton)	0	c Hildreth b Groenewald		34
H C Brook, b Overton	32	c Trescothick b Davey		15
C A Pujara, lbw b Groenewald	7	c Davies b Gregory		6
* G S Ballance, c Davies b Groenewald	11	c Davies b Gregory		19
J A Leaning, c Davies b Gregory	0	c Renshaw b Overton		68
M J Waite, c Trescothick b Groenewald	11	c and b Overton		6
§ A J Hodd, c Trescothick b Groenewald	0	lbw b Overton		1
T T Bresnan, c Davies b Davey	22	lbw b Abell		21
J A Brooks, b Gregory	0	c and b Groenewald		21
B O Coad, b Overton	8	c Trescothick b Abell		2
K Carver, not out	1	not out		0
Extras lb 2, nb 2	4	Extras b 2, lb 7		9
Total	96	Total		202

Bonus points — Somerset 3

FoW: 1-0 (Lyth), 2-30 (Pujara), 3-51 (Ballance), 4-53 (Brook), 5-64 (Waite),
1st   6-64 (Hodd), 7-64 (Leaning), 8-64 (Brooks), 9-82 (Coad), 10-96 (Bresnan)
FoW: 1-26 (Brook), 2-49 (Pujara), 3-67 (Lyth),4-81 (Ballance), 5-99 (Waite),
2nd   6-103 (Hodd), 7-159 (Bresnan), 8-188 (Brooks), 9-191 (Waite), 10-202 (Leaning)

	O	M	R	W		O	M	R	W
Gregory	13	4	30	3	Gregory	23	7	59	2
Overton	15	6	38	2	Overton	21.1	7	43	3
Davey	12.4	6	14	1	$ Davey	7.5	4	12	1
Groenewald	9	4	12	3	Groenewald	19	5	51	2
					$ Bess	9.1	5	13	0
					Abell	6	2	15	2

$ Davey was unable to complete his eighth over, which was finished by Bess.

Umpires: M Burns and A G Wharf   Scorers: J T Potter and L M Rhodes

Somerset v. Yorkshire
Brooks's haul in vain

The visitors opted to bowl on a pitch more like Headingley than the Taunton of 2017, but Yorkshire-born Renshaw took the game away from them with a 39-ball half-century, converted to three figures before lunch.

After a washed-out first day Yorkshire chose to go into this game with a specialist spinner and without Lees, which meant replacing Shaw with a bowling all-rounder in Waite.

Such was the Renshaw onslaught that Ballance was forced to turn briefly to spin, but opted for the Taunton specialist, Lyth.

Once the second-wicket stand worth 141 had been broken, however, Yorkshire's seamers reasserted themselves and dismissed the hosts for 216, Brooks taking 5-57.

Yorkshire's reply got off to the worst possible start. Lyth was run out backing up too far with no runs

JACK BROOKS: Fought back after onslaught

scored. When four wickets fell at 64 there was work to be done to avoid the follow-on, which Somerset would have enforced in the face of a poor final-day weather forecast. Bresnan steered Yorkshire to short-term safety, and next morning they were back in the game with Somerset four wickets down for only 24, a lead of 144. The support bowlers could not match the depth of Somerset's pace attack, and led by skipper Abell they reached 200 to leave Yorkshire wanting 321.

Bad light limited the reply to 49-1 at the close, but a revised forecast left Yorkshire needing to bat out the last day. Viewing from behind the arm still meant sitting in chilling conditions while those sheltered from the wind enjoyed shirt-sleeve warmth. Lyth and Ballance were victims of the pitch, and only Bresnan and Leaning managed a half-century stand. Davey broke down while bowling, but Abell stepped up as a more than useful fifth seamer, breaking the stand and taking a second wicket as Somerset closed out the game in mid-afternoon for their second win in two matches, this time by 116 runs.

Specsavers County Championship Division 1
Essex v. Yorkshire

Played at The Cloud FM County Ground, Chelmsford, on May 4, 5 and 6, 2018
Yorkshire won by 91 runs at 12.29pm on the Third Day

Toss won by Yorkshire   Yorkshire 19 points, Essex 3 points

Close of play: First Day, Yorkshire 2nd Inns 161-2 (Brook 57*, Pujara 22*); Second Day, Essex 97-4 (Lawrence 22*, ten Doeschate 27*)

First Innings	YORKSHIRE		Second innings	
A Lyth, c Foster b S J Cook	0		c Harmer b Siddle	27
H C Brook, c Harmer b S J Cook	0		(3) c Westley b Harmer	124
C A Pujara, lbw b Porter	9		(4) b Siddle	41
J E Root, c A N Cook b S J Cook	0		(5) b Bopara	35
* G S Ballance, c Browne b Siddle	22		(6) b Bopara	3
§ J M Bairstow, b S J Cook	7		(2) b Siddle	50
J A Leaning, lbw b Siddle	7		b Porter	29
T T Bresnan, lbw b S J Cook	1		lbw b Porter	0
S A Patterson, c Foster b Siddle	2		b Porter	7
J A Brooks, c Browne b Siddle	0		c Foster b Siddle	1
B O Coad, not out	0		not out	2
Extras nb 2	2		Extras b 4, lb 6	10
Total	50		Total	329

Bonus points — Essex 3

FoW: 1-0 (Brook), 2-9 (Lyth), 3-9 (Root), 4-11 (Pujara), 5-22 (Bairstow),
1st   6-41 (Leaning), 7-42 (Bresnan), 8-45 (Patterson), 9-45 (Patterson), 10-50 (Ballance)
FoW: 1-77 (Bairstow), 2-96 (Lyth), 3-190 (Pujara), 4-276 (Root), 5-288 (Brook),
2nd   6-290 (Ballance), 7-290 (Bresnan), 8-304 (Patterson), 9-305 (Brooks), 10-329 (Leaning)

	O	M	R	W		O	M	R	W
Porter	6	2	15	1	Porter	27.3	5	89	3
S J Cook	9	0	28	5	S J Cook	15	1	56	0
Siddle	3.4	0	7	4	Siddle	25	7	65	4
					Harmer	15	2	70	1
					Bopara	11	3	33	2
					Lawrence	1	0	6	0

First Innings	ESSEX		Second innings	
N J L Browne, b Coad	7		b Patterson	10
A N Cook, c Bairstow b Brooks	0		b Patterson	26
T Westley, b Brooks	0		lbw b Patterson	0
D W Lawrence, lbw b Bresnan	48		lbw b Patterson	32
R A Bopara, c Pujara b Patterson	9		c Brook b Patterson	0
* R N ten Doeschate, lbw b Bresnan	18		lbw b Coad	34
§ J S Foster, b Bresnan	3		c Bairstow b Coad	0
S R Harmer, c Bresnan b Coad	36		lbw b Coad	0
P M Siddle, c Ballance b Brooks	15		lbw b Bresnan	24
J A Porter, lbw b Coad	0		lbw b Patterson	3
S J Cook, not out	3		not out	5
Extras lb 3	3		Extras b 8, lb 4	12
Total	142		Total	146

Bonus points — Yorkshire 3

FoW: 1-2 (A N Cook), 2-2 (Westley), 3-12 (Browne), 4-58 (Bopara), 5-72 (Lawrence),
1st   6-80 (Foster), 7-93 (ten Doeschate), 8-120 (Siddle), 9-121 (Porter), 10-142 (Harmer)
FoW: 1-34 (A N Cook), 2-34 (Westley), 3-55 (Browne), 4-55 (Bopara), 5-114 (ten Doeschate),
2nd   6-114 (Foster), 7-114 (Harmer), 8-114 (Lawrence), 9-126 (Porter), 10-146 (Siddle)

	O	M	R	W		O	M	R	W
Coad	14.5	4	27	3	Coad	18	10	36	3
Brooks	14	1	63	3	Brooks	6	0	27	0
Patterson	8	2	23	1	Patterson	18	3	40	6
Bresnan	7	1	26	3	Bresnan	9	3	26	1

Umpires: R A Kettleborough and S J O'Shaughnessy   Scorers: J T Potter and A E Choat

Essex v. Yorkshire
Master stroke pays off

HARRY BROOK: Yorkshire's fourth-youngest centurion

Yorkshire welcomed back Bairstow, Root and Patterson, while Cook played for the Champions.

The England men contributed little in terms of runs.

Yorkshire elected to toss and bat on a brown track which concealed dangers that lurked beneath. The morning was painful to watch, and Yorkshire were fired out for 50 — well below their lowest score in Essex, which was set the previous year.

However, by lunch Brooks already had two wickets. The afternoon session was sufficient to dismiss Essex for 142, threatening a match completed in a single day. Gale produced a master stroke: he sent in Bairstow to open with Lyth. By the time Bairstow was bowled for 50 in the 15th over the initiative was with Yorkshire, and Harry Brook could play his natural game to great effect.

Yorkshire led by 72 at the close, and a productive second morning extended this by another hundred, Brook completing his ton before the break. He is the fourth youngest centurion for Yorkshire, but once he was dismissed for 124 the innings fell away, and Essex needed 238.

There were 32 overs to bowl on the second day, just enough for the pace bowlers to give their all. Bairstow now made a second telling intervention: by standing up not only to Patterson, but to Coad, he deprived the batsmen of the scope to attack from outside the crease. Patterson had shaken off any rustiness, and his second and fifth overs produced a brace of wickets. The fifth wicket added 42 before the close to restore a small advantage to the home side.

Coad was switched to the River end at the start of the third day, and he and Patterson prevented any dominance from the bat. When the score reached 114 Essex imploded, Patterson's fifth wicket uprooting the middle stump for the second time in the innings. The last hour and a half were as miserable for Essex as the first had been for Yorkshire.

Only once before, at Hove in 1924, had Yorkshire won with a smaller first-innings score.

Specsavers County Championship Division 1
Surrey v. Yorkshire

Played at The Kia Oval on May, 11, 12, 13 and 14, 2018
Surrey won by an innings and 17 runs at 11.44am on the Fourth Day

Toss: None. Yorkshire opted to field.   Surrey 24 points, Yorkshire 4 points

Close of play: First Day, Surrey 366-7 (Pope 131*, McKerr 27*); Second Day, Yorkshire 40-3 (Root 14*, Brook 1*); Third Day, Yorkshire 142-5 (Bairstow 25*, Leaning 13*)

SURREY

* R J Burns, c Pujara b Brooks		9
M D Stoneman, lbw b Bresnan		10
S G Borthwick, c Lyth b Shaw		5
D Elgar, b Root		61
§ B T Foakes, b Bairstow b Patterson		18
O J D Pope, not out		158
S M Curran, c Bairstow b Patterson		19
R Clarke, c Lyth b Brooks		71
C McKerr, c Pujara b Bresnan		29
J W Dernbach, c Root b Patterson		14
GS Virdi, c Leaning b Bresnan		1
Extras b 4, lb 10, w 1, nb 4		19
Total		414

Bonus points — Surrey 5, Yorkshire 3

FoW: 1-15 (Stoneman), 2-19 (Burns), 3-40 (Borthwick), 4-69 (Foakes), 5-137 (Elgar), 6-162 (Curran), 7-291 (Clarke), 8-373 (McKerr), 9-404 (Dernbach), 10-414 (Virdi)

	O	M	R	W
Bresnan	26.1	5	98	3
Brooks	18	0	91	2
Shaw	17	2	76	1
Patterson	27	2	107	3
Root	11	1	27	1
Brooks	2	1	1	0

First Innings	YORKSHIRE	Second Innings
A Lyth, lbw b Curran	6	c Clarke b Virdi	58
A Z Lees, c Elgar b Dernbach	0	c Borthwick b Dernbach	4
C A Pujara, c Borthwick b Curran	17	b Curran	0
* J E Root, lbw b Curran	14	b Virdi	23
H C Brook, c Foakes b Curran	17	lbw b Virdi	8
§ J M Bairstow, c Clarke b Dernbach	95	c Foakes b Clarke	29
J A Leaning, lbw b Curran	20	lbw b Clarke	28
T T Bresnan, c Borthwick b Curran	1	c Foakes b Curran	1
S A Patterson, c Pope b Clarke	5	b Curran	0
J Shaw, c Elgar b Curran	29	b Curran	0
J A Brooks, not out	5	not out	4
Extras b 6, lb 7, w 1, nb 6	20	Extras b 1, lb 3, w 1, nb 8	13
Total	229	Total	168

Bonus points — Yorkshire 1, Surrey 3

FoW: 1-1 (Lees), 2-7 (Lyth), 3-34 (Pujara), 4-41 (Root), 5-88 (Brook),
1st 6-155 (Leaning), 7-158 (Bresnan), 8-183 (Patterson), 9-203 (Bairstow), 10-229 (Shaw)
FoW: 1-9 (Lees), 2-10 (Pujara), 3-66 (Root), 4-99 (Lyth), 5-102 (Brook),
2nd 6-151 (Bairstow), 7-164 (Bresnan), 8-164 (Patterson), 9-164 (Shaw), 10-168 (Leaning)

	O	M	R	W		O	M	R	W
Dernbach	18	2	81	2	Dernbach	13	4	24	1
Curran	16.2	4	54	4	Curran	17	6	47	4
Clarke	16	2	47	2	Clarke	17.1	3	41	2
McKerr	3	0	16	0	Virdi	19	1	52	3
Virdi	4	1	18	0					

Umpires: D J Millns and M J Saggers   Scorers: J T Potter and P J Makepeace

Root out twice in day

Two changes were forced on Yorkshire by illness and injury, Root taking over the captaincy from Ballance, who was unwell, and paceman Coad standing down with a strain.

Yorkshire wisely invited Surrey to bat on a strip far more bowler friendly than in Surrey's previous drawn game. The visitors began well enough with four wickets before lunch and six for 162, but two dropped catches enabled the last recognised pair to prosper.

Moreover, by perhaps over-bowling Bresnan earlier in the day, there was no stamina to wipe out the last three with the second new ball.

It was not until the second day that Yorkshire managed to close the innings, and then a stuttering start left them 40-3 when rain intervened. The third day sealed Yorkshire's fate.

Root was out in the first over, and although Bairstow survived some terrifying risks, both in shot selection and running between the wickets, for his 95,

JONATHAN BAIRSTOW
Took risks, but hit 95

Yorkshire rarely looked like avoiding the follow-on, which was duly enforced. Lees again failed to take advantage of the opportunity afforded by Ballance's withdrawal.

Root was out for a second time in the day, seemingly unable to bat in the way that had become his trademark. Lyth and Bairstow survived to the end, courtesy of two missed stumpings, but after 20 minutes on the fourth day Lyth was caught in the cordon and the rest followed meekly — so meekly that 34 runs needed to make Surrey bat again proved beyond the last four wickets.

Lyth batted well for his first half-century of the season, but this was a disappointing performance. The only hope was that Pope (158 not out), Sam Curran (10 wickets in the match for 101) and Virdi (3-52 in the second innings) — all born in 1998 — might be sequestrated by the ECB before Scarborough.

Specsavers County Championship Division 1
Hampshire v. Yorkshire (Day/Night)

Played at The Ageas Bowl, West End, Southampton, on June 20, 21, 22 and 23, 2018
Match drawn at 7.50pm on the Fourth Day

Toss won by Yorkshire

Hampshire 11 points, Yorkshire 10 points

Close of play: First Day, Yorkshire 315-7 (Bresnan 33*, Patterson 18*); Second Day, Hampshire 245-3 (Adams 132*, Alsop 62*); Third Day, Yorkshire 91-2 (Pujara 14*, Ballance 18*)

YORKSHIRE

First Innings		Second Innings	
A Lyth, c Alsop b Berg	21	c Alsop b Rayner	17
A Z Lees, lbw b Edwards	0	lbw b Rayner	39
C A Pujara, b Steyn	0	b Holland	32
G S Ballance, c Northeast b Steyn	109	c Alsop b Rayner	21
H C Brook, lbw b Steyn	79	run out (Berg)	68
J A Leaning, b Edwards	39	not out	54
§ J A Tattersall, c Rayner b Steyn	6	b Rayner	22
T T Bresnan, b Edwards	35	not out	4
* S A Patterson, c Steyn b Abbott	37		
J A Brooks, c Rayner b Steyn	1		
B O Coad, not out	13		
Extras b 2, lb 4, nb 4	10	Extras lb 2, nb 4	6
Total	350	Total (6 wkts dec)	263

Bonus points — Yorkshire 4, Hampshire 3

FoW: 1-1 (Lees), 2-10 (Pujara), 3-21 (Lyth), 4-164 (Brook), 5-235 (Ballance), 6-245
1st (Tattersall). 7-277 (Leaning), 8-318 (Bresnan), 9-319 (Brooks), 10-350 (Patterson)

FoW: 1-49 (Lyth), 2-58 (Lees), 3-108 (Ballance), 4-112 (Pujara), 5-220 (Brook),
2nd 6-256 (Tattersall)

	O	M	R	W		O	M	R	W
Edwards	23	2	109	3	Steyn	21	6	47	0
Steyn	29	9	66	5	Edwards	13	2	53	0
Berg	17	2	51	1	Berg	14	8	26	0
Abbott	13.2	3	58	1	Holland	17	7	44	1
Holland	13	2	35	0	Rayner	33	9	54	4
Rayner	9	3	25	0	Abbott	14	5	34	0
					Adams	1	0	3	0

HAMPSHIRE

J J Weatherley, lbw b Brooks	7
J H K Adams, c Tattersall b Bresnan	147
* J M Vince, b Brooks	35
S A Northeast, b Patterson	4
§ T P Alsop, lbw b Brooks	63
I G Holland, c Tattersall b Brooks	31
G K Berg, not out	84
O P Rayner, c Tattersall b Patterson	0
K J Abbott, c sub (J A Thompson b Lyth	35
D W Steyn, b Patterson	23
F H Edwards, c Tattersall b Brooks	0
Extras b 1, lb 7, nb 6	14
Total	443

Bonus points — Hampshire 3, Yorkshire 1

Score at 110 overs: 302-5

FoW: 1-9 (Weatherley), 2-63 (Vince),3-68 (Northeast), 4-247 (Alsop), 5-286 (Adams),
6-309 (Holland), 7-310 (Rayner), 8-384 (Abbott), 9-42 (Steyn), 10-43 (Edwards)

	O	M	R	W
Coad	27	9	81	0
Brooks	30.4	3	124	5
Patterson	32	10	67	3
Bresnan	27	5	78	1
Lyth	19	3	54	1
Brook	1	0	8	0
Leaning	8	0	23	0

Umpires: J W Lloyds and R J Warren

Scorers: J T Potter and K R Baker

Brook twice in the pink

GARY BALLANCE: Sublime on return

Steven Patterson began his first-class captaincy career in this day-night match with a successful call at the toss.

Ironically it led to Yorkshire batting in the least batsman-friendly conditions of the game.

After the early loss of three wickets, Ballance, 109, and Brook, 79, batted sublimely until cloud cover made sighting the pink ball difficult. Patterson and Bresnan battled hard in the final session, occasionally rewarded in turn when the sighting issue transferred to the fielders.

After the first day, glorious sunny weather on the longest days of the year ensured that conditions were little different from those in a standard day match played under lights. Patterson and Coad carried Yorkshire to an unexpected fourth batting point, and then the skipper relished the new scoreboard which devoted its largest font to the message, MAIDEN OVER whenever appropriate — in Patterson's case on 10 occasions.

Hampshire's more cautious approach restricted them to three batting points but limited Yorkshire to one for bowling. Except when Yorkshire were able to take the second new ball five overs from the close of the second day the Kookaburra ball offered nothing to the bowlers, and Coad went wicketless for the first time in an innings since the match in which he made his debut.

Brooks eventually completed a five wicket haul.

Yorkshire were left with more than a day in which to bat to secure a draw. There was a minor tremor when the third and fourth wickets fell in successive overs 40 minutes into the final day, but Brook and Leaning batted serenely throughout the afternoon session.

Eventually, Berg induced Leaning to play two straight-drives in an over, both of which he deflected into the stumps at the non-striker's end. Brook was run out for 68, Tattersall unmoved. Until Adams bowled the final over Hampshire had relied exclusively on six men born overseas.

105

Specsavers County Championship Division 1
Yorkshire v. Surrey

Played at North Marine Road, Scarborough, on June 25, 26, 27 and 28, 2018
Surrey won by 7 wickets at 2.16pm on the Fourth Day

Toss won by Yorkshire   Surrey 21 points, Yorkshire 6 points

Close of play: First Day, Yorkshire 299-8 (Patterson 17*, Brooks 9*); Second Day, Surrey 219-7 (Pope 34*, Morkel 18*); Third Day, Surrey 2nd Inns 89-0 (Burns 55*, Stoneman 32*)

First Innings	YORKSHIRE		Second Innings	
A Lyth, c de Bruyn b Morkel		42	c Pope b Morkel	7
A Z Lees, c and b Dernbach		0	c Dernbach b Morkel	1
C A Pujara, c Jacks b Virdi		23	b Dernbach	17
G S Ballance, b Clarke		54	c Jacks b Morkel	15
H C Brook, lbw b Virdi		0	c Pope b Clarke	6
J A Leaning, c Jacks b Dernbach		21	c Pope b Morkel	15
§ J A Tattersall, c Borthwick b Morkel		70	lbw b Morkel	23
T T Bresnan, b Clarke		48	c Pope b Patel	18
* S A Patterson, b Dernbach		21	not out	25
J A Brooks, c Burns b Dernbach		27	c Clarke b Dernbach	13
B O Coad, not out		0	b Dernbach	4
Extras b 11, lb 6, nb 14		31	Extras lb 8	8
Total		337	Total	152

Penalties awarded following First Innings 5
Adjusted Total   342

Bonus points — Yorkshire 3, Surrey 3

FoW: 1-6 (Lees), 2-51 (Lyth), 3-107 (Pujara), 4-107 (Brook), 5-139 (Ballance),
1st 6-166 (Leaning), 7-266 (Bresnan), 8-276 (Tattersall), 9-337 (Brooks), 10-337 (Patterson)
FoW: 1-3 (Lees), 2-8 (Lyth), 3-24 (Ballance), 4-42 (Brook), 5-48 (Pujara),
2nd 6-70 (Leaning), 7-103 (Bresnan), 8-115 (Tattersall), 9-148 (Brooks), 1-152 (Coad)

	O	M	R	W		O	M	R	W
Morkel	26	7	63	2	Morkel	16	4	39	5
Dernbach	24.5	3	104	4	Dernbach	13.4	5	34	3
Clarke	20	6	52	2	Clarke	12	3	25	1
Patel	11	3	28	0	Virdi	18	6	32	0
Virdi	20	1	69	2	Patel	4	1	14	1
Borthwick	1	0	4	0					

First Innings	SURREY		Second Innings	
* R J Burns, c Tattersall b Coad		59	c Lees b Bresnan	97
M D Stoneman, c Tattersall b Coad		9	lbw b Coad	32
S G Borthwick, c Tattersall b Bresnan		20	b Leaning	62
R Patel, c Brook b Bresnan		32	not out	24
T B de Bruyn, c Tattersall b Patterson		38	not out	8
§ O J D Pope, not out		69		
W G Jacks, lbw b Patterson		7		
R Clarke, c and b Bresnan		0		
M Morkel, c Lyth b Coad		29		
J W Dernbach, c Leaning b Coad		0		
G S Virdi, b Coad		0		
Extras nb 4		4	Extras lb 4, nb 2	6
Total		267	Total (3 wkts)	229

Bonus points — Surrey 2, Yorkshire 3

FoW: 1-9 (Stoneman), 2-71 (Borthwick), 3-105 (Burns), 4-140 (Patel), 5-172 (de Bruyn),
1st 6-192 (Jacks), 7-197 (Clarke), 8-253 (Morkel), 9-253 (Dernbach), 10-267 (Virdi)
2nd 1-99 (Stoneman), 2-146 (Burns), 3-220 (Borthwick)

	O	M	R	W		O	M	R	W
Coad	20.2	5	53	5	Coad	17	6	47	1
Brooks	15	1	73	0	Brooks	14	2	53	0
Patterson	26	7	61	2	Patterson	14	4	39	0
Bresnan	21	2	77	3	Bresnan	9	0	51	1
Lyth	1	0	3	0	Lyth	3	1	10	0
					Leaning	8	3	16	1
					Brook	1.1	0	9	0

Umpires: P J Hartley and P R Pollard   Scorers: J T Potter and P J Makepeace

Game of mist opportunities!

JONATHAN TATTERSALL: Fine home Championship debut

Surrey won comfortably after Yorkshire had conceded first-innings advantage with a disappointing batting performance, admittedly against a fine Test bowler in Morne Morkel.

The weather was generally hot except on a distinctly chilly Tuesday, when sea mist disrupted play.

Yorkshire chose to bat and had a good first day, finishing on 299-8. Lyth cover-drove fluently, and Ballance made a stolid 50, but it was Tattersall, playing his first home Championship match, who top-scored with 70. Bresnan provided good support. Morkel bowled well, while Dernbach was more expensive but took most wickets. Clarke was his usual threat and Virdi, one of four of last year's Under-19 England players in the Surrey side, bowled his off-breaks skilfully. Yorkshire added 43 runs on Tuesday, including five penalty runs.

The Yorkshire seamers had seven Surrey wickets by the close on Tuesday, partly in sea-fretful conditions, and next morning Coad, still uncapped, finished them off with three wickets in four balls, taking five altogether. Pope, an Old Cranleighan like Jim Swanton, was having an excellent season, and was undefeated on 69.

Morkel, the South African Test bowler who played once for Yorkshire but was injured early on, now took control. He is very tall, gets disconcerting bounce, but he is also accurate, offering few opportunities to score. Yorkshire's batting in first-class cricket had been disappointing, but this time they had to deal with an outstanding cricketer at his best.

There was further disappointment from the home point of view as Surrey reached a competitive target of 228 with no difficulty. Burns made a fine 97 – he had scored the most first-class runs at this stage and led Surrey to the top of the Championship table with a strong prospect of winning it. Yorkshire were well beaten, but it is fair to state that they were without seven players currently representing England in a variety of limited-overs matches.

Specsavers County Championship Division 1
Lancashire v. Yorkshire

Played at Emirates Old Trafford, Manchester, on July 22, 23 and 24, 2018
Yorkshire won by 118 runs at 11.39am on the Third Day

Toss won by Yorkshire — Yorkshire 19 points, Lancashire 3-1 = 2 points
Close of play: First Day, Lancashire 109 all out: Second Day, Lancashire 194-6 (Bailey 38*, Onions 0*)

	First Innings	YORKSHIRE		Second Innings	
A Lyth, c Jennings b Anderson	70		c Vilas b Onions		4
H C Brook, b Onions	6		c Vilas b Bailey		55
J E Root, lbw b Clark	22		c Vilas b Anderson		3
K S Williamson, lbw b Clark	0		c Vilas b Onions		1
§ J M Bairstow, c Buttler b Clark	0		c Buttler b Onions		82
G S Ballance, b Onions	9		c Vilas b Bailey		9
T T Bresnan, run out (Clark)	22		b Clark		18
* S A Patterson, c Jennings b Bailey	22		not out		45
J A Brooks, b Hameed b Clark	14		st Vilas b Parkinson		5
J E Poysden, not out	20		c Hameed b Parkinson		1
B O Coad, b Clark	15		b Clark		0
Extras b 4, lb 6, nb 4	14		Extras b 6, lb 8, nb 2		16
Total	192		Total		239

Bonus points — Lancashire 3

FoW: 1-24 (Brook), 2-59 (Root), 3-59 (Williamson), 4-59 (Bairstow), 5-78 (Ballance),
1st 6-86 (Bresnan), 7-131 (Patterson), 8-131 (Lyth), 9-166 (Brooks), 10-192 (Coad)
FoW: 1-5 (Lyth), 2-18 (Root), 3-21 (Williamson), 4-154 (Brook), 5-160 (Bairstow),
2nd 6-170 (Ballance), 7-211 (Bresnan), 8-230 (Brooks), 9-238 (Poysden), 10-239 (Coad)

	O	M	R	W		O	M	R	W
Anderson	15	3	38	1	Anderson	9	0	52	1
Bailey	12	4	22	1	Onions	12	0	44	3
Onions	13	3	48	2	Bailey	9	1	47	2
Clark	12.1	1	58	5	Clark	10.3	0	39	2
Parkinson	5	1	16	0	Jennings	3	0	20	0
					Parkinson	8	2	23	2

	First Innings	LANCASHIRE		Second Innings	
K K Jennings, c Root b Bresnan	22		lbw b Coad		30
A L Davies, c Bairstow b Coad	51		lbw b Bresnan		32
H Hameed, b Patterson	1		c Bairstow b Patterson		31
§ D J Vilas, lbw b Patterson	0		lbw b Poysden		1
J C Buttler, c Bairstow b Bresnan	3		c Williamson b Root		59
J Clark, c Bresnan b Brooks	15		c Bairstow b Patterson		0
T E Bailey, b Coad	0		lbw b Patterson		45
G Onions, b Coad	0		c Bairstow b Root		0
M W Parkinson, not out	9		c Lyth b Root		2
J M Anderson, lbw b Brooks	8		b Root		0
* L S Livingstone, absent injured			not out		0
Extras	0		Extras b 1, lb 1, nb 2		4
Total	109		Total		204

Bonus points — Yorkshire 3

Over-rate deduction 1 point

FoW: 1-46(Jennings), 2-55 (Hameed), 3-55 (Vilas), 4-66 (Buttler), 5-92 (Davies),
1st 6-92 (Bailey), 7-92 (Onions), 8-92 (Clark), 9-109 (Anderson)
FoW: 1-54 (Davies), 2-86 (Jennings), 3-87(Vilas), 4-110 (Hameed), 5-110 (Clark),
2nd 6-190 (Buttler), 7-194 (Onions), 8-196 (Parkinson), 9-204 (Bailey), 10-204 (Anderson)

	O	M	R	W		O	M	R	W
Coad	9	3	28	3	Coad	11	3	29	1
Brooks	6.4	1	24	2	Brooks	8	0	50	0
Patterson	8	1	34	2	Bresnan	9	2	43	1
Bresnan	7	1	23	2	Patterson	18	6	38	3
					Poysden	7	0	37	1
					Root	7.4	5	5	4

Umpires: P R Pollard and A G Wharf   Scorers: J T Potter and C Rimmer

Lancashire v. Yorkshire
Rooted in tradition

Spectators debated for two sessions the efficacy of choosing to bat after unexpected rain as Yorkshire slumped to 86-6 and then 192 all out.

Jordan Clark's hat-trick — Root, Williamson and Bairstow — comprised three batsmen in the world top 20 Test players, and it was left to Patterson to give Lyth support in a crucial stand.

JOE ROOT: Career-best 4-5

The game turned on a spectacular catch by Root to break a stubborn first-wicket stand and open the floodgates. No hat-trick, but a double-wicket maiden for Patterson and a treble-wicket maiden for Coad were more effective, and before the scheduled close Lancashire's innings closed 83 in arrears. A serious injury to their skipper, Livingstone, was a mitigating circumstance.

Yorkshire's star batsmen again struggled, but Bairstow, reprieved on 22, and Brook combined in the only century stand of the match. It ended after one o'clock – lunch delayed by the addition of four overs lost on the first day. Bairstow departed soon after the interval, and Yorkshire needed the batting of Patterson to extend their lead beyond 300.

The revised hours left Yorkshire 48 overs to bowl in a hot evening session. The opening spells again went unrewarded, but Bresnan made the breakthrough. Once Patterson had settled into a rhythm his second double-wicket maiden looked to have sealed matters, but as the evening wore on Yorkshire tired, and Lancashire recovered from 110-5.

Patterson was obliged to return to stem the flow of runs, but it was the belated introduction of Root to the bowling crease that proved decisive: he suckered Buttler into edging a bad ball to leg-slip, ending a stand of 84, and next morning, with Coad off the field, the same two bowlers continued and wrapped up the innings in 40 minutes, Root taking career-best figures of 4-5.

In another role reversal Anderson, who struggled to maintain the over rate required in county cricket, showed commendable humanity with the bat. Having defended stoutly when Bailey was at the crease, he changed tack to ensure that Livingstone, who emerged in plaster with over a hundred needed, was not required to risk further injury.

Specsavers County Championship Division 1
Yorkshire v. Worcestershire

Played at North Marine Road, Scarborough, on August 19, 20, 21 and 22, 2018
Worcestershire won by an innings and 186 runs at 11.39am on the Fourth Day

Toss: None. Worcestershire opted to field   Worcestershire 24 points, Yorkshire 1 point
Close of play: First Day, Worcestershire 39-0 (Mitchell 16*, Fell 21*); Second Day, Worcestershire 310-1 (Mitchell 140*, Ali 107*); Third Day, Yorkshire 140-6 (Tattersall 7*, Willey 8*)

First Innings	YORKSHIRE		Second Innings	
A Lyth, lbw b Barnard		20	lbw b Ali	17
H C Brook, c Pennington b Tongue		6	c Tongue b Ali	16
K S Williamson, b Ali		87	c Cox b Parnell	61
G S Ballance, c Barnard b Pennington		3	c Clarke b Ali	19
T Kohler-Cadmore, c Barnard b Pennington		0	lbw b Ali	8
§ J A Tattersall, c Mitchell b Pennington		27	not out	15
T T Bresnan, c Fell b Pennington		2	c Mitchell b Parnell	0
* D J Willey, c Clarke b Ali		0	b Ali	5
M D Fisher, not out		20	c Cox b Ali	0
J A Brooks, c and b Barnard		38	b Pennington	9
J E Poysden, c Fell b Barnard		1	c Mitchell b Pennington	1
Extras b 2, lb 6, nb 4		12	Extras b 10, lb 5, nb 4	19
Total		216	Total	170

Bonus points — Yorkshire 1, Worcestershire 3

FoW: 1st: 1-8 (Brook), 2-42 (Lyth), 3-63 (Ballance), 4-63 (Kohler-Cadmore), 5-151 (Tattersall), 6-153 (Williamson), 7-155 (Bresnan), 8-155 (Willey), 9-211 (Brooks), 10-216 (Poysden)

FoW: 2nd: 1-37 (Lyth), 2-40 (Brook), 3-92 (Ballance), 4-116 (Kohler-Cadmore), 5-136 (Williamson), 6-138 (Bresnan), 7-149 (Willey), 8-149 (Fisher), 9-164 (Brooks), 10-170 (Poysden)

	O	M	R	W		O	M	R	W
Parnell	12	0	47	0	Parnell	16	5	33	2
Tongue	14	4	36	1	Tongue	10	2	28	0
Barnard	12.4	3	32	3	Barnard	5	0	18	0
Pennington	16	2	53	4	Pennington	8.1	3	27	2
Ali	7	0	40	2	Ali	23	7	49	6

WORCESTERSHIRE

D K H Mitchell, c Bresnan b Lyth		178
T C Fell, lbw b Brooks		45
* M M Ali, c Brook b Bresnan		219
J M Clarke, lbw b Lyth		34
§ O B Cox, lbw b Poysden		18
R A Whiteley, c Bresnan b Poysden		6
E G Barnard, c Fisher b Poysden		34
A G Milton, not out		9
W D Parnell		
J C Tongue	Did not bat	
D Y Pennington		
Extras b 10, lb 14, w 1, nb 4		29
Total (7 wkts dec)		572

Bonus points — Worcestershire 5   Score at 110 overs: 414-2

FoW: 1-111 (Fell), 2-405 (Mitchell), 3-473 (Clarke), 4-522 (Ali), 5-525 (Cox), 6-544 (Whiteley), 7-572 (Barnard)

	O	M	R	W
Brooks	23	5	77	1
Willey	24	3	71	0
Fisher	26	5	84	0
Bresnan	22	3	91	1
Poysden	25.2	1	128	3
Lyth	19	1	97	2

Umpires: N A Mallender and R T Robinson   Scorers: J T Potter and P M Mellish

Yorkshire v. Worcestershire

Moeen the magnificent

This was Yorkshire's heaviest defeat at Scarborough after an outstanding display by Worcestershire.

Moeen Ali's excellent 219 was the best by a visiting batsman on this ground, but Mitchell's dedicated endurance and massive 178 was just as impressive.

Moeen then took six wickets in the second innings with well flighted off-breaks,

In with a shout: wicket-keeper Jonathan Tattersall, Tim Bresnan and Harry Brook try to stop Moeen Ali's two-ton epic.

while the young Worcestershire bowlers, especially Pennington, all contributed to the success of the county coached by Kevin Sharp.

An uncontested toss put Yorkshire in, and only Williamson and a late stand by Brooks and Fisher enabled them to gain what would be their only point of the match. Williamson, dropped at slip, hit four successive boundaries off Parnell. Tattersall stayed patiently to add 88 with Williamson before four wickets fell for four runs, mainly to Pennington, a young fast bowler with a good action and considerable stamina.

Moeen Ali's 219 was an innings of genuine quality. For most of the second day he showed sensible restraint on a lively wicket, then accelerated on Tuesday morning with some fine clean hitting. He has the judgement, timing and power of a true Test batsman despite his difficult winter. Mitchell, who comes from Badsey near Evesham in the heart of Worcestershire, has not played Test cricket, but he had the temperament and technical skill to compile a large score and not surrender his wicket. He made his runs off 333 balls.

In mitigation it should be said that Yorkshire's seam attack did not bowl as badly as the score suggests. Fisher in particular deserved some wickets and Willey bowled well round the wicket from the Trafalgar Square end, but the two spinners conceded 225 for their five wickets.

Moeen now demonstrated his spin bowling skills, taking 6-49 to add to his two in the first innings. Only Williamson, and Tattersall at the end, showed the necessary resolution, and Brook will regret his impulsive drive when long-term survival was the objective.

Specsavers County Championship Division 1
Yorkshire v. Somerset

Played at Emerald Headingley, Leeds, on August 29, 30, 31 and September 1, 2018
Somerset won by 224 runs at 4.39pm on the Fourth Day

Toss won by Yorkshire

Somerset 23 points, Yorkshire 6 points

Close of play: First Day, Somerset 374-8 (J Overton 8*, Leach 3*); Second Day, Yorkshire 292-7 (Hodd 84*); Third Day, Yorkshire 8-2 (Shaw 4*, Williamson 0*)

First Innings		SOMERSET	Second Innings	
M E Trescothick, c Lyth b Willey	4		c Lyth b Willey	15
E J Byrom, c Hodd b Brooks	1		b Willey	4
Azhar Ali, b Shaw	89		c Ballance b Fisher	9
J C Hildreth, c Kohler-Cadmore b Willey	81		c Hodd b Lyth	72
* T B Abell, c Hodd b Brooks	12		not out	132
§ S M Davies, c Ballance b Brooks	80		c Lyth b Fisher	6
L Gregory, c Williamson b Brooks	65		c Williamson b Willey	57
C Overton, c Hodd b Shaw	15		run out (Shaw/Hodd)	27
J Overton, c Leaning b Brooks	8			
M J Leach, c Lyth b Willey	9			
J H Davey, not out	13			
Extras b 1, lb 17, nb 4	22		Extras b 4, lb 10, w 1, nb 2	17
Total	399		Total (7 wkts dec)	339

Bonus points — Somerset 4, Yorkshire 3

FoW: 1-5 (Byrom), 2-5 (Trescothick), 3-142 (Hildreth), 4-170 (Abell), 5-229 (Azhar Ali),
1st   6-343 (Gregory), 7-343 (Davies), 8-369 (C Overton), 9-375 (J Overton), 10-399 (Leach)
FoW: 1-8 (Byrom), 2-28 (Azhar Ali), 3-29 (Trescothick), 4-164 (Hildreth), 5-184 (Davies),
2nd   6-277 (Gregory), 7-339 (C Overton)

	O	M	R	W		O	M	R	W
Brooks	29	8	116	5	Brooks	17.1	2	81	0
Willey	26.2	8	74	3	Willey	17	2	72	3
Fisher	14	0	55	0	Fisher	14	1	80	2
Shaw	21	3	72	2	Shaw	9	0	42	0
Lyth	6	0	32	0	Brook	7	1	19	0
Williamson	2	0	9	0	Lyth	5	0	18	1
Brook	5	1	23	0	Leaning	1	0	13	0

First Innings		YORKSHIRE	Second Innings	
A Lyth, c Trescothick b Davey	45		c Davies b Gregory	4
H C Brook, b Gregory	2		b Gregory	0
K S Williamson, c Leach b C Overton	18		(4) c Davies b C Overton	51
G S Ballance, c Leach b C Overton	37		(5) b J Overton	4
J A Leaning, c and b Davey	4		(7) b J Overton	2
T Kohler-Cadmore, c Davies c Davey	81		lbw b C Overton	0
§ A J Hodd, c Hildreth b Gregory	85		(8) b Gregory	24
M D Fisher, lbw b Davey	14		(9) c Gregory b J Overton	19
* D J Willey, c Hildreth b Davey	3		(10) not out	34
J A Brooks, c Davey b C Overton	14		(11) c Trescothick b J Overton	4
J Shaw, not out	10		(3) lbw b Gregory	42
Extras lb 11, nb 10	21		Extras lb 8, nb 2	10
Total	320		Total	194

Bonus points — Yorkshire 3, Somerset 1

FoW: 1-5 (Brook), 2-52 (Williamson), 3-111 (Lyth), 4-119 (Ballance), 5-119 (Leaning),
1st   6-292 (Kohler-Cadmore), 7-292 (Fisher), 8-296 (Willey), 9-296 (Hodd), 10-320 (Brooks)
FoW: 1-3 (Brook), 2-4 (Lyth), 3-94 (Shaw), 4-99 (Williamson), 5-103 (Kohler-Cadmore),
2nd   6-103 (Ballance), 7-124 (Leaning), 8-143 (Hodd), 9-188 (Fisher), 10-194 (Brooks)

	O	M	R	W		O	M	R	W
Gregory	25	8	66	2	Gregory	18	8	33	4
Davey	23	7	65	5	Davey	14	6	27	0
C Overton	18.2	3	59	3	C Overton	16	4	45	2
J Overton	11	1	56	0	Leach	14	3	47	0
Abell	6	0	20	0	J Overton	14.3	6	25	4
Leach	14	1	43	0	Abell	2	0	9	0

Umpires: P J Hartley and G D Lloyd

Scorers: J T Potter and G A Stickley

Hodd seizes last chance

Yorkshire invited Somerset to bat first — and took two early wickets including that of Trescothick — but the advantage was soon lost on a good batting surface.

Azhar Ali made a solid 89, and Hildreth redeemed some past Headingley failures with an accomplished 81.

Yorkshire bowled reasonably well, and it was Brooks, destined next year for Somerset, who took most wickets, but as Davies and Gregory settled into a productive sixth-wicket partnership Somerset ended the day in command.

Having dismissed their opponents quickly on Thursday morning, Yorkshire lost five wickets for 119 to a lively Somerset attack, in which Scottish-born Davey eventually claimed a career-best 5-65.

Then Kohler-Cadmore and Hodd, recalled from the Second Eleven

ANDY HODD: Cheerful top-score 85 on his final recall

because of Tattersall's back spasms, initiated a revival, and were unlucky to miss centuries. Hodd will retire with many good wishes after his cheerful and effective contribution to Yorkshire, and one hopes Kohler-Cadmore will become a regular in the Championship order.

Somerset finished 79 ahead, but soon lost three wickets. When their young captain, Abell, joined Hildreth any prospect of a home win disappeared. Abell made 132 and Gregory a rapid 57 while Willey, off his long run, took three wickets and Fisher, handicapped by a toe injury, took two. By the close on Friday the hosts had lost Lyth and Brook, twice bowled by Gregory.

Next day Yorkshire were more resolute, so it took Somerset 76.3 overs to bowl them out. Williamson and Shaw batted almost to lunch, and Shaw should be commended on a career-best 42. Once Williamson was out wickets fell, and there was a mid-innings collapse, not as anticipated to spinner Leach but to the young seam attack of the Overton twins, Gregory and Davey. Selection availability and injury had made an impact on Yorkshire's season, so they now faced four matches against relegation contenders to ensure their survival in the First Division.

Specsavers County Championship Division 1
Nottinghamshire v. Yorkshire

Played at Trent Bridge, Nottingham, on September 4, 5, 6 and 7, 2018
Match drawn at 4.20pm on the Fourth Day

Toss: None. Yorkshire opted to field   Yorkshire 12 points, Nottinghamshire 12 points

Close of play: First Day, Nottinghamshire 332-7 (Patel 4*, Milnes 1*); Second Day, Yorkshire 258-4 (Kohler-Cadmore 57*, Tattersall 12*); Third Day, Yorkshire 357-5 (Kohler-Cadmore 92*, Bresnan 11*)

NOTTINGHAMSHIRE

First Innings		Second Innings	
K C Brathwaite, lbw b Waite	71	not out	42
B T Slater, c Tattersall b Waite	109	b Poysden	39
J D Libby, lbw b Waite	1	not out	0
B M Duckett, c Tattersall b Bresnan	80		
* S J Mullaney, b Brooks	39		
§ T J Moores, c Raval b Bresnan	8		
S R Patel, c Brooks b Poysden	54		
L Wood, c Tattersall b Brooks	9		
M E Milnes, lbw b Brooks	43		
H F Gurney, c Raval b Bresnan	14		
M H A Footitt, not out	1		
Extras b 1, lb 12, nb 6	19	Extras b 2, lb 2, nb 8	12
Total	448	Total (1 wkt dec)	93

Bonus points — Nottinghamshire 5, Yorkshire 2   Score at 110 overs: 412-7

FoW: 1-182 (Brathwaite), 2-188 (Libby), 3-205 (Slater), 4-292 (Mullaney), 5-318 (Duckett), 1st 6-321 (Moores), 7-331 (Wood), 8-421 (Milnes), 9-434 (Patel), 10-448 (Gurney)
2nd 1-91 (Slater)

	O	M	R	W		O	M	R	W
Bresnan	33.3	5	93	3	Bresnan	3	1	7	0
Brookes	21	2	79	2	Pillans	8	0	32	0
Waite	23	4	91	3	Waite	3	1	6	0
Pillans	22	5	98	0	Poysden	10	0	34	1
Poysden	10	0	60	2	Lyth	7	1	10	0
Brook	6	2	7	0					
Lyth	2	0	7	0					

YORKSHIRE

* A Lyth, c Wood b Footitt	0
J A Raval, b Gurney	15
H C Brook, c Wood b Patel	47
G S Ballance, c Slater b Patel	104
T Kohler-Cadmore, b Patel	106
§ J A Tattersall, c Moores b Gurney	51
T T Bresnan, c Footitt b Libby	80
M J Waite, c Milnes b Patel	42
M W Pillans, lbw b Patel	8
J A Brookes, c Libby b Patel	1
J E Poysden, not out	2
Extras b 11, lb 10, w 3, nb 18	42
Total	498

Bonus points — Yorkshire 5, Nottinghamshire 2   Score at 110 overs: 403-6

FoW: 1-0 (Lyth), 2-59 (Raval), 3-137 (Brook), 4-232 (Ballance), 5-334 (Tattersall), 6-395 (Kohler-Cadmore), 7-469 (Waite). 8-484 (Pillans), 9-492 (Brookes), 10-498 (Bresnan)

	O	M	R	W
Footitt	22	2	79	1
Milnes	21	2	96	0
Wood	15	1	51	0
Gurney $	33.5	4	114	2
Patel	47	12	114	6
Libby $	8.3	0	23	1

$ Gurney was unable to complete his 34th over. Libby took over

Umpires: R J Bailey and S J O'Shaughnessy   Scorers: J T Potter and R Marshall

Lyth captain No. 5

TOM KOHLER-CADMORE
Top-scorer with first century

Injury to Willey meant that Lyth became Yorkshire's fifth captain of the season.

He acquitted himself well, and Yorkshire looked a more professional side as they began with 18 overs in the first hour so that they were not having to catch up later in the game.

Like Yorkshire the hosts were bolstered by three autumn signings, two from other counties, and they were the top three scorers for the home side.

An early chance went begging, and 182 were on the board before Waite broke through with the first three wickets.

Nottinghamshire had to bat under lights all day, and the second new ball made further inroads to raise hopes of a third point on the second day. Those hopes were dashed in a poor opening session, but after lunch the visitors enjoyed a succession of six half-century partnerships and highest individual scores for Yorkshire, the chief being among these being Kohler-Cadmore's first century.

The greatest tension surrounded Yorkshire's bid for a fifth batting point. Waite came to the crease with five runs needed in two balls. Patel had conceded only four in 10 up to that point, but Waite took Yorkshire over the line with aplomb and went on to make 42, which put Yorkshire in front. There was moderate slow turn for Patel, who was rewarded with six wickets.

Bresnan was last out, his 80 signalling a welcome return to form. With little likelihood of victory in the time and 47 overs remaining, Yorkshire chose to rest Brooks. But for injuries he might have been rested for the game. Instead, he and Bresnan had shouldered a heavy workload in the first innings.

The players shook hands as soon as the playing conditions allowed. Twelve points for both sides were enough to make Nottinghamshire look safe, and enabled Yorkshire to gain a point on their *Red Rose* rivals, despite Lancashire's tied game at Taunton.

Specsavers County Championship Division 1
Yorkshire v. Lancashire

Played at Emerald Headingley, Leeds, on September 10, 11, 12 and 13, 2018
Yorkshire won by 95 runs at 11.09am on the Fourth Day

Toss: None. Lancashire opted to field.　　　　　Yorkshire 20 points, Lancashire 5 points

Close of play: First Day, Lancashire 105-0 (Brown 43*, Davies 57*); Second Day, Yorkshire 127-3 (Ballance 53*, Kohler-Cadmore 42*); Third Day, Lancashire 109-7 (Bohannon 6*, Maharaj 6*)

First Innings		YORKSHIRE	Second Innings	
A Lyth, c Vilas b Bailey	16		c Vilas b Onions	7
J A Raval, b Onions	8		lbw b Bailey	10
H C Brook, c Vilas b Bailey	3		b Bailey	5
G S Ballance, lbw b Bailey	5		lbw b Maharaj	85
T Kohler-Cadmore, not out	105		lbw b Maharaj	63
§ J A Tattersall, lbw b Onions	33		c Vilas b Bailey	22
T T Bresnan, c Vilas b Onions	0		c and b Maharaj	20
M J Waite, c Vilas b Onions	0		lbw b Onions	15
* S A Patterson, b Onions	17		b Bailey	9
J A Brooks, c Maharaj b Gleeson	6		c Croft b Gleeson	1
B O Coad, c Bohannon b Gleeson	12		not out	7
Extras b 2, lb 2	4		Extras b 4, lb 20, nb 4	28
Total	209		Total	272

Bonus points — Yorkshire 1, Lancashire 3

FoW: 1-20 (Raval), 2-23 (Brook), 3-32 (Lyth), 4-33 (Ballance), 5-138 (Tattersall),
1st　6-142 (Bresnan), 7-144 (Waite), 8-177 (Patterson), 9-187 (Brooks), 10-209 (Coad)
FoW: 1-17 (Raval), 2-19 (Lyth), 3-27 (Brook), 4-175 (Kohler-Cadmore), 5-192 (Ballance),
2nd　6-214 (Tattersall), 7-238 (Waite), 8-250 (Patterson), 9-254 (Bresnan), 10-272 (Brooks)

	O	M	R	W		O	M	R	W
Bailey	14	4	18	3	Bailey	29	6	69	4
Onions	21	6	76	4	Onions	24	5	77	2
Gleeson	15.4	2	74	3	Gleeson	10.2	3	31	1
Lamb	2	1	5	0	Maharaj	32	12	52	3
Maharaj	8	1	32	0	Lamb	2	0	13	0
					Livingstone	1	0	3	0
					Bohannon	3	1	3	0

First Innings		LANCASHIRE	Second Innings	
K R Brown, c Tattersall b Coad	43		lbw b Bresnan	10
A L Davies, lbw b Brooks	87		c Tattersall b Coad	8
S J Croft, c Lyth b Brooks	11		c Raval b Brooks	13
* L S Livingstone, b Brooks	7		b Brooks	28
§ D J Vilas, lbw b Brooks	0		b Coad	10
J J Bohannon, lbw b Brooks	10		c Bresnan b Coad	13
D J Lamb, c Tattersall b Bresnan	9		lbw b Coad	0
T E Bailey, c Tattersall b Waite	16		b Coad	7
K A Maharaj, c Patterson b Coad	38		b Brooks	18
G Onions, b Waite	3		b Brooks	4
R J Gleeson, not out	9		not out	0
Extras b 13, lb 2, nb 4	19		Extras b 2, lb 19, nb 2	23
Total	252		Total	134

Bonus points — Lancashire 2, Yorkshire 3

FoW: 1-105 (Brown), 2-145 (Croft), 3-153 (Livingstone), 4-157 (Vilas), 5-166 (Davies),
1st　6-175 (Bohannan), 7-198 (Bailey), 8-212 (Lamb), 9-221 (Onions), 10-252 (Maharaj)
FoW: 1-11 (Davies), 2-31 (Brown), 3-66 (Croft), 4-81 (Livingstone), 5-87 (Vilas),
2nd　6-87 (Lamb), 7-95 (Bailey), 8-122 (Maharaj), 9-134 (Onions), 10-134 (Bohannon)

	O	M	R	W		O	M	R	W
Coad	17.2	5	57	2	Coad	15.1	6	24	5
Brooks	17	4	66	5	Brooks	15	4	47	4
Patterson	22	6	40	0	Bresnan	7	0	17	1
Bresnan	17	3	58	1	Patterson	9	3	23	0
Waite	11	5	16	2	Waite	2	1	2	0

Umpires: R J Bailey and D J Millns　　　　　Scorers: J T Potter and C Rimmer

White Rose turn tables

JACK BROOKS: Nine-wicket bag in spells of constant pace

This was an important relegation contest between traditional rivals.

Yorkshire's chances of winning seemed remote at the end of the first day as in response to 209 by the home side Lancashire were 105-0.

Asked to bat on a cool, dark morning on a greenish wicket, Yorkshire were 33-4 as Bailey and Onions took advantage.

But an excellent undefeated 105 by Kohler-Cadmore, with steadfast support from Tattersall, gave Yorkshire a bonus point.

Bailey bowled very well to take three of the top four wickets. Onions claimed four and Gleeson, from Blackpool via Northamptonshire, had an encouraging debut. Lancashire's superiority was confirmed as Davies batted beautifully in the late afternoon to add 105 with Brown. Yorkshire now fought back in triplicate.

First, they dismissed Lancashire for 252, a lead of only 43. There was an inspired spell by Brooks, assisted by Coad, Bresnan and Waite, while Patterson controlled one end, going at fewer than two an over. Brown was out straight away next morning, and then Davies for an impressive 87, after which the Lancashire batting was disappointing. Brooks's pace was a constant problem, and his five wickets were all top order men.

The hosts again lost early wickets, but the most significant partnership of the match developed between Ballance and Kohler-Cadmore, whose 148 stand gave Yorkshire hope and a competitive lead of 229. Ballance's was a defensive innings, with some well timed boundaries, while Kohler-Cadmore, with studious defence and powerful hitting, looked an authentic first-class cricketer.

Lancashire needed 230. An engrossing match was finely balanced, but Brooks and Coad bowled very well, and Lancashire's batting let them down. Coad bowled fast and straight with his good high action, conceded only 24 runs for his five wickets, and Brooks's exuberance was sustained over both innings as he took a total of nine wickets in his last-but-one game for Yorkshire at Headingley.

Specsavers County Championship Division 1
Yorkshire v. Hampshire

Played at Emerald Headingley, Leeds, on September 18, 19, 20 and 21, 2018

Match drawn at noon on the Fourth Day

Toss: None. Hampshire opted to field · Yorkshire 8 points, Hampshire 8 points

Close of play: First Day, Hampshire 79-5 (Alsop 9*, Abbott 2*); Second Day, Yorkshire 172-4 (Lyth 60*, Tattersall 14*); Third Day, Yorkshire 287-5 (Lyth 134*, Bresnan 5*)

YORKSHIRE

First Innings		Second innings	
A Lyth, c Dawson b Holland	23	not out	134
J A Raval, b Abbott	8	c Alsop b Edwards	9
H C Brook, b Edwards	0	c Alsop b Dawson	28
G S Ballance, lbw b Berg	30	lbw b Dawson	11
T Kohler-Cadmore, b Berg	2	c Alsop b Holland	33
§ J A Tattersall, b Holland	19	c Adams b Dawson	43
T T Bresnan, b Edwards	25	not out	4
M J Waite, c Alsop b Edwards	22		
* S A Patterson, b Edwards	9		
J A Brooks, b Abbott	14		
B O Coad, not out	13		
Extras b 4, lb 1, nb 14	19	Extras b 7, lb 8, nb 10	25
Total	184	Total (5 wkts)	287

Bonus points — Hampshire 3

FoW: 1st 1-21 (Raval), 2-22 (Brook), 3-70 (Ballance), 4-72 (Kohler-Cadmore), 5-72 (Lyth), 6-110 (Tattersall), 7-136 (Waite), 8-149 (Bresnan), 9-160 (Patterson), 10-184 (Brooks)

2nd 1-26 (Raval), 2-65 (Brook), 3-81 (Ballance), 4-132 (Kohler-Cadmore), 5-265 (Tattersall)

	O	M	R	W		O	M	R	W
Abbott	14.1	4	50	2	Abbott	21	4	65	0
Edwards	16	2	83	4	Edwards	11	1	37	1
Holland	12	8	16	2	Berg	8	1	42	0
Berg	10	2	30	2	Holland	15	2	43	1
					Dawson	25	4	85	3

HAMPSHIRE

J J Weatherley, lbw b Brooks	21
O C Soames, c Tattersall b Coad	6
J H K Adams, c Brook b Brooks	0
* J M Vince, lbw b Bresnan	25
S A Northeast, c Brook b Bresnan	8
§ T P Alsop, c Lyth b Bresnan	24
K J Abbott, lbw b Bresnan	8
L A Dawson, c and b Bresnan	10
I G Holland, b Waite	9
G K Berg, lbw b Coad	25
F H Edwards, not out	9
Extras lb 4, nb 4	12
Total	157

Bonus points — Yorkshire 3

FoW: 1-29 (Weatherley), 2-33 (Soames), 3-33 (Adams), 4-63 (Northeast), 5-68 (Vince), 6-96 (Abbott), 7-107 (Alsop), 8-110 (Dawson), 9-140 (Holland), 10-157 (Berg)

	O	M	R	W
Coad	16.4	7	23	2
Brooks	15	3	60	2
Bresnan	13	4	28	5
Patterson	16	6	20	0
Lyth	1	0	1	0
Waite	5	2	17	1

Umpires: M A Gough and G D Lloyd · Scorers: J T Potter and K R Baker

Yorkshire v. Hampshire
Bresnan's best return

The early-autumn season at Headingley ended in rain and strong winds, but Yorkshire had done enough virtually to ensure survival in the first division.

The right of the visiting side to bowl first means that Yorkshire usually have to bat at Headingley in conditions favourable to seam and swing bowling.

They faced experienced Test bowlers in Edwards and Abbott, well supported by Berg and Holland, a Wisconsin-born Australian, but compiled a respectable total with Ballance top-scorer on 30, including his 10,000th first-class run.

Edwards concedes runs, as Brooks does, but he produced some fine deliveries off his long run like the yorker that accounted for Bresnan and the outswinger that bowled Brook. Coad was awarded his well earned Yorkshire cap.

TIM BRESNAN: A superb catch from his own bowling to dismiss Liam Dawson and complete a career-best 5-28

By the end of the first day Yorkshire had made inroads into the Hampshire batting. Brooks dismissed Weatherley, and then claimed the crucial wicket of Adams when Brook took a fine slip catch. He took another to remove Northeast off Bresnan, who also gained the important wicket of Vince before the close. It was Bresnan's day on Wednesday as he took a career-best 5-28, giving Yorkshire a modest lead of 27. Having made his debut at Headingley in 2001 in the Sunday League aged 16, he has bowled for 18 seasons and batted with distinction, and he should continue as a Yorkshire player into his 20th season.

Yorkshire had to bat well second time to avoid the possibility of defeat, and Lyth chose the occasion to play his best innings for a long time. He had reached a circumspect 60 by the end of the second day. Brook played some fine shots, but was out to the first ball from slow bowler Dawson. Ballance fell lbw, and Kohler-Cadmore was out just as he was beginning to dominate. It was left to Tattersall to provide the support Lyth needed. The weather on the third day gave Lyth time to complete an excellent century, but no play was possible on the final day.

Specsavers County Championship Division 1
Worcestershire v. Yorkshire

Played at Blackfinch New Road, Worcester, on September 24, 25 and 26, 2018

Yorkshire won by 7 wickets at 5.22pm on the Third Day

Toss: None. Yorkshire opted to field   Yorkshire 24 points, Worcestershire 6 points

Close of play: First Day, Worcestershire 319-8 (Twohig 30*, Tongue 20*); Second Day, Yorkshire 417-9 (Balance 189*, Coad 2*)

	First Innings		WORCESTERSHIRE			Second Innings	
D K H Mitchell, c Logan b Brooks			127	c Tattersall b Brooks			5
T C Fell, c Leaning b Bresnan			19	c Lyth b Coad			21
* M M Ali, c Kohler-Cadmore b Patterson			60	c and b Patterson			67
J M Clarke, b Brooks			8	b Patterson			16
A G Milton, c Kohler-Cadmore b Coad			1	c Tattersall b Coad			10
§ O B Cox, lbw b Brooks			9	b Patterson			18
E G Barnard, lbw b Brooks			34	c Leaning b Coad			0
W D Parnell, c Lyth b Brooks			6	(9) not out			58
B J Twohig, lbw b Coad			30	(8) c Bresnan b Coad			1
J C Tongue, not out			30	c Kohler-Cadmore b Bresnan			8
D Y Pennington, c Tattersall b Brooks			9	b Bresnan			9
Extras b 4, lb 6, w 1, nb 4			15	Extras b 3, lb 3, nb 2			8
Total			340	Total			221

Bonus points — Worcestershire 3, Yorkshire 3

FoW: 1-29 (Fell), 2-131 (Ali), 3-149 (Clarke), 4-154 (Milton), 5-167 (Cox), 1st 6-255 (Barnard), 7-255 (Parnell), 8-270 (Mitchell), 9-319 (Twohig), 10-340 (Pennington)
FoW: 1-15 (Mitchell), 2-33 (Fell), 3-63 (Clarke), 4-122 (Ali), 5-122 (Milton), 2nd 6-122 (Barnard), 7-132 (Twohig), 8-158 (Cox), 9-198 (Tongue), 10-221 (Pennington)

	O	M	R	W		O	M	R	W
Coad	26	10	65	2	Coad	11	1	56	4
Brooks	22	3	94	6	Brooks	13	0	69	1
Patterson	23	8	64	1	Bresnan	10	1	48	2
Bresnan	19	5	62	1	Patterson	14	3	38	3
Logan	10	2	40	0	Logan	2	1	4	0
Leaning	2	0	5	0					

	First Innings		YORKSHIRE			Second innings	
A Lyth, lbw b Parnell			27	c and b Barnard			20
J A Raval, b Twohig			21	b Pennington			13
J A Leaning, b Tongue			13	not out			22
G S Ballance, c Pennington b Barnard			194	c Pennington b Twohig			60
T Kohler-Cadmore, lbw b Twohig			8	not out			8
§ J A Tattersall, b Tongue			19				
T T Bresnan, c Mitchell b Pennington			7				
* S A Patterson, b Tongue			6				
J E G Logan, lbw b Ali			6				
J A Brooks, c Cox b Ali			82				
B O Coad, not out			8				
Extras b 22, lb 7, nb 8			37	Extras lb 7, w 1, nb 6			14
Total			428	Total (3 wkts)			137

Bonus points — Yorkshire 5, Worcestershire 3

FoW: 1-30 (Lyth), 2-45 (Leaning), 3-83 (Raval), 4-117 (Kohler-Cadmore), 5-161 (Tattersall), 1st 6-184 (Bresnan), 7-193 (Patterson), 8-232 (Logan), 9-403 (Brooks), 10-428 (Ballance)
2nd 1-39 (Raval), 2-47 (Lyth), 3-124 (Ballance)

	O	M	R	W		O	M	R	W
Parnell	14	1	84	1	Barnard	11.1	3	31	1
Tongue	14	5	31	3	Pennington	7	1	31	1
Barnard	13.5	0	76	1	Ali	6	1	31	0
Pennington	15	2	98	1	Twohig	6	0	37	1
Ali	16	3	44	2					
Twohig	15	2	47	2					
Mitchell	3	0	19	0					

Umpires: R K Illingworth and R J Warren   Scorers: J T Potter and S M Drinkwater

Worcestershire v. Yorkshire

Farewell six from Brooks

Leaning returned after back-to-back second-team centuries, and left-arm spinner James Logan made his debut.

Brook was unlucky to miss out on being ever-present — his bowling might have been handy in the rebalanced attack.

Events elsewhere ensured at least fifth place for Yorkshire, but at the start two points were needed to guarantee safety.

Yorkshire were held up by Mitchell and Moeen Ali as at Scarborough, and then for the crucial sixth wicket. Two catches were missed, one denying Logan

GARY BALLANCE: 194 and 60

a first wicket. Patterson outwitted his rival captain, and then Brooks embarked on yet another magical spell that brought a five-wicket haul. Yorkshire tired in the last session, but next morning Brooks made it six.

Yorkshire lost wickets regularly, and when Patterson joined Ballance seven runs were needed to save the follow-on. A first-innings deficit looked inevitable when Logan was dismissed, but Worcestershire had lost their best bowler to injury and, as at Old Trafford last year, Brooks found a slow wicket to his liking. He was soon outscoring Ballance.

Moeen was compelled to resort to seam bowling to dismiss him for 82, by which time maximum batting points had been secured. With the final shot of the day Ballance surpassed 200 runs in the session for Yorkshire, exactly 100 of which had been scored by himself.

By the time he was last out for 194 Yorkshire had a lead of 88 and the momentum to win the game. Brooks took an early wicket, but the main damage was done by Patterson and Coad. Moeen's skittish innings ended in the first over after lunch: Brooks narrowly failed to take a stunning catch running to deep backward-point, but two balls later the skipper made no mistake with a return catch.

Coad left the field, and Yorkshire struggled to take the last two wickets, but the target was only 134 in four sessions. One was sufficient as Ballance maintained his late-season form with another half-century. Worcestershire had both their opening bowlers off the field.

SPECSAVERS COUNTY CHAMPIONSHIP 2018

DIVISION 1

	P	W	L	D	Tied	Abdn	BAT	BOWL	Pen	Points
							Bonus Points			
1 Surrey (Div 1, 3)	14	10	1	3	0	0	41	38	0	254
2 Somerset (Div 1, 6)	14	7	2	4	1	0	33	35	0	208
3 Essex(Div 1, 1)	14	7	4	2	0	1	25	35	0	187
4 Yorkshire (Div 1, 4)	**14**	**5**	**5**	**3**	**0**	**1**	**25**	**33**	**0**	**158**
5 Hampshire (Div 1, 5)	14	4	5	5	0	0	16	39	0	144
6 Nottinghamshire (Div 2, 2)	14	4	8	2	0	0	21	38	0	133
7 Lancashire (Div 1, 2) * ...	14	3	7	3	1	0	23	40	1	133
8 Worcestershire (Div 2, 1) *	14	2	10	2	0	0	23	39	0	104

Abandoned matches — each team takes 5 points

Pen. 1 point deducted for each over short in a match based on a rate of 16 overs per hour

Nottinghamshire finished above Lancashire as they recorded more wins

* Relegated to Division 2 for 2019

DIVISION 2

	P	W	L	D	Tied	Abdn	BAT	BOWL	Pen	Points
							Bonus Points			
1 Warwickshire (Div 1, 8) *	14	9	2	3	0	0	41	42	0	242
2 Kent (Div 2, 5) *	14	10	3	1	0	0	16	40	0	221
3 Sussex (Div 2, 4)	14	6	4	4	0	0	32	38	0	186
4 Middlesex (Div 1, 7)	14	7	4	3	0	0	14	38	0	179
5 Gloucestershire (Div 2, 6)	14	5	4	5	0	0	15	37	0	157
6 Leicestershire Div 2, 10) .	14	5	7	2	0	0	22	40	3	149
7 Derbyshire (Div 2, 8)	14	4	7	3	0	0	30	38	0	147
8 Durham (Div 2, 9)	14	4	7	2	0	1	16	35	0	130
9 Northamptonshire (Div 2, 3	14	4	8	1	0	1	14	38	0	126
10 Glamorgan (Div 2, 7)	14	2	10	2	0	0	13	38	1	92

Abandoned matches — each team takes 5 points

Pen. 1 point deducted for each over short in a match based on a rate of 16 overs per hour

* Promoted to Division 1 for 2019.

(2017 positions in brackets)

University Match — First Class
Yorkshire v. Leeds/Bradford MCCU

At Emerald Headingley, Leeds, on April 7, 8 and 9, 2018
Match abandoned without a ball bowled on April 4

Umpires: N A Mallender and I N Ramage   Scorers: J T Potter and C N Rawson

YORKSHIRE AVERAGES 2018

SPECSAVERS COUNTY CHAMPIONSHIP

Played 13   Won 5   Lost 5   Drawn 3   Abandoned 1

BATTING AND FIELDING

(Qualification 10 completed innings)

Player	M.	I.	N.O.	Runs	H.S.	100s	50s	Avge	ct/st
G S Ballance	12	23	0	906	194	3	4	39.39	4
J A Tattersall	7	12	1	350	70	0	2	31.81	19/0
A Lyth	13	25	1	656	134*	1	2	27.33	16
J A Leaning	8	16	2	371	68	0	2	26.50	9
H C Brook	12	23	0	575	124	1	3	25.00	7
T T Bresnan	12	22	3	385	80	0	2	20.26	9
S A Patterson	8	13	2	205	45*	0	0	18.63	2
J A Brooks	13	22	3	303	82	0	1	15.94	1
C A Pujara	6	12	0	172	41	0	0	14.33	4
Also played									
T Kohler-Cadmore	6	11	2	414	106	2	2	46.00	4
J M Bairstow	3	6	0	263	95	0	3	43.83	9/0
K S Williamson	3	6	0	218	87	0	3	36.33	3
A J Hodd	3	6	0	175	85	0	2	29.16	12/0
J Shaw	3	6	1	104	42	0	0	20.80	0
J E Root	3	6	0	97	35	0	0	16.16	2
M J Waite	4	6	0	96	42	0	0	16.00	0
B O Coad	9	15	7	135	33	0	0	16.87	0
D J Willey	2	4	1	42	34*	0	0	14.00	0
M D Fisher	2	4	1	39	20*	0	0	13.00	1
J A Raval	4	7	0	84	21	0	0	12.00	3
J E Poysden	3	5	2	25	20*	0	0	8.33	0
M W Pillans	1	1	0	8	8	0	0	8.00	0
A Z Lees	4	8	0	50	39	0	0	6.25	1
J E G Logan	1	1	0	6	6	0	0	6.00	1
K Carver	1	2	2	1	1*	0	0	—	0

BOWLING

(Qualification 10 wickets)

Player	Overs	Mdns	Runs	Wkts	Avge	Best	5wI	10wM
B O Coad	272.5	87	784	48	16.33	6 -81	3	1
S A Patterson	235	63	594	24	24.75	6 -40	1	0
T T Bresnan	279.5	48	969	35	27.68	5 -28	1	0
J A Brooks	346.3	51	1430	51	28.03	6 -94	5	0
Also bowled								
J E Root	20.4	7	37	5	7.40	4 - 5	0	0
M J Waite	61	14	221	8	27.62	3 -91	0	0
D J Willey	67.2	13	217	6	36.16	3 -72	0	0
J E Poysden	52.2	1	259	7	37.00	3-128	0	0
J A Leaning	19	3	57	1	57.00	1 -16	0	0
A Lyth	68	8	246	4	61.50	2 -97	0	0
J Shaw	63	5	265	4	66.25	2 -72	0	0
M D Fisher	54	6	219	2	109.50	2 -80	0	0
H C Brook	22.1	5	67	0	—	0 - 2	0	0
M W Pillans	30	5	130	0	—	0 -98	0	0
J E G Logan	12	3	44	0	—	0 - 4	0	0
K S Williamson	2	0	9	0	—	0 - 9	0	0

Second NatWest Test Match
England v. Pakistan

Played at Emerald Headingley, Leeds, on June 1, 2 and 3, 2018
England won by an innings and 55 runs at 4.22pm on the Third Day
Toss won by Pakistan

Close of play: First Day, England 106-2 (Root 29*, Bess 0*); Second Day, England 302-7 (Buttler 34*, Curran 16*)

PAKISTAN

First Innings		Second Innings	
Azhar Ali, lbw b Broad	2	b Anderson	11
Imam-ul-Haq, c Root b Broad	0	lbw b Bess	34
Haris Sohail, c Malan b Woakes	28	c Bess b Anderson	8
Asad Shafiq, c Cook b Woakes	27	c Bairstow b Broad	5
Usman Salahuddin, lbw b Broad	4	c Root b Bess	33
* § Sarfraz Ahmed, b Anderson	14	lbw b Woakes	8
Shadab Khan, c Jennings b Curran	56	c Cook b Curran	4
Faheem Ashraf, lbw b Anderson	0	c Malan b Bess	3
Mohammad Amir, c Bairstow b Anderson	13	not out	7
Hasan Ali, c and b Woakes	24	c Bairstow b Broad	9
Mohammad Abbas, not out	1	c Root b Broad	1
Extras lb 5	5	Extras b 5, lb 5, nb 1	11
Total	174	Total	134

FoW: 1-0 (Imam), 2-17 (Azhar), 3-49 (Sohail), 4-62 (Shafiq), 5-78 (Sarfraz),
1st 6-78 (Salahuddin), 7-79 (Ashraf), 8-113 (Amir), 9-156 (Hasan), 10-174 (Shadab)
FoW: 1-20 (Azhar), 2-30 (Sohail), 3-42 (Shafiq), 4-84 (Imam), 5-97 (Sarfraz),
2nd 6-102 (Shadab), 7-111 (Ashraf), 8-115 (Salahuddin), 9-124 (Hasan), 10-134 (Abbas)

	O	M	R	W		O	M	R	W
Anderson	15	6	43	3	Anderson	10	2	35	2
Broad	15	6	38	3	Broad	12	2	28	3
Woakes	11	1	55	3	Curran	7	2	10	1
Curran	7.1	0	33	1	Woakes	6	0	18	1
					Bess	11	1	33	3

ENGLAND

A N Cook, c Sarfraz Ahmed b Hasan Ali	46
K K Jennings, c Sarfraz Ahmed b Faheem Ashraf	29
* J E Root, c Sarfraz Ahmed b M Amir	45
D M Bess, c Haris Sohail b Shadab Khan	49
D J Malan, c Haris Sohail b M Amir	28
§ J M Bairstow, c Sarfraz Ahmed b Faheem Ashraf	21
J C Buttler, not out	80
C R Woakes, c Sarfraz Ahmed b M Abbas	17
S M Curran, c Asad Shafiq b M Abbas	20
S C J Broad, c M Abbas b Faheem Ashraf	2
J M Anderson, c Haris Sohail b Hasan Ali	5
Extras b 8, lb 13	21
Total	363

FoW: 1-53 (Jennings), 2-104 (Cook), 3-138 (Root), 4-200 (Malan), 5-212 (Bess),
6-260 (Bairstow), 7-285 (Woakes), 8-319 (Curran), 9-344 (Broad), 10-363 (Anderson)

	O	M	R	W
Mohammad Amir	23	5	72	2
Mohammad Abbas	26	8	78	2
Hasan Ali	20.2	4	82	2
Faheem Ashraf	20	4	60	3
Shadab Khan	17	2	50	1

Man of the match: J C Buttler

Umpires: B N J Oxenford and R J Tucker Scorers: J T Potter and J R Virr
Third Umpire: P R Reiffel Fourth: M A Gough Match Referee: J J Crowe

2020

*WE ARE **SUMMER NIGHTS**, WE ARE **FIREWORKS**, WE ARE **MUSIC**, WE ARE **PINTS** AND **PIES**, WE ARE THE **WESTERN TERRACE**, WE ARE **ROOOOOOOT**, WE ARE **CROWD CATCHES**, WE ARE **REVERSE SWEEPS**, WE ARE **20 OVERS OF EVERYTHING YOU'VE GOT AND MORE.** WE ARE **EMERALD HEADINGLEY!***

ENGLAND V PAKISTAN

ENGLAND v AUSTRALIA

ROYAL LONDON ONE-DAY CUP HIGHLIGHTS OF 2018

WINNERS

Hampshire, who beat Kent by 61 runs

Win by 100 or more runs (1)

Yorkshire (328-4) defeated Durham (186) by 142 runs at Chester-le-Street

Win by 9 wickets (1)

Leicestershire (293-9) lost to Yorkshire (296-1) at Leicester

Totals of 250 and over (5)

379-7	v. Lancashire at Manchester (won)
346-9	v. Worcestershire at Leeds (lost)
328-4	v. Durham at Chester-le-Street (won)
296-1	v. Leicestershire at Leicester (won)
259-7	v. Essex at Chelmsford (won)

Match aggregates of 450 and over (8)

742	Yorkshire (379-7) defeated Lancashire (363) by 16 runs at Manchester
696	Worcestershire (350-6) defeated Yorkshire (346-9) by 4 runs at Leeds
589	Leicestershire (293-9) lost to Yorkshire (296-1) by 9 wickets at Leicester
589	Hampshire (348-9) defeated Yorkshire (241(by 107 runs at Southampton
514	Yorkshire (328-4) defeated Durham (186) by 142 runs at Chester-le-Street
495	Yorkshire (247-9) lost to Warwickshire (248-5) by 5 wickets at Leeds
493	Yorkshire (259-7) defeated Essex (234) by 25 runs at Chelmsford
486	Northamptonshire (241) lost to Yorkshire (245-6) by 4 wickets at Leeds

Century Partnerships (6)

For 1st wicket (1)

153	A Lyth and T Kohler-Cadmore v. Leicestershire at Leicester

For 2nd wicket (4)

235	A Lyth and D J Willey v. Lancashire at Manchester
176	T Kohler-Cadmore and C A Pujara v. Durham at Chester-le-Street
142*	A Lyth and C A Pujara v. Leicestershire at Leicester
101	T Kohler-Cadmore and C A Pujara v. Worcestershire at Leeds

For 5th wicket (1)

102	G S Balance and J A Leaning v. Essex at Chelmsford

Centuries (3)

A Lyth (2)

144	v. Lancashire at Manchester
132*	v. Leicestershire at Leicester

D J Willey (1)

131	v. Lancashire at Manchester

4 wickets in an innings (4)

D J Willey (2)

    4-47   v. Derbyshire at Derby

    4-59   v. Lancashire at Manchester

S A Patterson (1)

    4-36   v. Essex at Chelmsford

A U Rashid   (1)

    4-47   v. Durham at Chester-le-Street

3 catches in an innings (1)

T Kohler-Cadmore (1)

    3   v. Northamptonshire at Northampton

List A Debut for Yorkshire (1): C A Pujara

Match-By-Match Reports   PAUL E DYSON

Brook stays on

Prodigiously talented batsman Harry Brook has signed a new two-year contract extension with Yorkshire which will see him remain at Emerald Headingley until the end of 2021. Brook enjoyed an encouraging breakthrough season in Yorkshire's first team in 2018, his standout innings being a brilliant second innings century in an early season Specsavers County Championship win over Essex at Chelmsford. In first-class cricket, the 19-year-old scored 575 runs at an average of 25.00.

Royal London One-Day Cup — North Group
Durham v. Yorkshire

Played at Emirates Riverside, Chester-le-Street, on May 18, 2018
Yorkshire won by 142 runs

Toss won by Yorkshire   Yorkshire 2 points, Durham 0 points

YORKSHIRE

A Lyth, c Poynter b Potts		30
T Kohler-Cadmore, c Smith b Harding		164
C A Pujara, c Smith b Potts		82
H C Brook, b Potts		20
J A Leaning, not out		2
T T Bresnan, not out		9
§ A J Hodd		
A U Rashid		
* S A Patterson	Did not bat	
J C Wainman		
B O Coad		
Extras lb 5, w 6, nb 10		21
Total (4 wkts, 50 overs)		328

FoW: 1-80 (Lyth), 2-256 (Kohler-Cadmore), 3-316 (Pujara), 4-316 (Brook)

	O	M	R	W
Rimmington	10	0	60	0
Weighell	10	1	74	0
Potts	8	0	69	3
Collingwood	10	0	40	0
Harding	10	0	63	1
Pringle	2	0	17	0

DURHAM

G Clark, c Hodd b Coad	9
P D Collingwood, b Bresnan	12
M J Richardson, lbw b Rashid	43
* T W M Latham, c Brook b Patterson	11
W R Smith, run out (Lyth/Hodd)	16
R D Pringle, b Rashid	3
§ S W Poynter, b Bresnan	36
W J Weighell, b Rashid	3
M J Potts, b Rashid	30
N J Rimmington, c Hodd b Patterson	12
G H I Harding, not out	3
Extras lb 2, w 2, nb 4	8
Total (40 overs)	186

FoW: 1-12 (Clark), 2-22 (Collingwood), 3-53 (Latham), 4-90(Smith), 5-96 (Pringle), 6-107 (Richardson), 7-113 (Weighell), 8-160 (Poynter), 9-179 (Potts), 10-186 (Rimmington)

	O	M	R	W
Coad	7	0	32	1
Bresnan	10	1	39	2
Patterson	6	0	25	2
Wainman	7	0	41	0
Rashid	10	1	47	4

Umpires: R A Kettleborough and D J Millns   Scorers: J T Potter and W R Dobson
Third Umpire: S J O'Shaughnessy

K-C's great debut century

Yorkshire got off to the best possible start to their white-ball schedule with an emphatic win on a sunny day and on a greenish but firm pitch.

Steven Patterson was leading the county for the first time. and his first experience of captaincy could not have gone any better.

The victory was underpinned by a wonderful innings from Kohler-Cadmore, who became the first non-overseas batsman to score a century in his first List A game for Yorkshire.

He went on to make the county's fourth-highest such score as well as equal the one-day record at the Riverside.

His 164 came from 151 balls, containing 15 fours and

TOM KOHLER-CADMORE
Bludgeoned 164 ground record

all of Yorkshire's seven sixes. His stand of 176 in 172 balls for the second wicket with Pujara, who batted in an accomplished and supportive manner, gave Kohler-Cadmore the confidence to accelerate, once Collingwood's miserly spell was over, and his third 50 came from only 26 balls. His outstanding innings, which was characterised by some powerful clean hitting and savage stroke-play, had been set in motion during an opening stand with Lyth of 80 from 76 balls.

Durham were soon in trouble when Hodd held a brilliant right-handed catch, and Yorkshire's seamers took a firm grip on the innings, left-arm fast-medium Wainman playing his first county game for two years. The real damage was done by Rashid, when four wickets fell in 35 balls and only 13 runs were scored. Rashid, bowling an impeccable length, took three of those four, and his pressure contributed to the run-out of Smith, when he and Richardson found themselves together in the middle of the pitch. Poynter and Watts held things up for a while, but Rashid took his fourth wicket with his final ball and the end came with 10 overs left.

Royal London One-Day Cup — North Group
Yorkshire v. Warwickshire

Played at Emerald Headingley, Leeds, on May 20, 2018

Warwickshire won by 5 wickets

Toss won by Yorkshire

Warwickshire 2 points, Yorkshire 0 points

YORKSHIRE

A Lyth, lbw b Patel	38
T Kohler-Cadmore, c Stone b Thomason	39
C A Pujara, c Ambrose b Stone	73
H C Brook, c Ambrose b Stone	17
J A Leaning, c Ambrose b Patel	7
A U Rashid, c Ambrose b Patel	4
§ A J Hodd, b Patel	1
T T Bresnan, c Ambrose b Barker	25
J C Wainman, not out	18
* S A Patterson, run out (Patel)	7
B O Coad	Did not bat
Extras b 4, lb 1, w 11, nb 2	18
Total (9 wkts, 50 overs)	247

FoW: 1-80 (Kohler-Cadmore), 2-85 (Lyth), 3-112 (Brook), 4-123 (Leaning), 5-139 (Rashid), 6-149 (Hodd), 7-204 (Bresnan), 8-224 (Pujara), 9-247 (Patterson)

	O	M	R	W
Barker	10	1	40	1
Stone	10	1	45	2
Brookes	10	0	59	0
Thomason	8	0	51	1
Patel	10	2	33	4
Trott	2	0	14	0

WARWICKSHIRE

E J Pollock, b Coad	26
I J L Trott, run out (Bresnan/Wainman)	50
S R Hain, not out	102
I R Bell, c Kohler-Cadmore b Wainman	5
A J Hose, c Rashid b Coad	44
§ T R Ambrose, c Hodd b Wainman	2
A D Thomason, not out	8
K H D Barker	
* J S Patel	
O P Stone	Did not bat
H J H Brookes	
Extras b 2, lb 6, w 3	11
Total (5 wkts, 45.4 overs)	248

FoW: 1-39 (Pollock), 2-126 (Trott), 3-134 (Bell), 4-231 (Hose), 5-235 (Ambrose)

	O	M	R	W
Bresnan	5	0	44	0
Coad	10	0	40	2
Patterson	7.4	0	42	0
Rashid	10	0	46	0
Wainman	10	0	53	2
Lyth	3	0	15	0

Umpires: R A Kettleborough and G D Lloyd   Scorers: J T Potter and M D Smith

Pujara stands firm

The margins of victory – by five wickets and with 26 balls to spare – demonstrate how comfortable this win was for the visiting team.

Once Yorkshire had slipped to 149-6 in the 30th over it did not seem as though they would recover, and the gloomy predictions duly bore fruit.

The start was promising, though, with Lyth and Kohler-Cadmore again sharing a first-wicket stand of exactly 80 runs, just as they had against Durham, but

CHETESHWAR PUJARA: Showed how to play spin and build an innings

one ball slower in this match. Jeetan Patel removed Lyth two balls after his partner's dismissal from a high catch off Stone, and returned later to rip through the middle order, aided and abetted by some poor footwork and shot-selection.

Pujara stood firm, showing how to play spin as well as build an innings. He and Bresnan added 55, but in the modern era runs scored at less than five an over are rarely enough. Rashid completed 1,000 runs in List A cricket for Yorkshire, and Ambrose became the first Warwickshire player to take five catches in a List A match against Yorkshire.

Warwickshire's innings was dominated by a fine century from Hain. He came to the crease in the sixth over at the fall of the first wicket, and shared stands of 87 with Trott and 97 in only 83 balls with Hose. A direct hit from Wainman effected the run-out of Trott, who had just completed his 50th run but failed to make his ground for the second time.

Bell followed eight runs later, but there were no real alarms for the visitors, Hain taking only 110 balls to score his 102 not out. Coad was the best of Yorkshire's bowlers, but even though only one six was struck off them they just did not have enough runs to defend.

Royal London One-Day Cup — North Group
Yorkshire v. Worcestershire

Played at Emerald Headingley, Leeds, on May 23, 2018
Worcestershire won by 4 runs

Toss won by Yorkshire
Worcestershire 2 points, Yorkshire 0 points

WORCESTERSHIRE

D K H Mitchell, lbw b Coad		11
J M Clarke, run out (Rashid)		61
T M Head, c and b Rashid		77
T C Fell, b Rashid		32
B L D'Oliveira, c Kohler-Cadmore b Patterson		23
R A Whiteley, not out		66
§ O B Cox, c Hodd b Patterson		50
E G Barnard, not out		3
* J Leach		
C A J Morris	Did not bat	
P R Brown		
Extras b 3, lb 9, w 7, nb 8		27
Total (6 wkts, 50 overs)		350

FoW: 1-14 (Mitchell), 2-122 (Clarke), 3-188 (Fell), 4-218 (D'Oliveira), 5-220 (Head), 6-330 (Cox)

	O	M	R	W
Coad	9	0	55	1
Bresnan	10	0	78	0
Patterson	10	0	54	2
Wainman	8	0	56	0
Rashid	10	0	86	2
Lyth	3	0	9	0

YORKSHIRE

A Lyth, c Cox b Barnard		29
T Kohler-Cadmore, c Fell b D'Oliveira		89
C A Pujara, c Fell b Barnard		101
J C Wainman, c Cox b D'Oliveira		0
H C Brook, c Fell b Brown		5
J A Leaning, c D'Oliveira b Morris		25
T T Bresnan, c Cox b Barnard		26
A U Rashid, c Head b Leach		24
§ A J Hodd, not out		17
* S A Patterson, c Cox b Leach		17
B O Coad, not out		3
Extras b 1, w 9		10
Total (9 wkts, 50 overs)		346

FoW: 1-72 (Lyth), 2-173 (Kohler-Cadmore), 3-173 (Wainman), 4-184 (Brook), 5-253 (Leaning), 6-258 (Pujara), 7-296 (Rashid), 8-307 (Bresnan), 9-333 (Patterson)

	O	M	R	W
Leach	9	0	60	2
Morris	8	0	72	1
Barnard	10	0	75	3
D'Oliveira	8	0	48	2
Mitchell	7	0	34	0
Brown	8	0	56	1

Umpires: R K Illingworth and B V Taylor   Scorers: J T Potter and P M Mellish

Yorkshire v. Worcestershire
Brave bid all in vain

CHETESHWAR PUJARA
Century came in 92 balls

With Worcestershire recording Headingley's highest List A total, it was always going to be a tall order for Yorkshire to reach such a target.

Yet the hosts were ahead of their visitors in terms of overs used at each 50-run mark until the total reached 300. Both sides hit that mark after 46.1 overs, but Yorkshire had lost seven wickets to Worcestershire's five.

It was the onslaught of Whiteley, batting at No. 4 for Worcestershire, that made the essential difference, brave though Yorkshire's tail was. He smashed 66 from 41 balls and shared a stand of 110 with Cox in only 62 balls.

Patterson asked Worcestershire to bat on a cloudy morning, but the later 75 per cent of the match was bathed in sunshine, and the pitch played true and even throughout.

Worcestershire lost an early wicket, but Clarke and Head shared a century partnership before Clarke was unluckily run-out at the bowler's end backing up.

The Yorkshire bowling was inconsistent throughout. Lyth was very economical, but he bowled only three overs, while Rashid produced the second-most expensive spell in Yorkshire's List A history.

Lyth and Kohler-Cadmore gave Yorkshire's reply its now customary start, and Kohler-Cadmore shared a century stand with Pujara, who batted faster than in the previous games to score a century from 92 balls. When the stand was broken Wainman was sent in to press the accelerator, but this gamble failed. The momentum was lost, and the run-rate continued to mount as wickets fell.

It all came down to 12 being required from the final two balls. Hodd struck the first for six, but he could not repeat the feat and it was the end of a 696-run game, which was another record for Headingley.

133

Royal London One-Day Cup — North Group
Yorkshire v. Nottinghamshire
At Emerald Headingley, Leeds, on May 25, 2018
Match abandoned without a ball bowled

Toss: None

Umpires: I D Blackwell and J H Evans

Yorkshire 1 point, Nottinghamshire 1 point

Scorers: J T Potter and R Marshall

Leicestershire v. Yorkshire
Played at The Fischer County Ground, Grace Road, Leicester, on May 27, 2018
Yorkshire won by 9 wickets

Toss won by Leicestershire

Yorkshire 2 points, Leicestershire 0 points

LEICESTERSHIRE

C S Delport, lbw b Fisher		8
* P J Horton, c Patterson b Fisher		14
C N Ackerman, c and b Coad		8
M J Cosgrove, c Kohler-Cadmore b Rashid		84
§ E J H Eckersley, c Pujara b Plunkett		50
N J Dexter, not out		50
T J Wells, c Kohler-Cadmore b Rashid		8
B A Raine, c Rashid b Patterson		14
C F Parkinson, c Tattersall b Coad		21
R A Jones, c Tattersall b Fisher		0
V A Aaron, not out		14
Extras b 1, lb 10, w 9, nb 2		22
Total (9 wkts, 50 overs)		293

FoW: 1-10 (Delport), 2-21 (Ackermann), 3-39 (Horton), 4-167 (Eckersley, 5-185 (Cosgrove), 6-199 (Wells), 7-229 (Raine), 8-270 (Parkinson), 9-271 (Jones)

	O	M	R	W
Coad	9	0	46	2
Fisher	10	1	40	3
Plunkett	10	0	50	1
Patterson	10	0	64	1
Rashid	9	0	70	2
Lyth	2	0	12	0

YORKSHIRE

A Lyth, not out		132
T Kohler-Cadmore, c Horton b Delport		74
C A Pujara, not out		75
H C Brook		
G S Ballance		
A U Rashid		
§ J A Tattersall	Did not bat	
L E Plunkett		
* S A Patterson		
B O Coad		
M D Fisher		
Extras lb 3, w 11		14
Total (1 wkt, 46.3 overs)		295

FoW: 1-153 (Kohler-Cadmore)

	O	M	R	W
Raine	9	0	45	0
Jones	7	0	43	0
Aaron	10	0	63	0
Dexter	2	0	18	0
Parkinson	10	0	62	0
Delport	5.3	0	38	1
Ackerman	3	0	23	0

Umpires: J W Lloyds and J D Middlebrook

Scorers: J T Potter and P J Rogers

Top men are top men

ADAM LYTH: A century himself and in two century stands

Yorkshire made four changes to the team which had played in all of this competition's three matches so far, and were rewarded with a huge win.

The outstanding performance was an unbeaten century from Lyth, who was supported by Kohler-Cadmore and Pujara.

He shared century partnerships with each of them — 153 from 134 balls with Kohler-Cadmore and 142 with Pujara.

These were the only three batsmen the *White Rose* county needed to overhaul the hosts' 293-9.

Lyth made his runs from 127 balls with 15 fours and two sixes — 10 of his fours coming in his first 50, which used up only 36 balls.

He batted fluently, timed the ball well and took advantage of a fast-paced pitch and short, straight boundaries.

Earlier in the day Fisher, returning from injury — one originally suffered on this ground — for his first match of the season, took two wickets, including one with his third ball to help reduce Leicestershire to 39-3 inside 10 overs. He was easily Yorkshire's best bowler in terms of wicket-taking and economy.

Australian Cosgrove top-scored with 84, but neither he nor the middle-order's two other half-centurions batted faster than a run-a-ball. He shared a century partnership with Eckersley, and fell to a brilliant catch by Kohler-Cadmore on the long-on boundary. It was felt that the eventual Leicestershire total would not be enough, especially with it being played on a pitch which had produced 725 runs four days previously.

Yorkshire's top three, especially Lyth with the fourth List A century of his career, demonstrated how true this was, and reached the target with 21 balls to spare.

Royal London One-Day Cup — North Group
Derbyshire v. Yorkshire

Played at The 3aaa County Ground, Derby, on May 30, 2018
Yorkshire won by 2 wickets

Toss won by Yorkshire

Yorkshire 2 points, Derbyshire 0 points

DERBYSHIRE

B T Slater, not out	....	109
* B A Godleman, c Bresnan b Rashid	....	21
W L Madsen, c Pujara b Bresnan	....	20
L M Reece, retired hurt	....	16
G C Wilson, b Willey	....	3
M J J Critchley, c Tattersall b Willey	....	0
A L Hughes, c Plunkett b Willey	....	6
§ D Smit, c Kohler-Cadmore b Willey	....	2
G C Viljoen, not out	....	0
D Olivier		
R Rampaul	Did not bat	
Extras lb 3, w 9		12
Total (6 wkts, 24 overs)	....	189

FoW: 1-68 (Godleman), 2-101 (Madsen), 2-147 (Reece) rh, 3-157 (Wilson), 4-157 (Critchley), 5-171 (Hughes), 6-180 (Smit)

	O	M	R	W
Fisher	3	0	20	0
Willey	4	0	47	4
Patterson	3	0	26	0
Rashid	5	0	33	1
Plunkett	5	0	41	0
Bresnan	4	0	19	1

YORKSHIRE

T Kohler-Cadmore, c Wilson b Rampaul	....	81
A Lyth, c Slater b Rampaul	....	19
D J Willey, c Wilson b Olivier	....	0
C A Pujara, lbw b Critchley	....	14
G S Ballance, b Olivier	....	27
T T Bresnan, c Smit b Rampaul	....	0
§ J A Tattersall, lbw b Rampaul	....	2
A U Rashid, c Smit b Rampaul	....	13
L E Plunkett, not out	....	3
M D Fisher, not out	....	24
* S A Patterson	Did not bat	
Extras b 5, lb 4	....	9
Total (8 wkts, 23.5 overs)	....	192

FoW: 1-43 (Lyth), 2-43 (Willey), 3-71 (Pujara), 4-132 (Ballance), 5-133 (Bresnan), 6-135 (Tattersall), 7-155 (Rashid), 8-166 (Kohler-Cadmore)

	O	M	R	W
Madsen	2	1	15	0
Olivier	5	0	23	2
Rampaul	5	0	48	5
Viljoen	4.5	0	45	0
Critchley	5	0	38	1
Hughes	2	0	14	0

Umpires: P R Pollard and R T Robinson

Scorers: J T Potter and J M Brown

Derbyshire v. Yorkshire

Fisher's final flourish

The *White Rose* were still 24 runs short with 11 balls remaining when Kohler-Cadmore was eighth out after striking 81 from 63 balls.

It seemed that the game was up...but in strode Fisher, having starred with the ball in the previous game. He now struck Rampaul, who had just dismissed Kohler-Cadmore for his fifth wicket of the innings, for 13 from the five balls remaining in the 23rd and last-but-one over of a match reduced to 24 overs per side because of rain.

With Plunkett almost a spectator at the non-striker's end Fisher then smashed two boundaries in the final over and victory was achieved with one ball to spare, the match-winner having struck 24 not out including three fours and one six from a mere eight balls.

The reduction in playing time had ensured that Derbyshire attacked from the word go. Slater and skipper Godleman posted 68 from 49 balls for the first wicket, being particularly severe on Willey, who was playing in

MATTHEW FISHER: Three late fours and a six

his first match since returning from the Indian Premier League. Willey ended up as Yorkshire's leading wicket-taker, but he was also easily the most expensive of the visiting bowlers.

Bresnan was back to his economical best, and was the most frugal bowler of the innings as well as taking his 50th List A catch for Yorkshire. Slater dominated the innings with 109 not out from 82 balls, but the loss of four wickets for 23 runs during the final overs reduced the rate of acceleration.

Kohler-Cadmore and Lyth gave Yorkshire their customary rapid start with 43 from 29 balls, and Kohler-Cadmore also shared a 61-run stand with Ballance. The loss of three wickets for three runs in 10 balls made the home side favourites, but the bookies had reckoned without Fisher.

Royal London One-Day Cup — North Group
Lancashire v. Yorkshire

Played at Emirates Old Trafford, Manchester, on June 5, 2018
Yorkshire won by 16 runs

Toss won by Yorkshire   Yorkshire 2 points, Lancashire 0 points

YORKSHIRE

A Lyth, c Jones b Bailey		144
T Kohler-Cadmore, lbw b Bailey		0
D J Willey, b Livingstone		131
C A Pujara, run out (Hameed/Vilas)		19
G S Ballance, c Livingstone b Parkinson		38
H C Brook, b Parkinson		24
L E Plunkett, not out		6
M D Fisher, run out (Davies/Vilas/Bailey)		1
A U Rashid, not out		1
§ J A Tattersall		
* S A Patterson	Did not bat	
Extras lb 3, w 12		15
Total (7 wkts, 50 overs)		379

FoW: 1-12 (Kohler-Cadmore), 2-247 (Willey), 3-298 (Lyth), 4-299 (Pujara), 5-366 (Brook), 6-371 (Ballance), 7-377 (Fisher)

	O	M	R	W
Bailey	10	1	79	2
Clark	10	0	70	0
Livingstone	10	0	72	1
Jennings	4	0	33	0
Parkinson	10	0	71	2
Parry	4	0	34	0
Bohannon	2	0	17	0

LANCASHIRE

K K Jennings, c Kohler-Cadmore b Patterson	69
A L Davies, c Brook b Fisher	10
* L S Livingstone, c Fisher b Plunkett	79
§ D J Vilas, c Pujara b Rashid	47
H Hameed, b Willey	32
R P Jones, st Tattersall b Rashid	2
J Clark, c Patterson b Willey	23
J J Bohannon, c and b Rashid	16
T E Bailey, b Willey	33
S D Parry, lbw b Willey	20
M W Parkinson, not out	1
Extras b 9, lb 5, w 15, nb 2	31
Total (49 overs)	363

FoW: 1-20 (Davies), 2-144 (Livingstone), 3-218 (Jennings), 4-232 (Vilas), 5-238 (Jones), 6-259 (Hameed), 7-293 (Bohannon), 8-302 (Clark), 9-359 (Bailey), 10-363 (Parry)

	O	M	R	W
Willey	10	0	59	4
Fisher	9	1	74	1
Patterson	10	0	61	1
Plunkett	8	0	76	1
Rashid	10	0	64	3
Lyth	2	0	15	0

Umpires: R J Bailey and R J Warren   Scorers: J T Potter and C Rimmer

Willey the match-winner

Yorkshire's leading run-scorer so far, Kohler-Cadmore, went for a duck, but Lyth, who scored all of the first 42 runs to come from the bat and, more emphatically, Willey gave their innings its impetus.

This pair smashed Yorkshire's List A second-wicket record with a stand of 235 from 196 balls, propelling the county to their highest total against any first-

DAVID WILLEY: 11 fours and seven sixes in brutal 235 stand with Lyth

class county in the limited-overs format. Willey, with 11 fours and seven sixes, launched a brutal assault, his 131 using up only 95 balls, and Lyth, with 144 from 132 balls, made the highest innings for the *White Rose* against these rivals. Lancashire wilted from the onslaught; no bowler conceded fewer than seven runs an over; there were dropped catches and the display was epitomised by Bailey delivering four wides in one over.

Unbelievably, Lancashire made such an impressive response to their huge challenge that they lost by a mere 16 runs, and the day had produced a colossal 742 runs. It was skipper Livingstone whose 79, with 60 in boundaries, from 44 balls was the major contribution to his stand of 124 in 75 balls with England opener Keaton Jennings.

Livingstone fell to a brilliant catch by Fisher at mid-on, but Vilas kept up the pace, sharing 74 from 48 balls with Jennings.

At 218-2 in the 26th over the hosts were in a very good position, but wickets began to fall more regularly. Leg-spinner Rashid chipped in with three scalps including a caught-and-bowled, and six went down for 84 before Bailey and Parry with a half-century stand swung the momentum back towards the *Red Rose*.

With 21 needed from 10 balls, Willey returned to take the final two wickets in the last-but-one over, so adding four wickets to his earlier century. The day had contained several brilliant performances, but Willey's was the one which won the match.

Royal London One-Day Cup — North Group
Yorkshire v. Northamptonshire

Played at Emerald Headingley, Leeds, on June 7, 2018
Yorkshire won by 4 wickets

Toss won by Northamptonshire   Yorkshire 2 points, Northamptonshire 0 points

NORTHAMPTONSHIRE

§ A M Rossington, c Rashid b Fisher	7
B M Duckett, c Tattersall b Willey	2
R S Vasconcelos, c Kohler-Cadmore b Willey	10
* A G Wakely, c Fisher b Bresnan	42
R I Keogh, c Tattersall b Bresnan	13
C O Thurston, c Bresnan b Fisher	53
S A Zaib, c Kohler-Cadmore b Rashid	2
R K Kleinveldt, c Kohler-Cadmore b Rashid	29
G G White, not out	4
B A Hutton, c Rashid b Patterson	30
B D Cotton, c Patterson b Willey	8
Extras lb 2, w 2	4
Total (47.5 overs)	241

FoW: 1-5 (Duckett), 2-9 (Rossington), 3-23 (Vasconcelos), 4-68 (Keogh), 5-83 (Wakely), 6-101 (Zaib), 7-143 (Kleinveldt), 8-189 (Thurston), 9-228 (Hutton), 10-241 (Cotton)

	O	M	R	W
Willey	9.5	2	24	3
Fisher	7	0	32	2
Patterson	7	1	45	1
Rashid	10	0	59	2
Bresnan	8	1	40	2
Root	6	0	39	0

YORKSHIRE

A Lyth, c Rossington b Kleinveldt	9
T Kohler-Cadmore, c Rossington b Hutton	4
D J Willey, c Cotton b Zaib	71
J E Root, c Rossington b Keogh	18
C A Pujara, lbw b Keogh	6
G S Ballance, c Vasconcelos b Hutton	66
§ J R Tattersall, not out	52
T T Bresnan, not out	13
A U Rashid	
M D Fisher	Did not bat
* S A Patterson	
Extras	0
Total (6 wkts, 49 overs)	239

FoW: 1-14 (Lyth), 2-14 (Kohler-Cadmore), 3-89 (Root), 4-102 (Pujara), 5-134 (Willey), 6-221 (Ballance)

	O	M	R	W
Hutton	9	0	59	2
Kleinveldt	8	0	44	1
Cotton	5	0	24	0
Keogh	10	1	26	2
White	8	0	52	0
Zaib	9	0	38	1

Umpires: P J Hartley and S J O'Shaughnessy   Scorers: J T Potter and A C Kingston

Yorkshire v. Northamptonshire

Tattersall's maiden 50

Despite having won only one of their first four games in this competition Yorkshire had been victorious in their next three, and found themselves one win from a place in the play-offs.

Northamptonshire were pegged back almost immediately, slipping to 9-2 after 20 balls.

Charlie Thurston, in his first match for the visitors, scored an impressive half-century, but wickets kept falling

JONATHAN TATTERSALL: Saw his side into playoffs with over to spare

and it was not until Kleinveldt came to the crease at 101-6 in the 25th over that the accelerator was pressed. Graeme White made a career-best 41 from 39 balls, but the innings eventually petered out, Willey taking the final wicket with 13 balls remaining. The wickets were shared out among the Yorkshire bowlers, but Willey was the most impressive. All 10 wickets fell to catches, including three for Kohler-Cadmore.

Meanwhile, Nottinghamshire had humiliated Derbyshire and so increased their run-rate that for Yorkshire to be awarded a home tie their runs had to come in 41 overs. The loss of four cheap wickets, including that of Root, who was making one of his rare appearances for the county, and the dismissal of Willey – again in fine form with both bat and ball – for 71 meant that Tattersall came to the wicket with five down and 108 required from 106 balls.

Hopes of a home tie had disappeared, and Tattersall's List A record showed two innings, two runs. But with Ballance at the other end going well, the pair posted 87 together, the highest stand of the match, and both passed the half-century mark. So well did they bat together that when Ballance, with 66 from 61 balls, was caught the equation was a comfortable 21 from 26 balls. Tattersall went on to an undefeated 52 from 51 balls, and in the company of Bresnan saw Yorkshire into the play-offs with one over to spare.

Royal London One-Day Cup — Second Quarter-Final
Essex v. Yorkshire

Played at The Cloud FM County Ground, Chelmsford, on June 14, 2018
Yorkshire won by 25 runs

Toss won by Yorkshire

YORKSHIRE

A Lyth, c Zaidi b Porter		21
T Kohler-Cadmore, lbw b Porter		0
H C Brook, b Coles		2
G S Ballance, c Wheater b Wagner		91
§ J A Tattersall, lbw b Porter		0
J A Leaning, lbw b Harmer		57
T T Bresnan, b Coles		41
M D Fisher, not out		35
K Carver		
* S A Patterson	Did not bat	
B O Coad		
Extras lb 5, w 7		12
Total (7 wkts, 50 overs)		259

FoW: 1-1 (Kohler-Cadmore), 2-5 (Brook), 3-45 (Lyth), 4-45 (Tattersall), 5-174 (Ballance), 6-188 (Leaning), 7-259 (Bresnan)

	O	M	R	W
Porter	9	2	25	3
Coles	10	1	66	2
Wagner	10	0	54	1
Harmer	10	0	45	1
Bopara	8	1	47	0
Zaidi	3	0	17	0

ESSEX

V Chopra, c Leaning b Carver		37
A N Cook, c Patterson b Coad		11
* T Westley, run out (Coad)		2
D W Lawrence, lbw b Patterson		15
R S Bopara, c Brook b Patterson		8
§ A J A Wheater, b Patterson		78
S A A Zaidi, b Patterson		13
S R Harmer, b Carver		9
M T Coles, b Fisher		13
N Wagner, b Fisher		35
J A Porter, not out		2
Extras lb 4, w 5, nb 2		11
Total (49.1 overs)		234

FoW: 1-26 (Cook), 2-35 (Westley), 3-59 (Chopra), 4-74 (Lawrence), 5-89 (Bopara), 6-123 (Zaidi), 7-138 (Harmer), 8-159(Coles), 9-216 (Wheater), 10-234 (Wagner)

	O	M	R	W
Fisher	9.1	0	32	2
Coad	10	0	50	1
Bresnan	10	1	47	0
Carver	10	0	65	2
Patterson	10	1	36	4

TV Man of the Match: S A Patterson

Umpires: D J Millns and M J Saggers
Third: R T Robinson

Scorers: J T Potter and A E Choat
Fourth: J D Middlebrook

Patterson's four wicket haul

Shorn of six who would have been first choice, Yorkshire's team for this quarter-final contained only five capped players.

The inexperience was showing at 45-4, but the restored Leaning produced a watchful innings which complemented the stroke-play of Ballance, who passed 4,000 List A runs.

The pair mounted a rescue act in the shape of a stand of 129 from 168 balls.

The pitch, which had been used eight days previously for Essex's final group game, was not entirely reliable, but Bresnan, with 41 from 32 balls, and Fisher, with 35 from 29, hit out merrily in a stand of 71 off 49 balls to haul Yorkshire up to a competitive total.

STEVEN PATTERSON: Bowled understrength team to fine win

The bowling honours undoubtedly went to Porter. One of his three wickets was with the second ball of the match, and he conceded fewer than three runs per over.

It was felt that Yorkshire had to take 10 wickets, the target not appearing challenging enough, but when Bopara departed in the 25th over the scoreboard showed 89-5. Alastair Cook was dismissed with an uncharacteristic hoick to mid-off, and skipper Westley was unluckily run out backing up. Fisher bowled threateningly and economically, and Bresnan and skipper Patterson were strangling the progress of the innings in the middle overs, Bresnan's first spell consistently hitting a nagging length.

The required run rate increased. Wickets continued to fall, and when the eighth went down the target was 101 in 69 balls. Wicket-keeper Wheater and New Zealander Wagner began an onslaught which threatened the bowlers' composure, but their 57 from 39 balls was too little too late. Wheater was bowled by Patterson for 78 in 70 balls to give the fast-medium paceman his fourth wicket and the match award. Given the concerns over selection it was one of Yorkshire's best knockout wins.

Royal London One-Day Cup — Second Semi-Final
Hampshire v. Yorkshire

Played at The Ageas Bowl, West End, Southampton, on June 18, 2018
Hampshire won by 107 runs
Toss won by Yorkshire

HAMPSHIRE

J H K Adams, c Kohler-Cadmore b Coad		16
R R Rossouw, c Pujara b Bresnan		32
* J M Vince, c Kohler-Cadmore b Lyth		171
S A Northeast, c Patterson b Bresnan		58
J J Weatherley, b Coad		3
L A Dawson, c Lyth b Fisher		17
§ L D McManus, c Leaning b Patterson		25
G K Berg, not out		6
C P Wood, b Patterson		2
D W Steyn, run out (Tattersall)		6
R J W Topley, not out		6
Extras lb 2, w 2, nb 2		6
Total (9 wkts, 50 overs)		348

FoW: 1-30 (Adams), 2-76 (Rossouw), 3-218 (Northeast), 4-244 (Weatherley), 5-292 (Dawson), 6-313 (Vince), 7-333 (McManus), 8-336 (Wood), 9-342 (Steyn)

	O	M	R	W
Fisher	10	0	70	1
Coad	9	0	48	2
Bresnan	10	0	71	2
Patterson	10	0	56	2
Carver	6	0	66	0
Lyth	5	0	35	1

YORKSHIRE

A Lyth, lbw b Wood		11
T Kohler-Cadmore, c Berg b Dawson		21
C A Pujara, c Adams b Steyn		0
G S Ballance, c Northeast b Berg		25
§ J A Tattersall, c Berg b Topley		89
J A Leaning, b Dawson		23
T T Bresnan, b Wood		26
M D Fisher, lbw b Dawson		25
* S A Patterson, c McManus b Dawson		0
B O Coad, c Vince b Wood		9
K Carver, not out		3
Extras lb 2, w 5, nb 2		9
Total (43.4 overs)		241

FoW: 1-14 (Lyth), 2-15 (Pujara), 3-47 (Ballance), 4-73 (Kohler-Cadmore), 5-123 (Leaning), 6-173 (Bresnan), 7-223 (Tattersall), 8-227 (Fisher), 9-230 (Coad)

	O	M	R	W
Steyn	7	0	34	1
Wood	8.4	0	46	3
Berg	8	0	59	1
Topley	10	0	53	1
Dawson	10	0	47	4

TV Man of the Match: J M Vince

Umpires: M Burns and A G Wharf   Scorers: J T Potter and K R Baker
Third: P K Baldwin   Fourth: T Lungley

More semi-final sadness

ADAM LYTH: 50 up in List A catches

This match pitted together the two counties with the worst records in List A semi-finals, Hampshire's success-rate being 35 per cent and Yorkshire's a paltry 26.

Other than for the performance of Vince there may have been some justification for Patterson choosing to field first, but his magnificent 171 from 126 balls, strike rate 135, was the stand-out innings. Peppering the boundary with 20 fours and three sixes through beautifully timed orthodox strokes, he projected Hampshire towards their huge total. He shared a stand of 124 from 142 balls with Northeast, who reached 58 from 56 balls as Yorkshire's bowlers did their best not to wilt under the onslaught, but Carver suffered particularly badly. Their perseverance paid off when five wickets fell in the final 10 overs, but only Patterson and Coad emerged with much credit.

Yorkshire lost two early wickets: Lyth was, according to a TV replay, erroneously given out, and Pujara, rushed back from India, made a duck. Hampshire bowled a tight line and length, so wickets continued to fall, and the run rate continued to mount so much so that 200 were required from the last 19 overs with only five wickets remaining.

Bresnan completed his 2,000 runs in List A cricket for Yorkshire, Lyth having taken his 50th catch, but the main positive to take from the heavy defeat was the batting of Tattersall: his 89 came from only 81 balls, and he shared stands of exactly 50 with both Bresnan and Fisher. He batted attractively with strokes all round the wicket, but after his dismissal the innings and match, fizzled out.

Dawson was the best of Hampshire's bowlers, but the whole attack took advantage of Yorkshire's relatively inexperienced team, who were once again depleted by international calls at the time of an important match and, consequently, suffered yet another semi-final defeat.

Royal London One-Day Cup

FINAL TABLES 2018

NORTH GROUP

		P	W	L	T	NR/A	PTS	NRR
1	Worcestershire (1)	8	6	2	0	0	12	0.260
2	Nottinghamshire (3) *	8	5	2	0	1	11	0.675
3	**Yorkshire Vikings (2) * ....**	**8**	**5**	**2**	**0**	**1**	**11**	**0.513**
4	Warwickshire Bears (9)	8	4	2	0	2	10	0.446
5	Derbyshire Falcons (7)	8	4	4	0	0	8	-0.552
6	Lancashire Lightning (4)	8	3	4	0	1	7	0.969
7	Northamptonshire Steelbacks (8)	8	2	5	0	1	5	-0.339
8	Leicestershire Foxes (6)	8	2	6	0	0	4	-0.704
9	Durham (5)	8	2	6	0	0	4	-1.088

SOUTH GROUP

		P	W	L	T	NR/A	PTS	NRR
1	Hampshire Royals (6)	8	5	2	0	1	11	0.327
2	Essex Eagles (1) *	8	5	3	0	0	10	0.791
3	Kent Spitfires (9) *	8	5	3	0	0	10	0.010
4	Somerset (2)	8	4	3	0	1	9	0.548
5	Surrey (3)	8	4	3	0	1	9	-0.848
6	Middlesex Panthers (8)	8	4	4	0	0	8	0.089
7	Gloucestershire (7)	8	2	3	0	3	7	0.250
8	Sussex Sharks (5)	8	2	4	0	2	6	0.075
9	Glamorgan (4)	8	1	7	0	0	2	-0.784

* Qualified for Quarter-Finals

(2017 group positions in brackets)

146

YORKSHIRE AVERAGES 2018

ALL LIST A

Played 9   Won 6   Lost 3   Abandoned 1

BATTING AND FIELDING

(Qualification 4 completed innings)

Player	M.	I.	N.O.	Runs	H.S.	100s	50s	Avge	ct/st
A Lyth	9	9	1	433	144	2	0	54.12	1
C A Pujara	8	8	1	370	101	1	3	52.85	4
T Kohler-Cadmore	9	9	0	472	164	1	3	52.44	11
G S Ballance	6	5	0	247	91	0	2	49.40	0
J A Leaning	5	5	1	114	57	0	1	28.50	2
T T Bresnan	7	7	2	140	41	0	0	28.00	2
H C Brook	6	5	0	68	24	0	0	13.60	3
Also played									
D J Willey	3	3	0	202	131	1	1	67.33	0
J A Tattersall	6	4	1	143	89	0	2	47.66	5/1
M D Fisher	6	4	2	85	35*	0	0	42.50	2
A J Hodd	3	2	1	18	18*	0	0	18.00	0
J C Wainman	3	2	1	18	17*	0	0	18.00	4
J E Root	1	1	0	18	18	0	0	18.00	0
A U Rashid	7	4	1	42	24	0	0	14.00	6
B O Coad	6	2	1	12	9	0	0	12.00	1
S A Patterson	9	3	0	24	17	0	0	8.00	5
L E Plunkett	3	2	2	9	6*	0	0	—	1
K Carver	2	1	1	3	3*	0	0	—	0

BOWLING

(Qualification 4 wickets)

Player	Overs	Mdns	Runs	Wkts	Avge	Best	4wI	RPO
D J Willey	23.5	2	130	11	11.81	4-47	2	5.45
A U Rashid	64	1	405	14	28.92	4-47	1	6.32
M D Fisher	48.1	2	268	9	29.77	3-40	0	5.56
B O Coad	54	0	271	9	30.11	2-40	0	5.01
S A Patterson	73.4	2	409	13	31.46	4-36	1	5.55
T T Bresnan	57	3	338	7	48.28	2-39	0	5.92
Also bowled								
K Carver	16	0	131	2	65.50	2-65	0	8.18
J C Wainman	25	0	150	2	75.00	2-53	0	6.00
L E Plunkett	23	0	167	2	83.50	1-50	0	7.26
A Lyth	15	0	86	1	86.00	1-35	0	5.73
J E Root	6	0	39	0	—	0-39	0	6.50

Third Royal London One-Day International
England v. India

Played at Emerald Headingley, Leeds, on July 17, 2018

England won by 8 wickets

Toss won by England

INDIA

R G Sharma, c Wood b Willey		2
S Dhawan, run out (Stokes)		44
* V Kohli, b Rashid		71
K D Karthik, b Rashid		21
§ M S Dhoni, c Buttler b Willey		42
S K Raina, c Root b Rashid		1
H H Pandya, c Buttler b Wood		21
B Kumar, c Bairstow b Willey		21
S N Thakur, not out		22
K Yadav		
Y A Chahal	Did not bat	
Extras lb 6, w 5		11
Total (8 wkts, 50 overs)		256

FoW:- 1-13 (Sharma), 2-84 (Dhawan), 3-125 (Karthik), 4-156 (Kohli), 5-158 (Raina), 6-194 (Pandya), 7-221 (Dhoni), 8-256 (Kumar).

	O	M	R	W
Wood	10	2	30	1
Willey	9	0	40	3
Plunkett	5	0	41	0
Ali	10	0	47	0
Stokes	6	0	43	0
Rashid	10	0	49	3

ENGLAND

J M Vince, run out (Pandya/Dhoni)		27
J M Bairstow, c Raina b Thakur		30
J E Root, not out		100
* E J G Morgan, not out		88
B A Stokes		
§ J C Buttler		
M M Ali		
D J Willey	Did not bat	
A U Rashid		
L E Plunkett		
M A Wood		
Extras b 3, lb 6, w 5, nb 1		15
Total (2 wkts, 44.3 overs)		260

FoW: 1-53 (Bairstow), 3-74 (Vince)

	O	M	R	W
Kumar	7	0	49	0
Pandya	5.3	0	39	0
Thakur	10	0	51	1
Chahal	10	0	41	0
Yadav	10	0	55	0
Raina	2	0	16	0

Man of the Match: A U Rashid

Umpires: M A Gough and B N J Oxenford   Scorers: J T Potter and J R Virr
Third Umpire: R S A Palliyaguruge   Fourth: R T Robinson   Match Referee: D C Boon

First Royal London One-Day International
England v. New Zealand
ICC Women's Championship 2017/18 to 2020

Played at Emerald Headingley, Leeds, on July 7, 2018
England won by 142 runs

Toss won by England   England 2 points, New Zealand 0 points

ENGLAND

A E Jones, st Martin b Kerr		63
T T Beaumont, c Martin b Tahuhu		40
§ S J Taylor, c Martin b Kerr		26
* H C Knight, c Martin b Kasperek		63
N R Sciver, lbw b Tahuhu		37
K H Brunt, not out		30
L Winfield, not out		9
G A Elwiss		
S Ecclestone		
L A Marsh	Did not bat	
K L George		
Extras b 2, lb 3, w 15, nb 2		22
Total (5 wkts, 50 overs)		290

FoW: 1-111 (Beaumont), 2-129 (Jones), 3-148 (Taylor), 4-215 (Sciver), 5-269 (Knight)

	O	M	R	W
Tahuhu	9	0	57	2
Huddleston	6	0	34	0
Devine	8	0	54	0
Kasperek	9	0	51	1
Kerr	10	1	36	2
Bates	4	0	28	0
Watkin	4	0	25	0

NEW ZEALAND

* S W Bates, c George b Sciver	28
S F M Devine, c Ecclestone b Elwiss	33
A E Satterthwaite, lbw b Elwiss	2
§ K J Martin, c Jones b Sciver	1
M L Green, c Sciver b Ecclestone	21
A C Kerr, c Winfield b Sciver	8
K F Ebrahim, not out	16
J M Watkin, lbw b Marsh	1
L M Kasperek, lbw b Marsh	14
L M Tahuhu, b Marsh	6
H R Huddleston, lbw b George	1
Extras lb 8, w 9	17
Total (35.3 overs)	148

FoW: 1-70 (Devine), 2-71 (Bates), 3-73 (Martin), 4-75 (Satterthwaite), 5-101 (Kerr), 6-112 (Green), 7-115 (Watkin), 8-137 (Kasperek), 9-147 (Tahuhu), 10-148 (Huddleston)

	O	M	R	W
Brunt	5	1	15	0
George	5.3	0	34	1
Ecclestone	8	1	33	1
Elwiss	6	0	16	2
Sciver	4	0	18	3
Marsh	7	0	24	3

Umpires: M Burns and D J Millns

Tour Match — List A
ECB XI v. India A

Played at Emerald Headingley, Leeds, on June 17, 2018

India A won by 125 runs

Toss won by ECB XI

INDIA A

P P Shaw, c Davies b Higgins		70
M A Agarwal, c Jacks b Baber		4
G H Vihari, b Higgins		38
* S S Iyer, c Rawlins b Higgins		54
V Shankar, c Jacks b Rawlins		11
§ I Kishan, c Rawlins b Higgins		50
K H Pandya, c Jacks b Robinson		34
A R Patel, not out		28
D L Chahar, c Davies b Overton		10
M P Krishna, not out		9
K K Ahmed	Did not bat	
Extras b 1, lb 8, w 9, nb 2		20
Total (8 wkts, 50 overs)		328

FoW: 1-43 (Agarwal), 2-127 (Shaw), 3-128 (Vihari), 4-147 (Shankar), 5-246 (Kishan), 6-246 (Iyer), 7-302 (Pandya), 8-317 (Chahar).

	O	M	R	W
Robinson	10	0	65	1
Barber	7	0	51	1
Overton	10	0	67	1
Critchley	7	0	43	0
Higgins	10	0	50	4
Rawlins	5	0	33	1
Jacks	1	0	10	0

ECB XI

G T Hankins, c Shankar b Ahmed		27
* § A L Davies, c Ahmed b Chahar		4
B T Slater, c Kishan b Shankar		37
W G Jacks, lbw b Patel		28
H Z Finch, b Krishna		11
D M W Rawlins, b Patel		16
M J J Critchley, c Krishna b Chahar		40
R F Higgins, run out (Iyer)		9
O E Robinson, b Pandya		14
J Overton, not out		8
T E Barber, b Chahar		0
Extras lb 2, w 3, nb 4		9
Total (36.5 overs)		203

FoW: 1-15 (Davies), 2-62 (Hankins), 3-101 (Jacks), 4-107 (Slater), 5-126 (Rawlins), 6-134 (Finch), 7-147 (Higgins), 8-176 (Robinson), 9-202(Critchley), 10-203 (Barber).

	O	M	R	W
Chahar	7.5	0	48	3
Krishna	6	0	58	1
Ahmed	7	2	35	1
Shankar	5	0	18	1
Patel	5	0	21	2
Pandya	6	0	21	1

Umpires: I D Blackwell and T Lungley   Scorers: J T Potter and J R Virr

Yorkshire Premier Leagues Championship — Final
Great Ayton v. Wakefield Thornes

Played at Emerald Headingley, Leeds, on September 22, 2018

Wakefield Thornes won by 7 wickets

Toss won by Great Ayton

GREAT AYTON

C Batchelor, b Shaw	2
D Grainge, c Toft b Mahmood Rasool	12
P Holdsworth, c Shaw b Mahmood Rasool	6
J Thompson, c Medew-Ewan b Mahmood Rasool	0
A Jeewantha, run out (Toft/Froggett)	0
S Pennock, c Warner b Shaw	0
M Croft, b Shaw	4
T Leng, lbw b Morgan	7
§ * J Grainge, lbw b Morgan	17
A Liddle, not out	20
J Marsay, b Moran	0
Extras lb 6, w 19, nb 4	29
Total (26.3 overs)	97

FoW: 1-19 (Batchelor), 2-21 (D Grainge), 3-23 (Thompson), 4-23 (Jeewantha), 5-26 (Pennock), 6-42 (Croft), 7-43 (Holdsworth), 8-59 (Leng), 9-86 (J Grainge), 10-97 (Marsay)

	O	M	R	W
Shaw	9	3	27	3
Mahmood Rasool	11	2	33	3
Morgan	4.3	0	14	3
Warner	2	0	17	0

WAKEFIELD THORNES

J Wolfenden, b Jeewantha	20
J Warner, not out	28
D Toft, c J Graine b Batchelor	26
M Jordan, c Marsay b Liddle	6
J Shaw, not out	9
Faisel Irfan	
J Medew-Ewan	
G Wadsworth	Did not bat
§ * T Froggett	
S Morgan	
Mahmood Rasool	
Extras lb 5, w 3, nb 1	9
Total (3 wkts, 25 overs)	98

FoW: 1-29 (Wolfenden), 2-71 (Toft), 3-82 (Jordan)

	O	M	R	W
Marsay	7	2	22	0
Jeewantha	5	0	30	1
Leng	7	1	21	0
Batchelor	3	1	10	1
Liddle	3	0	10	1

Umpires: C Chaplin and S Malone   Scorers: B Cook, Miss K Batty and J T Potter

VITALITY BLAST AND ABU DHABI HIGHLIGHTS OF 2018

VITALITY BLAST WINNERS

Worcestershire Rapids, defeated Sussex Sharks by 5 wickets

Win by 9 wickets (1)

Hobart Hurricanes (140-7) lost to Yorkshire Vikings (144-1) at Abu Dhabi

Totals of 150 and over (12)

226-8	v. Birmingham at Leeds (won)
200-3	v. Durham at Leeds (won)
187-5	v. Leicestershire at Leeds (won)
184-5	v. Lahore Qalandars at Abu Dhabi (lost)
181-9	v. Lancashire at Leeds (lost)
179-7	v. Worcestershire at Worcester (won)
175-4	v. Lancashire at Manchester (lost)
166-8	v. Derbyshire at Chesterfield (lost)
165-3	v. Northamptonshire at Northampton (won)
163-6	v Nottinghamshire at Leeds (lost)
157-7	v. Durham at Chester-le-Street (won)
157-7	v. Birmingham at Birmingham (lost)

Match aggregates of 350 and over (6)

402	Yorkshire (226-8) defeated Birmingham (176-4) by 31 runs *(DLS method)* at Leeds
373	Yorkshire (184-5) lost to Lahore Qalandars (189-4) by 6 wickets at Abu Dhabi
366	Yorkshire (181-9) lost to Lancashire (185-4) by 6 wickets at Leeds
361	Nottinghamshire (212-5) defeated Yorkshire (149-7) by 63 runs at Nottingham
356	Yorkshire (200-3) defeated Durham (156-4) by 44 runs at Leeds
351	Lancashire (176-2) defeated Yorkshire (175-4) by 1 run at Manchester

Century Partnerships (3)

For the 2nd wicket (2)

150	A Lyth and D J Willey	v. Northamptonshire at Northampton
129	T Kohler-Cadmore and D J Willey	v. Lancashire at Leeds

For the 4th wicket (1)

110*	A Lyth and J A Tattersall	v. Durham at Leeds

4 wickets in an innings (none)

3 catches in an innings (1)

J A Tattersall (1)

3	v. Leicestershire at Leeds

4 dismissals in an innings (1)

J A Tattersall (1)

4 (2ct + 2st) v. Hobart Hurricanes at Abu Dhabi

Debuts (4)

T20: H C Brook, J A Tattersall and J A Thompson
For Yorkshire: J E Poysden

VITALITY BLAST in 2018

NORTH GROUP

		P	W	L	T	NR/A	PTS	NRR
1	Worcestershire Rapids (8) *	14	9	4	0	1	19	0.595
2	Durham Jets (9) *	14	9	4	0	1	19	0.556
3	Lancashire Lightning (7) *	14	8	5	0	1	17	0.683
4	Notts Outlaws (1) *	14	8	6	0	0	16	0.073
5	**Yorkshire Vikings**	**14**	**7**	**7**	**0**	**0**	**14**	**-0.035**
6	Birmingham Bears	14	6	7	1	0	13	0.033
7	Derbyshire Falcons	14	5	7	0	2	12	-0.047
8	Leicestershire Foxes	14	5	8	0	1	11	-0.380
9	Northamptonshire Steelbacks	14	2	11	1	0	5	-1.398

SOUTH GROUP

		P	W	L	T	NR/A	PTS	NRR
1	Somerset (4) *	14	10	4	0	0	20	0.786
2	Kent Spitfires (6) *	14	8	2	0	4	20	0.627
3	Sussex Sharks (5) *	14	7	3	0	4	18	0.737
4	Gloucestershire (9) *	14	8	4	0	2	18	0.381
5	Surrey (2)	14	7	5	0	2	16	0.989
6	Glamorgan (1)	14	7	6	0	1	15	-0.144
7	Essex Eagles (8)	14	2	8	1	3	8	-1.035
8	Hampshire Royals (3)	14	2	9	1	2	7	-0.824
9	Middlesex Panthers (7)	14	2	12	0	0	4	-1.128

* Qualified for the Quarter-Finals

(2017 group positions in brackets)

Vitality Blast — North Group
Yorkshire v. Durham

Played at Emerald Headingley, Leeds, on July 5, 2018
Yorkshire won by 44 runs

Toss won by Durham

Yorkshire 2 points, Durham 0 points

YORKSHIRE

T Kohler-Cadmore, c Collingwood b Rushworth	....	6
A Lyth, not out	....	92
H C Brook, c Latham b Imran Tahir	....	44
G S Ballance, c Latham b Pringle	....	0
§ J A Tattersall, not out	....	53
J A Leaning		
T T Bresnan		
Azeem Rafiq	Did not bat	
M D Fisher		
* S A Patterson		
J A Brooks		
Extras w 1, nb 4	....	5
Total (3 wkts, 20 overs)	....	200

FoW: 1-9 (Kohler-Cadmore), 2-90 (Brook), 3-90 (Ballance)

	O	M	R	W
Smith	1	0	5	0
Rushworth	3	0	31	1
Weighell	3	0	48	0
Rimmington	3	0	31	0
Collingwood	4	0	35	0
Pringle	2	0	17	1
Imran Tahir	4	0	33	1

DURHAM

G Clark, c Leaning b Brooks	....	8
B A Stokes, not out		90
PD Collingwood, lbw b Brooks	....	0
* T W M Latham, c Brooks b Patterson	....	12
W R Smith, c Azeem Rafiq b Brooks	....	22
R D Pringle, not out	....	19
W J Weighell		
§ S W Poynter		
N J Rimmington	Did not bat	
Imran Tahir		
C Rushworth		
Extras lb 3, w 2	....	5
Total (4 wkts, 20 overs)	....	156

FoW: 1-12 (Clark), 2-13 (Collingwood), 3-45 (Latham), 4-91 (Smith)

	O	M	R	W
Fisher	4	0	38	0
Brooks	4	0	21	3
Bresnan	4	0	37	0
Azeem Rafiq	4	0	31	0
Patterson	4	0	26	1

Man of the Match: A Lyth

Umpires: PK Baldwin and J H Evans

Scorers: J T Potter and W R Dobson

Vitality Blast — North Group
Birmingham v. Yorkshire

Played at Edgbaston, Birmingham, on July 8, 2018
Birmingham won by 8 wickets

Toss won by Birmingham   Birmingham 2 points, Yorkshire 0 points

YORKSHIRE

A Lyth, lbw b Brookes	0
T Kohler-Cadmore, c Hain b Hannon-Dalby	7
H C Brook, c Elliott b Brookes	20
G S Ballance, c Ambrose b Hannon-Dalby	79
§ J A Tattersall, b Sibley	15
J A Leaning, b Elliott	7
T T Bresnan, c Brookes b Hannon-Dalby	10
M D Fisher, not out	17
Azeem Rafiq	
* S A Patterson Did not bat	
J A Brooks	
Extras lb 1, w 1	2
Total (7 wkts, 20 overs)	157

FoW: 1-0 (Lyth), 2-28 (Kohler-Cadmore), 3-28 (Brook), 4-71 (Tattersall), 5-86 (Leaning), 6-114 (Bresnan), 7-157 (Ballance)

	O	M	R	W
Brookes	4	0	39	2
de Grandhomme	3	0	28	0
Hannon-Dalby	4	0	37	3
Patel	4	1	23	0
Sibley	4	0	25	1
Elliott	1	0	4	1

BIRMINGAM

E J Pollock, c Brooks b Patterson	39
I R Bell, not out	50
S R Hain, c Bresnan b Fisher	6
A J Hose, not out	51
* G D Elliott	
C de Grandhomme	
D P Sibley	
§ T R Ambrose Did not bat	
J S Patel	
H J H Brooks	
O J Hannon-Dalby	
Extras lb 2, w 6, nb 4	12
Total (2 wkts, 15.5 overs)	158

FoW: 1-55 (Pollock), 2-75 (Hain)

	O	M	R	W
Fisher	4	0	56	1
Brooks	2.5	0	35	0
Bresnan	3	0	14	0
Patterson	3	0	25	1
Azeem Rafiq	3	0	26	0

Man of the Match: E J Pollock

Umpires: B J Debenham and N G B Cook   Scorers: J T Potter and M D Smith

Vitality Blast — North Group
Durham v. Yorkshire

Played at Emirates Riverside, Chester-le-Street, on July 13, 2018
Yorkshire won by 10 runs

Toss won by Yorkshire

Yorkshire 2 points, Durham 0 points

YORKSHIRE

A Lyth, c Poynter b Collingwood	17
T Kohler-Cadmore, c Collingwood b Weighell	5
H C Brook, c Weighell b Collingwood	38
G S Ballance, c and b Collingwood	17
§ J A Tattersall, c Clark b Rimmington	36
J A Leaning, st Poynter b Imran Tahir	10
T T Bresnan, not out	28
M D Fisher, not out	0
Azeem Rafiq	
* S A Patterson Did not bat	
J A Brooks	
Extras lb 1, w 3, nb 2	6
Total (6 wkts, 20 overs)	157

FoW: 1-8 (Kohler-Cadmore), 2-50 (Lyth), 3-69 (Brook), 4-82 (Ballance), 5-104 (Leaning), 6-155 (Tattersall)

	O	M	R	W
Rushworth	4	0	25	0
Weighell	3	0	40	1
Rimmington	3	0	31	1
Collingwood	4	0	27	3
Smith	2	0	12	0
Imran Tahir	4	0	21	1

DURHAM

* T W M Latham, c Leaning b Fisher	42
G Clark, c Lyth b Fisher	39
P D Collingwood, c Patterson b Bresnan	22
L Trevaskis, run out (Ballance)	2
W R Smith, c and b Bresnan	13
W J Weighell, not out	7
§ S W Poynter, run out (Bresnan)	11
R C Davies, not out	0
N J Rimmington	
C Rushworth Did not bat	
Imran Tahir	
Extras lb 8, w 3	11
Total (6 wkts, 20 overs)	147

FoW: 1-77 (Latham), 2-99 (Clark), 3-102 (Trevaskis), 4-129 (Smith), 5-129 (Collingwood), 6-146 (Poynter)

	O	M	R	W
Fisher	4	0	26	2
Brooks	2	0	28	0
Bresnan	4	0	19	2
Patterson	4	0	27	0
Azeem Rafiq	4	0	24	0
Lyth	2	0	15	0

Man of the Match: T T Bresnan

Umpires: N A Mallender and J D Middlebrook   Scorers: J T Potter and W R Dobson

Vitality Blast — North Group
Worcestershire v. Yorkshire

Played at Blackfinch New Road, Worcester, on July 15, 2018
Yorkshire won by 12 runs

Toss won by Worcestershire   Yorkshire 2 points, Worcestershire 0 points

YORKSHIRE

A Lyth, c Whiteley b Brown		35
T Kohler-Cadmore, b Pennington		5
H C Brook, c Clarke b Mitchell		33
G S Ballance, c Mitchell b Head		40
§ J A Tattersall, c Guptill b Brown		29
J A Leaning, c Guptill b Wood		11
T T Bresnan, lbw b Brown		6
J A Thompson, not out		12
Azeem Rafiq, not out		1
* S A Patterson		
J A Brooks	Did not bat	
Extras b 1, lb 1, w 5		7
Total (7 wkts, 20 overs)		179

FoW: 1-41 (Lyth), 2-49 (Kohler-Cadmore), 3-111 (Ballance), 4-118 (Brook), 5-147 (Leaning), 6-164 (Tattersall), 7-164 (Bresnan)

	O	M	R	W
Pennington	3	0	26	1
Wood	3	0	21	1
Brown	4	0	34	3
Barnard	4	0	38	0
D'Oliveira	2	0	22	0
Mitchell	2	0	16	1
Head	2	0	20	1

WORCESTERSHIRE

M J Guptill, c Tattersall b Bresnan		0
J M Clarke, c Patterson b Bresnan		17
T M Head, c Ballance b Thompson		23
D K H Mitchell, c Brooks b Patterson		2
§ O B Cox, c Lyth b Azeem Rafiq		12
* B L D'Oliveira, c Brooks b Bresnan		24
R A Whiteley, c Leaning b Patterson		37
E G Barnard, not out		25
L Wood, c Thompson b Patterson		11
D Y Pennington, not out		6
P R Brown	Did not bat	
Extras b 1, lb 4, w 5		10
Total (8 wkts, 20 overs)		167

6-110 (D'Oliveira), 7-132 (Whiteley), 8-153 (Wood)

	O	M	R	W
Bresnan	4	0	38	3
Brooks	4	0	27	0
Patterson	4	0	35	3
Thompson	4	0	33	1
Azeem Rafiq	4	0	29	1

Man of the Match: T T Bresnan

Umpires: N L Bainton and G D Lloyd   Scorers: J T Potter and S M Drinkwater
Third Umpire: D J Millns

Vitality Blast — North Group
Lancashire v. Yorkshire

Played at Emirates Old Trafford, Manchester, on July 20, 2018
Lancashire won by 1 run

Toss won by Yorkshire

Lancashire 2 points, Yorkshire 0 points

LANCASHIRE

§ J C Buttler, run out (Plunkett)		16
* L S Livingstone, c Root b Patterson		79
A M Lilley, not out		42
J Clark, not out		36
A L Davies		
K K Jennings		
D J Vilas		
J P Faulkner	Did not bat	
S D Parry		
M W Parkinson		
T J Lester		
Extras w 1, nb 2		3
Total (2 wkts, 14 overs)		176

FoW: 1-55 (Buttler), 2-120 (Livingstone)

	O	M	R	W
Willey	3	0	41	0
Bresnan	2	0	24	0
Patterson	3	0	28	1
Plunkett	2	0	22	0
Rashid	3	0	44	0
Azeem Rafiq	1	0	17	0

YORKSHIRE

A Lyth, c Livingstone b Parkinson		60
D J Willey, st Buttler b Parkinson		20
J E Root, not out		51
L E Plunkett, b Clark		19
T T Bresnan, c Lilley b Faulkner		17
K S Williamson, not out		6
G S Ballance		
§ J A Tattersall	Did not bat	
Azeem Rafiq		
* S A Patterson		
Extras lb 1, w 1		2
Total (4 wkts, 14 overs)		175

FoW: 1-80 (Lyth), 2-90 (Willey), 3-131 (Plunkett), 4-151 (Bresnan)

	O	M	R	W
Livingstone	2	0	20	0
Lester	3	0	48	0
Faulkner	3	0	32	1
Parkinson	3	0	38	2
Clark	2	0	23	1
Parry	1	0	13	0

Man of the Match: L S Livingstone

Umpires: G D Lloyd and M J Saggers

Scorers: J T Potter and C Rimmer

Third Umpire: N L Bainton

Vitality Blast — North Group
Yorkshire v. Birmingham Bears

Played at Emerald Headingley, Leeds, on July 27, 2018
Yorkshire won by 31 runs (DLS method)

Toss won by Yorkshire   Yorkshire 2 points, Birmingham 0 points

YORKSHIRE

A Lyth, c Rankin b Woakes		40
T Kohler-Cadmore, b Stone		73
D J Willey, lbw b Patel		1
K S Williamson, c Rankin b Elliott		49
G S Ballance, c Hose b Woakes		35
T T Bresnan, c Ambrose b Elliott		10
L E Plunkett, not out		11
§ J A Tattersall, c Hose b Rankin		2
A U Rashid, c Woakes b Rankin		0
Azeem Rafiq, not out		0
* S A Patterson	Did not bat	
Extras lb 2, w 3		5
Total (8 wkts, 20 overs)		226

FoW: 1-63 (Lyth), 2-92 (Willey), 3-135 (Kohler-Cadmore), 4-188 (Ballance), 5-212 (Williamson), 6-212 (Bresnan), 7-221 (Tattersall), 8-224 (Rashid).

	O	M	R	W
Stone	4	0	34	1
Woakes	4	0	54	2
Patel	4	0	33	1
Rankin	4	0	56	2
Elliott	3	0	34	2
de Grandhomme	1	0	13	0

BIRMINGHAM
(Target to win: 208 off 18 overs)

E J Pollock, c Tattersall b Willey		22
I R Bell, c Bresnan b Plunkett		42
S R Hain, lbw b Rashid		16
A J Hose, c Bresnan b Plunkett		43
C de Grandhomme, not out		38
* G D Elliott, not out		5
C R Woakes		
§ T R Ambrose		
J S Patel	Did not bat	
W B Rankin		
O P Stone		
Extras lb 2, w 4, nb 4		10
Total (4 wkts, 18 overs)		176

FoW: 1-29 (Pollock), 2-58 (Hain), 3-99 (Bell), 4-147 (Hose).

	O	M	R	W
Willey	2	0	16	1
Bresnan	3	0	38	0
Patterson	4	0	48	0
Azeem Rafiq	2	0	22	0
Rashid	3	0	19	1
Plunkett	4	0	31	2

Man of the Match: T Kohler-Cadmore

Umpires: M Burns and P J Hartley   Scorers: J T Potter and M D Smith
Third Umpire: R J Bailey

Vitality Blast — North Group
Derbyshire v. Yorkshire

Played at Queen's Park, Chesterfield, on July 28, 2018
Derbyshire won by 5 wickets

Toss won by Yorkshire   Derbyshire 2 points, Yorkshire 0 points

YORKSHIRE

T Kohler-Cadmore, c Critchley b Rampaul	....	15
A Lyth, c Wilson b Rampaul	....	8
D J Willey, c MacLeod b Wahab Riaz	....	55
K S Williamson, c Dal b Wahab Riaz	....	35
G S Ballance, b Hughes	....	16
§ J A Tattersall, b Viljoen	....	5
T T Bresnan, c Wilson b Rampaul	....	16
L E Plunkett, b Rampaul	....	7
A U Rashid. not out	....	1
Azeem Rafiq, not out	....	2
* S A Patterson	Did not bat	
Extras b 1, lb 1, w 2, nb 2	....	6
Total (8 wkts, 20 overs)	....	166

FoW: 1-15 (Kohler-Cadmore), 2-37 (Lyth), 3-109 (Williamson), 4-128 (Willey), 5-139 (Ballance), 6-147 (Tattersall), 7-162 (Bresnan), 8-192 (Plunkett)

	O	M	R	W
Madsen	1	0	15	0
Rampaul	4	0	19	4
Wahab Riaz	4	0	34	2
Ferguson	4	0	29	0
Viljoen	4	0	34	1
Hughes	2	0	22	1
Critchley	1	0	11	0

DERBYSHIRE

B A Godleman, not out	....	71
C S MacLeod, c Willey b Azeem Rafiq	....	15
W L Madsen, run out (Williamson/Tattersall)	......	2
A K Dal, lbw b Rashid	....	8
* § G C Wilson, st Tattersall b Azeem Rafiq	....	18
G C Viljoen, b Rashid	....	5
M J J Critchley, not out	....	38
A L Hughes		
Wahab Riaz	Did not bat	
L H Ferguson		
R Rampaul		
Extras b 4, lb 6, w 3	....	13
Total (5 wkts, 19.5 overs)	....	170

FoW: 1-42 (MacLeod), 2-44 (Madsen), 3-60 (Dal), 4-95 (Wilson), 5-106 (Viljoen)

	O	M	R	W
Willey	2	0	17	0
Bresnan	1.5	0	39	0
Patterson	4	0	23	1
Azeem Rafiq	4	0	28	2
Plunkett	4	0	34	0
Rashid	4	0	19	1

Man of the Match: M J J Critchley

Umpires: J H Evans and R J Warren   Scorers: J T Potter and J M Brown

Vitality Blast — North Group
Yorkshire v. Derbyshire

Played at Emerald Headingley, Leeds, on July 30, 2018

Derbyshire won by 77 runs

Toss won by Yorkshire   Derbyshire 2 points, Yorkshire 0 points

DERBYSHIRE

B A Godleman, b Willey		0
C S MacLeod, c Azeem Rafiq b Thompson		28
Wahab Riaz, c Willey b Azeem Rafiq		42
W L Madsen, c Lyth b Thompson		66
G C Viljoen, c Patterson b Thompson		1
M J J Critchley, c Thompson b Azeem Rafiq		2
* § G C Wilson, c Ballance b Patterson		14
A L Hughes, not out		15
A K Dal, not out		0
L H Ferguson		
R Rampaul	Did not bat	
Extras lb 1, w 10		11
Total (7 wkts, 17 overs)		179

FoW: 1-0 (Godleman), 2-66 (MacLeod), 3-114 (Wahab Riaz), 4-146 (Viljoen), 5-147 (Madsen), 6-150 (Critchley), 7-176 (Wilson).

	O	M	R	W
Willey	4	0	36	1
Bresnan	3	0	30	0
Patterson	4	0	45	1
Thompson	3	0	23	3
Azeem Rafiq	3	0	44	2

YORKSHIRE

A Lyth, c Godleman b Ferguson	21
T Kohler-Cadmore, c Wilson b Ferguson	8
D J Willey, c MacLeod b Wahab Riaz	24
K S Williamson, c MacLeod b Hughes	4
G S Ballance, c Viljoen b Ferguson	13
H C Brook, c Wilson b Viljoen	18
T T Bresnan, c Wilson b Hughes	5
§ J A Tattersall, b Viljoen	2
J A Thompson, b Hughes	0
Azeem Rafiq, not out	2
* S A Patterson, b Viljoen	0
Extras lb 3, w 2	5
Total (14 overs)	102

FoW: 1-23 (Kohler-Cadmore), 2-37 (Lyth), 3-42 (Williamson), 4-67 (Ballance), 5-91 (Brook), 6-97 (Willey), 7-100 (Bresnan), 8-100 (Thompson), 9-102 (Tattersall), 10-102 (Patterson).

	O	M	R	W
Wahab Riaz	3	0	19	1
Rampaul	1	0	15	0
Ferguson	3	0	21	3
Hughes	3	0	12	3
Viljoen	4	0	32	3

Man of the Match: W L Madsen

Umpires: J H Evans and P J Hartley   Scorers: J T Potter and J M Brown

Vitality Blast — North Group
Yorkshire v. Leicestershire

Played at Emerald Headingley, Leeds, on July 31, 2018
Yorkshire won by 60 runs

Toss won by Yorkshire   Yorkshire 2 points, Leicestershire 0 points

YORKSHIRE

A Lyth, c Delport b Nabi		4
T Kohler-Cadmore, c Griffiths b Parkinson		53
D J Willey, c Cosgrove b Ackermann		31
K S Williamson, b Abbas		77
G S Ballance, c Cosgrove b Griffiths		6
H C Brook, not out		3
J A Thompson, not out		1
§ J A Tattersall		
J A Brooks	Did not bat	
Azeem Rafiq		
* S A Patterson		
Extras w 12		12
Total (5 wkts, 20 overs)		187

FoW: 1-12 (Lyth), 2-71 (Willey), 3-138 (Kohler-Cadmore), 4-173 (Ballance), 5-185 (Williamson)

	O	M	R	W
Mohammad Abbas	4	0	42	1
Mohammad Nabi	4	0	39	1
Raine	3	0	35	0
Griffiths	3	0	27	1
Parkinson	4	0	30	1
Ackermann	2	0	14	1

LEICESTERSHIRE

C S Delport, c Kohler-Cadmore b Willey		20
N J Dexter, c Tattersall b Brooks		20
M J Cosgrove, c Tattersall b Willey		4
B A Raine, c Thompson b Brooks		0
* C N Ackermann, b Brooks		0
Mohammad Nabi, c Lyth b Azeem Rafiq		18
§ E J H Eckersley, c Brooks b Azeem Rafiq		6
T J Wells, c Lyth b Patterson		17
C F Parkinson, not out		27
Mohammad Abbas, c Tattersall b Thompson		2
G T Griffiths, not out		3
Extras lb 5, w 3, nb 2		10
Total (9 wkts, 20 overs)		127

FoW: 1-24 (Delport), 2-28 (Cosgrove), 3-29 (Raine), 4-30 (Ackermann), 5-49 (Dexter), 6-66 (Eckersley), 7-76 (Nabi), 8-99 (Wells), 9-104 (Abbas)

	O	M	R	W
Willey	4	0	20	2
Azeem Rafiq	4	0	33	2
Brooks	4	0	23	3
Patterson	4	0	20	1
Thompson	4	0	26	1

Man of the Match: K S Williamson

Umpires: B J Debenham and S J O'Shaughnessy   Scorers: J T Potter and P J Rogers

Vitality Blast — North Group
Yorkshire v. Northamptonshire

Played at Emerald Headingley, Leeds, on August 3, 2018
Yorkshire won by 6 wickets

Toss won by Northamptonshire   Yorkshire 2 points, Northamptonshire 0 points

NORTHAMPTONSHIRE

R E Levi, c Tattersall b Brooks		4
§ B M Duckett, c Patterson b Thompson		21
J J Cobb, run out (Brooks)		6
* A G Wakely, c Kohler-Cadmore b Rafiq		19
S P Crook, c Kohler-Cadmore b Patterson		11
C O Thurston, c Thompson b Patterson		41
S Prasanna, c Brooks b Willey		5
L A Procter, not out		14
B A Hutton, not out		1
N L Buck		
R J Gleeson	Did not bat	
Extras lb 4, w 3		7
Total (7 wkts, 20 overs)		129

FoW: 1-5 (Levi), 2-16 (Cobb), 3-48 (Duckett), 4-62 (Crook), 5-79 (Wakely), 6-98 (Prasanna), 7-127 (Thurston).

	O	M	R	W
Willey	4	0	20	1
Brooks	4	0	31	1
Patterson	4	0	26	2
Thompson	4	0	24	1
Azeem Rafiq	4	0	24	1

YORKSHIRE

A Lyth, c Duckett b Gleeson		0
T Kohler-Cadmore, c Procter b Prasanna		27
D J Willey, run out (Thurston/Hutton)		15
K S Williamson, not out		52
G S Ballance, c Procter b Gleeson		24
H C Brook, not out		7
§ J A Tattersall		
J A Thompson		
Azeem Rafiq	Did not bat	
* S A Patterson		
J A Brooks		
Extras lb 1, w 6		7
Total (4 wkts, 18.4 overs)		132

FoW: 1-0 (Lyth), 2-23 (Willey), 3-57 (Kohler-Cadmore), 4-108 (Ballance)

	O	M	R	W
Gleeson	4	0	21	2
Buck	3	0	20	0
Hutton	3.4	0	23	0
Prasanna	4	0	31	1
Procter	4	0	36	0

Man of the Match: K S Williamson

Umpires: B J Debenham and M A Gough   Scorers: J T Potter and A C Kingston

Vitality Blast — North Group
Yorkshire v. Lancashire

Played at Emerald Headingley, Leeds, on August 9, 2018
Lancashire won by 6 wickets

Toss won by Yorkshire
Lancashire 2 points, Yorkshire 0 points

YORKSHIRE

T Kohler-Cadmore, c Croft b Parkinson	46
A Lyth, c and b Croft	0
D J Willey, c Watt b Lamb	80
K S Williamson, b Zahir Khan	1
G S Ballance, c Croft b Parkinson	13
§ J A Tattersall, c Davies c Zahir Khan	22
T T Bresnan, not out	9
J A Thompson, b Faulkner	1
Azeem Rafiq, c Watt b Faulkner	0
* S A Patterson, c Watt b Faulkner	0
J A Brooks	Did not bat
Extras lb 2, w 7	9
Total (9 wkts, 20 overs)	181

FoW: 1-1 (Lyth), 2-130 (Willey), 3-132 (Williamson), 4-141 (Kohler-Cadmore), 5-170 (Tattersall), 6-171 (Ballance), 7-181 (Thompson), 8-181 (Rafiq), 9-181 (Patterson)

	O	M	R	W
Croft	1	0	4	1
Faulkner	3	0	24	3
Watt	3	0	24	0
Clark	3	0	28	0
Lamb	2	0	23	1
Zahir Khan	4	0	45	2
Parkinson	4	0	31	2

LANCASHIRE

A L Davies, b Patterson	34
K R Brown, run out (Willey)	51
A M Lilley, c Willey b Thompson	47
* § D J Vilas, c Ballance b Patterson	20
J Clark, not out	17
S J Croft, not out	5
J P Faulkner	
D J Lamb	
M R J Watt	Did not bat
M W Parkinson	
Zahir Khan	
Extras lb 4, w 7	11
Total (4 wkts, 17.4 overs)	185

FoW: 1-57 (Davies), 2-114 (Lilley), 3-162 (Vilas), 4-162 (Brown)

	O	M	R	W
Willey	4	0	31	0
Brooks	2.4	0	26	0
Bresnan	2	0	31	0
Patterson	4	0	32	2
Thompson	3	0	32	1
Azeem Rafiq	2	0	29	0

Man of the Match: K R Brown

Umpires: J H Evans and S J O'Shaughnessy
Scorers: J T Potter and C Rimmer
Third Umpire: M Burns

Vitality Blast — North Group
Nottinghamshire v. Yorkshire

Played at Trent Bridge, Nottingham, on August 10, 2018

Nottinghamshire won by 63 runs

Toss won by Nottinghamshire   Nottinghamshire 2 points, Yorkshire 0 points

NOTTINGHAMSHIRE

M H Wessels, c Brooks b Fisher	16
A D Hales, c Williamson b Brooks	17
J D Libby, b Thompson	58
§ T J Moores, not out	80
* D T Christian, b Fisher	20
S J Mullaney, run out (Thompson)	1
S R Patel, not out	7
W T Root	
L J Fletcher	
I S Sodhi Did not bat	
H F Gurney	
Extras w 11, nb 2	13
Total (5 wkts, 20 overs)	212

FoW: 1-31 (Wessels), 2-43 (Hales), 3-155 (Libby), 4-185 (Christian), 5-187(Mullaney)

	O	M	R	W
Willey	4	0	38	0
Brooks	4	0	22	1
Fisher	4	0	52	2
Thompson	4	0	46	1
Brooks	1	0	13	0
Azeem Rafiq	2	0	27	0
Lyth	1	0	14	0

YORKSHIRE

A Lyth, c Mullaney b Christian	14
T Kohler-Cadmore, c Mullaney b Sodhi	72
* D J Willey, c Wessels b Patel	30
G S Ballance, b Gurney	10
K S Williamson, c Hales b Gurney	11
H C Brook, lbw b Fletcher	2
M D Fisher, b Gurney	1
J A Thompson, not out	6
§ J A Tattersall, not out	1
Azeem Rafiq	
J A Brooks Did not bat	
Extras w 2	2
Total (7 wkts, 20 overs)	149

FoW: 1-27(Lyth), 2-101 (Willey), 3-127 (Kohler-Cadmore), 4-138 (Ballance), 5-141 (Brook), 6-141 (Williamson), 7-143 (Fisher)

	O	M	R	W
Patel	2	0	16	1
Gurney	4	0	24	3
Fletcher	4	0	23	1
Christian	3	0	26	1
Sodhi	4	0	30	1
Mullaney	3	0	30	0

Man of the Match: T J Moores

Umpires: P K Baldwin and N G B Cook   Scorers: J T Potter and R Marshall

Vitality Blast — North Group
Northamptonshire v. Yorkshire

Played at Wantage Road, Northampton, on August 16, 2018
Yorkshire won by 7 wickets

Toss won by Northamptonshire　　　　　Yorkshire 2 points, Northamptonshire 0 points

NORTHAMPTONSHIRE

C O Thurston, c Williamson b Fisher	16
§ B M Duckett, c Lyth b Fisher	16
J J Cobb, not out	68
* A G Wakely, c Bresnan b Plunkett	14
S P Crook, c Fisher b Plunkett	18
S Prasanna, b Brooks	4
L A Procter, c Tattersall b Willey	14
G White, c Kohler-Cadmore b Willey	0
B A Hutton, c Tattersall b Willey	0
B W Sanderson, not out	7
R J Gleeson　　　　　Did not bat	
Extras lb 1, w 2, nb 2	5
Total (8 wkts, 20 overs)	162

FoW: 1-31 (Thurston), 2-33 (Duckett), 3-77 (Wakely), 4-97 (Crook), 5-105 (Prasanna), 6-148 (Procter), 7-148 (White), 8-148 (Hutton)

	O	M	R	W
Willey	4	1	30	3
Brooks	4	0	26	1
Fisher	4	0	29	2
Plunkett	4	0	25	2
Bresnan	3	0	42	0
Lyth	1	0	9	0

YORKSHIRE

A Lyth, c Wakely b Gleeson	66
T Kohler-Cadmore, c White b Hutton	0
* D J Willey, c Wakely b Sanderson	79
K S Williamson, not out	1
G S Balance, not out	9
M D Fisher	
T T Bresnan	
L E Plunkett　　　　　Did not bat	
J A Brooks	
§ J A Tattersall	
J A Thompson	
Extras w 6, nb 4	10
Total (3 wkts, 15.3 overs)	165

FoW: 1-3 (Kohler-Cadmore), 2-153 (Lyth), 3-153 (Willey)

	O	M	R	W
Hutton	3	0	29	1
Gleeson	3.3	0	46	1
Sanderson	3	0	26	1
Prasanna	3	0	19	0
Cobb	1	0	12	0
Procter	1	0	12	0
White	1	0	21	0

Man of the Match: D J Willey

Umpires: R J Bailey and M Burns　　　　　Scorers: J T Potter and A C Kingston

Vitality Blast — North Group
Yorkshire v. Nottinghamshire

Played at Emerald Headingley, Leeds, on August 17, 2018

Nottinghamshire won by 8 wickets

Toss won by Yorkshire

Nottinghamshire 2 points, Yorkshire 0 points

YORKSHIRE

T Kohler-Cadmore, c Mullaney b Carter	4
A Lyth, c Moores b Mullaney	44
* D J Willey, c Hales b Fletcher	51
K S Williamson, run out (Mullaney/Gurney)	44
G S Ballance, c Hales b Sodhi	7
J A Thompson, b Gurney	2
T T Bresnan, not out	5
§ J A Tattersall	
L E Plunkett	
M D Fisher	Did not bat
J A Brooks	
Extras b 3, lb 2, w 1	6
Total (6 wkts, 20 overs)	163

FoW: 1-4 (Kohler-Cadmore), 2-96 (Lyth), 3-106 (Willey), 4-136 (Ballance), 5-144 (Thompson), 6-163 (Williamson)

	O	M	R	W
Carter	3	0	25	1
Gurney	4	0	16	1
Fletcher	4	0	34	1
Christian	2	0	21	0
Sodhi	4	0	33	1
Mullaney	1	0	2	1
Patel	2	0	27	0

NOTTINGHAMSHIRE

M H Wessels, b Willey	16
A D Hales, not out	71
J D Libby, st Tattersall b Lyth	30
§ T J Moores, not out	43
S J Mullaney	
* D T Christian	
S R Patel	
L J Fletcher	Did not bat
I S Sodhi	
M Carter	
H F Gurney	
Extras lb 1, w 6, nb 2	9
Total (2 wkts, 19 overs)	169

FoW: 1-25 (Wessels), 2-98 (Libby)

	O	M	R	W
Willey	4	0	47	1
Brooks	3	0	29	0
Plunkett	4	0	26	0
Fisher	3	0	35	1
Thompson	1	0	8	0
Lyth	4	0	23	1

Man of the Match: A D Hales

Umpires: N L Bainton and M Burns

Scorers: J T Potter and R Marshall

Third Umpire: G D Lloyd

YORKSHIRE AVERAGES 2018

VITALITY BLAST

Played 14   Won 7   Lost 7

BATTING AND FIELDING

(Qualification 4 completed innings)

Player	M.	I.	N.O.	Runs	H.S.	100s	50s	Avge	ct/st
K S Williamson	10	10	3	280	77	0	2	40.00	2
D J Willey	10	10	0	386	80	0	4	38.60	3
A Lyth	14	14	1	401	92*	0	3	30.84	6
H C Brook	8	8	2	165	44	0	0	27.50	0
T Kohler-Cadmore	13	13	0	321	73	0	3	24.69	4
J A Tattersall	14	9	2	165	53*	0	1	23.57	8/2
G S Ballance	14	13	1	269	79	0	1	22.41	3
T T Bresnan	11	9	3	106	28*	0	0	17.66	5

Also played

Player	M.	I.	N.O.	Runs	H.S.	100s	50s	Avge	ct/st
L E Plunkett	5	3	1	37	19	0	0	18.50	0
M D Fisher	6	3	2	18	17*	0	0	18.00	1
J A Leaning	4	3	0	28	11	0	0	9.33	3
J A Thompson	8	6	3	22	12*	0	0	7.33	4
Azeem Rafiq	12	5	4	5	2*	0	0	5.00	2
A U Rashid	3	2	1	1	1*	0	0	1.00	0
S A Patterson	11	2	0	0	0	0	0	0.00	4
J E Root	1	1	1	51	51*	0	1	—	1
J A Brooks	10	0	0	0	—	0	0	—	7

BOWLING

(Qualification 4 wickets)

Player	Overs	Mdns	Runs	Wkts	Avge	Best	4wI	RPO
J A Thompson	23	0	192	8	24.00	3-23	0	8.34
S A Patterson	42	0	335	12	27.91	3-35	0	7.97
J A Brooks	34.3	0	268	9	29.77	3-21	0	7.76
D J Willey	35	1	296	9	32.88	3-30	0	8.45
M D Fisher	23	0	236	7	33.71	2-26	0	10.26
L E Plunkett	18	0	138	4	34.50	2-25	0	7.66
Azeem Rafiq	37	0	334	8	41.75	2-28	0	9.02
T T Bresnan	29.5	0	312	5	62.40	3-38	0	10.45

Also bowled

Player	Overs	Mdns	Runs	Wkts	Avge	Best	4wI	RPO
A U Rashid	10	0	82	3	27.33	2-19	0	8.20
A Lyth	8	0	61	1	61.00	1-23	0	7.62
H C Brook	1	0	13	0	—	0-13	0	13.00

Abu Dhabi T20 — Group A
Lahore Qalandars v. Yorkshire

Played at Sheikh Zayed Stadium, Abu Dhabi, on October 4, 2018

Lahore Qalandars won by 6 wickets

Toss won by Lahore Qalandars   Lahore 2 points, Yorkshire 0 points

YORKSHIRE

T Kohler-Cadmore, c Sohail Akhtar b Zulfiqar Babar .	2
A Lyth, lbw b Raja Farzan	32
H C Brook, b Shaheen Shah Afridi	37
G S Ballance, b Shaheen Shah Afridi	33
§ J A Tattersall, b Raja Farzan	26
J A Leaning, not out	26
T T Bresnan, not out	17
J Shaw	
* S A Patterson Did not bat	
J E Poysden	
J A Thompson	
Extras b 1, lb 5, w 2, nb 3	11
Total (5 wkts, 20 overs)	184

FoW: 1-2 (Kohler-Cadmore), 2-60 (Lyth), 3-80 (Brook), 4-130 (Ballance), 5-143 (Tattersall)

	O	M	R	W
Zulfiqar Babar	4	0	26	1
Majid Ali	4	0	31	0
Shaheen Shah Afridi	4	0	36	2
McClenaghan	4	0	46	0
Raja Farzan	4	0	39	2

LAHORE QALANDERS

Imran Nazir, c Leaning b Bresnan	2
* Sohail Akhtar, c Kohler-Cadmore b Bresnan	100
Bilal Arshad, c Lyth b Poysden	30
Faizan Khan, b Poysden	6
§ P D Salt, not out	37
Abdul Razzaq, not out	5
Zulfiqar Babar	
Majid Ali	
Shaheen Shah Afridi Did not bat	
M J McClenaghan	
Raja Farzan	
Extras lb 7, w 2	9
Total (4 wkts, 19.4 overs)	189

FoW: 1-12 (Imran Nazir), 2-82 (Bilal Irshad), 3-118 (Faizan Khan), 4-165 (Sohail Akhtar)

	O	M	R	W
Lyth	3	0	23	0
Bresnan	3.4	0	41	2
Shaw	4	0	28	0
Patterson	4	0	48	0
Poysden	4	0	26	2
Thompson	1	0	16	0

Man of the Match: Sohail Akhtar

Umpires: Iftikhar Ali and Rabiul Hoque

Abu Dhabi T20 — Group A
Hobart Hurricanes v. Yorkshire

Played at Sheikh Zayed Stadium, Abu Dhabi, on October 6, 2018
Yorkshire won by 9 wickets

Toss won by Hobart Hurricanes   Yorkshire 2 points, Hobart 0 points

HOBART HURRICANES

* C A Wakim, c Kohler-Cadmore b Coad	15
§ B M Duckett, c Tattersall b Shaw	2
S W Willis, c Poysden b Carver	35
C P Jewell, st Tattersall b Carver	38
J Botha, c Tattersall b Shaw	23
J Clark, b Poysden	2
K Oates, st Tattersall b Lyth	3
J R White, not out	12
M B Wright, not out	1
N T Ellis	
J E Taylor	Did not bat
Extras lb 7, w 1, nb 1	9
Total (7 wkts, 20 overs)	140

FoW: 1-23 (Wakim), 2-36 (Duckett), 3-88 (Jewell), 4-103 (Willis), 5-107 (Clark), 6-112 (Oates), 7-139 (Botha)

	O	M	R	W
Coad	3	0	8	1
Shaw	3	0	39	2
Lyth	4	0	21	1
Waite	2	0	14	0
Poysden	4	0	22	1
Carver	4	0	29	2

YORKSHIRE

T Kohler-Cadmore, not out	72
* A Lyth, c Wakim b Clark	21
H C Brook, not out	42
G S Ballance	
J A Leaning	
§ J A Tattersall	
M J Waite	Did not bat
B O Coad	
K Carver	
J Shaw	
J E Poysden	
Extras b 4, lb 4, w 1	9
Total (1 wkt, 12.5 overs)	144

FoW: 1-45 (Lyth)

	O	M	R	W
Botha	2	0	11	0
Taylor	2.5	0	25	0
Wakim	1	0	18	0
Clark	2	0	24	1
Ellis	2	0	24	0
Wright	2	0	25	0
White	1	0	9	0

Man of the Match: T Kohler-Cadmore

Umpires: I J Dixon and Iftikhar Ali

Second Eleven 2018

PLAYERS WHO APPEARED FOR YORKSHIRE SECOND ELEVEN IN 2018
(excluding First Eleven capped players)

Player	Date of Birth	Birthplace	Type
H C Brook *	February 22, 1999	Keighley	RHB/RM
K Carver *	March 26, 1996	Northallerton	LHB/SLA
B O Coad *	January 10, 1994	Harrogate	RHB/RM
M D Fisher *	November 9, 1997	York	RHB/RMF
T Kohler-Cadmore *	August 19, 1994	Chatham, Kent	RHB/OB
J Shaw *	January 3, 1996	Wakefield	RHB/RMF
J A Tattersall *	December 15, 1994	Knaresborough	RHB/WK
J C Wainman *	January 25, 1993	Harrogate	RHB/LM
M J Waite *	December 24, 1995	Leeds	RHB/RMF
Bilal Anjam	January 30, 1999	Rotherham	RHB/OB
E Barnes	November 26, 1997	York	RHB/RFM
B D Birkhead	October 28, 1998	Halifax	RHB/WK
H G Duke §	September 6, 2001	Wakefield	RHB/WK
G C H Hill	January 24, 2001	Keighley	RHB/RMF
S M Imtiaz §	March 16, 1996	Chigwell, London	RHB/WK
D Leech §	January 10, 2001	Midddlesbrough	RHB/RMF
J E G Logan	October 12, 1997	Wakefield	LHB/SLA
T W Loten	January 8, 1999	York	RHB/RMF
M L Revis §	November 15, 2001	Steeton, Keighley	RHB/RM
J R Sullivan §	August 4, 2000	Leeds	RHB/LB
M A Taylor	December 18, 1997	Wakefield	RHB/RFM
J A Thompson	October 9, 1996	Leeds	LHB/RMF
J D Warner	November 14, 1996	Wakefield	RHB/RFM
J Wharton §	February 1, 2001	Huddersfield	RHB/OB
B Whitford §	September 23, 1999	Keighley	RHB/RM
** C Wood §	November 18, 2001	York	RHB/OB

* Second Eleven cap

§ Debutants

** Christopher Wood was to make his debut against Lancashire at Southport and Birkdale CC, but the game was abandoned because of an unfit pitch, and he did not bat or bowl.

Safwaan Imtiaz is a triallist

SECOND ELEVEN HIGHLIGHTS OF 2018

CHAMPIONSHIP

Century partnerships (6)

For the 1st wicket (1)

105 by A Z Lees and T Kohler-Cadmore v. Northamptonshire at Desborough

For the 2nd wicket (1)

125 Azeem Rafiq and Safwaan Imtiaz v. Leicestershire at York

For the 3rd wicket (1)

194 T Kohler-Cadmore and J A Leaning v. Northamptonshire at Desborough

For the 4th wicket (1)

108 J A Tattersall and J A Thompson v. Warwickshire at Edgbaston Foundation Community Sports Ground

For the 6th wicket (2)

102 M D Fisher and E Barnes v. Durham at Scarborough
199 T W Loten and J C Wainman v. Worcestershire at Harrogate

Centuries (5)

T Kohler-Cadmore (1)

173 v. Northamptonshire at Desborough

J A Tattersall (1)

132 v. Warwickshire at Edgbaston Foundation Community Sport Ground

T W Loten (1)

131 v. Worcestershire at Harrogate

J C Wainman (1)

117 v. Worcestershire at Harrogate

H C Brook (1)

106 v. MCC Young Cricketers at York

Ten wickets in a match: – One instance. B O Coad registered match figures of 11-60 v. MCC Young Cricketers at York.

Five wickets in an innings (2)

B O Coad (1)

8-33 v. MCC Young Cricketers at York

K Carver (1)

6-26 v. Northamptonshire at Desborough

Five victims in an innings: No wicket-keeper managed this feat. The best return was three catches by Safwaan Imtiaz v. Nottinghamshire at the Nottinghamshire Sports Ground

CHAMPIONSHIP MILESTONES AND SPECIAL STATISTICS

J A Tattersall, J A Thompson and M J Waite each passed 1,000 runs for the Second Eleven. J C Wainman is the leading Second Eleven wicket-taker among present players with 99 victims. Thompson's Second Eleven Championship average of 73.57 was the second-best nationally for 2018. The sixth-wicket partnership of 199 by T W Loten and Wainman v. Worcestershire at Harrogate is a record for that wicket, beating a partnership of 193 by R A Kettleborough and Jamie Hood at Bradford in 1995. B O Coad's return of 8-33 is the best ever for Yorkshire v. MCC Young Cricketers. The previous best was 8-101 by James Lee at Stamford Bridge in 2009.

TROPHY

Century Partnerships (1)

For the 2nd wicket (1)

107 * B D Birkhead and J A Leaning v. MCC Young Cricketers at York

5 wickets in an innings: None

The best match figures were 4-17 by J A Thompson v. Derbyshire at Repton School. J C Wainman returned 4-42 v. Leicestershire at Stamford Bridge, and M D Fisher took 4-42 v. Warwickshire at Edgbaston.
J W Shutt took 4-47 v. MCC Young Cricketers at York.

Five victims in an innings: None

The best return was four catches by A J Hodd v. Lancashire at Liverpool.

TROPHY MILESTONES AND SPECIAL STATISTICS

J C Wainman's bowling average of 10.80 in the Second Eleven Trophy was the best nationally for those with a minimum of 10 wickets. Yorkshire have now played Lancashire 56 times in this competition. Their total of 51 in 2018 is the lowest they have ever recorded v. Yorkshire, beating the 89 they made at Old Trafford in 1998. Yorkshire's win by 155 runs is the largest winning margin by runs they have ever recorded over the *Red Rose*, beating the margin of 118 secured at Old Trafford in 1996.

T20 COMPETITION

Century Partnerships (1)

For the 1st wicket (1)

105 T Kohler-Cadmore and A Z Lees v. Northamptonshire at Finedon Dolben CC

Centuries (1)

H C Brook (1)

101* v. Derbyshire at Barnsley CC

5 wickets in an innings: None

Two bowlers recorded four-wicket hauls. J Shaw took 4-14 v. Northamptonshire at Finedon Dolben CC, and J A Thompson v. 4-27 v. Nottinghamshire at Worksop College.

Five victims in an innings: None

The best return was four victims by B D Birkhead v. Northamptonshire at Finedon Dolben CC

T20 MILESTONES AND SPECIAL STATISTICS

The 10th-wicket stand of 37 between J D Warner and J W Shutt v. Durham at Brandon CC was the highest nationally for the 10th wicket in the 2018 competition. Derbyshire's total of 67 is the lowest they have ever made v. Yorkshire in 53 encounters in this competition. The previous lowest by Derbyshire was 119 at Castleford in 2001. J A Leaning is the leading run-scorer among present players with 871 runs

Second Eleven Championship
Yorkshire v. Durham

Played at Emerald Headingley on May 9, 10 and 11, 2018

Match drawn at 5.02pm on the Third Day

Toss won by Durham   Yorkshire 11 points, Durham 11 points

Close of play: First Day, Durham 363-5 (Trevaskis 65, Potts 62) (89 overs); Second Day, Durham (2) 65-2 (Pringle 37, Davies 15) (18 overs)

First Innings	DURHAM	Second Innings	
R L Greenwell, c Kohler-Cadmore b Thompson	26	lbw b Thompson	7
* M A Jones, c Tattersall b Warner	45		
G J Harte, b Barnes	8		
R D Pringle, c Barnes b Shaw	28	c Leech b Warner	62
§ R C Davies, c Tattersall b Carver	109	(3) c Kohler-Cadmore b Barnes	63
L Trevaskis, not out	65	(5) c Fisher b Logan	16
M J Potts, not out	62	not out	42
O W Smithson		(9) not out	1
C F Hartley	Did not bat	(8) run out (Barnes)	13
S Steel		(2) lbw b Thompson	0
J Coughlin		(6) c Fisher b Logan	21

G H I Harding, O Gibson and A C Evans did not bat in either innings

Extras b 5, lb 11, nb 4	20	Extras b 9, lb 4, nb 4	17
Total (5 wkts dec, 89 overs)	363	Total (7 wkts dec, 50 overs)	242

FoW: 1-53 (Greenwell), 2-66 (Harte), 3-92 (Jones), 4-163 (Pringle), 5-267 (Davies)
2nd: 1-8 (Steel), 2-9 (Greenwell), 3-118 (Pringle), 4-137 (Davies), 5-158 (Trevaskis), 6-216 (Coughlin), 7-240 (Hartley)

	O	M	R	W		O	M	R	W
Shaw	18	2	75	1	Warner	7	2	19	1
Warner	13	2	49	1	Thompson	8	3	32	2
Thompson	15	2	58	1	Barnes	5	1	32	1
Barnes	11	3	34	1	Sullivan	8	1	53	0
Carver	16	0	55	1	Logan	13	5	46	2
Taylor	4	0	19	0	Leech	3	0	27	0
Logan	12	1	57	0	Taylor	6	1	20	0

First Innings	YORKSHIRE	Second Innings	
A Z Lees, c Davies b Hartley	64		
* T Kohler-Cadmore, b Hartley	38	lbw b Evans	0
§ J A Tattersall, c Trevaskis b Hartley	35	(5) lbw b Trevaskis	26
T W Loten, lbw b Hartley	0	(3) lbw b Pringle	22
J A Thompson, lbw b Trevaskis	20	(4) not out	77
M D Fisher, c Evans b Smithson	84	(1) c Potts b Smithson	0
E Barnes, not out	38	(6) b Smithson	14
J D Warner		not out	10

J Shaw, J E G Logan, M A Taylor, J R Sullivan, D Leech and K Carver did not bat in either innings

Extras b 10, lb 5, nb 14, w 1	30	Extras lb 1, w 1, nb 2	4
Total (6 wkts dec, 83.4 overs)	309	Total (5 wkts, 58 overs)	153

FoW: 1-93 (Kohler-Cadmore), 2-154 (Lees), 3-154 (Loten), 4-157 (Tattersall), 5-207 (Thompson),
1st: 6-309 (Fisher)
2nd: 1-0 (Fisher), 2-0 (Kohler-Cadmore), 3-71 (Loten), 4-108 (Tattersall), 5-127 (Barnes)

	O	M	R	W		O	M	R	W
Evans	13	1	49	0	Smithson	11	3	27	2
Smithson	16.4	3	59	1	Evans	11	4	40	1
Hartley	16	3	61	4	Potts	4	2	8	0
Gibson	6	0	29	0	Hartley	4	0	27	0
Pringle	12	1	32	0	Pringle	9	1	24	1
Potts	4	3	1	0	Trevaskis	9	1	26	1
Trevaskis	12	1	31	1					
Steel	4	0	32	0					

Umpires: M Newall and J Pitcher   Scorers: J R Virr and G Maddison

A Z Lees, K Carver and J Shaw were called to the Yorkshire first team to play Surrey at The Oval. J R Sullivan made his debut for the second team and B Whitford appeared as a fielder only. D Leech was also added to the side

Second Eleven Championship
Warwickhire v. Yorkshire

Played at Edgbaston Foundation Community Sports Ground on May 22, 23 and 24, 2018

Match drawn at 5.23pm on the Third Day

Toss won by Warwickshire

Warwickshire 12 points, Yorkshire 13 points

Close of play: First Day, Warwickshire 43-0 (Rhodes 24, Sibley 8) (8 overs); Second Day, Yorkshire (2) 95-1 (Wharton 36, Tattersall 10) (29 overs)

YORKSHIRE

First Innings			Second Innings	
* A Z Lees, b Thomson	41	(2) c Sibley b Thomson	36
J Wharton, c Mellor b Brookes	11	(1) lbw b Poysden	37
§ J A Tattersall, c Yates b Brookes	132	c Umeed b Brookes	23
T W Loten, run out (Brookes)	26	c Umeed b Brookes	11
J A Thompson, c Rhodes b Poysden	54	c Thomson b Rhodes	77
G C H Hill, c Banks b Thomson	1	lbw b Poysden	1
J Shaw, c Mellor b Wright	13	b Thomson	17
E Barnes, c Umeed b Wright	8		
K Carver, lbw b Wright	0	(8) not out	27
J D Warner, st Mellor b Poysden	9	(9) c Banks b Poysden	0
J E G Logan, not out	1	(10) b Poysden	6
M A Taylor	Did not bat	c Umeed b Sibley	17
Extras b 13, lb 5, nb 16, w 3, pen 5	42	Extras b 17, lb 7, nb 10	34

Five penalty runs were awarded in the Yorkshire first innings when the ball struck a fielding helmet

| Total (93.1 overs) | 338 | Total (95.3overs) | 286 |

FoW: 1-18 (Wharton), 2-86 (Lees), 3-139 (Loten), 4-247 (Thompson), 5-252 (Hill),
1st 6-304 (Shaw), 7-321 (Tattersall), 8-322 (Carver), 9-329 (Barnes), 10-338 (Warner)
FoW: 1-80 (Lees), 2-101 (Wharton), 3-115 (Tattersall), 4-132 (Loten), 5-139 (Hill),
2nd 6-193 (Shaw), 7-241 (Thompson), 8-249 (Warner), 9-255 (Logan), 10-286 (Taylor)

	O	M	R	W		O	M	R	W
Wright	20	3	32	3	Wright	12	3	29	0
Brookes	20	1	105	2	Brookes	16	3	73	2
Rankin	2	0	17	0	Thomson	17	4	48	2
Rhodes	12	4	22	0	Rhodes	10	5	19	1
Thomson	19	3	65	2	Poysden	30	9	51	4
Poysden	16.1	2	35	2	Sukhjit Singh	5	1	23	0
Sukhjit Singh	4	0	39	0	Sibley	5.3	1	19	1

WARWICKSHIRE

First innings		Second Innings	
W M H Rhodes, c Tattersall b Logan	95	c Logan b Shaw	4
* D P Sibley, c Tattersall b Warner	26	c Tattersall b Shaw	21
L Banks, lbw b Shaw	0	not out	8
A R I Umeed, c Lees b Carver	23	not out	1
R M Yates, c Lees b Carver	9		
A T Thomson, lbw b Carver	24		
§ A J Mellor, c Lees b Logan	64		
C J C Wright, run out (Hill)	9		
Sukhjit Singh, lbw b Carver	23		
J E Poysden, not out	7		
B L Brookes, c Hill b Shaw	0		
W B Rankin	Did not bat		
Extras b 8, lb 2, nb 8	18	Extras b 1, nb 2	3
Total (83 overs)	298	Total (2 wkts, 7 overs)	37

FoW: 1-84 (Sibley), 2-92 (Banks), 3-136 (Umeed), 4-152 (Yates), 5-166 (Rhodes),
1st 6-221 (Thomson), 7-239 (Wright), 8-287 (Sukhjit Singh), 9-287 (Mellor), 10-298 (Brookes)
FoW: 1-4 (Rhodes), 2-29 (Sibley)

	O	M	R	W		O	M	R	W
Shaw	15	1	96	2	Shaw	4	0	22	2
Thompson	4	0	20	0	Taylor	3	0	14	0
Warner	9	2	14	1					
Barnes	1.2	0	14	0					
Taylor	8.4	2	26	0					
Logan	20	5	38	2					
Carver	21	6	63	4					
Loten	4	0	17	0					

Umpires: J D Middlebrook and D J Gower

Scorers: S Smith and J R Virr

Second Eleven Championship
Yorkshire v. MCC Young Cricketers

Played at York CC on June 6, 7 and 8, 2018

Yorkshire won by 4 wickets at 4.55pm on the Third Day

Toss won by Yorkshire — Yorkshire 22 points, MCC Young Cricketers 5 points

Close of play: First Day, Yorkshire 157-5 (Loten 40, Shaw 11) (48 overs); Second Day, MCC Young Cricketers (2) 273-8 (Manthorpe 1) (75.2 overs)

MCC YOUNG CRICKETERS		
First Innings		Second Innings
B J Curran, lbw b Coad	0	c Hodd b Coad	74
* J H Barrett, c Thompson b Coad	8	c Lees b Coad	4
E Callis, lbw b Coad	4	b Wainman	5
§ S M Imtiaz, lbw b Brooks	13	b Carver	121
M D Lezar, c Leaning b Coad	65	c Hodd b Thompson	23
F J Hudson-Prentice, b Coad	40	c Hodd b Brookes	18
J J N P Bhula, lbw b Coad	38	c Brook b Wainman	10
B L Brookes, c Hodd b Coad	0	c Leaning b Wainman	4
D Manthorpe, not out	1	c Brook b Wainman	9
ODW Birts, c Leaning b Coad	0	not out	17
O W Smithson, lbw b Shaw	1	c Thompson b Coad	0
A J Willerton	Did not bat		
Extras b 4, lb 3, nb 14	21	Extras b 5, lb 5, nb 10	20
Total (53.1 overs)	191	Total (88.3 overs)	305

FoW: 1-0 (Curran), 2-4 (Callis), 3-23 (Imtiaz), 4-27 (Barrett), 5-101 (Hudson-Prentice), 1st 6-187 (Bhula), 7-187 (Brookes), 8-188 (Lezar), 9-188 (Birts), 10-191 (Smithson).
FoW: 1-9 (Barrett), 2-39 (Callis), 3-136 (Curran), 4-191 (Lezar), 5-255 (Hudson-Prentice), 2nd 6-259 (Imtiaz), 7-272 (Brookes), 8-273 (Bhula), 9-290 (Manthorpe), 10-305 (Smithson)

	O	M	R	W		O	M	R	W
Coad	12	3	33	8	Coad	15.3	6	27	3
Brooks	11	1	46	1	Brooks	16	2	59	1
Wainman	13	6	43	0	Shaw	14	5	29	0
Shaw	10.1	1	38	1	Wainman	17	0	69	4
Carver	5	2	11	0	Carver	13	2	63	1
Logan	2	0	13	0	Thompson	8	4	21	1
					Logan	5	0	27	0

YORKSHIRE		
First Innings		Second Innings
* A Z Lees, c Manthorpe b Smithson	4	(2) c Imtiaz b Hudson-Prentice	4
H C Brook, c Callis b Willerton	49	(1) c Callis b Birts	106
J A Leaning, c Imtiaz b Smithson	25	c Barrett b Manthorpe	11
T W Loten, c Imtiaz b Brookes	49	c Barrett b Manthorpe	23
§ A J Hodd, c Barrett b Hudson-Prentice	20	c Callis b Hudson-Prentice	28
J A Thompson, lbw b Hudson-Prentice	0	not out	36
J Shaw, c Callis b Manthorpe	25	lbw b Birts	28
J C Wainman, lbw b Birts	14	not out	4
J A Brooks, b Manthorpe	15		
B O Coad, c Brookes b Manthorpe	9		
K Carver, not out	7		
J E G Logan	Did not bat		
Extras lb 1, w 6, nb 6	13	Extras b 8, lb 3, w 5, nb 8, pen 5	29

Five penalty runs were awarded in the Yorkshire second innings when the ball struck a fielding helmet

Total (73.2 overs)	230	Total (6 wkts, 58.3 overs)	269

FoW: 1-27 (Lees), 2-85 (Leaning), 3-87 (Brook), 4-120 (Hodd), 5-120 (Thompson), 1st 6-173 (Loten), 7-199 (Wainman), 8-199 (Shaw), 9-217 (Coad), 10-230 (Brooks).
FoW: 1-10 (Lees), 2-29 (Leaning), 3-123 (Loten), 4-174 (Hodd), 5-211 (Brook), 2nd 6-258 (Shaw)

	O	M	R	W		O	M	R	W
Smithson	11	0	40	2	Hudson-Prentice	14	5	47	2
Brookes	5	0	43	1	Manthorpe	18	3	70	2
Hudson-Prentice	19	5	50	2	Birts	9.3	1	60	2
Manthorpe	7.2	2	31	3	Willerton	11	0	49	0
Willerton	14	4	19	1	Brookes	5	0	24	0
Birts	17	6	46	1	Bhula	1	0	3	0

Umpires: P R Pollard and S Richardson — Scorers: J R Virr and Miss S C Klyne

Second Eleven Championship
Lancashire v. Yorkshire

Played at Southport and Birkdale CC on June 12, 13 and 14, 2018
Match abandoned at 11.12am on the Second Day due to an unfit pitch

Toss won by Lancashire

Lancashire 12 points, Yorkshire 6 points

Close of play: First Day, Lancashire 266-3 (Guest 40, Bohannon 28) (67 overs)

First Innings	YORKSHIRE		Second Innings	
A J Hodd, b Hurt		16	c Guest b Lester	1
A Z Lees, b Hurt		0		
Bilal Anjam, lbw b Hurt		1	not out	5
T W Loten, b Lamb		10		
Azeem Rafiq, run out (Jones)		8	(2) not out	0
§ B D Birkhead, c Guest b Bohannon		10		
* J Shaw, b Lamb		0		
J C Wainman, c Guest b Lamb		12		
J D Warner, not out		2		
M A Taylor, c Guest b Hurt		3		
J E G Logan, c Guest b Hurt		0		
J W Shutt				
C Wood	Did not bat			
Extras b 1, lb 6, nb 6		13	Extras	0
Total (34.5 overs)		75	Total (1 wkt, 3.2 overs)	6

FoW: 1-1 (Lees), 2-16 (Hodd), 3-17 (Anjam), 4-34 (Rafiq), 5-49 (Loten),
1st 6-49 (Shaw), 7-53 (Birkhead), 8-61 (Wainman), 9-73 (Taylor), 10-75 (Logan)
2nd 1-1 (Hodd)

	O	M	R	W		O	M	R	W
Hurt	10.5	3	17	5	Hurt	2	1	1	0
Lester	8	3	16	0	Lester	1.2	0	5	1
Bohannon	7	4	8	1					
Lamb	9	3	27	3					

LANCASHIRE

R P Jones, c Birkhead b Wainman		76
K R Brown, c Anjam b Taylor		35
S J Croft, c Rafiq b Logan		38
J J Bohannon, not out		28
§ B D Guest, not out		40
D J Lamb		
* A J Lilley		
T J Lester		
L J Hurt	Did not bat	
J Watson		
S D Parry		
T G Lawson		
Extras b 21, lb 2, nb 26		49
Total (3 wkts dec, 67 overs)		266

FoW: 1-72 (Brown), 2-172 (Jones), 3-176 (Croft).

	O	M	R	W
Shaw	11	3	34	0
Wainman	14	2	61	1
Warner	8	1	33	0
Taylor	5	1	16	1
Azeem Rafiq	10	2	28	0
Logan	14	1	55	1
Shutt	5	0	16	0

Umpires: P R Pollard and I L Herbert

Scorers: G L Morgan and J R Virr

Second Eleven Championship
Yorkshire v. Leicestershire

Played at York CC on June 26, 27 and 28, 2018
Yorkshire won by 6 wickets at 4.42pm on the Third Day

Toss won by Leicestershire   Yorkshire 23 points, Leicestershire 8 points

Close of play: First Day, Yorkshire 11-2 (Imtiaz 1*) (5.3 overs); Second Day, Leicestershire (2) 109-7 (Mike 5*, Dickinson 2*) (30 overs)

LEICESTERSHIRE

First Innings		Second Innings	
§ H J Swindells, c Hodd b Wainman	9	b Carver	46
C T Lowen, c Hodd b Barnes	12	lbw b Wainman	0
A M Ali, c Taylor b Carver	114	lbw b Taylor	12
* T J Wells, b Carver	41	(5) c Taylor b Barnes	25
Z J Chappell, b Barnes	74	(6) b Carver	7
A Javid, lbw b Taylor	41	(4) lbw b Barnes	4
B W M Mike, not out	71	c Imtiaz b Carver	36
J H Funnell, c Birkhead b Taylor	0	lbw b Rafiq	0
J W Dickinson, c Birkhead b Taylor	0	b Barnes	14
M Ahmed, c Shaw b Taylor	3	not out	16
J E Bailey, not out	7	b Barnes	5
J W Graham	Did not bat		
Extras lb 1, w 2	3	Extras b 4, lb 2, nb 4	10
Total (9 wkts dec, 96 overs)	375	Total (46.1 overs)	170

FoW: 1-20 (Swindells), 2-27 (Lowen), 3-100 (Wells), 4-218 (Chappell), 5-274 (Ali),
1st   6-314 (Javid), 7-314 (Funnell), 8-326 (Dickinson), 9-347 (Ahmed).

FoW: 1-0 (Lowen), 2-38 (Ali), 3-91 (Swindells), 4-93 (Javid), 5-102 (Wells),
2nd   6-103 (Chappell), 7-106 (Funnell), 8-150 (Dickinson), 9-170 (Mike), 10-170 (Bailey)

	O	M	R	W		O	M	R	W
Wainman	15	3	56	1	Shaw	10	1	32	0
Shaw	19	3	68	0	Wainman	6	2	28	1
Barnes	9	3	19	2	Taylor	4	0	36	1
Thompson	7	0	28	0	Barnes	8.1	0	28	4
Carver	18	7	73	2	Carver	15	2	37	3
Azeem Rafiq	13	1	67	0	Azeem Rafiq	3	2	3	1
Taylor	11	3	44	4					
Loten	4	0	19	0					

YORKSHIRE

First Innings		Second Innings	
§ A J Hodd, c Graham b Funnell	7	c Wells b Mike	33
* Azeem Rafiq, c Javid b Funnell	0	c Funnell b Mike	90
S M Imtiaz, c Swindells b Mike	7	b Ahmed	93
B D Birkhead, c Javid b Wells	7		
M J Waite, b Wells	26	(4) not out	50
T W Loten, c Swindells b Mike	54	(5) lbw b Javid	4
J A Thompson, c Ali b Ahmed	10	(6) not out	16
J Shaw, c Wells b Ahmed	10		
J C Wainman, c Swindells b Graham	49		
E Barnes, c Swindells b Ahmed	38		
K Carver, not out	23		
M A Taylor	Did not bat		
Extras b 5, lb 10, w 1, nb 6	22	Extras lb 7	7
Total (79.2 overs)	253	Total (4 wkts, 55.2 overs)	293

FoW: 1-4 (Azeem Rafiq), 2-11 (Hodd), 3-25 (Imtiaz), 4-27 (Birkhead), 5-88 (Waite),
1st   6-120 (Thompson), 7-120 (Loten), 8-150 (Shaw), 9-209 (Wainman), 10-253 (Barnes)

2nd   1-46 (Hodd), 2-171 (Azeem Rafiq), 3-260 (Imtiaz), 4-265 (Loten)

	O	M	R	W		O	M	R	W
Mike	11	4	22	2	Mike	9	0	47	2
Funnell	2.3	0	8	2	Bailey	4	0	34	0
Wells	18.3	5	44	2	Wells	10	1	34	0
Bailey	6	1	24	0	Ahmed	16.2	1	88	1
Graham	11	0	39	1	Graham	4	0	14	0
Dickinson	11	1	37	0	Dickinson	5	0	40	0
Ahmed	12.2	1	37	3	Ali	4	0	17	0
Javid	7	1	27	0	Javid	3	0	12	1

Umpires: I N Ramage and S Widdup   Scorers: J R Virr and P N Johnson

Second Eleven Championship
Derbyshire v. Yorkshire

Played at Glossop CC on July 9, 10 and 11, 2018
Match drawn at 4.30pm on the Third Day

Toss won by Yorkshire   Derbyshire 12 points, Yorkshire 10 points
Close of play: First Day, Yorkshire 421 (Barnes 0*) (103.2 overs); Second Day, Yorkshire (2) 66-3
(T W Loten 5*, Hill 0*, 14 overs)

	First Innings		YORKSHIRE	Second Innings	
A Z Lees, c Wood b Thornton			10	c Kettleboough b Thortnton	0
B D Birkhead, c Coates b Brett			74	retired hurt	12
§ S M Imtiaz, b Sykes			43	c Brodrick b Thornton	40
M J Waite, c Hosein b Thornton			93	b Thornton	9
T W Loten, c Hughes b Brett			21	b Spencer	32
G C H Hill, c and b Brett			28	c Hosein b Zazai	34
J A Thompson, lbw b Zazai			71	not out	65
J Shaw, c Spencer b Brett			50	c Spencer b Ahmad Zazai	15
J C Wainman, c Wood b Brett			15	not out	39
E Barnes, not out			0		
* K Carver, c Brodrick b Brett			6		
J W Shutt	Did not bat				
Extras b 5, lb 1, nb 4			10	Extras	0
Total (103.2 overs)			421	Total (6 wkts dec, 66 overs)	246

FoW: 1-24 (Lees), 2-112 (Imtiaz), 3-134 (Birkhead), 4-190 (Loten), 5-248 (Hill),
1st 6-304 (Waite), 7-384 (Thompson), 8-411 (Shaw), 9-411 (Wainman), 10-421 (Carver).
FoW: 1-0 (Lees)., 2-53 (Waite), 3-66 (Imtiaz), 4-123 (Loten), 5-137 (Hill),
2nd 6-163 (Shaw)

	O	M	R	W		O	M	R	W
Thornton	16	4	72	2	Thornton	15	2	72	3
Spencer	17	2	92	0	Spencer	10	0	50	1
Coates	10	1	58	0	Brett	12	2	42	0
Zazai	17	4	71	1	Zazai	6	1	23	2
Sykes	16	4	52	1	Sykes	14	2	41	0
Brett	26.2	3	70	6	Kettleborough	1	1	0	0
					Coates	7	1	28	0

	First Innings		DERBYSHIRE	Second Innings	
* J M Kettleborough, b Waite			23	not out	63
§ H R Hosein, c Thompson b Wainman			26	c Thompson b Carver	26
C F Hughes, not out			166	not out	4
C A J Brodrick, c Thompson b Carver			26		
T A Wood, c Birkhead b Shaw			76		
S S Arthurton, not out			9		
J S Sykes					
T Brett					
M T Sencer	Did not bat				
G T Thornton					
A Zazai					
A Coates					
Extras lb 16, nb 10			26	Extras b 4	4
Total (4 wkts dec, 88 overs)			352	Total (1 wkt, 30 overs)	97

FoW: 1-34 (Kettleborough), 2-55 (Hosein), 3-98 (Brodrick), 4-333 (Wood)
2nd 1-78 (Hosein)

	O	M	R	W		O	M	R	W
Shaw	12	1	46	1	Shaw	4	4	0	0
Wainman	14	1	55	1	Wainman	3	0	14	0
Barnes	6	0	44	0	Carver	11	2	37	1
Waite	9	3	16	1	Thompson	1	0	5	0
Thompson	10	2	25	0	Hill	4	1	11	0
Shutt	12	0	56	0	Shutt	6	0	18	0
Carver	21	3	82	1	Lees	1	0	8	0
Hill	4	1	12	0					

Umpires: H Adnan and P J Hartley   Scorers: J A Wallis and J R Virr

Second Eleven Championship
Northamptonshire v. Yorkshire

Played at Desborough Town CC on July 24, 25 and 26, 2018
Yorkshire won by 180 runs at 4.48pm on the Third Day

Toss won by Yorkshire   Northamptonshire 6 points, Yorkshire 22 points
Close of play: First Day, Northamptonshire 36-1 (Claydon 12, Gay 2) (12 overs); Second Day, Yorkshire (2) 137-1 (Bilal Anjam 52, Loten 24) (35 overs)

First Innings	YORKSHIRE		Second Innings	
A Z Lees, c King b Heathfield	67		(2) c Heathfield b Zaib	55
T Kohler-Cadmore, b Zaib	173			
T W Loten, c King b Glover	0		run out (Brierley)	31
* J A Leaning, st King b Zaib	65		c Glover b Zaib	22
M J Waite, lbw b Zaib	1		c Glover b Zaib	32
J A Thompson, c Curran b Zaib	49		not out	40
§ B D Birkhead, c and b Brierley	5		run out (Claydon)	2
J Shaw, lbw b Zaib	0			
J C Wainman, not out	16			
K Carver, not out	8			
J E G Logan				
M A Taylor Did not bat				
Bilal Anjam			(1) b Glover	52
Extras b 1, lb 3, nb 2	6		Extras b 6, lb 2, nb 2	10
Total (8 wkts dec, 90 overs)	390		Total (6 wkts dec, 55 overs)	244

T Kohler-Cadmore was summoned back to Headingley before Yorkshire's second innings He was replaced by Bilal Anjam as a full substitute

FoW: 1-105 (Lees), 2-110 (Loten), 3-304 (Kohler-Cadmore), 4-306 (Waite), 5-319 (Leaning),
1st   6-364 (Thompson), 7-366 (Shaw), 8-366 (Birkhead)
FoW: 1-72 (Lees), 2-137 (Anjam), 3-164 (Loten), 4-170 (Leaning), 5-224 (Waite),
2nd   6-244 (Birkhead)

	O	M	R	W		O	M	R	W
Glover	13	2	52	1	Glover	12	1	61	1
Cotton	12	4	41	0	Cotton	16	6	42	0
Bhabra	10	0	47	0	Bhabra	7	1	38	0
Heathfield	8	1	40	1	Zaib	15	1	65	3
Zaib	27	5	103	5	Amjaid	5	1	30	0
Amjaid	16	2	92	0					
Brierley	4	0	11	1					

First Innings	NORTHAMPTONSHIRE		Second Innings	
B J Curran, c Birkhead b Carver	22		lbw b Wainman	43
B Claydon, c Leaning b Shaw	89		c Leaning b Logan	29
E Gay, c Carver b Shaw	57		lbw b Wainman	0
* C O Thurston, lbw b Thompson	28		c Thompson b Carver	21
S A Zaib, c Carver b Leaning	57		c Thompson b Logan	3
D D W Brierley, lbw b Logan	22		c Leaning b Carver	25
B D Cotton, not out	0		c and b Carver	0
§ A E King, not out	1		not out	2
B Glover			b Carver	0
U Amjaid Did not bat			c Leaning b Carver	9
T D Heathfield			b Carver	0
B J Bhabra				
Extras b 9, lb 5, nb 6	20		Extras b 24, nb 2	26
Total (6 wkts dec, 81 overs)	296		Total (49.3 overs)	158

FoW: 1-30 (Curran), 2-185 (Claydon), 3-198 (Gay), 4-225 (Thurston), 5-291 (Brierley),
1st   6-295 (Zaib)
FoW: 1-83 (Curran), 2-83 (Gay), 3-111 (Claydon), 4-111 (Thurston), 5-125 (Zaib),
2nd   6-139 (Brierley), 7-140 (Cotton), 8-140 (Glover), 9-154 (Umjaid), 10-158 (Heathfield)

	O	M	R	W		O	M	R	W
Shaw	13	8	23	2	Shaw	6	2	16	0
Wainman	15	2	65	0	Wainman	7	2	33	2
Carver	23	5	90	1	Thompson	5	1	14	0
Thompson	7	0	31	1	Logan	19	6	45	2
Taylor	4	0	26	0	Carver	12.3	3	26	6
Logan	15	3	27	1					
Leaning	4	0	20	1					

Umpires: N Pratt and M Dobbs   Scorers: T R Owen and J R Virr

Second Eleven Championship
Yorkshire v. Worcestershire

Played at Harrogate CC on July 31 and August 1 and 2, 2018
Match drawn at 5.18pm on the Third Day

Toss won by Worcestershire   Yorkshire 9 points, Worcestershire 8 points
Close of play: First Day, Yorkshire 427-8 (Taylor 36, Warner 49) (104 overs); Second Day, no play

YORKSHIRE
(Second Innings forfeited)

A Z Lees, c Fell b Holling		8
§ B D Birkhead, c Milton b Brewster		13
T W Loten, lbw b Westbury		131
* J A Leaning, b Carter		1
M J Waite, b Carter		1
J Shaw, c Milton b Brewster		1
J C Wainman, c Milton b Holling		117
E Barnes, b Carter		30
M A Taylor, not out		36
J D Warner, not out		49
K Carver		
J E G Logan	Did not bat	
Extras b 9, lb 15, nb 14, w 2		40
Total (8 wkts dec, 104 overs)		427

FoW: 1-24 (Birkhead), 2-30 (Lees), 3-42 (Leaning), 4-56 (Waite), 5-68 (Shaw), 6-267 (Loten), 7-320 (Barnes), 8-347 (Wainman).

	O	M	R	W
Carter	24	5	84	3
Brewster	19	7	49	2
Holling	11	2	54	2
Parker-Cole	13	1	53	0
Twohig	22	5	81	0
Rhodes	8	2	52	0
Westbury	7	1	30	1

WORCESTERSHIRE
(First Innings forfeited)

* O E Westbury, lbw b Barnes		20
G H Rhodes, c Warner b Wainman		47
T C Fell, b Shaw		75
J J Dell, b Carver		6
R Gibson, not out		37
B J Twohig, not out		4
R A Parker-Cole		
A Brewster		
J A Haynes, c and b Carver		50
§ A G Milton, c Birkhead b Shaw		14
A Carter		
J B A Holling		
Extras b 4, lb 6, nb 8		18
Total (6 wkts, 84 overs)		271

FoW: 1-32 (Westbury), 2-142 (Rhodes), 3-150 (Fell), 4-174 (Milton), 5-207 (Dell), 6-240 (Haynes)

	O	M	R	W
Shaw	15	5	51	2
Wainman	12	4	30	1
Barnes	12	2	45	1
Warner	8	2	21	0
Taylor	8	0	29	0
Carver	14	2	42	2
Logan	15	2	43	0

Umpires: MA Gough and G Roberts   Scorers: J R Virr and R M Wilks

Second Eleven Championship
Nottinghamshire v. Yorkshire

Played at Nottinghamshire Sports Ground on August 13, 14 and 15, 2018
Nottinghamshire won by 6 wickets at 2.08pm on the Third Day

Toss won by Yorkshire
Nottinghamshire 24 points, Yorkshire 6 points
Close of play: First Day, Yorkshire 70-0 (Brook 41, Birkhead 25) (16 overs); Second Day, Yorkshire (2) 157-4 (Waite 27, Loten 45) (46 overs)

First Innings	NOTTINGHAMSHIRE	Second Innings	
C F Gibson, c Brook b Warner	8	lbw b Wainman	0
L W James, c Waite b Warner	19	c Birkhead b Shaw	0
* C D Nash, lbw b Wainman	30	lbw b Wainman	6
W A R Fraine, c Wainman b Barnes	25	not out	12
P Coughlin, c Carver b Waite	86	c Barnes b Wainman	13
§ S D Budinger, c Imtiaz b Barnes	9	not out	0
L Wood, c Imtiaz b Barnes	92		
L A Patterson-White, c Brook b Leaning	50		
M Carter, not out	53		
M E Milnes, c Imtiaz b Wainman	8		
J M Blatherwick, b Shaw	24		
M H A Footitt	Did not bat		
Extras b 12, lb 3, nb 8, w 5	28	Extras nb 2	2
Total (85.4 overs)	432	Total (4 wkts, 6.3 overs)	33

FoW: 1-26 (Gibson), 2-33 (James), 3-82 (Nash), 4-108 (Fraine), 5-118 (Budinger), 6-259
1st (Coughlin), 7-317 (Wood), 8-364 (Patterson-White), 9-403 (Milnes), 10-432 (Blatherwick)
2nd 1-0 (Gibson), 2-8 (Nash), 3-12 (James), 4-29 (Coughlin)

	O	M	R	W		O	M	R	W
Shaw	14.4	1	73	1	Wainman	3.3	0	23	3
Wainman	14	2	60	2	Shaw	3	0	10	1
Warner	10	2	39	2					
Waite	10	0	64	1					
Barnes	12	2	65	3					
Brook	67	2	20	0					
Carver	9	0	49	0					
Shutt	6	0	30	0					
Leaning	4	0	17	1					

First Innings	YORKSHIRE	Second Innings *(following on)*	
H C Brook, b Blatherwick	71	lbw b Milnes	17
B D Birkhead, b Wood	25	§ run out (Milnes)	31
§ S M Imtiaz, c Budinger b Blatherwick	17	c Budinger b Blatherwick	3
* J A Leaning, c James b Footitt	6	lbw b Carter	18
M J Waite, c Blatherwick b Carter	7	c Carter b Blatherwick	33
T W Loten, c Carter	12	c Budinger b Blatherwick	74
J Shaw, c Budinger b Carter	2	c Fraine b Carter	8
J C Wainman, b Milnes	1	c Fraine b Carter	3
E Barnes, lbw b Carter	20	c Carter b Footitt	12
J D Warner, not out	10	lbw b Footitt	8
K Carver, b Carter	5		
J W Shutt	Did not bat		
J E G Logan		(11) not out	7
Extras b 18, lb 2, nb 10, w 5w	35	Extras b 10, lb 12, nb 16, w 1	39
Total (71.1 overs)	211	Total (76.5 overs)	253

J E G Logan replaced J W Shutt as a full substitute
§ S M Imtiaz kept wicket in Yorkshire's first innings and B D Birkhead in the second innings

FoW: 1-73 (Birkhead), 2-115 (Imtiaz), 3-131 (Leaning), 4-135 (Brook), 5-159 (Waite),
1st 6-162 (Shaw), 7-167 (Loten), 8-167 (Wainman), 9-195 (Barnes), 10-211 (Carver)
FoW: 1-35 (Brook), 2-56 (Imtiaz), 3-66 (Birkhead), 4-94 (Leaning), 5-178 (Waite),
2nd 6-217 (Loten), 7-217 (Shaw), 8-221 (Wainman), 9-237 (Warner), 10-253 (Barnes)

	O	M	R	W		O	M	R	W
Wood	14	2	45	1	Wood	11	1	39	0
Milnes	15	1	59	1	Milnes	8	2	24	1
Blatherwick	10	1	41	2	Blatherwick	16	2	49	3
Footitt	9	4	16	1	Carter	24	9	60	3
Carter	16.1	12	14	5	Footitt	9.5	3	24	2
Patterson-White	7	1	16	0	Coughlin	5	1	19	0
					Patterson-White	3	0	16	0

Umpires: W B Jones and I N Ramage
Scorers: Mrs A Cusworth and J R Virr

SECOND ELEVEN CHAMPIONSHIP 2018

FINAL

Durham beat Essex on first innings: Essex 130 and 380; Durham 263 and 144-9

NORTHERN GROUP FINAL TABLE

		P	W	L	D	Tied	Aban.	Bonus Points Bat	Bowl	Ded	Points
1	Durham (8)	9	6	1	2	0	0	26	26	0	158
2	Warwickshire (2)	9	4	2	3	0	0	26	30	0	135
3	Lancashire (1)	9	3	1	4	0	1	27	28	0	128
4	Nottinghamshire (6)	9	3	3	3	0	0	29	32	0	124
5	**Yorkshire (4)**	**9**	**3**	**1**	**5**	**0**	**0**	**27**	**22**	**0**	**122**
6	Leicestershire (7)	9	2	3	3	0	1	25	25	0	102
7	MCC Young Cricketers (9)	9	2	3	3	0	1	21	25	0	98
8	Northamptonshire (10) ..	9	2	5	2	0	0	22	32	0	96
9	Worcestershire (3)	9	1	4	4	0	0	26	28	0	90
10	Derbyshire (5)	9	1	4	3	0	1	21	21	0	78

SOUTHERN GROUP FINAL TABLE

		P	W	L	D	Tied	Aban.	Bonus Points Bat	Bowl	Ded	Points
1	Essex (10)	8	6	0	2	0	0	27	30	0	163
2	Hampshire (1)	8	4	1	3	0	0	22	27	0	128
3	Glamorgan (8)	8	2	1	5	0	0	25	20	0	102
4	Surrey (3)	8	2	2	4	0	0	24	23	0	99
5	Kent (4)	8	2	3	3	0	0	17	18	0	87
6	Gloucestershire (7)	8	1	3	4	0	0	24	23	0	78
7	Somerset (5)	8	0	2	6	0	0	22	23	0	75
8	Sussex (6)	8	2	5	1	0	0	17	20	0	74
9	Middlesex (2)	8	0	2	6	0	0	18	21	0	69

Ded. Points deducted for slow over-rates

(2017 group positions in brackets)

Since 2009 the Championship has been split into two groups, the winners of each group playing off for the title. These groups were deemed North and South for the 2012 season onwards.

The MCC Universities side, who finished ninth in the Southern Group in 2017, did not compete in 2018, so the Southern teams played only eight matches.

SECOND ELEVEN CHAMPIONS

In the seasons in which Yorkshire have competed. The Championship has been split into two groups since 2009, the group winners playing off for the Championship. These groups were deemed North and South from the 2012 season.

Season	Champions	Yorkshire's Position	Season	Champions	Yorkshire's Position
1959	Gloucestershire	7th	1996	Warwickshire	4th
1960	Northamptonshire	14th	1997	Lancashire	2nd
1961	Kent	11th	1998	Northamptonshire	9th
1975	Surrey	4th	1999	Middlesex	14th
1976	Kent	5th	2000	Middlesex	5th
1977	**Yorkshire**	**1st**	2001	Hampshire	2nd
1978	Sussex	5th	2002	Kent	3rd
1979	Warwickshire	3rd	**2003**	**Yorkshire**	**1st**
1980	Glamorgan	5th	2004	Somerset	8th
1981	Hampshire	11th	2005	Kent	10th
1982	Worcestershire	14th	2006	Kent	3rd
1983	Leicestershire	2nd	2007	Sussex	10th
1984	**Yorkshire**	**1st**	2008	Durham	5th
1985	Nottinghamshire	12th	2009	Surrey	A 2nd
1986	Lancashire	5th	2010	Surrey	A 8th
1987	**Yorkshire and Kent**	**1st**	2011	Warwickshire	A 10th
1988	Surrey	9th	2012	Kent	(North) 9th
1989	Middlesex	9th	2013	Lancashire & Middlesex	
1990	Sussex	17th			(North) 4th
1991	**Yorkshire**	**1st**	2014	Leicestershire	(North) 4th
1992	Surrey	5th	2015	Nottinghamshire	(North) 7th
1993	Middlesex	3rd	2016	Durham	(North) 5th
1994	Somerset	2nd	2017	Lancashire	(North) 4th
1995	Hampshire	5th	2018	Durham	(North) 5th

SECOND ELEVEN CHAMPIONSHIP
AVERAGES 2018

Played 9   Won 3   Lost 1   Drawn 5   Abandoned 0

BATTING AND FIELDING

(Qualification 5 innings)

Player	M.	I.	N.O.	Runs	H.S.	Avge	100s	50s	ct/st
J A Thompson	6	12	5	515	77*	73.57	0	5	7
J C Wainman	7	10	3	270	117	38.57	1	0	1
S M Imtiaz	3	6	0	203	93	33.83	0	1	4
M J Waite	5	9	1	252	93	31.50	0	2	1
T W Loten	9	16	0	500	131	31.25	1	2	0
J D Warner	5	7	4	88	49*	29.33	0	0	1
E Barnes	6	8	2	160	38*	26.66	0	0	2
A Z Lees	7	11	0	289	67	26.27	0	3	3
K Carver	8	7	4	76	27*	25.33	0	0	6
B D Birkhead	8	9	1	179	74	22.37	0	1	7
J A Leaning	4	7	0	148	65	21.14	0	1	7
A J Hodd	3	6	0	105	33	17.50	0	0	6
J Shaw	9	12	0	169	50	14.08	0	1	1
Also played									
T Kohler-Cadmore	2	3	0	211	173	70.33	1	0	2
H C Brook	2	4	0	243	106	60.75	1	1	4
J A Tattersall	2	4	0	216	132	54.00	1	0	5
M D Fisher	1	2	0	84	84	42.00	0	1	2
Azeem Rafiq	2	4	1	98	90	32.66	0	1	1
Bilal Anjam	2	3	1	58	52	29.00	0	1	1
M A Taylor	6	3	1	56	36*	28.00	0	0	2
J Wharton	1	2	0	48	37	24.00	0	0	1
G C H Hill	2	4	0	64	34	16.00	0	0	1
J A Brooks	1	1	0	15	15	15.00	0	0	0
B O Coad	1	1	0	9	9	9.00	0	0	0
J E G Logan	7	4	2	14	7*	—	0	0	1
J W Shutt	3	0	0	0	—	—	0	0	0
D Leech	1	0	0	0	—	—	0	0	0
J R Sullivan	1	0	0	0	—	—	0	0	0
B Whitford	1	0	0	0	—	—	0	0	0

SECOND ELEVEN CHAMPIONSHIP
AVERAGES 2018

BOWLING

(Qualification 10 wickets)

Player	Overs	Mdns	Runs	Wkts	Avge	Best	5wI	10wM
B O Coad	27.3	9	60	11	5.45	8-33	1	1
E Barnes	64.3	11	281	12	23.41	4-28	0	0
K Carver	178.3	34	628	22	28.54	6-26	1	0
J C Wainman	133.3	24	537	16	33.56	4-69	0	0
J Shaw	168.5	37	613	13	47.15	2-22	0	0
Also bowled								
J A Leaning	8	0	37	2	18.50	1-17	0	0
J D Warner	55	11	175	5	35.00	2-39	0	0
M A Taylor	53.4	7	230	6	38.33	4-44	0	0
M J Waite	19	3	80	2	40.00	1-16	0	0
J E G Logan	115	23	351	8	43.87	2-38	0	0
J A Thompson	65	12	234	5	46.80	2-32	0	0
J A Brooks	27	3	105	2	52.50	1-46	0	0
Azeem Rafiq	26	5	98	1	98.00	1-3	0	0
J W Shutt	29	0	120	0	—	—	0	0
G C H Hill	8	2	23	0	—	—	0	0
J R Sullivan	8	1	53	0	—	—	0	0
T W Loten	8	0	36	0	—	—	0	0
H C Brook	6	2	20	0	—	—	0	0
D Leech	3	0	27	0	—	—	0	0
A Z Lees	1	0	8	0	—	—	0	0

Second Eleven Trophy
Yorkshire v. Leicestershire

Played at Stamford Bridge on May 4, 2018
Leicestershire won by 163 runs at 4.54pm

Toss won by Leicestershire   Yorkshire 0 points, Leicestershire 2 points

LEICESTERSHIRE

M L Pettini, b Warner		137
* T J Wells, lbw b Rashid		35
A M Ali, c Anjam b Rafiq		15
Ateeq Javid, lbw b Rashid		18
H E Dearden, c Anjam b Wainman		26
Z J Chappell, c Thompson b Wainman		11
R J Sayer, c Rafiq b Wainman		1
T A I Taylor, not out		7
§ H J Swindells, c Rafiq b Wainman		0
B W M Mike, not out		0
J W Dickinson	Did not bat	
Extras b 4, lb 4, w 8, nb 2		18
Total (8 wickets, 50 overs)		268

FoW: 1-116 (Wells), 2-154 (Ali), 3-207 (Javid), 4-227 (Pettini), 5-259 (Dearden), 6-259 (Chappell), 7-267 (Sayer), 8-267 (Swindells)

	O	M	R	W
Wainman	8	0	42	4
Warner	9	0	42	1
Azeem Rafiq	10	0	47	1
Barnes	7	0	49	0
Thompson	6	0	24	0
Rashid	10	0	56	2

YORKSHIRE

* T Kohler-Cadmore, c Mike b Taylor	7
A Z Lees, c Dearden b Taylor	0
J A Thompson, lbw b Taylor	4
M J Waite, c Ali b Sayer	19
§ J A Tattersall, c Mike b Chappell	3
Bilal Anjam, c Mike b Sayer	17
A U Rashid, l;bw b Sayer	26
Azeem Rafiq, c Ali b Wells	1
J C Wainman, b Sayer	12
E Barnes, b Sayer	4
J D Warner, not out	0
Extras lb 4, w 4, nb 4	12
Total (29.1 overs)	105

FoW: 1-4 (Lees), 2-12 (Thompson), 3-14 (Kohler-Cadmore), 4-18 (Tattersall) 5-59 (Waite), 6-69 (Anjam), 7-73 (Rafiq), 8-92 (Wainman), 9-104 (Barnes), 10-105 (Rashid)

	O	M	R	W
Chappell	6	1	17	1
Taylor	5	0	13	3
Sayer	9.1	0	34	5
Mike	3	0	20	0
Wells	5	0	16	1
Dickinson	1	0	1	0

Umpires: M A Gough and S Richardson   Scorers: J R Virr and P N Johnson

Second Eleven Trophy
Yorkshire v. Durham

Played at Emerald Headingley, Leeds, on May 8, 2018

Yorkshire won by 66 runs (DLS method) at 6.45pm

Toss won by Yorkshire   * Yorkshire 2 points, Durham 0 points

* *It later transpired that a Yorkshire player had used a bat which infringed the new regulations for bat sizes. ECB penalized Yorkshire Second Eleven one point*

YORKSHIRE

A Z Lees, c Davies b Hartley	15
* T Kohler-Cadmore, c Trevaskis b Harding	63
T W Loten, lbw b Harte	42
J A Thompson, c Jones b Harte	17
§ J A Tattersall, lbw b Harding	39
A U Rashid, c Steel b Smithson	14
Azeem Rafiq, c Trevaskis b Hartley	36
J Shaw, run out	1
J C Wainman, c Trevaskis b Smithson	11
E Barnes, not out	5
J D Warner, not out	25
Extras lb 1, w 17, nb 2	20
Total (9 wkts, 50 overs)	288

FoW: 1-42 (Lees), 2-128 (Kohler-Cadmore), 3-132 (Loten), 4-159 (Thompson), 5-189 (Rashid), 6-225 (Tattersall), 7-227 (Shaw), 8-255 (Wainman), 9-256 (Azeem Rafiq)

	O	M	R	W
Smithson	10	0	50	2
Hartley	10	1	58	2
Harte	9	0	34	2
Pringle	9	0	62	0
Harding	8	0	54	2
Trevaskis	4	0	29	0

DURHAM

L Trevaskis, lbw b Rafiq	50
M A Jones, c Lees b Barnes	39
* G J Harte, c Tattersall b Warner	10
R D Pringle, c Thompson b Rashid	0
§ R C Davies, c Rashid b Shaw	43
S Steel, c Thompson b Rashid	11
C M McBride, not out	7
M J Potts	
G H I Harding	Did not bat
O W Smithson	
C F Hartley	
Extras b 4, lb 17, w 6, nb 4	31
Total (6 wkts, 33.2 overs)	191

FoW: 1-77 (Jones), 2-94 (Harte), 3-95 (Pringle), 4-146 (Trevaskis), 5-171 (Steel), 6-191 (Davies)

	O	M	R	W
Wainman	3	0	19	0
Shaw	4.2	0	36	1
Barnes	5	0	22	1
Azeem Rafiq	8	0	34	1
Warner	4	0	22	1
Rashid	9	2	37	2

Umpires: M Newall and S Widdop   Scorers: J R Virr and G Maddison

Second Eleven Trophy
Lancashire v. Yorkshire

Played at Aigburth, Liverpool, on May 15, 2018
Yorkshire won by 155 runs at 4.48pm

Toss won by Yorkshire   Lancashire 0 points, Yorkshire 2 points

YORKSHIRE

* T Kohler-Cadmore, c Lilley b Hurt		1
J A Tattersall, c Lavelle b Lester		0
J A Thompson, c Hameed b Lester		2
M D Fisher, b Lester		16
§ A J Hodd, c Hurt b Lamb		18
A U Rashid, c Hameed b Lamb		15
Azeem Rafiq, c and b Lilley		60
J C Wainman, c Hameed b Bohannon		13
K Carver, b Bohannon		0
E Barnes, not out		35
J D Warner, not out		18
Extras b 4, lb 6, w 18		28
Total (9 wkts, 50 overs)		206

FoW: 1-1 (Tattersall), 2-3 (Thompson), 3-8 (Kohler-Cadmore), 4-34 (Fisher), 5-59 (Hodd), 6-63 (Rashid), 7-109 (Wainman), 8-109 (Carver), 9-177 (Azeem Rafiq)

	O	M	R	W
Lester	10	1	35	3
Hurt	10	1	29	1
Lamb	7	0	31	2
Bohannon	10	1	49	2
Lilley	7	0	31	1
Morley	6	1	21	0

LANCASHIRE

K R Brown, c Hodd b Wainman		5
H Hameed, c Thompson b Wainman		1
R P Jones, b Barnes		11
D J Lamb, lbw b Barnes		2
J J Bohannon, c Hodd b Warner		3
* A M Lilley, c Hodd b Warner		5
S R Oldham, lbw b Rashid		1
§ G I D Lavelle, c Hodd b Rashid		2
T J Lester, c Kohler-Cadmore b Thompson		2
L J Hurt, lbw b Thompson		3
J P Morley, not out		1
Extras lb 2, nb 2, w 11		15
Total (20.3 overs)		51

FoW: 1-5 (Hameed), 2-21 (Brown), 3-28 (Lamb), 4-31 (Jones), 5-33 (Bohannon), 6-38 (Lilley), 7-44 (Oldham), 8-45 (Lavelle), 9-50 (Hurt), 10-51 (Lester)

	O	M	R	W
Wainman	5	1	13	2
Warner	6	0	21	2
Barnes	4	1	8	2
Rashid	3	1	5	2
Thompson	2.3	1	2	2

Umpires: I P Laurence and G D Lloyd   Scorers: G L Morgan and J R Virr

Second Eleven Trophy
Derbyshire v. Yorkshire

Played at Repton School on May 16, 2018
Yorkshire won by 8 wickets at 1.32pm

Toss won by Yorkshire   Derbyshire 0 points, Yorkshire 2 points

DERBYSHIRE

* J M Kettleborough, c Tattersall b Thompson	......	20
§ H R Hosein, c Kohler-Cadmore b Coad	....	0
C A J Brodrick, lbw b Wainman	....	0
T A Wood, b Wainman	....	1
A K Dal, lbw b Wainman	....	0
S Palumbo, c Tattersall b Thompson	....	15
Hamidullah Qadri, lbw b Warner	....	1
A F Gleadall, not out	....	7
W S Davis, b Thompson	....	4
J S Sykes, b Thompson	....	0
M Azarullah, run out (Thompson)	....	0
Extras b 12, lb 2, nb 2, w 3	....	19
Total (22.4 overs)		67

FoW: 1-2 (Hosein), 2-17 (Brodrick), 3-19 (Wood), 4-19 (Dal), 5-30 (Kettleborough), 6-39 (Qadri), 7-51 (Palumbo), 8-61 (Davis), 9-61 (Sykes), 10-67 (Azarullah)

	O	M	R	W
Coad	6	2	8	1
Wainman	5	2	10	3
Thompson	6	1	17	4
Warner	4	1	7	1
Azeem Rafiq	1.4	0	11	0

YORKSHIRE

A Z Lees, c Dal b Azarullah	....	3
T Kohler-Cadmore, c Qadri b Gleadall	....	0
H C Brook, not out	....	36
J A Leaning, not out	....	27
§ J A Tattersall		
J A Thompson		
* Azeem Rafiq		
B O Coad	Did not bat	
K Carver		
J C Wainman		
J D Warner		
Extras lb 1, w 1	....	2
Total (2 wkts, 10.2 overs)	....	68

FoW: 1-3 (Kohler-Cadmore), 2-3 (Lees)

	O	M	R	W
Gleadall	4	0	26	1
Azarullah	4	0	17	1
Davis	2.2	0	24	0

Umpires: A P Payne and R T Robinson   Scorers: J A Wallis and J R Virr

Second Eleven Trophy
Warwickshire v. Yorkshire

Played at Edgbaston on May 21, 2018
Warwickshire won by 12 runs at 6.50pm

Toss won by Yorkshire   Warwickshire 2 points, Yorkshire 0 points

WARWICKSHIRE

L Banks, c Tattersall b Fisher	....	2
* D P Sibley, c Lees b Warner	....	51
A R I Umeed, c Tattersall b Barnes	....	32
W M H Rhodes, c Warner b Shaw	....	101
A T Thomson, c Hill b Carver	....	30
§ A J Mellor, run out (Thompson)	....	1
G D Panayi, lbw b Fisher	....	1
C J C Wright, c Tattersall b Fisher	....	6
W B Rankin, lbw b Fisher	....	5
J E Poysden, b Thompson	....	27
O J Hannon-Dalby, not out	....	8
Extras lb 2, nb 10, w 5		17
Total (49.1 overs)		287

FoW: 1-2 (Banks), 2-56 (Umeed), 3-110 (Sibley), 4-167 (Thomson), 5-176 (Mellor), 6-177 (Panayi), 7-185 (Wright), 8-191 (Rankin), 9-257(Poysden), 10-287 (Rhodes)

	O	M	R	W
Fisher	10	0	42	4
Shaw	6.1	0	48	1
Barnes	6	0	44	1
Warner	7	0	54	1
Thompson	10	0	65	1
Carver	10	1	32	1

YORKSHIRE

§ J A Tattersall, c Sibley b Poysden	....	35
* A Z Lees, st Mellor b Poysden	....	45
J A Thompson, c Umeed b Rankin	....	67
T W Loten, b Poysden	....	1
M D Fisher, c Banks b Rankin	....	35
G C H Hill, c Hannon-Dalby b Sibley	....	28
J Shaw, c Panayi b Hannon-Dalby	....	18
E Barnes, c Panayi b Wright	....	11
K Carver, run out (Hannon-Dalby)	....	10
J D Warner, not out	....	1
J E G Logan, not out	....	2
Extras lb 7, nb 2, w 13		22
Total (9 wkts, 50 overs)	....	275

FoW: 1-71 (Tattersall), 2-104 (Lees), 3-112 (Loten), 4-172 (Fisher), 5-215 (Thompson), 6-237 (Hill), 7-249 (Shaw), 8-271 (Barnes), 9-272 (Carver)

	O	M	R	W
Hannon-Dalby	10	1	48	1
Wright	10	0	54	1
Rankin	10	0	56	2
Poysden	10	1	30	3
Thomson	4	0	28	0
Rhodes	2	0	19	0
Sibley	4	0	33	1

Umpires: N G C Cowley and D J Millns   Scorers: S Smith and J R Virr

Second Eleven Trophy
Yorkshire v. MCC Young Cricketers

Played at York CC on June 5, 2018
Yorkshire won by 9 wickets at 4.58pm

Toss won by MCC Young Cricketers   Yorkshire 2 points, MCC YC 0 points

MCC YOUNG CRICKETERS

B J Curran, lbw b Shutt	44
* J H Barrett, c Shutt b Shaw	40
§ S M Imtiaz, c Birkhead b Wainman	2
F J Hudson-Prentice, c Brooks b Shutt	10
J J N P Bhula, c Wainman b Shutt	14
M D Lezar, c Thompson b Shutt	30
B L Brookes, c Birkhead b Shaw	16
D Manthorpe, st Birkhead b Logan	2
B V Sears, b Brooks	9
O D W Birts, c Leaning b Brooks	15
O W Smithson, not out	0
Extras b 4, lb 1, w 6	11
Total (46.1 overs)	193

FoW: 1-80 (Barrett), 2-84 (Imtiaz), 3-91 (Curran), 4-100 (Hudson-Prentice), 5-133 (Bhula), 6-161 (Lezar), 7-164 (Manthorpe), 8-167 (Brookes), 9-193 (Birts), 10-193 (Sears)

	O	M	R	W
Brooks	6.1	0	31	2
Coad	7	0	34	0
Wainman	6	1	24	1
Shaw	7	0	25	2
Shutt	10	0	47	4
Logan	10	1	27	1

YORKSHIRE

* A Z Lees, b Birts		43
§ B D Birkhead, not out		94
J A Leaning, not out		43
J A Thompson		
T W Loten		
J Shaw		
J E G Logan	Did not bat	
J A Brooks		
B O Coad		
J W Shutt		
M A Taylor		
Extras lb 7, nb 2, w 5		14
Total (1 wkt, 37.2 overs)		194

FoW: 1-87 (Lees)

	O	M	R	W
Sears	6	0	38	0
Smithson	3	0	20	0
Hudson-Prentice	4	1	18	0
Birts	10	0	46	1
Bhula	6.2	1	29	0
Brookes	6	0	23	0
Manthorpe	2	0	13	0

Umpires: P R Pollard and S Widdup   Scorers: J R Virr and Miss S C Klyne

SECOND ELEVEN TROPHY 2018

SEMI-FINALS

Worcestershire (164) lost to Middlesex (168-5) by 5 wickets at Radlett

Somerset (300) beat Warwickshire (286) by 14 runs at Scorers, Shirley

FINAL

Somerset (250) lost to Middlesex (251-9) by 1 wicket

NORTHERN GROUP – FINAL TABLE *(2017 in brackets)*

		P	W	L	Aban/NR	Points	Net Run Rate
1	Warwickshire (4)	6	4	2	0	8	1.541
2	Worcestershire (3)	6	4	2	0	8	0.236
3	**Yorkshire (2)**	**6**	**4**	**2**	**0**	**7 ***	**1.053**
4	Lancashire (1)	6	3	3	0	6	-0.242
5	MCC Young Cricketers (8)	6	3	3	0	6	-0.590
6	Northamptonshire (6)	6	2	2	0	6	-0.312
7	Nottinghamshire (5)	6	3	3	2	5	-0.281
8	Leicestershire (10)	6	2	3	1	5	-0.215
9	Durham (9)	6	2	4	0	4	0.184
10	Derbyshire (7)	6	1	4	1	3	-1.429

SOUTHERN GROUP – FINAL TABLE *(2017 in brackets)*

		P	W	L	Aban/NR	Points	Net Run Rate
1	Middlesex	6	6	0	0	12	1.136
2	Somerset	6	4	2	0	8	1.164
3	Gloucestershire	6	4	2	0	8	0.648
4	Essex	6	3	2	1	7	0.605
5	Hampshire	6	3	2	1	7	0.604
6	Unicorns	6	1	2	3	5	-0.931
7	Kent	6	2	4	0	4	-0.150
8	Surrey	6	2	4	0	4	-0.767
9	Glamorgan	6	1	4	1	3	-1.167
10	Sussex	6	1	5	0	2	-1.868

* The point deducted because a Yorkshire player used a bat which infringed the new regulations for bat sizes in the Emerald Headingley match v. Durham cost the county a place in the semi-finals

SECOND ELEVEN TROPHY

PREVIOUS WINNERS

1986	**Northamptonshire**, who beat Essex by 14 runs
1987	**Derbyshire**, who beat Hampshire by 7 wickets
1988	**Yorkshire**, who beat Kent by 7 wickets
1989	**Middlesex**, who beat Kent by 6 wickets
1990	**Lancashire**, who beat Somerset by 8 wickets
1991	**Nottinghamshire**, who beat Surrey by 8 wickets
1992	**Surrey**, who beat Northamptonshire by 8 wickets
1993	**Leicestershire**, who beat Sussex by 142 runs
1994	**Yorkshire**, who beat Leicestershire by 6 wickets
1995	**Leicestershire**, who beat Gloucestershire by 3 runs
1996	**Leicestershire**, who beat Durham by 46 runs
1997	**Surrey**, who beat Gloucestershire by 3 wickets
1998	**Northamptonshire**, who beat Derbyshire by 5 wickets
1999	**Kent**, who beat Hampshire by 106 runs.
2000	**Leicestershire**, who beat Hampshire by 25 runs.
2001	**Surrey**, who beat Somerset by 6 wickets
2002	**Kent**, who beat Hampshire by 5 wickets
2003	**Hampshire**, who beat Warwickshire by 8 wickets
2004	**Worcestershire**, who beat Essex by 8 wickets
2005	**Sussex**, who beat Nottinghamshire by 6 wickets
2006	**Warwickshire**, who beat Yorkshire by 93 runs
2007	**Middlesex**, who beat Somerset by 1 run
2008	**Hampshire**, who beat Essex by 7 runs
2009	**Yorkshire**, who beat Lancashire by 2 wickets
2010	**Essex**, who beat Lancashire by 14 runs
2011	**Nottinghamshire**, who beat Lancashire by 4 wickets
2012	**Lancashire**, who beat Durham by 76 runs
2013	**Lancashire**, who beat Nottinghamshire by 76 runs
2014	**Leicestershire**, who beat Lancashire by 168 runs
2015	**Derbyshire**, who beat Durham by 10 runs
2016	**Lancashire**, who beat Somerset by 10 wickets *(DLS)*
2017	**Yorkshire**, who beat Middlesex by 99 runs *(DLS)*
2018	**Middlesex**, who beat Somerset by 1 wicket

SECOND ELEVEN TROPHY
AVERAGES 2018

Played 6   Won 4   Lost 2

BATTING AND FIELDING
(Qualification 3 innings)

Player	M.	I.	N.O.	Runs	H.S.	Avge	Strike Rate	100s	50s	ct/st
AzeemRafiq	4	3	0	97	60	32.33	84.34	0	1	2
E Barnes	4	4	2	55	35*	27.50	54.45	0	0	0
J A Thompson	6	4	0	90	67	22.50	78.94	0	1	5
A Z Lees	5	5	0	106	45	21.20	76.81	0	0	2
J A Tattersall	5	4	0	77	39	19.25	80.20	0	0	6
A U Rashid	3	3	0	55	26	18.33	77.46	0	0	1
T Kohler-Cadmore	4	4	0	71	63	17.75	63.39	0	1	2
J C Wainman	5	3	0	36	13	12.00	64.28	0	0	1
J D Warner	5	4	4	44	25*	—	102.32	0	0	1

Also played

G C H Hill	1	1	0	28	28	28.00	84.84	0	0	1
M D Fisher	2	2	0	51	35	25.50	98.07	0	0	0
T W Loten	4	2	0	43	42	21.50	63.23	0	0	0
M J Waite	1	1	0	19	19	19.00	47.50	0	0	0
A J Hodd	1	1	0	18	18	18.00	42.85	0	0	4
Bilal Anjam	1	1	0	17	17	17.00	62.96	0	0	2
J Shaw	3	2	0	19	18	9.50	111.78	0	0	0
K Carver	3	2	0	10	10	5.00	90.90	0	0	0
B D Birkhead	1	1	1	94	94*	—	87.85	0	1	2/1
H C Brook	1	1	1	36	36*	—	144.00	0	0	0
J A Leaning	2	2	2	70	43*	—	72.91	0	0	1
J E G Logan	4	1	1	2	2*	—	100.00	0	0	0
B O Coad	2	0	0	0	—	—	—	0	0	0
J A Brooks	1	0	0	0	—	—	—	0	0	1
J W Shutt	1	0	0	0	—	—	—	0	0	1
M A Taylor	1	0	0	0	—	—	—	0	0	0

BOWLING
(Qualification 4 wickets)

Player	Overs	Mdns	Runs	Wkts	Avge	Best	4wI	Strike Rate	Econ.
M D Fisher	10	0	42	4	10.50	4-42	1	15.00	4.20
J C Wainman	27	4	108	10	10.80	4-42	1	16.20	4.00
J W Shutt	10	0	47	4	11.75	4-47	1	15.00	4.70
J A Thompson	24.3	2	108	7	15.42	4-17	1	21.00	4.40
A U Rashid	22	3	98	6	16.33	2- 5	0	22.00	4.45
J D Warner	30	1	146	6	24.33	2-21	0	30.00	4.86
J Shaw	17.3	0	109	4	27.25	2-25	0	26.25	6.22
E Barnes	22	1	123	4	30.75	2- 8	0	33.00	5.59

Also bowled

J A Brooks	6.1	0	31	2	15.50	2-31	0	18.50	5.02
J E G Logan	10	1	27	1	27.00	1-27	0	60.00	2.70
K Carver	10	1	32	1	32.00	1-32	0	60.00	3.20
B O Coad	13	2	42	1	42.00	1- 8	0	78.00	3.23
Azeem Rafiq	19.4	0	92	2	46.00	1-34	0	59.00	4.67

Second Eleven Twenty20
Durham v. Yorkshire

Played at Brandon CC on June 19, 2018
Durham won by 22 runs at 2.09pm

Toss won by Yorkshire   Durham 2 points, Yorkshire 0 points

DURHAM

M A Jones, c Azeem Rafiq b Shutt		24
L Trevaskis, c Shutt b Shaw		29
* B A Carse, c Shaw b Azeem Rafiq		18
§ R C Davies, c Wainman b Shaw		0
S Steel, c Anjam b Warner		20
W J Weighell, st Birkhead b Logan		6
C M McBride, not out		15
B J McCarthy, c Warner b Shaw		8
R L Greenwell, not out		1
J O I Campbell		
B G Whitehead Did not bat		
Extras b 1, lb 4, w 2, nb 2		9
Total (7 wkts, 20 overs)		130

FoW: 1-50 (Jones), 2-71 (Trevaskis), 3-72 (Davies), 4-79 (Carse), 5-97 (Weighell), 6-109 (Steel), 7-119 (McCarthy)

	O	M	R	W
Azeem Rafiq	4	0	20	1
Warner	4	0	23	1
Barnes	1	0	18	0
Wainman	2	0	15	0
Shaw	4	0	17	3
Shutt	2	0	17	1
Logan	3	0	15	1

YORKSHIRE

Bilal Anjam, c Jones b Weighell		0
J C Wainman, c and b McCarthy		13
T W Loten, c Trevaskis b McCarthy		0
§ B D Birkhead, c Davies b Weighell		6
* Azeem Rafiq, c Carse b McCarthy		14
M L Revis, c Davies b Campbell		15
J Shaw, c Weighell b Greenwell		4
E Barnes, c Jones b Greenwell		8
J D Warner, run out (Weighell)		33
J E G Logan, lbw b Steel		3
J W Shutt, not out		7
Extras w 5		5
Total (19.2 overs)		108

FoW: 1-0 (Anjam), 2-3 (Loten), 3-11 (Birkhead), 4-35 (Wainman), 5-36 (Azeem Rafiq), 6-49 (Shaw), 7-61 (Barnes), 8-68 (Revis), 9-71 (Logan), 10-108 (Warner)

	O	M	R	W
Weighell	3	1	11	2
McCarthy	2.2	0	12	3
Campbell	4	0	24	1
Whitehead	4	0	21	0
Greenwell	4	0	28	2
Steel	2	0	12	1

Umpires: N Pratt and M Qureshi   Scorers: G Maddison and J R Virr

Second Eleven Twenty20
Durham v. Yorkshire

Played at Brandon CC on June 19, 2018
Durham won by 6 wkts at 5.42pm

Toss won by Durham   Durham 2 points, Yorkshire 0 points

YORKSHIRE

Bilal Anjam, b Harding	....	46
J C Wainman, c Carse b McCarthy	....	4
T W Loten, st Davies b Whitehead	....	21
* Azeem Rafiq, c Trevaskis b Steel	....	9
§ B D Birkhead, c Davies b Weighell	....	15
M L Revis, run out (Trevaskis)	....	3
J Shaw, b McCarthy	....	13
M A Taylor, not out	....	3
J D Warner, c Davies b Weighell	....	0
J E G Logan, not out	....	7
J W Shutt		
E Barnes	Did not bat	
Extras b 3, nb 1, w 7	....	11
Total (8 wkts, 20 overs)	....	132

FoW: 1-10 (Wainman), 2-75 (Loten), 3-81 (Anjam), 4-88 (Azeem Rafiq), 5-93 (Revis), 6-120 (Shaw), 7-124 (Birkhead), 8-124 (Warner)

	O	M	R	W
Weighell	3	0	18	2
McCarthy	4	0	29	2
Carse	3	0	18	0
Campbell	2	0	11	0
Whitehead	4	0	29	1
Harding	2	0	15	1
Steel	2	0	9	1

DURHAM

L Trevaskis, c Logan b Wainman	....	9
M A Jones, not out	....	50
* B A Carse, c Birkhead b Logan	....	43
§ R C Davies, c Barnes b Azeem Rafiq	....	7
S Steel, c Wainman b Logan	....	1
W J Weighell, not out	....	21
G H I Harding		
C M McBride		
B J McCarthy	Did not bat	
J O I Campbell		
B G Whitehead		
Extras nb 3, w 1	....	4
Total (4 wkts, 17.3 overs)	....	135

FoW: 1-12 (Trevaskis), 2-93 (Carse), 3-102 (Davies), 4-105 (Steel)

	O	M	R	W
Shaw	2	0	12	0
Wainman	3	0	26	1
Warner	4	0	26	0
Shutt	2	0	20	0
Azeem Rafiq	3.3	0	32	1
Logan	3	0	19	2

Umpires: N Pratt and M Qureshi   Scorers: G Maddison and J R Virr

Second Eleven Twenty20
Yorkshire v. Lancashire

Played at Harrogate CC on July 4, 2018
Lancashire won by 8 wickets at 2.16pm

Toss won by Yorkshire   Yorkshire 0 points, Lancashire 2 points

YORKSHIRE

Bilal Anjam, c Oldham b Lester	....	68
J C Wainman, c Bailey b Hurt	....	13
J A Thompson, c Guest b Hurt	....	5
M J Waite, b Hartley	....	1
T W Loten, c Jones b Hartley	....	11
§ B D Birkhead, b Hartley	....	5
J Shaw, c Lamb b Lester	....	6
E Barnes, run out (Bailey)	....	10
* K Carver, not out	....	6
J E G Logan, b Lamb	....	0
J W Shutt, not out	....	9
Extras lb 3, nb 6, w 2	....	11
Total (9 wkts, 20 overs)	....	145

FoW: 1-41 (Wainman), 2-54 (Thompson), 3-56 (Waite), 4-82 (Loten), 5-92 (Birkhead), 6-109 (Shaw), 7-129 (Barnes), 8-134 (Anjam), 9-135 (Logan)

	O	M	R	W
Bailey	2	0	24	0
Lester	4	0	27	2
Hurt	4	0	21	2
Lamb	4	0	31	1
Hartley	4	0	24	3
Bohannon	2	0	15	0

LANCASHIRE

* K R Brown, c Anjam b Wainman	....	11
J J Bohannon, not out	....	89
§ B D Guest, c Carver b Waite	....	40
H Hameed, not out	....	0
R P Jones		
D J Lamb		
T J Lester		
L J Hurt	Did not bat	
J P Morley		
T E Bailey		
T Hartley		
S R Oldham		
Extras lb 1, w 5	....	6
Total (2 wkts, 16.2 overs)	....	146

FoW: 1-32 (Brown), 2-139 (Guest)

	O	M	R	W
Shutt	4	0	26	0
Wainman	2	0	5	1
Shaw	2	0	31	0
Barnes	1	0	19	0
Thompson	1.2	0	17	0
Carver	3	0	25	0
Logan	2	0	17	0
Waite	1	0	5	1

Umpires: P K Baldwin and S Widdup   Scorers: J R Virr and G L Morgan

Second Eleven Twenty20
Yorkshire v. Lancashire

Played at Harrogate CC on July 14, 2018
Lancashire won by 31 runs at 5.27pm

Toss won by Lancashire

Yorkshire 0 points, Lancashire 2 points

LANCASHIRE

* K R Brown, b Shutt	....	75
J J Bohannon, b Waite	....	7
§ B D Guest, lbw b Thompson	....	0
H Hameed, c and b Carver	....	24
R P Jones, not out	....	20
D J Lamb, c Shutt b Shaw	....	7
T E Bailey, b Thompson	....	2
L J Hurt, not out	....	10
T J Lester		
J P Morley	Did not bat	
T Hartley		
S R Oldham		
Extras lb 6, w 4	....	10
Total (6 wkts, 20 overs)	....	155

FoW: 1-40 (Bohannon), 2-50 (Guest), 3-104 (Hameed), 4-132 (Brown), 5-142 (Lamb), 6-145 (Bailey)

	O	M	R	W
Shaw	3	0	14	1
Wainman	1	0	13	0
Waite	2	0	25	1
Barnes	2	0	8	0
Thompson	4	0	30	2
Carver	4	0	23	1
Shutt	4	0	36	1

YORKSHIRE

Bilal Anjam, c Guest b Hurt	....	22
J C Wainman, c Bailey b Lester	....	2
J A Thompson, c Brown b Bailey	....	2
M J Waite, st Guest b Hartley	....	13
T W Loten, c and b Hartley	....	23
§ B D Birkhead, c Bohannon b Hartley	....	11
J Shaw, c and b Lester	....	15
E Barnes, c Morley b Lester	....	15
M A Taylor, not out	....	6
* K Carver, not out	....	0
J W Shutt	Did not bat	
Extras b 4, lb 3, w 8	....	15
Total (8 wkts, 20 overs)	....	124

FoW: 1-20 (Wainman), 2-23 (Thompson), 3-50 (Anjam), 4-62 (Waite), 5-85 (Birkhead), 6-88 (Loten), 7-117 (Shaw), 8-117 (Barnes)

	O	M	R	W
Hartley	4	0	26	3
Bailey	4	1	17	1
Lester	4	0	21	3
Hurt	3	0	18	1
Morley	2	0	15	0
Lamb	3	0	20	0

Umpires: P K Baldwin and S Widdup

Scorers: J R Virr and G L Morgan

Played at Barnsley CC on July 12, 2018
Yorkshire won by 7 wickets at 2.32pm

Toss won by Derbyshire Yorkshire 2 points, Derbyshire 0 points

DERBYSHIRE

* B A Godleman, c Wainman b Brook		71
C F Hughes, b Shaw		0
C A J Brodrick, b Shaw		0
T A Wood, c Kohler-Cadmore b Hill		15
§ H R Hosein, c Leaning b Brook		19
J M Kettleborough, not out		17
D M Wheeldon, not out		39
Azarullah		
Hamidullah Qadri		
G T Thornton	Did not bat	
J S Sykes		
A Zazai		
Extras lb 3, nb 2, w 11		16
Total (5 wkts, 20 overs)		177

FoW: 1-5 Hughes, 2-5 (Brodrick), 3-62 (Wood), 4-111 (Godleman), 5-118 (Hosein)

	O	M	R	W
Shaw	3	0	34	2
Wainman	3	0	28	0
Thompson	3	0	13	0
Hill	2	0	13	1
Carver	4	0	41	0
Shutt	2	0	13	0
Leaning	1	0	5	0
Brook	2	0	27	2

YORKSHIRE

T Kohler-Cadmore, c Wood b Sykes		5
H C Brook, not out		101
J A Thompson, c Brodrick b Hughes		26
* J A Leaning, c Sykes b Azarullah		17
M J Waite, not out		22
J C Wainman		
J Shaw		
K Carver		
G C H Hill	Did not bat	
J W Shutt		
§ H G Duke		
E Barnes		
Extras lb 1, w 6		7
Total (3 wkts, 17.1 overs)		178

FoW: 1-6 (Kohler-Cadmore), 2-77 (Thompson), 3-112 (Leaning)

	O	M	R	W
Sykes	4	0	44	1
Wheeldon	1	0	16	0
Thornton	1	0	20	0
Azarullah	3	0	30	1
Hughes	4	0	20	1
Hamidullah Qadri	4	0	41	0
Brodrick	0.1	0	6	0

Umpires: P R Pollard and S Widdup Scorers: J R Virr and J A Wallis

Second Eleven Twenty20
Yorkshire v. Derbyshire

Played at Barnsley CC on July 12, 2018
Derbyshire won by 42 runs at 5.51pm

Toss won by Yorkshire   Yorkshire 0 points, Derbyshire 2 points

DERBYSHIRE

M J J Critchley, c Wainman b Thompson	36
* B A Godleman, b Wainman	6
C F Hughes, c Thompson b Wainman	1
A K Dal, c Thompson b Carver	66
C A J Brodrick, c Waite b Carver	33
M H McKiernan, c Waite b Shaw	6
T A Wood, c Brook b Shaw	18
§ H R Hosein, not out	3
D M Wheeldon, not out	1
Azarullah	
Hamidullah Qadri Did not bat	
G T Thornton	
Extras b 10, lb 2, nb 4, w 2	18
Total (7 wkts, 20 overs)	188

FoW: 1-12 (Godleman), 2-21 (Hughes), 3-78 (Critchley), 4-148 (Dal), 5-160 (Brodrick), 6-168 (McKiernan), 7-184 (Wood)

	O	M	R	W
Shaw	4	0	18	2
Wainman	4	0	39	2
Barnes	3	0	39	0
Thompson	3	0	28	1
Carver	4	0	32	2
Logan	2	0	20	0

YORKSHIRE

H C Brook, c Mc Kiernan b Thornton	2
A Z Lees, c Wheeldon b Critcheley	60
* J A Leaning, c Godleman b McKiernan	52
M J Waite, c Brodrick b Dal	4
J A Thompson, c Wheeldon b Dal	1
J Shaw, b McKienan	5
J C Wainman, not out	16
E Barnes, not out	1
K Carver	
§ A J Hodd Did not bat	
J E G Logan	
G C H Hill	
Extras lb 4, w 1	5
Total (6 wkts, 20 overs)	146

FoW: 1-12 (Brook), 2-94 (Lees), 3-99 (Waite), 4-110 (Thompson), 5-124 (Shaw), 6-143 (Leaning)

	O	M	R	W
Wheelson	2	0	16	0
Thornton	2	0	14	1
Azarullah	4	0	36	0
McKiernan	4	0	28	2
Dal	4	0	27	2
Critchley	4	0	21	1

Umpires: P R Pollard and S Widdup   Scorers: J R Virr and J A Wallis

Second Eleven Twenty20
Nottinghamshire v. Yorkshire

Played at Worksop College on July 18, 2018
Yorkshire won by 29 runs at 2.17pm

Toss won by Yorkshire

Nottinghamshire 0 points, Yorkshire 2 points

YORKSHIRE

T Kohler-Cadmore, c Patterson-White b Blatherwick .		27
A Z Lees, c Evison b Patterson-White		46
H C Brook, lbw b Carter		51
* J A Leaning, not out		23
M J Waite, c Budinger b Patterson-White		4
J A Thompson, not out		20
§ B D Birkhead		
J Shaw		
J C Wainman	Did not bat	
E Barnes		
K Carver		
J E G Logan		
Extras lb 6, nb 6, w 7		19
Total (4 wkts, 20 overs)		190

FoW: 1-45 (Kohler-Cadmore), 2-124 (Lees), 3-136 (Brook), 4-141 (Waite)

	O	M	R	W
Blatherwick	4	0	35	1
Footitt	4	0	37	0
Kitt	2	0	31	0
Carter	4	0	29	1
James	3	0	33	0
Patterson-White	3	0	19	2

NOTTINGHAMSHIRE

S D Budinger, c Birkhead b Wainman		0
L W James, c Barnes b Wainman		16
M Carter, c Birkhead b Thompson		6
* J D Libby, c Leaning b Thompson		8
J D M Evison, b Thompson		34
C R Marshall, b Shaw		40
L A Patterson-White, c Shaw b Barnes		33
§ T G Keast, c Brook b Thompson		2
J M Blatherwick, c Birkhead b Barnes		4
B M Kitt, not out		8
M H A Footitt, not out		1
J D Cook	Did not bat	
Extras lb 2, w 7		9
Total (9 wkts, 20 overs)		161

FoW: 1-0 (Budinger), 2-17 (James), 3-24 (Carter), 4-35 (Libby), 5-90 (Evison), 6-131(Marshall), 7-142 (Keast), 8-150 (Blatherwick), 9-153 (Patterson-White)

	O	M	R	W
Wainman	4	1	16	2
Shaw	2	0	29	1
Barnes	3	0	21	2
Thompson	4	0	27	4
Leaning	4	0	29	0
Carver	3	0	37	0

Umpires: D J Milnes and I G Rich

Scorers: Mrs A Cusworth and J R Virr

Second Eleven Twenty20
Nottinghamshire v. Yorkshire

Played at Worksop College on July 18, 2018
Yorkshire won by 6 wickets at 5.40pm

Toss won by Nottinghamshire   Nottinghamshire 0 points, Yortkshire 2 points

NOTTINGHAMSHIRE

S D Budinger, c Brook b Thompson		13
W A R Fraine, c Waite b Leaning		57
L W James, c Lees b Brook		26
*J D Libby, c Waite b Thompson		19
J D Cook, c Kohler-Cadmore b Wainman		8
L A Patterson-White, not out		18
J D M Evison, not out		0
C R Marshall		
J M Blatherwick	Did not bat	
M H A Footitt		
§ T G Keast		
Extras b 5, lb 1, nb 2, w 5		13
Total (5 wkts; 20 overs)		154

FoW: 1-38 (Budinger), 2-102 (Fraine), 3-107 (James), 4-132 (Cook), 5-153 (Libby)

	O	M	R	W
Wainman	4	0	30	1
Shaw	2	0	18	0
Thompson	4	0	27	2
Leaning	2	0	15	1
Logan	4	0	23	0
Carver	3	0	30	0
Brook	1	0	5	1

YORKSHIRE

T Kohler-Cadmore, c Keast b Footitt		27
A Z Lees, not out		72
H C Brook, c Blatherwick b Marshall		7
*J A Leaning, c Patterson-White b Blathwick		17
M J Waite, c Blatherwick b Marshall		11
J A Thompson, not out		10
§ B D Birkhead		
J Shaw		
J C Wainman	Did not bat	
K Carver		
J E G Logan		
E Barnes		
Extras b 2, lb 4, nb 2, w 3		11
Total (4 wkts, 18 overs)		155

FoW: 1-46 (Kohler-Cadmore), 2-60 (Brook), 3-122 (Leaning), 4-137 (Waite)

	O	M	R	W
Blatherwick	4	0	22	1
Footitt	3	0	29	1
James	2	0	18	0
Patterson-White	2	0	17	0
Marshall	4	0	31	2
Cook	3	0	32	0

Umpires: D J Milnes and I G Rich   Scorers: Mrs A Cusworth and J R Virr

Second Eleven Twenty20
Northamptonshire v. Yorkshire

Played at Finedon Dolben CC on July 23, 2018
Yorkshire won by 28 runs at 2.33pm

Toss won by Yorkshire   Northamptonshire 0 points, Yorkshire 2 points

YORKSHIRE

T Kohler-Cadmore, c C White b Zaib		75
A Z Lees, c Bartier b Zaib		60
M J Waite, c C White b Zaib		9
* J A Leaning, c Zaib b Kleinveldt		9
J A Thompson, c Home b Gleeson		31
§ B D Birkhead, not out		9
J Shaw, not out		1
J C Wainman		
E Barnes	Did not bat	
K Carver		
J E G Logan		
Extras b 1, w 6		7
Total (5 wkts, 20 overs)		201

FoW: 1-105 (Kohler-Cadmore), 2-131 (Waite), 3-156 (Lees), 4-159 (Leaning), 5-198 (Thompson)

	O	M	R	W
Kleinveldt	4	0	34	1
Gleeson	4	0	48	1
C White	2	0	18	0
Bartier	1	0	23	0
G G White	4	0	33	0
Zaib	4	0	33	3
Home	1	0	11	0

NORTHAMPTONSHIRE

B J Curran, b Shaw		7
* C O Thurston, c Birkhead b Shaw		0
S A Zaib, c Lees b Leaning		51
D D W Brierley, c Birkhead b Logan		32
C E Home, c Thompson b Carver		7
L W Bartier, b Leaning b Logan		8
R K Kleinveldt, c Birkhead b Thompson		42
G G White, c Kohler-Cadmore b Carver		0
C White, c Birkhead b Shaw		13
§ A E King, c Kohler-Cadmore b Shaw		0
R J Gleeson, not out		0
Extras b 5, lb 1, w 7		13
Total (20 overs)		173

FoW: 1-0 (Thurston), 2-8 (Curran), 3-86 (Zaib), 4-101 (Home), 5-102 (Brierley), 6-116 (Bartier), 7-119 (G G White), 8-167 (Kleinveldt), 9-169 (King), 10-173 (C White)

	O	M	R	W
Shaw	4	0	14	4
Wainman	3	0	25	0
Thompson	4	0	33	1
Carver	3	0	26	2
Taylor	2	0	25	0
Leaning	2	0	17	1
Logan	2	0	27	2

Umpires: A Davies and N Pratt   Scorers: R J Dickinson and J R Virr

Second Eleven Twenty20
Northamptonshire v. Yorkshire

Played at Finedon Dolben CC on July 23, 2018
Northamptonshire won by 6 runs at 6.28pm

Toss won by Northamptonshire   Northamptonshire 2 points, Yorkshire 0 points

NORTHAMPTONSHIRE

B J Curran, c Wainman b Thompson		94
* C O Thurston, b Thompson		40
S A Zaib, c Thompson b Logan		24
R K Kleinveldt, c Leaning b Wainman		10
G G White, c Wainman b Logan		4
L W Bartier, lbw b Logan		0
D D W Brierley, c Lees b Thompson		4
§ A E King, not out		22
C White, not out		6
R J Gleeson		
B J Bhabra	Did not bat	
Extras b 5, w 3		8
Total (7 wkts, 20 overs)		212

FoW: 1-75 (Thurston), 2-151 (Zaib), 3-164 (Curran), 4-176 (G G White), 5-176 (Bartier), 6-182 (Kleinveldt), 7-188 (Brierley)

	O	M	R	W
Shaw	4	0	36	0
Wainman	3	0	32	1
Leaning	3	0	39	0
Thompson	4	0	37	3
Carver	2	0	33	0
Taylor	2	0	20	0
Logan	2	0	10	3

YORKSHIRE

A Z Lees, c G G White b Zaib		69
* J A Leaning, c Zaib b Gleeson		8
T Kohler-Cadmore, c G G White b Zaib		58
M J Waite, b Bartier		8
J A Thompson, c Zaib b G G White		21
§ B D Birkhead, run out (Thurston)		0
J Shaw, b Bharbra		4
J C Wainman, c Thurston b Bhabra		0
M A Taylor, not out		4
K Carver, b Gleeson		10
J E G Logan, not out		7
Extras b 5, lb 2, nb 2, w 8		17
Total (9 wkts, 20 overs)		206

FoW: 1-58 (Leaning), 2-141 (Lees), 3-154 (Waite), 4-154 (Kohler-Cadmore), 5-154 (Birkhead), 6-179 (Thompson), 7-180 (Wainman), 8-185 (Shaw), 9-199 (Carver)

	O	M	R	W
Zaib	4	0	36	2
Gleeson	4	0	32	2
C White	2	0	20	0
G G White	4	0	40	1
Bhabra	3	0	23	2
Thurston	1	0	26	0
Bartier	2	0	22	1

Umpires: A Davies and N Pratt   Scorers: R J Dickinson and J R Virr

Second Eleven Twenty20
Yorkshire v. Worcestershire

Played at Marske-by-the-Sea CC on July 30, 2018
Yorkshire won by 4 runs at 2.20pm

Toss won by Worcestershire   Yorkshire 2 points, Worcestershire 0 points

YORKSHIRE

A Z Lees, c Simpson b Brewster		78
§ B D Birkhead, c Harvey b Parker-Cole		11
* J A Leaning, c Harvey b Gibson		30
M J Waite, not out		29
G C H Hill, not out		9
J Shaw		
J C Wainman		
K Carver	Did not bat	
J E G Logan		
T W Loten		
E Barnes		
Extras b 1, w 7		8
Total (3 wkts, 20 overs)		165

FoW: 1-25 (Birkhead), 2-119 (Leaning), 3-129 (Lees).

	O	M	R	W
Harvey	4	0	28	0
Simpson	3	0	28	0
Parker-Cole	2	0	15	1
Brewster	4	0	27	1
Twohig	3	0	40	0
Rhodes	2	0	17	0
Gibson	2	0	9	1

WORCESTERSHIRE

* O E Westbury, c Birkhead b Shaw		5
G H Rhodes, c Loten b Carver		19
§ T C Fell, b Barnes		65
J J Dell, c Leaning b Wainman		33
R Gibson, c Birkhead b Shaw		3
B J Twohig, c Logan b Shaw		9
A C Simpson, not out		9
R A Parker-Cole, c Logan b Hill		2
A Brewster		
C Harvey	Did not bat	
A P Sutton		
Extras b 6, lb 4, w 6		16
Total (7 wkts, 20 overs)		161

FoW: 1-8 (Westbury), 2-65 (Rhodes), 3-116 (Fell), 4-122 (Gibson), 5-147 (Dell) 6-155 (Twohig), 7-161 (Parker-Cole)

	O	M	R	W
Wainman	4	0	22	1
Shaw	4	0	28	3
Barnes	4	0	30	1
Hill	3	0	26	1
Carver	4	0	31	1
Logan	1	0	14	0

Umpires: M A Gough and G Roberts   Scorers: J R Virr and R M Wilks

Second Eleven Twenty20
Yorkshire v. Worcestershire

Played at Marske-by-the-Sea CC on July 30, 2018
Worcestershire won by 38 runs at 5.52pm

Toss won by Yorkshire   Yorkshire 0 points, Worcestershire 2 points

WORCESTERSHIRE

G H Rhodes, c Birkhead b Barnes		17
* O E Westbury, c Anjam b Carver		42
§ T C Fell, not out		120
J J Dell, c Wainman b Shaw		8
R Gibson, not out		5
B J Twohig		
R A Parker-Cole		
A C Simpson	Did not bat	
A D F Brewster		
C C Harvey		
A P Sutton		
Extras lb 1, nb 4, w 12		17
Total (3 wkts, 20 overs)		209

FoW: 1-24 (Rhodes), 2-129 (Westbury), 3-203 (Dell)

	O	M	R	W
Wainman	4	0	44	0
Shaw	4	0	26	1
Barnes	4	0	39	1
Carver	2	0	30	1
Hill	4	0	45	0
Logan	1	0	10	0
Leaning	1	0	14	0

YORKSHIRE

M J Waite, b Harvey		4
B D Birkhead, c Rhodes b Simpson		0
* J A Leaning, b Gibson		56
§ A J Hodd, b Parker-Cole		16
Bilal Anjam, c Simpson b Brewster		27
G C H Hill, b Gibson		15
J Shaw, c Dell b Twohig		19
J C Wainman, b Harvey		10
E Barnes, not out		5
K Carver, c and b Harvey		0
J E G Logan, not out		7
Extras b 1, lb 2, nb 2, w 7		12
Total (9 wkts, 20 overs)		171

FoW: 1-4 (Waite), 2-4 (Birkhead), 3-25 (Hodd), 4-107 (Anjam), 5-128 (Hill), 6-129 (Leaning), 7-156 (Shaw), 8-158 (Wainman), 9-159 (Carver)

	O	M	R	W
Harvey	4	0	41	3
Simpson	2	1	11	1
Parker-Cole	1	0	4	1
Brewster	4	0	23	1
Twohig	3	0	31	1
Gibson	4	0	33	2
Rhodes	1	0	17	0
Sutton	1	0	8	0

Umpires: M A Gough and G Roberts   Scorers: J R Virr and R M Wilks

SECOND ELEVEN
TWENTY20 2018

Two matches played against the same opponents at the same venue on the same day.

SEMI-FINALS

Durham (53-5)	lost to Essex (58-0)	by 10 wickets
Lancashire (66-4)	beat Gloucestershire (60-3)	by six runs

FINAL

Lancashire (66-9) beat Essex(41-7) by 25 runs

Finals Day at Arundel was severely disrupted by the weather

NORTHERN GROUP – FINAL TABLE *(2017 in brackets)*

		P	W	L	T	Aban/NR	Points	Net Run Rate
1	Lancashire (2)	12	10	2	0	0	20	1.200
2	Durham (5)	12	9	3	0	0	18	0.855
3	Derbyshire (10)	12	8	4	0	0	16	0.599
4	Leicestershire (8)	12	7	4	0	1	15	0.320
5	Warwickshire (4)	12	6	5	1	0	13	0.488
6	**Yorkshire (1)**	**12**	**5**	**7**	**0**	**0**	**10**	**-0.389**
7	Nottinghamshire (7)	12	4	7	1	0	9	-0.839
8	Northamptonshire (6)	12	3	8	0	1	7	-0.686
9	Worcestershire (9)	12	3	9	0	0	6	-0.458
10	MCC Young Cricketers (3)	12	3	9	0	0	6	-1.171

SOUTHERN GROUP – FINAL TABLE *(2017 in brackets)*

		P	W	L	T	Aban/NR	Points	Net Run Rate
1	Essex	12	8	2	0	2	18	1.586
2	Gloucestershire	12	7	5	0	0	14	0.915
3	Hampshire	12	7	5	0	0	14	0.463
4	Sussex	12	7	5	0	0	14	0.372
5	Kent	12	7	5	0	0	14	-0.284
6	Middlesex	12	6	6	0	0	12	-0.121
7	Somerset	12	4	6	0	2	10	-0.709
8	Surrey	12	4	8	0	0	8	-0.207
9	Glamorgan	12	4	8	0	0	8	-0.722
10	Unicorns	12	4	8	0	0	8	-1.078

PREVIOUS WINNERS

2011	**Sussex**, who beat Durham by 24 runs
2012	**England Under-19s**, who beat Sussex by eight wickets
2013	**Surrey**, who beat Middlesex by six runs
2014	**Leicesterhire**, who beat Somerset by 11 runs
2015	**Middlesex**, who beat Kent by four wickets
2016	**Middlesex**, who beat Somerset by two wickets
2017	**Sussex**, who beat Hampshire by 24 runs
2018	**Lancashire**, who beat Essex by 25 runs

SECOND ELEVEN TWENTY20
AVERAGES 2018

Played 12   Won 5   Lost 7

BATTING AND FIELDING

(Qualification 3 innings)

Player	M.	I.	N.O.	Runs	H.S.	Avge	Strike Rate	100s	50s	ct/st
A Z Lees	6	6	1	385	78	77.00	142.59	0	1	3
H C Brook	4	4	1	161	101*	53.66	169.47	1	1	3
T Kohler-Cadmore .	5	5	0	192	75	38.40	202.10	0	1	4
Bilal Anjam	5	5	0	163	68	32.60	110.13	0	1	1
J A Leaning	8	8	1	212	56	30.28	115.70	0	1	5
J A Thompson	8	8	2	116	31	19.33	165.71	0	0	4
T W Loten	5	4	0	55	23	13.75	85.93	0	0	1
M J Waite	10	10	2	105	29*	13.12	100.02	0	0	4
E Barnes	12	5	2	39	15	13.00	118.18	0	0	2
J E G Logan	11	5	3	24	7*	12.00	126.31	0	0	3
J C Wainman	12	7	1	58	16*	9.66	126.00	0	0	7
J Shaw	12	8	1	67	19	9.57	101.51	0	0	2
B D Birkhead	10	8	1	57	15	8.14	95.00	0	0	11/1
K Carver	10	4	2	16	10	8.00	114.28	0	0	2
M A Taylor	5	3	3	13	6*	—	108.33	0	0	0

Also played

Player	M.	I.	N.O.	Runs	H.S.	Avge	Strike Rate	100s	50s	ct/st
G C H Hill	4	2	1	24	15	24.00	104.34	0	0	0
J D Warner	3	2	0	33	33	16.50	157.14	0	0	1
A J Hodd	2	1	0	16	16	16.00	106.66	0	0	0
Azeem Rafiq	2	2	0	23	14	11.50	104.54	0	0	1
M L Revis	2	2	0	18	15	9.00	51.42	0	0	0
H G Duke	1	0	0	0	—	—	—	0	0	0
J W Shutt	5	2	2	16	9*	—	123.07	0	0	2

BOWLING

(Qualification 5 wickets)

Player	Overs	Mdns	Runs	Wkts	Avge	Best	Strike Rate	Econ.	4wI
J Shaw	38	0	277	17	16.29	4-14	13.41	7.28	1
J A Thompson.........	27.2	0	212	13	16.30	4-27	12.61	7.75	1
J E G Logan	20	0	155	8	19.37	3-10	15.00	7.75	0
J C Wainman	37	1	295	9	32.77	2-16	24.66	7.97	0
K Carver.................	32	0	295	7	42,14	2-26	27.42	9.21	0

Also bowled

Player	Overs	Mdns	Runs	Wkts	Avge	Best	Strike Rate	Econ.	4wI
H C Brook	3	0	32	3	10.66	2-27	6.00	10.66	0
M J Waite	3	0	30	2	15.00	1- 5	9.00	10.00	0
Azeem Rafiq...........	7.3	0	52	2	26.00	1-20	22.50	6.93	0
G C H Hill	9	0	84	2	42.00	1-13	27.00	9.33	0
E Barnes	18	0	174	4	43.50	2-21	27.00	9.66	0
J D Warner.............	8	0	49	1	49.00	1-23	48.00	6.12	0
J W Shutt...............	14	0	112	2	56.00	1-17	42.00	8.00	0
J A Leaning.............	13	0	119	2	59.50	1-15	39.00	9.15	0
M A Taylor	4	0	58	0	—	—	—	14.50	0

Other Second Eleven Matches
Gloucestershire v. Yorkshire

Played at Bristol on April 10, 11, 12 and 13, 2018

Match abandoned without a ball bowled   Toss: None

Lancashire v. Yorkshire

Played at Old Trafford, Manchester, on April 17, 18 and 19, 2018

Lancashire 198-3 (R P Jones 90, D J Lamb 58) and 197-6 dec (R P Jones 104, K Carver 3-41). **Yorkshire** 146-7 dec (T Kohler-Cadmore 48, M W Parkinson 4-26) and 253-7 (J A Tattersall 78, Azeem Rafiq 49, G P Balderson 3-26).

Yorkshire won by 3 wickets   Toss: Yorkshire

Yorkshire v. Nottinghamshire

Played at Scarborough on April 23, 24 and 25, 2018

Nottinghamshire 232 (T G Keast 59, S D Perera 52, C F Gibson 51, Bilal Anjam 4-12). **Yorkshire** 163-6 (J A Thompson 56, M E Milnes 4-62).

Match abandoned as a draw at 11am on the final day   Toss: Nottinghamshire

Yorkshire v. Nottinghamshire

Played at Scarborough on April 26, 2018

Nottinghamshire 235 (W T Root 56, S G Budinger 45, T G Keast 40, J C Wainman 4-31). **Yorkshire** 213 (J A Thompson 74, Bilal Anjam 58, W T Root 5-47).

Nottinghamshire won by 22 runs   Toss: Nottinghamshire

Somerset v. Yorkshire

Played at Taunton on August 28, 29 and 30, 2018

Yorkshire 329-8 dec (B D Birkhead 112, T W Loten 59, J A Ravel 50, C G Harrison 7-71) and 282-6 dec (J A Ravel 56, J D Warner 54*, E Barnes 50*, M J Waite 42). **Somerset** 341-6 dec (B G F Green 200*, W C Smeed 51).

Match drawn   Toss: Yorkshire

Leicestershire v. Yorkshire

Played at Kibworth CC on September 4, 5, 6 and 7, 2018

Yorkshire 401 (J Wharton 162, J A Thompson 53, J A Leaning 51, B O Coad 42*, B D Birkhead 41, M Ahmed 4-77) and 82-1 (J Wharton 46*). **Leicestershire** 416-9 dec (L J Hill 120, M H Azad 115*, A M Ali 46, K Carver 3-87).

Match drawn   Toss: Leicestershire

Surrey v. Yorkshire

Played at Guildford CC on September 12, 13 and 14, 2018

Surrey 239 (R S Patel 89, A E C Dahl 62, J Shaw 3-38) and 35-1. **Yorkshire** 289-6 dec (J A Leaning 115*, T W Loten 51, E Barnes 41, G J Batty 3-26).

Match drawn   Toss: Surrey

Yorkshire v. Durham

Played at Scarborough on September 18, 19 and 20, 2018

Yorkshire 472-7 dec (J A Leaning 126, J Shaw 103*, G C H Hill 79, T W Loten 44). **Durham** 295 (R C Davies 142, S Steel 66, J A Leaning 3-15).

Match drawn   Toss: Yorkshire

YORKSHIRE DIAMONDS

Captain: Lauren Winfield

General Manager: Jane Hildreth   Head Coach: Paul Grayson

KIA SUPER LEAGUE 2018 (T20)

2018 WINNERS: Surrey Stars, who beat Loughborough Lightning by 66 runs

LEAGUE TABLE

*4 points awarded for a win, plus 1 bonus point for any team that
achieves victory with a run rate 1.25 times that of the opposition*

		P	W	L	T	NR/A	PTS	NRR
1	Loughborough Lightning	10	7	3	0	0	33	+1.361
2	Western Storm	10	6	3	0	1	30	+0.919
3	Surrey Stars	10	5	4	0	1	24	-0.404
4	Lancashire Thunder	10	5	5	0	0	21	-0.825
5	**Yorkshire Diamonds**	**10**	**3**	**6**	**0**	**1**	**15**	**-0.290**
6	Southern Vipers	10	2	7	0	1	10	-0.490

YORKSHIRE DIAMONDS 2018 KIA SUPER LEAGUE SQUAD

Player	Date of Birth	Birthplace	Type
L Winfield (Captain)	August 16, 1990	York	RHB
C Athapaththu	February 9, 1990	Gokarella, Sri Lanka	LHB, OB
T F Brookes	February 15, 1993	Wordsley, Warwickshire	RHB,OB
K H Brunt	July 2, 1985	Barnsley	RHB, RAMF
A N Davidson-Richards	May 29, 1994	Tunbridge Wells	RHB, RAFM
G M Davies	May 12, 1994	Neath	LHB, RAFM
H L Fenby	November 23, 1998	Stockton, Co. Durham	RHB, LB
B A M Heath	August 20, 2001	Chesterfield	RHB, WK
D M Kimmince	May 14, 1989	Warwick, Queensland	RHB, RM
B A Langston	September 6, 1992	Harold Wood, Essex	RHB, RM
K A Levick	July 17, 1991	Sheffield	RHB, LB
A Z Monaghan	March 20, 2000	Basingstoke	RHB
B L Mooney	January 14, 1994	Shepperton, Victoria	LHB, WK
S Munro	August 31, 2001	Lincoln	RHB
K C Thompson	September 28, 1996	Harrogate	RHB, LAS

Kia Super League
Western Storm v Yorkshire Diamonds

Played at Cooper Associates County Ground, Taunton, on Sunday, July 22, 2018
Western Storm won by seven wickets (with 27 balls remaining)

Toss won by Western Storm   Western Storm 5 points, Yorkshire 0 points

YORKSHIRE

§ B L Mooney, run out (Taylor)		3
* L Winfield, lbw b Davies		41
C Athapaththu, lbw b Nicholas		0
A N Davidson-Richards, c and b Taylor		33
D M Kimmince, not out		55
B A Langston, b Davies		13
T F Brookes, not out		11
G M Davies		
A Z Monaghan	Did not bat	
K A Levick		
H L Fenby		
Extras lb 1, w 5		6
Total (5 wkts, 20 overs)		162

FoW: 1-12 (Mooney), 2-12 (Athapaththu), 3-60 (Winfield), 4-126 (Davidson-Richards), 5-150 (Langston)

	O	M	R	W
Shrubsole	4	0	32	0
Nicholas	4	0	29	1
Davies	4	0	28	2
Gibson	2	0	20	0
Taylor	3	0	23	1
Knight	3	0	29	0

WESTERN STORM

§ R H Priest, lbw b Fenby		0
S Mandhana, c Winfield b Davidson-Richards		48
* H C Knight, c Kimmince b Davidson-Richards		97
S R Taylor, not out		12
F C Wilson, not out		0
S N Luff		
N D Dattani		
A Shrubsole	Did not bat	
C Nicholas		
D R Gibson		
F R Davies		
Extras lb 1, w 6, nb 2		9
Total (3 wkts, 15.3 overs)		166

FoW: 1-0 (Priest), 2-80 (Mandhana), 3-161 (Knight)

	O	M	R	W
Fenby	4	1	38	1
Athapaththu	2	0	15	0
Langston	2	0	26	0
Kimmince	2	0	38	0
Davidson-Richards	3.3	0	31	2
Levick	2	0	17	0

Player of the Match: H C Knight

Umpires: R T Robinson, M J Saggers and N G B Cook (TV)

Scorers: L M Rhodes and K N Hutchinson

Kia Super League
Yorkshire Diamonds v. Lancashire Thunder

Played at Emerald Headingley, Leeds, on Friday, July 27, 2018
Lancashire Thunder won by 33 runs

Toss won by Yorkshire   Yorkshire 0 points, Lancashire 5points

LANCASHIRE

N E Bolton, c Monaghan b Davidson-Richards		11
E Jones, c Winfield b Athapaththu		5
G E B Boyce, c and b Davidson-Richards		2
A E Satterthwaite, not out		57
E L Lamb, st Mooney b Levick		1
§ E Threlkeld, not out		53
* D Hazell		
S Ecclestone		
K L Cross	Did not bat	
N Brown		
A Hartley		
Extras w 5		5
Total (4 wkts, 20 overs)		134

FoW: 1-17 (Jones), 2-21 (Bolton), 3-22 (Boyce), 4-25 (Lamb)

	O	M	R	W
Fenby	4	0	30	0
Brunt	4	0	26	0
Athapaththu	3	0	15	1
Levick	4	0	26	1
Davidson-Richards	3	0	15	2
Kimmince	2	0	22	0

YORKSHIRE

* L Winfield, c Satterthwaite b Ecclestone		28
§ B L Mooney, c Cross b Hartley		20
C Athapaththu, b Hartley		6
A N Davidson-Richards, st Threlkeld b Ecclestone		3
K H Brunt, run out (Hazell/Threlkeld)		4
D M Kimmince, run out (Ecclestone/Threlkeld)		12
T F Brookes, st Threlkeld b Hartley		21
B A Langston, not out		2
A Z Monaghan, run out (Threlkeld)		1
K A Levick, st Threlkeld b Hazell		0
H L Fenby, st Threlkeld b Ecclestone		0
Extras lb 2, w 2		4
Total (18.1 overs)		101

FoW: 1-43 (Winfield), 2-56 (Mooney), 3-59 (Davidson-Richards), 4-59 (Athapaththu), 5-71 (Brunt), 6-85 (Kimmince), 7-99 (Brookes), 8-100 (Monaghan), 9-100 (Levick), 10-101 (Fenby)

	O	M	R	W
Lamb	3	0	24	0
Cross	4	0	33	0
Hazell	4	1	12	1
Ecclestone	3.1	0	11	3
Hartley	4	0	19	3

Player of the Match: E Threlkeld

Umpires: R J Bailey, M Burns and P J Hartley (TV)
      Scorers: K N Hutchinson and M Cregan

Surrey Stars v. Yorkshire Diamonds

At Woodbridge Road, Guildford, on July 29, 2018
Match abandoned without a ball bowled

Surrey 2 points, Yorkshire 2 points   Umpires: T Lungley and M Newell

Kia Super League
Loughborough Lightning v. Yorkshire Diamonds

Played at Haselgrave Ground, Loughborough, on Tuesday, July 31, 2018

Loughborough Lightning won by 41 runs

Toss won by Loughborough   Loughborough 5 points, Yorkshire 0 points

LOUGHBOROUGH

R L Haynes, c Athapaththu b Levick		50
S F M Devine, c Mooney b Levick		30
§ A E Jones, c Davidson-Richards b Langston		8
E J Villani, run out (Langston)		17
* G A Elwiss, run out (Davidson-Richards/Brunt)		19
G L Adams, b Brunt		12
J L Gunn, not out		2
S Glenn, not out		0
L F Higham		
K L Gordon	Did not bat	
L C N Smith		
Extras lb 3, w 2		5
Total (6 wkts, 20 overs)		143

FoW: 1-80 (Devine), 2-85 (Haynes), 3-106 (Villani), 4-109 (Jones), 5-139 (Adams), 6-142 (Elwiss)

	O	M	R	W
Langston	4	0	28	1
Brunt	4	0	12	1
Davidson-Richards	4	0	35	0
Fenby	1	0	17	0
Kimmince	2	0	16	0
Athapaththu	1	0	8	0
Levick	4	0	24	2

YORKSHIRE

§ B L Mooney, c Devine b Gunn		7
* L Winfield, c Gunn b Devine		0
C Athapaththu, c Devine b Higham		3
A N Davidson-Richards, st Jones b Gordon		22
K H Brunt, lbw b Glenn		12
D M Kimmince, b Gordon		3
T F Brookes, c Gordon b Devine		30
B A Langston, c Villani b Gunn		16
A Z Monaghan, st Jones b Smith		1
K A Levick, not out		1
H L Fenby, not out		1
Extras lb 2, w 4		6
Total (9 wkts, 20 overs)		102

FoW: 1-5 (Winfield), 2-12 (Mooney), 3-19 (Athapaththu), 4-36 (Brunt), 5-42 (Kimmince), 6-57 (Davidson-Richards), 7-90 (Brookes), 8-98 (Monaghan), 9-100 (Langston)

	O	M	R	W
Gunn	4	1	12	2
Devine	4	1	19	2
Higham	1	0	2	1
Smith	4	0	26	1
Elwiss	2	0	17	0
Glenn	2	0	14	1
Gordon	3	0	10	2

Umpires: T J Lungley and S Redfern   Scorers: K N Hutchinson and K Gerrard

Kia Super League
Yorkshire Diamonds v. Southern Vipers

Played at York Cricket Club on Thursday, August 2, 2018
Yorkshire Diamonds won by 12 runs

Toss won by Yorkshire   Yorkshire 4 points, Southern Vipers 0 points

YORKSHIRE

* L Winfield, c du Preez b Farrant	64
§ B L Mooney, lbw b Bates	13
C Athapaththu, c Farrant b Kerr	43
A N Davidson-Richards, st Rudd b Kerr	17
K H Brunt, not out	21
D M Kimmince, c George b Farrant	7
B A Langston	
T F Brookes	
G M Davies Did not bat	
K A Levick	
H L Fenby	
Extras w 10	10
Total (5 wkts, 20 overs)	175

FoW: 1-56 (Mooney), 2-109 (Winfield), 3-142 (Davidson-Richards), 4-147 (Athapaththu), 5-175 (Kimmince)

	O	M	R	W
Farrant	4	0	44	2
Kerr	4	0	27	2
Brindle	2	0	18	0
Dean	2	0	27	0
Bates	4	0	33	1
George	4	0	26	0

SOUTHERN VIPERS

* S Bates, c Fenby b Davidson-Richards	34
D N Wyatt, c Mooney b Brunt	1
M du Preez b Langston b Davidson-Richards	25
S J McGlashan, c Kimmince b Brunt	21
M E Bouchier, lbw b Brunt	15
A Brindle, b Athapaththu	8
A C Kerr, not out	26
N E Farrant, c Winfield b Langston	2
K L George, lbw b Brunt	6
§ C E Rudd, lbw b Brunt	0
C E Dean, not out	0
Extras b 1, lb 5, w 19	25
Total (9 wkts, 20 overs)	163

FoW: 1-14 (Wyatt), 2-51 (Bates), 3-63 (du Preez), 4-104 (Bouchier), 5-111 (McGlashan), 6-140 (Brindle), 7-149 (Farrant), 8-163 (George), 9-163 (Rudd)

	O	M	R	W
Fenby	1	0	12	0
Brunt	4	0	26	5
Langston	3	0	24	1
Athapaththu	2	0	17	1
Davidson-Richards	4	0	37	2
Levick	4	0	28	0
Kimmince	2	0	13	0

Umpires: T J Lungley and S Redfern   Scorers: K N Hutchinson and K Rouse

Kia Super League
Yorkshire Diamonds v. Western Storm

Played at North Marine Road, Scarborough, on Sunday, August 5, 2018
Western Storm won by seven wickets (with four balls remaining)

Toss won by Yorkshire   Yorkshire 0 points, Western Storm 4 points

YORKSHIRE

* L Winfield, b Knight	....	48
§ B L Mooney, run out (Knight)	....	69
K H Brunt, c Nicholas b Dattani	....	9
C Athapaththu, c b (Shrubsole)	....	20
T F Brookes, run out (Shrubsole/Priest)	....	8
D M Kimmince, not out	....	6
A N Davidson-Richards, not out	....	0
B A Langston		
G M Davies		
K A Levick	Did not bat	
H L Fenby		
Extras lb 2, w 8, nb 2	....	12
Total (5 wkts, 20 overs)	....	172

FoW: 1-119 (Winfield), 2-128(Mooney), 3-135 (Brunt), 4-164 (Brookes), 5-165 (Athapaththu)

	O	M	R	W
Shrubsole	4	0	19	0
Nicholas	3	0	28	0
Davies	4	0	49	0
Dattani	3	0	28	1
Taylor	2	0	19	0
Knight	4	0	27	1

WESTERN STORM

§ R H Priest, c Winfield b Levick	....	37
S Mandhana, b Athapaththu	....	56
* H C Knight, not out	....	45
S R Taylor, run out (Davidson-Richards/Mooney)	...	4
F C Wilson, not out	....	14
S N Luff		
N D Dattani		
A Shrubsole	Did not bat	
F R Davies		
C Nicholas		
D R Gibson		
Extras w 18	....	18
Total (3 wkts, 19.2 overs)	....	174

FoW: 1-101 (Priest), 2-108 (Mandhana), 3-127 (Taylor)

	O	M	R	W
Langston	3	0	36	0
Brunt	3.2	0	25	0
Kimmince	1	0	21	0
Athapaththu	3	0	34	1
Levick	3	0	16	1
Davidson-Richards	3	0	25	0
Fenby	3	0	17	0

Umpires: J D Middlebrook and C M Watts   Scorers: K N Hutchinson and J Slater

Kia Super League
Southern Vipers v. Yorkshire Diamonds

Played at The Ageas Bowl, Southampton, on Wednesday, August 8, 2018
Southern Vipers won by 16 runs

Toss won by Yorkshire   Southern Vipers 4 points, Yorkshire 0 points

SOUTHERN VIPERS

* S W Bates, run out (Brunt)		27
T T Beaumont, c Brookes b Davidson-Richards		64
A C Kerr, c Kimmince b Levick		7
M du Preez, b Brookes		12
S J McGlashan, run out (Athapaththu/Kimmince)		2
M E Bouchier, st Mooney b Levick		6
P J Schofield, not out		22
F M K Morris, b Levick		3
C E Dean, not out		2
§ C E Rudd		
L K Bell	Did not bat	
Extras b 1, lb 5, w 8		14
Total (7 wkts, 20 overs)		159

FoW: 1-66 (Bates), 2-94 (Kerr), 3-111 (Beaumont), 4-116 (McGlashan), 5-125 (du Preez), 6-134 (Bouchier), 7-144 (Morris)

	O	M	R	W
Brunt	2	0	16	0
Langston	2	0	21	0
Athapaththu	1	0	17	0
Davidson-Richards	4	0	25	1
Kimmince	4	0	18	0
Levick	4	0	35	3
Fenby	2	0	17	0
Brookes	1	0	4	1

YORKSHIRE

§ B L Mooney, c Rudd b Kerr		10
A N Davidson-Richards, st Rudd b Kerr		29
C Athapaththu, c Bouchier b Bates		4
T F Brookes, c Bates b Schofiield		45
D M Kimmince, run out (Bates)		20
* K H Brunt, st Rudd b Bates		20
B A Langston, b Morris		5
G M Davies, not out		3
B A M Heath, c Kerr b Bates		0
K A Levick, c Bouchier b Bates		0
H L Fenby, run out (du Preez/Bates)		0
Extras lb 4, w 2, nb 1		7
Total (19.5 overs)		143

FoW: 1-11 (Mooney), 2-15 (Athapaththu), 3-76 (Brookes), 4-97 (Davidson-Richards), 5-130 (Brunt), 6-140 (Kimmince), 7-140 (Langston), 8-141 (Heath), 9-142 (Levick), 10-143 (Fenby)

	O	M	R	W
Bell	3	0	17	0
Kerr	4	0	22	2
Morris	4	0	29	1
Bates	3.5	0	26	4
Schofield	3	0	25	1
Dean	2	0	20	0
Kimmince	2	0	13	0

Player of the Match: TT Beaumont

Umpires: R T Robinson, N L Bainton, G D Lloyd (TV)

Scorers: K N Hutchinson and K Rouse

Kia Super League
Yorkshire Diamonds v. Surrey Stars

Played at York Cricket Club on Sunday, August 12, 2018

Yorkshire Diamonds won by nine wickets (with 63 balls remaining)

Toss won by Yorkshire   Yorkshire 5 points, Surrey 0 points

SURREY

L Lee, c Athapaththu b Davidson-Richards	13
B F Smith, b Brunt	1
M Kapp, c Davies b Kimmince	13
* N R Sciver, lbw b Kimmince	5
S R Dunkley-Brown, c Mooney b Langston	2
L A Marsh, b Levick	8
A Cranstone, b Levick	9
M K Villiers, b Langston	2
H V Jones, not out	2
E Gray, run out (Brunt)	1
§ R Southby, c Mooney b Langston	0
Extras b 1, lb 6, w 3	10
Total (16.4 overs)	66

FoW: 1-2 (Smith), 2-33 (Kapp), 3-34 (Lee), 4-41 (Sciver), 5-41 (Dunkley-Brown), 6-60 (Cranstone), 7-63 (Villiers), 8-65 (Marsh), 9-66 (Gray), 10-66 (Southby)

	O	M	R	W
Fenby	2	0	11	0
Brunt	3	1	5	1
Langston	3.4	0	14	3
Davidson-Richards	3	0	9	1
Kimmince	3	0	14	2
Levick	2	0	6	2

YORKSHIRE

* L Winfield, c Dunkley-Brown b Marsh		14
§ B L Mooney, not out		44
T F Brookes, not out		1
C Athapaththu		
A N Davidson-Richards		
D M Kimmince		
K H Brunt	Did not bat	
B A Langston		
G M Davies		
K A Levick		
H L Fenby		
Extras lb 1, w 7		8
Total (1 wkt, 9.3 overs)		67

FoW: 1-55 (Winfield)

	O	M	R	W
Kapp	3	0	14	0
Sciver	2	0	26	0
Marsh	3	0	20	1
Gray	1.3	0	6	0

Umpires: J D Middlebrook and S Redfern   Scorers: K N Hutchinson and S E Robinson

Kia Super League
Lancashire Thunder v. Yorkshire Diamonds

Played at Stanley Park, Blackpool, on Tuesday, August 14, 2018
Lancashire Thunder won by 9 runs

Toss won by Yorkshire

Lancashire 4 points, Yorkshire 0 points

LANCASHIRE

N E Bolton, c Levick b Brunt		46
G E B Boyce, c Davidson-Richards b Brunt		11
A E Satterthwaite, b Langston		7
H Kaur, c Davies b Brunt		74
§ E Threlkeld, c Brookes b Langston		3
E L Lamb, lbw b Levick		0
E Jones, c Davies b Levick		10
* D Hazell, run out (Davidson-Richards/Levick)		0
S Ecclestone, run out (Mooney/Brunt)		0
K L Cross, not out		0
A Hartley, not out		0
Extras lb 1, w 2		3
Total (9 wkts, 20 overs)		154

FoW: 1-26 (Boyce), 2-43 (Satterthwaite), 3-96 (Bolton), 4-116 (Threlkeld), 5-116 (Lamb), 6-130 (Jones), 7-137 (Hazell), 8-151 (Ecclestone), 9-154 (Kaur).

	O	M	R	W
Fenby	1	0	14	0
Brunt	4	0	22	3
Langston	4	0	12	2
Athapaththu	2	0	16	0
Kimmince	4	0	38	0
Davidson-Richards	2	0	26	0
Levick	3	0	25	2

YORKSHIRE

* L Winfield, lbw b Cross		2
§ B L Mooney, lbw b Hazell		25
T F Brookes, c Ecclestone b Hartley		22
C Athapaththu, c Satterthwaite b Hartley		9
A N Davidson-Richards, b Satterthwaite		33
K H Brunt, not out		44
D M Kimmince, c Cross b Ecclestone		2
B A Langston, run out (Cross)		0
G M Davies, run out (Cross/Satterthwaite)		4
K A Levick, not out		0
H Fenby	Did not bat	
Extras b 1, lb 1, w 2		4
Total (8 wkts, 20 overs)		145

FoW: 1-2 (Winfield), 2-49 (Brookes), 3-52 (Mooney), 4-70 (Athapaththu), 5-131 (Davidson-Richards), 6-134 (Kimmince), 7-136 (Langston), 8-142 (Davies).

	O	M	R	W
Cross	3	0	25	1
Lamb	3	0	29	0
Ecclestone	4	1	17	1
Hazell	3	0	25	1
Hartley	4	0	27	2
Satterthwaite	3	0	20	1

Umpires: J D Middlebrook and R A White   Scorers: M Cregan and K N Hutchinson

Kia Super League
Yorkshire Diamonds v. Loughborough Lightning

Played at Emerald Headingley, Leeds, on Saturday, August 18, 2018 *(Day/Night)*
Yorkshire Diamonds won by 3 runs

Toss won by Yorkshire   Yorkshire 4 points, Loughborough 0 points

YORKSHIRE

* L Winfield, b Smith		8
§ B L Mooney, c Haynes b Gordon		76
B A M Heath, c Jones b Gunn		24
T F Brookes, st Jones b Gordon		1
D M Kimmince, b Smith		2
A N Davidson-Richards, st Jones b Devine		11
B A Langston, not out		15
A Z Monaghan, not out		0
S Munro		
K A Levick	Did not bat	
K C Thompson		
Extras lb 3, w 8		11
Total (6 wkts, 20 overs)		148

FoW: 1-19 (Winfield), 2-84 (Heath), 3-97 (Brookes), 4-111 (Kimmince), 5-119 (Mooney), 6-146 (Davidson-Richards)

	O	M	R	W
Gunn	4	0	32	1
Devine	3	0	25	1
Smith	4	0	18	2
Elwiss	4	0	29	0
Gordon	4	0	29	2
Higham	1	0	12	0

LOUGHBOROUGH

R L Haynes, c Monaghan b Davidson-Richards		47
S F M Devine, c Dimmince b Brookes		22
§ A E Jones, c Winfield b Thompson		13
E J Villani, st Mooney b Thompson		26
* G A Elwiss, c Dimmince b Brookes		6
G L Adams, not out		7
J L Gunn, c Mooney b Davidson-Richards		4
L F Higham, not out		9
S Glenn		
K L Gordon	Did not bat	
L C N Smith		
Extras b 1, w 10		11
Total (6 wkts, 20 overs)		145

FoW: 1-30 (Devine), 2-83 (Jones), 3-95 (Haynes), 4-122 (Villani), 5-128 (Elwiss), 6-134 (Gunn)

	O	M	R	W
Thompson	4	0	18	2
Langston	3	0	29	0
Brookes	4	0	23	2
Levick	4	0	33	0
Kimmince	2	0	24	0
Davidson-Richards	3	0	17	2

Umpires: J D Middlebrook and T J Lungley   Scorers: K N Hutchinson and K Gerrard

KIA SUPER LEAGUE 2018

YORKSHIRE DIAMONDS AVERAGES

Played 9   Won 3   Lost 6   Abandoned 1

BATTING AND FIELDING

Player	M	I	N.O.	Runs	H.S.	50s	Avge	S.R	ct/st
B L Mooney	9	9	1	267	76	2	33.37	138.34	5/3
K H Brunt	7	6	2	1100	44*	0	27.50	120.87	0
L Winfield	8	8	0	2050	64	1	25.62	119.88	5
T F Brookes	9	8	2	1390	45	0	23.16	120.86	2
A N Davidson-Richards	9	8	1	1480	33	0	21.14	96.10	3
D M Kimmince	9	8	2	1070	55*	1	17.83	117.58	5
B A Langston	9	6	2	510	16	0	12.75	108.51	1
C Athapaththu	8	7	0	850	43	0	12.14	96.59	2
B A M Heath	2	2	0	240	24	0	12.00	77.41	0
G M Davies	6	2	1	70	4	0	07.00	116.66	3
A Z Monaghan	4	3	1	20	1	0	01.00	25.00	2
H L Fenby	8	3	1	10	1*	0	00.50	20.00	1
K A Levick	9	4	2	10	1*	0	00.50	11.11	1
S Munro	1	0	0	0	0	0	—	—	0
K C Thompson	1	0	0	0	—	0	—	—	0

BOWLING

Player	Overs	Mdns	Runs	Wkts	Avge	Best	4wI	Econ
T F Brookes	5	0	27	3	9.00	2-23	0	5.40
K C Thompson	4	0	18	2	9.00	2-18	0	4.50
K H Brunt	24.2	1	132	10	13.20	5-26	1	5.42
K A Levick	30	0	210	11	19.09	3-35	0	7.00
A N Davidson-Richards	29.3	0	220	10	22.00	2-15	0	7.45
B A Langston	24.4	0	190	7	27.14	3-14	0	7.70
C Athapaththu	14	0	122	3	40.66	1-15	0	8.71
D Kimmince	22	0	204	2	102.00	2-14	0	9.27
H L Fenby	18	1	156	1	156.00	1-38	0	8.66

RECORDS SECTION

All records in this section relate to First-Class Yorkshire matches except where stated

HONOURS

County Champions (34)
1867, 1870, 1893, 1896, 1898, 1900, 1901, 1902, 1905, 1908, 1912, 1919,
1922, 1923, 1924, 1925, 1931, 1932, 1933, 1935, 1937, 1938, 1939,
1946, 1959, 1960, 1962, 1963, 1966, 1967, 1968, 2001, 2014, 2015

Joint Champions (2)
1869, 1949

Promoted to Division 1
2005, 2012

Gillette Cup Winners (2)
1965, 1969

Cheltenham & Gloucester Trophy (1)
2002

Benson & Hedges Cup Winners (1)
1987

John Player Special League Winners (1)
1983

Fenner Trophy Winners (3)
1972, 1974, 1981

Asda Challenge Winners (1)
1987

Ward Knockout Cup (1)
1989

Joshua Tetley Festival Trophy (7)
1991, 1992 (Joint), 1993, 1994, 1996, 1997 and 1998

Tilcon Trophy Winners (2)
1978 and 1988

Pro-Arch Trophy (1)
2007-08

Emirates Airlines T20 (2)
2015 and 2016

Second Eleven Champions (4)
1977, 1984, 1991, 2003

Joint Champions (1)
1987

Minor Counties Champions (5)
1947, 1957, 1958, 1968, 1971

Under-25 Competition Winners (3)
1976, 1978, 1987

Bain Clarkson Trophy Winners (2)
1988 and 1994

Second Eleven Trophy (1)
2009

YORKSHIRE'S CHAMPIONSHIP CAPTAINS

1867 to 2018

* R Iddison (2)	1867, 1870
Lord Hawke (8)	1893, 1896, 1898, 1900, 1901, 1902, 1905, 1908
Sir Archibald White (1)	1912
D C F Burton (1)	1919
G Wilson (3)	1922, 1923, 1924
A W Lupton (1)	1925
F E Greenwood (2)	1931, 1932
A B Sellers (6)	1933, 1935, 1937, 1938, 1939, 1946
J R Burnet (1)	1959
J V Wilson (2)	1960, 1962
D B Close (4)	1963, 1966, 1967, 1968
D Byas (1)	2001
A W Gale (2)	2014, 2015

Joint Champions

* R Iddison (1)	1869
N W D Yardley (1)	1949

* R Iddison was captain when Yorkshire were Champion county, the County Championship starting in 1890.

RECORDS SECTION INDEX

CHAMPION COUNTIES SINCE 1873

The County Championship

The County Championship was officially constituted in 1890, and before that Yorkshire were generally considered Champions by the Press in 1867 and 1870, and equal top in 1869. From 1873 the list was generally accepted in the form as it is today.

		Yorkshire's Position
1873	{ Gloucestershire { Nottinghamshire	. . . . .7th
1874	Gloucestershire	4th
1875	Nottinghamshire	4th
1876	Gloucestershire	3rd
1877	Gloucestershire	7th
1878	Middlesex	6th
1879	Nottinghamshire/Lancashire	6th
1880	Nottinghamshire	5th
1881	Lancashire	3rd
1882	Nottinghamshire/Lancashire	3rd
1883	Nottinghamshire	2nd
1884	Nottinghamshire	3rd
1885	Nottinghamshire	2nd
1886	Nottinghamshire	4th
1887	Surrey	3rd
1888	Surrey	2nd
1889	{ Surrey/Lancashire { Nottinghamshire	. . . . .7th
1890	Surrey	3rd
1891	Surrey	8th
1892	Surrey	6th
1893	**Yorkshire**	**1st**
1894	Surrey	2nd
1895	Surrey	3rd
1896	**Yorkshire**	**1st**
1897	Lancashire	4th
1898	**Yorkshire**	**1st**
1899	Surrey	3rd
1900	**Yorkshire**	**1st**
1901	**Yorkshire**	**1st**
1902	**Yorkshire**	**1st**
1903	Middlesex	3rd
1904	Lancashire	2nd
1905	**Yorkshire**	**1st**
1906	Kent	2nd
1907	Nottinghamshire	2nd
1908	**Yorkshire**	**1st**

		Yorkshire's Position
1909	Kent	3rd
1910	Kent	8th
1911	Warwickshire	7th
1912	**Yorkshire**	**1st**
1913	Kent	2nd
1914	Surrey	4th
1919	**Yorkshire**	**1st**
1920	Middlesex	4th
1921	Middlesex	3rd
1922	**Yorkshire**	**1st**
1923	**Yorkshire**	**1st**
1924	**Yorkshire**	**1st**
1925	**Yorkshire**	**1st**
1926	Lancashire	2nd
1927	Lancashire	3rd
1928	Lancashire	4th
1929	Nottinghamshire	2nd
1930	Lancashire	3rd
1931	**Yorkshire**	**1st**
1932	**Yorkshire**	**1st**
1933	**Yorkshire**	**1st**
1934	Lancashire	5th
1935	**Yorkshire**	**1st**
1936	Derbyshire	3rd
1937	**Yorkshire**	**1st**
1938	**Yorkshire**	**1st**
1939	**Yorkshire**	**1st**
1946	**Yorkshire**	**1st**
1947	Middlesex	7th
1948	Glamorgan	4th
1949	**Yorkshire/Middlesex**	**1st**
1950	Lancashire/Surrey	3rd
1951	Warwickshire	2nd
1952	Surrey	2nd
1953	Surrey	12th
1954	Surrey	2nd
1955	Surrey	2nd
1956	Surrey	7th
1957	Surrey	3rd

CHAMPION COUNTIES SINCE 1873 *(Continued)*

	County	*Yorkshire's Position*		County	*Yorkshire's Position*
1958	Surrey	11th	1989	Worcestershire	16th
1959	**Yorkshire**	**1st**	1990	Middlesex	10th
1960	**Yorkshire**	**1st**	1991	Essex	14th
1961	Hampshire	2nd	1992	Essex	16th
1962	**Yorkshire**	**1st**	1993	Middlesex	12th
1963	**Yorkshire**	**1st**	1994	Warwickshire	13th
1964	Worcestershire	5th	1995	Warwickshire	8th
1965	Worcestershire	4th	1996	Leicestershire	6th
1966	**Yorkshire**	**1st**	1997	Glamorgan	6th
1967	**Yorkshire**	**1st**	1998	Leicestershire	3rd
1968	**Yorkshire**	**1st**	1999	Surrey	6th
1969	Glamorgan	13th	2000	Surrey	3rd
1970	Kent	4th	**2001**	**Yorkshire**	**1st**
1971	Surrey	13th	2002	Surrey	9th
1972	Warwickshire	10th	2003	Sussex	Div 2, 4th
1973	Hampshire	14th	2004	Warwickshire	Div 2, 7th
1974	Worcestershire	11th	2005	Nottinghamshire	Div 2, 3rd
1975	Leicestershire	2nd	2006	Sussex	Div 1, 6th
1976	Middlesex	8th	2007	Sussex	Div 1, 6th
1977	Kent/Middlesex	12th	2008	Durham	Div 1, 7th
1978	Kent	4th	2009	Durham	Div 1, 7th
1979	Essex	7th	2010	Nottinghamshire	Div 1, 3rd
1980	Middlesex	6th	2011	Lancashire	Div 1, 8th
1981	Nottinghamshire	10th	2012	Warwickshire	Div 2, 2nd
1982	Middlesex	10th	2013	Durham	Div 1, 2nd
1983	Essex	17th	**2014**	**Yorkshire**	**Div 1, 1st**
1984	Essex	14th	**2015**	**Yorkshire**	**Div 1, 1st**
1985	Middlesex	11th	2016	Middlesex	Div 1, 3rd
1986	Essex	10th	2017	Essex	Div 1, 4th
1987	Nottinghamshire	8th	2018	Surrey	Div 1, 4th
1988	Worcestershire	13th			

SEASON-BY-SEASON RECORD OF ALL FIRST-CLASS
MATCHES PLAYED BY YORKSHIRE 1863-2018

Season	Played	Won	Lost	Drawn	Abd§	Season	Played	Won	Lost	Drawn	Abd§
1863	4	2	1	1	0	1921	30	17	5	8	0
1864	7	2	4	1	0	1922	33	20	2	11	0
1865	9	0	7	2	0	1923	35	26	1	8	0
1866	3	0	2	1	0	1924	35	18	4	13	0
1867	7	7	0	0	0	1925	36	22	0	14	0
1868	7	4	3	0	0	1926	35	14	0	21	1
1869	5	4	1	0	0	1927	34	11	3	20	1
1870	7	6	0	1	0	1928	32	9	0	23	0
1871	7	3	3	1	0	1929	35	11	2	22	0
1872	10	2	7	1	0	1930	34	13	3	18	2
1873	13	7	5	1	0	1931	33	17	1	15	1
1874	14	10	3	1	0	1932	32	21	2	9	2
1875	12	6	4	2	0	1933	36	21	5	10	0
1876	12	5	3	4	0	1934	35	14	7	14	0
1877	14	2	7	5	0	1935	36	24	2	10	0
1878	20	10	7	3	0	1935-6	3	1	0	2	0
1879	17	7	5	5	0	1936	35	14	2	19	0
1880	20	6	8	6	0	1937	34	22	3	9	1
1881	20	11	6	3	0	1938	36	22	2	12	0
1882	24	11	9	4	0	1939	34	23	4	7	1
1883	19	10	2	7	0	1945	2	0	0	2	0
1884	20	10	6	4	0	1946	31	20	1	10	0
1885	21	8	3	10	0	1947	32	10	9	13	0
1886	21	5	8	8	0	1948	31	11	6	14	0
1887	20	6	5	9	0	1949	33	16	3	14	0
1888	20	7	7	6	0	1950	34	16	6	12	1
1889	16	3	11	2	1	1951	35	14	3	18	0
1890	20	10	4	6	0	1952	34	17	3	14	0
1891	17	5	11	1	2	1953	35	7	7	21	0
1892	19	6	6	7	0	1954	35	16	3	16*	0
1893	23	15	5	3	0	1955	33	23	6	4	0
1894	28	18	6	4	1	1956	35	11	7	17	0
1895	31	15	10	6	0	1957	34	16	5	13	1
1896	32	17	6	9	0	1958	33	10	8	15	2
1897	30	14	7	9	0	1959	35	18	8	9	0
1898	30	18	3	9	0	1960	38	19	7	12	0
1899	34	17	4	13	0	1961	39	19	5	15	0
1900	32	19	1	12	0	1962	37	16	5	16	0
1901	35	23	2	10	1	1963	33	14	4	15	0
1902	31	15	3	13	1	1964	33	12	4	17	0
1903	31	16	5	10	0	1965	33	12	4	17	0
1904	32	10	2	20	1	1966	32	16	6	10	1
1905	33	21	4	8	0	1967	31	16	5	10	2
1906	33	19	6	8	0	1968	32	13	4	15	0
1907	31	14	5	12	2	1969	29	4	7	18	0
1908	33	19	0	14	0	1970	26	10	5	11	0
1909	30	12	5	13	0	1971	27	5	8	14	0
1910	31	11	8	12	0	1972	21	4	5	12	1
1911	32	16	9	7	0	1973	22	3	5	14*	0
1912	35	14	3	18	1	1974	22	6	7	9	1
1913	32	16	5	11	0	1975	21	11	1	9	0
1914	31	16	4	11	2	1976	22	7	7	8	0
1919	31	12	5	14	0	1977	23	7	5	11	1
1920	30	17	6	7	0	1978	24	10	3	11	1

Season	Played	Won	Lost	Drawn	Abd§	Season	Played	Won	Lost	Drawn	Abd§
1979	22	6	3	13	1	1998	19	9	3	7	0
1980	24	5	4	15	0	1999	17	8	6	3	0
1981	24	5	9	10	0	2000	18	7	4	7	0
1982	22	5	1	16	1	2001	16	9	3	4	0
1983	23	1	5	17	1	2002	16	2	8	6	0
1984	24	5	4	15	0	2003	17	4	5	8	0
1985	25	3	4	18	1	2004	16	3	4	9	0
1986	25	4	6	15	0	2005	17	6	1	10	0
1986-7	1	0	0	1	0	2006	16	3	6	7	0
1987	24	7	4	13	1	2007	17	5	4	8	0
1988	24	5	6	13	0	2008	16	2	5	9	0
1989	22	3	9	10	0	2009	17	2	2	13	0
1990	24	5	9	10	0	2010	18	6	2	10	0
1991	24	4	6	14	0	2011	17	4	6	7	0
1991-2	1	0	1	0	0	2012	17	5	0	12	0
1992	22	4	6	12	1	2013	17	8	2	7	0
1992-3	1	0	0	1	0	2014	17	8	1	8	0
1993	19	6	4	9	0	2015	18	12	1	5	0
1994	20	7	6	7	0	2016	18	5	4	9	0
1995	20	8	8	4	0	2017	15	5	5	5	0
1995-6	2	2	0	0	0	2018	13	5	5	3	2
1996	19	8	5	6	0						
1997	20	7	4	9	0		3630	1526	663	1441	40

* Includes one tie each season

§ All these matches were abandoned without a ball being bowled, except Yorkshire v Kent at Harrogate, 1904, which was abandoned under Law 9. The two in 1914 and the one in 1939 were abandoned because of war. The four-day match, Yorkshire v. Essex at Leeds in 2018, was abandoned without a ball bowled, but each side received 5 points. All these matches are excluded from the total played. Of the 1,526 matches won 521 have been by an innings margin, 88 by 200 runs or more, and 134 by 10 wickets. Of the 663 lost 113 have been by an innings margin, 15 by 200 runs or more and 35 by 10 wickets.

ANALYSIS OF RESULTS VERSUS ALL FIRST-CLASS
TEAMS 1863-2018

COUNTY CHAMPIONSHIP

Opponents	Played	Won	Lost	Drawn	Tied
Derbyshire	205	103	19	83	0
Durham	36	16	8	12	0
Essex	163	85	27	51	0
Glamorgan	111	53	13	45	0
Gloucestershire	200	102	43	55	0
Hampshire	173	74	20	79	0
Kent	200	84	39	77	0
Lancashire	261	79	52	130	0
Leicestershire	166	84	15	66	1
Middlesex	235	82	59	93	1
Northamptonshire	142	67	26	49	0
Nottinghamshire	256	92	47	117	0
Somerset	177	91	26	60	0
Surrey	246	86	69	91	0
Sussex	199	85	33	81	0
Warwickshire	192	87	31	74	0
Worcestershire	142	71	22	49	0
Cambridgeshire	8	3	4	1	0
Total	3112	1344	553	1213	2

ANALYSIS OF RESULTS VERSUS ALL FIRST-CLASS
TEAMS 1863-2018 *(continued.)*

OTHER FIRST-CLASS MATCHES

Opponents	Played	Won	Lost	Drawn	Tied
Derbyshire	2	1	1	0	0
Essex	2	2	0	0	0
Hampshire	1	0	0	1	0
Lancashire	12	5	3	4	0
Leicestershire	2	1	1	0	0
Middlesex	1	1	0	0	0
Nottinghamshire	2	1	1	0	0
Surrey	1	0	0	1	0
Sussex	2	0	0	2	0
Warwickshire	2	0	0	2	0
Totals	27	11	6	10	0
Australians	55	6	19	30	0
Indians	14	5	1	8	0
New Zealanders	10	2	0	8	0
Pakistanis	4	1	0	3	0
South Africans	17	1	3	13	0
Sri Lankans	3	0	0	3	0
West Indians	17	3	7	7	0
Zimbabweans	2	0	1	1	0
Bangladesh A	1	1	0	0	0
India A	2	0	0	2	0
Pakistan A	2	1	0	1	0
South Africa A	1	0	0	1	0
Totals	128	20	31	77	0
Cambridge University/U C C E	88	42	17	29	0
Canadians	1	1	0	0	0
Combined Services	1	0	0	1	0
Durham MCCU	1	1	0	0	0
England XI's	6	1	2	3	0
Hon. M.B. Hawke's XI	1	0	1	0	0
International XI	1	1	0	0	0
Ireland	3	3	0	0	0
Jamaica	3	1	0	2	0
Leeds/Bradford MCCU	5	2	0	3	0
Liverpool and District*	3	2	1	0	0
Loughborough UCCE	2	1	0	1	0
MCC	155	55	40	60	0
Mashonaland	1	1	0	0	0
Matebeleland	1	1	0	0	0
Minor Counties	1	1	0	0	0
Oxford University	44	21	3	20	0
Philadelphians	1	0	0	1	0
Rest of England	16	4	5	7	0
Royal Air Force	1	0	0	1	0
Scotland**	11	7	0	4	0
South of England	2	1	0	1	0
C. I. Thornton's XI	5	2	0	3	0
United South of England	1	1	0	0	0
Western Province	2	0	1	1	0
Windward Islands	1	0	0	1	0
I Zingari	6	2	3	1	0
Totals	363	151	73	139	0
Grand Totals	3630	1526	663	1439	2

*Matches played in 1889, 1891, 1892 and 1893 are excluded. **Match played in 1878 is included

ABANDONED MATCHES (40)

1889	v. MCC at Lord's
1891 (2)	v. MCC at Lord's
	v. MCC at Scarborough
1894	v. Kent at Bradford
1901	v. Surrey at The Oval
1902	v. Leicestershire at Leicester (AR)
1904	v. Kent at Harrogate (Law 9
	— now Law 10)
1907 (2)	v. Derbyshire at Sheffield
	v. Nottinghamshire at Huddersfield
1912	v. Surrey at Sheffield
1914 (2)	v. England at Harrogate (due to war)
	v. MCC at Scarborough (due to war)
1926	v. Nottinghamshire at Leeds
1927	v. Kent at Bradford
1930 (2)	v. Derbyshire at Chesterfield*
	v. Northamptonshire at Harrogate*
1931	v. Sussex at Hull
1932 (2)	v. Derbyshire at Chesterfield
	v. Kent at Sheffield
1937	v. Cambridge University at Bradford
1939	v. MCC at Scarborough (due to war)
1950	v. Cambridge University at Cambridge
1957	v. West Indians at Bradford
1958 (2)	v. Nottinghamshire at Hull
	v. Worcestershire at Bradford
1966	v. Oxford University at Oxford
1967 (2)	v. Leicestershire at Leeds
	v. Lancashire at Manchester
1972	v. Australians at Bradford
1974	v. Hampshire at Bournemouth
1977	v. Gloucestershire at Bristol
1978	v. Pakistan at Bradford
1979	v. Nottinghamshire at Sheffield (AP)
1982	v. Nottinghamshire at Harrogate
1983	v. Middlesex at Lord's
1985	v. Essex at Sheffield (AP)
1987	v. Sussex at Hastings
1992	v. Oxford University at Oxford
2018	v. Leeds/Bradford MCCU at Leeds
2018	v. Essex at Leeds

*Consecutive matches

ANALYSIS OF RESULTS ON GROUNDS IN YORKSHIRE USED IN 2018

FIRST-CLASS MATCHES

Ground	Played	Won	Lost	Drawn	Tied
Leeds Headingley 1891-2018	462	176 (38.10%)	81 (17.53%)	205 (44.37%)	0 (0.00%)
Scarborough North Marine Road 1874-2018	257	103 (40.08%)	40 (15.56%)	114 (44.36%)	0 (0.00%)

HIGHEST MATCH AGGREGATES – OVER 1350 RUNS

Runs	Wkts	
1665	33	Yorkshire (351 and 481) lost to Warwickshire (601:9 dec and 232:4) by 6 wkts at Birmingham, 2002
1606	31	Yorkshire (438 and 363:5 dec) lost to Somerset (326 and 479:6) by 4 wkts at Taunton, 2009
1479	28	Yorkshire (405 and 333:4 dec) lost to Somerset (377 and 364:4) by 6 wkts at Taunton , 2010
1473	17	Yorkshire (600:4 dec. and 231:3 dec.) drew with Worcestershire (453:5 dec. and 189:5) at Scarborough, 1995.
1442	29	Yorkshire (501:6 dec. and 244:6 dec.) beat Lancashire (403:7 dec. and 294) by 48 runs at Scarborough, 1991.
1439	32	Yorkshire (536:8 dec. and 205:7 dec.) beat Glamorgan (482: 7 dec. and 216) by 43 runs at Cardiff, 1996.
1431	32	Yorkshire (388 and 312:6) drew with Sussex (398 and 333:6 dec) at Scarborough, 2011
1417	33	Yorkshire (422 and 193:7) drew with Glamorgan (466 and 336:6 dec) at Colwyn Bay, 2003
1406	37	Yorkshire (354 and 341:8) drew with Derbyshire (406 and 305:9 dec) at Derby, 2004
1400	32	Yorkshire (299 and 439: 4 dec.) drew with Hampshire (296 and 366:8) at Southampton, 2007
1393	35	Yorkshire (331 and 278) lost to Kent (377 and 407:5 dec) by 175 runs at Maidstone, 1994.
1390	34	Yorkshire (431:8 dec and 265:7) beat Hampshire (429 and 265) by 3 wkts at Southampton, 1995.
1390	33	Durham (573 and 124-3) beat Yorkahire (274 and 419) by 7 wkts at Scarborough, 2013.
1376	33	Yorkshire (531 and 158:3) beat Lancashire (373 and 314) by 7 wkts at Leeds, 2001
1376	20	Yorkshire (677: 7 dec.) drew with Durham (518 and 181:3 dec.) at Leeds, 2006
1374	36	Yorkshire (594: 9 dec. and 266:7 dec.) beat Surrey (344 and 170) by 346 runs at The Oval, 2007
1373	36	Yorkshire (520 and 114:6) drew with Derbyshire (216 and 523) at Derby, 2005
1364	35	Yorkshire (216 and 433) lost to Warwickshire (316 and 399:5 dec.) by 66 runs at Birmingham, 2006
1359	25	Yorkshire (561 and 138:3 dec.) drew with Derbyshire (412:4 dec. and 248:8) at Sheffield, 1996.
1359	30	Yorkshire (358 and 321) lost to Somerset (452 and 228:0) by 10 wkts at Taunton, 2011
1353	18	Yorkshire (377:2 dec. and 300:6) beat Derbyshire (475:7 dec. and 201:3 dec.) by 4 wkts at Scarborough, 1990.

LOWEST MATCH AGGREGATES – UNDER 225 RUNS
IN A COMPLETED MATCH

Runs	Wkts	
165	30	Yorkshire (46 and 37:0) beat Nottinghamshire (24 and 58 by 10 wkts at Sheffield, 1888.
175	29	Yorkshire (104) beat Essex (30 and 41) by an innings and 33 runs at Leyton, 1901.
182	15	Yorkshire (4:0 dec. and 88.5) beat Northamptonshire (4:0 dec. and 86) by 5 wkts at Bradford, 1931.
193	29	Yorkshire (99) beat Worcestershire (43 and 51) by an innings and 5 runs at Bradford, 1900.
219	30	Yorkshire (113) beat Nottinghamshire (71 and 35) by an innings and 7 runs at Nottingham, 1881.
222	32	Yorkshire (98 and 14:2) beat Gloucestershire (68 and 42) by 8 wkts at Gloucester, 1924.
223	40	Yorkshire (58 and 51) lost to Lancashire (64 and 50)

LOWEST MATCH AGGREGATES – UNDER 325 RUNS
IN A MATCH IN WHICH ALL 40 WICKETS FELL

Runs	Wkts	
223	40	Yorkshire (58 and 51) lost to Lancashire (64 and 50) by 5 runs at Manchester, 1893.
288	40	Yorkshire (55 and 68) lost to Lancashire (89 and 76) by 42 runs at Sheffield, 1872.
295	40	Yorkshire (71 and 63) lost to Surrey (56 and 105) by 27 runs at The Oval, 1886.
303	40	Yorkshire (109 and 77) beat Middlesex (63 and 54) by 69 runs at Lord's, 1891.
318	40	Yorkshire (96 and 96) beat Lancashire (39 and 87) by 66 runs at Manchester, 1874.
318	40	Yorkshire (94 and 104) beat Northamptonshire (61 and 59) by 78 runs at Bradford, 1955.
319	40	Yorkshire (84 and 72) lost to Derbyshire (106 and 57) by 7 runs at Derby, 1878.
320	40	Yorkshire (98 and 91) beat Surrey (72 and 59) by 58 runs at Sheffield, 1893.
321	40	Yorkshire (88 and 37) lost to I Zingari (103 and 93) by 71 runs at Scarborough, 1877.
321	40	Yorkshire (80 and 67) lost to Derbyshire (129 and 45) by 27 runs at Sheffield, 1879.

LARGE MARGINS OF VICTORY – BY AN INNINGS
AND OVER 250 RUNS

Inns and 397 runs	Yorkshire (548:4 dec.) beat Northamptonshire (58 and 93) at Harrogate, 1921
Inns and 387 runs	Yorkshire (662) beat Derbyshire (118 and 157) at Chesterfield, 1898.
Inns and 343 runs	Yorkshire (673:8 dec) beat Northamptonshire (184 and 146) at Leeds, 2003
Inns and 321 runs	Yorkshire (437) beat Leicestershire (58 and 58) at Leicester, 1908.
Inns and 314 runs	Yorkshire (356:8 dec) beat Northamptonshire (27 and 15) at Northampton, 1908. (Yorkshire's first match v. Northamptonshire).
Inns and 313 runs	Yorkshire (555:1 dec) beat Essex (78 and 164) at Leyton, 1932.
Inns and 307 runs	Yorkshire (681:5 dec.) beat Sussex (164 and 210) at Sheffield, 1897.
Inns and 302 runs	Yorkshire (660) beat Leicestershire (165 and 193) at Leicester, 1896.
Inns and 301 runs	Yorkshire (499) beat Somerset (125 and 73) at Bath, 1899.
Inns and 294 runs	Yorkshire (425:7 dec.) beat Gloucestershire (47 and 84) at Bristol, 1964.

LARGE MARGINS OF VICTORY – BY AN INNINGS
AND OVER 250 RUNS *(Continued)*

Inns and 284 runs	Yorkshire (467:7 dec) beat Leicestershire (111 and 72) at Bradford, 1932.
Inns and 282 runs	Yorkshire (481:8 dec) beat Derbyshire (106 and 93) at Huddersfield, 1901.
Inns and 280 runs	Yorkshire (562) beat Leicestershire (164 and 118) at Dewsbury, 1903.
Inns and 271 runs	Yorkshire (460) beat Hampshire (128 and 61) at Hull, 1900.
Inns and 271 runs	Yorkshire (495:5 dec) beat Warwickshire (99 and 125) at Huddersfield, 1922.
Inns and 266 runs	Yorkshire (352) beat Cambridgeshire (40 and 46) at Hunslet, 1869.
Inns and 260 runs	Yorkshire (521: 7dec.) beat Worcestershire (129 and 132) at Leeds, 2007.
Inns and 258 runs	Yorkshire (404:2 dec) beat Glamorgan (78 and 68) at Cardiff, 1922. (Yorkshire's first match v. Glamorgan).
Inns and 256 runs	Yorkshire (486) beat Leicestershire (137 and 93) at Sheffield, 1895.
Inns and 251 runs	Yorkshire (550) beat Leicestershire (154 and 145) at Leicester, 1933.

LARGE MARGINS OF VICTORY – BY OVER 300 RUNS

389 runs	Yorkshire (368 and 280:1 dec) beat Somerset (125 and 134) at Bath, 1906.
370 runs	Yorkshire (194 and 274) beat Hampshire (62 and 36) at Leeds, 1904.
351 runs	Yorkshire (280 and 331) beat Northamptonshire (146 and 114) at Northampton, 1947.
346 runs	Yorkshire (594: 9 dec. and 266: 7 dec.) beat Surrey (344 and 179) at The Oval, 2007.
328 runs	Yorkshire (186 and 318:1 dec) beat Somerset (43 and 133) at Bradford, 1930.
328 runs	Yorkshire (280 and 277:7 dec) beat Glamorgan (104 and 105) at Swansea, 2001.
320 runs	Yorkshire (331 and 353:9 dec) beat Durham (150 and 214) at Chester-le-Street, 2004
308 runs	Yorkshire (89 and 420) beat Warwickshire (72 and 129) at Birmingham, 1921.
308 runs	Yorkshire (89 and 420) beat Warwickshire (72 and 129)
305 runs	Yorkshire (370 and 305:4 dec) beat Hampshire (227 and 143) at Leeds, 2015
305 runs	Yorkshire (282 and 263:4 dec) beat Nottinghamshire (94 and 146) at Scarborough 2016

LARGE MARGINS OF VICTORY – BY 10 WICKETS
(WITH OVER 100 RUNS SCORED IN THE 4th INNINGS)

4th Innings

167:0 wkt	Yorkshire (247 and 167:0) beat Northamptonshire 233 and 180) at Huddersfield, 1948.
147:0 wkt	Yorkshire (381 and 147:0) beat Middlesex (384 and 142) at Lord's, 1896.
142:0 wkt	Yorkshire (304 and 142:0) beat Sussex (254 and 188) at Bradford, 1887.
139:0 wkt	Yorkshire (163:9 dec and 139:0) beat Nottinghamshire (234 and 67) at Leeds, 1932.
138:0 wkt	Yorkshire (293 and 138:0) beat Hampshire (251 and 179) at Southampton, 1897.
132:0 wkt	Yorkshire (328 and 132:0) beat Northamptonshire (281 and 175) at Leeds, 2005
129:0 wkt	Yorkshire (355 and 129:0) beat Durham MCCU (196 and 287) at Durham, 2011
127:0 wkt	Yorkshire (258 and 127:0) beat Cambridge University (127 and 257) at Cambridge, 1930.
119:0 wkt	Yorkshire (109 and 119:0) beat Essex (108 and 119) at Leeds, 1931.
118:0 wkt	Yorkshire (121 and 118:0) beat MCC (125 and 113) at Lord's, 1883.
116:0 wkt	Yorkshire (147 and 116:0) beat Hampshire (141 and 120) at Bournemouth, 1930.
114:0 wkt	Yorkshire (135 and 114:0) beat Hampshire (71 and 176) at Bournemouth, 1948.
114:0 wkt	Yorkshire (135 and 114:0) beat Hampshire (71 and 176)
105:0 wkt	Yorkshire (307 and 105:0) beat Worcestershire (311 and 100) at Worcester, 2015

HEAVY DEFEATS – BY AN INNINGS
AND OVER 250 RUNS

Inns and 272 runs	Yorkshire (78 and 186) lost to Surrey (536) at The Oval, 1898.
Inns and 261 runs	Yorkshire (247 and 89) lost to Sussex (597: 8 dec.) at Hove, 2007.
Inns and 255 runs	Yorkshire (125 and 144) lost to All England XI (524) at Sheffield, 1865.

HEAVY DEFEATS – BY OVER 300 RUNS

376 runs	Essex (227 and 334-7 dec) defeated Yorkshire (111 and 74) at Chelmsford 2017
324 runs	Yorkshire (247 and 204) lost to Gloucestershire (291 and 484) at Cheltenham, 1994.
305 runs	Yorkshire (119 and 51) lost to Cambridge University (312 and 163) at Cambridge, 1906.

HEAVY DEFEATS – BY 10 WICKETS
(WITH OVER 100 RUNS SCORED IN THE 4th INNINGS)

4th Innings

228:0 wkt	Yorkshire (358 and 321) lost to Somerset (452 and 228:0) at Taunton, 2011
148:0 wkt	Yorkshire (83 and 216) lost to Lancashire (154 and 148:0) at Manchester, 1875.
119:0 wkt	Yorkshire (92 and 109) lost to Nottinghamshire (86 and 119:0 wkt) at Leeds, 1989.
108:0 wkt	Yorkshire (236 and 107) lost to Hampshire (236 and 108:0 wkt) at Southampton, 2008
100:0 wkt	Yorkshire (95 and 91) lost to Gloucestershire (88 and 100:0) at Bristol, 1956.

NARROW VICTORIES – BY 1 WICKET

Yorkshire (70 and 91:9) beat Cambridgeshire (86 and 74) at Wisbech, 1867.
Yorkshire (91 and 145:9) beat MCC (73 and 161) at Lord's, 1870.
Yorkshire (265 and 154:9) beat Derbyshire (234 and 184) at Derby, 1897.
Yorkshire (177 and 197:9) beat MCC (188 and 185) at Lord's, 1899.
Yorkshire (391 and 241:9) beat Somerset (349 and 281) at Taunton, 1901.
Yorkshire (239 and 168:9) beat MCC (179 and 226) at Scarborough, 1935.
Yorkshire (152 and 90:9) beat Worcestershire (119 and 121) at Leeds, 1946.
Yorkshire (229 and 175:9) beat Glamorgan (194 and 207) at Bradford, 1960.
Yorkshire (265.9 dec and 191:9) beat Worcestershire (227 and 227) at Worcester, 1961.
Yorkshire (329:6 dec and 167:9) beat Essex (339.9 dec and 154) at Scarborough, 1979.
Yorkshire (Innings forfeited and 251:9 beat Sussex (195 and 55.1 dec) at Leeds, 1986.
Yorkshire (314 and 150:9) beat Essex (200 and 261) at Scarborough, 1998.

NARROW VICTORIES – BY 5 RUNS OR LESS

By 1 run	Yorkshire (228 and 214) beat Middlesex (206 and 235) at Bradford, 1976.
By 1 run	Yorkshire (383 and inns forfeited) beat Loughborough UCCE (93: 3 dec. and 289) at Leeds, 2007.
By 2 runs	Yorkshire (108 and 122) beat Nottinghamshire (56 and 172) at Nottingham, 1870.
By 2 runs	Yorkshire (304:9 dec and 135) beat Middlesex (225:2 dec and 212) at Leeds, 1985.
By 3 runs	Yorkshire (446:9 dec and 172:4 dec) beat Essex (300:3 dec and 315) at Colchester, 1991.
By 3 runs	Yorkshire (202 and 283) beat Somerset (224 and 258) at Taunton, 2017
By 5 runs	Yorkshire (271 and 147:6 dec) beat Surrey (198 and 215) at Sheffield, 1950.
By 5 runs	Yorkshire (151 and 176) beat Hampshire (165 and 157) at Bradford, 1962.
By 5 runs	Yorkshire (376:4 and 106) beat Middlesex (325:8 and 152) at Lord's, 1975
By 5 runs	Yorkshire (323:5 dec and inns forfeited) beat Somerset (inns forfeited and 318) at Taunton, 1986.

NARROW DEFEATS – BY 1 WICKET

Yorkshire (224 and 210) lost to Australian Imperial Forces XI (265 and 170:9) at Sheffield, 1919
Yorkshire (101 and 159) lost to Warwickshire (45 and 216:9) at Scarborough, 1934.
Yorkshire (239 and 184:9 dec.) lost to Warwickshire (125 and 302:9) at Birmingham, 1983.
Yorkshire (289 and 153) lost to Surrey (250:2 dec and 193:9) at Guildford, 1991.
Yorkshire (341 and Inns forfeited) lost to Surrey (39:1 dec and 306:9) at Bradford, 1992.

NARROW DEFEATS – BY 5 RUNS OR LESS

By 1 run   Yorkshire (135 and 297) lost to Essex (139 and 294) at Huddersfield, 1897.
By 1 run   Yorkshire (159 and 232) lost to Gloucestershire (164 and 228) at Bristol, 1906.
By 1 run   Yorkshire (126 and 137) lost to Worcestershire (101 and 163)
            at Worcester, 1968.
By 1 run   Yorkshire (366 and 217) lost to Surrey (409 and 175) at The Oval, 1995.
By 2 runs   Yorkshire (172 and 107) lost to Gloucestershire (157 and 124)
            at Sheffield, 1913.
By 2 runs   Yorkshire (179:9 dec and 144) lost to MCC (109 and 216) at Lord's, 1957.
By 3 runs   Yorkshire (126 and 181) lost to Sussex (182 and 128) at Sheffield, 1883.
By 3 runs   Yorkshire (160 and 71) lost to Lancashire (81 and 153) at Huddersfield, 1889.
By 3 runs   Yorkshire (134 and 158) lost to Nottinghamshire (200 and 95) at Leeds, 1923.
By 4 runs   Yorkshire (169 and 193) lost to Middlesex (105 and 261) at Bradford, 1920.
By 5 runs   Yorkshire (58 and 51) lost to Lancashire (64 and 50) at Manchester, 1893.
By 5 runs   Yorkshire (119 and 115) lost to Warwickshire (167 and 72) at Bradford, 1969.

HIGH FOURTH INNINGS SCORES – 300 AND OVER

By Yorkshire

To Win: 406:4   beat Leicestershire by 6 wkts at Leicester, 2005
            402:6   beat Gloucestershire by 4 wkts at Bristol, 2012
            400:4   beat Leicestershire by 6 wkts at Scarborough, 2005
            339:6   beat Durham by 4 wkts at Chester-le-Street, 2013
            331:8   beat Middlesex by 2 wkts at Lord's, 1910.
            327:6   beat Nottinghamshire by 4 wkts at Nottingham, 1990.*
            323:5   beat Nottinghamshire by 5 wkts at Nottingham, 1977.
            318:3   beat Glamorgan by 7 wkts at Middlesbrough, 1976.
            316:8   beat Gloucestershire by 2 wkts at Scarborough, 2012
            309:7   beat Somerset by 3 wkts at Taunton, 1984.
            305:8   beat Nottinghamshire by 2 wkts at Worksop, 1982.
            305:5   beat Hampshire by 5 wkts at West End, Southampton, 2015
            305:3   beat Lancashire by 7 wkts at Manchester, 1994.
            304:4   beat Derbyshire by 6 wkts at Chesterfield, 1959.
            300:4   beat Derbyshire by 6 wkts at Chesterfield, 1981.
            300:6   beat Derbyshire by 6 wkts at Scarborough, 1990.*

To Draw: 341:8   (set 358) drew with Derbyshire at Derby, 2004.
            333:7   (set 369) drew with Essex at Chelmsford, 2010
            316:6   (set 326) drew with Oxford University at Oxford, 1948.
            312:6   (set 344) drew with Sussex at Scarborough 2011
            316:7   (set 320) drew with Somerset at Scarborough, 1990.
            300:5   (set 392) drew with Kent at Canterbury, 2010

To Lose: 433   (set 500) lost to Warwickshire by 66 runs at Birmingham, 2006
            380   (set 406) lost to MCC. by 25 runs at Lord's, 1937.
            343   (set 490) lost to Durham by 146 runs at Leeds 2011
            324   (set 485) lost to Northamptonshire by 160 runs at Luton, 1994.
            322   (set 344) lost to Middlesex by 21 runs at Lord's, 1996.
            309   (set 400) lost to Middlesex by 90 runs at Lord's 1878.

                     *Consecutive matches

By Opponents:

To Win: 479:6   Somerset won by 4 wkts at Taunton, 2009
            472:3   Middlesex won by 7 wkts at Lord's, 2014
            404:5   Hampshire won by 5 wkts at Leeds, 2006
            392:4   Gloucestershire won by 6 wkts at Bristol, 1948.
            364:4   Somerset won by 6 wkts at Taunton, 2010
            354:5   Nottinghamshire won by 5 wkts at Scarborough, 1990
            337:4   Worcestershire won by 6 wkts at Kidderminster, 2007
            334:6   Glamorgan won by 4 wkts at Harrogate, 1955
            329:5   Worcestershire won by 5 wkts at Worcester, 1979
            321:6   Hampshire won by 4 wickets at Leeds, 2017
            306:9   Surrey won by 1 wkt at Bradford, 1992
            305:7   Lancashire won by 3 wkts at Manchester, 1980
            302:9   Warwickshire won by 1 wkt at Birmingham, 1983

HIGH FOURTH INNINGS SCORES – 300 AND OVER *(Continued)*

By Opponents:

To Draw:	366:8	(set 443) Hampshire drew at Southampton, 2007.
	334:7	(set 339) MCC. drew at Scarborough, 1911.
	322:9	(set 334) Middlesex drew at Leeds, 1988.
	317:6	(set 355) Nottinghamshire drew at Nottingham, 1910.
	300:9	(set 314) Northamptonshire drew at Northampton, 1990.
To Lose:	370	(set 539) Leicestershire lost by 168 runs at Leicester, 2001
	319	(set 364) Gloucestershire lost by 44 runs at Leeds, 1987.
	318	(set 324) Somerset lost by 5 runs at Taunton, 1986.
	315	(set 319) Essex lost by 3 runs at Colchester, 1991.
	314	(set 334) Lancashire lost by 19 runs at Manchester, 1993.
	310	(set 417) Warwickshire lost by 106 runs at Scarborough, 1939.
	306	(set 413) Kent lost by 106 runs at Leeds, 1952.
	300	(set 330) Middlesex lost by 29 runs at Sheffield, 1930.

TIE MATCHES

Yorkshire (351:4 dec and 113) tied with Leicestershire (328 and 136) at Huddersfield, 1954.
Yorkshire (106:9 dec and 207) tied with Middlesex (102 and 211) at Bradford, 1973.

HIGHEST SCORES BY AND AGAINST YORKSHIRE

Yorkshire versus: —

	By Yorkshire:	Against Yorkshire:
Derbyshire:		
In Yorkshire:	677:7 dec at Leeds 2013	491 at Bradford, 1949
Away:	662 at Chesterfield, 1898	523 at Derby, 2005
Durham:		
In Yorkshire:	677:7 dec. at Leeds, 2006	573 at Scarborough, 2013
Away	589-8 dec at Chester-le-Street, 2014	507:8 dec at Chester-le-Street, 2016
Essex:		
In Yorkshire:	516 at Scarborough, 2010	622:8 dec. at Leeds, 2005
Away:	555:1 dec. at Leyton, 1932	521 at Leyton, 1905
Glamorgan:		
In Yorkshire:	580:9 dec at Scarborough, 2001	498 at Leeds, 1999
Away:	536:8 dec. at Cardiff, 1996	482:7 dec. at Cardiff, 1996
Gloucestershire:		
In Yorkshire:	504:7 dec. at Bradford, 1905	411 at Leeds, 1992
Away:	494 at Bristol, 1897	574 at Cheltenham, 1990
Hampshire:		
In Yorkshire:	593:9 dec. at Leeds 2016	498:6 dec at Scarborough, 2010
Away	585:3 dec at Portsmouth 1920	599:3 at Southampton, 2011
Kent:		
In Yorkshire:	550:9 at Scarborough, 1995	537:9 dec at Leeds, 2012
Away:	559 at Canterbury, 1887	580: 9 dec. at Maidstone, 1998
Lancashire:		
In Yorkshire:	590 at Bradford, 1887	517 at Leeds, 2007.
Away:	616:6 dec at Manchester, 2014	537 at Manchester, 2005
Leicestershire:		
In Yorkshire	562 { at Scarborough, 1901 / at Dewsbury, 1903	681:7 dec. at Bradford, 1996
Away:	660 at Leicester, 1896	425 at Leicester, 1906

Yorkshire versus: —

Middlesex:	**By Yorkshire:**	**Against Yorkshire:**
In Yorkshire:	575:7 dec. at Bradford, 1899	527 at Huddersfield, 1887
Away	538:6 dec at Lord's, 1925	573:8 dec at Lord's, 2015

Northamptonshire:
In Yorkshire:	673:8 dec at Leeds, 2003	517:7 dec at Scarborough, 1999
Away	546:3 dec at Northampton, 2014	531:4 dec at Northampton, 1996

Nottinghamshire:
In Yorkshire:	572:8 dec at Scarborough, 2013	545:7 dec at Leeds, 2010
Away	534:9 dec at Nottingham, 2011	490 at Nottingham, 1897

Somerset:
In Yorkshire:	525:4 dec. at Leeds, 1953	630 at Leeds, 1901
Away:	589:5 dec at Bath, 2001	592 at Taunton, 1892

Surrey:
In Yorkshire:	582:7 dec. at Sheffield, 1935	516-7 dec at Leeds, 2017
Away:	704 at The Oval, 1899	634:5 dec at The Oval, 2013

Sussex:
In Yorkshire:	681:5 dec. at Sheffield, 1897	566 at Sheffield, 1937
Away:	522:7 dec. at Hastings, 1911	597:8 dec. at Hove, 2007

Warwickshire:
In Yorkshire	561:7 dec at Scarborough 2007	482 at Leeds, 2011
Away:	887 at Birmingham, 1896	601:9 dec. at Birmingham, 2002
	(Highest score by a First-Class county)	

Worcestershire:
In Yorkshire:	600: 4 dec. at Scarborough, 1995	572:7 dec. at Scarborough 2018
Away:	560:6 dec. at Worcester, 1928	456:8 at Worcester, 1904

Australians:
In Yorkshire:	377 at Sheffield, 1953	470 at Bradford, 1893

Indians:
In Yorkshire:	385 at Hull, 1911	490:5 dec. at Sheffield, 1946

New Zealanders:
In Yorkshire:	419 at Bradford, 1965	370:7 dec. at Bradford, 1949

Pakistanis:
In Yorkshire:	433:9 dec. at Sheffield, 1954	356 at Sheffield, 1954

South Africans:
In Yorkshire:	579 at Sheffield, 1951	454:8 dec at Sheffield, 1951

Sri Lankans:
In Yorkshire:	314:8 dec. at Leeds, 1991	422:8 dec. at Leeds, 1991

West Indians:
In Yorkshire:	312:5 dec. at Scarborough, 1973	426 at Scarborough, 1995

Zimbabweans:
In Yorkshire:	298:9 dec at Leeds, 1990	235 at Leeds, 2000

Cambridge University:
In Yorkshire:	359 at Scarborough, 1967	366 at Leeds, 1998
Away:	540 at Cambridge, 1938	425:7 at Cambridge, 1929

Durham MCCU:
Away:	355 at Durham, 2011	287 at Durham, 2011

Leeds/Bradford MCCU:
In Yorkshire	543-5 dec at Leeds, 2017	211 at Leeds, 2012

Loughborough MCCU:
In Yorkshire:	383:6 dec at Leeds, 2007	289 at Leeds, 2007

HIGHEST SCORES BY AND AGAINST YORKSHIRE *(Continued)*

Yorkshire versus: —

MCC:	**By Yorkshire:**	**Against Yorkshire:**
In Yorkshire:	557:8 dec. at Scarborough, 1933	478:8 at Scarborough, 1904
Away:	528:8 dec. at Lord's, 1919	488 at Lord's, 1919

Oxford University:		
In Yorkshire:	173 at Harrogate, 1972	190:6 dec at Harrogate, 1972
Away:	468:6 dec. at Oxford, 1978	422:9 dec. at Oxford, 1953

LOWEST SCORES BY AND AGAINST YORKSHIRE

Yorkshire versus:

Derbyshire:	**By Yorkshire:**	**Against Yorkshire:**
In Yorkshire:	50 at Sheffield, 1894	20 at Sheffield, 1939
Away:	44 at Chesterfield, 1948	26 at Derby, 1880

Durham:		
In Yorkshire:	93 at Leeds, 2003	125 at Harrogate, 1995
Away:	108 at Durham, 1992	74 at Chester-le-Street, 1998

Essex:		
In Yorkshire:	31 at Huddersfield, 1935	52 at Harrogate, 1900
Away:	50 at Chelmsford, 2018	30 at Leyton, 1901

Glamorgan:		
In Yorkshire:	83 at Sheffield, 1946	52 at Hull, 1926
Away:	92 at Swansea, 1956	48 at Cardiff, 1924

Gloucestershire:		
In Yorkshire:	61 at Leeds, 1894	36 at Sheffield, 1903
Away:	35 at Bristol, 1959	42 at Gloucester, 1924

Hampshire:		
In Yorkshire:	23 at Middlesbrough, 1965	36 at Leeds, 1904
Away:	96 at Bournemouth, 1971	36 at Southampton, 1898

Kent:		
In Yorkshire:	30 at Sheffield, 1865	39 { at Sheffield, 1882 { at Sheffield, 1936
Away:	62 at Maidstone, 1889	63 at Canterbury, 1901

Lancashire:		
In Yorkshire:	33 at Leeds, 1924	30 at Holbeck, 1868
Away:	51 { at Manchester, 1888 { at Manchester, 1893	39 at Manchester, 1874

Leicestershire:	By Yorkshire:	Against Yorkshire:
In Yorkshire:	93 at Leeds, 1935	34 at Leeds, 1906
Away:	47 at Leicester, 1911	57 at Leicester, 1898

Middlesex:		
In Yorkshire:	45 at Leeds, 1898	45 at Huddersfield, 1879
Away:	43 at Lord's, 1888	49 at Lord's in 1890

Northamptonshire:		
In Yorkshire:	85 at Sheffield, 1919	51 at Bradford, 1920
Away	64 at Northampton, 1959	15 at Northampton, 1908 (and 27 in first innings)

Nottinghamshire:		
In Yorkshire:	32 at Sheffield, 1876	24 at Sheffield, 1888
Away:	43 at Nottingham, 1869	13 at Nottingham, 1901 (second smallest total by a First-Class county)

Yorkshire versus:

Somerset: **By Yorkshire:**   **Against Yorkshire:**

	By Yorkshire:	Against Yorkshire:
In Yorkshire:	73 at Leeds, 1895	43 at Bradford, 1930
Away:	83 at Wells, 1949	35 at Bath, 1898

Surrey:

In Yorkshire:	54 at Sheffield, 1873	31 at Holbeck, 1883
Away:	26 at The Oval, 1909	44 at The Oval, 1935

Sussex:

In Yorkshire:	61 at Dewsbury, 1891	20 at Hull, 1922
Away:	42 at Hove, 1922	24 at Hove, 1878

Warwickshire:

In Yorkshire:	49 at Huddersfield, 1951	35 at Sheffield, 1979
Away:	54 at Birmingham, 1964	35 at Birmingham, 1963

Worcestershire:

In Yorkshire:	62 at Bradford, 1907	24 at Huddersfield, 1903
Away:	72 at Worcester, 1977	65 at Worcester, 1925

Australians:

In Yorkshire:	48 at Leeds, 1893	23 at Leeds, 1902

Indians:

In Yorkshire:	146 at Bradford, 1959	66 at Harrogate, 1932

New Zealanders:

In Yorkshire:	189 at Harrogate, 1931	134 at Bradford, 1965

Pakistanis:

In Yorkshire:	137 at Bradford, 1962	150 at Leeds, 1967

South Africans:

In Yorkshire:	113 at Bradford, 1907	76 at Bradford, 1951

Sri Lankans:

In Yorkshire:	Have not been dismissed. Lowest is 184:1 dec at Leeds, 1991	287:5 dec at Leeds, 1988

West Indians:

In Yorkshire:	50 at Harrogate, 1906	58 at Leeds, 1928

Zimbabweans:

In Yorkshire:	124 at Leeds, 2000	68 at Leeds, 2000

Cambridge University:

In Yorkshire:	110 at Sheffield, 1903	39 at Sheffield, 1903
Away:	51 at Cambridge, 1906	30 at Cambridge, 1928

Durham MCCU:

Away	355 at Durham, 2011	196 at Durham, 2011

Leeds/Bradford MCCU:

In Yorkshire	135 at Leeds, 2012	118 at Leeds, 2013

Loughborough MCCU:

In Yorkshire	348:5 dec at Leeds, 2010	289 at Leeds, 2007

MCC:

In Yorkshire:	46 { at Scarborough, 1876 / at Scarborough, 1877	31 at Scarborough, 1877
Away:	44 at Lord's, 1880	27 at Lord's, 1902

Oxford University:

In Yorkshire:	Have not been dismissed. Lowest is 115:8 at Harrogate, 1972	133 at Harrogate, 1972
Away:	141 at Oxford, 1949	46 at Oxford, 1956

INDIVIDUAL INNINGS OF 150 AND OVER

A complete list of all First-class Centuries up to and including 2007 is to be found in the 2008 edition

J M BAIRSTOW (7)

205	v. Nottinghamshire	Nottingham	2011
182	v. Leicestershire	Scarborough	2012
186	v. Derbyshire	Leeds	2013
161*	v. Sussex	Arundel	2014
219*	v. Durham	Chester-le-Street	2015
246	v. Hampshire	Leeds	2016
198	v. Surrey	Leeds	2016

G S BALLANCE (4)

203 *	v. Hampshire	West End	2017
194	v. Worcestershire	Worcester	2018
174	v. Northamptonshire	Leeds	2014
165	v. Sussex	Hove	2015

W BARBER (7)

162	v. Middlesex	Sheffield	1932
168	v. MCC	Lord's	1934
248	v. Kent	Leeds	1934
191	v. Sussex	Leeds	1935
255	v. Surrey	Sheffield	1935
158	v. Kent	Sheffield	1936
157	v. Surrey	Sheffield	1938

M G BEVAN (2)

153*	v. Surrey	The Oval	1995
160*	v. Surrey	Middlesbrough	1996

H D BIRD (1)

181*	v. Glamorgan	Bradford	1959

R J BLAKEY (3)

204*	v. Gloucestershire	Leeds	1987
196	v. Oxford University	Oxford	1991
223*	v. Northamptonshire	Leeds	2003

G BLEWETT (1)

190	v. Northamptonshire	Scarborough	1999

M W BOOTH (1)

210	v. Worcestershire	Worcester	1911

G BOYCOTT (32)

165*	v. Leicestershire	Scarborough	1963
151	v. Middlesex	Leeds	1964
151*	v. Leicestershire	Leicester	1964
177	v. Gloucestershire	Bristol	1964
164	v. Sussex	Hove	1966
220*	v. Northamptonshire	Sheffield	1967
180*	v. Warwickshire	Middlesbrough	1968
260*	v. Essex	Colchester (Garrison Ground)	1970
169	v. Nottinghamshire	Leeds	1971
233	v. Essex	Colchester (Garrison Ground)	1971
182*	v. Middlesex	Lord's	1971
169	v. Lancashire	Sheffield	1971
151	v. Leicestershire	Bradford	1971
204*	v. Leicestershire	Leicester	1972

G BOYCOTT *(Continued)*

152*	v. Worcestershire	Worcester	1975
175*	v. Middlesex	Scarborough	1975
201*	v. Middlesex	Lord's	1975
161*	v. Gloucestershire	Leeds	1976
207*	v. Cambridge University	Cambridge	1976
156*	v. Glamorgan	Middlesbrough	1976
154	v Nottinghamshire	Nottingham	1977
151*	v Derbyshire	Leeds	1979
167	v Derbyshire	Chesterfield	1979
175*	v Nottinghamshire	Worksop	1979
154*	v Derbyshire	Scarborough	1980
159	v Worcestershire	Sheffield (Abbeydale Park)	1982
152*	v Warwickshire	Leeds	1982
214*	v Nottinghamshire	Worksop	1983
163	v Nottinghamshire	Bradford	1983
169*	v Derbyshire	Chesterfield	1983
153*	v Derbyshire	Harrogate	1984
184	v Worcestershire	Worcester	1985

T T BRESNAN *(1)*

169*	v. Durham	Chester-le-Street	2015

G L BROPHY *(1)*

177*	v Worcestershire	Worcester	2011

J T BROWN *(8)*

168*	v Sussex	Huddersfield	1895
203	v Middlesex	Lord's	1896
311	v Sussex	Sheffield	1897
300	v Derbyshire	Chesterfield	1898
150	v Sussex	Hove	1898
168	v Cambridge University	Cambridge	1899
167	v Australians	Bradford	1899
192	v Derbyshire	Derby	1899

D BYAS *(5)*

153	v Nottinghamshire	Worksop	1991
156	v Essex	Chelmsford	1993
181	v Cambridge University	Cambridge	1995
193	v Lancashire	Leeds	1995
213	v Worcestershire	Scarborough	1995

D B CLOSE *(5)*

164	v Combined Services	Harrogate	1954
154	v Nottinghamshire	Nottingham	1959
198	v Surrey	The Oval	1960
184	v Nottinghamshire	Scarborough	1960
161	v Northamptonshire	Northampton	1963

D DENTON *(11)*

153*	v Australians	Bradford	1905
165	v Hampshire	Bournemouth	1905
172	v Gloucestershire	Bradford	1905
184	v Nottinghamshire	Nottingham	1909
182	v Derbyshire	Chesterfield	1910

INDIVIDUAL INNINGS OF 150 AND OVER *(Continued)*

D DENTON *(Continued)*

200*	v Warwickshire	Birmingham	1912
182	v Gloucestershire	Bristol	1912
221	v Kent	Tunbridge Wells	1912
191	v Hampshire	Southampton	1912
168*	v Hampshire	Southampton	1914
209*	v Worcestershire	Worcester	1920

A W GALE (4)

150	v. Surrey	The Oval	2008
151*	v. Nottinghamshire	Nottingham	2010
272	v. Nottinghamshire	Scarborough	2013
164	v. Worcestershire	Scarborough	2015

P A GIBB (1)

157*	v. Nottinghamshire	Sheffield	1935

S HAIGH (1)

159	v. Nottinghamshire	Sheffield	1901

L HALL (1)

160	v. Lancashire	Bradford	1887

J H HAMPSHIRE (5)

150	v. Leicestershire	Bradford	1964
183*	v. Sussex	Hove	1971
157*	v. Nottinghamshire	Worksop	1974
158	v. Gloucestershire	Harrogate	1974
155*	v. Gloucestershire	Leeds	1976

I J HARVEY (1)

209*	v. Somerset	Leeds	2005

LORD HAWKE (1)

166	v. Warwickshire	Birmingham	1896

G H HIRST (15)

186	v. Surrey	The Oval	1899
155	v. Nottinghamshire	Scarborough	1900
214	v. Worcestershire	Worcester	1901
153	v. Leicestershire	Dewsbury	1903
153	v. Oxford University	Oxford	1904
152	v. Hampshire	Portsmouth	1904
157	v. Kent	Tunbridge Wells	1904
341	v. Leicestershire	Leicester (Aylestone Road)	1905
232*	v. Surrey	The Oval	1905
169	v. Oxford University	Oxford	1906
158	v. Cambridge University	Cambridge	1910
156	v. Lancashire	Manchester	1911
218	v. Sussex	Hastings	1911
166*	v. Sussex	Hastings	1913
180*	v. MCC	Lord's	1919

P HOLMES (16)

302*	v. Hampshire	Portsmouth	1920
150	v. Derbyshire	Chesterfield	1921
277*	v. Northamptonshire	Harrogate	1921
209	v. Warwickshire	Birmingham	1922

INDIVIDUAL INNINGS OF 150 AND OVER *(Continued)*

P HOLMES *(Continued)*

220*	v. Warwickshire	Huddersfield	1922
199	v. Somerset	Hull	1923
315*	v. Middlesex	Lord's	1925
194	v. Leicestershire	Hull	1925
159	v. Hampshire	Southampton	1925
180	v. Gloucestershire	Gloucester	1927
175*	v. New Zealanders	Bradford	1927
179*	v. Middlesex	Leeds	1928
275	v. Warwickshire	Bradford	1928
285	v. Nottinghamshire	Nottingham	1929
250	v. Warwickshire	Birmingham	1931
224*	v. Essex	Leyton	1932

L HUTTON (31)

196	v. Worcestershire	Worcester	1934
163	v. Surrey	Leeds	1936
161	v. MCC	Lord's	1937
271*	v. Derbyshire	Sheffield	1937
153	v. Leicestershire	Hull	1937
180	v. Cambridge University	Cambridge	1938
158	v. Warwickshire	Birmingham	1939
280*	v. Hampshire	Sheffield	1939
151	v. Surrey	Leeds	1939
177	v. Sussex	Scarborough	1939
183*	v. Indians	Bradford	1946
171*	v. Northamptonshire	Hull	1946
197	v. Glamorgan	Swansea	1947
197	v. Essex	Southend-on-Sea	1947
270*	v. Hampshire	Bournemouth	1947
176*	v. Sussex	Sheffield	1948
155	v. Sussex	Hove	1948
167	v. New Zealanders	Bradford	1949
201	v. Lancashire	Manchester	1949
165	v. Sussex	Hove	1949
269*	v. Northamptonshire	Wellingborough	1949
156	v. Essex	Colchester (Castle Park)	1950
153	v. Nottinghamshire	Nottingham	1950
156	v. South Africans	Sheffield	1951
151	v. Surrey	The Oval	1951
194*	v. Nottinghamshire	Nottingham	1951
152	v. Lancashire	Leeds	1952
189	v. Kent	Leeds	1952
178	v. Somerset	Leeds	1953
163	v. Combined Services	Harrogate	1954
194	v. Nottinghamshire	Nottingham	1955

R A HUTTON (1)

189	v. Pakistanis	Bradford	1971

R ILLINGWORTH (2)

150	v. Essex	Colchester (Castle Park)	1959
162	v. Indians	Sheffield	1959

Hon F S JACKSON (3)

160	v. Gloucestershire	Sheffield	1898
155	v. Middlesex	Bradford	1899
158	v. Surrey	Bradford	1904

P A JAQUES (7)

243	v. Hampshire	Southampton (Rose Bowl)	2004
173	v. Glamorgan	Leeds	2004
176	v. Northamptonshire	Leeds	2005
219	v. Derbyshire	Leeds	2005
172	v. Durham	Scarborough	2005
160	v. Gloucestershire	Bristol	2012
152	v. Durham	Scarborough	2013

R KILNER (5)

169	v. Gloucestershire	Bristol	1914
206*	v. Derbyshire	Sheffield	1920
166	v. Northamptonshire	Northampton	1921
150	v. Northamptonshire	Harrogate	1921
150	v. Middlesex	Lord's	1926

F LEE (1)

165	v. Lancashire	Bradford	1887

A Z LEES (1)

275*	v. Derbyshire	Chesterfield	2013

D S LEHMANN (13)

177	v. Somerset	Taunton	1997
163*	v. Leicestershire	Leicester	1997
182	v. Hampshire	Portsmouth	1997
200	v. Worcestershire	Worcester	1998
187*	v. Somerset	Bath	2001
252	v. Lancashire	Leeds	2001
193	v. Leicestershire	Leicester	2001
216	v. Sussex	Arundel	2002
187	v. Lancashire	Leeds	2002
150	v. Warwickshire	Birmingham	2006
193	v. Kent	Canterbury	2006
172	v. Kent	Leeds	2006
339	v. Durham	Leeds	2006

E I LESTER (5)

186	v. Warwickshire	Scarborough	1949
178	v. Nottinghamshire	Nottingham	1952
157	v. Cambridge University	Hull	1953
150	v. Oxford University	Oxford	1954
163	v. Essex	Romford	1954

M LEYLAND (17)

191	v. Glamorgan	Swansea	1926
204*	v. Middlesex	Sheffield	1927
247	v. Worcestershire	Worcester	1928
189*	v. Glamorgan	Huddersfield	1928
211*	v. Lancashire	Leeds	1930
172	v. Middlesex	Sheffield	1930
186	v. Derbyshire	Leeds	1930
189	v. Middlesex	Sheffield	1932
153	v. Leicestershire	Leicester (Aylestone Road)	1932
166	v. Leicestershire	Bradford	1932
153*	v. Hampshire	Bournemouth	1932
192	v. Northamptonshire	Leeds	1933
210*	v. Kent	Dover	1933

M LEYLAND *(Continued)*

263	v. Essex	Hull	1936
163*	v. Surrey	Leeds	1936
167	v. Worcestershire	Stourbridge	1937
180*	v. Middlesex	Lord's	1939

E LOCKWOOD (1)

208	v. Kent	Gravesend	1883

J D LOVE (4)

163	v. Nottinghamshire	Bradford	1976
170*	v. Worcestershire	Worcester	1979
161	v. Warwickshire	Birmingham	1981
154	v. Lancashire	Manchester	1981

F A LOWSON (10)

155	v. Kent	Maidstone	1951
155	v. Worcestershire	Bradford	1952
166	v. Scotland	Glasgow	1953
259*	v. Worcestershire	Worcester	1953
165	v. Sussex	Hove	1954
164	v. Essex	Scarborough	1954
150*	v. Kent	Dover	1954
183*	v. Oxford University	Oxford	1956
154	v. Somerset	Taunton	1956
154	v. Cambridge University	Cambridge	1957

R G LUMB (2)

159	v. Somerset	Harrogate	1979
165*	v. Gloucestershire	Bradford	1984

A LYTH (5)

248 *	v. Leicestershire	Leicester	2012
230	v. Northamptonshire	Northampton	2014
251	v. Lancashire	Manchester	2014
202	v. Surrey	The Oval	2016
194	v. Leeds/Bradford MCCU	Leeds	2017

A McGRATH (7)

165	v. Lancashire	Leeds	2002
174	v. Derbyshire	Derby	2004
165*	v. Leicestershire	Leicester	2005
173*	v. Worcestershire	Leeds	2005
158	v. Derbyshire	Derby	2005
188*	v. Warwickshire	Birmingham	2007
211	v. Warwickshire	Birmingham	2009

D R MARTYN (1)

238	v. Gloucestershire	Leeds	2003

A A METCALFE (7)

151	v. Northamptonshire	Luton	1986
151	v. Lancashire	Manchester	1986
152	v. MCC	Scarborough	1987
216*	v. Middlesex	Leeds	1988
162	v. Gloucestershire	Cheltenham	1990
150*	v. Derbyshire	Scarborough	1990
194*	v. Nottinghamshire	Nottingham	1990

A MITCHELL (7)

189	v. Northamptonshire	Northampton	1926
176	v. Nottinghamshire	Bradford	1930
177*	v. Gloucestershire	Bradford	1932
150*	v. Worcestershire	Worcester	1933
158	v. MCC	Scarborough	1933
152	v. Hampshire	Bradford	1934
181	v. Surrey	Bradford	1934

F MITCHELL (2)

194	v. Leicestershire	Leicester	1899
162*	v. Warwickshire	Birmingham	1901

M D MOXON (14)

153	v. Lancashire	Leeds	1983
153	v. Somerset	Leeds	1985
168	v. Worcestershire	Worcester	1985
191	v. Northamptonshire	Scarborough	1989
162*	v. Surrey	The Oval	1989
218*	v. Sussex	Eastbourne	1990
200	v. Essex	Colchester (Castle Park)	1991
183	v. Gloucestershire	Cheltenham	1992
171*	v. Kent	Leeds	1993
161*	v. Lancashire	Manchester	1994
274*	v. Worcestershire	Worcester	1994
203*	v. Kent	Leeds	1995
213	v. Glamorgan	Cardiff (Sophia Gardens)	1996
155	v. Pakistan 'A'	Leeds	1997

E OLDROYD (5)

151*	v. Glamorgan	Cardiff	1922
194	v. Worcestershire	Worcester	1923
162*	v. Glamorgan	Swansea	1928
168	v. Glamorgan	Hull	1929
164*	v. Somerset	Bath	1930

D E V PADGETT (1)

161*	v. Oxford University	Oxford	1959

R PEEL (2)

158	v. Middlesex	Lord's	1889
210*	v. Warwickshire	Birmingham	1896

A U RASHID (3)

157*	v. Lancashire	Leeds	2009
180	v. Somerset	Leeds	2013
159*	v. Lancashire	Manchester	2014

W RHODES (8)

196	v. Worcestershire	Worcester	1904
201	v. Somerset	Taunton	1905
199	v. Sussex	Hove	1909
176	v. Nottinghamshire	Harrogate	1912
152	v. Leicestershire	Leicester (Aylestone Road)	1913
167*	v. Nottinghamshire	Leeds	1920
267*	v. Leicestershire	Leeds	1921
157	v. Derbyshire	Leeds	1925

INDIVIDUAL INNINGS OF 150 AND OVER *(Continued)*

P E ROBINSON (2)

150*	v. Derbyshire	Scarborough	1990
189	v. Lancashire	Scarborough	1991

J E ROOT (5)

160	v. Sussex	Scarborough	2011
222 *	v. Hampshire	Southampton (West End)	2012
182	v. Durham	Chester-le-Street	2013
236	v. Derbyshire	Leeds	2013
	2013 innings consecutive		
213	v.Surrey	Leeds	2016

J W ROTHERY (1)

161	v. Kent	Dover	1908

J A RUDOLPH (5)

220	v. Warwickshire	Scarborough	2007
155	v. Somerset	Taunton	2008
198	v. Worcestershire	Leeds	2009
191	v. Somerset	Taunton	2009
228*	v. Durham	Leeds	2010

H RUDSTON (1)

164	v. Leicestershire	Leicester (Aylestone Rd)	1904

J J SAYERS (3)

187	v. Kent	Tunbridge Wells	2007
173	v. Warwickshire	Birmingham	2009
152	v. Somerset	Taunton	2009

A B SELLERS (1)

204	v. Cambridge University	Cambridge	1936

K SHARP (2)

173	v. Derbyshire	Chesterfield	1984
181	v. Gloucestershire	Harrogate	1986

P J SHARPE (4)

203*	v. Cambridge University	Cambridge	1960
152	v. Kent	Sheffield	1960
197	v. Pakistanis	Leeds	1967
172*	v. Glamorgan	Swansea	1971

G A SMITHSON (1)

169	v. Leicestershire	Leicester	1947

W B STOTT (2)

181	v. Essex	Sheffield	1957
186	v. Warwickshire	Birmingham	1960

H SUTCLIFFE (39)

174	v. Kent	Dover	1919
232	v. Surrey	The Oval	1922
213	v. Somerset	Dewsbury	1924
160	v. Sussex	Sheffield	1924
255*	v. Essex	Southend-on-Sea	1924
235	v. Middlesex	Leeds	1925
206	v. Warwickshire	Dewsbury	1925
171	v. MCC	Scarborough	1925

H SUTCLIFFE *(Continued)*

200	v. Leicestershire	Leicester (Aylestone Road)	1926
176	v. Surrey	Leeds	1927
169	v. Nottinghamshire	Bradford	1927
228	v. Sussex	Eastbourne	1928
150	v. Northamptonshire	Northampton	1929
150*	v. Essex	Dewsbury	1930
173	v. Sussex	Hove	1930
173*	v. Cambridge University	Cambridge	1931
230	v. Kent	Folkestone	1931
183	v. Somerset	Dewsbury	1931
195	v. Lancashire	Sheffield	1931
187	v. Leicestershire	Leicester (Aylestone Road)	1931
153*	v. Warwickshire	Hull	1932
313	v. Essex	Leyton	1932
270	v. Sussex	Leeds	1932
182	v. Derbyshire	Leeds	1932
194	v. Essex	Scarborough	1932
205	v. Warwickshire	Birmingham	1933
177	v. Middlesex	Bradford	1933
174	v. Leicestershire	Leicester (Aylestone Road)	1933
152	v. Cambridge University	Cambridge	1934
166	v. Essex	Hull	1934
203	v. Surrey	The Oval	1934
187*	v. Worcestershire	Bradford	1934
200*	v. Worcestershire	Sheffield	1935
212	v. Leicestershire	Leicester (Aylestone Road)	1935
202	v. Middlesex	Scarborough	1936
189	v. Leicestershire	Hull	1937
165	v. Lancashire	Manchester	1939
234*	v. Leicestershire	Hull	1939
175	v. Middlesex	Lord's	1939

W H H SUTCLIFFE (3)

171*	v. Worcestershire	Worcester	1952
181	v. Kent	Canterbury	1952
161*	v. Glamorgan	Harrogate	1955

K TAYLOR (8)

168*	v. Nottinghamshire	Nottingham	1956
159	v. Leicestershire	Sheffield	1961
203*	v. Warwickshire	Birmingham	1961
178*	v. Oxford University	Oxford	1962
163	v. Nottinghamshire	Leeds	1962
153	v. Lancashire	Manchester	1964
160	v. Australians	Sheffield	1964
162	v. Worcestershire	Kidderminster	1967

T L TAYLOR (1)

156	v. Hampshire	Harrogate	1901

J TUNNICLIFFE (2)

243	v. Derbyshire	Chesterfield	1898
158	v. Worcestershire	Worcester	1900

G ULYETT (1)

199*	v. Derbyshire	Sheffield	1887

M P VAUGHAN (7)

183	v. Glamorgan	Cardiff (Sophia Gardens)	1996
183	v. Northamptonshire	Northampton	1996
161	v. Essex	Ilford	1997
177	v. Durham	Chester-le-Street	1998
151	v. Essex	Chelmsford	1999
153	v. Kent	Scarborough	1999
155*	v. Derbyshire	Leeds	2000

E WAINWRIGHT (3)

171	v. Middlesex	Lord's	1897
153	v. Leicestershire	Leicester	1899
228	v. Surrey	The Oval	1899

W WATSON (7)

153*	v. Surrey	The Oval	1947
172	v. Derbyshire	Scarborough	1948
162*	v. Somerset	Leeds	1953
163	v. Sussex	Sheffield	1955
174	v. Lancashire	Sheffield	1955
214*	v. Worcestershire	Worcester	1955
162	v. Northamptonshire	Harrogate	1957

C WHITE (6)

181	v. Lancashire	Leeds	1996
172*	v. Worcestershire	Leeds	1997
186	v. Lancashire	Manchester	2001
183	v. Glamorgan	Scarborough	2001
161	v. Leicestershire	Scarborough	2002
173*	v. Derbyshire	Derby	2003

K S WILLIAMSON (1)

189	v. Sussex	Scarborough	2014

B B WILSON (2)

150	v. Warwickshire	Birmingham	1912
208	v. Sussex	Bradford	1914

J V WILSON (7)

157*	v. Sussex	Leeds	1949
157	v. Essex	Sheffield	1950
166*	v. Sussex	Hull	1951
223*	v. Scotland	Scarborough	1951
154	v. Oxford University	Oxford	1952
230	v. Derbyshire	Sheffield	1952
165	v. Oxford University	Oxford	1956

M J WOOD (5)

200*	v. Warwickshire	Leeds	1998
157	v. Northamptonshire	Leeds	2003
207	v. Somerset	Taunton	2003
155	v. Hampshire	Scarborough	2003
202*	v. Bangladesh 'A'	Leeds	2005

N W D YARDLEY (2)

177	v. Derbyshire	Scarborough	1947
183*	v. Hampshire	Leeds	1951

YOUNUS KHAN (2)

202*	v. Hampshire	Southampton (Rose Bowl)	2007
217*	v. Kent	Scarborough	2007

CENTURIES BY CURRENT PLAYERS

A complete list of all First-class Centuries up to and including 2007 is to be found in the 2008 edition

J M BAIRSTOW (15)

205	v. Nottinghamshire	Nottingham	2011
136	v. Somerset	Taunton	2011
182	v. Leicestershire	Scarborough	2012
118	v. Leicestershire	Leicester	2012
107	v. Kent	Leeds	2012
186	v. Derbyshire	Leeds	2013
123	v. Leeds/Bradford	Leeds	2014
161*	v. Sussex	Arundel	2014
102	v. Hampshire	Leeds	2015
125*	v. Middlesex	Leeds	2015
219*	v. Durham	Chester-le-Street **	2015
108	v. Warwickshire	Birmingham **	2015

(** consecutive innings)

139	v. Worcestershire	Scarborough	2015
246	v. Hampshire	Leeds	2016
198	v. Surrey	Leeds	2016

G S BALLANCE (21)

111	v. Warwickshire	Birmingham	2011
121*	v. Gloucestershire	Bristol	2012
112	v. Leeds/Bradford MCCU	Leeds	2013
107	v. Somerset	Leeds	2013
141	v. Nottinghamshire	Scarborough	2013
112	v. Warwickshire	Leeds	2013
148	v. Surrey 1st inns	The Oval **	2013
108*	v. Hampshire 1st inns	West End, Southampton	2013
101	v. Leeds/Bradford MCCU	Leeds **	2014
174	v. Northamptonshire	Leeds	2014
130	v. Middlesex	Lord's	2014
165	v. Sussex	Hove	2015
105	v. MCC	Abu Dhabi	2016
132	v. Middlesex	Scarborough	2016
101*	v. Nottinghamshire	Scarborough	2016
120	v. Hampshire	Leeds	2017
108	v. Hampshire (1st innings)	West End, Southampton	2017
203*	v. Hampshire (2nd innings)	West End, Southampton	2017
109	v. Hampshire	West End, Southampton	2018
104	v. Nottinghamshire	Nottingham	2018
194	v. Worcestershire	Worcester	2018

T T BRESNAN (5)

116	v. Surrey	The Oval	2007
101*	v. Warwickshire	Scarborough	2007
100*	v. Somerset	Taunton	2015
169*	v. Durham	Chester-le-Street	2015
142*	v. Middlesex	Lord's	2016

H C BROOK (1)

124	v. Essex	Chelmsford	2018

T KOHLER-CADMORE (2)

106	v. Nottinghamshire	Nottingham	2018
105*	v. Lancashire	Leeds	2018

J A LEANING (4)

116	v. Nottinghamshire	Nottingham	2015
123	v. Somerset	Taunton	2015
110	v. Nottinghamshire	Leeds	2015
118	v. Lancashire	Manchester	2017

A LYTH (22)

132	v. Nottinghamshire	Nottingham	2008
142	v. Somerset	Taunton	2010
133	v. Hampshire	Southampton	2010
100	v. Lancashire	Manchester	2010
248*	v. Leicestershire	Leicester	2012
111	v. Leeds/Bradford	Leeds	2013
105	v. Somerset	Taunton	2013
130	v. Leeds/Bradford MCCU	Leeds	2014
104	v. Durham	Chester-le-Street	2014
230	v. Northamptonshire	Northampton	2014
143	v. Durham	Leeds	2014
117	v. Middlesex	Scarborough	2014
251	v. Lancashire	Manchester	2014
122	v. Nottinghamshire	Nottingham	2014
113	v. MCC	Abu Dhabi	2015
111	v. Hampshire	Leeds	2016
106	v. Somerset	Taunton	2016
202	v. Surrey	The Oval	2016
114*	v. Durham	Leeds	2016
194	v. Leeds/Bradford MCCU	Leeds	2017
100	v. Lancashire	Leeds	2017
134*	v. Hampshire	Leeds	2018

A U RASHID (10)

108	v. Worcestershire	Kidderminster	2007
111	v. Sussex	Hove	2008
117*	v. Hampshire	Basingstoke	2009
157*	v. Lancashire	Leeds	2009
180	v. Somerset	Leeds	2013
110*	v. Warwickshire	Birmingham	2013
103	v. Somerset	Taunton	2013
108	v. Somerset	Taunton	2014
159*	v. Lancashire	Manchester	2014
127	v. Durham	Scarborough	2015

(2013 consecutive innings)

J E ROOT (6)

160	v. Sussex	Scarborough	2011
222 *	v. Hampshire	Southampton (West End)	2012
125	v. Northamptonshire	Leeds	2012
182	v. Durham	Chester-le-Street	2013
236	v. Derbyshire	Leeds	2013
213	v. Surrey	Leeds	2016

CENTURIES

(Including highest score)

112	H Sutcliffe	313	v. Essex	at Leyton	1932
103	G Boycott	260*	v. Essex	at Colchester (Garrison Gd)	1970
85	L Hutton	280*	v. Hampshire	at Sheffield	1939
62	M Leyland	263	v. Essex	at Hull	1936
61	D Denton	221	v. Kent	at Tunbridge Wells	1912
60	P Holmes	315*	v. Middlesex	at Lord's	1925
56	G H Hirst	341	v. Leicestershire	at Leicester (Aylestone Rd)	1905
46	W Rhodes	267*	v. Leicestershire	at Leeds	1921
41	M D Moxon	274*	v. Worcestershire	at Worcester	1994
39	A Mitchell	189	v. Northamptonshire	at Northampton	1926
37	E Oldroyd	194	v. Worcestershire	at Worcester	1923
34	J H Hampshire	183*	v. Sussex	at Hove	1971
34	A McGrath	211	v. Warwickshire	at Birmingham	2009
33	D B Close	198	v. Surrey	at The Oval	1960
30	F A Lowson	259*	v. Worcestershire	at Worcester	1953
29	D E V Padgett	161*	v. Oxford University	at Oxford	1959
29	J V Wilson	230	v. Derbyshire	at Sheffield	1952
28	D Byas	213	v. Worcestershire	at Scarborough	1995
27	W Barber	255	v. Surrey	at Sheffield	1935
26	D S Lehmann	339	v. Durham	at Leeds	2006
26	W Watson	214*	v. Worcestershire	at Worcester	1955
25	A A Metcalfe	216*	v. Middlesex	at Leeds	1988
24	E I Lester	186	v. Warwickshire	at Scarborough	1949
23	J T Brown	311	v. Sussex	at Sheffield	1897
23	P J Sharpe	203*	v. Cambridge University	at Cambridge	1960
22	R G Lumb	165*	v. Gloucestershire	at Bradford	1984
22	A Lyth	251	v. Lancashire	at Manchester	2014
22	J Tunnicliffe	243	v. Derbyshire	at Chesterfield	1898
21	G S Ballance	203*	v. Hampshire	at West End, Southampton	2017
21	Hon F S Jackson	160	v. Gloucestershire	at Sheffield	1898
20	M P Vaughan	183	v. Glamorgan	at Cardiff (Sophia Gardens)	1996
and		183	v. Northamptonshire	at Northampton	1996
19	A W Gale	272	v. Nottinghamshire	at Scarborough	2013
19	C White	186	v. Lancashire	at Manchester	2001
18	J A Rudolph	228*	v. Durham	at Leeds	2010
18	E Wainwright	228	v. Surrey	at The Oval	1899
17	W B Stott	186	v. Warwickshire	at Birmingham	1960
17	N W D Yardley	183*	v. Hampshire	at Leeds	1951
16	K Taylor	203*	v. Warwickshire	at Birmingham	1961
16	M J Wood	207	v. Somerset	at Taunton	2003
15	J M Bairstow	246	v. Hampshire	at Leeds	2016
15	R Kilner	206*	v. Derbyshire	at Sheffield	1920
15	G Ulyett	199*	v. Derbyshire	at Sheffield	1887
15	B B Wilson	208	v. Sussex	at Bradford	1914
14	R Illingworth	162	v. Indians	at Sheffield	1959
13	J D Love	170*	v. Worcestershire	at Worcester	1979
12	R J Blakey	223*	v. Northamptonshire	at Leeds	2003
12	H Halliday	144	v. Derbyshire	at Chesterfield	1950
11	P A Jaques	243	v. Hampshire	at Southampton (Rose Bowl)	2004
11	A Z Lees	275*	v. Derbyshire	at Chesterfield	2013
11	K Sharp	181	v. Gloucestershire	at Harrogate	1986
10	C W J Athey	134	v. Derbyshire	at Derby	1982
10	Lord Hawke	166	v. Warwickshire	at Birmingham	1896
10	F Mitchell	194	v. Leicestershire	at Leicester	1899
10	A U Rashid	180	v. Somerset	at Leeds	2013
9	D L Bairstow	145	v. Middlesex	at Scarborough	1980

9	M G Bevan	160*	v. Surrey	at Middlesbrough	1996
9	L Hall	160	v. Lancashire	at Bradford	1887
9	J J Sayers	187	v. Kent	at Tunbridge Wells	2007
8	W Bates	136	v. Sussex	at Hove	1886
8	M J Lumb	144	v. Middlesex	at Southgate	2006
8	T L Taylor	156	v. Hampshire	at Harrogate	1901
7	J B Bolus	146*	v. Hampshire	at Portsmouth	1960
7	E Robinson	135*	v. Leicestershire	at Leicester (Aylestone Rd)	1921
7	P E Robinson	189	v. Lancashire	at Scarborough	1991
6	E Lockwood	208	v. Kent	at Gravesend	1883
6	R Peel	210*	v. Warwickshire	at Birmingham	1896
6	J E Root	236	v. Derbyshire	at Leeds	2013
6	W H H Sutcliffe	181	v. Kent	at Canterbury	1952
5	T T Bresnan	169*	v. Durham	at Chester-le-Street	2015
5	C M Old	116	v. Indians	at Bradford	1974
4	I Grimshaw	129*	v. Cambridge University	at Sheffield	1885
4	S Haigh	159	v. Nottinghamshire	at Sheffield	1901
4	S N Hartley	114	v. Gloucestershire	at Bradford	1982
4	R A Hutton	189	v. Pakistanis	at Bradford	1971
4	J A Leaning	123	v. Somerset	at Taunton	2015
4	A B Sellers	204	v. Cambridge University	at Cambridge	1936
3	G L Brophy	177*	v. Worcestershire	at Worcester	2011
3	P Carrick	131*	v. Northamptonshire	at Northampton	1980
3	A J Dalton	128	v. Middlesex	at Leeds	1972
3	A Drake	147*	v. Derbyshire	at Chesterfield	1911
3	F Lee	165	v. Lancashire	at Bradford	1887
3	G G Macaulay	125*	v. Nottinghamshire	at Nottingham	1921
3	R Moorhouse	113	v. Somerset	at Taunton	1896
3	R M Pyrah	134*	v. Loughborough MCCU	at Leeds	2010
3	J W Rothery	161	v. Kent	at Dover	1908
3	J Rowbotham	113	v. Surrey	at The Oval	1873
3	T F Smailes	117	v. Glamorgan	at Cardiff	1938
3	Younus Khan	217*	v. Kent	at Scarborough	2007
2	M W Booth	210	v. Worcestershire	at Worcester	1911
2	D C F Burton	142*	v. Hampshire	at Dewsbury	1919
2	K R Davidson	128	v. Kent	at Maidstone	1934
2	P A Gibb	157*	v. Nottinghamshire	at Sheffield	1935
2	P J Hartley	127*	v. Lancashire	at Manchester	1988
2	I J Harvey	209*	v. Somerset	at Leeds	2005
2	C Johnson	107	v. Somerset	at Sheffield	1973
2	S A Kellett	125*	v. Derbyshire	at Chesterfield	1991
2	N Kilner	112	v. Leicestershire	at Leeds	1921
2	T Kohler-Cadmore	106	v. Nottinghamshire	at Nottingham	2018
2	B Parker	138*	v. Oxford University	at Oxford	1997
2	A Sellers	105	v. Middlesex	at Lord's	1893
2	E Smith (Morley)	129	v. Hampshire	at Bradford	1899
2	G A Smithson	169	v. Leicestershire	at Leicester	1947
2	G B Stevenson	115*	v. Warwickshire	at Birmingham	1982
2	F S Trueman	104	v. Northamptonshire	at Northampton	1963
2	C Turner	130	v. Somerset	at Sheffield	1936
2	D J Wainwright	104*	v. Sussex	at Hove	2008
2	T A Wardall	106	v. Gloucestershire	at Gloucester (Spa Ground)	1892
1	Azeem Rafiq	100	v. Worcestershire	at Worcester	2009

1	A T Barber	100	v. England XI	at Sheffield	1929
1	H D Bird	181*	v. Glamorgan	at Bradford	1959
1	T J D Birtles	104	v. Lancashire	at Sheffield	1914
1	G S Blewett	190	v. Northamptonshire	at Scarborough	1999
1	H C Brook	124	v. Essex	at Chelmsford	2018
1	J A Brooks	109*	v. Lancashire	at Manchester	2017
1	M T G Elliott	127	v, Warwickshire	at Birmingham	2002
1	T Emmett	104	v. Gloucestershire	at Clifton	1873
1	G M Fellows	109	v. Lancashire	at Manchester	2002
1	A J Finch	110	v. Warwickshire	at Birmingham	2014
1	J N Gillespie	123*	v. Surrey	at The Oval	2007
1	D Gough	121	v. Warwickshire	at Leeds	1996
1	A K D Gray	104	v. Somerset	at Taunton	2003
1	A P Grayson	100	v. Worcestershire	at Worcester	1994
1	F E Greenwood	104*	v. Glamorgan	at Hull	1929
1	G M Hamilton	125	v. Hampshire	at Leeds	2000
1	P S P Handscomb	101*	v. Lancashire	at Manchester	2017
1	W E Harbord	109	v. Oxford University	at Oxford	1930
1	R Iddison	112	v. Cambridgeshire	at Hunslet	1869
1	W G Keighley	110	v. Surrey	at Leeds	1951
1	R A Kettleborough	108	v. Essex	at Leeds	1996
1	B Leadbeater	140*	v. Hampshire	at Portsmouth	1976
1	J S Lehmann	116	v. Somerset	at Leeds	2016
1	D R Martyn	238	v. Gloucestershire	at Leeds	2003
1	G J Maxwell	140	v. Durham	at Scarborough	2015
1	S E Marsh	125*	v. Surrey	at The Oval	2017
1	J T Newstead	100*	v. Nottinghamshire	at Nottingham	1908
1	L E Plunkett	126	v. Hampshire	at Leeds	2016
1	C A Pujara	133*	v. Hampshire	at Leeds	2015
1	R B Richardson	112	v. Warwickshire	at Birmingham	1993
1	H Rudston	164	v. Leicestershire	at Leicester (Aylestone Rd)	1904
1	A Sidebottom	124	v. Glamorgan	at Cardiff (Sophia Gardens)	1977
1	I G Swallow	114	v. MCC	at Scarborough	1987
1	S R Tendulkar	100	v. Durham	at Durham	1992
1	J Thewlis	108	v. Surrey	at The Oval	1868
1	C T Tyson	100*	v. Hampshire	at Southampton	1921
1	H Verity	101	v. Jamaica	at Kingston (Sabina Park)	1935/36
1	A Waddington	114	v. Worcestershire	at Leeds	1927
1	W A I Washington	100*	v. Surrey	at Leeds	1902
1	H Wilkinson	113	v. MCC	at Scarborough	1904
1	W H Wilkinson	103	v. Sussex	at Sheffield	1909
1	K S Williamson	189	v. Sussex	at Scarborough	2014
1	E R Wilson	104*	v. Essex	at Bradford	1913
1	A Wood	123*	v. Worcestershire	at Sheffield	1935
1	J D Woodford	101	v. Warwickshire	at Middlesbrough	1971

SUMMARY OF CENTURIES
FOR AND AGAINST YORKSHIRE 1863-2018

FOR YORKSHIRE				AGAINST YORKSHIRE		
Total	In Yorkshire	Away		Total	In Yorkshire	Away
110	65	45	Derbyshire	57	27	30
32	16	16	Durham	24	13	11
76	34	42	Essex	46	21	25
68	38	30	Glamorgan	23	13	10
87	41	46	Gloucestershire	53	27	26
99	43	56	Hampshire	61	27	34
81	37	44	Kent	60	29	31
117	58	59	Lancashire	116	58	58
97	52	45	Leicestershire	46	23	23
97	49	48	Middlesex	92	38	54
81	35	46	Northamptonshire	53	25	28
129	60	69	Nottinghamshire	85	33	52
102	50	52	Somerset	62	23	39
119	50	69	Surrey	113	40	73
90	42	48	Sussex	77	33	44
105	36	69	Warwickshire	75	29	46
75	32	43	Worcestershire	45	17	28
1	1	0	Cambridgeshire	0	0	0
1566	739	827	**Totals**	1088	476	612
9	9	0	Australians	16	16	0
9	9	0	Indians	7	7	0
8	8	0	New Zealanders	3	3	0
5	5	0	Pakistanis	1	1	0
9	9	0	South Africans	7	7	0
5	5	0	Sri Lankans	1	1	0
5	5	0	West Indians	6	6	0
1	1	0	Zimbabweans	0	0	0
3	3	0	Bangladesh 'A'	1	1	0
0	0	0	India 'A'	3	3	0
1	1	0	Pakistan 'A'	1	1	0
45	1	44	Cambridge University	20	2	18
2	2	0	Combined Services	0	0	0
1	0	1	Durham MCCU	1	0	1
4	3	1	England XIs	3	2	1
0	0	0	International XI	1	1	0
1	0	1	Ireland	0	0	0
3	0	3	Jamaica	3	0	3
8	8	0	Leeds/Bradford MCCU	0	0	0
1	0	1	Liverpool and District	0	0	0
2	2	0	Loughborough MCCU	1	1	0
1	0	1	Mashonaland	0	0	0
2	0	2	Matabeleland	1	0	1
54	38	16	MCC	52	34	18
39	0	39	Oxford University	11	0	11
6	0	6	Rest of England	15	0	15
9	5	4	Scotland	1	0	1
3	3	0	C L Thornton's XI	4	4	0
0	0	0	Western Province	1	0	1
1	1	0	I Zingari	1	1	0
237	118	119	**Totals**	161	91	70
1803	857	946	**Grand Totals**	1249	567	682

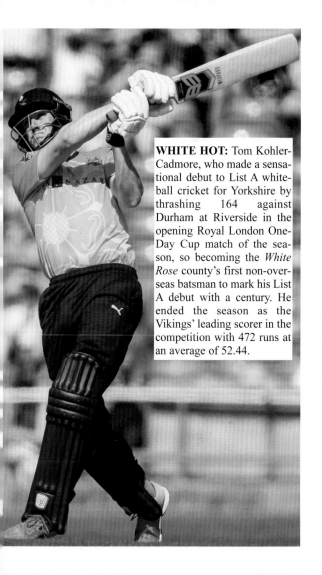

WHITE HOT: Tom Kohler-Cadmore, who made a sensational debut to List A white-ball cricket for Yorkshire by thrashing 164 against Durham at Riverside in the opening Royal London One-Day Cup match of the season, so becoming the *White Rose* county's first non-overseas batsman to mark his List A debut with a century. He ended the season as the Vikings' leading scorer in the competition with 472 runs at an average of 52.44.

TABLE-TOPPERS: The Yorkshire squad who clinched the Under-17 County Championship title in 2018. Back row, left to right: Vikram Sharma, Josh Sullivan, Finlay Bean, Dominic Leech, George Hill, Matthew Revis, Archie Greaves, James Mukherjee, Harry Sullivan, Harrison Quarmby and Harry Harding. Front row: Sam Wisniewski, Chris Wood, Richard Damms, Academy Coach; James Wharton, captain; Graham Tipping, Assistant Coach to Yorkshire Under-17s; Pete Sim, Strength and Conditioning Coach; Harry Duke and Arjun Ramkumar.

FUTURE HOPE: George Hill, left, who was to come third in both the batting and bowling averages for Yorkshire Academy in Yorkshire League North and Cup matches in 2018, marches into the winter nets at Emerald Headingley.

ROSES GEMS: Yorkshire Diamonds line up for their clash with Lancashire Thunder at Emerald Headingley. Back row, left to right: Katie Thompson, Thea Brookes, Sophie Munro, Helen Fenby, Alice Monaghan and Bess Heath. Front row: Gwen Davies, Beth Langston, Katie Levick, Lauren Winfield, captain; Alice Davidson-Richards, Delissa Kimmince and Beth Mooney. Not present: Katherine Brunt.

WELL BOWLED: Katherine Brunt congratulates a laughing Alice Davidson-Richards, but the *Red Rose* were to prevail.

PRESIDENT'S MEN: President Richard Hutton, centre, awarded YCCC President's Medals to David S Hall CBE, TD, extreme left, and J C David Allan, right, at the Club's 2018 Annual General Meeting. Both have served as chairman of the Archives Committee, and David Hall was curator of the Emerald Museum.

FAREWELL GIFTS: Canon Max Wigley, right, retired after serving as Yorkshire CCC chaplain for 15 years, and he received gifts on behalf of the Club from Chairman Robin Smith, left, who also presented a bouquet to Max's wife, Judith. Also pictured is Max's successor as chaplain, the Right Reverend Chris Edmondson, the former Bishop of Bolton.

REMEMBERING BRIAN: Items of memorabilia belonging to Brian Close, who captained Yorkshire and Somerset, are presented by Brian's widow, Vivien, to the two clubs at Emerald Headingley. Vivien hands silverware and a shield to Yorkshire Chairman Robin Smith, above, and to Somerset President Richard Parsons, below, as Yorkshire President Richard Hutton looks on. The pieces will be added to Brian's collection available for display in the cricket museums at Headingley and Taunton.

VERITY HONOURED: Yorkshire Vice-President Bryan Stott, an "old boy" of Rawdon Cricket Club, unveils a blue plaque at the club in tribute to Yorkshire and England's left-arm spinner Hedley Verity, one of Rawdon's most distinguished players, 75 years after his death. Captain Verity, of the Green Howards, was leading an infantry attack in Sicily in July 1943 when he was hit in the chest. He died 12 days later. Below, left to right: Peter Smith, Rawdon co-cricket chairman; Bryan Stott, John Davies, Parish Council chairman, and Clive Woods, chairman of Aireborough Civic Society. *(Photos: John Hughes)*

REMEMBERING DC: Pat Callaghan, right, widow of BBC Radio Leeds ball-by-ball commentator Dave Callaghan, who died earlier in the year, is pictured with their daughter, Julia, outside the boxes at Scarborough from which Dave broadcast to the nation and beyond. Dave's family were invited to the first day of the Yorkshire v. Worcestershire match to mark the unveiling of a plaque which reads: *Dave Callaghan 1955-2018 "The Voice of Yorkshire Cricket."* Obituary — Page 75. BELOW: North Marine Road still shows how it can attract a first-class crowd.

I'M IN CHARGE: Steven Patterson, above, will be keen to make his mark in 2019 as he again leads the Yorkshire first team after being appointed to the captaincy during last summer.

FOUR CENTURIES IN ONE INNINGS

		F S Jackson 117
		E Wainwright 126
1896	v. Warwickshire	Lord Hawke 166
	at Birmingham	R Peel *210

(First instance in First-Class cricket)

THREE CENTURIES IN ONE INNINGS

1884	v. Cambridge University	L Hall 116
	at Cambridge	W Bates 133
		I Grimshaw 115
1887	v. Kent	G Ulyett 124
	at Canterbury	L Hall 110
		F Lee 119
1897	v. Sussex	J T Brown 311
	at Sheffield	J Tunnicliffe 147
		E Wainwright *104
1899	v. Middlesex	F S Jackson 155
	at Bradford	D Denton 113
		F Mitchell 121
1904	v. Surrey	D Denton 105
	at The Oval	G H Hirst 104
		J Tunnicliffe *139
1919	v. Gloucestershire	H Sutcliffe 118
	at Leeds	D Denton 122
		R Kilner *115
1925	v. Glamorgan	P Holmes 130
	at Huddersfield	H Sutcliffe 121
		E Robinson *108
1928	v. Middlesex	P Holmes 105
	at Lord's	E Oldroyd 108
		A Mitchell 105
1928	v. Essex	H Sutcliffe 129
	at Leyton	P Holmes 136
		M Leyland *133
1929	v. Glamorgan	E Oldroyd 168
	at Hull	W Barber 114
		F E Greenwood *104
1933	v. MCC	H Sutcliffe 107
	at Scarborough	A Mitchell 158
		M Leyland 133
1936	v. Surrey	H Sutcliffe 129
	at Leeds	L Hutton 163
		M Leyland *163
1937	v. Leicestershire	H Sutcliffe 189
	at Hull	L Hutton 153
		M Leyland *118
1947	v. Leicestershire	L Hutton 137
	at Leicester	N W D Yardley 100
		G.A Smithson 169
1971	v. Oxford University	J H Hampshire *116
	at Oxford	R A Hutton 101
		A J Dalton 111
1975	v. Gloucestershire	G Boycott 141
	at Bristol	R G Lumb 101
		J H Hampshire *106

THREE CENTURIES IN ONE INNINGS *(Continued)*

		M D Moxon	.130
1995	v. Cambridge University	D Byas	.181
	at Cambridge	M G Bevan	*113
		M J Wood	.102
2001	v. Leicestershire	M J Lumb	.122
	at Leeds	D S Lehmann	.104
		C White	.183
2001	v. Glamorgan	M J Wood	.124
	at Scarborough	D Byas	.104
		J A Rudolph	.122
2007	v. Surrey	T T Bresnan	.116
	at The Oval	J N Gillespie	*123
		A Lyth	.130
2014	v. Leeds/Bradford MCCU	G S Ballance	.101
	at Leeds	J M Bairstow	.123
		A Lyth	.111
2016	v. Hampshire	J M Bairstow	.246
	at Leeds	L E Plunkett	.126

CENTURY IN EACH INNINGS

D Denton	107 and 109*	v. Nottinghamshire at Nottingham, 1906
G H Hirst	111 and 117*	v. Somerset at Bath, 1906
D Denton	133 and 121	v. MCC at Scarborough, 1908
W Rhodes	128 and 115	v. MCC at Scarborough, 1911
P Holmes	126 and 111*	v. Lancashire at Manchester, 1920
H Sutcliffe	107 and 109*	v. MCC at Scarborough, 1926
H Sutcliffe	111 and 100*	v. Nottinghamshire at Nottingham, 1928
E I Lester	126 and 142	v. Northamptonshire at Northampton, 1947
L Hutton	197 and 104	v. Essex at Southend, 1947
E I Lester	125* and 132	v. Lancashire at Manchester, 1948
L Hutton	165 and 100	v. Sussex at Hove, 1949
L Hutton	103 and 137	v. MCC at Scarborough, 1952
G Boycott	103 and 105	v. Nottinghamshire at Sheffield, 1966
G Boycott	163 and 141*	v. Nottinghamshire at Bradford, 1983
M D Moxon	123 and 112*	v. Indians at Scarborough, 1986
A A Metcalfe	194* and 107	v. Nottinghamshire at Nottingham, 1990
M P Vaughan	100 and 151	v. Essex at Chelmsford, 1999
Younus Khan	106 and 202*	v. Hampshire at Southampton, 2007
G S Ballance	148 and 108*	v. Surrey at The Oval, 2013
G S Ballance	108 and 203*	v. Hampshire at West End, 2017

HIGHEST INDIVIDUAL SCORES
FOR AND AGAINST YORKSHIRE

Highest For Yorkshire:
341 G H Hirst v. Leicestershire at Leicester, 1905

Highest Against Yorkshire:
318* W G Grace for Gloucestershire at Cheltenham, 1876

Yorkshire versus:

Derbyshire	*For Yorkshire:*	300 — J T Brown at Chesterfield, 1898
	Against:	270* — C F Hughes at Leeds, 2013
Most Centuries	*For Yorkshire:*	G Boycott 9
	Against:	K J Barnett and W Storer 4 each
Durham	*For Yorkshire:*	339 — D S Lehmann at Leeds, 2006
	Against:	221* — K K Jennings at Chester-le-Street, 2016
Most Centuries	*For Yorkshire:*	A McGrath 5
	Against:	M J Di Venuto 4

Yorkshire versus

Essex

	For Yorkshire:	313 — H Sutcliffe at Leyton, 1932
	Against:	219* — D J Insole at Colchester, 1949
Most Centuries	For Yorkshire:	H Sutcliffe 9
	Against:	F L Fane, K W R Fletcher, G A Gooch and D J Insole 3 each

Glamorgan

	For Yorkshire:	213 — M D Moxon at Cardiff, 1996
	Against:	202* — H Morris at Cardiff, 1996
Most Centuries	For Yorkshire:	G Boycott, P Holmes and H Sutcliffe 5 each
	Against:	H Morris 5

Gloucestershire

	For Yorkshire:	238 — D R Martyn at Leeds, 2003
	Against:	318* — W G Grace at Cheltenham, 1876
Most Centuries	For Yorkshire:	G Boycott 6
	Against:	W G Grace 9

Hampshire

	For Yorkshire:	302* — P Holmes at Portsmouth, 1920
	Against:	300* — M A Carberry at Southampton, 2011
Most Centuries	For Yorkshire:	H Sutcliffe 6
	Against:	C P Mead 10

Kent

	For Yorkshire:	248 — W Barber at Leeds, 1934.
	Against:	207 — D P Fulton at Maidstone, 1998
Most Centuries	For Yorkshire:	A McGrath 6
	Against:	F E Woolley 5

Lancashire

	For Yorkshire:	252 — D S Lehmann at Leeds, 2001
	Against:	225 — G D Lloyd at Leeds, 1997 (Non-Championship)
		206 — S G Law at Leeds, 2007
Most Centuries	For Yorkshire:	G Boycott and H Sutcliffe 9 each
	Against:	M A Atherton and C H Lloyd 6 each.

Leicestershire

	For Yorkshire:	341— G H Hirst at Leicester, 1905
	Against:	218— J J Whitaker at Bradford, 1996
Most Centuries	For Yorkshire:	H Sutcliffe 10
	Against:	J J Whitaker and C J B Wood 5 each

Middlesex

	For Yorkshire:	315* — P Holmes at Lord's, 1925
	Against:	243* — A J Webbe at Huddersfield, 1887
Most Centuries	For Yorkshire:	P Holmes and H Sutcliffe 7 each
	Against:	M W Gatting 8

Northamptonshire

	For Yorkshire:	277* — P Holmes at Harrogate, 1921
	Against:	235 — A J Lamb at Leeds, 1990
Most Centuries	For Yorkshire:	H Sutcliffe 5
	Against:	W Larkins 5

Nottinghamshire

	For Yorkshire:	285 — P Holmes at Nottingham, 1929
	Against:	251* — D J Hussey at Leeds, 2010
Most Centuries	For Yorkshire:	G Boycott 15
	Against:	R T Robinson 6

Somerset

	For Yorkshire:	213 — H Sutcliffe at Dewsbury, 1924
	Against:	297 — M J Wood at Taunton, 2005
Most Centuries	For Yorkshire:	G Boycott 6
	Against:	L C H Palairet, IVA. Richards, M E Trescothick 5 each

Surrey

	For Yorkshire:	255 — W Barber at Sheffield, 1935
	Against:	273 — T W Hayward at The Oval, 1899
Most Centuries	For Yorkshire:	H Sutcliffe 9
	Against:	J B Hobbs 8

Yorkshire versus

Sussex	*For Yorkshire:*	311 — J T Brown at Sheffield, 1897
	Against:	274* — M W Goodwin at Hove, 2011
Most Centuries	*For Yorkshire:*	L Hutton 8
	Against:	C B Fry 7

Warwickshire	*For Yorkshire:*	275 — P Holmes at Bradford, 1928
	Against:	225 — D P Ostler at Birmingham, 2002
Most Centuries	*For Yorkshire:*	G Boycott and H Sutcliffe 8 each
	Against:	D L Amiss, H E Dollery, R B Khanhai and W G Quaife 4 each.

Worcestershire	*For Yorkshire:*	274* — M D Moxon at Worcester, 1994
	Against:	259 — D Kenyon at Kidderminster, 1956
Most Centuries	*For Yorkshire:*	M Leyland 6
	Against:	D Kenyon and G M Turner 5 each

Australians	*For Yorkshire:*	167 — J T Brown at Bradford, 1899
	Against:	193* — B C Booth at Bradford, 1964
Most Centuries	*For Yorkshire:*	G Boycott and D Denton 2 each
	Against:	N C O'Neill 2

Indians	*For Yorkshire:*	183* — L Hutton at Bradford, 1946
	Against:	244* — V S Hazare at Sheffield, 1946
Most Centuries	*For Yorkshire:*	M D Moxon 2
	Against:	V S Hazare, VMankad, PR Umrigar D K Gaekwad, G A Parkar and R Lamba 1 each

New Zealanders	*For Yorkshire:*	175 — P Holmes at Bradford, 1927
	Against:	126 — W M Wallace at Bradford, 1949
Most Centuries	*For Yorkshire:*	L Hutton and DB Close 2 each
	Against:	H G Vivian, WM Wallace and J G Wright 1 each

Pakistanis	*For Yorkshire:*	197 — P J Sharpe at Leeds, 1967
	Against:	139 — A H Kardar at Sheffield, 1954
Most Centuries	*For Yorkshire:*	P J Sharpe 2
	Against:	A H Kardar 1

South Africans	*For Yorkshire:*	156 — L Hutton at Sheffield, 1951
	Against:	168 — I J Seidle at Sheffield, 1929
Most Centuries	*For Yorkshire:*	L Hutton 2
	Against:	H B Cameron, J D Lindsay, B Mitchell, D P B Morkel, I J Seidle, L J Tancred, C B van Ryneveld 1 each

Sri Lankans	*For Yorkshire:*	132 — M D Moxon at Leeds, 1988
	Against:	112 — S A R Silva at Leeds, 1988
Most Centuries	*For Yorkshire:*	K Sharp 2
	Against:	S A R Silva 1

West Indians	*For Yorkshire:*	112* — D Denton at Harrogate, 1906
	Against:	164 — S F A Bacchus at Leeds, 1980
Most Centuries	*For Yorkshire:*	M G Bevan, D Denton, L Hutton, R G Lumb and A A Metcalfe 1 each
	Against:	S F A Bacchus, C O Browne, S Chanderpaul P A Goodman, C L Hooper and G St A Sobers 1 each

HIGHEST INDIVIDUAL SCORES FOR AND AGAINST
YORKSHIRE *(continued)*

Yorkshire versus

Zimbabweans	*For Yorkshire:*	113 — M D Moxon at Leeds, 1990
	Against:	89 — G J Whittall at Leeds, 2000
Most Centuries	*For Yorkshire:*	M D Moxon 1
	Against:	None
Cambridge	*For Yorkshire:*	207* — G Boycott at Cambridge, 1976
University	*Against:*	171* — G L Jessop at Cambridge, 1899
		171 — P B H May at Cambridge, 1952
Most Centuries	*For Yorkshire:*	H Sutcliffe 4
	Against:	G M Kemp 2
Durham MCCU	*For Yorkshire:*	139 — J J Sayers at Durham, 2011
	Against:	127 — T Westley at Durham, 2011
Most Centuries	*For Yorkshire:*	J J Sayers 1
	Against:	T Westley 1
Leeds Bradford MCCU	*For Yorkshire:*	194 — A Lyth at Leeds, 2017
	Against:	69 — A MacQueen at Leeds, 2012
Most Centuries	*For Yorkshire:*	A Lyth, 3
Loughborough MCCU	*For Yorkshire:*	134* — R M Pyrah at Leeds, 2010
	Against:	107 — C P Murtagh at Leeds, 2007
Most Centuries	*For Yorkshire:*	R M Pyrah 2
	Against:	C P Murtagh 1
MCC	*For Yorkshire:*	180* — G H Hirst at Lord's, 1919
	Against:	214 — E H Hendren at Lord's, 1919
Most Centuries	*For Yorkshire:*	L Hutton 8
	Against:	R E S Wyatt 5
Oxford University	*For Yorkshire:*	196 — R J Blakey at Oxford, 1991
	Against:	201 — J E Raphael at Oxford, 1904
Most Centuries	*For Yorkshire:*	M Leyland 4
	Against:	A A Baig and Nawab of Pataudi (Jun.) 2 each

J B Hobbs scored 11 centuries against Yorkshire – the highest by any individual (8 for Surrey and 3 for the Rest of England).

Three players have scored 10 centuries against Yorkshire – W G Grace (9 for Gloucestershire and 1 for MCC). E H Hendren (6 for Middlesex, 3 for MCC and 1 for the Rest of England) and C P Mead (all 10 for Hampshire).

CARRYING BAT THROUGH A COMPLETED INNINGS

Batsman	Score	Total	Against	Season
G R Atkinson	30*	73	Nottinghamshire at Bradford	1865
L Hall	31*	94	Sussex at Hove	1878
L Hall	124*	331	Sussex at Hove	1883
L Hall	128*	285	Sussex at Huddersfield	1884
L Hall	32*	81	Kent at Sheffield	1885
L Hall	79*	285	Surrey at Sheffield	1885
L Hall	37*	96	Derbyshire at Derby	1885
L Hall	50*	173	Sussex at Huddersfield	1886
L Hall	74*	172	Kent at Canterbury	1886
G Ulyett	199*	399	Derbyshire at Sheffield	1887
L Hall	119*	334	Gloucestershire at Dewsbury	1887
L Hall	82*	218	Sussex at Sheffield	1887
L Hall	34*	104	Surrey at The Oval	1888
L Hall	129*	461	Gloucestershire at Clifton	1888
L Hall	85*	259	Middlesex at Lord's	1889
L Hall	41*	106	Nottinghamshire at Sheffield	1891
W Rhodes	98*	184	MCC at Lord's	1903
W Rhodes	85*	152	Essex at Leyton	1910
P Holmes	145*	270	Northamptonshire at Northampton	1920
H Sutcliffe	125*	307	Essex at Southend	1920
P Holmes	175*	377	New Zealanders at Bradford	1927
P Holmes	110*	219	Northamptonshire at Bradford	1929
H Sutcliffe	104*	170	Hampshire at Leeds	1932
H Sutcliffe	114*	202	Rest of England at The Oval	1933
H Sutcliffe	187*	401	Worcestershire at Bradford	1934
H Sutcliffe	135*	262	Glamorgan at Neath	1935
H Sutcliffe	125*	322	Oxford University at Oxford	1939
L Hutton	99*	200	Leicestershire at Sheffield	1948
L Hutton	78*	153	Worcestershire at Sheffield	1949
F A Lowson	76*	218	MCC at Lord's	1951
W B Stott	144*	262	Worcestershire at Worcester	1959
D E V Padgett	115*	230	Gloucestershire at Bristol	1962
G Boycott	114*	297	Leicestershire at Sheffield	1968
G Boycott	53*	119	Warwickshire at Bradford	1969
G Boycott	182*	320	Middlesex at Lord's	1971
G Boycott	138*	232	Warwickshire at Birmingham	1971
G Boycott	175*	360	Nottinghamshire at Worksop	1979
G Boycott	112*	233	Derbyshire at Sheffield	1983
G Boycott	55*	183	Warwickshire at Leeds	1984
G Boycott	55*	131	Surrey at Sheffield	1985
M J Wood	60*	160	Somerset at Scarborough	2004
J J Sayers	122*	326	Middlesex at Scarborough	2006
J J Sayers	149*	414	Durham at Leeds	2007
A Lyth	248*	486	Leicestershire at Leicester	2012

44 instances, of which L Hall (14 times), G Boycott (8) and H Sutcliffe (6) account for 28 between them.

The highest percentage of an innings total is 61.17% by H. Sutcliffe (104* v. Hampshire at Leeds in 1932) but P Holmes was absent ill, so only nine wickets fell.

Other contributions exceeding 55% are:

59.48%	G Boycott	(138*	v. Warwickshire at Birmingham, 1971)
56.87%	G Boycott	(182*	v. Middlesex at Lord's, 1971)
56.43%	H Sutcliffe	(114*	v. Rest of England at The Oval, 1933)
55.92%	W Rhodes	(85*	v. Essex at Leyton, 1910)

2,000 RUNS IN A SEASON

Batsman	Season	M	I	NO	Runs	HS	Avge	100s
G H Hirst	1904	32	44	3	2257	157	55.04	8
D Denton	1905	33	52	2	2258	172	45.16	8
G H Hirst	1906	32	53	6	2164	169	46.04	6
D Denton	1911	32	55	4	2161	137*	42.37	6
D Denton	1912	36	51	4	2088	221	44.23	6
P Holmes	1920	30	45	6	2144	302*	54.97	7
P Holmes	1925	35	49	9	2351	315*	58.77	6
H Sutcliffe	1925	34	48	8	2236	235	55.90	7
H Sutcliffe	1928	27	35	5	2418	228	80.60	11
P Holmes	1928	31	40	4	2093	275	58.13	6
H Sutcliffe	1931	28	33	8	2351	230	94.04	9
H Sutcliffe	1932	29	41	5	2883	313	80.08	12
M Leyland	1933	31	44	4	2196	210*	54.90	7
A Mitchell	1933	34	49	10	2100	158	53.84	6
H Sutcliffe	1935	32	47	3	2183	212	49.61	8
L Hutton	1937	28	45	6	2448	271*	62.76	8
H Sutcliffe	1937	32	52	5	2054	189	43.70	4
L Hutton	1939	29	44	5	2316	280*	59.38	10
L Hutton	1947	19	31	2	2068	270*	71.31	10
L Hutton	1949	26	44	6	2640	269*	69.47	9
F A Lowson	1950	31	54	5	2067	141*	42.18	5
D E V Padgett	1959	35	60	8	2158	161*	41.50	4
W B Stott	1959	32	56	2	2034	144*	37.66	3
P J Sharpe	1962	36	62	8	2201	138	40.75	7
G Boycott	1971	18	25	4	2221	233	105.76	11
A A Metcalfe	1990	23	44	4	2047	194*	51.17	6

1,000 RUNS IN A SEASON

Batsman		Runs scored	Runs scored	Runs scored
C W J Athey	(2)	1113 in 1980	1339 in 1982	—
D L Bairstow	(3)	1083 in 1981	1102 in 1983	1163 in 1985
J M Bairstow	(2)	1015 in 2011	1108 in 2015	—
G S Ballance	(2)	1363 in 2013	1023 in 2017	—
W Barber	(8)	1000 in 1932	1595 in 1933	1930 in 1934
		1958 in 1935	1466 in 1937	1455 in 1938
		1501 in 1939	1170 in 1946	—
M G Bevan	(2)	1598 in 1995	1225 in 1996	—
R J Blakey	(5)	1361 in 1987	1159 in 1989	1065 in 1992
		1236 in 1994	1041 in 2002	—
J B Bolus	(2)	1245 in 1960	1970 in 1961	—
M W Booth	(2)	1189 in 1911	1076 in 1913	—
G Boycott	(19)	1628 in 1963	1639 in 1964	1215 in 1965
		1388 in 1966	1530 in 1967	1004 in 1968
		1558 in 1970	2221 in 1971	1156 in 1972
		1478 in 1974	1915 in 1975	1288 in 1976
		1259 in 1977	1074 in 1978	1160 in 1979
		1913 in 1982	1941 in 1983	1567 in 1984
		1657 in 1985	—	—
J T Brown	(9)	1196 in 1894	1260 in 1895	1755 in 1896
		1634 in 1897	1641 in 1898	1375 in 1899
		1181 in 1900	1627 in 1901	1291 in 1903
D Byas	(5)	1557 in 1991	1073 in 1993	1297 in 1994
		1913 in 1995	1319 in 1997	—

Batsman	Runs scored	Runs scored	Runs scored
D B Close .... (13)	1192 in 1952	1287 in 1954	1131 in 1955
	1315 in 1957	1335 in 1958	1740 in 1959
	1699 in 1960	1821 in 1961	1438 in 1962
	1145 in 1963	1281 in 1964	1127 in 1965
	1259 in 1966	—	—
K R Davidson .... (1)	1241 in 1934	—	—
D Denton .... (20)	1028 in 1896	1357 in 1897	1595 in 1899
	1378 in 1900	1400 in 1901	1191 in 1902
	1562 in 1903	1919 in 1904	2258 in 1905
	1905 in 1906	1128 in 1907	1852 in 1908
	1765 in 1909	1106 in 1910	2161 in 1911
	2088 in 1912	1364 in 1913	1799 in 1914
	1213 in 1919	1324 in 1920	—
A Drake .... (2)	1487 in 1911	1029 in 1913	—
A W Gale .... (2)	1076 in 2013	1045 in 2015	—
A P Grayson .... (1)	1046 in 1994	—	—
S Haigh .... (1)	1031 in 1904	—	—
L Hall .... (1)	1120 in 1887	—	—
H Halliday .... (4)	1357 in 1948	1484 in 1950	1351 in 1952
	1461 in 1953	—	—
J H Hampshire .... (12)	1236 in 1963	1280 in 1964	1424 in 1965
	1105 in 1966	1244 in 1967	1133 in 1968
	1079 in 1970	1259 in 1971	1124 in 1975
	1303 in 1976	1596 in 1978	1425 in 1981
Lord Hawke .... (1)	1005 in 1895	—	—
G H Hirst .... (19)	1110 in 1896	1248 in 1897	1546 in 1899
	1752 in 1900	1669 in 1901	1113 in 1902
	1535 in 1903	2257 in 1904	1972 in 1905
	2164 in 1906	1167 in 1907	1513 in 1908
	1151 in 1909	1679 in 1910	1639 in 1911
	1119 in 1912	1431 in 1913	1655 in 1914
	1312 in 1919	—	—
P Holmes .... (14)	1876 in 1919	2144 in 1920	1458 in 1921
	1614 in 1922	1884 in 1923	1610 in 1924
	2351 in 1925	1792 in 1926	1774 in 1927
	2093 in 1928	1724 in 1929	1957 in 1930
	1431 in 1931	1191 in 1932	—
L Hutton .... (12)	1282 in 1936	2448 in 1937	1171 in 1938
	2316 in 1939	1322 in 1946	2068 in 1947
	1792 in 1948	2640 in 1949	1581 in 1950
	1554 in 1951	1956 in 1952	1532 in 1953
R Illingworth .... (5)	1193 in 1957	1490 in 1959	1029 in 1961
	1610 in 1962	1301 in 1964	—
F S Jackson .... (4)	1211 in 1896	1300 in 1897	1442 in 1898
	1468 in 1899	—	—
P A Jaques .... (2)	1118 in 2004	1359 in 2005	—
S A Kellett .... (2)	1266 in 1991	1326 in 1992	—
R Kilner .... (10)	1586 in 1913	1329 in 1914	1135 in 1919
	1240 in 1920	1137 in 1921	1132 in 1922
	1265 in 1923	1002 in 1925	1021 in 1926
	1004 in 1927	—	—
A Z Lees .... (2)	1018 in 2014	1285 in 2016	—
D S Lehmann .... (5)	1575 in 1997	1477 in 2000	1416 in 2001
....	1136 in 2002	1706 in 2006	—

1,000 RUNS IN A SEASON *(Continued)*

Batsman	Runs scored	Runs scored	Runs scored
E I Lester	(6) 1256 in 1948	1774 in 1949	1015 in 1950
	1786 in 1952	1380 in 1953	1330 in 1954
M Leyland	(17) 1088 in 1923	1203 in 1924	1560 in 1925
	1561 in 1926	1478 in 1927	1554 in 1928
	1407 in 1929	1814 in 1930	1127 in 1931
	1821 in 1932	2196 in 1933	1228 in 1934
	1366 in 1935	1621 in 1936	1120 in 1937
	1640 in 1938	1238 in 1939	
J D Love	(2) 1161 in 1981	1020 in 1983	—
F A Lowson	(8) 1678 in 1949	2067 in 1950	1607 in 1951
	1562 in 1952	1586 in 1953	1719 in 1954
	1082 in 1955	1428 in 1956	—
M J Lumb	(1) 1038 in 2003	—	—
R G Lumb	(5) 1002 in 1973	1437 in 1975	1070 in 1978
	1465 in 1979	1223 in 1980	
A Lyth	(3) 1509 in 2010	1619 in 2014	1153 in 2016
A McGrath	(3) 1425 in 2005	1293 in 2006	1219 in 2010
A A Metcalfe	(6) 1674 in 1986	1162 in 1987	1320 in 1988
	1230 in 1989	2047 in 1990	1210 in 1991
A Mitchell	(10) 1320 in 1928	1633 in 1930	1351 in 1932
	2100 in 1933	1854 in 1934	1530 in 1935
	1095 in 1936	1602 in 1937	1305 in 1938
	1219 in 1939	—	—
F Mitchell	(2) 1678 in 1899	1801 in 1901	—
R Moorhouse	(1) 1096 in 1895	—	—
M D Moxon	(11) 1016 in 1984	1256 in 1985	1298 in 1987
	1430 in 1988	1156 in 1989	1621 in 1990
	1669 in 1991	1314 in 1992	1251 in 1993
	1458 in 1994	1145 in 1995	—
E Oldroyd	(10) 1473 in 1921	1690 in 1922	1349 in 1923
	1607 in 1924	1262 in 1925	1197 in 1926
	1390 in 1927	1304 in 1928	1474 in 1929
	1285 in 1930	—	—
D E V Padgett	(12) 1046 in 1956	2158 in 1959	1574 in 1960
	1856 in 1961	1750 in 1962	1380 in 1964
	1220 in 1965	1194 in 1966	1284 in 1967
	1163 in 1968	1078 in 1969	1042 in 1970
R Peel	(1) 1193 in 1896	—	—
W Rhodes	(17) 1251 in 1904	1353 in 1905	1618 in 1906
	1574 in 1908	1663 in 1909	1355 in 1910
	1961 in 1911	1030 in 1912	1805 in 1913
	1325 in 1914	1138 in 1919	1329 in 1921
	1368 in 1922	1168 in 1923	1030 in 1924
	1256 in 1925	1071 in 1926	—
E Robinson	(2) 1104 in 1921	1097 in 1929	—
P E Robinson	(3) 1173 in 1988	1402 in 1990	1293 in 1991
J A Rudolph	(4) 1078 in 2007	1292 in 2008	1366 in 2009
	1375 in 2010	—	—
J J Sayers	(1) 1150 in 2009	—	—
A B Sellers	(1) 1109 in 1938	—	—
K Sharp	(1) 1445 in 1984	—	—

1,000 RUNS IN A SEASON *(Continued)*

Batsman		*Runs scored*	*Runs scored*	*Runs scored*
P J Sharpe	(10)	1039 in 1960	1240 in 1961	2201 in 1962
		1273 in 1964	1091 in 1965	1352 in 1967
		1256 in 1968	1012 in 1969	1149 in 1970
		1320 in 1973	—	—
W B Stott	(5)	1362 in 1957	1036 in 1958	2034 in 1959
		1790 in 1960	1409 in 1961	—
H Sutcliffe	(21)	†1839 in 1919	1393 in 1920	1235 in 1921
		1909 in 1922	1773 in 1923	1720 in 1924
		2236 in 1925	1672 in 1926	1814 in 1927
		2418 in 1928	1485 in 1929	1636 in 1930
		2351 in 1931	2883 in 1932	1986 in 1933
		1511 in 1934	2183 in 1935	1295 in 1936
		2054 in 1937	1660 in 1938	1416 in 1939

† First season in First-Class cricket – The record for a debut season.

Batsman		*Runs scored*	*Runs scored*	*Runs scored*
W H H Sutcliffe	(1)	1193 in 1955	—	—
K Taylor	(6)	1306 in 1959	1107 in 1960	1494 in 1961
		1372 in 1962	1149 in 1964	1044 in 1966
T L Taylor	(2)	1236 in 1901	1373 in 1902	—
S R Tendulkar	(1)	1070 in 1992	—	—
J Tunnicliffe	(12)	1333 in 1895	1368 in 1896	1208 in 1897
		1713 in 1898	1434 in 1899	1496 in 1900
		1295 in 1901	1274 in 1902	1650 in 1904
		1096 in 1905	1232 in 1906	1195 in 1907
C Turner	(1)	1153 in 1934	—	—
G Ulyett	(4)	1083 in 1878	1158 in 1882	1024 in 1885
		1285 in 1887	—	—
M P Vaughan	(4)	1066 in 1994	1235 in 1995	1161 in 1996
		1161 in 1998	—	—
E Wainwright	(3)	1492 in 1897	1479 in 1899	1044 in 1901
W A I Washington	(1)	1022 in 1902	—	—
W Watson	(8)	1331 in 1947	1352 in 1948	1586 in 1952
		1350 in 1953	1347 in 1954	1564 in 1955
		1378 in 1956	1455 in 1957	—
W H Wilkinson	(1)	1282 in 1908	—	—
B B Wilson	(5)	1054 in 1909	1455 in 1911	1453 in 1912
		1533 in 1913	1632 in 1914	—
J V Wilson	(12)	1460 in 1949	1548 in 1950	1985 in 1951
		1349 in 1952	1531 in 1953	1713 in 1954
		1799 in 1955	1602 in 1956	1287 in 1957
		1064 in 1960	1018 in 1961	1226 in 1962
A Wood	(1)	1237 in 1935	—	—
M J Wood	(4)	1080 in 1998	1060 in 2001	1432 in 2003
		1005 in 2005	—	—
N W D Yardley	(4)	1028 in 1939	1299 in 1947	1413 in 1949
		1031 in 1950	—	—

BATSMEN WHO HAVE SCORED OVER 10,000 RUNS

Player	M	I	NO	Runs	HS	Av'ge	100s
H Sutcliffe	602	864	96	38558	313	50.20	112
D Denton	676	1058	61	33282	221	33.38	61
G Boycott	414	674	111	32570	260*	57.85	103
G H Hirst	717	1050	128	32024	341	34.73	56
W Rhodes	883	1195	162	31075	267*	30.08	46
P Holmes	485	699	74	26220	315*	41.95	60
M Leyland	548	720	82	26180	263	41.03	62
L Hutton	341	527	62	24807	280*	53.34	85
D B Close	536	811	102	22650	198	31.94	33
J H Hampshire	456	724	89	21979	183*	34.61	34
J V Wilson	477	724	75	20548	230	31.66	29
D E V Padgett	487	774	63	20306	161*	28.55	29
J Tunnicliffe	472	768	57	19435	243	27.33	22
M D Moxon	277	476	42	18973	274*	43.71	41
A Mitchell	401	550	69	18189	189	37.81	39
P J Sharpe	411	666	71	17685	203*	29.72	23
E Oldroyd	383	509	58	15891	194	35.23	37
J T Brown	345	567	41	15694	311	29.83	23
W Barber	354	495	48	15315	255	34.26	27
R Illingworth	496	668	131	14986	162	27.90	14
D Byas	268	449	42	14398	213	35.37	28
G Ulyett	355	618	31	14157	199*	24.11	15
R J Blakey	339	541	84	14150	223*	30.96	12
A McGrath	242	405	29	14091	211	37.47	34
W Watson	283	430	65	13953	214*	38.22	26
F A Lowson	252	404	31	13897	259*	37.25	30
Lord Hawke	510	739	91	13133	166	20.26	10
R Kilner	365	478	46	13018	206*	30.13	15
D L Bairstow	429	601	113	12985	145	26.60	9
K Taylor	303	505	35	12864	203*	27.37	16
N W D Yardley	302	420	56	11632	183*	31.95	17
R G Lumb	239	395	30	11525	165*	31.57	22
E Wainwright	352	545	30	11092	228	21.53	18
S Haigh	513	687	110	10993	159	19.05	4
E I Lester	228	339	27	10616	186	34.02	24
A A Metcalfe	184	317	19	10465	216*	35.11	25
C White	221	350	45	10376	186	34.01	19
Hon F S Jackson	207	328	22	10371	160	33.89	21
J D Love	247	388	58	10263	170*	31.10	13

PLAYERS WHO HAVE SCORED CENTURIES
FOR AND AGAINST YORKSHIRE

Player		For	Venue	Season
C W J Athey (5)	114*	Gloucestershire	Bradford	1984
(10 for Yorkshire)	101	Gloucestershire	Gloucester	1985
	101*	Gloucestershire	Leeds	1987
	112	Sussex	Scarborough	1993
	100	Sussex	Eastbourne	1996
M G Bevan (1)	142	Leicestershire	Leicester	2002
(9 for Yorkshire)				
J B Bolus (2)	114	Nottinghamshire	Bradford	1963
(7 for Yorkshire)	138	Derbyshire	Sheffield	1973
D B Close (1)	102	Somerset	Taunton	1971
(33 for Yorkshire)				
M T G Elliott (1)	125	Glamorgan	Leeds	2004
(1 for Yorkshire)				
P A Gibb (1)	107	Essex	Brentwood	1951
(2 for Yorkshire)				
P A Jaques (1)	222	Northamptonshire	Northampton	2003
(7 for Yorkshire)				
N Kilner (2)	119	Warwickshire	Hull	1932
(2 for Yorkshire)	197	Warwickshire	Birmingham	1933
M J Lumb (1)	135	Nottinghamshire	Scarborough	2013
(8 for Yorkshire)				
P J Sharpe (1)	126	Derbyshire	Chesterfield	1976
(23 for Yorkshire)				

RECORD PARTNERSHIPS FOR YORKSHIRE

1st wkt	555	P Holmes (224*)	and H Sutcliffe (313)	v. Essex at Leyton	1932
2nd wkt	346	W Barber (162)	and M Leyland (189)	v. Middlesex at Sheffield	1932
3rd wkt	346	J J Sayers (173)	and A McGrath (211)	v. Warwickshire at Birmingham	2009
4th wkt	372	J E Root (213)	and J M Bairstow (198)	v. Surrey at Leeds	2016
5th wkt	340	E Wainwright (228)	and G H Hirst (186)	v. Surrey at The Oval	1899
6th wkt	296	A Lyth (251)	and A U Rashid (159*)	v. Lancashire at Manchester,	2014
7th wkt	366*	J M Bairstow (219*)	and T T Bresnan (169*)	v, Durham at Chester-le-Street	2015
8th wkt	292	R Peel (210*)	and Lord Hawke (166)	v. Warwickshire at Birmingham	1896
9th wkt	246	T T Bresnan (116)	and J N Gillespie (123*)	v. Surrey at The Oval	2007
10th wkt	149	G Boycott (79)	and G B Stevenson (115*)	v. Warwickshire at Birmingham	1982

RECORD PARTNERSHIPS AGAINST YORKSHIRE

1st wkt	372	R R Montgomerie (127)	and M B Loye (205)	for Northamptonshire at Northampton	1996
2nd wkt	417	K J Barnett (210*)	and TA Tweats (189)	for Derbyshire at Derby	1997
3rd wkt	523	M A Carberry (300*)	and N D McKenzie (237)	for Hampshire at Southampton	2011
4th wkt	447	R Abel (193)	and T Hayward (273)	for Surrey at The Oval	1899
5th wkt	261	W G Grace (318*)	and W O Moberley (103)	for Gloucestershire at Cheltenham	1876
6th wkt	294	D R Jardine (157)	and P G H Fender (177)	for Surrey at Bradford	1928
7th wkt	315	D M Benkenstein (151)	and O D Gibson (155)	for Durham at Leeds	2006
8th wkt	178	A P Wells (253*)	and B T P Donelan (59)	for Sussex at Middlesbrough	1991
9th wkt	233	I J L Trott (161*)	and J S Patel (120)	for Warwickshire at Birmingham	2009
10th wkt	132	A Hill (172*)	and M Jean-Jacques (73)	for Derbyshire at Sheffield	1986

CENTURY PARTNERSHIPS FOR THE FIRST WICKET IN BOTH INNINGS

128	108	G Ulyett (82 and 91)	and L Hall (87 and 37)	v. Sussex at Hove	1885
		(First instance in First-Class cricket)			
138	147*	J T Brown (203 and 81*)	and J Tunnicliffe (62 and 63*)	v. Middlesex at Lord's	1896
		(Second instance in First-Class cricket)			
105	265*	P Holmes (51 and 127*)	and H Sutcliffe (71 and 131*)	v. Surrey at The Oval	1926
184	210*	P Holmes (83 and 101*)	and H Sutcliffe (111 and 100*)	v. Nottinghamshire at Nottingham	1928
110	117	L Hutton (95 and 86)	and W Watson (34 and 57)	v. Lancashire at Manchester	1947
122	230	W B Stott (50 and 114)	and K Taylor (79 and 140)	v. Nottinghamshire at Nottingham	1957
136	138	J B Bolus (108 and 71)	and K Taylor (89 and 75)	v. Cambridge University at Cambridge	1962
105	105	G Boycott (38 and 64)	and K Taylor (85 and 49)	v. Leicestershire at Leicester	1963
116	112*	K Taylor (45 and 68)	and J H Hampshire (68 and 67*)	v. Oxford University at Oxford	1964
104	104	G Boycott (117 and 49*)	and R G Lumb (47 and 57)	v. Sussex at Leeds	1974
134	185*	M D Moxon (57 and 89*)	and A A Metcalfe (216* and 78*)	v. Middlesex at Leeds	1988
118	129*	G S Ballance (72 and 73*)	and J J Sayers (139 and 53*)	v. Durham MCCU at Durham	2011

CENTURY PARTNERSHIPS FOR THE FIRST WICKET IN BOTH INNINGS BUT WITH CHANGE OF PARTNER

109		W H H Sutcliffe (82) and F A Lowson (46)
	143	W H H Sutcliffe (88) and W Watson (52) v. Canadians at Scarborough, 1954
109		G Boycott (70) and R G Lumb (44)
	135	G Boycott (74) and JH Hampshire (58) v. Northamptonshire at Bradford, 1977

CENTURY PARTNERSHIPS

FIRST WICKET (Qualification 200 runs)

555	P Holmes (224*) and H Sutcliffe (313) v. Essex at Leyton, 1932	
554	J T Brown (300) and J Tunnicliffe (243) v. Derbyshire at Chesterfield, 1898	
378	J T Brown (311) and J Tunnicliffe (147) v. Sussex at Sheffield, 1897	
375	A Lyth (230) and (A Z Lees (138) v. Northamptonshire at Northampton, 2014	
362	M D Moxon (213) and M P Vaughan (183) v. Glamorgan at Cardiff, 1996	
351	G Boycott (184) and M D Moxon (168) v. Worcestershire at Worcester, 1985	
347	P Holmes (302*) and H Sutcliffe (131) v. Hampshire at Portsmouth, 1920	
323	P Holmes (125) and H Sutcliffe (195) v. Lancashire at Sheffield, 1931	
315	H Sutcliffe (189) and L Hutton (153) v. Leicestershire at Hull, 1937	
315	H Sutcliffe (116) and L Hutton (280*) v. Hampshire at Sheffield, 1939	
309	P Holmes (250) and H Sutcliffe (129) v. Warwickshire at Birmingham, 1931	
309	C White (186) and M J Wood (115) v. Lancashire at Manchester, 2001	
290	P Holmes (179*) and H Sutcliffe (104) v. Middlesex at Leeds, 1928	
288	G Boycott (130*) and R G Lumb (159) v. Somerset at Harrogate, 1979	
286	L Hutton (156) and F A Lowson (115) v. South Africans at Sheffield, 1951	
282	M D Moxon (147) and A A Metcalfe (151) v. Lancashire at Manchester, 1986	
281*	W B Stott (138*) and K Taylor (130*) v. Sussex at Hove, 1960	
279	P Holmes (133) and H Sutcliffe (145) v. Northamptonshire at Northampton, 1919	
274	P.Holmes (199) and H Sutcliffe (139) v. Somerset at Hull, 1923	
274	P Holmes (180) and H Sutcliffe (134) v. Gloucestershire at Gloucester, 1927	
272	P Holmes (194) and H Sutcliffe (129) v. Leicestershire at Hull, 1925	
272	M J Wood (202*) and J J Sayers (115) v. Bangladesh 'A' at Leeds, 2005	
270	A Lyth (143) and A Z Lees (108) v. Durham at Leeds, 2014	
268	P Holmes (136) and H Sutcliffe (129) v. Essex at Leyton, 1928	
267	W Barber (248) and L Hutton (70) v. Kent at Leeds, 1934	
265*	P Holmes (127*) and H Sutcliffe (131*) v. Surrey at The Oval, 1926	
264	G Boycott (161*) and R G Lumb (132) v. Gloucestershire at Leeds, 1976	
253	P Holmes (123) and H Sutcliffe (132) v. Lancashire at Sheffield, 1919	
248	G Boycott (163) and A A Metcalfe (122) v. Nottinghamshire at Bradford, 1983	
245	L Hutton (152) and F A Lowson (120) v. Lancashire at Leeds, 1952	
244	J A Rudolph (149) and J J Sayers (86) v Nottinghamshire at Nottingham, 2009	
241	P Holmes (142) and H Sutcliffe (123*) v. Surrey at The Oval, 1929	
240	G Boycott (233) and P J Sharpe (92) v. Essex at Colchester, 1971	
238*	P Holmes (126*) and H Sutcliffe (105*) v. Cambridge University at Cambridge, 1923	
236	G Boycott (131) and K Taylor (153) v. Lancashire at Manchester, 1964	
235	P Holmes (130) and H Sutcliffe (132*) v. Glamorgan at Sheffield, 1930	
233	G Boycott (141*) and R G Lumb (90) v. Cambridge University at Cambridge, 1973	
233	H Halliday (116) and W Watson (108) v. Northamptonshire at Northampton, 1948	
231	M P Vaughan (151) and D Byas (90) v. Essex at Chelmsford, 1999	
230	H Sutcliffe (129) and L Hutton (163) v. Surrey at Leeds, 1936	
230	W B Stott (114) and K Taylor (140*) v. Nottinghamshire at Nottingham, 1957	
228	H Halliday (90) and J V Wilson (223*) v. Scotland at Scarborough, 1951	
228	G Boycott (141) and R G Lumb (101) v. Gloucestershire at Bristol, 1975	
227	P Holmes (110) and H Sutcliffe (119) v. Leicestershire at Leicester, 1928	
225	R G Lumb (101) and C W J Athey (125*) v. Gloucestershire at Sheffield, 1980	
224	C W J Athey (114) and J D Love (104) v. Warwickshire at Birmingham, 1980	
222	W B Stott (141) and K Taylor (90) v. Sussex at Bradford, 1958	
221	P Holmes (130) and H Sutcliffe (121) v. Glamorgan at Huddersfield, 1925	
221	M D Moxon (141) and A A Metcalfe (73) v. Surrey at The Oval, 1992	
221	A Lyth (111) and A Z Lees (121) v. Leeds/Bradford MCCU at Leeds, 2013	
219	P Holmes (102) and A Mitchell (130*) v. Somerset at Bradford, 1930	
218	M Leyland (110) and H Sutcliffe (235) v. Middlesex at Leeds, 1925	
218	R G Lumb (145) and M D Moxon (111) v. Derbyshire at Sheffield, 1981	
210*	P Holmes (101*) and H Sutcliffe (100*) v. Nottinghamshire at Nottingham, 1928	
210	G Boycott (128) and P J Sharpe (197) v. Pakistanis at Leeds, 1967	
209	F A Lowson (115) and D E V Padgett (107) v. Scotland at Hull, 1956	

CENTURY PARTNERSHIPS *(Continued)*

208	A Mitchell (85) and E Oldroyd (111) v. Cambridge University at Cambridge, 1929
207	A Mitchell (90) and W Barber (107) v. Middlesex at Lord's, 1935
206	G Boycott (118) and R G Lumb (87) v. Glamorgan at Sheffield, 1978
204	M D Moxon (66) and A A Metcalfe (162) v. Gloucestershire at Cheltenham, 1990
203	L Hutton (119) and F A Lowson (83) v. Somerset at Huddersfield, 1952
203	M D Moxon (117) and S A Kellett (87) v. Somerset at Middlesbrough, 1992
203	M D Moxon (134) and M P Vaughan (106) v. Matebeleland at Bulawayo, 1996
200*	P Holmes (107*) and H Sutcliffe (80*) v. Oxford University at Oxford, 1930

Note: P Holmes and H Sutcliffe shared 69 century opening partnerships for Yorkshire;
G Boycott and R G Lumb 29; L Hutton and F A Lowson 22; M D Moxon and A A Metcalfe 21;
J T Brown and J Tunnicliffe 19; H Sutcliffe and L Hutton 15, and L Hall and G Ulyett 12.

SECOND WICKET (Qualification 200 runs)

346	W Barber (162) and M Leyland (189) v. Middlesex at Sheffield, 1932
343	F A Lowson (183*) and J V Wilson (165) v. Oxford University at Oxford, 1956
333	P Holmes (209) and E Oldroyd (138*) v. Warwickshire at Birmingham, 1922
314	H Sutcliffe (255*) and E Oldroyd (138) v. Essex at Southend-on-Sea, 1924
311	A Z Lees (275*) and P A Jaques (139) v. Derbyshire at Chesterfield, 2013
305	J W.Rothery (134) and D Denton (182) v. Derbyshire at Chesterfield, 1910
302	W Watson (172) and J V Wilson (140) v. Derbyshire at Scarborough, 1948
301	P J Sharpe (172*) and D E V Padgett (133) v. Glamorgan at Swansea, 1971
288	H Sutcliffe (165) and A Mitchell (126) v. Lancashire at Manchester, 1939
280	L Hall (160) and F Lee (165) v. Lancashire at Bradford, 1887
266*	K Taylor (178*) and D E V Padgett (107*) v. Oxford University at Oxford, 1962
264	P A Jaques (152) and K S Williamson (97) v. Durham at Scarborough, 2013
261*	L Hutton (146*) and J V Wilson (110*) v. Scotland at Hull, 1949
260	R G Lumb (144) and K Sharp (132) v. Glamorgan at Cardiff, 1984
258	H Sutcliffe (230) and E Oldroyd (93) v. Kent at Folkestone, 1931
253	B B Wilson (150) and D Denton (200*) v. Warwickshire at Birmingham, 1912
248	H Sutcliffe (200) and M. Leyland (116) v. Leicestershire at Leicester, 1926
244	P. Holmes (138) and E Oldroyd (151*) v. Glamorgan at Cardiff, 1922
243	G Boycott (141) and J D Love (163) v. Nottinghamshire at Bradford, 1976
243	C White (183) and M J Wood (124) v. Glamorgan at Scarborough, 2001
237	H Sutcliffe (118) and D Denton (122) v. Gloucestershire at Leeds, 1919
237	M D Moxon (132) and K Sharp (128) v. Sri Lankans at Leeds, 1988
236	F A Lowson (112) and J V Wilson (157) v. Essex at Leeds, 1950
235	M D Moxon (130) and D Byas (181) v. Cambridge University at Cambridge, 1995
230	L Hutton (180) and A Mitchell (100) v. Cambridge University at Cambridge, 1938
230	M P Vaughan (109) and B Parker (138*) v. Oxford University at Oxford, 1997.
227	M J Wood (102) and M J Lumb (122) v. Leicestershire at Leeds, 2001
225	H Sutcliffe (138) and E Oldroyd (97) v. Derbyshire at Dewsbury, 1928
223	M D Moxon (153) and R J Blakey (90) v. Somerset at Leeds, 1985
222	H Sutcliffe (174) and D Denton (114) v. Kent at Dover, 1919
219	F S Jackson (155) and D Denton (113) v. Middlesex at Bradford, 1899
217	R G Lumb (107) and J D Love (107) v. Oxford University at Oxford, 1978
216	M P Vaughan (105) and D Byas (102) v. Somerset at Bradford, 1994
215	A W Gale (136) and A McGrath (99) v. Lancashire at Manchester, 2008
215	S E Marsh (125*) and A Z Lees (102) v. Surrey at The Oval, 2017
211	J A Rudolph (141) and A McGrath (80) v Nottinghamshire at Leeds, 2010
207	P A Jaques (115) and A McGrath (93) v. Essex at Chelmsford, 2004
206	J Tunnicliffe (102) and F S Jackson (134*) v. Lancashire at Sheffield, 1898
206	H Sutcliffe (187) and M Leyland (90) v. Leicestershire at Leicester, 1931
205	H Sutcliffe (174) and A Mitchell (95) v. Leicestershire at Leicester, 1933
205	G Boycott (148) and P J Sharpe (108) v. Kent at Sheffield, 1970
203	A T Barber (100) and E Oldroyd (143) v. An England XI at Sheffield, 1929
203	J J Sayers (187) and A McGrath (100) v. Kent at Tunbridge Wells, 2007
202*	W Rhodes (115*) and G H Hirst (117*) v. Somerset at Bath, 1906
202	G Boycott (113) and C W J Athey (114) v. Northamptonshire at Northampton, 1978

271

CENTURY PARTNERSHIPS *(Continued)*

THIRD WICKET (Qualification 200 runs)

346	J J Sayers (173) and A McGrath (211) v. Warwickshire at Birmingham, 2009	
323*	H Sutcliffe (147*) and M Leyland (189*) v. Glamorgan at Huddersfield, 1928	
317	A McGrath (165) and D S Lehmann (187) v. Lancashire at Leeds, 2002	
310	A McGrath (134) and P A Jaques (219) v. Derbyshire at Leeds, 2005	
301	H Sutcliffe (175) and M Leyland (180*) v. Middlesex at Lord's, 1939	
293*	A A Metcalfe (150*) and P E Robinson (116*) v. Derbyshire at Scarborough, 1990	
269	D Byas (101) and R J Blakey (196) v. Oxford University at Oxford, 1991	
258*	J T Brown (134*) and F Mitchell (116*) v. Warwickshire at Bradford, 1901	
252	D E V Padgett (139*) and D B Close (154) v. Nottinghamshire at Nottingham, 1959	
249	D E V Padgett (95) and D B Close (184) v. Nottinghamshire at Scarborough, 1960	
248	C Johnson (102) and J H Hampshire (155*) v. Gloucestershire at Leeds, 1976	
247	P Holmes (175*) and M Leyland (118) v. New Zealanders at Bradford, 1927	
244	D E V Padgett (161*) and D B Close (144) v. Oxford University at Oxford, 1959	
240	L Hutton (151) and M Leyland (95) v. Surrey at Leeds, 1939	
237	J A Rudolph (198) and A McGrath (120) v. Worcestershire at Leeds, 2009	
236	H Sutcliffe (107) and R Kilner (137) v. Nottinghamshire at Nottingham, 1920	
236	M J Wood (94) and D S Lehmann (200) v. Worcestershire at Worcester, 1998	
234*	D Byas (126*) and A McGrath (105*) v. Oxford University at Oxford, 1997.	
233	L Hutton (101) and M Leyland (167) v. Worcestershire at Stourbridge, 1937	
230	D Byas (103) and M J Wood (103) v. Derbyshire at Leeds, 1998	
229	L Hall (86) and R Peel (158) v. Middlesex at Lord's, 1889	
228	A Mitchell (142) and M Leyland (133) v. Worcestershire at Sheffield, 1933	
228	W Barber (141) and M Leyland (114) v. Surrey at The Oval, 1939	
228	J V Wilson (132*) and D E V Padgett (115) v. Warwickshire at Birmingham, 1955	
226	D E V Padgett (117) and D B Close (198) v. Surrey at The Oval, 1960	
224	J V Wilson (110) and D B Close (114) v. Cambridge University at Cambridge, 1955	
224	G Boycott (140*) and K Sharp (121) v. Gloucestershire at Cheltenham, 1983	
221	A Mitchell (138) and M Leyland (134) v. Nottinghamshire at Bradford, 1933	
219	L Hall (116) and W Bates (131) v. Cambridge University at Cambridge, 1884	
218	J A Rudolph (127) and A W Gale (121) v. Lancashire at Manchester, 2009	
217	A McGrath (144) and J A Rudolph (129) v. Kent at Canterbury, 2008	
216	R G Lumb (118) and J H Hampshire (127) v. Surrey at The Oval, 1975	
215	A Mitchell (73) and M Leyland (139) v. Surrey at Bradford, 1928	
213	E Oldroyd (168) and W Barber (128) v. Glamorgan at Hull, 1929	
208	J V Wilson (157*) and E I Lester (112) v. Sussex at Leeds, 1949	
206	A McGrath (105) and J A Rudolph (228*) v Durham at Leeds, 2010	
205*	E Oldroyd (122*) and M Leyland (100*) v. Hampshire at Harrogate, 1924	
205	F S Jackson (124) and D Denton (112) v. Somerset at Taunton, 1897	
205	D E V Padgett (83) and D B Close (128) v. Somerset at Bath, 1959	
204	M P Vaughan (113) and A McGrath (70) v. Essex at Scarborough, 2001	
203	D Denton (132) and J Tunnicliffe (102) v. Warwickshire at Birmingham, 1905	
203	A A Metcalfe (216*) and P E Robinson (88) v. Middlesex at Leeds, 1988	
201	J Tunnicliffe (101) and T L Taylor (71) v. Surrey at The Oval, 1900	
201	H Sutcliffe (87) and W Barber (130) v. Leicestershire at Leicester, 1938	
200	M D Moxon (274*) and A P Grayson (100) v. Worcestershire at Worcester, 1994	

FOURTH WICKET (Qualification 175 runs)

372	J E Root (213) and J M Bairstow (198) v. Surrey at Leeds, 2016	
358	D S Lehmann (339) and M J Lumb (98) v. Durham at Leeds, 2006	
330	M J Wood (116) and D R Martyn (238) v. Gloucestershire at Leeds, 2003	
312	D Denton (168*) and G H Hirst (146) v. Hampshire at Southampton, 1914	
299	P Holmes (277*) and R Kilner (150) v. Northamptonshire at Harrogate, 1921	
272	D Byas (138) and A McGrath (137) v. Hampshire at Harrogate, 1996	
271	B B Wilson (208) and W Rhodes (113) v. Sussex at Bradford, 1914	
259	A Drake (115) and G H Hirst (218) v. Sussex at Hastings, 1911	
258	J Tunnicliffe (128) and G H Hirst (152) v. Hampshire at Portsmouth, 1904	
258	P E Robinson (147) and D Byas (117) v. Kent at Scarborough, 1989	

255	A W Gale (148) and J A Leaning (110) v. Nottinghamshire at Leeds, 2015
254	A W Gale (164) and J M Bairstow (139) v. Worcestershire at Scarborough, 2015
249	W B Stott (143) and G Boycott (145) v. Lancashire at Sheffield, 1963
247*	R G Lumb (165*) and S N Hartley (104*) v. Gloucestershire at Bradford, 1984
247	M Leyland (263) and L Hutton (83) v. Essex at Hull, 1936
238	D S Lehmann (216) and M J Lumb (92) v. Sussex at Arundel, 2002
233	D Byas (120) and P E Robinson (189) v. Lancashire at Scarborough, 1991
231	J E Root (236) and J M Bairstow (186) v. Derbyshire at Leeds, 2013
226	W H Wilkinson (89) and G H Hirst (140) v. Northamptonshire at Hull, 1909
225	C H Grimshaw (85) and G H Hirst (169) v. Oxford University at Oxford, 1906
212	B B Wilson (108) and G H Hirst (166*) v. Sussex at Hastings, 1913
212	G Boycott (260*) and J H Hampshire (80) v. Essex at Colchester, 1970
211	J V Wilson (120) and W Watson (108) v. Derbyshire at Harrogate, 1951
210*	A Mitchell (150*) and M Leyland (117*) v. Worcestershire at Worcester, 1933
210	E. I. Lester (178) and W Watson (97) v. Nottinghamshire at Nottingham, 1952
207	D Byas (213) and C White (107*) v. Worcestershire at Scarborough, 1995
206	J A Rudolph (121) and A W Gale (150) v. Surrey at The Oval, 2008
205*	G Boycott (151*) and P J Sharpe (79*) v. Leicestershire at Leicester, 1964
205	E Oldroyd (121) and R Kilner (117) v. Worcestershire at Dudley, 1922
205	W Watson (162*) and E I Lester (98) v. Somerset at Leeds, 1953
205	A Lyth (111) and J M Bairstow (246) v. Hampshire at Leeds, 2016
204	A W Gale (148) and G S Ballance (90) v. Surrey at Leeds, 2013
201*	J H Hampshire (105*) and D B Close (101*) v. Surrey at Bradford, 1965
203	P A Jaques (160) and G S Ballance (121*) v. Gloucestershire at Bristol, 2012
201	W H H Sutcliffe (181) and L Hutton (120) v. Kent at Canterbury, 1952
200	J V Wilson (92) and W Watson (122) v. Somerset at Taunton, 1950
198	A A Metcalfe (138) and D Byas (95) v. Warwickshire at Leeds, 1989
198	A W Gale (124) and J M Bairstow (95) v. Durham at Chester-le-Street, 2014
197	N W D Yardley (177) and A Coxon (58) v. Derbyshire at Scarborough, 1947
197	A Lyth (248*) and J M Bairstow (118) v. Leicestershire at Leicester, 2012
196	M D Moxon (130) and D L Bairstow (104) v. Derbyshire at Harrogate, 1987
193	A Drake (85) and G H Hirst (156) v. Lancashire at Manchester, 1911
192	J V Wilson (132) and W Watson (105) v. Essex at Bradford, 1955
191	M Leyland (114) and C Turner (63) v. Essex at Ilford, 1938
190	A W Gale (125) and J A Leaning (76) v. Hampshire at West End, Southampton, 2015
188	H Myers (60) and G H Hirst (158) v. Cambridge University at Cambridge, 1910
187	E Oldroyd (168) and F E Greenwood (104*) v. Glamorgan at Hull, 1929
187	K Taylor (203*) and W B Stott (57) v. Warwickshire at Birmingham, 1961
186	D S Lehmann (193) and D Byas (100) v. Leicestershire at Leicester, 2001
184	J H Hampshire (96) and R Illingworth (100*) v. Leicestershire at Sheffield, 1968
182*	E I Lester (101*) and W W Watson (103*) v. Nottinghamshire at Bradford, 1952
180*	G Boycott (207*) and B Leadbeater (50*) v. Cambridge University at Cambridge, 1976
180	J Tunnicliffe (139*) and G H Hirst (108) v. Surrey at The Oval, 1904
179	J H Hampshire (179) and S N Hartley (63) v. Surrey at Harrogate, 1981
179	M D Moxon (171*) and R J Blakey (71) v. Kent at Leeds, 1993
178	E I Lester (186) and J V Wilson (71) v. Warwickshire at Scarborough, 1949
177	J D Love (105*) and J H Hampshire (89) v. Lancashire at Manchester, 1980
175	L Hutton (177) and W Barber (84) v. Sussex at Scarborough, 1939
175	A McGrath (188*) and J A Rudolph (82) v. Warwickshire at Birmingham, 2007

FIFTH WICKET (Qualification 150 runs)

340	E Wainwright (228) and G H Hirst (186) v. Surrey at The Oval, 1899
329	F Mitchell (194) and E Wainwright (153) v. Leicestershire at Leicester, 1899
297	A W Gale (272) and G S Ballance (141) v. Nottinghamshire at Scarborough, 2013
276	W Rhodes (104*) and R Kilner (166) v. Northamptonshire at Northampton, 1921
273	L Hutton (270*) and N W D Yardley (136) v. Hampshire at Bournemouth, 1947
245*	H Sutcliffe (107*) and W Barber (128*) v. Northamptonshire at Northampton, 1939

229	D S Lehmann (193) and C White (79) v. Kent at Canterbury, 2006
217	D B Close (140*) and R Illingworth (107) v. Warwickshire at Sheffield, 1962
207	G S Ballance (107) and A U Rashid (180) v. Somerset at Leeds, 2013
198	E Wainwright (145) and R Peel (111) v. Sussex at Bradford, 1896
198	W Barber (168) and K R Davidson (101*) v. MCC at Lord's, 1934
196*	R Kilner (115*) and G H Hirst (82*) v. Gloucestershire at Leeds, 1919
195	M J Lumb (93) and C White (173*) v. Derbyshire at Derby, 2003
194*	Younus Khan (202*) and G L Brophy (100*) v. Hampshire at Southampton, 2007
193	A Mitchell (189) and W Rhodes (88) v. Northamptonshire at Northampton, 1926
193	J D Love (106) and S N Hartley (108) v. Oxford University at Oxford, 1985
192	C W J Athey (114*) and J D Love (123) v. Surrey at The Oval, 1982
191*	L Hutton (271*) and C Turner (81*) v. Derbyshire at Sheffield, 1937
191	M G Bevan (105) and A A Metcalfe (100) v. West Indians at Scarborough, 1995
190*	R J Blakey (204*) and J D Love (79*) v. Gloucestershire at Leeds, 1987
189	J E Root (160) and G S Ballance (87) v. Sussex at Scarborough 2011
188	D E V Padgett (146) and J V Wilson (72) v. Sussex at Middlesbrough, 1960
187	J V Wilson (230) and H Halliday (74) v. Derbyshire at Sheffield, 1952
185	G Boycott (104*) and K Sharp (99) v. Kent at Tunbridge Wells, 1984
182	E Lockwood (208) and E Lumb (40) v. Kent at Gravesend, 1882
182	B B Wilson (109) and W Rhodes (111) v. Sussex at Hove, 1910
182	D B Close (164) and J V Wilson (55) v. Combined Services at Harrogate, 1954
182	A W Gale (126*) and J A Leaning (76) v. Middlesex at Scarborough, 2014
181	A A Metcalfe (149) and J D Love (88) v. Glamorgan at Leeds, 1986
177	Hon F S Jackson (87) and G H Hirst (232*) v. Surrey at The Oval, 1905
176	L Hutton (176*) and A Coxon (72) v. Sussex at Sheffield, 1948
175	A Drake (108) and R Kilner (77) v. Cambridge University at Cambridge, 1913
173	H Sutcliffe (206) and R Kilner (124) v. Warwickshire at Dewsbury, 1925
170	W Rhodes (157) and R Kilner (67) v. Derbyshire at Leeds, 1925
170	J V Wilson (130*) and N W D Yardley (67) v. Lancashire at Manchester, 1954
169	W Watson (147) and A B Sellers (92) v. Worcestershire at Worcester, 1947
168	A T Barber (63) and A Mitchell (122*) v. Worcestershire at Worcester, 1929
167	J M Bairstow (136) and G S Ballance (61) v. Somerset at Taunton 2011
165	E Oldroyd (143) and W Rhodes (110) v. Glamorgan at Leeds, 1922
165	K Sharp (100*) and P Carrick (73) v. Middlesex at Lord's, 1980
164	A A Metcalfe (151) and D L Bairstow (88) v. Northamptonshire at Luton, 1986
159*	J D Love (170*) and D L Bairstow (52*) v. Worcestershire at Worcester, 1979
159	D B Close (128) and R Illingworth (74) v. Lancashire at Sheffield, 1959
159	J H Hampshire (183*) and C Johnson (53) v. Sussex at Hove, 1971
158*	G Boycott (153*) and P E Robinson (74*) v. Derbyshire at Harrogate, 1984
157	T L Taylor (135*) and G H Hirst (72) v. An England XI at Hastings, 1901
157	G H Hirst (142) and F Smith (51) v. Somerset at Bradford, 1903
157	W Barber (87) and N W D Yardley (101) v. Surrey at The Oval, 1937
156	A McGrath (158) and I J Harvey (103) v. Derbyshire at Derby, 2005
155	J M Bairstow (102) and J A Leaning (82) v. Hampshire at Leeds, 2015
153	S N Hartley (87) and M D Moxon (112*) v. Indians at Scarborough, 1986
152	J H Hampshire (83) and S N Hartley (106) v. Nottinghamshire at Nottingham, 1981
151*	G H Hirst (102*) and R Kilner (50*) v. Kent at Bradford, 1913
151	G H Hirst (120) and F Smith (55) v. Kent at Leeds, 1903
151	W Rhodes (57) and R Kilner (90) v. Nottinghamshire at Nottingham, 1925

SIXTH WICKET (Qualification 150 runs)

296	A Lyth (251) and A U Rashid (159*) v. Lancashire at Manchester, 2014
276	M Leyland (191) and E Robinson (124*) v. Glamorgan at Swansea, 1926
252	C White (181) and R J Blakey (109*) v. Lancashire at Leeds, 1996
248	G J Maxwell (140) and A U Rashid (127) v. Durham at Scarborough, 2015
233	M W Booth (210) and G H Hirst (100) v. Worcestershire at Worcester, 1911
229	W Rhodes (267*) and N Kilner (112) v. Leicestershire at Leeds, 1921
225	E Wainwright (91) and Lord Hawke (127) v. Hampshire at Southampton, 1899

217*	H Sutcliffe (200*) and A Wood (123*) v. Worcestershire at Sheffield, 1935
214	W Watson (214*) and N W D Yardley (76) v. Worcestershire at Worcester, 1955
205	G H Hirst (125) and S Haigh (159) v. Nottinghamshire at Sheffield, 1901
200	D Denton (127) and G H Hirst (134) v. Essex at Bradford, 1902
198	M Leyland (247) and W Rhodes (100*) v. Worcestershire at Worcester, 1928
190	W Rhodes (126) and M Leyland (79) v. Middlesex at Bradford, 1923
190	J A Rudolph (122) and A U Rashid (86) v. Surrey at The Oval, 2007
188	W Watson (174) and R Illingworth (53) v. Lancashire at Sheffield, 1955
188	M P Vaughan (161) and R J Blakey (92) v. Essex at Ilford, 1997.
188	G S Ballance (111) and A U Rashid (82) v. Warwickshire at Birmingham 2011
184	R Kilner (104) and M W Booth (79) v. Leicestershire at Leeds, 1913
183	G H Hirst (131) and E Smith (129) v. Hampshire at Bradford, 1899
183	W Watson (139*) and R Illingworth (78) v. Somerset at Harrogate, 1956
178*	D Denton (108*) and G H Hirst (112*) v. Lancashire at Manchester, 1902
178*	N W D Yardley (100*) and R Illingworth (71*) v. Gloucestershire at Bristol, 1955
178	E Robinson (100) and D C F Burton (83) v. Derbyshire at Hull, 1921
178	H Sutcliffe (135) and P A Gibb (157*) v. Nottinghamshire at Sheffield, 1935
175	G M Fellows (88) and R J Blakey (103) v. Warwickshire at Birmingham, 2002
174	D S Lehmann (136) and G M Hamilton (73) v. Kent at Maidstone, 1998
173	T Kohler-Cadmore (81) and A J Hodd (85) v. Somerset at Leeds, 2018
172	A J Dalton (119*) and D L Bairstow (62) v. Worcestershire at Dudley, 1971
170*	A U Rashid 103*) and A J Hodd (68*) v. Somerset at Taunton, 2013
170	A W Gale (101) and T T Bresnan (97) v. Worcestershire at Worcester, 2009
169	W Barber (124) and H Verity (78*) v. Warwickshire at Birmingham, 1933
169	R Illingworth (162) and J Birkenshaw (37) v. Indians at Sheffield, 1959
166	E Wainwright (116) and E Smith (61) v. Kent at Catford, 1900
166	D B Close (161) and F S Trueman (104) v. Northamptonshire at Northampton, 1963
162*	G Boycott (220*) and J G Binks (70*) v. Northamptonshire at Sheffield, 1967
161*	D L Bairstow (100*) and P Carrick (59*) v. Middlesex at Leeds, 1983
159*	D S Lehmann (187*) and R J Blakey (78*) v. Somerset at Bath, 2001
159	J M Bairstow (182) and A McGrath (90) v. Leicestershire at Scarborough, 2012
156	W Rhodes (82*) and E Robinson (94) v. Derbyshire at Chesterfield, 1919
154	C Turner (84) and A Wood (79) v. Glamorgan at Swansea, 1936
153*	J A Rudolph (92*) and A U Rashid (73*) v. Worcestershire at Kidderminster, 2007
153	J A Rudolph (69*) and J M Bairstow (81) v. Warwickshire at Birmingham, 2010
151	D Denton (91) and W Rhodes (76) v. Middlesex at Sheffield, 1904
151	G Boycott (152*) and P Carrick (75) v. Warwickshire at Leeds, 1982
150	G Ulyett (199*) and J M Preston (93) v. Derbyshire at Sheffield, 1887

SEVENTH WICKET (Qualification 125 runs)

366*	J M Bairstow (219*) and T T Bresnan (169*) v. Durham at Chester-le-Street, 2015
254	W Rhodes (135) and D C F Burton (142*) v. Hampshire at Dewsbury, 1919
247	P Holmes (285) and W Rhodes (79) v. Nottinghamshire at Nottingham, 1929
227	J M Bairstow (246) and L E Plunkett (126) v. Hampshire at Leeds, 2016
215	E Robinson (135*) and D C F Burton (110) v. Leicestershire at Leicester, 1921
197	G S Ballance (165*) and T T Bresnan (78) v. Sussex at Hove, 2015
185	E Wainwright (100) and G H Hirst (134) v. Gloucestershire at Bristol, 1897
183	G H Hirst (341) and H Myers (57) v. Leicestershire at Leicester, 1905
183	J A Rudolph (220) and T T Bresnan (101*) v. Warwickshire at Scarborough, 2007
180	C Turner (130) and A Wood (97) v. Somerset at Sheffield, 1936
170	G S Blewett (190) and G M Hamilton (84*) v. Northamptonshire at Scarborough, 1999
168	G L Brophy (99) and A U Rashid (157*) v. Lancashire at Leeds, 2009
166	R Peel (55) and I Grimshaw (122*) v. Derbyshire at Holbeck, 1886
162	E Wainwright (109) and S Haigh (73) v. Somerset at Taunton, 1900
162	R J Blakey (90) and R K J Dawson (87) v. Kent at Canterbury, 2002
162	A W Gale (149) and G L Brophy (97) v. Warwickshire at Scarborough, 2006
161	R G Lumb (118) and C M Old (89) v. Worcestershire at Bradford, 1980

160	J Tunnicliffe (158) and D Hunter (58*)	v. Worcestershire at Worcester, 1900
157*	F A Lowson (259*) and R Booth (53*)	v. Worcestershire at Worcester, 1953
157	K S Wiiliamson (189) and T T Bresnan (61)	v. Sussex at Scarborough, 2014
155	D Byas (122*) and P Carrick (61)	v. Leicestershire at Leicester.1991.
154*	G H Hirst (76*) and J T Newstead (100*)	v. Nottinghamshire at Nottingham, 1908
148	J Rowbotham (113) and J Thewlis (50)	v. Surrey at The Oval, 1873
147	E Wainwright (78) and G Ulyett (73)	v. Somerset at Taunton, 1893
147	M P Vaughan (153) and R J Harden (64)	v. Kent at Scarborough, 1999
143	C White (135*) and A K D Gray (60)	v. Durham at Chester-le-Street, 2003
141	G H Hirst (108*) and S Haigh (48)	v. Worcestershire at Worcester, 1905
141	J H Hampshire (149*) and J G Binks (72)	v. MCC at Scarborough, 1965
140	E Wainwright (117) and S Haigh (54)	v. CI Thornton's XI at Scarborough, 1900
140	D Byas (67) and P J Hartley (75)	v. Derbyshire at Chesterfield, 1990
138	D Denton (78) and G H Hirst (103*)	v. Sussex at Leeds, 1905
136	GH Hirst (93) and S Haigh (138)	v. Warwickshire at Birmingham, 1904
136	E Robinson (77*) and A Wood (65)	v. Glamorgan at Scarborough, 1931
133*	W Rhodes (267*) and M Leyland (52*)	v. Leicestershire at Leeds, 1921
133*	E I Lester (86*) and A B Sellers (73*)	v. Northamptonshire at Northampton, 1948
133	D Byas (100) and P W Jarvis (80)	v. Northamptonshire at Scarborough, 1992
132	W Rhodes (196) and S Haigh (59*)	v. Worcestershire at Worcester, 1904
132	A J Hodd (96*) and Azeem Rafiq (74)	v. Nottinghamshire at Scarborough, 2016
131*	D L Bairstow (79*) and A Sidebottom (52*)	v. Oxford University at Oxford, 1981
130	P J Sharpe (64) and J V Wilson (134)	v. Warwickshire at Birmingham, 1962
128	W Barber (66) and T F Smailes (86)	v. Cambridge University at Cambridge, 1938
128	D B Close (88*) and A Coxon (59)	v. Essex at Leeds, 1949
126	E Wainwright (171) and R Peel (46)	v. Middlesex at Lord's, 1897
126	W Rhodes (91) and G G Macaulay (63)	v. Hampshire at Hull, 1925
126	J C Balderstone (58) and J G Binks (95)	v. Middlesex at Lord's, 1964
126	J M Bairstow (70) and A U Rashid (59)	v. Kent at Canterbury, 2010
125	A B Sellers (109) and T F Smailes (65)	v. Kent at Bradford, 1937

EIGHTH WICKET (Qualification 125 runs)

292	R Peel (210*) and Lord Hawke (166)	v. Warwickshire at Birmingham, 1896
238	I J Harvey (209*) and T T Bresnan (74)	v. Somerset at Leeds, 2005
192*	W Rhodes (108*) and G G Macaulay (101*)	v. Essex at Harrogate, 1922
192	A U Rashid (117*) and A Shahzad (78)	v. Hampshire at Basingstoke, 2009
180	W Barber (191) and T F Smailes (89)	v. Sussex at Leeds, 1935
167	J A Leaning (118) and J A Brooks (109*)	v. Lancashire at Manchester, 2017
165	S Haigh (62) and Lord Hawke (126)	v. Surrey at The Oval, 1902
163	G G Macaulay (67) and A Waddington (114)	v. Worcestershire at Leeds, 1927
159	E Smith (95) and W Rhodes (105)	v. MCC at Scarborough, 1901
159	A Shahzad (88) and D J Wainwright (85*)	v. Sussex at Hove, 2009
156	G S Ballance (112) and R J Sidebottom (40)	v. Leeds/Bradford MCCU at Leeds, 2013
152	W Rhodes (98) and J W Rothery (70)	v. Hampshire at Portsmouth, 1904
151	W Rhodes (201) and Lord Hawke (51)	v. Somerset at Taunton, 1905
151	R J Blakey (80*) and P J Hartley (69)	v. Sussex at Eastbourne, 1996
149	G L Brophy (177*) and R J Sidebottom (61)	v. Worcestershire at Worcester 2011
147	J P G Chadwick (59) and F S Trueman (101)	v. Middlesex at Scarborough, 1965
146	S Haigh (159) and Lord Hawke (89)	v. Nottinghamshire at Sheffield, 1901
144	G L Brophy (85) and D J Wainwright (102*)	v. Warwickshire at Scarborough, 2009
138	E Wainwright (100) and Lord Hawke (81)	v. Kent at Tonbridge, 1898
137	E Wainwright (171) and Lord Hawke (75)	v. Middlesex at Lord's, 1897
135	P W Jarvis (55) and P J Hartley (69)	v. Nottinghamshire at Scarborough, 1992
133	R Illingworth (61) and F S Trueman (74)	v. Leicestershire at Leicester, 1955
132	G H Hirst (103) and E Smith (59)	v. Middlesex at Sheffield, 1904
132	W Watson (119) and J H Wardle (65)	v. Leicestershire at Leicester, 1949
131	P E Robinson (85) and P Carrick (64)	v. Surrey at Harrogate, 1990
130	E Smith (98) and Lord Hawke (54)	v. Lancashire at Leeds, 1904
128	H Verity (96*) and T F Smailes (77)	v. Indians at Bradford, 1936
128	D L Bairstow (145) and G B Stevenson (11)	v. Middlesex at Scarborough, 1980

127	E Robinson (70*) and A Wood (62) v. Middlesex at Leeds, 1928
126	R Peel (74) and E Peate (61) v. Gloucestershire at Bradford, 1883
126	M W Booth (56) and E R Wilson (104*) v. Essex at Bradford, 1913
126	J D Middlebrook (84) and C E W Silverwood (70) v. Essex at Chelmsford, 2001
126	M J Lumb (115*) and D Gough (72) v. Hampshire at Southampton, 2003

NINTH WICKET (Qualification 100 runs)

246	T T Bresnan (116) and J N Gillespie (123*) v. Surrey at The Oval, 2007
192	G H Hirst (130*) and S Haigh (85) v. Surrey at Bradford, 1898
179	R A Hutton (189) and G A Cope (30*) v. Pakistanis at Bradford, 1971
176*	R Moorhouse (59*) and G H Hirst (115*) v. Gloucestershire at Bristol, 1894
173	S Haigh (85) and W Rhodes (92*) v. Sussex at Hove, 1902
171	G S Ballance (194) and J A Brooks (82) v. Worcestershire at Worcester, 2018
167	H Verity (89) and T F Smailes (80) v. Somerset at Bath, 1936
162	W Rhodes (94*) and S Haigh (84) v. Lancashire at Manchester, 1904
161	E Smith (116*) and W Rhodes (79) v. Sussex at Sheffield, 1900
154	R M Pyrah (117) and R J Sidebottom (52) v.Lancashire at Leeds 2011
151	J M Bairstow (205) and R J Sidebottom (45*) v. Nottinghamshire at Nottingham 2011
150	Azeem Rafiq (100) and M J Hoggard (56*) v. Worcestershire at Worcester, 2009
149*	R J Blakey (63*) and A K D Gray (74*) v. Leicestershire at Scarborough, 2002
149	G H Hirst (232*) and D Hunter (40) v. Surrey at The Oval, 1905
146	G H Hirst (214) and W Rhodes (53) v. Worcestershire at Worcester, 1901
144	T T Bresnan (91) and J N Gillespie (44) v. Hampshire at Leeds, 2006
140	A U Rashid (111) and D J Wainwright (104) v. Sussex at Hove, 2008
136	R Peel (210*) and G H Hirst (85) v. Warwickshire at Birmingham, 1896
125*	L Hutton (269*) and A Coxon (65*) v. Northamptonshire at Wellingborough, 1949
124	P J Hartley (87*) and P W Jarvis (47) v. Essex at Chelmsford, 1986
120	G H Hirst (138) and W Rhodes (38) v. Nottinghamshire at Nottingham, 1899
119	A B Sellers (80*) and E P Robinson (66) v. Warwickshire at Birmingham, 1938
118	S Haigh (96) and W Rhodes (44) v. Somerset at Leeds, 1901
114	E Oldroyd (194) and A Dolphin (47) v. Worcestershire at Worcester, 1923
114	N Kilner (102*) and G G Macaulay (60) v. Gloucestershire at Bristol, 1923
113	G G Macaulay (125*) and A Waddington (44) v. Nottinghamshire at Nottingham, 1921
113	A Wood (69) and H.Verity (45*) v. MCC at Lord's, 1938
112	G H Hirst (78) and Lord Hawke (61*) v. Essex at Leyton, 1907
109	Lees Whitehead (60) and W Rhodes (81*) v. Sussex at Harrogate, 1899
108	A McGrath (133*) and C E W Silverwood (80) v. Durham at Chester-le-Street, 2005
106	L E Plunkett (86) and S A Patterson (43) v. Warwickshire at Leeds, 2014
105	J V Wilson (134) and A G Nicholson (20*) v. Nottinghamshire at Leeds, 1962
105	C M Old (100*) and H P Cooper (30) v. Lancashire at Manchester, 1978
105	C White (74*) and J D Batty (50) v. Gloucestershire at Sheffield, 1993
104	L Hall (129*) and R Moorhouse (86) v. Gloucestershire at Clifton, 1888
100	G Pollitt (51) and Lees Whitehead (54) v. Hampshire at Bradford, 1899

TENTH WICKET (Qualification 100 runs)

149	G Boycott (79) and G B Stevenson (115*) v. Warwickshire at Birmingham, 1982
148	Lord Hawke (107*) and D Hunter (47) v. Kent at Sheffield, 1898
144	A Sidebottom (124) and A L Robinson (30*) v. Glamorgan at Cardiff, 1977
121	J T Brown (141) and D Hunter (25*) v. Liverpool & District at Liverpool, 1894
118	Lord Hawke (110*) and D Hunter (41) v. Kent at Leeds, 1896
113	P J Hartley (88*) and R D Stemp (22) v. Middlesex at Lord's, 1996
110	C E W. Silverwood (45*) and R D Stemp (65) v. Durham at Chester-le-Street, 1996
109	A Shahzad (70) and R J Sidebottom (28*) v. Worcestershire at Scarborough, 2011
108	Lord Hawke (79) and Lees Whitehead (45*) v. Lancashire at Manchester, 1903
108	G Boycott (129) and M K Bore (37*) v. Nottinghamshire at Bradford, 1973
106	A B Sellers (79) and D V Brennan (30) v. Worcestershire at Worcester, 1948
103	A Dolphin (62*) and E Smith (49) v. Essex at Leyton, 1919
102	D Denton (77*) and D Hunter (45) v. Cambridge University at Cambridge, 1895

FIFTEEN WICKETS OR MORE IN A MATCH

**A complete list of 12, 13 and 14 wickets in a match up to and including 2007
is to be found in the 2008 edition**

W E BOWES (1)

16 for 35 (8 for 18 and 8 for 17) v. Northamptonshire at Kettering, 1935

A DRAKE (1)

15 for 51 (5 for 16 and 10 for 35) v. Somerset at Weston-super-Mare, 1914

T EMMETT (1)

16 for 38 (7 for 15 and 9 for 23) v. Cambridgeshire at Hunslet, 1869

G H HIRST (1)

15 for 63 (8 for 25 and 7 for 38) v. Leicestershire at Hull, 1907

R ILLINGWORTH (1)

15 for 123 (8 for 70 and 7 for 53) v. Glamorgan at Swansea, 1960

R PEEL (1)

15 for 50 (9 for 22 and 6 for 28) v. Somerset at Leeds, 1895

W RHODES (1)

15 for 56 (9 for 28 and 6 for 28) v. Essex at Leyton, 1899

H VERITY (4)

17 for 91 (8 for 47 and 9 for 44) v. Essex at Leyton, 1933
15 for 129 (8 for 56 and 7 for 73) v. Oxford University at Oxford, 1936
15 for 38 (6 for 26 and 9 for 12) v. Kent at Sheffield, 1936
15 for 100 (6 for 52 and 9 for 48) v. Essex at Westcliffe-on-Sea, 1936

J H WARDLE (1)

16 for 112 (9 for 48 and 7 for 64) v. Sussex at Hull, 1954

TEN WICKETS IN A MATCH
(including best analysis)

61	W Rhodes	15 for	56	v Essex	at Leyton	1899
48	H Verity	17 for	91	v Essex	at Leyton	1933
40	G H Hirst	15 for	63	v Leicestershire	at Hull	1907
31	G G Macaulay	14 for	92	v Gloucestershire	at Bristol	1926
28	S Haigh	14 for	43	v Hampshire	at Southampton	1898
27	R Peel	14 for	33	v Nottinghamshire	at Sheffield	1888
25	W E Bowes	16 for	35	v Northamptonshire	at Kettering	1935
25	J H Wardle	16 for	112	v Sussex	at Hull	1954
22	E Peate	14 for	77	v Surrey	at Huddersfield	1881
20	F S Trueman	14 for	123	v Surrey	at The Oval	1960
19	T Emmett	16 for	38	v Cambridgeshire	at Hunslet	1869
17	R Appleyard	12 for	43	v Essex	at Bradford	1951
15	E Wainwright	14 for	77	v Essex	at Bradford	1896
11	R Illingworth	15 for	123	v Glamorgan	at Swansea	1960
10	A Waddington	13 for	48	v Northamptonshire	at Northampton	1920
9	M W Booth	14 for	160	v Essex	at Leyton	1914
9	R Kilner	12 for	55	v Sussex	at Hove	1924
8	W Bates	11 for	47	v Nottinghamshire	at Nottingham	1881
8	G Freeman	13 for	60	v Surrey	at Sheffield	1869
7	E P Robinson	13 for	115	v Lancashire	at Leeds	1939
7	D Wilson	13 for	52	v Warwickshire	at Middlesbrough	1967
6	G A Cope	12 for	116	v Glamorgan	at Cardiff (Sophia Gardens)	1968

6 A Hill	12 for 59	v Surrey	at The Oval	1871
6 T F Smailes	14 for 58	v Derbyshire	at Sheffield	1939
5 P Carrick	12 for 89	v Derbyshire	at Sheffield (Abbeydale Pk)	1983
5 J M Preston	13 for 63	v MCC	at Scarborough	1888
5 E Robinson	12 for 95	v Northamptonshire	at Huddersfield	1927
4 J T Newstead	11 for 72	v Worcestershire	at Bradford	1907
3 T W Foster	11 for 93	v Liverpool & District	at Liverpool	1894
3 G P Harrison	11 for 76	v Kent	at Dewsbury	1883
3 F S Jackson	12 for 80	v Hampshire	at Southampton	1897
3 P W Jarvis	11 for 92	v Middlesex	at Lord's	1986
3 S P Kirby	13 for 154	v Somerset	at Taunton	2003
3 A G Nicholson	12 for 73	v Glamorgan	at Leeds	1964
3 R K Platt	10 for 87	v Surrey	at The Oval	1959
3 A Sidebottom	11 for 64	v Kent	at Sheffield (Abbeydale Pk)	1980
3 R J Sidebottom	11 for 43	v Kent	at Leeds	2000
3 G Ulyett	12 for 102	v Lancashire	at Huddersfield	1889
2 T Armitage	13 for 46	v Surrey	at Sheffield	1876
2 R Aspinall	14 for 65	v Northamptonshire	at Northampton	1947
2 J T Brown (Darfield)	12 for 109	v Gloucestershire	at Huddersfield	1899
2 R O Clayton	12 for 104	v Lancashire	at Manchester	1877
2 D B Close	11 for 116	v Kent	at Gillingham	1965
2 B O Coad	10 for 102	v. Warwickshire	at Birmingham	2017
2 M J Cowan	12 for 87	v Warwickshire	at Birmingham	1960
2 A Coxon	10 for 57	v Derbyshire	at Chesterfield	1949
2 D Gough	10 for 80	v Lancashire	at Leeds	1995
2 G M Hamilton	11 for 72	v Surrey	at Leeds	1998
2 P J Hartley	11 for 68	v Derbyshire	at Chesterfield	1995
2 R A Hutton	11 for 62	v Lancashire	at Manchester	1971
2 E Leadbeater	11 for 162	v Nottinghamshire	at Nottingham	1950
2 M A Robinson	12 for 124	v Gloucestershire	at Harrogate	1993
2 M Ryan	10 for 77	v Leicestershire	at Bradford	1962
2 E Smith (Morley)	10 for 97	v MCC	at Scarborough	1893
2 G B Stevenson	11 for 74	v Nottinghamshire	at Nottingham	1980
2 S Wade	11 for 56	v Gloucestershire	at Cheltenham	1886
2 E R Wilson	11 for 109	v Sussex	at Hove	1921
1 A B Bainbridge	12 for 111	v Essex	at Harrogate	1961
1 J Birkenshaw	11 for 134	v Middlesex	at Leeds	1960
1 A Booth	10 for 91	v Indians	at Bradford	1946
1 H P Cooper	11 for 96	v Northamptonshire	at Northampton	1976
1 A Drake	15 for 51	v Somerset	at Weston-Super-Mare	1914
1 L Greenwood	11 for 71	v Surrey	at The Oval	1867
1 P M Hutchison	11 for 102	v Pakistan 'A'	at Leeds	1997
1 L Hutton	10 for 101	v Leicestershire	at Leicester (Aylestone Rd)	1937
1 R Iddison	10 for 68	v Surrey	at Sheffield	1864
1 M Leyland	10 for 94	v Leicestershire	at Leicester (Aylestone Rd)	1933
1 J D Middlebrook	10 for 170	v Hampshire	at Southampton	2000
1 F W Milligan	12 for 110	v Sussex	at Sheffield	1897
1 H Myers	12 for 192	v Gloucestershire	at Dewsbury	1904
1 C M Old	11 for 46	v Gloucestershire	at Middlesbrough	1969
1 D Pickles	12 for 133	v Somerset	at Taunton	1957
1 A U Rashid	11 for 114	v Worcestershire	at Worcester	2011
1 W Ringrose	11 for 135	v Australians	at Bradford	1905
1 C E W Silverwood	12 for 148	v Kent	at Leeds	1997
1 W Slinn	12 for 53	v Nottinghamshire	at Nottingham	1864
1 J Waring	10 for 63	v Lancashire	at Leeds	1966
1 F Wilkinson	10 for 129	v Hampshire	at Bournemouth	1938
1 A C Williams	10 for 66	v Hampshire	at Dewsbury	1919

TEN WICKETS IN AN INNINGS

Bowler				Year
A Drake	10 for 35	v.	Somerset at Weston-super-Mare	1914
H Verity	10 for 36	v.	Warwickshire at Leeds	1931
*H Verity	10 for 10	v.	Nottinghamshire at Leeds	1932
T F Smailes	10 for 47	v.	Derbyshire at Sheffield	1939

*Includes the hat trick.

EIGHT WICKETS OR MORE IN AN INNINGS

(Ten wickets in an innings also listed above)

A complete list of seven wickets in an innings up to and including 2007 is to be found in the 2008 edition

R APPLEYARD (1)

8 for 76 v. MCC at Scarborough, 1951

R ASPINALL (1)

8 for 42 v. Northamptonshire at Northampton, 1947

W BATES (2)

8 for 45 v. Lancashire at Huddersfield, 1878
8 for 21 v. Surrey at The Oval, 1879

M W BOOTH (4)

8 for 52 v. Leicestershire at Sheffield, 1912
8 for 47 v. Middlesex at Leeds, 1912
8 for 86 v. Middlesex at Sheffield, 1913
8 for 64 v. Essex at Leyton, 1914

W E BOWES (9)

8 for 77 v. Leicestershire at Dewsbury, 1929
8 for 69 v. Middlesex at Bradford, 1930
9 for 121 v. Essex at Scarborough, 1932
8 for 62 v. Sussex at Hove, 1932
8 for 69 v. Gloucestershire at Gloucester, 1933
8 for 40 v.Worcestershire at Sheffield, 1935
8 for 18 v. Northamptonshire at Kettering, 1935
8 for 17 v. Northamptonshire at Kettering, 1935
8 for 56 v. Leicestershire at Scarborough, 1936

J T BROWN (Darfield) (1)

8 for 40 v. Gloucestershire at Huddersfield, 1899

P CARRICK (2)

8 for 33 v. Cambridge University at Cambridge, 1973
8 for 72 v. Derbyshire at Scarborough, 1975

R O CLAYTON (1)

8 for 66 v. Lancashire at Manchester, 1877

D B CLOSE (2)

8 for 41 v. Kent at Leeds, 1959
8 for 43 v. Essex at Leeds, 1960

H P COOPER (1)

8 for 62 v. Glamorgan at Cardiff, 1975

280

EIGHT WICKETS OR MORE IN AN INNINGS *(Continued)*

G A COPE (1)

8 for 73 v. Gloucestershire at Bristol, 1975

M J COWAN (1)

9 for 43 v. Warwickshire at Birmingham, 1960

A COXON (1)

8 for 31 v. Worcestershire at Leeds, 1946

A DRAKE (2)

8 for 59 v. Gloucestershire at Sheffield, 1913
10 for 35 v. Somerset at Weston-super-Mare, 1914

T EMMETT (8)

9 for 34 v. Nottinghamshire at Dewsbury, 1868
9 for 23 v. Cambridgeshire at Hunslet, 1869
8 for 31 v. Nottinghamshire at Sheffield, 1871
8 for 46 v. Gloucestershire at Clifton, 1877
8 for 16 v. MCC at Scarborough, 1877
8 for 22 v. Surrey at The Oval, 1881
8 for 52 v. MCC at Scarborough, 1882
8 for 32 v. Sussex at Huddersfield, 1884

S D FLETCHER (1)

8 for 58 v. Essex at Sheffield, 1988

T W FOSTER (1)

9 for 59 v. MCC at Lord's, 1894

G FREEMAN (2)

8 for 11 v. Lancashire at Holbeck, 1868
8 for 29 v. Surrey at Sheffield, 1869

L GREENWOOD (1)

8 for 35 v. Cambridgeshire at Dewsbury, 1867

S HAIGH (5)

8 for 78 v. Australians at Bradford, 1896
8 for 35 v. Hampshire at Harrogate, 1896
8 for 21 v. Hampshire at Southampton, 1898
8 for 33 v. Warwickshire at Scarborough, 1899
9 for 25 v. Gloucestershire at Leeds, 1912

P J HARTLEY (2)

8 for 111 v. Sussex at Hove, 1992
9 for 41 v. Derbyshire at Chesterfield, 1995

G H HIRST (8)

8 for 59 v. Warwickshire at Birmingham, 1896
8 for 48 v. Australians at Bradford, 1899
8 for 25 v. Leicestershire at Hull, 1907
9 for 45 v. Middlesex at Sheffield, 1907
9 for 23 v. Lancashire at Leeds, 1910
8 for 80 v. Somerset at Sheffield, 1910
9 for 41 v. Worcestershire at Worcester, 1911
9 for 69 v. MCC at Lord's, 1912

R ILLINGWORTH (5)

8 for 69 v. Surrey at The Oval, 1954
9 for 42 v. Worcestershire at Worcester, 1957
8 for 70 v. Glamorgan at Swansea, 1960
8 for 50 v. Lancashire at Manchester, 1961
8 for 20 v. Worcestershire at Leeds, 1965

R KILNER (2)

8 for 26 v. Glamorgan at Cardiff, 1923
8 for 40 v. Middlesex at Bradford, 1926

S P KIRBY (1)

8 for 80 v. Somerset at Taunton, 2003

E LEADBEATER (1)

8 for 83 v. Worcestershire at Worcester, 1950

M LEYLAND (1)

8 for 63 v. Hampshire at Huddersfield, 1938

G G MACAULAY (3)

8 for 43 v. Gloucestershire at Bristol, 1926
8 for 37 v. Derbyshire at Hull, 1927
8 for 21 v. Indians at Harrogate, 1932

H MYERS (1)

8 for 81 v. Gloucestershire at Dewsbury, 1904

A G NICHOLSON (2)

9 for 62 v. Sussex at Eastbourne, 1967
8 for 22 v. Kent at Canterbury, 1968

E PEATE (6)

8 for 24 v. Lancashire at Manchester, 1880
8 for 30 v. Surrey at Huddersfield, 1881
8 for 69 v. Sussex at Hove, 1881
8 for 32 v. Middlesex at Sheffield, 1882
8 for 5 v. Surrey at Holbeck, 1883
8 for 63 v. Kent at Gravesend, 1884

R PEEL (6)

8 for 12 v. Nottinghamshire at Sheffield, 1888
8 for 60 v. Surrey at Sheffield, 1890
8 for 54 v. Cambridge University at Cambridge, 1893
9 for 22 v. Somerset at Leeds, 1895
8 for 27 v. South of England XI at Scarborough, 1896
8 for 53 v. Kent at Halifax, 1897

J M PRESTON (2)

8 for 27 v. Sussex at Hove, 1888
9 for 28 v. MCC at Scarborough, 1888

EIGHT WICKETS OR MORE IN AN INNINGS *(Continued)*

W RHODES (18)

9 for 28 v. Essex at Leyton, 1899
8 for 38 v. Nottinghamshire at Nottingham, 1899
8 for 68 v. Cambridge University at Cambridge, 1900
8 for 43 v. Lancashire at Bradford, 1900
8 for 23 v. Hampshire at Hull, 1900
8 for 72 v. Gloucestershire at Bradford, 1900
8 for 28 v. Essex at Harrogate, 1900
8 for 53 v. Middlesex at Lord's, 1901
8 for 55 v. Kent at Canterbury, 1901
8 for 26 v. Kent at Catford, 1902
8 for 87 v. Worcestershire at Worcester, 1903
8 for 61 v. Lancashire at Bradford, 1903
8 for 90 v. Warwickshire at Birmingham, 1905
8 for 92 v. Northamptonshire at Northampton, 1911
8 for 44 v. Warwickshire at Bradford, 1919
8 for 39 v. Sussex at Leeds, 1920
8 for 48 v. Somerset at Huddersfield, 1926
9 for 39 v. Essex at Leyton, 1929

W RINGROSE (1)

9 for 76 v. Australians at Bradford, 1905

E ROBINSON (3)

9 for 36 v. Lancashire at Bradford, 1920
8 for 32 v. Northamptonshire at Huddersfield, 1927
8 for 13 v. Cambridge University at Cambridge, 1928

E P ROBINSON (2)

8 for 35 v. Lancashire at Leeds, 1939
8 for 76 v. Surrey at The Oval, 1946

M A ROBINSON (1)

9 for 37 v. Northamptonshire at Harrogate, 1993

A SIDEBOTTOM (1)

8 for 72 v. Leicestershire at Middlesbrough, 1986

T F SMAILES (2)

8 for 68 v. Glamorgan at Hull, 1938
10 for 47 v. Derbyshire at Sheffield, 1939

G B STEVENSON (2)

8 for 65 v. Lancashire at Leeds, 1978
8 for 57 v. Northamptonshire at Leeds, 1980

F S TRUEMAN (8)

8 for 70 v. Minor Counties at Lord's, 1949
8 for 68 v. Nottinghamshire at Sheffield, 1951
8 for 53 v. Nottinghamshire at Nottingham, 1951
8 for 28 v. Kent at Dover, 1954
8 for 84 v. Nottinghamshire at Worksop, 1962
8 for 45 v. Gloucestershire at Bradford, 1963
8 for 36 v. Sussex at Hove, 1965
8 for 37 v. Essex at Bradford, 1966

EIGHT WICKETS OR MORE IN AN INNINGS *(Continued)*

H VERITY (20)

9 for 60 v. Glamorgan at Swansea, 1930
10 for 36 v. Warwickshire at Leeds, 1931
8 for 33 v. Glamorgan at Swansea, 1931
8 for 107 v. Lancashire at Bradford, 1932
8 for 39 v. Northamptonshire at Northampton, 1932
10 for 10 v. Nottinghamshire at Leeds, 1932
8 for 47 v. Essex at Leyton, 1933
9 for 44 v. Essex at Leyton, 1933
9 for 59 v. Kent at Dover, 1933
8 for 28 v. Leicestershire at Leeds, 1935
8 for 56 v. Oxford University at Oxford, 1936
8 for 40 v. Worcestershire at Stourbridge, 1936
9 for 12 v. Kent at Sheffield, 1936
9 for 48 v. Essex at Westcliff-on-Sea, 1936
8 for 42 v. Nottinghamshire at Bradford, 1936
9 for 43 v. Warwickshire at Leeds, 1937
8 for 80 v. Sussex at Eastbourne, 1937
8 for 43 v. Middlesex at The Oval, 1937
9 for 62 v. MCC at Lord's, 1939
8 for 38 v. Leicestershire at Hull, 1939

A WADDINGTON (3)

8 for 34 v. Northamptonshire at Leeds, 1922
8 for 39 v. Kent at Leeds, 1922
8 for 35 v. Hampshire at Bradford, 1922

E WAINWRIGHT (3)

8 for 49 v. Middlesex at Sheffield, 1891
9 for 66 v. Middlesex at Sheffield, 1894
8 for 34 v. Essex at Bradford, 1896

J H WARDLE (4)

8 for 87 v. Derbyshire at Chesterfield, 1948
8 for 26 v. Middlesex at Lord's, 1950
9 for 48 v. Sussex at Hull, 1954
9 for 25 v. Lancashire at Manchester, 1954

C WHITE (1)

8 for 55 v. Gloucestershire at Gloucester, 1998

A C WILLIAMS (1)

9 for 29 v. Hampshire at Dewsbury, 1919

R WOOD (1)

8 for 45 v. Scotland at Glasgow, 1952

SIX WICKETS IN AN INNINGS AT LESS THAN FOUR RUNS EACH

A complete list of 5 wickets at less than 4 runs each up to and including 2007 is to be found in the 2008 edition

R APPLEYARD (2)

6 for 17 v. Essex at Bradford, 1951
6 for 12 v. Hampshire at Bournemouth, 1954

T ARMITAGE (1)

6 for 20 v. Surrey at Sheffield, 1876

R ASPINALL (1)

6 for 23 v. Northamptonshire at Northampton, 1947

W BATES (5)

6 for 11 v. Middlesex at Huddersfield, 1879
6 for 22 v. Kent at Bradford, 1881
6 for 17 v. Nottinghamshire at Nottingham, 1881
6 for 12 v. Kent at Sheffield, 1882
6 for 19 v. Lancashire at Dewsbury, 1886

A BOOTH (1)

6 for 21 v. Warwickshire at Birmingham, 1946

W E BOWES (4)

6 for 17 v. Middlesex at Lord's, 1934
6 for 16 v. Lancashire at Bradford, 1935
6 for 20 v. Gloucestershire at Sheffield, 1936
6 for 23 v. Warwickshire at Birmingham, 1947

J T BROWN (Darfield) (1)

6 for 19 v. Worcestershire at Worcester, 1899

R.O CLAYTON (1)

6 for 20 v. Nottinghamshire at Sheffield, 1876

A COXON (1)

6 for 17 v. Surrey at Sheffield, 1948

T EMMETT (6)

6 for 7 v. Surrey at Sheffield, 1867
6 for 13 v. Lancashire at Holbeck, 1868
6 for 21 v. Middlesex at Scarborough, 1874
6 for 12 v. Derbyshire at Sheffield, 1878
6 for 19 v. Derbyshire at Bradford, 1881
6 for 22 v. Australians at Bradford, 1882

H FISHER (1)

6 for 11 v. Leicestershire at Bradford, 1932

SIX WICKETS IN AN INNINGS AT LESS THAN FOUR
RUNS EACH *(Continued)*

S HAIGH (10)

6 for 18 v. Derbyshire at Bradford, 1897
6 for 22 v. Hampshire at Southampton, 1898
6 for 21 v. Surrey at The Oval, 1900
6 for 23 v. Cambridge University at Cambridge, 1902
6 for 19 v. Somerset at Sheffield, 1902
6 for 22 v. Cambridge University at Sheffield, 1903
6 for 21 v. Hampshire at Leeds, 1904
6 for 21 v. Nottinghamshire at Sheffield, 1905
6 for 13 v. Surrey at Leeds, 1908
6 for 14 v. Australians at Bradford, 1912

A HILL (2)

6 for 9 v. United South of England XI at Bradford, 1874
6 for 18 v. MCC at Lord's, 1881

G H HIRST (7)

6 for 23 v. MCC at Lord's, 1893
6 for 20 v. Lancashire at Bradford, 1906
6 for 12 v. Northamptonshire at Northampton, 1908
6 for 7 v. Northamptonshire at Northampton, 1908
6 for 23 v. Surrey at Leeds, 1908
6 for 23 v. Lancashire at Manchester, 1909
6 for 20 v. Surrey at Sheffield, 1909

R ILLINGWORTH (2)

6 for 15 v. Scotland at Hull, 1956
6 for 13 v. Leicestershire at Leicester, 1963

F S JACKSON (1)

6 for 19 v. Hampshire at Southampton, 1897

R KILNER (5)

6 for 22 v. Essex at Harrogate, 1922
6 for 13 v. Hampshire at Bournemouth, 1922
6 for 14 v. Middlesex at Bradford, 1923
6 for 22 v. Surrey at Sheffield, 1923
6 for 15 v. Hampshire at Portsmouth, 1924

G G MACAULAY (10)

6 for 10 v. Warwickshire at Birmingham, 1921
6 for 3 v. Derbyshire at Hull, 1921
6 for 8 v. Northamptonshire at Northampton, 1922
6 for 12 v. Glamorgan at Cardiff, 1922
6 for 18 v. Northamptonshire at Bradford, 1923
6 for 19 v. Northamptonshire at Northampton, 1925
6 for 22 v. Leicestershire at Leeds, 1926
6 for 11 v. Leicestershire at Hull, 1930
6 for 22 v. Leicestershire at Bradford, 1933
6 for 22 v. Middlesex at Leeds, 1934

SIX WICKETS IN AN INNINGS AT LESS THAN FOUR
RUNS EACH *(Continued)*

E PEATE (5)

6 for 14 v. Middlesex at Huddersfield, 1879
6 for 12 v. Derbyshire at Derby, 1882
6 for 13 v. Gloucestershire at Moreton-in-Marsh, 1884
6 for 16 v. Sussex at Huddersfield, 1886
6 for 16 v. Cambridge University at Sheffield, 1886

R PEEL (4)

6 for 21 v. Nottinghamshire at Sheffield, 1888
6 for 19 v. Australians at Huddersfield, 1888
6 for 22 v. Gloucestershire at Bristol, 1891
6 for 19 v. Leicestershire at Scarborough, 1896

A C RHODES (1)

6 for 19 v. Cambridge University at Cambridge, 1932

W RHODES (12)

6 for 21 v. Somerset at Bath, 1898
6 for 16 v. Gloucestershire at Bristol, 1899
6 for 4 v. Nottinghamshire at Nottingham, 1901
6 for 15 v. MCC at Lord's, 1902
6 for 16 v. Cambridge University at Cambridge, 1905
6 for 9 v. Essex at Huddersfield, 1905
6 for 22 v. Derbyshire at Glossop, 1907
6 for 17 v. Leicestershire at Leicester, 1908
6 for 13 v. Sussex at Hove, 1922
6 for 23 v. Nottinghamshire at Leeds, 1923
6 for 22 v. Cambridge University at Cambridge, 1924
6 for 20 v. Gloucestershire at Dewsbury, 1927

W RINGROSE (1)

6 for 20 v. Leicestershire at Dewsbury, 1903

R J SIDEBOTTOM (1)

6 for 16 v. Kent at Leeds, 2000

W SLINN (1)

6 for 19 v. Nottinghamshire at Nottingham, 1864

G B STEVENSON(1)

6 for 14 v. Warwickshire at Sheffield, 1979

F S TRUEMAN (4)

6 for 23 v. Oxford University at Oxford, 1955
6 for 23 v. Oxford University at Oxford, 1958
6 for 18 v. Warwickshire at Birmingham, 1963
6 for 20 v. Leicestershire at Sheffield, 1968

H VERITY (5)

6 for 11 v. Surrey at Bradford, 1931
6 for 21 v. Glamorgan at Swansea, 1931
6 for 12 v. Derbyshire at Hull, 1933
6 for 10 v. Essex at Ilford, 1937
6 for 22 v. Hampshire at Bournemouth, 1939

SIX WICKETS IN AN INNINGS AT LESS THAN FOUR
RUNS EACH *(Continued)*

A WADDINGTON (2)

6 for 21 v. Northamptonshire at Harrogate, 1921
6 for 21 v. Northamptonshire at Northampton, 1923

S WADE (1)

6 for 18 v. Gloucestershire at Dewsbury, 1887

E WAINWRIGHT (4)

6 for 16 v. Sussex at Leeds, 1893
6 for 23 v. Sussex at Hove, 1893
6 for 18 v. Sussex at Dewsbury, 1894
6 for 22 v. MCC at Scarborough, 1894

J H WARDLE (8)

6 for 17 v. Sussex at Sheffield, 1948
6 for 10 v. Scotland at Edinburgh, 1950
6 for 12 v. Gloucestershire at Hull, 1950
6 for 20 v. Kent at Scarborough, 1950
6 for 23 v. Somerset at Sheffield, 1951
6 for 21 v. Glamorgan at Leeds, 1951
6 for 18 v. Gloucestershire at Bristol, 1951
6 for 6 v. Gloucestershire at Bristol, 1955

D WILSON (3)

6 for 22 v. Sussex at Bradford, 1963
6 for 15 v. Gloucestershire at Middlesbrough, 1966
6 for 22 v. Middlesex at Sheffield, 1966

FOUR WICKETS IN FOUR BALLS

A Drake v. Derbyshire at Chesterfield, 1914

FOUR WICKETS IN FIVE BALLS

F S Jackson v. Australians at Leeds, 1902
A Waddington v. Northamptonshire at Northampton, 1920
G G Macaulay v. Lancashire at Manchester, 1933
P J Hartley v. Derbyshire at Chesterfield, 1995
D Gough v. Kent at Leeds, 1995
J D Middlebrook v. Hampshire at Southampton, 2000

BEST BOWLING ANALYSES IN A MATCH
FOR AND AGAINST YORKSHIRE

Best For Yorkshire:
17 for 91 (8 for 47 and 9 for 44) H Verity v Essex at Leyton, 1933

Against Yorkshire:
17 for 91 (9 for 62 and 8 for 29) H Dean for Lancashire at Liverpool, 1913
(non-championship)

County Championship
16 for 114 (8 for 48 and 8 for 66) G Burton for Middlesex at Sheffield, 1888

Yorkshire versus:

Derbyshire	*For Yorkshire:*	14 for 58 (4 for 11 and 10 for 47) T F Smailes at Sheffield, 1939
	Against:	13 for 65 (7 for 33 and 6 for 32) W Mycroft at Sheffield, 1879
Most 10 wickets in a match	*For Yorkshire:*	P Carrick and E Peate 4 each
	Against:	W Mycroft 3
Durham	*For Yorkshire:*	10 for 101 (6 for 57 and 4 for 44) M A Robinson at Durham, 1992
	Against:	10 for 144 (7 for 81 and 3 for 63) O D Gibson at Chester-le-Street, 2007
Most 10 wickets in a match	*For Yorkshire:*	M A Robinson 1
	Against:	G R Breese and O D Gibson 1 each
Essex	*For Yorkshire:*	17 for 91 (8 for 47 and 9 for 44) H Verity at Leyton, 1933
	Against:	14 for 127 (7 for 37 and 7 for 90) W Mead at Leyton, 1899
Most 10 wickets in a match	*For Yorkshire:*	W Rhodes 7
	Against:	J K Lever, W Mead 2 each
Glamorgan	*For Yorkshire:*	15 for 123 (8 for 70 and 7 for 53) R Illingworth at Swansea, 1960
	Against:	12 for 76 (7 for 30 and 5 for 46) D J Shepherd at Cardiff, 1957
Most 10 wickets in a match	*For Yorkshire:*	H Verity 5
	Against:	D J Shepherd, J S Pressdee 1 each
Gloucestershire	*For Yorkshire:*	14 for 64 (7 for 58 and 7 for 6) R Illingworth at Harrogate, 1967
	Against:	15 for 79 (8 for 33 and 7 for 46) W G Grace at Sheffield, 1872
Most 10 wickets in a match	*For Yorkshire:*	W Rhodes 8
	Against:	E G Dennett 5
Hampshire	*For Yorkshire:*	14 for 43 (8 for 21 and 6 for 22) S Haigh at Southampton, 1898
	Against:	12 for 145 (7 for 78 and 5 for 67) D Shackleton at Bradford, 1962
Most 10 wickets in a match	*For Yorkshire:*	W Rhodes, E Robinson, H Verity 3 each
	Against:	A S Kennedy 3

Yorkshire versus

Kent	*For Yorkshire:*	15 for 38 (6 for 26 and 9 for 12) H Verity at Sheffield, 1936
	Against:	13 for 48 (5 for 13 and 8 for 35) A Hearne at Sheffield, 1885
Most 10 wickets in a match	*For Yorkshire:* *Against:*	E Peate and J H Wardle 4 each C Blythe 6
Lancashire	*For Yorkshire:*	14 for 80 (6 for 56 and 8 for 24) E Peate at Manchester, 1880
	Against:	17 for 91 (9 for 62 and 8 for 29) H Dean at Liverpool, 1913 (non-championship) 14 for 90 (6 for 47 and 8 for 43) R Tattersall at Leeds, 1956 (championship)
Most 10 wickets in a match	*For Yorkshire:* *Against:*	T Emmett 5 J Briggs 8
Leicestershire	*For Yorkshire:*	15 for 63 (8 for 25 and 7 for 38) G H Hirst at Hull, 1907
	Against:	12 for 139 (8 for 85 and 4 for 54) A D Pougher at Leicester, 1895
Most 10 wickets in a match	*For Yorkshire:* *Against:*	G H Hirst 5 A D Pougher 2
Middlesex	*For Yorkshire:*	13 for 94 (6 for 61 and 7 for 33) S Haigh at Leeds, 1900
	Against:	16 for 114 (8 for 48 and 8 for 66) G Burton at Sheffield, 1888
Most 10 wickets in a match	*For Yorkshire:* *Against:*	W Rhodes 5 J T Hearne 7
Northamptonshire	*For Yorkshire:*	16 for 35 (8 for 18 and 8 for 17) W E Bowes at Kettering, 1935
	Against:	15 for 31 (7 for 22 and 8 for 9) G E Tribe at Northampton, 1958
Most 10 wickets in a match	*For Yorkshire:* *Against:*	W E Bowes, G G Macaulay, H Verity, A Waddington 3 each G E Tribe 3
Nottinghamshire	*For Yorkshire:*	14 for 33 (8 for 12 and 6 for 21) R Peel at Sheffield, 1888
	Against:	14 for 94 (8 for 38 and 6 for 56) F Morley at Nottingham, 1878
Most 10 wickets in a match	*For Yorkshire:* *Against:*	G H Hirst 5 F Morley, J C Shaw 4 each
Somerset	*For Yorkshire:*	15 for 50 (9 for 22 and 6 for 28) R Peel at Leeds, 1895
	Against:	15 for 71 (6 for 30 and 9 for 41) L C Braund at Sheffield, 1902
Most 10 wickets in a match	*For Yorkshire:* *Against:*	G H Hirst 7 L C Braund 3

BEST BOWLING ANALYSES IN A MATCH
FOR AND AGAINST YORKSHIRE *(continued)*

Yorkshire versus

Surrey

	For Yorkshire:	14 for 77 (6 for 47 and 8 for 30)
		E Peate at Huddersfield, 1881
	Against:	15 for 154 (7 for 55 and 8 for 99)
		T Richardson at Leeds, 1897
Most 10 wickets	*For Yorkshire:*	W Rhodes 7
in a match	*Against:*	G A Lohmann, T Richardson 6 each

Sussex

	For Yorkshire:	16 for 112 (9 for 48 and 7 for 64)
		J H Wardle at Hull, 1954
	Against:	12 for 110 (6 for 71 and 6 for 39)
		G R Cox at Sheffield, 1907
Most 10 wickets	*For Yorkshire:*	R Peel, E Wainwright 3 each
in a match	*Against:*	Twelve players 1 each

Warwickshire

	For Yorkshire:	14 for 92 (9 for 43 and 5 for 49)
		H Verity at Leeds, 1937
	Against:	12 for 55 (5 for 21 and 7 for 34)
		T W Cartwright at Bradford, 1969
Most 10 wickets	*For Yorkshire:*	S Haigh 4
in a match	*Against:*	E F Field 4

Worcestershire

	For Yorkshire:	14 for 211 (8 for 87 and 6 for 124)
		W Rhodes at Worcester, 1903
	Against:	13 for 76 (4 for 38 and 9 for 38)
		J A Cuffe at Bradford, 1907
Most 10 wickets	*For Yorkshire:*	S Haigh, G G Macaulay 4 each
in a match	*Against:*	N Gifford 2

Australians

	For Yorkshire:	13 for 149 (8 for 48 and 5 for 101)
		G H Hirst at Bradford, 1899
	Against:	13 for 170 (6 for 91 and 7 for 79)
		J M Gregory at Sheffield, 1919
Most 10 wickets	*For Yorkshire:*	S Haigh 2
in a match	*Against:*	C V Grimmett, F R Spofforth, C T B Turner, H Trumble 2 each

BEST BOWLING ANALYSES IN AN INNINGS
FOR AND AGAINST YORKSHIRE

Best For Yorkshire:
10 for 10 H Verity v Nottinghamshire at Leeds, 1932

Against Yorkshire:
10 for 37 C V Grimmett for Australians at Sheffield, 1930
(non-championship)

County Championship
10 for 51 H Howell for Warwickshire at Birmingham, 1923

Yorkshire versus:

Derbyshire

	For Yorkshire:	10 for 47	T F Smailes at Sheffield, 1939
	Against:	9 for 27	J J Hulme at Sheffield, 1894
Most 5 wickets	*For Yorkshire:*	S Haigh, E Peat, W Rhodes 11 each	
in an innings	*Against:*	W Mycroft 10	

BEST BOWLING ANALYSES IN AN INNINGS
FOR AND AGAINST YORKSHIRE *(continued)*

Yorkshire versus

Durham	*For Yorkshire:*	6 for 37	R D Stemp at Durham, 1994
		6 for 37	J N Gillespie at Chester-le-Street, 2006
	Against:	7 for 58	J Wood at Leeds, 1999
Most 5 wickets	*For Yorkshire:*	D Gough and M J Hoggard 2 each	
in an innings	*Against:*	G R Breese, S J E Brown, S J Harmison and G Onions 2 each	
Essex	*For Yorkshire:*	9 for 28	W Rhodes at Leyton, 1899
	Against:	8 for 44	F G Bull at Bradford, 1896
Most 5 wickets	*For Yorkshire:*	W Rhodes 18	
in an innings	*Against:*	W Mead 14	
Glamorgan	*For Yorkshire:*	9 for 60	H Verity at Swansea, 1930
	Against:	9 for 43	J S Pressdee at Swansea, 1965
Most 5 wickets	*For Yorkshire:*	H Verity 12	
in an innings	*Against:*	D J Shepherd 6	
Gloucestershire	*For Yorkshire:*	9 for 25	S Haigh at Leeds, 1912
	Against:	9 for 36	C W L Parker at Bristol, 1922
Most 5 wickets	*For Yorkshire:*	W Rhodes 22	
in an innings	*Against:*	T W J Goddard 17	
Hampshire	*For Yorkshire:*	9 for 29	A C Williams at Dewsbury, 1919
	Against:	8 for 49	O W Herman at Bournemouth, 1930
Most 5 wickets	*For Yorkshire:*	G H Hirst 10	
in an innings	*Against:*	A S Kennedy 10	
Kent	*For Yorkshire:*	9 for 12	H Verity at Sheffield, 1936
	Against:	8 for 35	A Hearne at Sheffield, 1885
Most 5 wickets	*For Yorkshire:*	W Rhodes 12	
in an innings	*Against:*	A P Freeman 14	
Lancashire	*For Yorkshire:*	9 for 23	G H Hirst at Leeds, 1910
	Against:	9 for 41	A Mold at Huddersfield, 1890
Most 5 wickets	*For Yorkshire:*	T Emmett 16	
in an innings	*Against:*	J Briggs 19	
Leicestershire	*For Yorkshire:*	8 for 25	G H Hirst at Hull, 1907
	Against:	9 for 63	C T Spencer at Huddersfield, 1954
Most 5 wickets	*For Yorkshire:*	G H Hirst 15	
in an innings	*Against:*	H A Smith 7	
Middlesex	*For Yorkshire:*	9 for 45	G H Hirst at Sheffield 1907
	Against:	9 for 57	F A Tarrant at Leeds, 1906
Most 5 wickets	*For Yorkshire:*	W Rhodes 18	
in an innings	*Against:*	J T Hearne 21	
Northamptonshire	*For Yorkshire:*	9 for 37	M A Robinson at Harrogate, 1993
	Against:	9 for 30	A E Thomas at Bradford, 1920
Most 5 wickets	*For Yorkshire:*	G G Macaulay 14	
in an innings	*Against:*	G E Tribe, W Wells 7 each	
Nottinghamshire	*For Yorkshire:*	10 for 10	H Verity at Leeds, 1932
	Against:	8 for 32	J C Shaw at Nottingham, 1865
Most 5 wickets	*For Yorkshire:*	W Rhodes 17	
in an innings	*Against:*	F Morley 17	

BEST BOWLING ANALYSES IN AN INNINGS
FOR AND AGAINST YORKSHIRE *(continued)*

Yorkshire versus

Somerset
	For Yorkshire:	10 for 35	A Drake at Weston-super-Mare, 1914
	Against:	9 for 41	L C Braund at Sheffield, 1902
Most 5 wickets	*For Yorkshire:*	G H Hirst 16	
in an innings	*Against:*	E J Tyler 8	

Surrey
	For Yorkshire:	8 for 5	E Peate at Holbeck, 1883
	Against:	9 for 47	T Richardson at Sheffield, 1893
Most 5 wickets	*For Yorkshire:*	W Rhodes 17	
in an innings	*Against:*	W Southerton 19	

Sussex
	For Yorkshire:	9 for 48	J H Wardle at Hull, 1954
	Against:	9 for 34	James Langridge at Sheffield, 1934
Most 5 wickets	*For Yorkshire:*	W Rhodes 14	
in an innings	*Against:*	G R Cox, J A Snow 6 each	

Warwickshire
	For Yorkshire:	10 for 36	H Verity at Leeds, 1930
	Against:	10 for 51	H Howell at Birmingham, 1923
Most 5 wickets	*For Yorkshire:*	W Rhodes 18	
in an innings	*Against:*	E F Field, W E Hollies 7 each	

Worcestershire
	For Yorkshire:	9 for 41	G H Hirst at Worcester, 1911
	Against:	9 for 38	J A Cuffe at Bradford, 1907
Most 5 wickets	*For Yorkshire:*	S Haigh, W Rhodes 11 each	
in an innings	*Against:*	R T D Perks 7	

Australians
	For Yorkshire:	9 for 76	W Ringrose at Bradford, 1905
	Against:	10 for 37	C V Grimmett at Sheffield, 1930
Most 5 wickets	*For Yorkshire:*	R Peel 7	
in an innings	*Against:*	F R Spofforth 7	

HAT-TRICKS

G Freeman v. Lancashire at Holbeck, 1868
G Freeman v. Middlesex at Sheffield, 1868
A Hill v. United South of England XI at Bradford, 1874
A Hill v. Surrey at The Oval, 1880
E Peate v. Kent at Sheffield, 1882
G Ulyett v. Lancashire at Sheffield, 1883
E Peate v. Gloucestershire at Moreton-in-Marsh, 1884
W Fletcher v. MCC at Lord's, 1892
E Wainwright v. Sussex at Dewsbury, 1894
G H Hirst v. Leicestershire at Leicester, 1895
J T Brown v. Derbyshire at Derby, 1896
R Peel v. Kent at Halifax, 1897
S Haigh v. Derbyshire at Bradford, 1897
W Rhodes v. Kent at Canterbury, 1901
S Haigh v. Somerset at Sheffield, 1902
H A Sedgwick v. Worcestershire at Hull, 1906
G Deyes v. Gentlemen of Ireland at Bray, 1907
G H Hirst v. Leicestershire at Hull, 1907
J T Newstead v. Worcestershire at Bradford, 1907
S Haigh v. Lancashire at Manchester, 1909
M W Booth v. Worcestershire at Bradford, 1911
A Drake v. Essex at Huddersfield, 1912

HAT-TRICKS *(Continued)*

M W Booth v. Essex at Leyton, 1912
A Drake v. Derbyshire at Chesterfield, 1914 (4 in 4)
W Rhodes v. Derbyshire at Derby, 1920
A Waddington v. Northamptonshire at Northampton, 1920 (4 in 5)
G G Macaulay v. Warwickshire at Birmingham, 1923
E Robinson v. Sussex at Hull, 1928
G G Macaulay v. Leicestershire at Hull, 1930
E Robinson v. Kent at Gravesend, 1930
H Verity v. Nottinghamshire at Leeds, 1932
H Fisher v. Somerset at Sheffield, 1932 (all lbw)
G G Macaulay v. Glamorgan at Cardiff, 1933
G G Macaulay v. Lancashire at Manchester, 1933 (4 in 5)
M.Leyland v. Surrey at Sheffield, 1935
E Robinson v. Kent at Leeds, 1939
A Coxon v. Worcestershire at Leeds, 1946
F S Trueman v. Nottinghamshire at Nottingham, 1951
F S Trueman v. Nottinghamshire at Scarborough, 1955
R Appleyard v. Gloucestershire at Sheffield, 1956
F S.Trueman v. MCC at Lord's, 1958
D Wilson v. Nottinghamshire at Middlesbrough, 1959
F S Trueman v. Nottinghamshire at Bradford, 1963
D Wilson v. Nottinghamshire at Worksop, 1966
D Wilson v. Kent at Harrogate, 1966
G A Cope v. Essex at Colchester, 1970
A L Robinson v. Nottinghamshire at Worksop, 1974
P W Jarvis v. Derbyshire at Chesterfield, 1985
P J Hartley v. Derbyshire at Chesterfield, 1995 (4 in 5)
D Gough v. Kent at Leeds, 1995 (4 in 5)
C White v. Gloucestershire at Gloucester, 1998
M J Hoggard v. Sussex at Hove, 2009

52 Hat-Tricks: G G Macaulay and F S Trueman took four each, S Haigh and D Wilson three each. There have been seven hat-tricks versus Kent and Nottinghamshire, and six versus Derbyshire.

200 WICKETS IN A SEASON

Bowler	Season	Overs	Maidens	Runs	Wickets	Average
W Rhodes	1900	1366.4	411	3054	240	12.72
W Rhodes	1901	1455.3	474	3497	233	15.00
G H Hirst	1906	1111.1	262	3089	201	15.36
G G Macaulay	1925	1241.2	291	2986	200	14.93
R Appleyard†	1951	1323.2	394	2829	200	14.14

† First full season in First-Class cricket.

100 WICKETS IN A SEASON

Bowler		Wickets taken	Wickets taken	Wickets taken
R Appleyard	(3)	200 in 1951	141 in 1954	110 in 1956
A Booth	(1)	111 in 1946	—	—
M W Booth	(3)	104 in 1912	167 in 1913	155 in 1914
W E Bowes	(8)	117 in 1931	168 in 1932	130 in 1933
		109 in 1934	154 in 1935	113 in 1936
		106 in 1938	107 in 1939	—

Bowler		Wickets taken	Wickets taken	Wickets taken
D B Close	(2)	105 in 1949	114 in 1952	—
A Coxon	(2)	101 in 1949	129 in 1950	—
A Drake	(2)	115 in 1913	158 in 1914	—
T Emmett	(1)	112 in 1886	—	—
S Haigh	(10)	100 in 1898	160 in 1900	154 in 1902
		102 in 1903	118 in 1904	118 in 1905
		161 in 1906	120 in 1909	100 in 1911
		125 in 1912	—	—
G H Hirst	(12)	150 in 1895	171 in 1901	121 in 1903
		114 in 1904	100 in 1905	201 in 1906
		169 in 1907	164 in 1908	138 in 1910
		130 in 1911	113 in 1912	100 in 1913
R Illingworth	(5)	103 in 1956	120 in 1961	116 in 1962
		122 in 1964	105 in 1968	—
R Kilner	(4)	107 in 1922	143 in 1923	134 in 1924
		123 in 1925	—	—
G G Macaulay	(10)	101 in 1921	130 in 1922	163 in 1923
		184 in 1924	200 in 1925	133 in 1926
		130 in 1927	117 in 1928	102 in 1929
		141 in 1933	—	—
J T Newstead	(1)	131 in 1908	—	—
A G Nicholson	(2)	113 in 1966	101 in 1967	—
E Peate	(3)	131 in 1880	133 in 1881	165 in 1882
R Peel	(6)	118 in 1888	132 in 1890	106 in 1892
		134 in 1894	155 in 1895	108 in 1896
W Rhodes	(22)	141 in 1898	153 in 1899	240 in 1900
		233 in 1901	174 in 1902	169 in 1903
		118 in 1904	158 in 1905	113 in 1906
		164 in 1907	100 in 1908	115 in 1909
		105 in 1911	117 in 1914	155 in 1919
		156 in 1920	128 in 1921	100 in 1922
		127 in 1923	102 in 1926	111 in 1928
		100 in 1929	—	—
E Robinson	(1)	111 in 1928	—	—
E P Robinson	(4)	104 in 1938	120 in 1939	149 in 1946
		108 in 1947	—	—
T F Smailes	(4)	105 in 1934	125 in 1936	120 in 1937
		104 in 1938	—	—
F S Trueman	(8)	129 in 1954	140 in 1955	104 in 1959
		150 in 1960	124 in 1961	122 in 1962
		121 in 1965	107 in 1966	—
H Verity	(9)	169 in 1931	146 in 1932	168 in 1933
		100 in 1934	199 in 1935	185 in 1936
		185 in 1937	137 in 1938	189 in 1939
A Waddington	(5)	100 in 1919	140 in 1920	105 in 1921
		132 in 1922	105 in 1925	—
E Wainwright	(3)	114 in 1893	157 in 1894	102 in 1896
J H Wardle	(10)	148 in 1948	100 in 1949	172 in 1950
		122 in 1951	169 in 1952	126 in 1953
		122 in 1954	159 in 1955	146 in 1956
		106 in 1957	—	—
D Wilson	(3)	100 in 1966	107 in 1968	101 in 1969

BOWLERS WHO HAVE TAKEN OVER 500 WICKETS

Player	M	Runs	Wkts	Av'ge	Best
W Rhodes	883	57634	3598	16.01	9 for 28
G H Hirst	717	44716	2481	18.02	9 for 23
S Haigh	513	29289	1876	15.61	9 for 25
G G Macaulay	445	30554	1774	17.22	8 for 21
F S Trueman	459	29890	1745	17.12	8 for 28
H Verity	278	21353	1558	13.70	10 for 10
J H Wardle	330	27917	1539	18.13	9 for 25
R Illingworth	496	26806	1431	18.73	9 for 42
W E Bowes	301	21227	1351	15.71	9 for 121
R Peel	318	20638	1311	15.74	9 for 22
T Emmett	299	15465	1216	12.71	9 for 23
D Wilson	392	22626	1104	20.49	7 for 19
P Carrick	425	30530	1018	29.99	8 for 33
E Wainwright	352	17744	998	17.77	9 for 66
D B Close	536	23489	967	24.29	8 for 41
Emmott Robinson	413	19645	893	21.99	9 for 36
A G Nicholson	.282	17296	876	19.74	9 for 62
R Kilner	365	14855	857	17.33	8 for 26
A Waddington	255	16203	835	19.40	8 for 34
T F Smailes	262	16593	802	20.68	10 for 47
E Peate	154	9986	794	12.57	8 for 5
Ellis P Robinson	208	15141	735	20.60	8 for 35
C M Old	222	13409	647	20.72	7 for 20
R Appleyard	133	9903	642	15.42	8 for 76
W Bates	202	10692	637	16.78	8 for 21
G A Cope	230	15627	630	24.80	8 for 73
P J Hartley	195	17438	579	30.11	9 for 41
A Sidebottom	216	13852	558	24.82	8 for 72
M W Booth	144	11017	557	19.17	8 for 47
A Hill	140	7002	542	12.91	7 for 14
Hon F S Jackson	207	9690	506	19.15	7 for 42

BOWLERS UNCHANGED IN A MATCH

(IN WHICH THE OPPONENTS WERE DISMISSED TWICE)

There have been 31 instances. The first and most recent are listed below.

A complete list is to be found in the 2008 edition.

First: L Greenwood (11 for 71) and G Freeman (8 for 73) v. Surrey
at The Oval, 1867
Yorkshire won by an innings and 111 runs

Most Recent: E Robinson (8 for 65) and G G Macaulay (12 for 50) v. Worcestershire
at Leeds, 1927
Yorkshire won by an innings and 106 runs

FIELDERS (IN MATCHES FOR YORKSHIRE)

MOST CATCHES IN AN INNINGS

6	E P Robinson	v. Leicestershire	at Bradford, 1938
5	J Tunnicliffe	v. Leicestershire	at Leeds, 1897
5	J Tunnicliffe	v. Leicestershire	at Leicester, 1900
5	J Tunnicliffe	v. Leicestershire	at Scarborough, 1901
5	A B Sellers	v. Essex	at Leyton, 1933
5	D Wilson	v. Surrey	at The Oval, 1969
5	R G Lumb	v. Gloucestershire	at Middlesbrough, 1972

MOST CATCHES IN A MATCH

7	J Tunnicliffe	v. Leicestershire	at Leeds, 1897
7	J Tunnicliffe	v. Leicestershire	at Leicester, 1900
7	A B Sellers	v Essex	at Leyton, 1933
7	E P Robinson	v. Leicestershire	at Bradford, 1938
7	A Lyth	v. Middlesex	at Scarborough, 2014

MOST CATCHES IN A SEASON

70	J Tunnicliffe	in 1901
70	P J Sharpe	in 1962
61	J Tunnicliffe	in 1895
60	J Tunnicliffe	in 1904
59	J Tunnicliffe	in 1896
57	J V Wilson	in 1955
54	J V Wilson	in 1961
53	J V Wilson	in 1957
51	J V Wilson	in 1951

MOST CATCHES IN A CAREER

665	J Tunnicliffe	(1.40 per match)
586	W Rhodes	(0.66 per match)
564	D B Close	(1.05 per match)
525	P J Sharpe	(1.27 per match)
520	J V Wilson	(1.09 per match)
518	G H Hirst	(0.72 per match)

WICKET-KEEPERS IN MATCHES FOR YORKSHIRE

MOST DISMISSALS IN AN INNINGS

7	(7ct)	D L Bairstow	v. Derbyshire	at Scarborough	1982
6	(6ct)	J Hunter	v. Gloucestershire	at Gloucester	1887
6	(5ct,1st)	D Hunter	v. Surrey	at Sheffield	1891
6	(6ct)	D Hunter	v. Middlesex	at Leeds	1909
6	(2ct,4st)	W R Allen	v. Sussex	at Hove	1921
6	(5ct,1st)	J G Binks	v. Lancashire	at Leeds	1962
6	(6ct)	D L Bairstow	v. Lancashire	at Manchester	1971
6	(6ct)	D L Bairstow	v. Warwickshire	at Bradford	1978
6	(5ct,1st)	D L Bairstow	v. Lancashire	at Leeds	1980
6	(6ct)	D L Bairstow	v. Derbyshire	at Chesterfield	1984
6	(6ct)	R J Blakey	v. Sussex	at Eastbourne	1990
6	(5ct,1st)	R J Blakey	v. Gloucestershire	at Cheltenham	1992
6	(5ct,1st)	R J Blakey	v. Glamorgan	at Cardiff	1994
6	(6ct)	R J Blakey	v. Glamorgan	at Leeds	2003
6	(6ct)	G L Brophy	v. Durham	at Chester-le-Street	2009
6	(6ct)	J M Bairstow	v. Middlesex	at Leeds	2013
6	(6ct)	J M Bairstow	v. Sussex	at Arundel	2014

MOST DISMISSALS IN A MATCH

11	(11ct)	D L Bairstow	v. Derbyshire	at Scarborough	1982
		(Equalled World Record)			
9	(9ct)	J.Hunter	v. Gloucestershire	at Gloucester	1887
9	(8ct,1st)	A Dolphin	v. Derbyshire	at Bradford	1919
9	(9ct)	D L Bairstow	v. Lancashire	at Manchester	1971
9	(9ct)	R J Blakey	v. Sussex	at Eastbourne	1990
8	(2ct,6st)	G Pinder	v. Lancashire	at Sheffield	1872
8	(2ct,6st)	D Hunter	v. Surrey	at Bradford	1898
8	(7ct,1st)	A Bairstow	v. Cambridge University	at Cambridge	1899
8	(8ct)	A Wood	v. Northamptonshire	at Huddersfield	1932
8	(8ct)	D L Bairstow	v. Lancashire	at Leeds	1978
8	(7ct,1st)	D L Bairstow	v. Derbyshire	at Chesterfield	1984
8	(6ct,2st)	D L Bairstow	v. Derbyshire	at Chesterfield	1985
8	(8ct)	R J Blakey	v. Hampshire	at Southampton	1989
8	(8ct)	R J Blakey	v. Northamptonshire	at Harrogate	1993
8	(8ct)	A J Hodd	v. Glamorgan	at Leeds	2012
8	(8ct)	J M Bairstow	v. Middlesex	at Leeds	2013

MOST DISMISSALS IN A SEASON   MOST DISMISSALS IN A CAREER

107	(96ct,11st)	J G Binks, 1960	1186	(863ct,323st)	D Hunter (2.29 per match)
94	(81ct,13st)	JG Binks, 1961	1044	(872ct,172st)	J G Binks (2.12 per match)
89	(75ct,14st)	A Wood, 1934	1038	(907ct,131st)	D L Bairstow (2.41 per match)
88	(80ct,8st)	J G Binks, 1963	855	(612ct,243st)	A Wood (2.09 per match)
86	(70ct,16st)	J G Binks, 1962	829	(569ct,260st)	A Dolphin (1.94 per match)
82	(52ct,30st)	A Dolphin, 1919	824	(768ct, 56st)	R J Blakey (2.43 per match)
80	(57ct,23st)	A. Wood, 1935			

YORKSHIRE PLAYERS WHO HAVE COMPLETED THE "DOUBLE"

(all First-Class matches)

Player	Year	Runs	Average	Wickets	Average
M W Booth (1)	1913	1,228	27.28	181	18.46
D B Close (2)	†1949	1,098	27.45	113	27.87
	1952	1,192	33.11	114	24.08
A Drake (1)	1913	1,056	23.46	116	16.93
S Haigh (1)	1904	1,055	26.37	121	19.85
G H Hirst (14)	1896	1,122	28.20	104	21.64
	1897	1,535	35.69	101	23.22
	1901	1,950	42.39	183	16.38
	1903	1,844	47.28	128	14.94
	1904	2,501	54.36	132	21.09
	1905	2,266	53.95	110	19.94
	††1906	2,385	45.86	208	16.50
	1907	1,344	28.38	188	15.20
	1908	1,598	38.97	114	14.05
	1909	1,256	27.30	115	20.05
	1910	1,840	32.85	164	14.79
	1911	1,789	33.12	137	20.40
	1912	1,133	25.75	118	17.37
	1913	1,540	35.81	101	20.13
R Illingworth (6)	1957	1,213	28.20	106	18.40
	1959	1,726	46.64	110	21.46
	1960	1,006	25.79	109	17.55
	1961	1,153	24.53	128	17.90
	1962	1,612	34.29	117	19.45
	1964	1,301	37.17	122	17.45
F S Jackson (1)	1898	1,566	41.21	104	15.67
R Kilner (4)	1922	1,198	27.22	122	14.73
	1923	1,404	32.24	158	12.91
	1925	1,068	30.51	131	17.92
	1926	1,187	37.09	107	22.52
R Peel (1)	1896	1,206	30.15	128	17.50
W Rhodes (16)	1903	1,137	27.07	193	14.57
	1904	1,537	35.74	131	21.59
	1905	1,581	35.93	182	16.95
	1906	1,721	29.16	128	23.57
	1907	1,055	22.93	177	15.57
	1908	1,673	31.56	115	16.13
	1909	2,094	40.26	141	15.89
	1911	2,261	38.32	117	24.07
	1914	1,377	29.29	118	18.27
	1919	1,237	34.36	164	14.42
	1920	1,123	28.07	161	13.18
	1921	1,474	39.83	141	13.27
	1922	1,511	39.76	119	12.19
	1923	1,321	33.02	134	11.54
	1924	1,126	26.18	109	14.46
	1926	1,132	34.30	115	14.86
T F Smailes (1)	1938	1,002	25.05	113	20.84
E Wainwright (1)	1897	1,612	35.82	101	23.06

† First season in First-Class cricket.
†† The only instance in First-Class cricket of 2,000 runs and 200 wickets in a season.

H Sutcliffe (194) and M Leyland (45) hit 102 off six consecutive overs for Yorkshire v. Essex at Scarborough in 1932.

From 1898 to 1930 inclusive, Wilfred Rhodes took no less than 4,187 wickets, and scored 39,969 runs in First-Class cricket at home and abroad, a remarkable record. He also took 100 wickets and scored 1,000 in a season 16 times, and G H Hirst 14 times.

Of players with a qualification of not less than 50 wickets, Wilfred Rhodes was first in bowling in First-Class cricket in 1900, 1901, 1919, 1920, 1922, 1923 and 1926; Schofield Haigh in 1902, 1905, 1908 and 1909; Mr E R Wilson in 1921; G G Macaulay in 1924; H Verity in 1930, 1933, 1935, 1937 and 1939; W E Bowes in 1938; A Booth in 1946; R Appleyard in 1951 and 1955, and F S Trueman in 1952 and 1963.

The highest aggregate of runs made in one season in First-Class cricket by a Yorkshire player is 3,429 by L Hutton in 1949. This total has been exceeded three times, viz: D C S Compton 3,816 and W J Edrich 3,539 in 1947, and 3,518 by T Hayward in 1906. H Sutcliffe scored 3,336 in 1932.

Three players have taken all 10 Yorkshire wickets in an innings. G Wootton, playing for All England XI at Sheffield in 1865, took all 10 wickets for 54 runs. H Howell performed the feat for Warwickshire at Edgbaston in 1923 at a cost of 51 runs; and C V Grimmett, Australia, took all 10 wickets for 37 runs at Sheffield in 1930.

The match against Sussex at Dewsbury on June 7th and 8th, 1894, was brought to a summary conclusion by a remarkable bowling performance on the part of Edward Wainwright. In the second innings of Sussex, he took the last five wickets in seven balls, including the "hat trick". In the whole match he obtained 13 wickets for only 38 runs.

M D Moxon has the unique distinction of scoring a century in each of his first two First-Class matches in Yorkshire — 116 (2nd inns.) v. Essex at Leeds and 111 (1st inns.) v. Derbyshire at Sheffield, June 1981).

In the Yorkshire v. Norfolk match — played on the Hyde Park Ground, Sheffield, on July 14th to 18th, 1834 — 851 runs were scored in the four innings, of which no fewer than 128 were extras: 75 byes and 53 wides. At that time wides were not run out, so that every wide included in the above total represents a wide actually bowled. This particular achievement has never been surpassed in the annals of county cricket.

L Hutton reached his 1,000 runs in First-Class cricket in 1949 as early as June 9th.

W Barber reached his 1,000 runs in 1934 on June 13th. P Holmes reached his 1,000 in 1925 on June 16th, as also did H Sutcliffe in 1932. J T Brown reached his 1,000 in 1899 on June 22nd. In 1905, D Denton reached his 1,000 runs on June 26th; and in 1906 G H Hirst gained the same total on June 27th.

In 1912, D Denton scored over 1,000 runs during July, while M Leyland and H Sutcliffe both scored over 1,000 runs in August 1932.

L Hutton scored over 1,000 in June and over 1,000 runs in August in 1949.

H Verity took his 100th wicket in First-Class cricket as early as June 19th in 1936 and on June 27th in 1935. In 1900, W Rhodes obtained his 100th wicket on June 21st, and again on the same date in 1901, while G H Hirst obtained his 100th wicket on June 28th, 1906.

In 1930, Yorkshiremen (H Sutcliffe and H Verity) occupied the first places by English players in the batting and the bowling averages of First-Class cricket, which is a record without precedent. H Sutcliffe was also first in the batting averages in 1931 and 1932.

G Boycott was the first player to have achieved an average of over 100 in each of two English seasons. In 1971, he scored 2,503 runs for an average of 100.12, and in 1979 he scored 1,538 runs for an average of 102.53.

FIRST-CLASS MATCHES BEGUN AND FINISHED IN ONE DAY

Yorkshire v. Somerset, at Huddersfield, July 9th, 1894.

Yorkshire v. Hampshire, at Southampton, May 27th, 1898

Yorkshire v. Worcestershire, at Bradford, May 7th, 1900

YORKSHIRE TEST CRICKETERS 1877-2018 (Correct to November 28, 2018)

Player	M.	I	NO	Runs	HS.	Av'ge	100s	50s	Balls	R	W	Av'ge	Best	5wI	10wM	c/st
APPLEYARD, R ...1954-56	9	9	6	51	19*	17.00	—	—	1,596	554	31	17.87	5-51	1	—	4
ARMITAGE, T ...1877	2	3	0	33	21	11.00	—	—	12	15	0	—	—	—	—	0
ATHEY, C W J ...1980-88	23	41	1	919	123	22.97	1	4	—	—	—	—	—	—	—	13
BAIRSTOW, D L ...1979-81	4	7	1	125	59	20.83	—	1	—	—	—	—	—	—	—	12/1
BAIRSTOW, J M ...2012-18	60	104	6	3,696	167*	37.71	6	19	—	—	—	—	—	—	—	57/9
BALLANCE, G S 2013/14-17	23	42	2	1,498	156	37.45	4	7	—	—	—	—	—	—	—	22
BARBER, W ...1935	2	4	0	83	44	20.75	—	—	12	5	0	—	—	—	—	1
BATES, W ...1881-87	15	26	2	656	64	27.33	—	5	2,364	821	50	16.42	7-28	4	1	9
BINKS, J G ...1964	2	4	0	91	55	22.75	—	1	—	—	—	—	—	—	—	8/0
BLAKEY, R J ...1993	2	2	0	7	6	1.75	—	—	—	—	—	—	—	—	—	2/0
BOOTH, M W ...1913-14	2	2	0	46	32	23.00	—	—	312	130	7	18.57	4-49	—	—	0
BOWES, W E ...1932-46	15	11	5	28	10*	4.66	—	—	3,655	1,519	68	22.33	6-33	6	—	2
†BOYCOTT, G ...1964-82	108	193	23	8,114	246*	47.72	22	42	944	382	7	54.57	3-47	—	—	33
BRENNAN, D V ...1951	2	2	0	16	16	8.00	—	—	—	—	—	—	—	—	—	0/1
BRESNAN, T T ...2009-13/14	23	26	4	575	91	26.13	—	3	4,674	2,357	72	32.73	5-48	1	—	8
BROWN, J T ...1894-99	8	16	3	470	140	36.15	1	1	35	22	0	—	—	—	—	7
†CLOSE, D B ...1949-76	22	37	2	887	70	25.34	—	4	1,212	532	18	29.55	4-35	—	—	24
COPE, G A ...1977-78	3	3	0	40	22	13.33	—	—	864	277	8	34.62	3-102	—	—	1
COXON, A ...1948	1	2	0	19	19	9.50	—	—	378	172	3	57.33	2-90	—	—	0
DAWSON, R K J ...2002-03	7	13	3	114	19*	11.40	—	—	1,116	677	11	61.54	4-134	—	—	3
DENTON, D ...1905-10	11	22	1	424	104	20.19	1	—	—	—	—	—	—	—	—	8
DOLPHIN, A ...1921	1	2	0	1	1	0.50	—	—	—	—	—	—	—	—	—	1/0
EMMETT, T ...1877-82	7	13	1	160	48	13.33	—	—	728	284	9	31.55	7-68	1	—	9
GIBB, P A ...1938-46	8	13	0	581	120	44.69	2	3	—	—	—	—	—	—	—	3/1
GOUGH, D ...1994-2003	58	86	18	855	65	12.57	—	2	11,821	6,503	229	28.39	6-42	9	—	13

For England

YORKSHIRE TEST CRICKETERS 1877-2018 (Continued)

Player	M.	I	NO	Runs	HS.	Av'ge.	100s	50s	Balls	R	W	Av'ge	Best	5wI	10wM	c/st
GREENWOOD, A 1877	2	4	0	77	49	19.25	—	—	—	—	—	—	—	—	—	2
HAIGH, S 1899-1912	11	18	3	113	25	7.53	—	—	1,294	622	24	25.91	6-11	1	—	8
HAMILTON, G.M. 1999	1	2	0	0	0	0.00	—	—	90	63	0	—	—	—	—	0
HAMPSHIRE, J H ...1969-75	8	16	1	403	107	26.86	1	2	—	—	—	—	—	—	—	9
†HAWKE, LORD ...1896-99	5	8	1	55	30	7.85	—	—	—	—	—	—	—	—	—	3
HILL, A 1877	2	4	2	101	49	50.50	—	—	—	—	—	—	—	—	—	1
HIRST, G H ...1897-1909	24	38	3	790	85	22.57	—	5	3,967	1,770	59	30.00	5-48	3	—	18
HOGGARD, M J ..2000-2008	67	92	27	473	38	7.27	—	—	13,909	7,564	248	30.50	7-61	7	1	24
HOLMES, P 1921-32	7	14	1	357	88	27.46	—	4	—	—	—	—	—	—	—	3
HUNTER, J 1884-85	5	7	2	93	39*	18.60	—	—	—	—	—	—	—	—	—	8/3
†HUTTON, L 1937-55	79	138	15	6,971	364	56.67	19	33	260	232	3	77.33	1-2	—	—	57
HUTTON, R A 1971	5	8	2	219	81	36.50	—	2	738	257	9	28.55	3-72	—	—	9
†ILLINGWORTH, R .1958-73	61	90	11	1,836	113	23.24	2	5	11,934	3,807	122	31.20	6-29	3	—	45
JACKSON, Hon F S1893-1905	20	33	4	1,415	144*	48.79	5	6	1,587	799	24	33.29	5-52	1	—	10
JARVIS, P W 1988-93	9	15	2	132	29*	10.15	—	—	1,912	965	21	45.95	4-107	—	—	2
KILNER, R 1924-26	9	8	1	233	74	33.28	—	2	2,368	734	24	30.58	4-51	—	—	6
LEADBEATER, E .1951-52	2	2	0	40	38	20.00	—	—	289	218	2	109.00	1-38	—	—	3
LEYLAND, M ...1928-38	41	65	5	2,764	187	46.06	9	10	1,103	585	6	97.50	3-91	—	—	13
LOWSON, F A ...1951-55	7	13	1	245	68	18.84	—	2	—	—	—	—	—	—	—	5
LYTH A 2015	7	13	0	265	107	20.38	1	—	6	0	0	—	—	—	—	8
McGRATH, A 2003	4	5	0	201	81	40.20	—	2	102	56	4	14.00	3-16	—	—	3
MACAULAY, G G ...1923-33	8	10	4	112	76	18.66	—	1	1,701	662	24	27.58	5-64	1	—	5
MILLIGAN, F W 1899	2	4	0	58	38	14.50	—	—	45	29	0	—	—	—	—	1
MITCHELL, A ...1933-36	6	10	0	298	72	29.80	—	2	6	4	0	—	—	—	—	9
*MITCHELL, F 1899	2	4	0	88	41	22.00	—	—	—	—	—	—	—	—	—	2

For England

YORKSHIRE TEST CRICKETERS 1877-2018 (Continued)

Player	M.	I	NO	Runs	HS.	Av'ge.	100s	50s	Balls	R	W	Av'ge	Best	5wI	10wM	c/st
MOXON, M D 1986-89	10	17	1	455	99	28.43	—	3	48	30	0	—	—	—	—	10
OLD, C M 1972-81	46	66	9	845	65	14.82	—	2	8,858	4,020	143	28.11	7-50	4	—	22
PADGETT, D E V 1960	2	4	0	51	31	12.75	—	—	12	8	0	—	—	—	—	2
PEATE, E 1881-86	9	14	8	70	13	11.66	—	—	2,096	682	31	22.00	6-85	2	—	2
PEEL, R 1884-96	20	33	4	427	83	14.72	—	3	5,216	1,715	101	16.98	7-31	5	1	17
PLUNKETT, L E 2005/6-2014	13	20	5	238	55*	15.86	—	1	2,659	1,536	41	37.46	5-64	1	—	3
RASHID, A U 2015/16-18	18	31	5	527	61	20.26	—	2	3,660	2,273	60	37.88	5-49	2	—	4
RHODES, W 1899-1930	58	98	21	2,325	179	30.19	2	11	8,231	3,425	127	26.96	8-68	6	1	60
ROOT, J E 2012-18	77	141	12	6,508	254	50.44	15	41	1,878	939	20	46.95	2- 9	—	—	85
SHARPE, P J 1963-69	12	21	4	786	111	46.23	1	4	—	—	—	—	—	—	—	17
SHAHZAD, A 2010	1	1	0	5	5	5.00	—	—	102	63	4	15.75	3-45	—	—	2
SIDEBOTTOM, A 1985	1	1	0	2	2	2.00	—	—	112	65	1	65.00	1-65	—	—	0
SIDEBOTTOM, R J .2001-10	22	31	11	313	31	15.65	—	—	4,812	2,231	79	28.24	7-47	5	1	5
SILVERWOOD, CEW1997-2003	6	7	3	29	10	7.25	—	—	828	444	11	40.36	5-91	1	—	2
SMAILES, T F 1946	1	1	0	25	25	25.00	—	—	120	62	3	20.66	3-44	—	—	0
SMITHSON, G A 1948	2	3	0	70	35	23.33	—	—	—	—	—	—	—	—	—	0
†STANYFORTH, R T 1927-28	4	6	1	13	6*	2.60	—	—	—	—	—	—	—	—	—	7/2
STEVENSON, G B .1980-81	2	2	1	28	27*	28.00	—	—	312	183	5	36.60	3-111	—	—	0
SUTCLIFFE, H 1924-35	54	84	9	4,555	194	60.73	16	23	—	—	—	—	—	—	—	23
TAYLOR, K 1959-64	3	5	0	57	24	11.40	—	—	12	6	0	—	—	—	—	1
TRUEMAN, F S ..1952-65	67	85	14	981	39*	13.81	—	—	15,178	6,625	307	21.57	8-31	17	3	64
ULYETT, G 1877-90	25	39	0	949	149	24.33	1	7	2,627	1,020	50	20.40	7-36	1	—	19
†VAUGHAN M P .1999-2008	82	147	9	5,719	197	41.44	18	18	978	561	6	93.50	2-71	—	—	44
VERITY, H 1931-39	40	44	12	669	66*	20.90	—	3	11,173	3,510	144	24.37	8-43	5	2	30
WADDINGTON, A .1920-21	2	4	0	16	7	4.00	—	—	276	119	1	119.00	1-35	—	—	1
WAINWRIGHT, E .1893-98	5	9	0	132	49	14.66	—	—	127	73	0	—	—	—	—	2

For England

Player	M.	I	NO	Runs	HS.	Av'ge	100s	50s	Balls	R	W	Av'ge	Best	5wI	10wM	c/st
WARDLE, J H 1948-57	28	41	8	653	66	19.78		2	6,597	2,080	102	20.39	7-36	5	1	12
WATSON, W ...1951-59	23	37	3	879	116	25.85	2	3	—	—	—	—	—	—	—	8
WHITE, C ...1994-2002	30	50	7	1,052	121	24.46	1	5	3,959	2,220	59	37.62	5-32	3	—	14
WILSON, C E M ...1899	2	4	1	42	18	14.00			—	—	—	—	—	—	—	0
WILSON, D ...1964-71	6	7	1	75	42	12.50			1,472	466	11	42.36	2-17	—	—	1
WILSON, E R ...1921	1	2	0	10	5	5.00			123	36	3	12.00	2-28	—	—	0
WOOD, A ...1938-39	4	5	1	80	53	20.00		1	—	—	—	—	—	—	—	10/1
†YARDLEY, N W D ...1938-50	20	34	2	812	99	25.37		4	1,662	707	21	33.66	3-67	—	—	14

*Also represented and captained South Africa
†Captained England

For South Africa

Player	M.	I	NO	Runs	HS.	Av'ge	100s	50s	Balls	R	W	Av'ge	Best	5wI	10wM	c/st
†MITCHELL, F 1912	3	6	0	28	12	4.66			—				—			0

†Captained South Africa

Overseas Players

(Qualification: 20 first-class matches for Yorkshire)

For Australia

Player	M.	I	NO	Runs	HS.	Av'ge	100s	50s	Balls	R	W	Av'ge	Best	5wI	10wM	c/st
BEVAN, M G ...1994-98	18	30	3	785	91	29.07		6	1,285	703	29	24.24	6-82	1	1	8
GILLESPIE, J N ...1996-2006	71	93	28	1,218	201*	18.73	1	2	14,234	6,770	259	26.13	7-37	8	—	27
JAQUES, P A ...2005-2008	11	19	0	902	150	47.47	3	6	—	—	—	—	—	—	—	7
LEHMANN, D S ...1999-2004	27	42	2	1,798	177	44.95	5	10	974	412	15	27.46	3-42	—	—	11

For South Africa

Player	M.	I	NO	Runs	HS.	Av'ge	100s	50s	Balls	R	W	Av'ge	Best	5wI	10wM	c/st
RUDOLPH, J A ...2003-12/13	48	83	9	2,622	222*	35.43	6	11	664	432	4	108.00	1-1	—	—	29

For West Indies

Player	M.	I	NO	Runs	HS.	Av'ge	100s	50s	Balls	R	W	Av'ge	Best	5wI	10wM	c/st
RICHARDSON, R B 1983-84/95	86	146	12	5,949	194	44.39	16	27	66	18	0	—	—	—	—	90

CENTURIES FOR ENGLAND

C W J ATHEY (1)

123 v. Pakistan at Lord's, 1987

J M BAIRSTOW (6)

150* v. South Africa at Cape Town, 2016
167* v. Sri Lanka at Lord's, 2016
101 v. New Zealand at Christchurch, 2018

140 v. Sri Lanka at Leeds, 2016
119 v. Australia at Perth, 2017
110 v. Sri Lanka at Colombo (SSC), 2018

G S BALLANCE (4)

104* v. Sri Lanka at Lord's, 2014
256 v. India at Southampton, 2014

110 v. India at Lord's, 2014
122 v. West Indies at North Sound, 2015

G BOYCOTT (22)

113 v. Australia at The Oval, 1964
117 v. South Africa at Port Elizabeth, 1965
246* v. India at Leeds, 1967
116 v. West Indies at Georgetown, 1968
128 v. West Indies at Manchester, 1969
106 v. West Indies at Lord's, 1969
142* v. Australia at Sydney, 1971
119* v. Australia at Adelaide, 1971
121* v. Pakistan at Lord's, 1971
112 v. Pakistan at Leeds, 1971
115 v. New Zealand at Leeds, 1973

112 v West Indies at Port-of-Spain, 1974
107 v. Australia at Nottingham, 1977
191 v. Australia at Leeds, 1977
100* v. Pakistan at Hyderabad, 1978
131 v. New Zealand at Nottingham, 1978
155 v. India at Birmingham, 1979
125 v. India at The Oval, 1979
128* v. Australia at Lord's, 1980
104* v. West Indies at St John's, 1981
137 v. Australia at The Oval, 1981
105 v. India at Delhi, 1981

J T BROWN (1)

140 v. Australia at Melbourne, 1895

D DENTON (1)

104 v. South Africa at Old Wanderers, Johannesburg, 1910

P A GIBB (2)

106 v. South Africa at Old Wanderers, Johannesburg, 1938
120 v. South Africa at Kingsmead, Durban, 1939

J H HAMPSHIRE (1)

107 v. West Indies at Lord's, 1969

L HUTTON (19)

100 v. New Zealand at Manchester, 1937
100 v. Australia at Nottingham, 1938
364 v. Australia at The Oval, 1938
196 v. West Indies at Lord's, 1939
165* v. West Indies at The Oval, 1939
122* v. Australia at Sydney, 1947
100 v. South Africa at Leeds, 1947
158 v. South Africa at Ellis Park, J'b'rg, 1948
123 v. South Africa at Ellis Park, J'b'rg, 1949
101 v. New Zealand at Leeds, 1949

206 v. New Zealand at The Oval, 1949
202* v. West Indies at The Oval, 1950
156* v. Australia at Adeladide, 1951
100 v. South Africa at Leeds, 1951
150 v. India at Lord's, 1952
104 v. India at Manchester, 1952
145 v. Australia at Lord's, 1953
169 v. West Indies at Georgetown, 1954
205 v. West Indies at Kingston, 1954

R ILLINGWORTH (2)

113 v. West Indies at Lord's, 1969

107 v. India at Manchester, 1971

Hon. F S JACKSON (5)

103 v. Australia at The Oval, 1893
118 v. Australia at The Oval, 1899
128 v. Australia at Manchester, 1902

144* v. Australia at Leeds, 1905
113 v. Australia at Manchester, 1905

CENTURIES FOR ENGLAND

M LEYLAND (9)

137 v. Australia at Melbourne, 1929
102 v. South Africa at Lord's, 1929
109 v. Australia at Lord's, 1934
153 v. Australia at Manchester, 1934
110 v. Australia at The Oval, 1934

161 v. South Africa at The Oval, 1935
126 v. Australia at Woolloongabba, Brisbane, 1936
111* v. Australia at Melbourne, 1937
187 v. Australia at The Oval, 1938

A LYTH (1)

107 v. New Zealand at Leeds 2015

W RHODES (2)

179 v. Australia at Melbourne, 1912
152 v. South Africa at Old Wanderers, Johannesburg, 1913

J E ROOT (15)

104 v. New Zealand at Leeds, 2013
200* v. Sri Lanka at Lord's, 2014
149* v. India at The Oval, 2014
134 v. Australia at Cardiff 2015
110 v. South Africa at Johannesburg, 2016
124 v. India at Rajkot, 2016
136 v. West Indies at Birmingham, 2017
124 v. Sri Lanka at Pallekele, 2018

180 v. Australia at Lord's, 2013
154* v. India at Nottingham, 2014
182* v. West Indies at St George's, 2015
130 v. Australia at Nottingham, 2015
254 v. Pakistan at Manchester, 2016
190 v. South Africa at Lord's, 2017
125 v. India at The Oval, 2018

P J SHARPE (1)

111 v. New Zealand at Nottingham, 1969

H SUTCLIFFE (16)

122 v. South Africa at Lord's, 1924
115 v. Australia at Sydney, 1924
176 v. Australia at Melbourne, 1925 (1st Inns)
127 v. Australia at Melbourne, 1925 (2nd Inns)
143 v. Australia at Melbourne, 1925
161 v. Australia at The Oval, 1926
102 v. South Africa at Old Wanderers, Jbg.1927
135 v. Australia at Melbourne, 1929

114 v. South Africa at Birmingham, 1929
100 v. South Africa at Lord's, 1929
104 v. South Africa at The Oval, 1929 (1st inns)
109* v. South Africa at The Oval, 1929 (2nd inns)
161 v. Australia at The Oval, 1930
117 v. New Zealand at The Oval, 1931
109* v. New Zealand at Manchester, 1931
194 v. Australia at Sydney, 1932

G ULYETT (1)

149 v. Australia at Melbourne, 1882

M P VAUGHAN (18)

120 v. Pakistan at Manchester, 2001
115 v. Sri Lanka at Lord's, 2002
100 v. India at Lord's, 2002
197 v. India at Nottingham, 2002
195 v. India at The Oval, 2002
177 v. Australia at Adelaide, 2002
145 v. Australia at Melbourne, 2002
183 v. Australia at Sydney, 2003
156 v. South Africa at Birmingham, 2003

105 v. Sri Lanka at Kandy, 2003
140 v. West Indies at Antigua, 2004
103 v. West Indies at Lord's (1st inns) 2004
101* v. West Indies at Lord's (2nd inns) 2004
120 v. Bangladesh at Lord's, 2005
166 v. Australia at Manchester,2005
103 v. West Indies at Leeds, 2007
124 v. India at Nottingham, 2007
106 v. New Zealand at Lord's, 2008

CENTURIES FOR ENGLAND *(Continued)*

W WATSON (2)

109   v. Australia at Lord's, 1953   116 v. West Indies at Kingston, 1954

C WHITE (1)

121 v. India at Ahmedabad, 2001

Summary of the Centuries

versus	Total	In England	Away
Australia	43	23	20
Bangladesh	1	1	0
India	18	15	3
New Zealand	12	11	1
Pakistan	6	5	1
South Africa	21	11	10
Sri Lanka	8	5	3
West Indies	20	11	9
Totals	129	82	47

For Australia

J N GILLESPIE (1)

201* v. Bangladesh at Chittagong, 2006

P A JAQUES (3)

100   v. Sri Lanka at Brisbane, 2007   108   v. West Indies at Bridgetown, 2008
150   v. Sri Lanka at Hobart, 2007

D S LEHMANN (5)

160   v. West Indies at Port of Spain, 2003   129   v. Sri Lanka at Galle, 2004
110   v. Bangladesh at Darwin, 2003   153   v. Sri Lanka at Columbo, 2004
177   v. Bangladesh at Cairns, 2003

For South Africa

J A RUDOLPH (6)

222* v. Bangladesh at Chittagong, 2003   102   v. Sri Lanka at Galle, 2004
101   v West Indies at Cape Town, 2004   102* v Australia at Perth, 2005
154* v. New Zealand at Auckland, 2004   105* v. New Zealand at Dunedin, 2012

10 WICKETS IN A MATCH FOR ENGLAND

W BATES (1)
14 for 102 (7 for 28 and 7 for 74) v. Australia at Melbourne, 1882

M J HOGGARD (1)
12 for 205 (5 for 144 and 7 for 61) v. South Africa at Johannesburg, 2005

R PEEL (1)
11 for 68 (7 for 31 and 4 for 37) v. Australia at Mancester, 1888

Note: The scorebook for the Australia v. England Test match at Sydney in February 1888
shows that the final wicket to fall was taken by W Attewell, and not by Peel
Peel therefore took 9, and not 10 wickets, in the match
His career totals have been amended to take account of this alteration

W RHODES (1)
15 for 124 (7 for 56 and 8 for 68) v. Australia at Melbourne, 1904

R J SIDEBOTTOM (1)
10 for 139 (4 for 90 and 6 for 49) v. New Zealand at Hamilton, 2008

F S TRUEMAN (3)
11 for 88 (5 for 58 and 6 for 30) v. Australia at Leeds, 1961
11 for 152 (6 for 100 and 5 for 52) v. West Indies at Lord's, 1963*
12 for 119 (5 for 75 and 7 for 44) v. West Indies at Birmingham, 1963*
consecutive Tests

H VERITY (2)
11 for 153 (7 for 49 and 4 for 104) v. India at Chepauk, Madras, 1934
15 for 104 (7 for 61 and 8 for 43) v. Australia at Lord's, 1934

J H WARDLE (1)
12 for 89 (5 for 53 and 7 for 36) v. South Africa at Cape Town, 1957

Summary of Ten Wickets in a Match

versus	Total	In England	Away
Australia	5	3	2
India	1	—	1
New Zealand	1	—	1
Pakistan	—	—	—
South Africa	2	—	2
Sri Lanka	—	—	—
West Indies	2	2	—
Totals	11	5	6

For Australia

M G BEVAN (1)
10 for 113 (4 for 31and 6 for 82) v. West Indies at Adelaide, 1997

5 WICKETS IN AN INNINGS FOR ENGLAND

R APPLEYARD (1)
5 for 51 v. Pakistan at Nottingham, 1954

W BATES (4)
7 for 28 v. Australia at Melbourne, 1882   5 for 31 v. Australia at Adelaide, 1884
7 for 74 v. Australia at Melbourne, 1882   5 for 24 v. Australia at Sydney, 1885

5 WICKETS IN AN INNINGS FOR ENGLAND *(Continued)*

W E BOWES (6)

6-34	v. New Zealand	at Auckland	1933	5-100	v. South Africa	at Manchester	1935
6-142	v. Australia	at Leeds	1934*	5-49	v. Australia	at The Oval	1938
5-55	v. Australia	at The Oval	1934*	6-33	v. West Indies	at Manchester	1939

consecutive Test matches

T T BRESNAN (1)

5-48   v. India   at Nottingham   2011

T EMMETT (1)

7-68   v. Australia   at Melbourne   1879

D GOUGH (9)

6-49	v. Australia	at Sydney	1995	5-70	v. South Africa	at Johannesburg	1999
5-40	v.New Zealand	at Wellington	1997	5-109	v. West Indies	at Birmingham	2000
5-149	v. Australia	at Leeds	1997	5-61	v. Pakistan	at Lord's	2001
6-42	v.South Africa	at Leeds	1998	5-103	v. Australia	at Leeds	2001
5-96	v. Australia	at Melbourne	1998				

S HAIGH (1)

6-11   v. South Africa   at Cape Town   1909

G H HIRST (3)

5-77	v. Australia	at The Oval	1902	5-58	v. Australia	at Birmingham 1909
5-48	v. Australia	at Melbourne	1904			

M J HOGGARD (7)

7-63	v. New Zealand	at Christchurch	2002	5-73	v. Bangladesh	at Chester-le-Street
5-92	v. Sri Lanka	at Birmingham	2002			2005
5-144	v. South Africa	at Johannesburg	2005*	6-57	v. India	at Nagpur 2006
7-61	v. South Africa	at Johannesburg	2005*	7-109	v. Australia	at Adelaide 2006

Consecutive Test innings

R ILLINGWORTH (3)

6-29	v. India	at Lord's	1967	5-70	v. India	at The Oval 1971
6-87	v. Australia	at Leeds	1968			

Hon F S JACKSON (1)

5-52   v. Australia   at Nottingham   1905

G G MACAULAY (1)

5-64   v. South Africa   at Cape Town   1923

C M OLD (4)

5-113	v. New Zealand	at Lord's	1973	6-54	v. New Zealand	at Wellington 1978
5-21	v. India	at Lord's	1976	7-50	v. Pakistan	at Birmingham 1978

E PEATE (2)

5-43   v. Australia   at Sydney 1882   6-85   v. Australia   at Lord's   1884

R PEEL (5)

5-51	v. Australia	at Adelaide	1884	6-67	v. Australia	at Sydney 1894
5-18	v. Australia	at Sydney	1888	6-23	v. Australia	at The Oval 1896
7-31	v. Australia	at Manchester	1888			

L E PLUNKETT (1)

5-64   v. Sri Lanka   at Leeds   2014

A U RASHID (2)

5-64   v. Pakistan   at Abu Dhabi   2015   5-49   v. Sri Lanka   at Colombo (SSC) 2018

5 WICKETS IN AN INNINGS FOR ENGLAND *(Continued)*

W RHODES (6)

7-17	v. Australia	at Birmingham	1902	7-56	v. Australia	at Melbourne	1904*
5-63	v. Australia	at Sheffield	1902	8-68	v. Australia	at Melbourne	1904*
5-94	v. Australia	at Sydney	1903*	5-83	v. Australia	at Manchester	1909

consecutive Test innings

C E W SILVERWOOD (1)

5-91 v. South Africa at Cape Town 2000

R J SIDEBOTTOM (5)

5-88	v. West Indies	at Chester-le-Street		5-105	v. New Zealand	at Wellington	2008
			2007	7-47	v. New Zealand	at Napier	2008
6-49	v. New Zealand	at Hamilton	2008	6-47	v. New Zealand	at Nottingham	2008

F S TRUEMAN (17)

8-31	v. India	at Manchester	1952	6-31	v. Pakistan	at Lord's	1962
5-48	v. India	at The Oval	1952	5-62	v. Australia	at Melbourne	1963
5-90	v. Australia	at Lord's	1956	7-75	v. New Zealand	at Christchurch	1963
5-63	v. West Indies	at Nottingham	1957	6-100	v. West Indies	at Lord's	1963*
5-31	v. New Zealand	at Birmingham	1958	5-52	v. West Indies	at Lord's	1963*
5-35	v. West Indies	at Port-of-Spain	1960	5-75	v. West Indies	at Birmingham	1963*
5-27	v. South Africa	at Nottingham	1960	7-44	v. West Indies	at Birmingham	1963*
5-58	v. Australia	at Leeds	1961*	5-48	v. Australia	at Lord's	1964
6-30	v. Australia	at Leeds	1961*				

G ULYETT (1)

7-36 v. Australia at Lord's 1884

H VERITY (5)

5-33	v. Australia	at Sydney	1933	8-43	v. Australia	at Lord's	1934*
7-49	v. India	at Chepauk, Madras	1934	5-70	v. South Africa	at Cape Town	1939
7-61	v. Australia	at Lord's	1934*				

J H WARDLE (5)

7-56	v. Pakistan	at The Oval	1954	7-36	v. South Africa	at Cape Town	1957*
5-79	v. Australia	at Sydney	1955	5-61	v. South Africa	at Kingsmead Durban	1957*
5-53	v. South Africa	at Cape Town	1957*				

C WHITE (3)

5-57	v. West Indies	at Leeds	2000	5-32	v. West Indies	at The Oval	2000
	5-127	v. Australia	at Perth	2002			

consecutive Test innings

Summary of Five Wickets in an Innings

versus	Total	In England	Away
Australia	42	22	20
Bangladesh	1	1	0
India	8	6	2
New Zealand	11	3	8
Pakistan	6	5	1
South Africa	13	3	10
Sri Lanka	3	2	1
West Indies	11	10	1
Totals	95	52	43

5 WICKETS IN AN INNINGS

M G BEVAN (1)

6-82	v. West Indies	at Adelaide	1997

J N GILLESPIE (8)

5-54	v. South Africa	at Port Elizabeth	1997
7-37	v. England	at Leeds	1997
5-88	v. England	at Perth	1998
5-89	v. West Indies	at Adelaide	2000
6-40	v. West Indies	at Melbourne	2000
5-53	v. England	at Lord's	2001
5-39	v. West Indies	at Georgetown	2003
5-56	v. India	at Nagpur	2004

HAT-TRICKS

W Bates	v. Australia	at Melbourne	1882
D Gough	v. Australia	at Sydney	1998
M J Hoggard	v. West Indies	at Bridgetown	2004
R J Sidebottom	v. New Zealand	at Hamilton	2008

FOUR WICKETS IN FIVE BALLS

C M Old	v. Pakistan	at Birmingham	1978

THREE WICKETS IN FOUR BALLS

R Appleyard	v. New Zealand	at Auckland	1955
D Gough	v. Pakistan	at Lord's	2001

YORKSHIRE PLAYERS WHO PLAYED ALL THEIR TEST CRICKET AFTER LEAVING YORKSHIRE

For England

Player	M.	I	NO	Runs	HS.	Av'ge	100s	50s	Balls	R	W	Av'ge	Best	5wI	10wM	c/st
BALDERSTONE, J C ...1976	2	4	0	39	35	9.75	—	—	96	80	1	80.00	1:80	—	—	1
BATTY G J ...2003/4-16/17	9	12	2	149	38	14.90	—	1	1,714	914	15	60.93	3-55	—	—	3
BIRKENSHAW, J ...1973-74	5	7	0	148	64	21.14	—	1	1,017	469	13	36.07	5:57	1	—	3
BOLUS, J B ...1963-64	7	12	0	496	88	41.33	—	4	18	16	0	—	—	—	—	2
†PARKIN, C H ...1920-24	10	16	3	160	36	12.30	—	—	2,095	1,128	32	35.25	5:38	2	—	3
RHODES, S J ...1994-95	11	17	5	294	65*	24.50	—	1	—	—	—	—	—	—	—	46/3
†SUGG, F H ...1888	2	2	0	55	31	27.50	—	—	—	—	—	—	—	—	—	0
WARD, A ...1893-95	7	13	0	487	117	37.46	1	3	—	—	—	—	—	—	—	1
WOOD, B ...1972-78	12	21	0	454	90	21.61	—	2	98	50	0	—	—	—	—	6
For South Africa																
THORNTON, P G ...1902	1	1	1	1	1*	—	—	—	24	20	1	20.00	1:20	—	—	1

†Born outside Yorkshire

CENTURIES FOR ENGLAND

A WARD (1)

117 v. Australia at Sydney, 1894

5 WICKETS IN AN INNINGS FOR ENGLAND

J BIRKENSHAW (1)

5 : 57 v. Pakistan at Karachi, 1973

C H PARKIN (2)

5 : 60 v. Australia at Adelaide, 1921

5 : 38 v. Australia at Manchester, 1921

YORKSHIRE'S TEST CRICKET RECORDS

R APPLEYARD

Auckland 1954-55: took 3 wickets in 4 balls as New Zealand were dismissed for the lowest total in Test history (26).

C W J ATHEY

Perth 1986-87: shared an opening stand of 223 with B C Broad – England's highest for any wicket at the WACA Ground.

J M BAIRSTOW

Cape Town, January 2016: scored his maiden Test Century (150*). His sixth- wicket partnership of 399 with B A Stokes (258) was the highest in Test cricket and the highest First Class partnership for any wicket at Newlands. There was only one higher partnership for England. This was 411 by P B H May and M C Cowdrey for the fourth wicket against the West Indies at Birmingham in 1957.

Chittagong, October 2016: scored 52 in the first innings, which passed his 1,000 Test runs in a calendar year. He became only the third Yorkshire player to do this after M P Vaughan with 1,481 in 2002 and J E Root 1,385 in 2015. He was only the second Test wicket-keeper to pass this mark. His first scoring shot in the second inning broke a 16-year record set by Zimbabwe's A Flower (1,045 in 2000) to give him the highest total of runs scored in a calendar year by a Test wicket-keeper. His final tally for 2016 was 1,470.

Mohali, November 2016: his third catch of India's first innings (U T Yadav) was his 68th dismissal of the year to pass the previous best in a calendar year (67) by I A Healy (Australia) in 1991 and M V Boucher (South Africa) in 1998. Bairstow's final tally for the calendar year was 70 (66 caught and 4 stumped).

W BATES

Melbourne 1882-83 (Second Test): achieved the first hat-trick for England when he dismissed P S McDonnell, G Giffen and G J Bonnor in Australia's first innings. Later in the match, he became the first player to score a fifty (55) and take 10 or more wickets (14 for 102) in the same Test.

W E BOWES

Melbourne 1932-33: enjoyed the unique satisfaction of bowling D G Bradman first ball in a Test match (his first ball to him in Test cricket).

G BOYCOTT

Leeds 1967: scored 246 not out off 555 balls in 573 minutes to establish the record England score against India. His first 100 took 341 minutes (316 balls) and he was excluded from the next Test as a disciplinary measure; shared in hundred partnerships for three successive wickets.

Adelaide 1970-71: with J H Edrich, became the third opening pair to share hundred partnerships in both innings of a Test against Australia.

Port-of-Spain 1973-74: first to score 99 and a hundred in the same Test.

Nottingham 1977: with A P E Knott, equalled England v. Australia sixth-wicket partnership record of 215 – the only England v. Australia stand to be equalled or broken since 1938. Batted on each day of the five-day Test (second after M L Jaisimha to achieve this feat).

Leeds 1977: first to score his 100th First Class hundred in a Test; became the fourth England player to be on the field for an entire Test.

G BOYCOTT *(Continued)*

Perth: 1978-79: eighth to score 2,000 runs for England against Australia.

Birmingham 1979: emulated K F Barrington by scoring hundreds on each of England's six current home grounds.

Perth: 1979-80: fourth to carry his bat through a completed England innings (third v. Australia) and the first to do so without scoring 100; first to score 99 not out in a Test.

Lord's 1981: 100th Test for England – second after M C Cowdrey (1968).

The Oval, 1981: second after Hon F S Jackson to score five hundreds v. Australia in England.

Gained three Test records from M C Cowdrey: exceeded England aggregate of 7,624 runs in 11 fewer Tests (Manchester 1981); 61st fifty – world record (The Oval 1981); 189th innings – world record (Bangalore 1981-82).

Delhi, 4.23p.m. on 23 December 1981: passed G St.A Sobers's world Test record of 8,032 runs, having played 30 more innings and batted over 451 hours (cf. 15 complete five-day Tests); his 22nd hundred equalled the England record.

J T BROWN

Melbourne 1894-95: his 28-minute fifty remains the fastest in Test cricket, and his 95-minute hundred was a record until 1897-98; his third-wicket stand of 210 with A Ward set a Test record for any wicket.

D B CLOSE

Manchester 1949: at 18 years 149 days he became – and remains – the youngest to represent England.

Melbourne 1950-51: became the youngest (19 years 301 days) to represent England against Australia.

T EMMETT

Melbourne 1878-79: first England bowler to take seven wickets in a Test innings.

P A GIBB

Johannesburg 1938-39: enjoyed a record England debut, scoring 93 and 106 as well as sharing second-wicket stands of 184 and 168 with E Paynter.

Durban 1938-39: shared record England v. South Africa second-wicket stand of 280 with W J Edrich, his 120 in 451 minutes including only two boundaries.

D GOUGH

Sydney 1998-99: achieved the 23rd hat-trick in Test cricket (ninth for England and first for England v. Australia since 1899).

Lord's 2001: took 3 wickets in 4 balls v. Pakistan.

S HAIGH

Cape Town 1898-99: bowled unchanged through the second innings with A E Trott, taking 6 for 11 as South Africa were dismissed for 35 in the space of 114 balls.

J H HAMPSHIRE

Lord's 1969: became the first England player to score 100 at Lord's on his debut in Tests.

A HILL

Melbourne 1876-77: took the first wicket to fall in Test cricket when he bowled N Thompson, and held the first catch when he dismissed T P Horan.

YORKSHIRE'S TEST CRICKET RECORDS *(Continued)*

G H HIRST

The Oval 1902: helped to score the last 15 runs in a match-winning tenth-wicket partnership with W Rhodes.

Birmingham 1909: shared all 20 Australian wickets with fellow left-arm spinner C Blythe (11 for 102).

M J HOGGARD

Bridgetown 2004: became the third Yorkshire player to take a hat-trick in Test cricket (see W Bates and D Gough). It was the 10th hat-trick for England and the third for England versus West Indies.

L HUTTON

Nottingham 1938: scored 100 in his first Test against Australia.

The Oval 1938: his score (364) and batting time (13 hours 17 minutes – the longest innings in English First-Class cricket) remain England records, and were world Test records until 1958. It remains the highest Test score at The Oval. His stand of 382 with M Leyland is the England second-wicket record in all Tests and the highest for any wicket against Australia. He also shared a record England v. Australia sixth-wicket stand of 216 with J Hardstaff Jr. – the first instance of a batsman sharing in two stands of 200 in the same Test innings. 770 runs were scored during his innings (Test record) which was England's 100th century against Australia, and contained 35 fours. England's total of 903 for 7 declared remains the Ashes Test record.

Lord's 1939: added 248 for the fourth wicket with D C S Compton in 140 minutes.

The Oval 1939: shared (then) world-record third-wicket stand of 264 with W R Hammond, which remains the record for England v. West Indies. Hutton's last eight Tests had brought him 1,109 runs.

The Oval 1948: last out in the first innings, he was on the field for all but the final 57 minutes of the match.

Johannesburg 1948-49: shared (then) world-record first-wicket stand of 359 in 310 minutes with C Washbrook on the opening day of Test cricket at Ellis Park; it remains England's highest opening stand in all Tests.

The Oval 1950: scored England's first 200 in a home Test v. West Indies, and remains alone in carrying his bat for England against them; his 202 not out (in 470 minutes) is the highest score by an England batsman achieving this feat.

Adelaide 1950-51: only England batsman to carry his bat throughout a complete Test innings twice, and second after R Abel (1891-92) to do so for any country against Australia.

Manchester 1951: scored 98 not out, just failing to become the first to score his 100th First Class hundred in a Test match.

The Oval 1951: became the only batsman to be out 'obstructing the field' in Test cricket.

1952: first professional to be appointed captain of England in the 20th Century.

The Oval 1953: first captain to win a rubber after losing the toss in all five Tests.

Kingston 1953-54: scored the first 200 by an England captain in a Test overseas.

R ILLINGWORTH

Manchester 1971: shared record England v. India eighth-wicket stand of 168 with P Lever.

315

YORKSHIRE'S TEST CRICKET RECORDS *(Continued)*

Hon. F S JACKSON

The Oval 1893: his 100 took 135 minutes, and was the first in a Test in England to be completed with a hit over the boundary (then worth only four runs).

The Oval 1899: his stand of 185 with T W Hayward was then England's highest for any wicket in England, and the record opening partnership by either side in England v. Australia Tests.

Nottingham 1905: dismissed M A Noble, C Hill and J Darling in one over (W01W0W).

Leeds 1905: batted 268 minutes for 144 not out – the first hundred in a Headingley Test.

Manchester 1905: first to score five Test hundreds in England.

The Oval 1905: first captain to win every toss in a five-match rubber.

M LEYLAND

Melbourne 1928-29: scored 137 in his first innings against Australia.

1934: first to score three hundreds in a rubber against Australia in England.

Brisbane 1936-37: scored England's only 100 at 'The Gabba' before 1974-75.

The Oval 1938: contributed 187 in 381 minutes to the record Test total of 903 for 7 declared, sharing in England's highest stand against Australia (all wickets) and record second-wicket stand in all Tests: 382 with L Hutton. First to score hundreds in his first and last innings against Australia.

G G MACAULAY

Cape Town 1922-23: fourth bowler (third for England) to take a wicket (G A L Hearne) with his first ball in Test cricket. Made the winning hit in the fourth of only six Tests to be decided by a one-wicket margin.

Leeds 1926: shared a match-saving ninth-wicket stand of 108 with G Geary.

C M OLD

Birmingham 1978: took 4 wickets in 5 balls in his 19th over (0WW no-ball WW1) to emulate the feat of M J C Allom.

R PEEL

Took his 50th wicket in his ninth Test and his 100th in his 20th Test – all against Australia.

Kingston 1929-30: ended the world's longest Test career (30 years 315 days) as the oldest Test cricketer (52 years 165 days).

W RHODES

Birmingham 1902: his first-innings analysis of 7 for 17 remains the record for all Tests at Edgbaston.

The Oval 1902: helped to score the last 15 runs in a match-winning tenth-wicket partnership with G H Hirst.

Sydney 1903-04: shared record England v. Australia tenth-wicket stand of 130 in 66 minutes with R E Foster.

Melbourne 1903-04: first to take 15 wickets in England v. Australia Tests; his match analysis of 15 for 124 remains the record for all Tests at Melbourne.

Melbourne 1911-12: shared record England v. Australia first-wicket stand of 323 in 268 minutes with J B Hobbs.

YORKSHIRE'S TEST CRICKET RECORDS (Continued)

W RHODES (Continued)

Johannesburg 1913-14: took his 100th wicket and completed the first 'double' for England (in 44 matches).

Sydney 1920-21: first to score 2,000 runs and take 100 wickets in Test cricket.

Adelaide 1920-21: third bowler to take 100 wickets against Australia.

The Oval 1926: set (then) record of 109 wickets against Australia.

J E ROOT

Chittagong, October 2016: his score (40) in England's first innings took him passed 1,000 runs in a calendar year. He also did this in 2015 (1,385) and became the first Yorkshire player to do this twice. His final tally (1,477) in 2016 left him four short of M P Vaughan's total in 2002

Visakhapatnam, November 2016: Played his 50th Test match, which was also his 100th first-class match

Lord's, July 2017 v. West Indies: His first innings (190) was the highest by an England captain in his first innings in this role.

H SUTCLIFFE

Birmingham 1924: shared the first of 15 three-figure partnerships with J B Hobbs at the first attempt.

Lord's 1924: shared stand of 268 with J B Hobbs, which remains the first-wicket record for all Lord's Tests, and was then the England v. South Africa record.

Sydney 1924-25: his first opening stands against Australia with J B Hobbs realised 157 and 110.

Melbourne 1924-25 (Second Test): with J B Hobbs achieved the first instance of a batting partnership enduring throughout a full day's Test match play; they remain the only England pair to achieve this feat, and their stand of 283 in 289 minutes remains the longest for the first wicket in this series. Became the first to score 100 in each innings of a Test against Australia, and the first Englishman to score three successive hundreds in Test cricket.

Melbourne 1924-25 (Fourth Test): first to score four hundreds in one rubber of Test matches; it was his third 100 in successive Test innings at Melbourne. Completed 1,000 runs in fewest Test innings (12) – since equalled.

Sydney 1924-25: his aggregate of 734 runs was the record for any rubber until 1928-29.

The Oval 1926: shared first-wicket stand of 172 with J B Hobbs on a rain-affected pitch.

The Oval 1929: first to score hundreds in each innings of a Test twice; only England batsman to score four hundreds in a rubber twice.

Sydney 1932-33: his highest England innings of 194 overtook J B Hobbs's world record of 15 Test hundreds.

F S TRUEMAN

Leeds 1952: reduced India to 0 for 4 in their second innings by taking 3 wickets in 8 balls on his debut.

Manchester 1952: achieved record England v. India innings analysis of 8 for 31.

The Oval 1952: set England v. India series record with 29 wickets.

Leeds 1961: took 5 for 0 with 24 off-cutters at a reduced pace v. Australia.

Lord's 1962: shared record England v. Pakistan ninth-wicket stand of 76 with T W Graveney.

YORKSHIRE'S TEST CRICKET RECORDS *(Continued)*

F S TRUEMAN *(Continued)*

Christchurch 1962-63: passed J B Statham's world Test record of 242 wickets; his analysis of 7-75 remains the record for Lancaster Park Tests and for England in New Zealand.

Birmingham 1963: returned record match analysis (12-119) against West Indies in England and for any Birmingham Test, ending with a 6-4 spell from 24 balls.

The Oval 1963: set England v. West Indies series record with 34 wickets.

The Oval 1964: first to take 300 wickets in Tests.

G ULYETT

Sydney 1881-82: with R G Barlow shared the first century opening partnership in Test cricket (122).

Melbourne 1881-82: his 149 was the first Test hundred for England in Australia, and the highest score for England on the first day of a Test in Australia until 1965-66.

M P VAUGHAN

Scored 1481 runs in 2002 – more than any other England player in a calendar year, surpassing the 1379 scored by D L Amiss in 1979. It was the fourth highest in a calendar year.

Scored 633 runs in the 2002-3 series versus Australia – surpassed for England in a five Test series versus Australia only by W R Hammond, who scored 905 runs in 1928-29, H Sutcliffe (734 in 1924-25), J B Hobbs (662 in 1911-12) and G Boycott (657 in 1970-71), when he played in five of the six Tests.

Scored six Test Match centuries in 2002 to equal the record set for England by D C S Compton in 1947.

Lord's 2004: scored a century in each innings (103 and 101*) versus West Indies and so became the third player (after G A Headley and G A Gooch) to score a century in each innings of a Test match at Lord's.

Lord's 2005: only the second player (J B Hobbs is the other) to have scored centuries in three consecutive Test match innings at Lord's. Scored the 100th century for England by a Yorkshire player.

H VERITY

Lord's 1934: took 14 for 80 on the third day (six of them in the final hour) to secure England's first win against Australia at Lord's since 1896. It remains the most wickets to fall to one bowler in a day of Test cricket in England. His match analysis of 15 for 104 was then the England v. Australia record, and has been surpassed only by J C Laker.

W WATSON

Lord's 1953: scored 109 in 346 minutes in his first Test against Australia.

N W D YARDLEY

Melbourne 1946-47: dismissed D G Bradman for the third consecutive innings without assistance from the field. Became the first to score a fifty in each innings for England and take five wickets in the same match.

Nottingham 1947: shared record England v. South Africa fifth-wicket stand of 237 with D C S Compton.

* * *

Facts adapted by Bill Frindall from his *England Test Cricketers – The Complete Record from 1877* (Collins Willow, 1989). With later additions.

TEST MATCHES AT HEADINGLEY, LEEDS 1899-2018

1899 **Australia 172** (J Worrall 76) and **224** (H Trumble 56, J T Hearne hat-trick). **England 220** (A F A Lilley 55, H Trumble 5 for 60) and **19 for 0 wkt.**
Match drawn   Toss: Australia

1905 **England 301** (Hon F S Jackson 144*) and **295 for 5 wkts dec** (J T Tyldesley 100, T W Hayward 60, W W. Armstrong 5 for 122). **Australia 195** (W W Armstrong 66, A R Warren 5 for 57) and **224 for 7 wkts** (M A Noble 62).
Match drawn   Toss: England

1907 **England 76** (G A Faulkner 6 for 17) and **162** (C B Fry 54). **South Africa 110** (C Blythe 8 for 59) and **75** (C Blythe 7 for 40).
England won by 53 runs   Toss: England

1909 **Australia 188** and **207** (S F Barnes 6 for 63). **England 182** (J Sharp 61, J T Tyldesley 55, C G Macartney 7 for 58) and **87** (A Cotter 5 for 38).
Australia won by 126 runs   Toss: Australia

1912 **England 242** (F E Woolley 57) and **238** (R H Spooner 82, J B Hobbs 55). **South Africa 147** (S F Barnes 6 for 52) and **159**.
England won by 174 runs   Toss: England

1921 **Australia 407** (C G Macartney 115, W W Armstrong 77, C E Pellew 52, J M Taylor 50) and **273 for 7 wkts dec** (T J E Andrew 92). **England 259** (J W H T Douglas 75, Hon L H Tennyson 63, G Brown 57) and **202.**
Australia won by 219 runs   Toss: Australia

1924 **England 396** (E H Hendren 132, H Sutcliffe 83) and **60 for 1 wkt.** **South Africa 132** (H W Taylor 59*, M W Tate 6 for 42) and **323** (H W Taylor 56, R H Catterall 56).
England won by 9 wickets   Toss: England

1926 **Australia 494** (C G Macartney 151, W M Woodfull 141, A J Richardson 100). **England 294** (G G Macaulay 76, C V Grimmett 5 for 88) and **254 for 3 wkts** (H Sutcliffe 94, J B Hobbs 88).
Match drawn   Toss: England

1929 **South Africa 236** (R H Catterall 74, C L Vincent 60, A P Freeman 7 for 115) and **275** (H G Owen-Smith 129). **England 328** (F E Woolley 83, W R Hammond 65, N A Quinn 6 for 92) and **186 for 5 wkts** (F E Woolley 95*).
England won by 5 wickets   Toss: South Africa

1930 **Australia 566** (D G Bradman 334, A F Kippax 77, W M Woodfull 50, M W Tate 5 for 124). **England 391** (W R Hammond 113, C V Grimmett 5 for 135) and **95 for 3 wkts.**
Match drawn   Toss: Australia

1934 **England 200** and **229 for 6 wkts.** **Australia 584** (D G Bradman 304, W H Ponsford 181, W E Bowes 6 for 142).
Match drawn   Toss: England

1935 **England 216** (W R Hammond 63, A Mitchell 58) and **294 for 7 wkts dec** (W R Hammond 87*, A Mitchell 72, D Smith 57). **South Africa 171** (E A B Rowan 62) and **194 for 5 wkts** (B Mitchell 58).
Match drawn   Toss: England

1938 **England 223** (W R Hammond 76, W J O'Reilly 5 for 66) and **123** (W J O'Reilly 5 for 56). **Australia 242** (D G Bradman 103, B A Barnett 57) and **107 for 5 wkts.**
Australia won by 5 wickets   Toss: England

1947 **South Africa 175** (B Mitchell 53, A Nourse 51) and **184** (A D Nourse 57). **England 317 for 7 wkts dec** (L Hutton 100, C Washbrook 75) and **47 for 0 wkt.**
England won by 10 wickets   Toss: South Africa

1948 **England 496** (C Washbrook 143, W .J Edrich 111, L Hutton 81, A V Bedser 79) and **365 for 8 wkts dec** (D C S. Compton 66, C Washbrook 65, L Hutton 57, W J Edrich 54). **Australia 458** (R N Harvey 112, S J E Loxton 93, R R Lindwall 77, K R Miller 58) and **404 for 3 wkts** (A R Morris 182, D G Bradman 173*).
Australia won by 7 wickets   Toss: England

1949 **England 372** (D C S Compton 114, L Hutton 101, T B Burtt 5 for 97, J Cowie 5 for 127) and **267 for 4 wkts dec** (C Washbrook 103*, W J Edrich 70). **New Zealand 341** (F B Smith 96, M P Donnelly 64, T E Bailey 6 for 118) and **195 for 2 wkts** (B Sutcliffe 82, F Smith 54*).
Match drawn   Toss: England

1951 **South Africa 538** (E A B Rowan 236, P N F Mansell 90, C B. van Ryneveld 83, R A McLean 67) and **87 for 0 wkt** (E A B Rowan 60*). **England 505** (P B H May 138, L Hutton 100, T E Bailey 95, F A Lowson 58, A M B Rowan 5 for 174).
Match drawn   Toss: South Africa

1952 **India 293** (V L Manjrekar 133, V S Hazare 89) and 165 (D G Phadkar 64, V S Hazare 56). **England 334** (T W Graveney 71, T G Evans 66, Ghulam Ahmed 5 for 100) and **128 for 3 wkts** (R T Simpson 51).
England won by 7 wickets   Toss: India

1953 **England 167** (T W Graveney 55, R R Lindwall 5 for 54) and **275** (W J Edrich 64, D C S Compton 61). **Australia 266** (R N Harvey 71, G B Hole 53, A V Bedser 6 for 95) and **147 for 4 wkts.**
Match drawn   Toss: Australia

1955 **South Africa 171** and **500** (D J McGlew 133, W R Endean 116*, T L Goddard 74, H J Keith 73). **England 191** (D C S Compton 61) and **256** (P B H May 97, T L Goddard 5 for 69, H J Tayfield 5 for 94).
South Africa won by 224 runs   Toss: South Africa

1956 **England 325** (P B H May 101, C Washbrook 98). **Australia 143** (J C Laker 5 for 58) and **140** (R N Harvey 69, J C Laker 6 for 55).
England won by an innings and 42 runs   Toss: England

1957 **West Indies 142** (P J Loader 6 for 36, including hat-trick) and **132**. **England 279** (P B H May 69, M C Cowdrey 68, Rev D S Sheppard 68, F M M Worrell 7 for 70).
England won by an innings and 5 runs   Toss: West Indies

1958 **New Zealand 67** (J C Laker 5 for 17) and **129** (G A R Lock 7 for 51). **England 267 for 2 wkts dec** (P B H May 113*, C A Milton 104*).
England won by an innings and 71 runs   Toss: New Zealand

1959 **India 161** and **149**. **England 483 for 8 wkts dec** (M C Cowdrey 160, K F Barrington 80, W G A Parkhouse 78, G Pullar 75).
England won by an innings and 173 runs   Toss: India

1961 **Australia 237** (R N Harvey 73, C C McDonald 54, F S Trueman 5 for 58) and **120** (R N Harvey 53, F S Trueman 6 for 30); **England 299** (M C Cowdrey 93, G Pullar 53, A K Davidson 5 for 63) and **62 for 2 wkts.**
England won by 8 wickets   Toss: Australia

1962 **England 428** (P H Parfitt 119, M J Stewart 86, D A Allen 62, Munir Malik 5 for 128). **Pakistan 131** (Alimuddin 50) and **180** (Alimuddin 60, Saeed Ahmed 54).
England won by an innings and 117 runs   Toss: Pakistan

1963 **West Indies 397** (G St A Sobers 102, R B Kanhai 92, J S Solomon 62) and **229** (B F Butcher 78, G St.A Sobers 52). **England 174** (G A R Lock 53, C C Griffith 6 for 36) and **231** (J M Parks 57, D B Close 56).
West Indies won by 221 runs   Toss: West Indies

1964 **England 268** (J M Parks 68, E R Dexter 66, N J N Hawke 5 for 75) and 229 (K F Barrington 85). **Australia 389** (P J P Burge 160, W M Lawry 78) and **111 for 3 wkts** (I R Redpath 58*).
Australia won by 7 wickets   Toss: England

1965 **England 546 for 4 wkts dec** (J H Edrich 310*, K F Barrington 163). **New Zealand 193** (J R Reid 54) and 166 (V Pollard 53, F J Titmus 5 for 19).
England won by an innings and 187 runs   Toss: England

1966 **West Indies 500 for 9 wkts dec** (G St A Sobers 174, S M Nurse 137). **England 240** (B L D'Oliveira 88, G St A Sobers 5 for 41) and **205** (R W Barber 55, L R Gibbs 6 for 39).
West Indies won by an innings and 55 runs   Toss: West Indies

320

1967 **England 550 for 4 wkts dec** (G Boycott 246*, B L D'Oliveira 109, K F Barrington 93, T W Graveney 59) and **126 for 4 wkts. India 164** (Nawab of Pataudi jnr 64) and **510** (Nawab of Pataudi jnr 148, A L Wadekar 91, F M Engineer 87, Hanumant Singh 73).
England won by 6 wickets   Toss: England

1968 **Australia 315** (I R Redpath 92, I M Chappell 65) and **312** (I M Chappell 81, K D Walters 56, R Illingworth 6 for 87). **England 302** (R M Prideaux 64, J H Edrich 62, A N Connolly 5 for 72) and **230 for 4 wkts** (J H Edrich 65).
Match drawn   Toss: Australia

1969 **England 223** (J H Edrich 79) and **240** (G.St A Sobers 5 for 42). **West Indies 161** and **272** (B F Butcher 91, G S Camacho 71).
England won by 30 runs   Toss: England

1971 **England 316** (G Boycott 112, B L D'Oliveira 74) and **264** (B L D'Oliveira 72, D L Amiss 56) **Pakistan 350** (Zaheer Abbas 72, Wasim Bari 63, Mushtaq Mohammad 57) and **205** (Sadiq Mohammad 91).
England won by 25 runs   Toss: England

1972 **Australia 146** (K R Stackpole 52) and **136** (D L Underwood 6 for 45). **England 263** (R Illingworth 57, A A Mallett 5 for 114) and **21 for 1 wkt.**
England won by 9 wickets   Toss: Australia

1973 **New Zealand 276** (M G Burgess 87, V Pollard 62) and **142** (G M Turner 81, G G Arnold 5 for 27). **England 419** (G Boycott 115, K W R Fletcher 81, R Illingworth 65, RO Collinge 5 for 74).
England won by an innings and 1 run   Toss: New Zealand

1974 **Pakistan 285** (Majid Khan 75, Safraz Nawaz 53) and **179. England 183** and **238 for 6 wkts** (J H Edrich 70, K W R Fletcher 67*).
Match drawn   Toss: Pakistan

1975 **England 288** (D S Steele 73, J H Edrich 62, A W Greig 51, G J Gilmour 6 for 85) and **291** (D S Steele 92). **Australia 135** (P H Edmonds 5 for 28) and **220 for 3 wkts** (R B McCosker 95*, I M Chappell 62).
Match drawn   Toss: England

1976 **West Indies 450** (C G Greenidge 115, R C Fredericks 109, I V A Richards 66, L G Rowe 50) and **196** (C L King 58, R G D Willis 5 for 42). **England 387** (A W Greig 116, A P E Knott 116) and **204** (A W Greig 76*).
West Indies won by 55 runs   Toss: West Indies

1977 **England 436** (G Boycott 191, A P E Knott 57). **Australia 103** (I T Botham 5 for 21) and **248** (R W Marsh 63).
England won by an innings and 85 runs   Toss: England

1978 **Pakistan 201** (Sadiq Mohammad 97). **England 119 for 7 wkts** (Safraz Nawaz 5 for 39).
Match drawn   Toss: Pakistan

1979 **England 270** (I T Botham 137). **India 223 for 6 wkts** (S M Gavaskar 78, D B Vengsarkar 65*).
Match drawn   Toss: England

1980 **England 143 and 227 for 6 wkts dec** (G A Gooch 55). **West Indies 245.**
Match drawn   Toss: West Indies

1981 **Australia 401 for 9 wkts dec** (J Dyson 102, K J Hughes 89, G N Yallop 58, I T Botham 6 for 95) and **111** (R G D Willis 8 for 43). **England 174** (I T Botham 50) and **356** (I T Botham 149*, G R Dilley 56, T M Alderman 6 for 135).
England won by 18 runs   Toss: Australia

1982 **Pakistan 275** (Imran Khan 67*, Mudassar Nazar 65, Javed Miandad 54) and **199** (Javed Miandad 52, I T Botham 5 for 74). **England 256** (D I Gower 74, I T Botham 57, Imran Khan 5 for 49) and **219 for 7 wkts** (G Fowler 86).
England won by 3 wickets   Toss: Pakistan

1983 **England 225** (C J Tavaré 69, A J Lamb 58, B L Cairns 7 for 74) and **252** (D I Gower 112*, E J Chatfield 5 for 95). **New Zealand 377** (J G Wright 93, B A Edgar 84, R J Hadlee 75) and **103 for 5 wkts** (R G D Willis 5 for 35).
New Zealand won by 5 wickets   Toss: New Zealand

1984 **England 270** (A J Lamb 100) and **159** (G Fowler 50, M D Marshall 7 for 53). **West Indies 302** (H A Gomes 104*, M A Holding 59, P J W Allott 6 for 61) and **131 for 2 wkts.**
West Indies won by 8 wickets   Toss: England

1985 **Australia 331** (A M J Hilditch 119) and **324** (W B Phillips 91, A M J Hilditch 80, K C Wessels 64, J E Emburey 5 for 82). **England 533** (R T Robinson 175, I T Botham 60, P R Downton 54, M W Gatting 53) and **123 for 5 wkts.**
England won by 5 wickets   Toss: Australia

1986 **India 272** (D B Vengsarkar 61) and **237** (D B Vengsarkar 102*). **England 102** (R M H Binny 5 for 40) and **128.**
India won by 279 runs   Toss: India

1987 **England 136** (D J Capel 53) and **199** (D I Gower 55, Imran Khan 7 for 40). **Pakistan 353** (Salim Malik 99, Ijaz Ahmed 50, N A Foster 8 for 107).
Pakistan won by an innings and 18 runs   Toss: England

1988 **England 201** (A J Lamb 64*) and **138** (G A Gooch 50). **West Indies 275** (R A Harper 56, D L Haynes 54, D R Pringle 5 for 95) and **67 for 0 wkt.**
West Indies won by 10 wickets   Toss: West Indies

1989 **Australia 601 for 7 wkts dec** (S R Waugh 177*, M A Taylor 136, D M Jones 79, M G Hughes 71, A R Border 66) and **230 for 3 wkts dec** (M A Taylor 60, A R Border 60*). **England 430** (A J Lamb 125, K J Barnett 80, R A Smith 66, T M Alderman 5 for 107) and **191.** (G A Gooch 68, T M Alderman 5 for 44).
Australia won by 210 runs   Toss: England

1991 **England 198** (R A Smith 54) and **252** (G A Gooch 154*, C E L Ambrose 6 for 52). **West Indies 173** (I V A Richards 73) and **162** (R B Richardson 68).
England won by 115 runs   Toss: West Indies

1992 **Pakistan 197** (Salim Malik 82*) and **221** (Salim Malik 84*, Ramiz Raja 63, N A Mallinder 5 for 50). **England 320** (G A Gooch 135, M A Atherton 76, Waqar Younis 5 for 117) and **99 for 4 wkts.**
England won by 6 wickets   Toss: Pakistan

1993 **Australia 653 for 4 wkts dec** (A R Border 200*, S R Waugh 157*, D C Boon 107, M J Slater 67, M E Waugh 52). **England 200** (G A Gooch 59, M A Atherton 55, P R Reiffel 5 for 65) and **305** (A J Stewart 78, M A Atherton 63).
Australia won by an innings and 148 runs   Toss: Australia

1994 **England 477 for 9 wkts dec** (M A Atherton 99, A J Stewart 89, G P Thorpe 72, S J Rhodes 65*) and **267 for 5 wkts dec** (G A Hick 110, G P Thorpe 73). **South Africa 447** (P N Kirsten 104, B M McMillan 78, C R Matthews 62*) and **116 for 3 wkts** (G Kirsten 65).
Match drawn   Toss: England

1995 **England 199** (M A Atherton 81, I R Bishop 5 for 32) and **208** (G P Thorpe 61). **West Indies 282** (S L Campbell 69, J C Adams 58, B C Lara 53) and **129 for 1 wkt** (C L Hooper 73*).
West Indies won by 9 wickets   Toss: West Indies

1996 **Pakistan 448** (Ijaz Ahmed 141, Mohin Khan 105, Salim Malik 55, Asif Mujtaba 51, D G Cork 5 for 113) and **242 for 7 wkts dec** (Inzamam-ul-Haq 65, Ijaz Ahmed sen 52) **England 501** (A J Stewart 170, N V Knight 113, J P Crawley 53).
Match drawn   Toss: England

1997 **England 172** (J N. Gillespie 7 for 37) and **268** (N Hussain 105, J P Crawley 72, P R Reiffel 5 for 49). **Australia 501 for 9 wkts dec** (M T G Elliott 199, R T Ponting 127, P R Reiffel 54*, D Gough 5 for 149).
Australia won by an innings and 61 runs   Toss: Australia

1998 **England 230** (M A Butcher 116) and **240** (N Hussain 94, S M Pollock 5 for 53, A A Donald 5 for 71). **South Africa 252** (W J. Cronje 57, A R C Fraser 5 for 42) and **195** (J N Rhodes 85, B M McMillan 54, D Gough 6 for 42).
England won by 23 runs   Toss: England

2000 **West Indies 172** (R R Sarwan 59*, C White 5 for 57) and **61** (A R Caddick 5 for 14). **England 272** (M P Vaughan 76, G A Hick 59).
England won by an innings and 39 runs   Toss: West Indies

2001 **Australia 447** (R T Ponting 144, D R Martyn 118, M E Waugh 72, D Gough 5 for 103) and **176 for 4 wkts dec** (R T Ponting 72). **England 309** (A J Stewart 76*, G D McGrath 7 for 76) and **315 for 4 wkts** (M A Butcher 173*, N Hussain 55).
England won by 6 wickets   Toss: Australia

2002 **India 628 for 8 wkts dec** (S R Tendulkar 193, R S Dravid 148, S C Ganguly 128, S B Bangar 68). **England 273** (A J Stewart 78*, M P Vaughan 61) and **309** (N Hussain 110.)
India won by an innings and 46 runs   Toss: India

2003 **South Africa 342** (G Kirsten 130, M Zondeki 59, J A Rudolph 55) and **365** (A J Hall 99*, G Kirsten 60). **England 307** (M A Butcher 77, M E Trescothick 59, A Flintoff 55) and **209** (M A Butcher 61, A Flintoff 50, J H Kallis 6 for 54.)
South Africa won by 191 runs   Toss: South Africa

2004 **New Zealand 409** (S P Fleming 97, M H W Papps 86, B B McCullum 54) and **161.** **England 526** (M E Trescothick 132, G O Jones 100, A Flintoff 94, A J Strauss 62) and **45 for 1 wkt**
England won by 9 wickets   Toss: England

2006 **England 515** (K P Pietersen 135, I R Bell 119, Umar Gul 5 for 123) and **345** (A J Strauss 116, M E Trescothick 58, C M W Reid 55). **Pakistan 538** (Mohammad Yousuf 192, Younis Khan 173) and **155.**
England won by 167 runs   Toss: England

2007 **England 570 for 7 wkts dec** (K P Pietersen 226, M P Vaughan 103, M J Prior 75). **West Indies 146** and **141** (D J Bravo 52).
England won by an innings and 283 runs   Toss: England

2008 **England 203** and **327** (S C J Broad 67*, A N Cook 60). **South Africa 522** (A B de Villiers 174, A G Prince 149) and **9 for 0 wkt.**
South Africa won by 10 wickets   Toss: South Africa

2009 **England 102** (P M Siddle 5 for 21) and **263** (G P Swann 62, S C J Broad 61, M G Johnson 5 for 69). **Australia 445** (M J North 110, M J Clarke 93, R T Ponting 78, S R Watson 51, S C J Broad 6 for 91).
Australia won by an innings and 80 runs   Toss: England

2010 **Australia 88** and **349** (R T Ponting 66, M J Clarke 77, S P D Smith 77). **Pakistan 258** (S R Watson 6-33) and **180-7** (Imran Farhat 67, Azhar Ali 51).
Pakistan won by 3 wickets   Toss: Australia
(This was a Home Test Match for Pakistan)

2012 **South Africa 419** (A N Petersen 182, G C Smith 52) and **258-9 dec** (J A Rudolph 69, GC Smith 52, S C J Broad 5-69). **England 425** (K P Pietersen 149, M J Prior 68) and **130-4.**
Match drawn   Toss: England

2013 **England 354** (J E Root 104, J M Bairstow 64, T A Boult 5-57) and **287-5 dec** (A N Cook 130, I J L Trott 76). **New Zealand 174** and **220** (L R P L Taylor 70, G P Swann 6-90)
England won by 247 runs   Toss: England

2014 **Sri Lanka 257** (K C Sangakkara 79, L E Plunkett 5-64) and **457** (K C Sangakkara 55, DPMD Jayawardene 79, A D Mathews 160). **England 365** (S D Robson 127, G S Ballance 74, I R Bell 64) and **249** (M M Ali 108*, K T G D Prasad 5-50)
Sri Lanka won by 100 runs   Toss: England

2015 **New Zealand 350** (T W M Latham 84, L Ronchi 88, S C J Broad 5-109) and **454-8 dec** (M J Guptill 70, B B McCullum 55, B J Watling 120, M D Craig 58*). **England 350** (A Lyth 107, A N Cook 75) and **255** (A N Cook 56, J C Buttler 73)
New Zealand won by 199 runs   Toss: England

2016 **England 298** (A D Hales 86, J M Bairstow 140). **Sri Lanka 91** (J M Anderson 5-16) and **119** (B K G Mendis 53, J N Anderson 5-29)
England won by an innings and 88 runs   Toss: Sri Lanka

323

2017 **England 258** (J E Root 58, B A Stokes100) and **490-8 dec** (M D Stoneman 52, J E Root 72, D J Malan 61, B A Stokes 58, M M Ali 84, C R Woakes 61*). **West Indies** 427 (K C Brathwaite 134, S D Hope 147, J M Anderson 5-76) and 322-5 (K C Brathwaite 95, S D Hope 118*).

West Indies won by 5 wickets Toss: England

2018 **Pakistan** 174 (Shadab Khan 56) and 134. **England** 363 (J C Buttler 80*)

England won by an innings and 55 runs Toss: Pakistan

SUMMARY OF RESULTS

ENGLAND	First played	Last played	Played	Won	Lost	Drawn
v. Australia	1899	2009	24	7	9	8
v. India	1952	2002	6	3	2	1
v. New Zealand	1949	2015	8	5	2	1
v. Pakistan	1962	2018	10	6	1	3
v. South Africa	1907	2012	13	6	3	4
v. Sri Lanka	2014	2016	2	1	1	0
v. West Indies	1957	2017	13	5	7	1
Totals	1899	2018	76	33	25	18

SIX HIGHEST AGGREGATES

Runs *Wkts*

1723	31	in 1948 (England 496 and 365 for 8 wkts dec; Australia 458 and 404 for 3 wkts)
1553	40	in 2006 (England 515 and 345; Pakistan 538 and 155)
1497	33	in 2017 (England 258 and 490-8 dec; West Indies 427 and 322-5)
1452	30	in 1989 (Australia 601 for 7 wkts dec and 230 for 3 wkts dec; England 430 and 191)
1409	40	in 2015 (New Zealand 350 and 454 for 8 wkts dec; England 350 and 255)
1350	28	in 1967 (England 550 for 4 wkts dec and 126 for 4 wkts; India 164 and 510)

Note: The highest aggregate prior to the Second World War

1141	37	in 1921 (Australia 407 and 272 for 7 wkts dec; England 259 and 202)

SIX LOWEST AGGREGATES

Runs	*Wkts*	
423	40	in 1907 (England 76 and 162; South Africa 110 and 75)
463	22	in 1958 (New Zealand 67 and 129; England 267 for 2 wkts)
505	30	in 2000 (West Indies 172 and 61; England 272)
508	30	in 2016 (England 298; Sri Lanka 91 and 119)
553	30	in 1957 (West Indies 142 and 279; England 279)
566	31	in 1972 (Australia 146 and 136; England 263 and 21 for 1 wkt)

SIX HIGHEST TOTALS

653 for 4 wkts dec	Australia v. England, 1993
608 for 8 wkts dec	India v. England, 2002
601 for 7 wkts dec	Australia v. England, 1989
584	Australia v. England, 1934
570 for 7 wkts dec	England v. West Indies, 2007
566	Australia v. England, 1930

SIX LOWEST TOTALS

61	West Indies v. England, 2000
67	New Zealand v. England, 1958
75	South Africa v. England, 1907
76	England v. South Africa, 1907
87	England v Australia, 1909
88	Australia v. Pakistan, 2010

SIX HIGHEST INDIVIDUAL SCORES

For England

310*	J H Edrich versus New Zealand, 1965
246*	G Boycott versus India, 1967
226	K P Pietersen versus West Indies, 2007
191	G Boycott versus Australia, 1977
175	R T Robinson versus Australia, 1985
173*	M A Butcher versus Australia, 2001

For Australia

334	D G Bradman, 1930
304	D G Bradman, 1934
200*	A R Border, 1993
199	M T G Elliott, 1997
182	A R Morris, 1948
181	W H Ponsford, 1934

For Pakistan

192	Mohammad Yousuf, 2006
173	Younis Khan, 2006
141	Ijaz Ahmed, 1996
105	Moin Khan, 1996
99	Salim Malik, 1987
97	Sadiq Mohammad, 1978

For India

193	S R Tendulkar, 2002
148	Nawab of Pataudi jnr, 1967
148	R S Dravid, 2002
133	V L Manjrekar, 1952
128	S C Ganguly, 2002
102*	D B Vengsarkar, 1986

For South Africa

236	E A B Rowan, 1951
182	A N Petersen, 2012
174	A B de Villiers, 2008
149	A G Prince, 2008
133	D J McGlew, 1955
130	G Kirsten, 2003

For New Zealand

120	B J Watling , 2015
97	S P Fleming, 2004
96	F B Smith, 1949
93	J G Wright, 1983
88	L Ronchi, 2015
87	M G Burgess, 1973

For Sri Lanka

160*	A D Mathews, 2014
79	K C Sangakkara, 2014
55	K C Sangakkara, 2014
53*	B K G Mendis, 2016
48	H M R K B Herath, 2014
45	L D Chandimal, 2014
45	F D M Karunaratne, 2014

For West Indies

174	G St.A Sobers, 1966
147	S D Hope, 2017 (1st innings)
137	S M Nurse, 1966
134	K C Brathwaite, 2017
118*	S D Hope, 2017 (2nd innings)
115	C G Greenidge, 1976

S D Hope was the first player to score centuries in both innings of a First Class match at Headingley

HUNDRED BEFORE LUNCH

First day

112*	C G Macartney for Australia, 1926
105*	D G Bradman for Australia, 1930

Third day

102	(from 27* to 129) H G Owen-Smith for South Africa, 1929

CARRYING BAT THROUGH A COMPLETED INNINGS

154* out of 252 G A Gooch, England v. West Indies, 1991

MOST CENTURIES IN AN INNINGS

3	1926	C G Macartney (151), W M Woodfull (141) and A J Richardson for Australia
3	1993	A R Border (200*), S R Waugh (157*) and D C Boon (107) for Australia
3	2002	S R Tendulkar (193), R S Dravid (148) and S C Ganguly (128) for India

MOST CENTURIES IN A MATCH

5	1948	C Washbrook (143) and W J Edrich (111) for England; R N Harvey (112), A R Morris (182) and D G Bradman (173*) for Australia
5	2006	K P Pietersen (135), I R Bell (119) and A J Strauss (116) for England: Younis Khan (173) and Mohammad Yousuf (192) for Pakistan
4	1976	C G Greenidge (134) and R C Fredericks (109) for West Indies; A W Greig (116) and A P E Knott (116) for England
4	1996	Ijaz Ahmed (141) and Moin Khan (105) for Pakistan; A J Stewart (170) and N V Knight (113) for England
4	2002	S R Tendulkar (193), R S Dravid (148) and S C Gangulay (128) for India; N Hussain (110) for England
4	2017	B A Stokes (100) for England; K C Brathwaite (134), S D Hope (147 and 118*) for West Indies

CENTURY PARTNERSHIPS

For England
(six highest)
For the 1st wicket

177	A Lyth (107) and A N Cook (75) v. New Zealand, 2015
168	L Hutton (81) and C Washbrook (143) v. Australia, 1948 (1st inns)
168	G A Gooch (135) and M A Atherton (76) v. Pakistan, 1992
158	M E Trescothick (58) and A J Strauss (116) v. Pakistan, 2006
156	J B Hobbs (88) and H Sutcliffe (94) v. Australia, 1926
153	M E Trescothick (132) and A J Strauss (62) v. New Zealand, 2004

For all other wickets

369	(2nd wkt) J H Edrich (310*) and K F Barrington (163) v. New Zealand, 1965
252	(4th wkt) G Boycott (246*) and B L D'Oliveira (109) v. India, 1967
194*	(3rd wkt) C A Milton (104*) and P B H May (113*) v. New Zealand, 1958
193	(4th wkt) M C Cowdrey (160) and K F Barrington (80) v. India, 1959
187	(4th wkt) P B H May (101) and C Washbrook (98) v. Australia, 1956
181	(3rd wkt) M A Butcher (173*) and N Hussain (55) v. Australia, 2001

For Australia
(six highest)
For the 1st wkt – none
For all other wickets

388	(4th wkt) W H Ponsford (181) and D G Bradman (304), 1934
332*	(5th wkt) A R Border (200*) and S R Waugh (157*), 1993
301	(2nd wkt) A R Morris (182) and D G Bradman (173*), 1948
268	(5th wkt) M T G Elliott (199) and R T Ponting (127), 1997
235	(2nd wkt) W M Woodfull (141) and C G Macartney (151), 1926
229	(3rd wkt) D G Bradman (334) and A F Kippax (77), 1930

For other countries in total
India

249	(4th wkt) S R Tendulkar (193) and S C Gangulay (128), 2002
222	(4th wkt) V S Hazare (89) and V L Manjrekar (133), 1952
170	(2nd wkt) S B Bangar (68) and R S Dravid (148), 2002
168	(2nd wkt) F M Engineer (87) and A L Wadekar (91), 1967
150	(3rd wkt) R S Dravid (148) and S R Tendulkar (193), 2002
134	(5th wkt) Hanumant Singh (73) and Nawab of Pataudi jnr (148), 1967
105	(6th wkt) V S Hazare (56) and D G Phadkar (64), 1952

CENTURY PARTNERSHIPS *(Continued)*

New Zealand

169	(2nd wkt)	M H W Papps (86) and S P Fleming (97), 2004
121	(5th wkt)	B B McCullum (55) and B J Watling (120), 2015
120	(5th wkt)	M P Donnelly (64) and F B Smith (96), 1949
120	(6th wkt)	T W M Latham (84) and L Ronchi (88), 2015
116	(2nd wkt)	J G Wright (93) and M D Crowe (37), 1983
112	(1st wkt)	B Sutcliffe (82) and V J Scott (43), 1949
106	(5th wkt)	M G Burgess (87) and V Pollard (62), 1973

Pakistan

363	(3rd wkt)	Younis Khan (173) and Mohammad Yousuf (192), 2006
130	(4th wkt)	Ijaz Ahmed (141) and Salim Malik (55), 1996
129	(3rd wkt)	Zaheer Abbas (72) and Mushtaq Mohammed (57), 1971
112	(7th wkt)	Asif Mujtaba (51) and Moin Khan (105), 1996
110	(2nd wkt)	Imran Farhat (67) and Azhar Ali (51), 2010 v. Australia
100	(3rd wkt)	Mudassar Nazar (65) and Javed Miandad (54), 1982
100	(4th wkt)	Majid Khan (75) and Zaheer Abbas (48), 1974

South Africa

212	(5th wkt)	A G Prince (149)	and A B de Villiers (174)	2008
198	(2nd wkt)	E A B Rowan (236)	and C B van Ryneveld (83)	1951
176	(1st wkt)	D J McGlew (133)	and T L Goddard (74)	1955
150	(8th wkt)	G Kirsten (130)	and M Zondeki (59)	2003
120	(1st wkt)	A N Petersen (182)	and G C Smith (52)	2012
120	(1st wkt)	J A Rudolph (69)	and G C Smith (52)	2012
117	(6th wkt)	J N Rhodes (85)	and B M McMillan (54)	1998
115	(7th wkt)	P N Kirsten (104)	and B M McMillan (78)	1994
108	(5th wkt)	E A B Rowan (236)	and R A McLean (67)	1951
103	(10th wkt)	H G Owen-Smith (129)	and A J Bell (26*)	1929

Sri Lanka

149	(8th wkt)	A D Mathews (160)	and H M R K B Herath (48)	2014

West Indies

265	(5th wkt)	S M Nurse (137)	and G St A Sobers (174)	1966
246	(4th wkt)	K C Brathwaite (134)	and S D Hope (147)	2017
192	(1st wkt)	R C Fredericks (109)	and C G Greenidge (115)	1976
144	(3rd wkt)	K C Brathwaite (95)	and S D Hope (118*)	2017
143	(4th wkt)	R B Kanhai (92)	and G St A Sobers (102)	1963
118*	(2nd wkt)	C L Hooper (73*)	and B C Lara (48*)	1995
108	(3rd wkt)	G S Camacho (71)	and B F Butcher (91)	1969
106	(1st wkt)	C G Greenidge (49)	and D L Haynes (43)	1984

6 BEST INNINGS ANALYSES

For England

8-43	R G D Willis	v. Australia	1981
8-59	C Blythe	v. South Africa	1907 (1st inns)
8-107	N A Foster	v. Pakistan	1987
7-40	C Blythe	v. South Africa,	1907 (2nd inns)
7-51	G A R Lock	v. New Zealand	1958
7-115	A P Freeman	v. South Africa	1929

For Australia

7-37	J N Gilliespie	1997	
7-58	C G Macartney	1909	
7-76	G D McGrath	2001	
6-33	S R Watson	2010	v. Pakistan
6-85	G J Gilmour	1975	
6-135	T M Alderman	1981	

5 WICKETS IN AN INNINGS

For India (2)
5-40	R M H Binny	1986
5-100	Ghulam Ahmed	1952

For New Zealand (6)
7-74	B L Cairns	1983
5-57	T A Boult	2013
5-74	R O Collinge	1973
5-95	E J Chatfield	1983
5-97	T B Burtt	1949
5-127	J Cowie	1949

For Pakistan (6)
7-40	Imran Khan	1987
5-39	Sarfraz Nawaz	1978
5-49	Imran Khan	1982
5-117	Waqar Younis	1992
5-123	Umar Gul	2006
5-128	Munir Malik	1962

For South Africa (8)
6-17	G A Faulkner	1907
6-92	N A Quinn	1929
6-54	J H Kallis	2003
5-53	S M Pollock	1998
5-69	T L Goddard	1955
5-71	A A Donald	1998
5-94	H J Tayfield	1955
5-174	A M B Rowan	1951

For Sri Lanka
5-50	K T G D Prasad	2014

For West Indies (8)
7-53	M D Marshall	1984
7-70	F M Worrell	1957
6-36	C C Griffith	1963
6-39	L R Gibbs	1996
6-52	C E L Ambrose	1991
5-32	I R Bishop	1995
5-41	G.St.A Sobers	1966
5-42	G.St A Sobers	1969

10 WICKETS IN A MATCH

For England (8)
15-99	(8-59 and 7-40)	C Blythe	v. South Africa	1907
11-65	(4-14 and 7-51)	G A R Lock	v. New Zeland	1958
11-88	(5-58 and 6-30)	F S Trueman	v. Australia	1961
11-113	(5-58 and 6-55)	J C Laker	v. Australia	1956
10-45	(5-16 and 5-29)	J M Anderson	v. Sri Lanka	2016
10-82	(4-37 and 6-45)	D L Underwood	v. Australia	1972
10-115	(6-52 and 4-63)	S F Barnes	v. South Africa	1912
10-132	(4-42 and 6-90)	G P Swann	v. New Zealand	2013
10-207	(7-115 and 3-92)	A P Freeman	v. South Africa	1929

For Australia (3)
11-85	(7-58 and 4-27)	C G Macartney	1909
10-122	(5-66 and 5-56)	W J O'Reilly	1938
10-151	(5-107 and 5-44)	T M Alderman	1989

For New Zealand (1)
10-144	(7-74 and 3-70)	B L Cairns	1983

For Pakistan (1)
10-77	(3-37 and 7-40)	Imran Khan	1987

Note: Best bowling in a match for:

India	7-58	(5-40 and 2-18)	R M H Binney	1986
Sri Lanka	6-125	(1-75 and 5-50)	K T G D Prasad	2014
South Africa	9-75	(6-17 and 3-58)	G A Faulkner	1907
West Indies	9-81	(6 -36 and 3-45)	C C Griffith	1963

HAT-TRICKS

J T Hearne	v. Australia	1899
P J Loader	v. West Indies	1957
S C J Broad	v. Sri Lanka	2014

TEST MATCH AT BRAMALL LANE, SHEFFIELD 1902

1902 **Australia 194** (S F Barnes 6 for 49) and **289** (C Hill 119, V T Trumper 62, W Rhodes 5 for 63) **England 145** (J V Saunders 5 for 50, M A Noble 5 for 51) and **195** (A C MacLaren 63, G L Jessop 55, M A Noble 6 for 52).
Australia won by 143 runs

Toss: Australia

For England

YORKSHIRE ONE-DAY INTERNATIONAL CRICKETERS 1971-2018 (Correct to October 25, 2018)

Player	M	I	NO	Runs	HS	Av'ge	100s	50s	Balls	Runs	W	Av'ge	Best	4wI	Ct/St
ATHEY, C W J 1980-88	31	30	3	848	142*	31.40	2	4	—	—	—	—	—	0	16
BAIRSTOW, D L 1979-84	21	20	6	206	23*	14.71	0	0	—	—	—	—	—	0	17/4
BAIRSTOW, J M 2011-18	54	50	8	2017	141*	48.02	6	7	—	—	—	—	—	0	18/2
BALLANCE, G S .2013-14/15	16	15	1	297	79	21.21	0	2	—	—	—	—	—	0	8
BLAKEY, R J 1992-93	3	2	0	25	25	12.50	0	0	—	—	—	—	—	0	2/1
BOYCOTT, G 1971-81	36	34	4	1,082	105	36.06	1	9	—	—	—	—	—	0	5
BRESNAN, T T ...2006-15	85	64	20	871	80	19.79	0	0	4,221	3,813	109	34.98	5-48	4	20
COPE, G A 1977-78	2	1	1	1	1*	—	0	0	112	35	2	17.50	1-16	0	0
GOUGH, D 1994-2006	158	81	38	609	46*	12.42	0	0	8,422	6,154	234	26.29	5-44	10	24
HAMPSHIRE, J H .1971-72	3	3	1	48	25*	24.00	0	0	—	—	—	—	—	0	0
HOGGARD, M J ..2001-06	26	6	2	17	7	4.25	0	0	1,306	1,152	32	36.00	5-49	1	5
JARVIS, P W 1988-93	16	8	2	31	16*	5.16	0	0	879	672	24	28.00	5-35	2	1
LOVE, J D 1981	3	3	1	61	43	20.33	0	0	—	—	—	—	—	0	1
McGRATH, A ...2003-04	14	12	0	166	52	16.60	0	1	228	175	4	43.75	1-13	0	4
MOXON, M D ...1985-88	8	8	0	174	70	21.75	0	1	—	—	—	—	—	0	5
OLD, C M 1973-81	32	25	7	338	51*	18.77	0	1	1,755	999	45	22.20	4-8	2	8
PLUNKETT, L E 2005/6-2018	74	44	15	582	56	20.06	0	1	3501	3424	115	29.77	5-52	6	24
RASHID, A U 2009-18	78	34	9	514	69	20.56	0	1	3940	3620	119	30.42	5-27	8	24
ROOT, J E 2012/13-18	121	115	19	4946	133*	51.52	13	29	1342	1299	20	64.95	3-52	0	56
SHAHZAD, A 2010-11	11	8	2	39	9		0	0	588	490	17	28.82	3-41	0	4
SIDEBOTTOM, R J .2001-10	25	18	8	133	24	13.30	0	0	1,277	1,039	29	35.82	3-19	0	6
SILVERWOOD, C E W 1996-2001	7	4	0	17	12	4.25	0	0	306	244	6	40.66	3-43	0	0
STEVENSON, G B .1980-81	4	4	0	43	28*	43.00	0	0	192	125	7	17.85	4-33	1	2
VAUGHAN, M P ...2001-07	86	83	3	1,982	90*	27.15	0	16	796	649	16	40.56	4-22	1	25
WHITE, C ...1994-2003	51	41	5	568	57*	15.77	0	1	2,364	1,726	65	26.55	5-21	2	12
WILLEY, D J ...2015-2018	42	25	12	245	50	18.84	0	1	1761	1665	48	34.68	4-34	2	19
For Scotland															
BLAIN, J A R ...1999-2009	33	25	6	284	41	14.94	0	0	1,329	1,173	41	28.60	5-22	4	8
HAMILTON, G M 1999-2010	38	38	3	1,231	119	35.17	2	7	220	160	3	53.33	2-36	0	6/1
WARDLAW, I ...2012/14/15	22	14	8	21	7*	3.50	0	0	1,108	1,036	36	28.77	4-22	2	1

For England

Player	M	I	NO	Runs	HS	Av'ge	100s	50s	Balls	Runs	W	Av'ge	Best	4wI	Ct/St
BATTY, G J 2002-09	10	8	2	30	17	5.00	0	0	440	366	5	73.20	2-40	—	4
CLOSE, D B 1972	3	3	0	49	43	16.33	0	0	18	21	0	—	—	—	1
GRAYSON, A P 2000-01	2	2	0	6	6	3.00	0	0	90	60	3	20.00	3-40	—	1
ILLINGWORTH, R .1971-72	3	2	0	5	4	2.50	0	0	130	84	4	21.00	3-50	—	1
LUMB, M J 2013/14	3	3	0	165	106	55.00	1	0	—	—	—	—	—	—	—
RHODES, S J 1989-95	9	8	2	107	56	17.83	0	1	—	—	—	—	—	—	9/2
WHARF, A G 2004-05	13	5	3	19	9	9.50	0	0	584	428	18	23.77	4-24	1	1
WOOD, B 1972-82	13	12	2	314	78*	31.40	0	2	420	224	9	24.88	2-14	—	6

Overseas Players

(Qualification: 24 List A matches for Yorkshire)

For Australia

Player	M	I	NO	Runs	HS	Av'ge	100s	50s	Balls	Runs	W	Av'ge	Best	4wI	Ct/St
BEVAN, M G ...1994-2004	232	196	67	6,912	108*	53.58	6	46	1,966	1,655	36	45.97	3-36	—	128
HARVEY, I J .1997/98-2004	73	51	11	715	48*	17.87	0	11	3,279	2,577	85	30.31	4-16	4	17
JAQUES, P A 2006-2007	6	6	0	125	94	20.83	0	1	—	—	—	—	—	—	3
LEHMANN, D S .1996-2005	117	101	22	3,078	119	38.96	4	17	1,793	1,445	52	27.78	4-7	1	26

For South Africa

Player	M	I	NO	Runs	HS	Av'ge	100s	50s	Balls	Runs	W	Av'ge	Best	4wI	Ct/St
RUDOLPH, J A 2003-06	43	37	6	1,157	81	37.32	0	7	24	26	0	—	—	—	11

For West Indies

Player	M	I	NO	Runs	HS	Av'ge	100s	50s	Balls	Runs	W	Av'ge	Best	4wI	Ct/St
RICHARDSON, R B 1983-96	224	217	30	6,248	122	33.41	5	44	58	46	1	46.00	1-4	—	75

LIMITED-OVERS INTERNATIONAL MATCHES
AT HEADINGLEY, LEEDS 1973-2018

1973 **West Indies 181** (54 overs) (R B Kanhai 55). **England 182 for 9 wkts** (54.3 overs) (M H Denness 66).
England won by 1 wicket   **Award: M H Denness**

1974 **India 265** (53.5 overs) (B P Patel 82, A L Wadekar 67). **England 266 for 6 wkts** (51.1 overs) (J H Edrich 90).
England won by 4 wickets   **Award: J H Edrich**

1975 **Australia 278 for 7 wkts** (60 overs) (R Edwards 80*). **Pakistan 205** (53 overs) (Majid Khan 65, Asif Iqbal 53, D K Lillee 5 for 34).
Australia won by 73 runs   **Award: D K Lillee**

1975 **East Africa 120** (55.3 overs). **India 123 for 0 wkt** (29.5 overs) (S M Gavaskar 65* F M Engineer 54*).
India won by 10 wickets   **Award: F M Engineer**

1975 **England 93** (36.2 overs) (G J Gilmour 6 for 14). **Australia 94 for 6 wkts** (28.4 overs).
Australia won by 4 wickets   **Award: G J Gilmour**

1979 **Canada 139 for 9 wkts** (60 overs). **Pakistan 140 for 2 wkts** (40.1 overs) (Sadiq Mohammed 57*).
Pakistan won by 8 wickets   **Award: Sadiq Mohammed**

1979 **India 182 (55.5 overs)** (S M Gavaskar 55). **New Zealand 183 for 2 wkts** (57 overs) (B A Edgar 84*).
New Zealand won by 8 wickets   **Award: B A Edgar**

1979 **England 165 for 9 wkts** (60 overs). **Pakistan 151** (56 overs) (Asif Iqbal 51, M Hendrick 4 for 15)
England won by 14 runs   **Award: M Hendrick**

1980 **West Indies 198** (55 overs) (C G Greenidge 78). **England 174** (51.2 overs) (C J Tavaré 82*).
West Indies won by 24 runs   **Award: C J Tavaré**

1981 **Australia 236 for 8 wkts** (55 overs) (G M Wood 108). **England 165** (46.5 overs) (R M Hogg 4 for 29).
Australia won by 71 runs   **Award: G M Wood**

1982 **India 193** (55 overs) (Kapil Dev 60, I T Botham 4 for 56). **England 194 for 1 wkt** (50.1 overs) (B Wood 78*, C J Tavaré 66).
England won by 9 wickets   **Award: B Wood**

1983 **West Indies 252 for 9 wkts** (60 overs) (H A Gomes 78). **Australia 151** (30.3 overs) (W W Davis 7 for 51).
West Indies won by 101 runs   **Award: W W Davis**

1983 **Pakistan 235 for 7 wkts** (60 overs) (Imran Khan 102*, Shahid Mahboob 77, A L F de Mel 5 for 39). **Sri Lanka 224** (58.3 overs) (S Wettimuny 50, Abdul Qadir 5 for 44).
Pakistan won by 11 runs   **Award: Abdul Qadir**

1983 **Sri Lanka 136** (50.4 overs). **England 137 for 1 wkt** (24.1 overs) (G Fowler 81*).
England won by 9 wickets   **Award: R G D Willis**

1986 **New Zealand 217 for 8 wkts** (55 overs) (J J Crowe 66). **England 170** (48.2 overs).
New Zealand won by 47 runs   **Award: J J Crowe**

1988 **England 186 for 8 wkts** (55 overs). **West Indies 139** (46.3 overs).
England won by 47 runs   **Award: D R Pringle**

1990 **England 295 for 6 wkts** (55 overs) (R A Smith 128, G A Gooch 55). **New Zealand 298 for 6 wkts** (54.5 overs) (M J Greatbatch 102*, J G Wright 52, A H Jones 51).
New Zealand won by 4 wickets   **Award: M J Greatbatch**

1990 **England 229** (54.3 overs) (A J Lamb 56, D I Gower 50). **India 233 for 4 wkts** (53 overs) (S V Manjrekar 82, M Azharuddin 55*).
India won by 6 wickets   **Award: A Kumble**

1996 **India 158** (40.2 overs). **England 162 for 4 wkts** (39.3 overs) (G P Thorpe 79*).
England won by 6 wickets   Award: G P Thorpe

1997 **Australia 170 for 8 wkts** (50 overs).**England 175 for 4 wkts** (40.1 overs) (G P Thorpe 75*, A J Hollioake 66*).
England won by 6 wickets   Award: G P Thorpe

1998 **South Africa 205 for 8 wkts** (50 overs) (S M Pollock 56). **England 206 for 3 wkts** (35 overs) (A D Brown 59, N V Knight 51).
England won by 7 wickets   Award: A D Brown

1999 **Pakistan 275 for 8 wkts** (50 overs) (Inzamam-ul-Haq 81, Abdur Razzaq 60). **Australia 265** (49.5 overs) (M G Bevan 61, Wasim Akram 4-40).
Pakistan won by 10 runs   Award: Inazmam-ul-Haq

1999 **Zimbabwe 175** (49.3 overs) (M A Goodwin 57). **New Zealand 70 for 3 wkts** (15 overs).
No result   No Award

1999 **South Africa 271 for 7 wkts** (50 overs) (H H Gibbs 101, D J Cullinan 50). **Australia 275 for 5 wkts** (49.4 overs) (S R Waugh 120*, R T Ponting 69).
Australia won by 5 wickets   Award: S R Waugh

2001 **England 156 (45.2 overs)** (B C Hollioake 53, Waqar Younis 7 for 36). **Pakistan 153 for 4 wkts** (39.5 overs) (Abdur Razzaq 75).
Pakistan won — England conceding the match following a pitch invasion.
       Award: Waqar Younis

2002 **Sri Lanka 240 for 7 wkts** (32 overs) (S T Jayasuriya 112). **England 241 for 7 wkts** (31.2 overs) (M E Trescothick 82).
England won by 3 wkts   Award: S T Jayasuriya

2003 **England 81 for 4 wkts. Zimbabwe** did not bat.
No result   No Award

2004 **West Indies 159** (40.1 overs). **England 160 for 3 wkts** (22 overs) (M E Trescothick 55).
England won by 7 wickets   Award: S J Harmison

2005 **Bangladesh 208 for 7 wkts** (50 overs) (Belim 81, A Flintoff 4-29). **England 209 for 5 wkts** (38.5 overs) (A J Strauss 98)
England won by 5 wickets   Award: A J Strauss

Australia 219 for 7 wkts (50 overs) (P D Collingwood 4-34). **England 221 for 1 wkt** (46 overs) (M E Trescothick 104*, M P Vaughan 59*).
England won by 9 wickets   Award: M E Trescothick

2006 **England 321 for 7 wkts** (50 overs) (M E Trescothick 121, S L Malinga 4-44). **Sri Lanka 324 for 2 wkts** (37.3 overs) (S T Jayasuriya 152, W U Tharanga 109).
Sri Lanka won by 8 wickets   Award: S T Jayasuriya

2007 **India 324 for 6 wkts** (50 overs) (Yuvraj Singh 72, S R Tendulkar 71, S C Ganguly 59, G Gambhir 51). **England 242 for 8 wkts** (39 overs) (P D Collingwood 91*)
India won by 38 runs *(D/L Method)*   Award: S C Ganguly

2008 **England 275 for 4 wkts** (50 overs) (K P Pietersen 90*, A Flintoff 78). **South Africa 255** (J H Kallis 52).
England won by 20 runs   Award: K P Pietersen

2009 **England v. West Indies**   **Match abandoned without a ball bowled**

2010 **Pakistan 294 for 8 wkts** (50 overs) (Kamran Akmal 74, Asad Shafiq 50, S C J Broad 4-81). **England 295 for 6 wkts** (A J Strauss 126, I J L Trott 53)
England won by 4 wickets   Award: A J Strauss

2011 **Sri Lanka 309 for 5 wkts** (50 overs) (D P M D Jayawardene 144, K C Sangakkara 69) **England** 240 all out (E J G Morgan 52)
Sri Lanka won by 69 runs   Award: D P M D Jayawardene

2012 **England v. West Indies**   **Match abandoned without a ball bowled**

2013 **England v. Australia**   **Match abandoned without a ball bowled**

LIMITED-OVERS INTERNATIONAL MATCHES
AT HEADINGLEY, LEEDS 1973-2018 *(Continued)*

2014 **England 294 for 7 wkts** (50 overs) (J E Root 113). **India** 253 all out (48.4 overs) (R A Jadeja 87)
England won by 41 runs   **Award: J E Root**

2015 **Australia 299 for 7 wkts** (50 overs) (G J Bailey 75, G J Maxwell 85, M S Wade 50*). **England 304 for 7 wkts** (48.2 overs) (E J G Morgan 92, P J Cummins 4-49)
England won by 7 wickets   **Award: E J G Morgan**

2016 **Pakistan 247 for 8 wkts** (50 overs) (Azhar Ali 80, Imad Wasim 57*); **England 252 for 6 wkts** (48 overs) (B A Stokes 69, J M Bairstow 61)
England won by 6 wickets   **Award: J M Bairstow**

2017 **England 339 for 6 wkts** (50 overs) (A D Hales 61, E J G Morgan 107, M M Ali 77*) **South Africa 267** (45 overs) (H M Amla 72, F du Plessis 67, C R Woakes 4-38)
England won by 72 runs   **Award M M Ali**

2018 **India 256 for 8 wkts** (50 overs) (V Kohli 71). **England 260 for 2 wkts** (44.3 overs) (J E Root 100*, E J G Morgan 88*)
England won by 8 wickets   **Award: A U Rashid**

SUMMARY OF RESULTS

ENGLAND	Played	Won	Lost
v. Australia	5	3	2
v. Bangladesh	1	1	0
v. India	7	5	2
v. New Zealand	2	0	2
v. Pakistan	4	3	1
v. South Africa	3	3	0
v. Sri Lanka	4	2	2
v. West Indies	4	3	1
v. Zimbabwe	1*	0	0
Totals	31	20	10

*No result. In addition to two matches v. West Indies abandoned and one match v. Australia abandoned

AUSTRALIA	Played	Won	Lost
v. England	5	2	3
v. Pakistan	2	1	1
v. South Africa	1	1	0
v. West Indies	1	0	1
Totals	9	4	5

In addition to one match abandoned

BANGLADESH	Played	Won	Lost
v. England	1	0	1

INDIA	Played	Won	Lost
v. England	7	2	5
v. East Africa	1	1	0
v. New Zealand	1	0	1
Totals	9	3	6

NEW ZEALAND	Played	Won	Lost
v. England	2	2	0
v. India	1	1	0
v. Zimbabwe	1*	0	0
Totals	4	3	0

*No result

PAKISTAN	Played	Won	Lost
v. Australia	2	1	1
v. Canada	1	1	0
v. England	4	1	3
v. Sri Lanka	1	1	0
Totals	8	4	4

SOUTH AFRICA	Played	Won	Lost
v. Australia	1	0	1
v. England	2	0	2
Totals	3	0	3

SRI LANKA	Played	Won	Lost
v. England	4	2	2
v. Pakistan	1	0	1
Totals	5	2	3

WEST INDIES	Played	Won	Lost
v. Australia	1	1	0
v. England	4	1	3
Totals	5	2	3

In addition to two matches abandoned

ZIMBABWE	Played	Won	Lost
v. England	1*	0	0
v. New Zealand	1*	0	0
Totals	2*	0	0

*No result

CANADA	Played	Won	Lost
v. Pakistan	1	0	1
EAST AFRICA	Played	Won	Lost
v. India	1	0	1

CENTURIES

152	S J Jayasuriya	for Sri Lanka	v. England	2006
144	D P M D Jayawardene	for Sri Lanka	v. England	2011
128	R A Smith	for England	v. New Zealand	1990
126	A J Strauss	for England	v. Pakistan	2010
121	M E Trescothick	for England	v. Sri Lanka	2006
120*	S R Waugh	for Australia	v. South Africa	1999
113	J E Root	for England	v. India	2014
112	S J Jayasuriya	for Sri Lanka	v. England	2002
109	W U Tharanga	for Sri Lanka	v. England	2006
108	G M Wood	for Australia	v. England	1981
104*	M E Trescothick	for England	v. Australia	2005
102*	Imran Khan	for Pakistan	v. Sri Lanka	1983
102*	M J Greatbatch	for New Zealand	v. England	1990
101	H H Gibbs	for South Africa	v. Australia	1999
100*	J E Root	for England	v. India	2018

4 WICKETS IN AN INNINGS

7-36	Waqar Younis	for Pakistan	v. England	2001
7-51	W W Davis	for West Indies	v. Australia	1983
6-14	G J Gilmour	for Australia	v. England	1975
5-34	D K Lillee	for Australia	v. Pakistan	1975
5-39	A L F de Mel	for Sri Lanka	v. Pakistan	1983
5-44	Abdul Qadir	for Pakistan	v. Sri Lanka	1983
4-15	M Hendrick	for England	v. Pakistan	1979
4-29	R M Hogg	for Australia	v England	1981
4-29	A Flintoff	for England	v. Bangladesh	2005
4-34	P D Collingwood	for England	v. Australia	2005
4-40	Wasim Akram	for Pakistan	v. Australia	1999
4-44	S L Malinga	for Sri Lanka	v. England	2006
4-49	P J Cummins	Australia	v. England	2015
4-56	I T Botham	for England	v. India	1982
4-81	S J C Broad	for England	v. Pakistan	2010

LIMITED-OVERS INTERNATIONAL MATCHES AT NORTH MARINE ROAD, SCARBOROUGH 1976-1978

1976 **England 202 for 8 wkts** (55 overs) (G D Barlow 80*, A M E Roberts 4 for 32).
West Indies 207 for 4 wkts (41 overs) (I V A Richards 119*).
West Indies won by 6 wickets   **Award: I V A Richards**

1978 **England 206 for 8 wkts** (55 overs) (G A Gooch 94, B L Cairns 5 for 28).
New Zealand 187 for 8 wkts (55 overs) (B E Congdon 52*).
England won by 19 runs   **Award: G A Gooch**

LIST OF PLAYERS AND CAREER AVERAGES IN ALL FIRST-CLASS MATCHES FOR YORKSHIRE 1863-2018

Based on research by John T Potter, Paul E Dyson, Mick Pope and the late Roy D Wilkinson and Anthony Woodhouse

Career records date from the foundation of Yorkshire County Cricket Club in 1863. The Club welcome any help in keeping this list up to date. The compilers do not believe that we should alter the status of matches from that determined when they were played. These averages include the match versus Gentlemen of Scotland in 1878, and exclude those versus Liverpool and District in 1889, 1891, 1892 and 1893 in line with what appear to have been the decisions of the Club.

* Played as an amateur   © Awarded County Cap   § Born outside Yorkshire

Player	Date of Birth	Date of Death (if known)	First Played	Last Played	M	Inns	NO	Runs	HS	Av'ge	100s	Runs	Wkts	Av'ge	Ct/St
Ackroyd, A *	Aug. 29, 1858	Oct. 3, 1927	1879	1879	1	1	1	2	2*		0	7	0	—	0
Allen, S *	Dec. 20, 1893	Oct 9, 1978	1924	1924	1	2	0	8	6	4.00	0	116	2	58.00	0
Allen, W R	Apr14, 1893	Oct 14, 1950	1921	1925	30	32	10	475	95*	21.59	0	—	0	—	45/21
Ambler, J	Feb 12, 1860	Feb 10, 1899	1886	1886	4	7	0	68	25	9.71	0	22	0	—	2
Anderson, G	Jan 20, 1826	Nov 27, 1902	1863	1869	19	31	6	520	99*	20.80	0	—	—	—	19
Anderson, P N	Apr. 28, 1966		1988	1988	1	1	1	0	0	0.00	0	47	1	47.00	0
Anson, C E *	Oct 14, 1889	Mar 26, 1969	1924	1924	1	2	0	27	14	13.50	0	—	—	—	1
Appleton, C *	May15, 1844	Feb 26, 1925	1865	1865	3	6	1	56	56	11.20	0	—	—	—	0
Appleyard, R ©	June 27, 1924	Mar 17, 2015	1950	1958	133	122	43	679	63	8.59	0	9,903	642	15.42	70
Armitage, C I *	Apr 28, 1849	Apr 24, 1917	1873	1878	3	5	0	26	29	5.20	0	29	0	—	0
Armitage, T	Apr 25, 1848	Sept 21, 1922	1872	1878	52	85	8	1,053	95	13.67	0	1,614	107	15.08	20
Ash, D L	Feb 18, 1944		1965	1965	3	3	0	22	12	7.33	0	22	0	—	0
Ashman, J R	May 20, 1926		1951	1951	1	1	1	0	0*		0	116	4	29.00	0
Ashraf, Moin A	Jan 5, 1992		2010	2013	21	19	5	56	56	4.00	0	1,268	43	29.48	2
Aspinall, R ©	Oct 26, 1918	Aug 16, 1999	1946	1950	36	48	8	763	75*	19.07	0	2,670	131	20.38	18
Aspinall, W	Mar 24, 1858	Jan 27, 1910	1880	1880	2	3	0	16	14	5.33	0	—	—	—	0
Asquith, F T	Feb 5, 1870	Jan 11, 1916	1903	1903	1	1	1	0	0*		0	—	—	—	2
Athey, C W J ©	Sept 27, 1957		1976	1983	151	246	21	6,320	134	28.08	10	1,003	21	47.76	144/2
Atkinson, G R	Sept 21, 1830	May 3, 1906	1863	1870	27	38	8	399	44	13.30	0	1,146	54	21.22	14
Atkinson, H T	Feb 1, 1881	Dec 23, 1959	1907	1907	1	2	0	0	0	0.00	0	17	0	—	0
§ Azeem Rafiq ©	Feb 27, 1991		2009	2017	35	41	4	814	100	22.00	1	2,511	63	39.85	14
Backhouse, E N	May 13, 1901	Nov 1, 1936	1931	1931	1	1	0	2	2	2.00	0	4	0	—	0
Badger, H D *	Mar 7, 1900	Aug 10, 1975	1921	1922	2	4	2	6	6*	3.00	0	145	6	24.16	1
Bainbridge, A B	Oct 15, 1932		1961	1963	5	10	0	93	24	9.30	0	358	20	17.90	3

LIST OF PLAYERS AND CAREER AVERAGES IN ALL FIRST-CLASS MATCHES FOR YORKSHIRE (Continued)

Player	Date of Birth	Date of Death (if known)	First Played	Last Played	M	Inns	NO	Runs	HS	Av'ge	100s	Runs	Wkts	Av'ge	Ct/St
Baines, F E *	June 18, 1864	Nov 17, 1948	1888	1888	1	1	0	0	0	0.00	0	—	—	—	—
Bairstow, A ......©	Aug 14, 1868	Dec 7, 1945	1896	1900	24	24	10	69	12	4.92	0	—	—	—	41/18
Bairstow, D L ......©	Sept 1, 1951	Jan 5, 1998	1970	1990	429	601	113	12,985	145	26.60	9	192	6	32.00	907/131
Bairstow, J M ......©	**Sept 26, 1989**		2009	2018	92	146	22	6,343	246	51.15	15	1	0		246/10
Baker, G R	Apr 18, 1862	Feb 6, 1938	1884	1884	7	7	3	42	13	4.20	0	43	0		5
Baker, R *	July 3, 1849	June 21, 1896	1874	1875	3	5	1	45	22	11.25	0	—	—	—	3
Balderstone, J C	Nov 16, 1940	Mar 6, 2000	1961	1969	68	81	6	1,332	82	17.76	0	790	37	21.35	24
§ Ballance, G S ......©	**Nov 22, 1989**		2008	2018	102	164	18	6,899	203*	47.25	21	143	0		63
Barber, A T *	June 17, 1905	Mar 10, 1985	1929	1930	42	54	3	1,050	100	20.58	1	0	0		40
Barber, W ......©	Apr 18, 1901	Sept 10, 1968	1926	1947	354	495	48	15,315	255	34.26	27	404	14	28.85	169
Barraclough, E S	Mar 30, 1923	Jan 17, 1999	1949	1950	2	4	2	43	24*	21.50	0	136	4	34.00	0
Bates, W	Nov 19, 1855	Jan 8, 1900	1877	1887	202	331	21	6,499	136	20.37	8	10,692	637	16.78	163
Bates, W E ......©	Mar 5, 1884	Jan 17, 1957	1907	1913	113	167	15	2,634	81	17.32	0	57	2	28.50	64
Batty, G J	Oct 13, 1977		1997	1997	1	1	0	18	18	18.00	0	70	2	35.00	0
Batty, J D	May 15, 1971		1989	1994	64	67	20	703	50	14.95	0	5,286	140	37.75	25
Bayes, G W	Feb 27, 1884	Dec 6, 1960	1910	1921	18	24	11	165	36	12.69	0	1,534	48	31.95	7
Beaumont, H	Oct 14, 1916	Nov 15, 2003	1946	1947	28	46	6	716	60	17.90	0	236	9	26.22	11
Beaumont, J	Sept 16, 1854	May 1, 1920	1877	1878	5	9	3	60	24	10.00	0	50	2	25.00	2
Bedford, H	July 17, 1907	July 5, 1968	1928	1928	5	5	1	57	24	14.25	0	179	8	22.37	0
Bedford, W	Feb 24, 1879	July, 28 1939	1903	1903	2	7	1	38	30*	38.00	0	117	2	58.50	1
Bell, J T	June 16, 1895	Aug 8, 1974	1921	1923	18	32	2	492	78	16.40	0	—	—	—	12
Berry, John	Jan 10, 1823	Feb 26, 1895	1864	1867	3	4	0	68	30	17.00	0	149	8	18.62	1
Berry, Joseph	Nov 29, 1829	Apr 20, 1894	1863	1874	7	7	0	76	31*	17.00	0	—	—	—	6
Berry, P J	Dec 28, 1966		1986	1990	3	4	0	86	40	9.55	0	401	7	57.28	4
§ Best T L	Aug 26, 1981		2010	2010	2	4	1	56	44*	18.66	0	793	18	44.05	0
Betts, G	Sept 19, 1841	Sept 26, 1902	1873	1874	2	4	1	44	30	14.66	0	720	10	72.00	4
§ Bevan, M G ......©	May 8, 1970		1995	1996	32	56	8	2,823	160*	58.81	9	66	0		
Binks, J G	Oct 5, 1935		1955	1969	491	587	128	6,745	95	14.69	0	—	—	—	872/172
Binns, D	Mar 31, 1870	Dec 8, 1934	1898	1898	1	1	0	4	4	4.00	0	—	—	—	0/3
Bird, H D	Apr 19, 1933		1956	1959	14	25	2	613	181*	26.65	1	—	—	—	3
Birkenshaw, J	Nov 13, 1940		1958	1960	30	42	7	588	42	16.80	0	1,819	69	26.36	21

Player	Date of Birth	Date of Death (if known)	First Played	Last Played	M	Inns	NO	Runs	HS	Av'ge	100s	Runs	Wkts	Av'ge	Ct/St
Birtles, T J D	Oct 26, 1886	Jan 13, 1971	1913	1924	37	57	11	876	104	19.04	1	20	0	—	19
Blackburn, J D H *	Oct 27, 1924	Feb 19, 1987	1956	1956	1	2	0	18	18	9.00	0	—	—	—	1
Blackburn, J S	Sept 24, 1852	July 8, 1922	1876	1877	6	11	1	102	28	10.20	0	173	45	24.71	4
§ Blackburn, W E *	Nov 24, 1888	June 3, 1941	1919	1920	10	13	6	26	6*	3.71	0	1,113	45	24.73	9
§ Blain J A R	Jan 4, 1979		2004	2010	15	17	7	137	28*	13.70	0	1,312	38	34.52	4
Blake, W	Nov 29, 1854		1880	1880	2	3	0	44	21	14.66	0	17	1	17.00	0
Blakey, R J	Jan 15, 1967		1985	2003	339	541	84	14,150	223*	30.96	12	68	1	68.00	768/56
Blamires, E	July 31, 1850	Mar 22, 1886	1877	1877	1	2	0	23	17	11.50	0	82	5	16.40	0
§ Blewett, G S	Oct 28, 1971		1999	1999	12	23	2	655	190	31.19	1	212	5	42.40	5
Bloom, G R	Sept 13, 1941		1964	1964	1	1	0	2	2	2.00	0	—	—	—	2
Bocking, H	Dec 10, 1835	Feb 22, 1907	1865	1865	2	2	0	14	11	7.00	0	—	—	—	0
Boden, J G*	Dec 27, 1848	Jan 3, 1928	1878	1878	1	1	0	6	6	6.00	0	—	—	—	1
Bolton, B C *	Sept 23, 1861	Nov 18, 1910	1890	1891	4	6	0	25	11	4.16	0	252	13	19.38	2
Bolus, J B	Jan 31, 1934		1956	1962	107	179	18	4,712	146*	29.26	7	407	13	31.30	45
Booth, A	Nov 3, 1902	Aug 17, 1974	1931	1947	36	36	16	114	29	5.70	0	1,684	122	13.80	10
Booth, M W	Dec 10, 1886	July 1, 1916	1908	1914	144	218	31	4,244	210	22.69	2	11,017	557	19.77	114
Booth, P A	Sept 5, 1965		1982	1989	23	29	9	193	33*	9.65	0	1,517	35	43.34	7
Booth, R K	Oct 1, 1926		1951	1955	65	76	28	730	53*	15.20	0	—	—	—	79/29
Bore, M K	June 2, 1947	May 2, 2017	1969	1977	74	78	21	481	37*	8.43	0	4,866	162	30.03	27
Borrill, P D	July 4, 1951		1971	1971	2	—	—	—	—	—	—	61	5	12.20	0
Bosomworth W E	Mar 8, 1847	June 7, 1891	1872	1880	4	7	1	20	7	3.33	0	140	9	15.55	2
Bottomley, I H *	Apr 9, 1855	Apr 23, 1922	1878	1880	9	12	0	166	32	13.83	0	75	1	75.00	1
Bottomley, T	Dec 26, 1910	Feb 19, 1977	1934	1935	6	7	0	142	51	20.28	0	188	1	188.00	5
Bower, W	Oct 17, 1857	Jan 31, 1943	1883	1883	1	2	0	10	5	5.00	0	—	—	—	0
Bowes, W E	July 25, 1908	Sept 4, 1987	1929	1947	301	257	117	1,251	43*	8.93	0	21,227	1,351	15.71	118
Boycott, G	Oct 21, 1940		1962	1986	414	674	111	32,570	260*	57.85	103	665	28	23.75	200
Bracken, T	Jan 5, 1859	Oct 7, 1924	1882	1882	3	6	0	12	9	2.00	0	—	—	—	2
§ Brathwaite, K C	Dec 1, 1992		2017	2017	2	4	0	40	18	10.00	0	—	—	—	1
Brayshay, P B *	Oct 14, 1916	July 6, 2004	1952	1952	2	3	0	20	13	6.66	0	104	3	34.66	0
Brearley, H *	June 26, 1913	Aug 14, 2007	1937	1937	1	2	0	17	9	8.50	0	—	—	—	0

Player	Date of Birth	Date of Death (if known)	First Played	Last Played	M	Inns	NO	Runs	HS	Av'ge	100s	Runs	Wkts	Av'ge	Ct/St
Brennan, D V *©	Feb 10, 1920	Jan 9, 1985	1947	1953	204	221	66	1,653	47	10.66	0				280/100
Bresnan, T T ©	**Feb 28, 1985**		**2003**	**2018**	**159**	**224**	**35**	**5,451**	**169***	**28.84**	**5**	**13,401**	**439**	**30.52**	**88**
Britton, G	Feb 7, 1843	Jan 3, 1910	1867	1867	3	3	0	3	3	1.50	0				0
Broadbent, A	June 7, 1879	July 19, 1958	1909	1910	3	5	0	66	29	13.20	0	252	5	50.40	1
Broadhead, W B	May 31, 1903	Apr 2, 1986	1929	1929	3	2	0	5	5	2.50	0				1
Broadhurst, M	June 20, 1974		1991	1994	5	3	0	7	6	2.33	0	231	7	33.00	0
Brook, H C	**Feb 22, 1999**		**2016**	**2018**	**17**	**30**	**0**	**657**	**124**	**21.90**	**1**	**132**	**1**	**132.00**	**8**
Brook, J W	Feb 1, 1897		1923	1923	1	1	0	0	0	0.00	0				0
Brooke, B	Mar 3, 1930	Mar.3 1989	1950	1950	2	1	0	16	14	4.00	0	191	2	95.50	0
§ Brooks, J A ©	June 4, 1984		2013	2018	81	102	34	1,229	109*	18.07	0	8,341	316	26.39	21
§ Brophy, G L ©	Nov 26, 1975		2006	2012	73	112	12	3,012	177*	30.12	3	6	0		176/15
Broughton, P N	Oct 22, 1935		1956	1956	6	5	2	19	12	6.33	0	365	16	22.81	4
Brown, A	June 10, 1854	Nov 2, 1900	1872	1872	3	3	0	9	5	3.00	0	47	3	15.66	3
Brown, J T (Driffield) ©	Aug 20, 1869	Nov 4, 1904	1889	1904	345	567	41	15,694	311	29.83	23	5,183	177	29.28	188
Brown, J T (Darfield) ©	Nov 24, 1874	Apr 12, 1950	1897	1903	30	32	3	333	37*	11.48	0	2,071	97	21.35	18
Brown, W	Nov 19, 1876	July 27, 1945	1902	1908	2	2	1	2	2	2.00	0	84	4	21.00	0
Brownhill, J *	Feb 18, 1838	Jan 6, 1915	1863	1871	14	20	3	185	25	10.88	0				7
Brumfitt, J *	Feb 18, 1917	Mar 16, 1987	1938	1938	1	1	0	9	9	9.00	0				0
Buller, J S	Aug 23, 1909	Aug 7, 1970	1930	1930	1	2	0	5	3	2.50	0				2
Bulmer, J R L	Dec 28, 1867	Jan 20, 1917	1891	1891	1	2	1	5	0*	5.00	0	79	1	79.00	2
Burgess, T	Oct 1, 1859	Feb 15, 1922	1895	1895	1	2	0	0	0*	0.00	0				0
Burgin, E	Jan 4, 1924		1952	1953	12	10	3	92	32	13.14	0	795	31	25.64	2
Burman, J	Oct 5, 1838	Nov 14, 1900	1867	1867	2	2	1	1	1*	1.00	0				0
Burnet, J R *	Oct 11, 1918	Mar 6, 1999	1958	1959	54	75	6	889	54	12.88	0	26	1	26.00	2
§ Burrows, M	Aug 18, 1855	May 29, 1893	1880	1880	6	10	0	82	23	8.20	0				2
Burton, D C F *©	Sept 13, 1887	Sept 24, 1971	1907	1921	104	130	15	2,273	142*	19.76	2				44
Burton, R C *	Apr 11, 1891	Apr 30, 1971	1914	1914	2	2	0	47	47	23.50	0				0
Butterfield, E B *	Oct 22, 1848	May 6, 1899	1870	1870	1	2	0	18	10	9.00	0	73	6	12.16	2
Byas, D ©	Aug 26, 1963		1986	2001	268	449	42	14,398	213	35.37	28	727	12	60.58	351
Byrom, J L *	July 20, 1851	Aug 24, 1931	1874	1874	2	4	0	19	11	4.75	0				1

LIST OF PLAYERS AND CAREER AVERAGES IN ALL FIRST-CLASS MATCHES FOR YORKSHIRE (Continued)

Player	Date of Birth	Date of Death (if known)	First Played	Last Played	M	Inns	NO	Runs	HS	Av'ge	100s	Runs	Wkts	Av'ge	Ct/St
Callis, E	Nov 8, 1994		2016	2017	2	3	1	131	84	65.50	0	155	3	51.66	1
Cammish, J W	May 21, 1934	July 16, 1974	1954	1954	2	1	0	0	0	0.00	0				0
Carrick, P	© July, 16 1952	Jan 11, 2000	1970	1993	425	543	102	9,994	131*	22.66	3	30,530	1,018	29.99	183
Carter, Rev E S *	Feb 3, 1845	May 23, 1923	1876	1881	14	21	2	210	39*	11.05	0	104	8	13.00	8
Carman, W H	June 20, 1861	Jan 16, 1935	1891	1891	3	6	0	57	49	9.50	0				0
Carver, K	**Mar 26, 1996**		**2014**	**2018**	**8**	**13**	**6**	**108**	**20**	**15.42**	**0**	**543**	**18**	**30.16**	**4**
Cawthray, G	Sept 28, 1913	Jan 5, 2001	1939	1952	4	6	0	114	59	19.00	0	304	4	76.00	1
Chadwick, J P G	Nov 8, 1934		1960	1965	6	9	3	106	59	17.66	0				7
Champion, A	Dec 27, 1851	June 26, 1909	1876	1879	14	23	4	148	80	7.78	0	67	2	33.50	7
Chapman, C A	June 8, 1971		1990	1998	8	13	2	238	80	21.63	0	17	1	17.00	13/3
Charlesworth, A P	Feb 19, 1865	May 11, 1926	1894	1895	7	12	1	241	63	21.90	0				2
§ Chichester-Constable, R C J *	Dec 21, 1890	May 26, 1963	1919	1919	1	1	0	0	0	0.00	0	6	0	—	1
Clarkson, A	Sept 5, 1939		1963	1963	4	8	1	80	30	11.42	0	92	5	18.40	5
Claughton, H M	Dec 24, 1891	Oct 17, 1980	1914	1919	4	2	0	39	15	6.50	0	176	3	58.66	1
§ Claydon, M E	Nov 25, 1982		2005	2006	3	2	0	38	19	19.00	0	263	3	87.66	0
§ Clayton, R O	Jan 1, 1844	Nov 26, 1901	1870	1879	70	115	23	992	62	10.78	0	2,478	153	16.19	26
§ Cleary, M F	July 19, 1980		2005	2005	2	2	0	23	12	11.50	0	250	8	31.25	2
Clegg, H	Dec 8, 1850	Dec 30, 1920	1881	1881	6	8	1	63	25*	9.00	0				2
Clifford, C C	July, 5, 1942		1972	1972	11	12	4	39	12*	4.87	0	666	26	25.61	5
Close, D B	© June 24, 1931	Sept 14, 2015	1949	1970	536	811	102	22,650	198	31.94	33	23,489	967	24.29	564
Clough, G D	May 23, 1978		1998	1998	1	2	0	34	33	17.00	0	11	0	—	1
Coad, B O	© **Jan 10, 1994**		**2016**	**2018**	**24**	**33**	**13**	**281**	**33**	**14.05**	**0**	**2030**	**103**	**19.70**	**1**
Collinson, R W *	Nov 6, 1875	Dec 26, 1963	1897	1897	2	3	0	58	34	19.33	0				0
Cooper, H P	Apr 17, 1949		1971	1980	98	107	29	1,159	56	14.85	0	6,327	227	27.87	60
Cooper, P E *	Feb 19, 1885	May 21, 1950	1910	1910	1	2	0	0	0	0.00	0				0
Cope, G A	© Feb 23, 1947		1966	1980	230	249	89	2,241	78	14.00	0	15,627	630	24.80	64
Corbett, A M	Nov 25, 1855	Oct 7, 1934	1881	1881	1	2	0	31	18	15.50	0				2
Coverdale, S P	Nov 20, 1954		1973	1980	6	4	0	31	18	7.75	0				11/4
§ Coverdale, W *	July 8, 1862	Sept 23, 1934	1888	1888	6	2	0	2	1	1.00	0				2

LIST OF PLAYERS AND CAREER AVERAGES IN ALL FIRST-CLASS MATCHES FOR YORKSHIRE (Continued)

Player	Date of Birth	Date of Death (if known)	First Played	Last Played	M	Inns	NO	Runs	HS	Av'ge	100s	Runs	Wkts	Av'ge	Ct/St
Cowan, M J	©June 10, 1933		1953	1962	91	84	48	170	19*	4.72	0	6,389	266	24.01	37
Cownley, J M	Feb 24, 1929	Nov 7, 1998	1952	1952	2	2	1	19	19	19.00	0	119	1	119.00	0
Coxon, A	©Jan 18, 1916	Jan 22, 2006	1945	1950	142	182	33	2,747	83	18.43	0	9,528	464	20.53	124
Craven, V J	July 31, 1980		2000	2004	33	55	6	1,206	81*	24.61	0	584	15	38.93	18
Crawford, G H	Dec 15, 1890	June 28, 1975	1914	1926	9	8	0	46	21	5.75	0	541	21	25.76	3
Crawford, M G *	July 30, 1920	Dec 2, 2012	1951	1951	1	2	0	22	13	11.00	0	—	—	—	1
Creighton, E	July 9, 1859	Feb 17, 1931	1888	1888	4	8	0	33	10	5.50	0	181	10	18.10	0
Crick, H	Jan 29, 1910	Feb 10, 1960	1937	1947	8	10	2	88	20	8.80	0	—	—	—	18/4
Crookes, R	Oct 9, 1846	Feb 15, 1897	1879	1879	1	2	1	2	2*	2.00	0	14	0	—	1
Crossland, S M	Aug 16, 1851	April 11, 1906	1883	1886	4	6	2	32	20	8.00	0	—	—	—	3/5
Crowther, A	Aug 1, 1878	June 4, 1946	1905	1905	1	2	0	0	0	0.00	0	—	—	—	1
Cuttell, W	Jan 28, 1835	June 10, 1896	1863	1871	15	27	6	271	56	12.90	0	596	36	16.55	4
Dalton, A J	Mar 14, 1947		1969	1972	21	31	2	710	128	24.48	3	—	—	—	6
§ Darnton, T	Feb 12, 1836	Oct 18, 1874	1864	1868	13	22	1	314	81*	14.95	0	349	12	29.08	3
Davidson, K R	©Dec 24, 1905	Dec 25, 1954	1933	1935	30	46	5	1,331	128	32.46	2	—	—	—	18
Dawes, J	Feb 14, 1836	Not known	1865	1865	5	9	2	93	28*	13.28	0	196	5	39.20	3
Dawood, I	July 23, 1976		2004	2005	20	31	7	636	75	26.50	0	—	—	—	46/3
Dawson, E	May 1, 1835	Dec 1, 1888	1863	1874	16	25	1	224	20	9.33	0	—	—	—	5
Dawson, R K J	©Aug 4, 1980		2001	2006	72	106	9	2,179	87	22.46	0	6,444	157	41.04	39
Dawson, W A *	Dec 3, 1850	Mar 6, 1916	1870	1870	1	2	0	10	10	5.00	0	—	—	—	1
Day, A G *	Sept 20, 1865	Oct 16, 1908	1885	1888	6	10	0	78	25	7.80	0	—	—	—	3
Dennis, F	©June 11, 1907	Nov 21, 2000	1928	1933	89	117	28	1,332	67	18.50	0	4,517	156	28.95	58
Dennis, S J	©Oct 18, 1960		1980	1988	67	62	24	338	53*	8.89	0	5,548	173	32.06	19
Denton, D	©July 4, 1874	Feb 16, 1950	1894	1920	676	1,058	61	33,282	221	33.38	61	957	34	28.14	360/1
Denton, J	Feb 3, 1865	July 19, 1946	1887	1888	15	24	1	222	59	9.65	0	22	1	22.00	6
Dewse, H	Feb 23, 1836	July 8, 1910	1873	1873	1	2	0	14	12	7.00	0	15	1	15.00	1
Deyes, G	Feb 11, 1878	Jan 11, 1963	1905	1907	17	24	4	44	24	2.20	0	944	41	23.02	6
Dick, R D *	Apr 16, 1889	Dec 14, 1983	1911	1911	1	1	0	2	2	2.00	0	37	2	18.50	1
Dobson, M J	Feb 22, 1854	Sept 17, 1932	1879	1879	2	1	0	1	1	2.00	0	—	—	—	1
Doidge, M J	July 2, 1970		1990	1990	1	3	0	—	—	0.33	0	106	0	—	0

341

LIST OF PLAYERS AND CAREER AVERAGES IN ALL FIRST-CLASS MATCHES FOR YORKSHIRE (Continued)

Player	Date of Birth	Date of Death (if known)	First Played	Last Played	M	Inns	NO	Runs	HS	Av'ge	100s	Runs	Wkts	Av'ge	Ct/St
Dolphin, A ©	Dec 24, 1885	Oct 5, 1942	1905	1927	427	446	157	3,325	66	11.50	0	28	1	28.00	569/260
Douglas, J S	Apr 4, 1903	Dec 27, 1971	1925	1934	23	26	8	125	19	6.94	0	1,310	49	26.73	14
Drake, A ©	Apr 16, 1884	Feb 14, 1919	1909	1914	156	244	24	4,789	147*	21.76	3	8,623	479	18.00	93
Drake, J	Sept 1, 1893	May 22, 1967	1923	1924	2	4	1	21	10	7.00	0	117	1	117.00	1
Driver, J	May 16, 1861	Dec 10, 1946	1889	1889	2	4	1	24	8	8.00	0	—	—	—	3
Dury, T S *	June 12, 1854	Mar 20, 1932	1878	1881	13	24	1	329	46	14.30	0	21	0	—	3
Dyson, W L	Dec 11, 1857	May 1, 1936	1887	1887	2	4	0	8	6	2.00	0	—	—	—	2
Earnshaw, W	Sept 20, 1867	Nov 24, 1941	1893	1896	6	7	3	44	23	11.00	0	—	—	—	6/2
Eastwood, D	Mar 30, 1848	Mar 17, 1903	1870	1877	29	51	2	591	68	12.06	0	349	11	31.72	16
Eckersley, R	Sept 4, 1925	May 30, 2009	1945	1945	1	1	0	9	9*	—	0	62	0	—	0
Elam, F W *	Sept 13, 1871	Mar 19, 1943	1900	1902	2	3	1	48	28	24.00	0	—	—	—	0
Elliott, M T G §	Sept 28, 1971		2002	2002	5	10	1	487	127	54.11	1	77	1	77.00	7
Ellis, J E	Nov 10, 1864	Dec 1, 1927	1888	1892	11	15	6	14	4*	1.55	0	—	—	—	11/10
Ellis, S *	Nov 23, 1851	Oct 28, 1930	1880	1880	2	3	0	12	9	4.00	0	—	—	—	0
Elms, J E	Dec 24, 1874	Nov 1, 1951	1905	1905	1	2	0	20	10	10.00	0	28	1	28.00	1
Eistub, C J	Feb 3, 1981		2000	2002	6	7	0	28	18*	4.00	0	356	9	39.55	2
Emmett, T ©	Sept 3, 1841	June 29, 1904	1866	1888	299	484	65	6,315	104	15.07	1	15,465	1,216	12.71	179
Farrar, A	Apr 29, 1883	Dec 25, 1954	1906	1906	1	1	0	2	2	2.00	0	—	—	—	1
Fearnley, M C	Aug 21, 1936	July 7, 1979	1962	1964	3	4	2	19	11*	9.50	0	133	6	22.16	1
Featherby, W D	Aug 18, 1888	Nov 20, 1958	1920	1920	2	—	—	—	—	—	—	12	0	—	0
Fellows, G M §	July 30, 1978		1998	2003	46	71	6	1,526	109	23.47	1	1,202	32	37.56	23
Fiddling, K	Oct 13, 1917	June 19, 1992	1938	1946	18	24	6	182	25	10.11	0	—	—	—	24/13
Finch, A J ©	Nov 17, 1986		2014	2015	8	10	1	415	110	46.11	1	40	1	40.00	11
Firth, A *	Sept 3, 1847	Jan 16, 1927	1869	1869	1	1	0	4	4	4.00	0	—	—	—	0
Firth, Rev E B *	Apr 11, 1863	July 25, 1905	1894	1894	1	2	1	1	1*	1.00	0	—	—	—	0
Firth, E L *	Mar 7, 1886	Jan 8, 1949	1912	1912	2	4	0	43	37	10.75	0	1	0	—	1
Firth, J	June 26, 1917	Sept 6, 1981	1949	1950	8	8	5	134	67*	44.66	0	—	—	—	14/2
Fisher, H ©	Aug 3, 1903	Apr 16, 1974	1928	1936	52	58	14	681	76*	15.47	0	2,621	93	28.18	22
Fisher, I D	Mar 31, 1976		1996	2001	24	32	9	545	68*	23.69	0	1,382	43	32.13	1
Fisher, M D	**Nov 9, 1997**		**2015**	**2018**	**7**	**10**	**2**	**125**	**37**	**15.62**	**0**	**657**	**15**	**43.80**	**2**

LIST OF PLAYERS AND CAREER AVERAGES IN ALL FIRST-CLASS MATCHES FOR YORKSHIRE (Continued)

Player	Date of Birth	Date of Death (if known)	First Played	Last Played	M	Inns	NO	Runs	HS	Av'ge	100s	Runs	Wkts	Av'ge	Ct/St
Flaxington, S	Oct 14, 1860	Mar 10, 1895	1882	1882	4	8	0	121	57	15.12	0	—	—	—	1
§ Fleming, S P	Apr 1, 1973		2003	2003	7	14	2	469	88*	39.08	0	—	—	—	13
Fletcher, S D	June 8, 1964		1983	1991	107	91	31	414	28*	6.90	0	7,966	234	34.04	25
Fletcher, C W	Feb 16, 1866	June 1, 1935	1892	1892	5	5	1	80	31*	11.42	0	157	7	22.42	4
Foord, C W	June 11, 1924	July 8, 2015	1947	1953	51	34	16	114	35	6.33	0	3,412	126	27.07	19
Foster, E	Nov 23, 1873	April 16, 1956	1901	1901	1	1	0	2	2	2.00	0	27	0	—	0
Foster, M J	Sept 17, 1972		1993	1994	5	7	1	165	63*	27.50	0	150	6	25.00	6
§ Foster, T W *	Nov 12, 1871	Jan 31, 1947	1894	1895	14	20	5	138	25*	9.20	0	952	58	16.41	6
Frank, J *	Dec 27, 1857	Oct 22, 1940	1881	1881	1	2	0	10	7	5.00	0	17	1	17.00	3
Frank, R W *	May 29, 1864	Sept 9, 1950	1889	1903	18	28	4	298	58	12.41	0	9	0	—	8
Freeman, G	July 27, 1843	Nov 18, 1895	1865	1880	32	54	2	752	53	14.46	0	2,079	209	9.94	16
Gale, A W	Nov 28, 1983		2004	2016	149	235	17	7,726	272	35.44	19	238	1	238.00	46
Geldart, C J	Dec 17, 1991		2010	2011	2	2	0	51	34	25.50	0	—	—	—	1
Gibb, P A *	July 11, 1913	Dec 7, 1977	1935	1946	36	54	7	1,545	157*	32.87	2	82	3	27.33	25/8
Gibson, B P **	Mar 31, 1996		2011	2011	1	1	0	0	1*	—	0	—	—	—	6/0
Gibson, R	Jan 22, 1996		2016	2016	1	1	0	0	0	0.00	0	42	1	42.00	0
§ Gifkins, C J *	Feb 19, 1856	Jan 31, 1897	1880	1880	2	3	0	30	23	10.00	0	—	—	—	1
Gilbert, C R	Apr 16, 1984		2007	2007	1	1	0	64	64	64.00	0	11	0	—	1
Gill, F	Sept 3, 1883	Nov 1, 1917	1906	1906	2	4	0	18	11	4.50	0	—	—	—	4
§ Gillespie, J N	April 19, 1975		2006	2007	26	34	11	640	123*	27.82	1	2,013	59	34.11	4
Gillhouley, K	Aug 8, 1934		1961	1961	24	31	7	323	56*	13.45	0	1,702	77	22.10	16
Gough, D	Sept 18, 1970		1989	2008	146	188	29	2,922	121	18.37	1	12,487	453	27.56	30
Goulder, A	Aug 16, 1907	June 11, 1986	1929	1929	2	1	0	3	3	3.00	0	90	3	30.00	0
§ Gray, A K D	May 19, 1974		2001	2004	18	26	3	649	104	28.21	0	1,357	30	45.23	16
Grayson, A P	Mar 31, 1971		1990	1995	52	80	10	1,958	100	27.97	1	846	13	65.07	36
Greenwood, A	Aug 20, 1847	Feb 12, 1889	1869	1880	95	166	12	2,762	91	17.93	0	9	0	—	33
Greenwood, F E *	Sept 28, 1905	July 30, 1963	1929	1932	57	66	8	1,558	104*	26.86	1	36	2	18.00	37
Greenwood, G	July 13, 1834	Nov 1, 1909	1864	1874	50	84	12	885	83	12.29	0	1,615	85	19.00	24

** At 15 years and 27 days on April 27, 2011, First Day of Yorkshire's match v. Durham MCCU, he became the youngest ever English First Class cricketer.

LIST OF PLAYERS AND CAREER AVERAGES IN ALL FIRST-CLASS MATCHES FOR YORKSHIRE (Continued)

Player	Date of Birth	Date of Death (if known)	First Played	Last Played	M	Inns	NO	Runs	HS	Av'ge	100s	Runs	Wkts	Av'ge	Ct/St
Grimshaw, C H	May 12, 1880	Sept 25, 1947	1904	1908	54	75	7	1,219	85	17.92	0	221	7	31.57	42
Grimshaw, I	May 4, 1857	Jan 18, 1911	1880	1887	125	194	14	3,354	129*	18.63	4	—	0	—	76/3
Guy S M	Nov 17, 1978		2000	2011	37	52	6	742	52*	16.13	0	8	0	—	98/12
Haggas, S	Apr 18, 1856	Mar 14, 1926	1878	1882	31	47	3	478	43	10.86	0				10
Haigh, S	◎ Mar 19, 1871	Feb 27, 1921	1895	1913	513	687	110	10,993	159	19.05	4	29,289	1,876	15.61	276
Hall, B	Sept 16, 1929	Feb 27, 1989	1952	1952	1	2	0	14	10	7.00	0	55	1	55.00	1
Hall, C H	Apr 5, 1906	Dec 11, 1976	1928	1934	23	22	9	67	15*	5.15	0	1,226	45	27.24	11
§ Hall, J	Nov 11, 1815	Apr 17, 1888	1863	1863	1	2	0	4	2	2.00	0				2
Hall, L	◎ Nov 1, 1852	Nov 19, 1915	1873	1894	275	477	58	9,757	160	23.28	9	781	15	52.06	173
Halliday, H	◎ Feb 9, 1920	Aug 27, 1967	1938	1953	182	279	18	8,361	144	32.03	12	3,119	101	30.88	140
Halliley, C	Dec 5, 1852	Mar 23, 1929	1872	1872	3	5	0	27	17	5.40	0				2
Hamer, A	Dec 8, 1916	Nov 3, 1993	1938	1938	2	2	0	3	3	1.50	0	64	1	64.00	2
§ Hamilton, G M	◎ Sept 16, 1974		1994	2003	73	108	18	2,228	125	24.75	1	5,479	222	24.68	25
Hampshire, A W	Oct 18, 1950		1975	1975	2	2	0	18	15	9.00	0				1
Hampshire, J	Oct 5, 1913	May 23, 1997	1937	1937	3	2	0	5	2	2.50	0	109	5	21.80	1
§ Hampshire, J H	◎ Feb 10, 1941	March 1, 2017	1961	1981	456	724	89	21,979	183*	34.61	34	1,108	24	46.16	367
§ Handscomb, P S P	Apr 26, 1991		2017	2017	9	14	1	441	141*	33.92	1				3
Hannon-Dalby, O J	Jun 20, 1989		2008	2012	24	25	10	45	11*	3.00	0	1,938	43	45.06	7
§ Harbord, W E *	Dec 15, 1908	July 28, 1992	1929	1935	16	21	2	411	69	20.55	0				7
§ Harden, R J	Aug 16, 1965		1999	2000	12	22	3	439	69	23.10	0				2
Hardisty, C H	Dec 10, 1885	Mar 2, 1968	1906	1909	38	55	5	991	84	19.82	0	1,145	55	20.81	18
Hargreaves, H S	Mar 22, 1912	Sept 29, 1990	1934	1938	18	20	6	51	9	3.64	0	195	8	24.37	3
§ Harmison, S J	Oct 23, 1978		2012	2012	3	3	0	25	23	8.33	0	18	2	7.50	1
Harris, W	Nov 21, 1861	May 23, 1923	1884	1887	4	8	2	45	25	7.50	0				1
Harrison, G P	◎ Feb 11, 1862	Sept 14, 1940	1883	1892	59	87	26	407	28	6.67	0	3,276	226	14.49	36
Harrison, H	Jan 26, 1885	Feb 11, 1962	1907	1907	2	1	0	4	4*	—	0	39	2	19.50	2
Harrison, W H	May 27, 1863	July 15, 1939	1888	1888	1	6	1	12	7	2.40	0		0		0
Hart, H W *	Sept 21, 1859	Nov 2, 1895	1888	1888	1	3	0	6	6	3.00	0	32	2	16.00	0
Hart, P R	Jan 12, 1947		1981	1981	3	5	0	23	11	4.60	0	140	2	70.00	1
Hartington, H E	Sept 18, 1881	Feb 16, 1950	1910	1911	10	10	4	51	16	8.50	0	764	23	33.21	2

LIST OF PLAYERS AND CAREER AVERAGES IN ALL FIRST-CLASS MATCHES FOR YORKSHIRE (Continued)

Player	Date of Birth	Date of Death (if known)	First Played	Last Played	M	Inns	NO	Runs	HS	Av'ge	100s	Runs	Wkts	Av'ge	Ct/St
Hartley, P J ©	Apr 18, 1960		1985	1997	195	237	51	3,844	127*	20.66	2	17,438	579	30.11	60
Hartley, S N ©	Mar 18, 1956		1978	1988	133	199	27	4,193	114	24.37	4	2,052	42	48.85	47
§ Harvey, I J	Apr 10, 1972		2004	2005	20	31	1	1,045	209*	36.03	2	1,218	37	32.91	12
Hatton, A G	Mar 25, 1937		1960	1961	3	3	1	4	4*	—		202	6	33.66	1
§ Hawke, Lord * ©	Aug 16, 1860	Oct 10, 1938	1881	1911	510	739	91	13,133	166	20.26	10	16	0	—	159
Hayley, H	Feb 22, 1860	June 3, 1922	1884	1898	7	12	1	122	24	11.09	0	48	0	—	3
Haywood, W J	Feb 25, 1841	Jan 7, 1912	1878	1878	1	2	0	7	7	3.50	0	14	1	14.00	0
§ Head, T M	Dec 29, 1993		2016	2016	1	2	0	56	54	28.00	0	16	0	—	0
Hicks, J	Dec 10, 1850	June 10, 1912	1872	1876	15	25	3	313	66	14.22	0	17	0	—	12
Higgins, J	Mar 13, 1877	July 19, 1954	1901	1905	9	14	5	93	28*	10.33	0				10/3
Hill, A	Nov 15, 1843	Aug 28, 1910	1871	1882	140	223	25	1,705	49	8.61	0	7,002	542	12.91	91
Hill, H *	Nov 29, 1858	Aug 14, 1935	1888	1891	14	27	2	337	34	13.48	0				10
Hill, L G *	Nov 2, 1860	Aug 27, 1940	1882	1882	1	2	0	13	8	6.50	0				1
Hirst, E T *	May 6, 1857	Oct 26, 1914	1877	1888	21	33	2	328	87*	10.58	0				7
Hirst, E W *	Feb 27, 1855	Oct 24, 1933	1881	1881	2	3	0	33	28	11.00	0	3	0	—	0
Hirst, G H ©	Sept 7, 1871	May 10, 1954	1891	1921*	717	1,050	128	32,024	341	34.73	56	44,716	2,481	18.02	518
Hirst, T H	May 21, 1865	Apr 3, 1927	1899	1899	1	1	0	5	5*	—	0	27	0	—	0
§ Hodd, A J	Jan 12, 1984		2014	2018	57	79	10	1,803	96*	26.13	0	14	0	—	165/11
Hodgson, D M	Feb 26, 1990		2015	2015	2	3	0	72	35	24.00	0				2
Hodgson, G	July 24, 1938		1964	1964	1	1	0	4	4	4.00	0				0/2
Hodgson, I	Nov 15, 1828	Nov 24, 1867	1863	1866	21	35	14	164	21*	7.80	0	1,537	88	17.46	11
Hodgson, L J	Jun 29, 1986		2009	2010	3	3	0	99	34	33.00	0	158	2	79.00	2
Hodgson, P	Sept 21, 1935	Mar 30, 2015	1954	1956	13	6	2	33	8*	8.25	0	648	22	29.45	6
© Hoggard, M J	Dec 31, 1976		1996	2009	102	120	34	956	89*	11.11	0	8,956	331	27.05	23
Holdsworth, W E N	Sept 17, 1928	July 31, 2016	1952	1953	27	26	12	111	22*	7.92	0	1,598	53	30.15	7
Holgate, G	June 23, 1839	July 11, 1895	1865	1867	12	19	0	174	38	9.15	0				17/1
© Holmes, P	Nov 25, 1886	Sept 3, 1971	1913	1933	485	699	74	26,220	315*	41.95	60	124	1	124.00	319
Horner, N F	May 10, 1926	Dec 24, 2003	1950	1950	2	4	1	114	43	28.50	0				2
Houseman I J	Oct 12, 1969		1989	1991	5	2	0	18	18	18.00	0	311	3	103.66	0
Hoyle, T H	Mar 19, 1884	June 2, 1953	1919	1919	1	2	0	7	7	3.50	0				0/1

LIST OF PLAYERS AND CAREER AVERAGES IN ALL FIRST-CLASS MATCHES FOR YORKSHIRE (Continued)

Player	Date of Birth	Date of Death (if known)	First Played	Last Played	M	Inns	NO	Runs	HS	Av'ge	100s	Runs	Wkts	Av'ge	Ct/St
Hudson, B	June 29, 1851	Nov 11, 1901	1880	1880	5	4	0	13	5	3.25	0	43	0	—	2
Hunter, B	Feb 23, 1860	Jan 11, 1927	1888	1909	517	681	323	4,177	58*	11.66	0	—	0	—	863/323
Hunter, J	Aug 3, 1855	Jan 4, 1891	1878	1888	143	213	61	1,183	60*	7.78	0	—	—	—	207/102
Huchison, P M ◎	June 9, 1977		1996	2001	39	39	23	187	30	11.68	0	3,244	143	22.68	8
Hutton, L ◎	June 23, 1916	Sept, 6, 1990	1934	1955	341	527	62	24,807	280*	53.34	85	4,221	154	27.40	278
Hutton, R A ◎	Sept 6, 1942		1962	1974	208	292	45	4,986	189	20.18	4	10,254	468	21.91	160
Iddison, R	Sept 15, 1834	Mar 19, 1890	1863	1876	72	108	15	1,916	112	20.60	0	1,540	102	15.09	70
Illingworth, R ◎	June 8, 1932		1951	1983	496	668	131	14,986	162	27.90	14	26,806	1,431	18.73	286
§ Imran Tahir	Mar 27, 1979		2007	2007	1	2	0	5	5	2.50	0	141	0	—	0
Ingham, P G	Sept 28, 1956		1979	1981	8	14	0	290	64	20.71	0	—	—	—	0
Inglis, J W	Oct 19, 1979		2000	2000	1	2	0	4	2	2.00	0	—	—	—	0
§ Inzamam-ul-Haq ◎	Mar 3, 1970		2007	2007	3	4	0	89	51	22.25	0	—	—	—	5
Jackson, Hon F S *	Nov 21, 1870	Mar 9, 1947	1890	1907	207	328	22	10,371	160	33.89	21	9,690	506	19.15	129
Jackson, S R *	July 15, 1859	July 19, 1941	1891	1891	1	2	0	9	9	4.50	0	—	—	—	0
Jacques, T A *	Feb 19, 1905	Feb 23, 1995	1927	1936	28	20	7	162	35*	12.46	0	1,786	57	31.33	12
Jakeman, F	Jan 10, 1921	May 17, 1986	1946	1947	10	16	1	262	64	18.71	0	—	—	—	3
James, B	Apr 23, 1934		1954	1954	4	5	3	22	11*	11.00	0	228	8	28.50	0
§ Jaques, P A ◎	May 3, 1979		2004	2013	53	82	3	4,039	243	51.12	11	112	1	112.00	46
Jarvis, P W ◎	June 29, 1965		1981	1993	138	160	46	1,898	80	16.64	0	11,990	449	26.70	36
Johnson, C	Sept 5, 1947		1969	1979	100	152	14	2,960	107	21.44	2	265	4	66.25	50
Johnson, J	May 16, 1916	Jan 16, 2011	1936	1939	3	3	2	5	4*	5.00	0	27	5	5.40	1
Johnson, M	Apr 23, 1958		1981	1981	4	4	2	2	1	1.00	0	301	7	43.00	1
Joy, J	Dec 29, 1825	Sept 27, 1889	1863	1867	3	5	0	107	74	21.40	0	5	0	—	3
Judson, A	July 10, 1885	Apr 8, 1975	1920	1920	1	1	0				0	5	0	—	1
§ Katich, S M	Aug 21, 1975		2002	2002	1	2	0	37	21	18.50	0	25	0	—	1
Kaye, Harold S *	May 9, 1953	Nov 6, 1953	1907	1908	18	25	1	243	37	10.12	0	—	—	—	9
Kaye, Haven	June 11, 1846	Jan 24, 1892	1872	1873	8	14	0	117	33	8.35	0	—	—	—	3
Keedy, G	Nov 27, 1974		1994	1994	1	1	0	1	1	1.00	0	—	—	—	0
§ Keighley, W G * ◎	Jan 10, 1925	June 14, 2005	1947	1951	35	51	5	1,227	110	26.67	1	18	0	—	12

LIST OF PLAYERS AND CAREER AVERAGES IN ALL FIRST-CLASS MATCHES FOR YORKSHIRE (Continued)

Player	Date of Birth	Date of Death (if known)	First Played	Last Played	M	Inns	NO	Runs	HS	Av'ge	100s	Runs	Wkts	Av'ge	Ct/St
Kellett, S A ...... ©	Oct 16, 1967		1989	1995	86	147	10	4,204	125*	30.68	2	7	0	—	74
Kemmie, G	May 17, 1904	Apr 11, 1994	1927	1927	1	2	0	6	6	3.00	0	—	—	—	1
Kettleborough, R A ...	Mar 15, 1973		1994	1997	13	19	2	446	108	26.23	1	153	3	51.00	9
Kilburn, S	Oct 16, 1868	Sept 25, 1940	1896	1896	1	1	0	8	8	8.00	0	—	—	—	0
Kilner, N	July 21, 1895	Apr 28, 1979	1919	1923	69	73	7	1,253	112	18.98	2	8	0	—	34
Kilner, R ...... ©	Oct 17, 1890	Apr 5, 1928	1911	1927	365	478	46	13,018	206*	30.13	15	14,855	857	17.33	231
King, A M	Oct 8, 1932		1955	1955	1	1	0	12	12	12.00	0	—	—	—	0
Kippax, P J	Oct 15, 1940		1961	1962	4	7	2	37	37	7.40	0	279	8	34.87	0
§ Kirby, S P ...... ©	Oct 4, 1977		2001	2004	47	61	14	342	57	7.27	0	5,143	182	28.25	11
§ Kohler-Cadmore T .	Apr 19, 1994		2017	2018	9	17	2	565	106	37.66	2	—	—	—	5
§ Kruis, G J	May 9, 1974		2005	2009	54	64	31	617	50*	18.69	0	5,431	154	35.26	11
§ Lambert, G A	Jan 4, 1980		2000	2000	2	3	2	6	3*	6.00	0	133	4	33.25	1
Lancaster, W W	Feb 4, 1873	Dec 30, 1938	1895	1895	7	10	0	163	51	16.30	0	29	0	—	1
§ Landon, C W *	May 30, 1850	Mar 5, 1903	1878	1882	9	13	0	51	18	3.92	0	74	0	—	7
§ Law, W *	Apr 9, 1851	Dec 20, 1892	1871	1873	4	7	0	51	22	7.28	0	—	—	—	7
Lawson, M A K	Oct 24, 1985		2004	2007	15	21	4	197	44	12.31	0	1,699	42	40.45	7
Leadbeater, B ...... ©	Aug 14, 1943		1966	1979	144	236	27	5,247	140*	25.10	1	5	1	5.00	80
Leadbeater, E	Aug 15, 1927	Apr 17, 2011	1949	1956	81	94	29	898	91	13.81	0	5,657	201	28.14	49
Leadbeater, H *	Dec 31, 1863	Oct 9, 1928	1884	1890	6	10	2	141	65	17.62	0	11	0	—	4
§ Leaning, J A ...... ©	Oct 18, 1993		2013	2018	59	95	10	2,640	123	31.05	4	327	4	81.75	48
Leatham, G A B * ...	Apr 30, 1851	June 19, 1932	1874	1886	12	18	5	61	14	4.69	0	—	—	—	21/7
Leather, R S *	Aug 17, 1880	Jan 3, 1913	1906	1906	1	2	0	19	14	9.50	0	—	—	—	0
Lee, C	Mar 17, 1924	Sept 4, 1999	1952	1952	2	4	0	98	74	24.50	0	—	—	—	1
Lee, F ...... ©	Nov 18, 1856	Sept 13, 1896	1882	1890	105	182	10	3,622	165	21.05	3	—	—	—	53/1
Lee, G H	Aug 24, 1854	Oct 4, 1919	1879	1879	1	2	0	13	6	6.50	0	—	—	—	0
Lee, Herbert	July 2, 1856	Feb 4, 1908	1885	1885	5	6	0	20	12	3.33	0	—	—	—	2
Lee, J E *	Mar 23, 1858	Apr 2, 1880	1867	1867	2	3	0	9	6	3.00	0	—	—	—	0
Lee, J E	Dec 23, 1988		2006	2009	2	3	1	24	21*	12.00	0	149	2	74.50	1
Lees, A Z ...... ©	Apr 14, 1993		2010	2018	82	140	11	4,528	275*	35.10	11	77	2	38.50	56
Legard, A D *	June 19, 1878	Aug 15, 1939	1910	1910	4	5	0	50	15	10.00	0	26	0	—	1

LIST OF PLAYERS AND CAREER AVERAGES IN ALL FIRST-CLASS MATCHES FOR YORKSHIRE (Continued)

Player	Date of Birth	Date of Death (if known)	First Played	Last Played	M	Inns	NO	Runs	HS	Av'ge	100s	Runs	Wkts	Av'ge	Ct/St
§ Lehmann, D S ....©	Feb 5, 1970		1997	2006	88	137	8	8,871	339	68.76	26	1,952	61	32.00	35
§ Lehmann, J S	Jul 8, 1992		2016	2016	5	8	1	384	116	54.85	1				2
Lester, E I	Feb 18, 1923		1945	1956	228	339	27	10,616	186	34.02	24	160	3	53.33	106
Leyland, M	July 20, 1900	Jan 1, 1967	1920	1946	548	720	82	26,180	263	41.03	62	11,079	409	27.08	204
Lilley, A E	Apr 17, 1992		2011	2011	1	1	0	0	0	0.00	0	34	0	—	0
Linaker, L	Apr 8, 1885	Nov 17, 1961	1909	1909	1	2	1	0	0	0.00	0	28	1	28.00	—
Lister, J	Dec 9, 1850	Dec 3, 1919	1874	1878	7	11	1	36	10	3.60	0				2
Lister, J *	May 14, 1930	Jan 28, 1991	1954	1954	2	4	1	35	16	8.75	0				2
§ Lister-Kaye, K A *	Mar 27, 1892	Feb 28, 1955	1928	1928	2	2	1	13	7*	13.00	0	64	1	64.00	2
Lockwood, E	Apr 4, 1845	Dec 19, 1921	1868	1884	214	364	29	7,789	208	23.25	6	2,265	141	16.06	164/2
Lockwood, H	Oct 20, 1855	Feb 18, 1930	1877	1882	16	27	2	408	90	16.32	0	37	0	—	8
Lodge, J T	Apr 16, 1921	July 9, 2002	1948	1948	2	3	0	48	30	16.00	0	17	0	—	1
Logan, J E G ...©	Oct 12, 1997		2018	2018	1	1	0	6	6	6.00	0	44	0	—	1
Love, J D ...©	Apr 22, 1955		1975	1989	247	388	58	10,263	170*	31.10	13	835	12	69.58	123
Lowe, G E	Jan 12, 1877	Aug 15, 1932	1902	1902	1	1	0	5	5*	5.00	0				0
Lowe J R	Oct 19,1991		2010	2010	1	1	0	5	5*	5.00	0	15	0	—	0
Lowson, F A ...©	Aug 19, 1925	Sept 8, 1984	1949	1958	252	404	31	13,897	259*	37.25	30	84	8	10.50	180
§ Lucas, D S	Aug 19, 1978		2005	2005	1							15	0	—	5
Lumb, E *	Sept 12, 1852	Apr 5, 1891	1872	1886	14	23	4	311	70*	16.36	0				5
§ Lumb, M J ...©	Feb 12, 1980		2000	2006	78	135	12	4,194	144	34.09	8	199	5	39.80	43
Lumb, R G ...©	Feb 27, 1950		1970	1984	239	395	30	11,525	165*	31.57	22	5	0	—	129
Lupton, A W * ...©	Feb 23, 1879	Apr 14, 1944	1908	1927	104	79	15	668	43*	10.43	0	88	0	—	25
Lynas, G G	Sept 7, 1832	Dec 8, 1896	1867	1867	2	3	1	4	4*	2.00	0				2
Lyth, A ...©	Sept 25, 1987		2007	2018	146	245	12	9,230	251	39.61	22	1,464	32	45.75	192
Macaulay, G G ...©	Dec 7, 1897	Dec 13, 1940	1920	1935	445	430	112	5,717	125*	17.97	3	30,554	1,774	17.22	361
McGrath, A ...©	Oct 6, 1975		1995	2012	242	405	29	14,091	211	37.47	34	4,652	128	36.34	168
McHugh, F P	Nov 15, 1925		1949	1949	3	3	0	0	0	0.00	0	147	4	36.75	1
§ Marsh, S E	Jul 9, 1983		2017	2017	2	3	1	225	125*	112.50	1				—
Marshall, A	July 10, 1849	Aug 3, 1891	1874	1874	1	2	0	11	11	1.00	0				1
§ Martyn, D R	Oct 21, 1971		2003	2003	2	3	1	342	238	171.00	1				2

LIST OF PLAYERS AND CAREER AVERAGES IN ALL FIRST-CLASS MATCHES FOR YORKSHIRE (Continued)

Player	Date of Birth	Date of Death (if known)	First Played	Last Played	M	Inns	NO	Runs	HS	Av'ge	100s	Runs	Wkts	Av'ge	Ct/St
Mason, A	May 2, 1921	Mar 22, 2006	1947	1950	18	19	3	105	22	6.56	0	1,473	51	28.88	6
Maude, E *	Dec 31, 1839	July 2, 1876	1866	1866	2	2	1	17	16	8.50	0				0
§ Maxwell, G J	Oct 14, 1988		2015	2015	4	2	0	244	140	40.66	1	144	4	36.00	0
Metcalfe, A A ....©	Dec 25, 1963		1983	1995	184	317	19	10,465	216*	35.11	25	344	3	114.66	72
Micklethwait, W H * ..	Dec 13, 1885	Oct 7, 1947	1911	1911	1	1	0	44	44	44.00	0				0
Middlebrook, J D	May 13, 1977		1998	2015	29	38	7	534	84	15.25	0	1,899	66	28.77	1
Middlebrook, W	May 23, 1858	Apr 26, 1919	1888	1889	17	27	7	88	19*	4.40	0	895	50	17.90	17
Midgley, C A *	Nov 13, 1877	June 24, 1942	1906	1906	4	6	2	115	59*	28.75	0	149	8	18.62	3
Milburn, S M	Sept 29, 1972		1992	1995	6	8	2	22	7	3.66	0	431	14	30.78	0
§ Milligan, F W * ...©	Mar 19, 1870	Mar 31, 1900	1894	1898	81	113	10	1,879	74	18.24	0	2,736	112	24.42	40
Mitchell, A	Sept 13, 1902	Dec 25, 1976	1922	1945	401	550	69	18,189	189	37.81	39	291	5	58.20	406
Mitchell, F * .....©	Aug 13, 1872	Oct 11, 1935	1894	1904	83	125	5	4,104	194	34.20	10	16	1	16.00	52
Monks, G D	Sept 3, 1929		1952	1952	1			3	3	3.00	0				0
Moorhouse, R ......©	Sept 7, 1866	Jan 7, 1921	1888	1899	206	315	45	5,217	113	19.32	3	1,232	43	28.65	92
§ Morkel, M	Oct 6, 1984		2008	2008	1	2	0	8	8	4.00	0	33	1	33.00	0
Morris, A C	Oct 4, 1976		1995	1997	16	23	4	362	60	17.23	0	508	9	56.44	12
Mosley, H	Mar 8, 1850	Nov 29, 1933	1881	1881	2	4	2	1	1	0.25	0	34	3	11.33	1
Motley, A *	Feb 5, 1858	Sept 28, 1897	1879	1879	2	2	1	10	8*	10.00	0	135	7	19.28	1
Mounsey, J T ......©	Aug 30, 1871	Apr 6, 1949	1891	1897	92	145	21	1,939	64	15.63	0	444	10	44.40	45
Moxon, M D ....©	May 4, 1960		1981	1997	277	476	41	18,973	274*	43.71	41	1,213	22	55.13	190
Myers, H	Jan 2, 1875	June 12, 1944	1901	1910	201	289	46	4,450	91	18.31	0	7,095	282	25.15	106
Myers, M	Apr 12, 1847	Dec 8, 1919	1876	1878	22	40	4	537	49	14.91	0	20	0		11
§ Naved-ul-Hasan, Rana	Feb 28, 1978		2008	2009	11	16	3	207	32	15.92	0	1,018	26	39.15	3
Naylor, J E	Dec 11, 1930	June 27, 1996	1953	1953	1						—	88			—
Newstead, J T .....©	Sept 8, 1877	Mar 25, 1952	1903	1913	96	128	17	1,791	100*	16.13	1	5,555	297	18.70	75
Nicholson, A G ....©	June 25, 1938	Nov 3, 1985	1962	1975	282	267	125	1,667	50	11.73	0	17,296	876	19.74	85
Nicholson, N G	Oct 17, 1963		1988	1989	5	8	3	134	56*	26.80	0	25	0		5
Oates, William	Jan 1, 1852	Dec 9, 1940	1874	1875	7	13	7	34	14*	5.66	0				5/1
Oates, W F	June 11, 1929	May 15, 2001	1956	1956	3	3	0	20	9	6.66	0				0

LIST OF PLAYERS AND CAREER AVERAGES IN ALL FIRST-CLASS MATCHES FOR YORKSHIRE (Continued)

Player	Date of Birth	Date of Death (if known)	First Played	Last Played	M	Inns	NO	Runs	HS	Av'ge	100s	Runs	Wkts	Av'ge	Ct/St
Old, C M ©	Dec 22, 1948		1966	1982	222	262	56	4,785	116	23.22	5	13,409	647	20.72	131
Oldham, S	Jan 26, 1948		1974	1985	59	39	18	212	50	10.09	0	3,849	130	29.60	18
Oldroyd, E	Oct 1, 1888	Dec 27, 1964	1910	1931	383	509	58	15,891	194	35.23	37	1,658	42	39.47	203
Oyston, C	May 12, 1869	July 15, 1942	1900	1909	15	21	8	96	22	7.38	0	872	31	28.12	3
Padgett, D E V ©	July 20, 1934		1951	1971	487	774	63	20,306	161*	28.55	29	208	6	34.66	250
Padgett, G H	Oct 9, 1931		1952	1952	6	7	4	56	32*	18.66	0	336	4	84.00	5
Padgett, J	Nov 21, 1860		1882	1889	6	9	0	92	22	10.22	0	—	—	—	2
Parker, B	June 23, 1970		1992	1998	44	71	10	1,839	138*	30.14	2	3	0	—	19
§ Parkin, C H	Feb 18, 1886	June 15, 1943	1906	1906	1	1	0	0	0	0.00	0	25	2	12.50	0
Parratt, J	Mar 24, 1859	May 6, 1905	1888	1890	2	2	0	11	11	5.50	0	75	1	75.00	4
§ Parton, J W	Jan 31, 1863	Jan. 30, 1906	1889	1889	1	2	0	16	14	8.00	0	4	1	4.00	0
Patterson, H E ©	**Oct 3, 1983**		**2005**	**2018**	**140**	**165**	**41**	**2,044**	**63***	**16.48**	**0**	**10,359**	**372**	**27.84**	**25**
Pearson, H E	Aug 7, 1851	July 8, 1903	1878	1880	4	7	5	31	10*	15.50	0	90	5	18.00	1
Pearson, J H	May 14, 1915	May 13, 2007	1934	1936	3	3	0	54	44	18.00	0	—	—	—	0
§ Peate, E	Mar 2, 1855	Mar 11, 1900	1879	1887	154	226	61	1,793	95	10.86	0	9,986	794	12.57	97
§ Peel, R	Feb 12, 1857	Aug 12, 1941	1882	1897	318	510	42	9,322	210*	19.91	6	20,638	1,311	15.74	141
Penny, J H	Sept 29, 1856	July 29, 1902	1891	1891	1	1	0	8	8*	8.00	0	31	2	15.50	1
Pickles, C S	Jan 30, 1966		1985	1992	58	76	21	1,336	66	24.29	0	3,638	83	43.83	24
Pickles, D	Nov 16, 1935		1957	1960	41	40	20	74	12	3.70	0	2,062	96	21.47	10
§ Pillans, M W	**Jul 4, 1991**		**2018**	**2018**	**1**	**1**	**0**	**8**	**8**	**8.00**	**0**	**130**	**7**	**18.57**	**0**
Pinder, G	July 15, 1841	Jan 15, 1903	1867	1880	125	199	44	1,639	57	10.57	0	325	19	17.10	145/102
§ Platt, R K	Dec 26, 1932		1955	1963	96	103	47	405	57*	7.23	0	6,389	282	22.65	35
§ Plunkett, L E ©	Apr 6, 1985		2013	2017	36	51	7	1,241	126	28.20	1	2,925	98	29.84	20
Pollard, G	Aug 7, 1835	Mar 26, 1909	1865	1865	1	2	0	3	3	1.50	0	19	0	—	0
Pollitt, G	June 3, 1874	May 19, 1942	1899	1899	1	1	0	51	51	51.00	0	—	—	—	0
§ Poysden, J E ©	**Aug 8, 1991**		**2018**	**2018**	**3**	**5**	**2**	**25**	**20***	**8.33**	**0**	**259**	**7**	**37.00**	**0**
Prest, C H *	Dec 9, 1841	Mar 4, 1875	1864	1864	2	4	0	57	31	14.25	0	—	—	—	3
Preston, J M	Aug 23, 1864	Nov 26, 1890	1885	1889	79	134	11	1,935	93	15.73	0	3,232	178	18.15	36
Pride, T	July 23, 1864	Feb 16, 1919	1887	1887	1	1	0	1	1	1.00	0	—	—	—	4/3
Priestley, I M	Sept 25, 1967		1989	1989	2	4	2	25	23	12.50	0	119	4	29.75	1

Player	Date of Birth	Date of Death (if known)	First Played	Last Played	M	Inns	NO	Runs	HS	Av'ge	100s	Runs	Wkts	Av'ge	Ct/St
Pullan, P	Mar 29, 1857	Mar 3, 1901	1884	1884	1	1	0	14	14	14.00	0	5	0	—	1
§ Pujara, C A	Jan 25, 1988		2015	2015	4	6	1	264	133*	52.80	1	0	0	—	2
Pyrah, R M ©	Nov 1, 1982		2004	2015	51	61	8	1,621	134*	30.58	3	2527	55	45.94	22
§ Radcliffe, E J R H * ©	Jan 27, 1884	Nov 23, 1969	1909	1911	64	89	13	826	54	10.86	0	134	2	67.00	21
Ramage, A	Nov 29, 1957		1979	1983	23	22	3	219	52	16.84	0	1,649	44	37.47	4
Ramsden, G	Mar 2, 1983		2000	2000	1			0	0*	—	0	68	1	68.00	0
Randhawa, G S	Jan 25, 1992		2011	2011	1	1	0	5	5	5.00	0	62	2	31.00	0
Raper, J R S *	Aug 9, 1909	Mar 9, 1997	1936	1947	3	4	0	24	15	6.00	0	—		—	0
Rashid, A U ©	Feb 17, 1988		2006	2017	140	196	33	5,620	180	34.47	10	14,136	420	33.65	70
§ Raval, J A	May 22, 1988		2018	2018	4	7	0	84	21	12.00	0	—		—	3
Rawlin, E R	Oct 4, 1897	Jan 11, 1943	1927	1936	8	10	1	72	35	8.00	0	498	21	23.71	2
Rawlin, J T	Nov 10, 1856	Jan 19, 1924	1880	1885	27	36	2	274	35	8.05	0	258	11	23.45	13
Rawlinson, E B	Apr 10, 1837	Feb 17, 1892	1867	1875	37	68	5	991	55	15.73	0	62	5	12.40	16
Read, J	Feb 2, 1998		2016	2016	1	1	0	14	14	14.00	0	—		—	4
Redfearn, J	May 13, 1862	Jan 14, 1931	1890	1890	1	1	0	5	5	5.00	0	—		—	0
Render, G W A	Jan 5, 1887	Sept 17, 1922	1919	1919	1	1	0	5	5	5.00	0	—		—	0
Rhodes, A C ©	Oct 14, 1906	May 21, 1957	1932	1934	61	70	19	917	64*	17.98	0	3,026	107	28.28	45
§ Rhodes, H E *	Jan 11, 1852	Sept 10, 1889	1878	1883	10	16	1	269	64	17.93	0	—		—	1
Rhodes, S J	June 17, 1964		1981	1984	3	2	1	41	35	41.00	0	—		—	3
Rhodes, Wilfred ©	Oct 29, 1877	July 8, 1973	1898	1930	883	1,195	162	31,075	267*	30.08	46	57,634	3,598	16.01	586
Rhodes, William	Mar 4, 1883	Aug 5, 1941	1911	1911	1	1	0	1	1*	1.00	0	40	0	—	0
§ Rhodes, W M H	Mar 2, 1995		2015	2016	15	25	2	689	95	29.95	0	551	16	34.43	8
Richardson, J A *	Aug 4, 1908	Apr 2, 1985	1936	1947	7	12	2	308	61	30.80	0	90	2	45.00	3
§ Richardson, R B ©	Jan 12, 1962		1993	1994	23	39	1	1,310	112	34.47	1	23	1	23.00	18
§ Richardson, S A	Sept 5, 1977		2000	2003	13	23	2	377	69	17.95	0	—		—	11
Riley, H *	Aug 17, 1875	Nov 6, 1922	1895	1900	4	5	1	36	25*	9.00	0	54	1	54.00	1
Riley, M *	Apr 5, 1851	June 1, 1899	1878	1882	17	28	1	361	92	13.37	0	10	0	—	3
Ringrose, W ©	Sept 2, 1871	Sept 14, 1943	1901	1906	57	66	9	353	23	6.19	0	3,224	155	20.80	25
§ Robinson, A L ©	Aug 17, 1946		1971	1977	84	69	31	365	30*	9.60	0	4,927	196	25.13	48
Robinson, B L H	May 12, 1858	Dec 14, 1909	1879	1879	1	2	0	5	4	2.50	0	20	1	20.00	0

LIST OF PLAYERS AND CAREER AVERAGES IN ALL FIRST-CLASS MATCHES FOR YORKSHIRE (Continued)

Player	Date of Birth	Date of Death (if known)	First Played	Last Played	M	Inns	NO	Runs	HS	Av'ge	100s	Runs	Wkts	Av'ge	Ct/St
Robinson, Edward *	Dec 27, 1862	Sept 3, 1942	1887	1887	1	2	1	23	23*	23.00	0				0
Robinson, Emmott ...Ⓒ	Nov 16, 1883	Nov 17, 1969	1919	1931	413	455	77	9,651	135*	25.53	7	19,645	893	21.99	318
Robinson, E P ......Ⓒ	Aug 10, 1911	Nov 10, 1998	1934	1949	208	253	46	2,596	75*	12.54	0	15,141	735	20.60	189
Robinson, M A ......Ⓒ	Nov 23, 1966		1991	1995	90	93	36	240	18	4.21	0	6,866	218	31.49	17
Robinson, P E ......Ⓒ	Aug 3, 1963		1984	1991	132	217	31	6,668	189	35.84	7	238	1	238.00	96
Robinson, W	Nov 29, 1851	Aug 14, 1919	1876	1877	7	14	1	151	68	11.61	0				3
Roebuck J C G	Aug 14, 1991		2010	2010	1	1	0	23	23	23.00	0				0
Root, J E ....Ⓒ	Dec 30, 1990		2010	2018	45	75	8	2,822	236	42.11	6	669	17	39.35	26
Roper, E *	Apr 8, 1851	Apr 27, 1921	1878	1880	5	7	1	85	68	14.16	0				2
Rothery, J W	Sept 5, 1876	June 2, 1919	1903	1910	150	236	18	4,614	161	21.16	3	44	2	22.00	45
Rowbotham, J	July 8, 1831	Dec 22, 1899	1863	1876	94	162	9	2,624	113	17.15	3	37	3	12.33	52
§ Rudolph J A	May 4, 1981		2007	2011	68	112	8	5,429	228*	52.20	18	311	1	311.00	79
Rudston J A	Nov 22, 1878		1902	1907	21	30	0	609	164	20.30	1				3
Ryan, M	June 23, 1933	Apr 14, 1962	1954	1965	150	149	58	682	26*	7.49	0	9,466	413	22.92	59
Ryder, L	Aug 28, 1900	Jan 24, 1955	1924	1924	2	2	1	1	1	1.00	0	151	4	37.75	2
Sanderson B W	Jan 3, 1989		2008	2010	3	2	1	6	6	6.00	0	190	6	31.66	0
Savile, G *	Apr 26, 1847	Sept 4, 1904	1867	1874	5	5	1	140	65	20.00	0				2
Sayers, J J	Nov 5, 1983		2004	2013	97	161	13	4,855	187	32.80	9	166	6	27.66	60
Schofield, C J	Mar 21, 1976		1996	1996	1			25	25	25.00	0				0
Schofield, D	Oct 9, 1947		1970	1974	3	4	4	13	6*		0	112	5	22.40	0
Scott, E	July 6, 1834	Dec 3, 1898	1864	1864	1	1	0	8	8	8.00	0	27	2	13.50	1
Sedgwick, H A	Apr 8, 1883	Dec 28, 1957	1906	1906	3	5	2	53	34	17.66	0	327	16	20.43	2
Sellers, Arthur *	May 31, 1870	Sept 25, 1941	1890	1899	49	88	1	1,643	105	18.88	2	84	2	42.00	40
Sellers, A B * ......Ⓒ	Mar 5, 1907	Feb 20, 1981	1932	1948	334	437	51	8,949	204	23.18	4	653	8	81.62	264
Shackleton, W A	Mar 9, 1908	Nov 16, 1971	1928	1934	5	6	0	49	25	8.16	0	130	6	21.66	3
Shahzad, Ajmal ....Ⓒ	July 27, 1985		2006	2012	45	58	14	1,145	88	26.02	0	4,196	125	33.56	5
Sharp, K ....Ⓒ	Apr 6, 1959		1976	1990	195	320	35	8,426	181	29.56	11	836	12	69.66	95
§ Sharp, C M *	Sept 6, 1851	June 25, 1935	1875	1875	1	1	0	15	15	15.00	0	17			0
Sharpe, P J ....Ⓒ	Dec 27, 1936	May 19, 2014	1958	1974	411	666	71	17,685	203*	29.72	23	140	2	70.00	526
Shaw C	Feb 17, 1964		1984	1988	61	58	27	340	31	10.96	0	4,101	123	33.34	9

LIST OF PLAYERS AND CAREER AVERAGES IN ALL FIRST-CLASS MATCHES FOR YORKSHIRE (Continued)

Player	Date of Birth	Date of Death (if known)	First Played	Last Played	M	Inns	NO	Runs	HS	Av'ge	100s	Runs	Wkts	Av'ge	Ct/St
Shaw, James	Mar 12, 1865	Jan 22, 1921	1896	1897	3	3	0	8	8	2.66	0	181	7	25.85	2
Shaw, Joshua	**Jan 3, 1996**		**2016**	**2018**	**7**	**10**	**2**	**138**	**42**	**17.25**	**0**	**593**	**12**	**49.41**	**1**
Sheepshanks, E R *	Mar 22, 1910	Dec 31, 1937	1929	1929	1	1	0	26	26	26.00	0	—	—	—	0
Shepherd, D A *	Mar 10, 1916	May 29, 1998	1938	1938	1	1	0	0	0	0.00	0	—	—	—	0
Shotton, W	Dec 1, 1840	May 26, 1909	1865	1874	2	4	0	13	7	3.25	0	—	—	—	0
Sidebottom, A	Apr 1, 1954		1973	1991	216	249	50	4,243	124	22.33	1	13,852	558	24.82	60
Sidebottom, R J	Jan 15, 1978		1997	2017	137	172	55	1,674	61	14.30	0	10,128	450	22.50	37
Sidgwick, R *	Aug 7, 1851		1882	1882	9	13	0	64	17	4.92	0	—	—	—	7
Silverwood, C E W ⊚	Mar 5, 1975		1993	2005	131	179	33	2,369	80	16.22	0	11,413	427	27.62	30
Silvester, S	Mar 12, 1951		1976	1977	6	7	4	30	14	10.00	0	313	12	26.08	2
Simpson, E T B *	Mar 5, 1867		1889	1889	1	2	1	1	1	0.50	0	—	—	—	2
§ Sims, Rev H M *	Mar 15, 1853	Oct 5, 1885	1875	1877	5	10	1	109	35*	12.11	0	—	—	—	5
Slinn, W	Dec 13, 1826	June 19, 1888	1863	1864	9	14	3	22	11	2.00	0	742	48	15.45	5
Smailes, T F	Mar 27, 1910	Mar 10, 2015	1932	1948	262	339	42	5,686	117	19.14	3	16,593	802	20.68	153
Smales, K ⊚	Sept 15, 1927		1948	1950	13	19	3	165	45	10.31	0	766	22	34.81	4
Smith, A F	Mar 7, 1847	Jan 6, 1915	1868	1874	28	49	4	692	89	15.37	0	—	—	—	11
Smith, E (Morley) * ⊚	Oct 19, 1869	April 9, 1945	1888	1907	154	234	18	4,453	129	20.61	2	6,278	248	25.31	112
Smith, E (Barnsley)	July 11, 1888	Jan 2, 1972	1914	1926	16	21	5	169	49	10.56	0	1,090	46	23.69	5
Smith, Fred (Yeadon)	Dec 18, 1879	Oct 20, 1905	1903	1903	13	19	1	292	55	16.22	0	—	—	—	3
Smith, Fred (Idle)	Dec 26, 1885	Not known	1911	1911	1	1	0	11	11	11.00	0	45	2	22.50	0
Smith, G	Jan 19, 1875	Jan 16, 1929	1901	1906	2	1	0	7	7	7.00	0	62	2		0
Smith, J	Mar 23, 1833	Feb 12, 1909	1865	1865	2	3	0	28	16	9.33	0	72	6	12.00	3
Smith, N	Apr 1, 1949	Mar 4, 2003	1970	1971	8	11	5	82	20	13.66	0	—	—	—	14/3
Smith, R	Apr 6, 1942		1969	1970	5	8	3	99	37*	19.80	0	—	—	—	0
Smith, Walter	Aug 19, 1845	June 2, 1926	1874	1874	5	9	0	152	59	16.88	0	—	—	—	3
§ Smith, William	Nov 1, 1839	Apr 19, 1897	1865	1874	11	19	3	260	90	16.25	0	84	1	84.00	8
Smithson, G A ⊚	Nov 1, 1926	Sept 6, 1970	1946	1950	39	60	5	1,449	169	26.34	2	237	12	19.75	21
Smurthwaite, J	Oct 17, 1916	Oct 20, 1989	1938	1939	7	9	5	29	20*	7.25	0	—	—	—	4
Sowden, A	Dec 1, 1853	July 5, 1921	1878	1887	8	11	0	137	37	12.45	0	22	0	—	1
Squire, D	Dec 31, 1864	Apr 28, 1922	1893	1893	1	2	0	0	0	0.00	0	25	0	—	0

Player	Date of Birth	Date of Death (if known)	First Played	Last Played	M	Inns	NO	Runs	HS	Av'ge	100s	Runs	Wkts	Av'ge	Ct/St
Squires, P J	Aug 4, 1951		1972	1976	49	84	8	1,271	70	16.72	0	32	0	—	14
Stanley, H C *	Feb 16, 1888	May 18, 1934	1911	1913	8	13	0	155	42	11.92	0				6
§ Stanyforth, R T *	May 30, 1892	Feb 20, 1964	1928	1928	3	3	0	26	10	8.66	0				2
Starc, M A	Jan 30, 1990		2012	2012	2	1	1	28	28*	—	0	153	7	21.85	2
Stead, B	June 21, 1939	Apr 15, 1980	1959	1959	2	3	0	8	8	2.66	0	115	7	16.42	0
§ Stemp, R D	© Dec 11, 1967		1993	1998	104	135	36	1,267	65	12.79	0	8,557	241	35.50	49
Stephenson, E	June 5, 1832	July 5, 1898	1863	1873	36	61	5	803	60	14.33	0				30/27
Stephenson, J S *	Nov 10, 1903	Oct 7, 1975	1923	1926	16	19	2	182	60	10.70	0	65	0	—	6
Stevenson, G B	© Dec 16, 1955	Jan 21, 2014	1973	1986	177	217	32	3,856	115*	20.84	2	13,254	464	28.56	73
Stott, W B	© July 18, 1934		1952	1963	187	329	19	9,168	186	31.61	17	112	7	16.00	91
Stringer, P M	Feb 23, 1943		1967	1969	19	17	8	101	15*	11.22	0	696	32	21.75	7
Stuchbury, S	June 22, 1954		1978	1981	3	3	2	7	4*	7.00	0	236	8	29.50	0
§ Sugg, F H	Jan 11, 1862	May 29, 1933	1883	1883	8	12	4	80	13*	10.00	0				4/1
§ Sugg, W	May 21, 1860	May 21, 1933	1881	1881	1	2	0	9	9	9.00	0	43	0	—	0
Sullivan, J H B *	Sept 21, 1890	Feb 8, 1932	1912	1912	1	2	0	41	26	20.50	0	9	0	—	0
Sutcliffe, H	© Nov 24, 1894	Jan 22, 1978	1919	1945	602	864	96	38,558	313	50.20	112	381	8	47.62	402
Sutcliffe, W H H *	Oct 10, 1926	Sept 16, 1998	1948	1957	177	273	34	6,247	181	26.13	6	152	6	25.33	80
Swallow, I G	Dec 18, 1962		1983	1989	61	82	18	1,296	114	20.25	1	3,270	64	51.09	28
§ Swanepoel, P J	Mar 30, 1977		2003	2003	2	3	0	20	17	6.66	0	129	3	43.00	1
§ Tait, T	Oct 7, 1872	Sept 6, 1954	1898	1899	2	3	1	7	3	3.50	0				1
Tasker, J *	© Feb 4, 1887	Aug 24, 1975	1912	1913	31	43	4	586	67	15.02	0				14
Tattersall, G *	Apr 21, 1882	June 29, 1972	1905	1905	1	2	0	26	26	13.00	0				0
Tattersall, J A	**Dec 15, 1994**		**2018**	**2018**	**7**	**12**	**1**	**350**	**70**	**31.81**	**0**				**19**
Taylor, C R	Feb 21, 1981		2001	2008	16	27	3	416	52*	17.33	0				8
Taylor, H	Dec 18, 1900	Oct 28, 1988	1924	1925	9	13	0	153	36	11.76	0				1
Taylor, H S	Dec 11, 1856	Nov 16, 1896	1879	1879	3	5	0	36	22	7.20	0				0
Taylor, J	Apr 2, 1850	May 27, 1924	1880	1881	9	13	1	107	44	8.91	0				4
Taylor, K	© Aug 21, 1935		1953	1968	303	505	35	12,864	203*	27.37	16	3,680	129	28.52	146
Taylor, N S	June 2, 1963		1982	1983	8	6	1	10	10	2.00	0	720	22	32.72	2

LIST OF PLAYERS AND CAREER AVERAGES IN ALL FIRST-CLASS MATCHES FOR YORKSHIRE (Continued)

Player	Date of Birth	Date of Death (if known)	First Played	Last Played	M	Inns	NO	Runs	HS	Av'ge	100s	Runs	Wkts	Av'ge	Ct/St
Taylor, T L *	© May 25, 1878	Mar. 16, 1960	1899	1906	82	122	10	3,933	156	35.11	8	—	—	—	47/2
§ Tendulkar, S R	© Apr 24, 1973		1992	1992	16	25	2	1,070	100	46.52	1	195	4	48.75	10
Thewlis, H	Aug 31, 1865	Nov 30, 1920	1888	1888	2	4	1	4	2*	1.33	0	—	—	—	2
Thewlis, John Sen.	Mar 11, 1828	Dec 29, 1899	1863	1875	44	80	3	1,280	108	16.62	1	—	—	—	21/1
Thewlis, John Jun.	Sept 21, 1850	Aug 9, 1901	1879	1879	3	4	0	21	10	5.25	0	—	—	—	0
Thornicroft, N D	Jan 23, 1985		2002	2007	7	10	4	50	30	8.33	0	545	16	34.06	2
Thornton, A	July 20, 1854	Apr 18, 1915	1881	1881	3	4	0	21	7	5.25	0	—	—	—	2
Thornton, G *	Dec 24, 1867	Jan 31, 1939	1891	1891	3	4	0	21	16	5.25	0	74	2	37.00	2
Thorpe, G	Feb 20, 1834	Mar 2, 1899	1864	1864	1	2	1	14	9*	14.00	0	—	—	—	0
Threapleton, J W	July 20, 1857	July 30, 1918	1881	1881	1	1	1	8	8*	—	0	—	—	—	2/1
Tinsley, H J	Feb 20, 1865	Dec 10, 1938	1890	1891	9	13	0	56	15	4.30	0	57	4	14.25	1
Townsley, R A J	June 24, 1952		1974	1975	2	4	0	22	12	5.50	0	0	0	—	1
Towse, A D	Apr 22, 1968		1988	1988	1	1	0	1	1	1.00	0	50	3	16.66	1
Trueman, F S	© Feb 6, 1931	July 1, 2006	1949	1968	459	533	81	6,852	104	15.15	2	29,890	1,745	17.12	325
Tunnicliffe, J	© Aug 26, 1866	July 1, 1948	1891	1907	472	768	57	19,435	243	27.33	22	388	7	55.42	665
Turner, A	Sept 2, 1885	Aug 29, 1951	1910	1911	9	16	1	163	37	10.86	0	—	—	—	7
Turner, B	Sept 25, 1938	Dec 27, 2015	1960	1961	2	4	2	7	3*	3.50	0	47	4	11.75	2
Turner, C	Jan 11, 1902	Nov 19, 1968	1925	1946	200	266	32	6,132	130	26.20	2	5,320	173	30.75	181
Turner, F I	Sept 3, 1894	Oct 18, 1954	1924	1924	5	7	0	33	12	4.71	0	—	—	—	2
Tyson, C T	Jan 24, 1889	Apr 3, 1940	1921	1921	3	5	2	232	100*	77.33	1	—	—	—	1
Ullathorne, C E	Apr 11, 1845	May 2, 1904	1868	1875	27	46	8	283	28	7.44	0	—	—	—	19
Ullyett, G	© Oct 21, 1851	June 18, 1898	1873	1893	355	618	31	14,157	199*	24.11	15	8,181	457	17.90	235
§ Usher, J	Feb 26, 1859	Dec 10, 1938	1888	1888	2	2	0	7	5	3.50	0	31	2	15.50	1
van Geloven, J	Jan 4, 1934	Aug 21, 2003	1955	1955	3	2	1	17	16	17.00	0	224	6	37.33	2
§ Vaughan, M P	© Oct 29, 1974		1993	2009	151	267	14	9,160	183	36.20	20	4,268	92	46.39	55
§ Verelst, H W *	July 2, 1846	Apr 5, 1918	1868	1869	3	4	1	66	33*	22.00	0	—	—	—	2
Verity, H	© May 18, 1905	July 31, 1943	1930	1939	278	294	77	3,898	101	17.96	1	21,353	1,558	13.70	191
Waddington, A	© Feb 4, 1893	Oct 28, 1959	1919	1927	255	250	65	2,396	114	12.95	1	16,203	835	19.40	222

LIST OF PLAYERS AND CAREER AVERAGES IN ALL FIRST-CLASS MATCHES FOR YORKSHIRE (Continued)

Player	Date of Birth	Date of Death (if known)	First Played	Last Played	M	Inns	NO	Runs	HS	Av'ge	100s	Runs	Wkts	Av'ge	Ct/St
Wade, S ©	Feb 8, 1858	Nov 5, 1931	1886	1890	65	11	20	1,438	74*	15.80	0	2,498	133	18.78	31
Wainwright, D J ©	Mar 21, 1985		2004	2011	29	36	11	914	104*	36.56	2	2,480	69	35.94	6
Wainwright, E ©	Apr 8, 1865	Oct 28, 1919	1888	1902	352	545	30	11,092	228	21.53	18	17,744	998	17.77	327
Wainwright, W	Jan 21, 1882	Dec 31, 1961	1903	1905	24	36	3	648	62	19.63	0	582	19	30.63	21
Waite, M J §	Dec 24, 1995		2017	2018	5	8	0	118	42	14.75	0	291	11	26.45	0
Wake, W R *	May 21, 1852	Mar 14, 1896	1881	1881	3	3	0	13	11	4.33	0				2
Walker, A *	June 22, 1844	May 26, 1927	1863	1870	9	16	1	138	26	9.20	0	74	1	74.00	3
Walker, C	June 27, 1919	Dec 3, 1992	1947	1948	5	9	2	268	91	38.28	0	71	2	35.50	1
Walker, T	Apr 3, 1854	Aug 28, 1925	1879	1880	14	22	2	179	30	8.95	0	7			3
Waller, G	Dec 3, 1864	Dec 11, 1937	1893	1894	3	4	0	17	13	4.25	0	70	4	17.50	1
Wallgate, L *	Nov 12, 1849	May 9, 1887	1875	1878	3	3	0	9	6	3.00	0	17	1	17.00	3
Ward, A	Nov 21, 1865	Jan 6, 1939	1886	1886	4	7	1	41	22	6.83	0	1	0	—	1
Ward, F	Aug 31, 1881	Feb 28, 1948	1903	1903	1	1	1	0	0*	0.00	0	16	0	—	0
Ward, H P *	Jan 20, 1899	Dec 16, 1946	1920	1920	1	1	0	10	10*		0				1
Wardall, T A ©	Apr 19, 1862	Dec 20, 1932	1884	1894	43	73	2	1,003	106	14.12	2	489	23	21.26	25
Wardlaw, I	Jun 29, 1985		2011	2012	4	3	2	31	31*	31.00	0	368	4	92.00	2
Wardle, J H ©	Jan 8, 1923	July 23, 1985	1946	1958	330	418	57	5,765	79	15.96	0	27,917	1,539	18.13	210
Waring, J S	Oct 1, 1942		1963	1966	28	27	15	137	9	11.41	0	1,122	53	21.16	17
Waring, S *	Nov 4, 1838	Apr 17, 1919	1870	1870	1	1	0	9	9	9.00	0				0
Washington, W A I ©	Dec 11, 1879	Oct 20, 1927	1900	1902	44	62	6	1,290	100*	23.03	1				18
Watson, H	Sept 26, 1880	Nov 24, 1951	1908	1914	29	35	11	141	41	5.87	0				46/10
Watson, W ©	Mar 7, 1920	Apr 24, 2004	1939	1957	283	430	65	13,953	214*	38.22	26	75	0	—	170
Waud, B W *	June 4, 1837	May 31, 1889	1863	1864	6	10	1	165	42	18.33	0				2
Webster, C	June 9, 1838	Jan 6, 1881	1868	1868	3	5	1	30	10	7.50	0				1
Webster, H H	May 8, 1844	Mar 5, 1915	1868	1868	2	3	0	10	10	3.33	0				0
§ Weekes, L C	July 19, 1971		1994	2000	2	2	0	20	10	10.00	0	191	10	19.10	1
West, J	Oct 16, 1844	Jan 27, 1890	1868	1876	38	64	13	461	41	9.03	0	853	53	16.09	14
Wharf, A G	June 4, 1975		1994	1997	7	9	1	186	62	23.25	0	454	11	41.27	2

Player	Date of Birth	Date of Death (if known)	First Played	Last Played	M	Inns	NO	Runs	HS	Av'ge	100s	Runs	Wkts	Av'ge	Ct/St
Whatmough, F J	Dec 4, 1856	June 3, 1904	1878	1882	7	11	1	51	20	5.10	0	111	5	22.20	4
Wheater, C H *	Mar 4, 1860	May 11, 1885	1880	1880	2	4	1	45	27	15.00	0	—	0	—	3
White, Sir A W *	Oct 14, 1877	Dec 16, 1945	1908	1920	97	128	28	1,457	55	14.57	0	7	0	—	50
White, C	Dec 16, 1969		1990	2007	221	350	45	10,376	186	34.01	19	7,649	276	27.71	140
Whitehead, J P	Sept 3, 1925	Aug 15, 2000	1946	1951	37	38	17	387	58*	18.42	0	2,610	96	27.47	11
Whitehead, Lees	Mar 14, 1864	Nov 22, 1913	1889	1904	119	172	38	2,073	67*	15.47	0	2,408	99	24.32	68
Whitehead, Luther	June 25, 1869	Jan 17, 1931	1893	1893	2	4	0	21	13	5.25	0				0
Whiteley, J P	Feb 28, 1955		1978	1982	45	38	17	231	20	11.00	0	2,410	70	34.42	21
Whiting, C P	Apr 18, 1888	Jan 14, 1959	1914	1920	6	10	2	92	26	11.50	0	416	15	27.73	2
Whitwell, J F *	Feb 22, 1869	Nov 6, 1932	1890	1890	10	14	12	8	4	4.00	0	11	1	11.00	2
§ Whitwell, W F *	Dec 12, 1867	Apr 12, 1942	1890	1890	11	18	6	67	26	5.58	0	518	25	20.72	2
Widdup, S	Nov 10, 1977		2000	2001	1	1	0	19	15	19.00	0	22	1	22.00	5
Wigley, D H	Oct 26, 1981		2002	2002	1	1	0	9	9	9.00	0	116	1	116.00	
§ Wilkinson, A J A *	May 28, 1835	Dec 11, 1905	1865	1868	5	6	0	129	53	21.50	0	57	0	—	1
Wilkinson, F	May 23, 1914	Mar 26, 1984	1937	1939	14	14	1	73	18*	5.61	0	590	26	22.69	12
Wilkinson, H *	Dec 11, 1877	Apr 15, 1967	1903	1905	48	75	3	1,382	113	19.19	1	121	3	40.33	19
Wilkinson, R.	Nov 11, 1977		1998	1998	1	1	0	9	9	9.00	0	35	1	35.00	0
§ Wilkinson, W H	Mar 12, 1881	June 4, 1961	1903	1910	126	192	14	3,812	104	21.41	1	971	31	31.32	93
§ Willey D J	**Feb 28, 1990**		**2016**	**2018**	**8**	**11**	**1**	**127**	**34***	**12.70**	**0**	**699**	**19**	**36.78**	**0**
Williams, A C	Mar 1, 1887	June 1, 1966	1911	1919	12	14	10	95	48*	23.75	0	678	30	22.60	6
§ Williamson, K S	Aug 8, 1990		2013	2018	19	32	3	1,292	189	44.55	4	475	11	43.18	20
Wilson, B B	Dec 11, 1879	Sept 14, 1957	1906	1914	185	308	15	8,053	208	27.50	15	278	2	139.00	53
Wilson, C E M *	May 15, 1875	Feb 8, 1944	1896	1899	9	13	3	256	91*	25.60	0	257	12	21.41	3
Wilson, D	Aug 7, 1937	July 21, 2012	1957	1974	392	502	85	5,788	83	13.88	0	22,626	1,104	20.49	235
Wilson, E R *	Mar 25, 1879	July 21, 1957	1899	1923	66	72	18	902	104	16.70	1	3,106	197	15.76	30
Wilson, Geoffrey *	Aug 21, 1895	Nov 29, 1960	1919	1924	92	94	14	983	70	12.28	0	11	0	—	33
Wilson, G A *	Feb 2, 1916	Sept 24, 2002	1936	1939	15	25	5	352	55*	17.60	0	138	1	138.00	7
Wilson, John *	June 30, 1857	Nov 11, 1931	1887	1888	4	5	1	17	13*	4.25	0	165	12	13.75	3

LIST OF PLAYERS AND CAREER AVERAGES IN ALL FIRST-CLASS MATCHES FOR YORKSHIRE (Continued)

Player	Date of Birth	Date of Death (if known)	First Played	Last Played	M	Inns	NO	Runs	HS	Av'ge	100s	Runs	Wkts	Av'ge	Ct/St
Wilson, J P *	Apr 3, 1889	Oct 3, 1959	1911	1912	9	14	1	81	36	6.23	0	24	1	24.00	2
Wilson, J V	Jan 17, 1921 ©	June 5, 2008	1946	1962	477	724	75	20,548	230	31.66	29	313	3	104.33	520
Wood, A	Aug 25, 1898 ©	Apr 1, 1973	1927	1946	408	481	80	8,579	123*	21.39	1	33	1	33.00	612/243
Wood, B	Dec 26, 1942		1964	1964	5	7	2	63	35	12.60	0				4
Wood, C H	July 23, 1934	June 28, 2006	1959	1959	4	4	1	22	10	7.33	0	319	11	29.00	1
Wood, G W	Nov 18, 1862	Dec 4, 1948	1895	1895	2	2	0	2	2	1.00	0				0/1
Wood, H *	Mar 22, 1855	July 31, 1941	1879	1880	10	16	1	156	36	10.40	0	212	10	21.20	8
Wood, J H *			1881	1881	2	1	0	14	14	14.00	0				0
Wood, M J	Apr 6, 1977 ©		1997	2007	128	222	20	6,742	207	33.37	16	27	2	13.50	113
Wood, R	June 3, 1929	May 22, 1990	1952	1956	22	18	4	60	17	4.28	0	1,346	51	26.39	5
Woodford, J D	Sept 9, 1943		1968	1972	38	61	2	1,204	101	20.40	1	185	4	46.25	12
Woodhead, F E *	May 29, 1868	Aug 25, 1943	1893	1894	4	8	0	57	18	7.12	0				3
Woodhouse, W H *	Apr 16, 1856	Mar 4, 1938	1884	1885	9	13	0	218	63	16.76	0				6
Wormald, A	May 10, 1855	Feb 6, 1940	1885	1891	7	11	3	161	80	20.12	0				10/2
Worsley, W A *	Apr 5, 1890 ©	Dec 4, 1973	1928	1929	60	50	4	722	60	15.69	0				32
Wrathmell, L F	Jan 22, 1855	Sept 16, 1928	1886	1886	1	2	0	18	17	9.00	0				0
Wright, R	July 19, 1852	Jan 2, 1891	1877	1877	2	4	1	28	22	9.33	0				0
Wright, T J *	Mar 5, 1900	Nov 7, 1962	1919	1919	1	1	0	12	12	12.00	0				0
Yardley, N W D *	Mar 19, 1915 ©	Oct 3, 1989	1936	1955	302	420	56	11,632	183*	31.95	17	5,818	195	29.83	220
Yeadon, J	Dec 10, 1861	May 30, 1914	1888	1888	3	6	2	41	22	10.25	0				5/3
§ Younus Khan	Nov 29, 1977 ©		2007	2007	13	19	2	824	217*	48.47	3	342	8	42.75	11
§ Yuvraj Singh	Dec 12, 1981		2003	2003	7	12	2	145	56	14.50	0	130	3	43.33	12

358

In the career averages it should be noted that the bowling analysis for the second Cambridgeshire innings at Ashton-under-Lyne in 1865 has not been found. G R Atkinson took 3 wickets, W Cuttell 2, G Freeman 4 and R Iddison 1. The respective bowling averages have been calculated excluding these wickets.

MOST FIRST-CLASS APPEARANCES FOR YORKSHIRE

Matches	Player	Matches	Player
883	W Rhodes (1898-1930)	477	J V Wilson (1946-1962)
717	G H Hirst (1891-1929)	472	J Tunnicliffe (1891-1907)
676	D Denton (1894-1920)	459	F S Trueman (1949-1968)
602	H Sutcliffe (1919-1945)	456	J H Hampshire (1961-1981)
548	M Leyland (1920-1947)	445	G G Macaulay (1920-1935)
536	D B Close (1949-1970)	429	D L Bairstow (1970-1990)
517	D Hunter (1888-1909)	427	A Dolphin (1905-1927)
513	S Haigh (1895-1913)	425	P Carrick (1970-1993)
510	Lord Hawke (1881-1911)	414	G Boycott (1962-1986)
496	R Illingworth (1951-1983)	413	E. Robinson (1919-1931)
491	† J G Binks (1955-1969)	411	P J Sharpe (1958-1974)
487	D E V Padgett (1951-1971)	408	A Wood (1927-1946)
485	P Holmes (1913-1933)	401	A Mitchell (1922-1945)

† Kept wicket in 412 consecutive Championship matches 1955-1969

MOST TOTAL APPEARANCES FOR YORKSHIRE
(First-Class, Domestic List A and t20)

Matches	Player	Matches	Player
883	W Rhodes (1898-1930)	513	S Haigh (1895-1913)
832	D L Bairstow (1970-1990)	510	Lord Hawke (1881-1911)
729	P Carrick (1970-1993)	502	P J Sharpe (1958-1974)
719	R J Blakey (1985-2004)	485	P Holmes (1913-1933)
717	G H Hirst (1891-1929)	477	J V Wilson (1946-1962)
690	J H Hampshire (1961-1981)	472	J Tunnicliffe (1891-1907)
678	G Boycott (1962-1986)	470	F S Trueman (1949-1968)
676	D Denton (1894-1920)	467	J D Love (1975-1989)
602	H Sutcliffe (1919-1945)	453	D Wilson (1957-1974)
583	A McGrath (1995-2012)	452	A Sidebottom (1973-1991)
581	D Byas (1986-2001)	445	G G Macaulay (1920-1935)
568	D B Close (1949-1970)	443	C M Old (1966-1982)
548	M Leyland (1920-1947)	427	A Dolphin (1905-1927)
546	C White (1990-2007)	414	P J Hartley (1985-1997)
544	D E V Padgett (1951-1971)	413	E Robinson (1919-1931)
537	R Illingworth (1951-1983)	408	A Wood (1927-1946)
521	J G Binks (1955-1969)	402	A G Nicholson (1962-1975)
517	D Hunter (1888-1909)	401	A Mitchell (1922-1945)
514	M D Moxon (1980-1997)		

ONE DAY RECORDS SECTION

Yorkshire County Cricket Club thanks Statistician JOHN T. POTTER, who in 2014 revamped and streamlined Yorkshire's One-Day Records Section. John's symbols in the pages that follow are:

$ = Sunday and National Leagues, Pro 40, Clydesdale Bank 40 and Yorkshire Bank 40

\# = Benson & Hedges Cup

\+ = Gillette Cup, NatWest Trophy, Cheltenham & Gloucester Trophy, Friends Provident Trophy and Royal London Cup

LIST A
WINNERS OF THE GILLETTE CUP, NATWEST TROPHY, CHELTENHAM & GLOUCESTER TROPHY FRIENDS PROVIDENT TROPHY AND ROYAL LONDON ONE-DAY CUP

		Yorkshire's Position
GILLETTE CUP		
1963	Sussex	Quarter-Final
1964	Sussex	Round 2
1965	**Yorkshire**	**Winner**
1966	Warwickshire	Round 2
1967	Kent	Quarter-Final
1968	Warwickshire	Round 2
1969	**Yorkshire**	**Winner**
1970	Lancashire	Round 1
1971	Lancashire	Round 2
1972	Lancashire	Round 1
1973	Gloucestershire	Round 1
1974	Kent	Quarter-Final
1975	Lancashire	Round 2
1976	Northamptonshire	Round 1
1977	Middlesex	Round 2
1978	Sussex	Quarter-Final
1979	Somerset	Quarter-Final
1980	Middlesex	Semi-Final
NATWEST TROPHY		
1981	Derbyshire	Round 1
1982	Surrey	Semi-Final
1983	Somerset	Round 2
1984	Middlesex	Round 1
1985	Essex	Round 2
1986	Sussex	Quarter-Final
1987	Nottinghamshire	Quarter-Final
1988	Middlesex	Round 2
1989	Warwickshire	Round 2
1990	Lancashire	Quarter-Final

		Yorkshire's Position
1991	Hampshire	Round 1
1992	Northamptonshire	Round 2
1993	Warwickshire	Quarter-Final
1994	Worcestershire	Round 2
1995	Warwickshire	Semi-Final
1996	Lancashire	Semi-Final
1997	Essex	Quarter-Final
1998	Lancashire	Round 2
1999	Gloucestershire	Semi-Final
2000	Gloucestershire	Round 4
CHELTENHAM & GLOUCESTER TROPHY		
2001	Somerset	Quarter-Final
2002	**Yorkshire**	**Winner**
2003	Gloucestershire	Round 4
2004	Gloucestershire	Semi-Final
2005	Hampshire	Semi-Final
2006	Sussex	North 7 (10)
FRIENDS PROVIDENT TROPHY		
2007	Durham	North 5 (10)
2008	Essex	Semi-Final
2009	Hampshire	Group C 3 (5)
ROYAL LONDON ONE-DAY CUP		
2014	Durham	Quarter-Final
2015	Gloucestershire	Semi-Final
2016	Warwickshire	Semi-Final
2017	Nottinghamshire	Quarter-Final
2018	Hampshire	Semi-Final

WINNERS OF THE NATIONAL AND SUNDAY LEAGUES, PRO 40, CLYDESDALE BANK 40 AND YORKSHIRE BANK 40 1969-2014

		Yorkshire's Position			Yorkshire's Position
	SUNDAY LEAGUE		1993	Glamorgan	9th
1969	Lancashire	8th	1994	Warwickshire	5th
1970	Lancashire	14th	1995	Kent	12th
1971	Worcestershire	15th	1996	Surrey	3rd
1972	Kent	4th	1997	Warwickshire	10th
1973	Kent	2nd	1998	Lancashire	9th
1974	Leicestershire	=6th		**NATIONAL LEAGUE**	
1975	Hampshire	=5th	1999	Lancashire	5th Div 1
1976	Kent	15th	2000	Gloucestershire	2nd Div 1
1977	Leicestershire	=13th	2001	Kent	6th Div 1
1978	Hampshire	7th	2002	Glamorgan	4th Div 1
1979	Somerset	=4th	2003	Surrey	8th Div 1
1980	Warwickshire	=14th	2004	Glamorgan	4th Div 2
1981	Essex	=7th	2005	Essex	8th Div 2
1982	Sussex	16th	2006	Essex	9th Div 2
1983	**Yorkshire**	**1st**	2007	Worcestershire	6th Div 2
1984	Essex	=14th	2008	Sussex	2nd Div 2
1985	Essex	6th	2009	Sussex	7th Div 1
1986	Hampshire	8th		**CLYDESDALE BANK 40**	
1987	Worcestershire	=13th	2010	Warwickshire	Group B 1 (7) (Semi-Final)
1988	Worcestershire	8th			
1989	Lancashire	11th	2011	Surrey	Group A 6 (7)
1990	Derbyshire	6th	2012	Hampshire	Group C 5 (7)
1991	Nottinghamshire	7th	2013	Nottinghamshire	Group C 6 (7)
1992	Middlesex	15th			

BENSON & HEDGES WINNERS 1972-2002

		Yorkshire's Position			Yorkshire's Position
1972	Leicestershire	Final	1988	Hampshire	Group B 4 (5)
1973	Kent	Group N 3 (5)	1989	Nottinghamshire	Group C 3 (5)
1974	Surrey	Quarter-Final	1990	Lancashire	Group C 3 (5)
1975	Leicestershire	Quarter-Final	1991	Worcestershire	Semi-Final
1976	Kent	Group D 3 (5)	1992	Hampshire	Group C 5 (5)
1977	Gloucestershire	Group D 3 (5)	1993	Derbyshire	Round One
1978	Kent	Group D 4 (5)	1994	Warwickshire	Round One
1979	Essex	Semi-Final	1995	Lancashire	Quarter-Final
1980	Northamptonshire	Group B 4 (5)	1996	Lancashire	Semi-Final
1981	Somerset	Quarter-Final	1997	Surrey	Quarter-Final
1982	Somerset	Group A 5 (5)	1998	Essex	Semi-Final
1983	Middlesex	Group B 5 (5)	1999	Gloucestershire	Final
1984	Lancashire	Semi-Final	2000	Gloucestershire	Quarter-Final
1985	Leicestershire	Group B 3 (5)	2001	Surrey	Semi-Final
1986	Middlesex	Group B 3 (5)	2002	Warwickshire	Quarter-Final
1987	**Yorkshire**	**Winner**			

SEASON-BY-SEASON RECORD OF ALL LIST A MATCHES PLAYED BY YORKSHIRE 1963-2018

Season	Played	Won	Lost	Tie	N R	Abd	Season	Played	Won	Lost	Tie	N R	Abd
1963	2	1	1	0	0	0	1992	21	8	13	0	0	2
1964	1	0	1	0	0	0	1993	21	10	10	0	1	0
1965	4	4	0	0	0	1	1994	19	11	8	0	0	1
1966	1	0	1	0	0	0	1995	27	15	11	0	1	1
1967	2	1	1	0	0	0	1996	27	18	9	0	0	0
1968	1	0	1	0	0	0	1997	25	14	10	1	0	1
1969	19	12	7	0	0	2	1998	25	14	10	0	1	0
1970	17	5	10	0	2	0	1999	23	13	10	0	0	0
1971	15	5	10	0	0	2	2000	24	13	10	0	1	0
1972	25	15	8	0	2	1	2001	26	13	13	0	0	0
1973	21	14	7	0	0	0	2002	27	16	11	0	0	1
1974	22	12	9	0	1	1	2003	18	6	12	0	0	0
1975	22	12	10	0	0	0	2004	23	13	8	0	2	0
1976	22	9	13	0	0	0	2005	22	8	14	0	0	0
1977	19	5	10	0	4	2	2006	15	4	10	0	1	2
1978	22	10	11	0	1	2	2007	17	8	7	0	2	1
1979	21	12	6	0	3	3	2008	18	10	4	1	3	0
1980	23	9	14	0	0	0	2009	16	6	9	0	1	0
1981	19	9	8	0	2	3	2010	13	10	3	0	0	0
1982	23	7	14	1	1	1	2011	12	5	7	0	0	0
1983	19	11	7	0	1	3	2012	11	4	7	0	0	1
1984	23	10	13	0	0	0	2013	13	4	9	0	0	0
1985	19	9	9	0	1	3	2014	10	6	4	0	0	0
1986	22	11	9	1	1	1	2015	10	5	3	0	2	0
1987	24	14	9	0	1	2	2016	10	5	4	0	1	0
1988	21	9	9	0	3	1	2017	10	6	3	0	1	0
1989	23	10	13	0	0	0	2018	9	6	3	0	0	1
1990	22	13	9	0	0	1							
1991	24	13	10	0	1	0		990	493	452	4	41	40

Abandoned matches are not included in the list of matches played.

ABANDONED LIST A MATCHES (40)

1965	v. South Africa at Bradford $
1969 (2)	v. Warwickshire at Harrogate $
	v. Lancashire at Manchester $
1971 (2)	v. Gloucestershire at Sheffield $
	v. Somerset at Weston-Super-Mare $
1972	v. Sussex at Leeds $
1974	v. Warwickshire at Leeds $
1977 (2)	v. Warwickshire at Birmingham $
	v. Surrey at Leeds $
1978 (2)	v. Essex at Bradford $
	v. Gloucestershire at Hull $
1979 (3)	v. Leicestershire at Middlesbrough $
	v. Kent at Huddersfield $
	v. Worcestershire at Worcester $
1981 (3)	v. Warwickshire at Birmingham $
	v. Lancashire at Leeds #
	v. Sussex at Hove $
1982	v. Glamorgan at Bradford $
1983 (3)	v. Derbyshire at Chesterfield #
	v. Surrey at Leeds $
	v. Essex at Chelmsford $

1985 (3)	v. Derbyshire at Scarborough $
	v. Warwickshire at Birmingham $
	v. Lancashire at Leeds $
1986	v. Kent at Canterbury $
1987 (2)	v. Sussex at Hull $
	v. Hampshire at Leeds $
1988	v. Northamptonshire at Northampton $
1990	v. Glamorgan at Newport $
1992 (2)	v. Sussex at Hove $
	v. Durham at Darlington $
1994	v. Essex at Leeds $
1995	v. Derbyshire at Chesterfield #
1997	v. Sussex at Scarborough $
2002	v. Nottinghamshire at Nottingham $
2006 (2)	v. Nottinghamshire at Leeds +
	v. Derbyshire at Derby $
2007	v. Warwickshire at Birmingham +
2012	v. Northamptonshire at Leeds $
2018	v. Nottinghamshire at Leeds +

ANALYSIS OF LIST A RESULTS V. ALL TEAMS 1963-2018
DOMESTIC MATCHES

		HOME				AWAY				
Opponents	Played	Won	Lost	Tied	N. R	Won	Lost	Tied	N. R	Abd
Derbyshire	64	20	9	0	1	20	9	1	4	4
Durham	30	10	5	0	0	7	7	0	1	1
Essex	47	12	12	0	0	11	12	0	0	3
Glamorgan	39	9	8	0	0	9	13	0	0	2
Gloucestershire	55	12	12	0	2	8	19	0	2	2
Hampshire	45	11	9	0	1	9	15	0	0	1
Kent	55	13	11	0	1	10	20	0	0	2
Lancashire	63	10	16	0	2	15	18	0	2	3
Leicestershire	67	19	16	0	0	13	16	1	2	1
Middlesex	48	14	4	0	3	9	16	0	2	0
Northamptonshire	59	18	11	0	3	19	7	0	1	2
Nottinghamshire	59	19	8	1	2	10	16	0	3	3
Somerset	54	13	14	0	1	11	15	0	0	1
Surrey	56	12	15	0	0	11	18	0	0	2
Sussex	46	11	11	0	1	11	12	0	0	5
Warwickshire	62	11	18	1	2	13	17	0	0	6
Worcestershire	64	13	20	0	2	17	12	0	0	1
Bedfordshire	1	0	0	0	0	1	0	0	0	0
Berkshire	2	0	0	0	0	2	0	0	0	0
Cambridgeshire	3	2	0	0	0	1	0	0	0	0
Cheshire	1	0	0	0	0	1	0	0	0	0
Combined Universities	3	0	2	0	0	1	0	0	0	0
Devon	4	0	0	0	0	4	0	0	0	0
Dorset	1	0	0	0	0	1	0	0	0	0
Durham (M C)	3	1	1	0	0	1	0	0	0	0
Herefordshire	1	0	0	0	0	1	0	0	0	0
Ireland	4	3	0	0	0	1	0	0	0	0
Minor Counties	11	6	0	0	0	5	0	0	0	0
Netherlands	4	1	1	0	0	1	1	0	0	0
Norfolk	2	1	0	0	0	1	0	0	0	0
Northumberland	1	1	0	0	0	0	0	0	0	0
Scotland	16	8	0	0	0	8	0	0	0	0
Shropshire	2	0	0	0	0	1	1	0	0	0
Unicorns	4	2	0	0	0	2	0	0	0	0
Wiltshire	1	0	0	0	0	1	0	0	0	0
Yorkshire Cricket Board	1	0	0	0	0	1	0	0	0	0
Total	**978**	**252**	**203**	**2**	**21**	**237**	**244**	**2**	**17**	**39**

OTHER MATCHES

Australia	3	0	1	0	2	0	0	0	0	0
Bangladesh A	1	1	0	0	0	0	0	0	0	0
South Africa	0	0	0	0	0	0	0	0	0	1
South Africa A	1	0	0	0	1	0	0	0	0	0
Sri Lanka A	3	0	3	0	0	0	0	0	0	0
West Indies	1	1	0	0	0	0	0	0	0	0
West Indies A	1	0	1	0	0	0	0	0	0	0
Young Australia	1	1	0	0	0	0	0	0	9	0
Zimbabwe	1	1	0	0	0	0	0	0	0	0
Total	**12**	**4**	**5**	**0**	**3**	**0**	**0**	**0**	**0**	**1**
Grand Total	**990**	**256**	**208**	**2**	**24**	**237**	**244**	**2**	**17**	**40**

Abandoned matches are not included in the list of matches played.

LIST A HIGHEST AND LOWEST SCORES BY AND AGAINST YORKSHIRE
PLUS INDIVIDUAL BEST BATTING AND BOWLING

The lowest score is the lowest all-out total or the lowest score at completion of the allotted overs, 10-over matches not included

Yorkshire versus:

Derbyshire

		By Yorkshire		Against Yorkshire	
Highest Score:	In Yorkshire	349:7	at Leeds 2017 +	334:8	at Leeds 2017 +
	Away	288:6	at Derby 2002 #	268:8	at Chesterfield 2010 $
Lowest Score:	In Yorkshire	117	at Huddersfield 1978 $	87	at Scarborough 1973 $
	Away	132	at Chesterfield 1986 $	127	at Chesterfield 1972 #
Best Batting:	In Yorkshire	140	P S P Handscomb at Leeds 2017 +	112	W L Madsen at Leeds 2017 +
	Away	115*	M J Wood at Derby 2002 #	109*	C J Adams at Derby 1997 $
Best Bowling:	In Yorkshire	6-32	S A Patterson at Leeds 2010 $	4-20	F E Rumsey at Bradford 1973 +
	Away	5-35	C W J Athey at Chesterfield 1981 $	5-24	C J Tunnicliffe at Derby 1981 #

Durham

		By Yorkshire		Against Yorkshire	
Highest Score:	In Yorkshire	339:4	at Leeds 2017 +	335:5	at Leeds 2017 +
	Away	328:4	at Chester-le-Street 2018 +	281:7	at Chester-le-Street 2016 +
Lowest Score:	In Yorkshire	133	at Leeds 1995 $	121	at Scarborough 1997 $
	Away	122	at Chester-le-Street 2007 $	136	at Chester-le-Street 1996 $
Best Batting:	In Yorkshire	164	J M Bairstow at Leeds 2017 +	114	W Larkins at Leeds 1993 $
	Away	174	T Kohler-Cadmore at Chester-le-Street 2018 +	124*	J P Maher at Chester-le-Street 2006 +
Best Bowling:	In Yorkshire	4-18	C White at Scarborough 1997 $	4-20	S J E Brown at Leeds 1995 $
	Away	4-26	C E W Silverwood at Chester-le-Street 1996 $	4-31	P D Collingwood at Chester-le-Street 2000 #

Essex

		By Yorkshire		Against Yorkshire	
Highest Score:	In Yorkshire	290:6	at Scarborough 2014 +	291:5	at Scarborough 2014 +
	Away	307:3	at Chelmsford 1995 +	285:8	at Chelmsford 2008 +
Lowest Score:	In Yorkshire	54	at Leeds 2003 $	108	at Leeds 1996 $
	Away	119:8	at Colchester 1987 $	123	at Colchester 1974 $
Best Batting:	In Yorkshire	111*	J A Leaning at Scarborough 2014 +	119*	R N ten Doeschate at Scarborough 2014 +
	Away	125*	A W Gale at Chelmsford 2010 $	136*	N Hussain at Chelmsford 2002 #
Best Bowling:	In Yorkshire	4-20	G B Stevenson at Barnsley 1977 #	6-18	R E East at Hull 1969 $
	Away	4-31	A L Robinson at Leyton 1976 $	5-20	R E East at Colchester 1979 $

LIST A HIGHEST AND LOWEST SCORES BY AND AGAINST YORKSHIRE
PLUS INDIVIDUAL BEST BATTING AND BOWLING (Continued)

Yorkshire versus:

Glamorgan

		By Yorkshire		Against Yorkshire	
Highest Score:	In Yorkshire	253:4	at Leeds 1991 $	216:6	at Leeds 2013 $
	Away	257	at Colwyn Bay 2013 $	285:7	at Colwyn Bay 2013 $
Lowest Score:	In Yorkshire	139	at Hull 1981 $	83	at Leeds 1987 +
	Away	93-8	at Swansea 1985 $	90	at Neath 1969 $
Best Batting:	In Yorkshire	96 A A Metcalfe	at Leeds 1991 $	97* G P Ellis	at Leeds 1976 $
	Away	141* M D Moxon	at Cardiff 1991 #	127 A R Butcher	at Cardiff 1991 #
Best Bowling:	In Yorkshire	5-22 P Carrick	at Leeds 1991 $	5-26 D S Harrison	at Leeds 2002 $
	Away	6-40 R J Sidebottom	at Cardiff 1998 $	5-16 G C Holmes	at Swansea 1985 $

Gloucestershire

		By Yorkshire		Against Yorkshire	
Highest Score:	In Yorkshire	263:9	at Leeds 2015 +	269	at Leeds 2009 +
	Away	262:7	at Bristol 1996 $	294-6	at Cheltenham 2010 $
Lowest Score:	In Yorkshire	115	at Leeds 1973 $	91	at Scarborough 2001 $
	Away	133	at Cheltenham 1999 $	90	at Tewkesbury 1972 $
Best Batting:	In Yorkshire	118 J A Rudolph	at Leeds 2009 +	146* S Young	at Leeds 1997 $
	Away	100* J D Love	at Gloucester in 1985 $	143* C M Spearman	at Bristol 2004 $
		100* R J Blakey	at Cheltenham 1990 $		
Best Bowling:	In Yorkshire	5-42 N D Thornicroft	at Leeds 2003 $	5-33 M C J Ball	at Leeds 2003 $
	Away	4-25 R D Stemp	at Bristol 1996 $	5-42 M C J Ball	at Cheltenham 1999 $

Hampshire

		By Yorkshire		Against Yorkshire	
Highest Score:	In Yorkshire	259.4	at Middlesbrough 1985 $	257:6	at Middlesbrough 1985 $
	Away	264:2	at Southampton 1995 $	348:9	at West End, Southampton, 2018 +
Lowest Score:	In Yorkshire	74:9	at Hull 1970 $	50	at Leeds 1991 $
	Away	118	at Southampton 1990 +	133	at Bournemouth 1976 $
Best Batting:	In Yorkshire	104* D Byas	at Hull 1999 #	155* B A Richards	at Hull 1970 $
	Away	97* M G Bevan	at Southampton 1995 $	171 J M Vince	at West End, Southampton, 2018 +
Best Bowling:	In Yorkshire	5-16 G M Hamilton	at Leeds 1998 $	5-33 A J Murtagh	at Huddersfield 1977 $
	Away	5-33 A U Rashid	at Southampton 2014 +	5-31 D W White	at Southampton 1969 $

LIST A HIGHEST AND LOWEST SCORES BY AND AGAINST YORKSHIRE PLUS INDIVIDUAL BEST BATTING AND BOWLING (*Continued*)

Yorkshire versus:

Kent

		By Yorkshire			Against Yorkshire		
Highest Score:	In Yorkshire	299:3		at Leeds 2002 $	232:8		at Leeds 2011 $
	Away	263:3		at Maidstone 1998 $	266:5		at Maidstone 1998 $
Lowest Score:	In Yorkshire	75		at Leeds 1995 $	133		at Leeds 1974 $
					133		at Leeds 1979 #
Best Batting:	Away	114		at Canterbury 1978 #	105		at Canterbury 1969 $
	In Yorkshire	130*	R J Blakey	at Scarborough 1991 $	118*	M H Denness	at Scarborough 1976 $
	Away	102	A McGrath	at Canterbury 2001 $	118*	C J Tavare	at Canterbury 1981 +
Best Bowling:	In Yorkshire	4-15	A G Nicholson	at Canterbury 1974 $	6-32	M T Coles	at Canterbury 2012 $
	Away	6-18	D Wilson	at Canterbury 1969 $	5-25	B D Julien	at Canterbury 1971 +

Lancashire

		By Yorkshire			Against Yorkshire		
Highest Score:	In Yorkshire	296:9		at Leeds 2017 +	287:9		at Leeds 2006 +
	Away	379:7		at Manchester 2018 +	363		at Manchester 2018 +
Lowest Score:	In Yorkshire	81		at Leeds 1998 $	68		at Leeds 2000 $
	In Yorkshire	81		at Leeds 2002 #			
Best Batting:	Away	125		at Manchester 1973 #	84		at Manchester 2016 +
	In Yorkshire	111*	D Byas	at Leeds 1996 $	102*	N J Speak	at Leeds 1992 $
	Away	144	A Lyth	at Manchester 2018 +	141*	B J Hodge	at Manchester 2007 +
Best Bowling:	In Yorkshire	5-25	C White	at Manchester 2000 +	6-25	G Chapple	at Leeds 1998 $
	Away	4-18	G S Blewett	at Manchester 1999 +	5-49	M Watkinson	at Manchester 1991 #

Leicestershire

		By Yorkshire			Against Yorkshire		
Highest Score:	In Yorkshire	303:4		at Leeds 2008 $	302:7		at Leeds 2008 $
	Away	376:3		at Leicester 2016 +	298:9		at Leicester 1997 $
Lowest Score:	In Yorkshire	93		at Leeds 1998 $	141		at Hull 1975 $
	Away	89:9		at Leicester 1989 $	53		at Leicester 2000 $
Best Batting:	In Yorkshire	120	J A Rudolph	at Leeds 2008 $	108	N E Briers	at Bradford 1984 $
	Away	176	T M Head	at Leicester 2016 +	108	E J H Eckersley	at Leicester 2013 $
Best Bowling:	In Yorkshire	4-18	H P Cooper	at Leeds 1975 +	5-24	C W Henderson	at Leicester 2004 $
	Away	5-16	S Stuchbury	at Leicester 1982 $	4-25	J Ormond	at Leicester 2001 #

LIST A HIGHEST AND LOWEST SCORES BY AND AGAINST YORKSHIRE PLUS INDIVIDUAL BEST BATTING AND BOWLING (*Continued*)

Yorkshire versus:

Middlesex

		By Yorkshire		Against Yorkshire	
Highest Score:	In Yorkshire	271:7	at Scarborough 2010 $	245:8	at Scarborough 1990 $
	Away	275:4	at Southgate 2004 $	273:6	at Lord's 2011 $
Lowest Score:	In Yorkshire	148	at Leeds 1974 $	23	at Leeds 1974 $
	Away	90	at Lord's 1979 #	107	at Lord's 1964 +
Best Batting:	In Yorkshire	124* J A Rudolph	at Leeds 1996 +	104 P N Weekes	at Scarborough 2010 $
	Away	116 A A Metcalfe	at Southgate 2004 $	125* O A Shah	at Lord's 1991
Best Bowling:	In Yorkshire	4-6 R Illingworth	at Leeds 1986 $	4-24 N G Cowans	at Hull 1983 $
	Away	4-28 H P Cooper	at Lord's 1975 #	5-44 T M Lamb	at Lord's 1979 +

Northamptonshire

		By Yorkshire		Against Yorkshire	
Highest Score:	In Yorkshire	314:8	at Leeds 2007 +	314:4	at Scarborough 2016 +
	Away	341:3	at Northampton 2006 +	339:7	at Northampton 2006 +
Lowest Score:	In Yorkshire	129	at Huddersfield 1974 $	127	at Leeds 2000 $
	Away	112	at Northampton 2000 $	109	at Northampton 1975 $
Best Batting:	In Yorkshire	125 A Lyth	at Leeds 2007 +	132 U Afzaal	at Scarborough 2016 +
	Away	152* G S Ballance	at Northampton 2006 +	161 D J G Sales	at Northampton in 2017 +
Best Bowling:	In Yorkshire	5-38 C M Old	at Bradford 1969 $	5-16 B S Crump	at Sheffield 1972 $
	Away	5-29 P W Jarvis	at Northampton 1975 $	5-15 Sarfraz Nawaz	at Northampton 1992 $

Nottinghamshire

		By Yorkshire		Against Yorkshire	
Highest Score:	In Yorkshire	352:6	at Scarborough 2001 $	251:5	at Scarborough 2001 $
	Away	280:4	at Nottingham 2007 +	251:9	at Scarborough 2016 +
Lowest Score:	In Yorkshire	120:9	at Scarborough 1998 $	291:6	at Nottingham 2004 $
	Away	147	at Nottingham 1975 $	66	at Bradford 1969 $
Best Batting:	In Yorkshire	191 D S Lehmann	at Scarborough 2001 $	101 M J Harris	at Hull 1973 #
	Away	103 R B Richardson	at Nottingham 1993 $	123 D W Randall	at Nottingham 1987 $
Best Bowling:	In Yorkshire	5-17 A G Nicholson	at Hull 1972 $	5-41 C L Cairns	at Scarborough 1996 $
	Away	4-12 C M Old	at Nottingham 1977 $	5-30 F D Stephenson	at Nottingham 1991 #

LIST A HIGHEST AND LOWEST SCORES BY AND AGAINST YORKSHIRE PLUS INDIVIDUAL BEST BATTING AND BOWLING (Continued)

Yorkshire versus:

		By Yorkshire		Against Yorkshire	
Somerset					
Highest Score:	In Yorkshire	283:9	at Scarborough 2002 $	338:5	at Leeds 2013 $
	Away	343:9	at Taunton 2005 $	345:4	at Taunton 2005 $
Lowest Score:	In Yorkshire	110	at Scarborough 1977 $	103	at Sheffield 1972 $
	Away	120	at Taunton 1992 #	63	at Taunton 1965 +
Best Batting:	In Yorkshire	127 J A Rudolph	at Scarborough 2007 $	113 R T Ponting	at Scarborough 2004 $
	Away	148 A McGrath	at Taunton 2006 $	140* P D Trego	at Taunton 2013 $
Best Bowling:	In Yorkshire	6-36 A G Nicholson	at Sheffield 1972 $	4-10 I T Botham	at Scarborough 1979 $
	Away	6-15 F S Trueman	at Taunton 1965 +	5-27 J Garner	at Bath 1985 $
Surrey					
Highest Score:	In Yorkshire	289:9	at Leeds 2017 +	375:4	at Scarborough 1994 $
	Away	334:5	at The Oval 2005 $	329:8	at The Oval 2009 +
Lowest Score:	In Yorkshire	76	at Harrogate 1970 +	90	at Leeds 1996 $
	Away	128:8	at The Oval 1971 $	134	at The Oval 1969 +
Best Batting:	In Yorkshire	118* J D Love	at Leeds 1987 $	136 M A Lynch	at Bradford 1985 $
	Away	146 G Boycott	at Lord's 1965 +	177 S A Newman	at The Oval 2009 +
Best Bowling:	In Yorkshire	5-25 D Gough	at Leeds 1998 $	7-33 R D Jackman	at Harrogate 1970 +
	Away	5-29 R Illingworth	at Lord's 1965 +	5-22 R D Jackman	at The Oval 1978 $
Sussex					
Highest Score:	In Yorkshire	302:4	at Scarborough 2011 $	267	at Scarborough 2011 $
	Away	270	at Hove 1963 +	292	at Hove 1963 +
Lowest Score:	In Yorkshire	89:7	at Huddersfield 1969 $	85	at Bradford 1972 #
	Away	89	at Hove 1998 $	108	at Hove 1971 $
Best Batting:	In Yorkshire	132* J A Rudolph	at Scarborough 2011 $	129 A W Greig	at Scarborough 1976 $
	Away	111* J H Hampshire	at Hastings 1973 $	103 L J Wright	at Hove 2012 $
Best Bowling:	In Yorkshire	5-34 G M Hamilton	at Scarborough 2000 $	4-15 Imran Khan	at Sheffield 1985 $
	Away	5-13 D Gough	at Hove 1994 $	4-10 M H Yardy	at Hove 2011 $

LIST A HIGHEST AND LOWEST SCORES BY AND AGAINST YORKSHIRE PLUS INDIVIDUAL BEST BATTING AND BOWLING *(Continued)*

Yorkshire versus:

Warwickshire

		By Yorkshire		Against Yorkshire	
Highest Score:	In Yorkshire	274:3	at Leeds 2003 $	283:6	at Leeds 2016 +
	Away	281:8	at Birmingham 2017 +	309-3	at Birmingham 2005 $
Lowest Score:	In Yorkshire	158	at Scarborough 2012 $	59	at Leeds 2001 $
	Away	56	at Birmingham 1995 $	158:9	at Birmingham 2003 $
Best Batting:	In Yorkshire	139* S P Fleming	at Leeds 2003 $	118 I J L Trott	at Leeds 2016 +
	Away	100* J H Hampshire	at Birmingham 1975 $	137 I R Bell	at Birmingham 2005 $
Best Bowling:	In Yorkshire	5-31 M D Moxon	at Leeds 1991 #	4-16 N M Carter	at Scarborough 2012 $
	Away	4-27 H P Cooper	at Birmingham 1973 $	7-32 R G D Willis	at Birmingham 1981 #

Worcestershire

		By Yorkshire		Against Yorkshire	
Highest Score:	In Yorkshire	346:9	at Leeds 2018 +	350:6	at Leeds 2018 +
	Away	346:6	at Worcester 2015 +	342	at Worcester 2017 +
Lowest Score:	In Yorkshire	88	at Leeds 1995 $	86	at Leeds 1969 $
	Away	90	at Worcester 1987 $	122	at Worcester 1975 $
Best Batting:	In Yorkshire	101 M G Bevan	at Scarborough 1995 $	113* G A Hick	at Scarborough 1995 $
		101 C A Pujara	at Leeds 2018 +		
	Away	142 G Boycott	at Worcester 1980 #	115 Younis Ahmed	at Worcester 1980 #
Best Bowling:	In Yorkshire	7-15 R A Hutton	at Leeds 1969 $	5-36 Kabir Ali	at Leeds 2002 $
	Away	6-14 H P Cooper	at Worcester 1975 $	5-30 R J Chapman	at Worcester 1998 $

Bedfordshire +

		By Yorkshire		Against Yorkshire	
Highest Score:	Away	212:6	at Luton 2001	211:9	at Luton 2001
Best Batting:	Away	88 D S Lehmann	at Luton 2001	34 O J Clayton	at Luton 2001
Best Bowling:	Away	4-39 R J Sidebottom	at Luton 2001	4-54 S R Rashid	at Luton 2001

Berkshire +

		By Yorkshire		Against Yorkshire	
Highest Score:	Away	131:3	at Reading 1983	128:9	at Reading 1983
Lowest Score:	Away			105	at Finchampstead 1988
Best Batting:	Away	74* A A Metcalfe	at Reading 1983	29 G R J Roope	at Reading 1983
Best Bowling:	Away	5-27 G B Stevenson	at Reading 1983	1-15 M Lickley	at Reading 1983

LIST A HIGHEST AND LOWEST SCORES BY AND AGAINST YORKSHIRE PLUS INDIVIDUAL BEST BATTING AND BOWLING (Continued)

Yorkshire versus:

Cambridgeshire +

		By Yorkshire			Against Yorkshire		
Highest Score:	In Yorkshire	177:1		at Leeds 1986	176: 8		at Leeds 1986
	Away	299:5		at March 2003	214:8		at March 2003
Lowest Score:	In Yorkshire	299:5		at March 2003	176: 8		at Leeds 1986
	Away				214:8		at March 2003
Best Batting:	In Yorkshire	75	M D Moxon	at Leeds 1986	85	J D R Benson	at Leeds 1986
	Away	118*	M J Wood	at March 2003	53	N T Gadsby	at March 2003
Best Bowling:	In Yorkshire	3-11	A G Nicholson	at Castleford 1967	2-8	D H Fairey	at Castleford 1967
	Away	3-37	A K D Gray	at March 2003	3-53	Ajaz Akhtar	at March 2003

Cheshire +

		By Yorkshire			Against Yorkshire		
Highest Score:	Away	160:0		at Oxton 1985	159:7		at Oxton 1985
Best Batting:	Away	82*	M D Moxon	at Oxton 1985	46	K Teasdale	at Oxton 1985
Best Bowling:	Away	2-17	G B Stevenson	at Oxton 1985			

Combined Universities

		By Yorkshire			Against Yorkshire		
Highest Score:	In Yorkshire	197:8		at Leeds 1990	200:8		at Leeds 1990
	Away	151:1		at Oxford 1980	150:7		at Oxford 1980
Lowest Score:	In Yorkshire	197:8		at Leeds 1990	200:8		at Leeds 1990
	Away	151:1		at Oxford 1980	150:7		at Oxford 1980
Best Batting:	In Yorkshire	74*	C W J Athey	at Oxford 1980	63	S P James	at Leeds 1990
	Away				63	J O D Orders	at Oxford 1980
Best Bowling:	In Yorkshire	3-34	P J Hartley	at Leeds 1990	3-44	M E W Brooker	at Barnsley 1976
	Away	2-43	H P Cooper	at Oxford 1980	1-16	C J Ross	at Oxford 1980

Devon +

		By Yorkshire			Against Yorkshire		
Highest Score:	Away	411:6		at Exmouth 2004	279-8		at Exmouth 2004
Lowest Score:	Away	259:5		at Exmouth 2002	80		at Exmouth 1998
Best Batting:	Away	160	M J Wood	at Exmouth 1994	83	P M Roebuck	at Exmouth 1994
Best Bowling:	Away	4-26	D S Lehmann	at Exmouth 2002	2-42	A O F Le Fleming	at Exmouth 1994

LIST A HIGHEST AND LOWEST SCORES BY AND AGAINST YORKSHIRE PLUS INDIVIDUAL BEST BATTING AND BOWLING *(Continued)*

Yorkshire versus:

		By Yorkshire			Against Yorkshire	
Dorset +						
Highest Score:	Away	101:2		at Bournemouth 2004	97	at Bournemouth 2004
Best Batting:	Away	71*	M J Wood	at Bournemouth 2004	23	C L Park	at Bournemouth 2004
Best Bowling:	Away	4-18	C E W Silverwood	at Bournemouth 2004	2-31	D J Worrad	at Bournemouth 2004
Durham M C +						
Highest Score:	In Yorkshire	249:6		at Middlesbrough 1978	138:5	at Middlesbrough 1978
	Away	214:6		at Chester-le-Street 1979	213-9	at Chester-le-Street 1979
Lowest Score:	In Yorkshire	135		at Harrogate 1973	136:7	at Harrogate 1973
	Away				213-9	at Chester-le-Street 1979
Best Batting:	In Yorkshire	110	J H Hampshire	at Middlesbrough 1978	52	N A Riddell	at Middlesbrough 1978
	Away	92	G Boycott	at Chester-le-Street 1979	52	Wasim Raja	at Chester-le-Street 1979
Best Bowling:	In Yorkshire	4-9	C M Old	at Middlesbrough 1978	5-15	B R Lander	at Harrogate 1978
	Away	3-39	H P Cooper	at Chester-le-Street 1979	2-35	B L Cairns	at Chester-le-Street 1979
Herefordshire +						
Highest Score:	Away	275:8		at Kington 1999	124:5	at Kington 1999
Best Batting:	Away	77	G S Blewett	at Kington 1999	39	R D Hughes	at Kington 1999
Best Bowling:	Away	2-22	G M Hamilton	at Kington 1999	2-41	C W Boroughs	at Kington 1999
Ireland +						
Highest Score:	In Yorkshire	299:6		at Leeds 1995	228:7	at Leeds 1995
	Away	202:4		at Belfast 2005	201:7	at Belfast 2005
Lowest Score:	In Yorkshire	249		at Leeds 1997	53	at Leeds 1997
	Away				201:7	at Belfast 2005
Best Batting:	In Yorkshire	113	C White	at Leeds 1995	82	S J S Warke	at Leeds 1995
	Away	58	M P Vaughan	at Belfast 2005	59	E J G Morgan	at Belfast 2005
Best Bowling:	In Yorkshire	7-27	D Gough	at Leeds 1997	3-26	P McCrum	at Leeds 1997
	Away	4-43	C White	at Belfast 2005	1-29	W K McCallan	at Belfast 2005

LIST A HIGHEST AND LOWEST SCORES BY AND AGAINST YORKSHIRE
PLUS INDIVIDUAL BEST BATTING AND BOWLING *(Continued)*

Yorkshire versus:

Minor Counties

Metric	Ground	By Yorkshire		Against Yorkshire	
Highest Score:	In Yorkshire	309:5	at Leeds 1997	206:6	at Leeds 1988
	Away	218:3	at Scunthorpe 1975	182	at Scunthorpe 1975
	In Yorkshire	218:9	at Jesmond 1979		
Lowest Score:	In Yorkshire	309:5	at Leeds 1997	109	at Leeds 1974
	Away	218:3	at Scunthorpe 1975	85	at Jesmond 1979
		218:9	at Jesmond 1979		
Best Batting:	In Yorkshire	109* A McGrath	at Leeds 1997	80* J D Love	at Leeds 1991
	Away	83* G Boycott	at Chester-le-Street 1973	61 N A Folland	at Jesmond 1989
Best Bowling:	In Yorkshire	6-27 A G Nicholson	at Middlesbrough 1972	3-37 S Oakes	at Leeds 1997
	Away	5-32 S Oldham	at Scunthorpe 1975	3-27 I E Conn	at Jesmond 1989

Netherlands $

Metric	Ground	By Yorkshire		Against Yorkshire	
Highest Score:	In Yorkshire	204:6	at Leeds 2010	200:8	at Leeds 2010
	Away	158:5	at Rotterdam 2010	154:9	at Rotterdam 2010
Lowest Score:	In Yorkshire	188:9	at Leeds 2011	190:8	at Leeds 2011
	Away	123	at Amsterdam 2011	154:9	at Amsterdam 2011
Best Batting:	In Yorkshire	83* J A Rudolph	at Leeds 2010	62 M G Dighton	at Leeds 2010
	Away	46* J M Bairstow	at Rotterdam 2010	34 P W Borren	at Rotterdam 2010
Best Bowling:	In Yorkshire	3-34 S A Patterson	at Leeds 2010	3-26 Mudassar Bukhari	at Leeds 2011
	Away	4-24 R M Pyrah	at Rotterdam 2010	3-28 Mudassar Bukhari	at Amsterdam 2011

Norfolk +

Metric	Ground	By Yorkshire		Against Yorkshire	
Highest Score:	In Yorkshire	106:0	at Leeds 1990	104	at Leeds 1990
	Away	167	at Lakenham 1969	78	at Lakenham 1969
Lowest Score:	In Yorkshire			104	at Leeds 1990
	Away	167	at Lakenham 1969	78	at Lakenham 1969
Best Batting:	In Yorkshire	56* M D Moxon	at Leeds 1990	25 R J Finney	at Leeds 1990
	Away	55 J H Hampshire	at Lakenham 1969	21 G J Donaldson	at Lakenham 1969
Best Bowling:	In Yorkshire	3-8 P Carrick	at Leeds 1990		
	Away	3-14 C M Old	at Lakenham 1969	6-48 T I Moore	at Lakenham 1969

Yorkshire versus:

Northumberland +

		By Yorkshire		Against Yorkshire	
Highest Score:	In Yorkshire	138:2	at Leeds 1992	137	at Leeds 1992
Best Batting:	In Yorkshire	38 S A Kellett	at Leeds 1992	47 G R Morris	at Leeds 1992
Best Bowling:	In Yorkshire	3-18 M A Robinson	at Leeds 1992	2-22 S Greensword	at Leeds 1992

Scotland

		By Yorkshire		Against Yorkshire	
Highest Score:	In Yorkshire	317:5	at Leeds 1986 #	244	at Leeds 2008 +
	Away	259:8	at Edinburgh 2007 +	217	at Edinburgh 2007 +
Lowest Score:	In Yorkshire	228:6	at Bradford 1981 #	142	at Leeds 1996 #
	Away	199:8	at Edinburgh 2004 $	129	at Glasgow 1995 #
Best Batting:	In Yorkshire	118* J D Love	at Bradford 1981 #	73 I L Philip	at Leeds 1989 +
	Away	91 A A Metcalfe	at Glasgow 1987 #	78 J A Beukes	at Edinburgh 2005 $
Best Bowling:	In Yorkshire	5-28 C E W Silverwood	at Leeds 1996 #	2-22 P J C Hoffman	at Leeds 2006 +
	Away	4-20 R K J Dawson	at Edinburgh 2004 $	3-42 Asim Butt	at Linlithgow 1998 #

Shropshire +

		By Yorkshire		Against Yorkshire	
Highest Score:	Away	192	at Telford 1984	229:5	at Telford 1984
Lowest Score:	Away	192	at Telford 1984	185	at Wellington 1976
Best Batting:	Away	59 J H Hampshire	at Wellington 1976	80 Mushtaq Mohammad	at Telford 1984
Best Bowling:	Away	3-17 A L Robinson	at Wellington 1976	3-26 Mushtaq Mohammad	at Telford 1984

Unicorns $

		By Yorkshire		Against Yorkshire	
Highest Score:	In Yorkshire	266:6	at Leeds 2013	234	at Leeds 2013
	Away	191:5	at Chesterfield 2013	189:9	at Chesterfield 2013
Lowest Score:	In Yorkshire			150:6	at Leeds 2012
	Away			184	at Scarborough 2012
Best Batting:	In Yorkshire	139 G S Ballance	at Leeds 2013	107 M S Lineker	at Leeds 2013
	Away	103* G S Ballance	at Scarborough 2012	83* T J New	at Scarborough 2012
Best Bowling:	In Yorkshire	5-22 J A Leaning	at Leeds 2012	2-25 R J Woolley	at Leeds 2012
	Away	3-34 R M Pyrah	at Chesterfield 2013	2-31 W W Lee	at Chesterfield 2013

LIST A HIGHEST AND LOWEST SCORES BY AND AGAINST YORKSHIRE
PLUS INDIVIDUAL BEST BATTING AND BOWLING (Continued)

Yorkshire versus:

		By Yorkshire		Against Yorkshire	
Wiltshire +					
Highest Score:	Away	304:7	at Trowbridge 1987	175	at Trowbridge 1987
Best Batting:	Away	85 A A Metcalfe	at Trowbridge 1987	62 J J Newman	at Trowbridge 1987
Best Bowling:	Away	4-40 K Sharp	at Trowbridge 1987	2-38 R C Cooper	at Trowbridge 1987
Yorkshire Cricket Board +					
Highest Score:	Away	240:5	at Harrogate 2000	110	at Harrogate 2000
Best Batting:	Away	70 M P Vaughan	at Harrogate 2000	31 R A Kettleborough	at Harrogate 2000
Best Bowling:	Away	5-30 D Gough	at Harrogate 2000	1-25 A E McKenna	at Harrogate 2000
Australians					
Highest Score:	In Yorkshire	188	at Leeds 1989	297:3	at Leeds 1989
Lowest Score:	In Yorkshire	140	at Bradford 1972	297:3	at Leeds 1989
Best Batting:	In Yorkshire	105 G Boycott	at Bradford 1972	172 D C Boon	at Leeds 1989
Best Bowling:	In Yorkshire	2-23 D Wilson	at Bradford 1972	3-30 D J Colley	at Bradford 1972
Bangladesh A					
Highest Score:	In Yorkshire	198	at Leeds 2013	191	at Leeds 2013
Best Batting:	In Yorkshire	47* L E Plunkett	at Leeds 2013	69 Anamul Haque	at Leeds 2013
Best Bowling:	In Yorkshire	5-30 Azeem Rafiq	at Leeds 2013	3-25 Elias Sunny	at Leeds 2013
South Africa A					
Highest Score:	In Yorkshire			129:4	at Leeds 2017
Best Batting:	In Yorkshire			56* K Zonda	at Leeds 2017
Best Bowling:	In Yorkshire	2-16 S A Patterson	at Leeds 2017		
Sri Lanka A					
Highest Score:	In Yorkshire	249	at Leeds 2014	275:9	at Leeds 2014
Lowest Score:	In Yorkshire	179:7	at Leeds 2004		
Best Batting:	In Yorkshire	81 A W Gale	at Leeds 2007	100 L D Chandimal	at Leeds 2014
Best Bowling:	In Yorkshire	5-51 A Shahzad	at Leeds 2007	4-42 S Prasanna	at Leeds 2014

LIST A HIGHEST AND LOWEST SCORES BY AND AGAINST YORKSHIRE PLUS INDIVIDUAL BEST BATTING AND BOWLING *(Continued)*

Yorkshire versus:

		By Yorkshire				Against Yorkshire		
West Indians								
Highest Score:	In Yorkshire	253:4		at Scarborough 1995		242		at Scarborough 1995
Best Batting:	In Yorkshire	106	A McGrath	at Scarborough 1995		54	R B Richardson	at Scarborough 1995
Best Bowling:	In Yorkshire	3-42	G M Hamilton	at Scarborough 1995		3-48	R Dhanraj	at Scarborough 1995
West Indians A								
Highest Score:	In Yorkshire	139		at Leeds 2002		140:2		at Leeds 2002
Best Batting:	In Yorkshire	48	M J Wood	at Leeds 2002		57	D Ganga	at Leeds 2002
Best Bowling:	In Yorkshire	1-31	C J Elstub	at Leeds 2002		4-24	J J C Lawson	at Leeds 2002
Young Australians								
Highest Score:	In Yorkshire	224:6		at Leeds 1995		156		at Leeds 1995
Best Batting:	In Yorkshire	76	M P Vaughan	at Leeds 1995		51	A C Gilchrist	at Leeds 1995
Best Bowling:	In Yorkshire	5-32	A C Morris	at Leeds 1995		2-21	S Young	at Leeds 1995
Zimbabwe								
Highest Score:	In Yorkshire	203:7		at Sheffield 1982		202		at Sheffield 1982
Best Batting:	In Yorkshire	98*	G Boycott	at Sheffield 1982		53	D A G Fletcher	at Sheffield 1982
Best Bowling:	In Yorkshire	3-47	P W Jarvis	at Sheffield 1982		3-30	D A G Fletcher	at Sheffield 1982

375

LIST A HIGHEST TEAM TOTALS

BY YORKSHIRE

411:6	v.	Devon at Exmouth	2004 +
379:7	v.	Lancashire at Manchester	2018 +
376:3	v.	Leicestershire at Leicester	2016 +
352:6	v.	Nottinghamshire at Scarborough	2001 $
349:7	v.	Derbyshire at Leeds	2017 +
346:9	v.	Worcestershire at Leeds	2018 +
345:5	v.	Nottinghamshire at Leeds	1996 +
345:6	v.	Worcestershire at Worcester	2015 +
343:9	v.	Somerset at Taunton	2005 $
341:3	v.	Northamptonshire at Northampton	2006 +
339:4	v.	Durham at Leeds	2017 +
334:5	v	Surrey at The Oval	2005 $
330:6	v	Surrey at The Oval	2009 +
328:4	v.	Durham at Chester-le-Street	2018 +
325:7	v.	Lancashire at Manchester	2016 +
324:7	v.	Lancashire at Manchester	2014 +
318:7	v.	Leicestershire at Leicester	1993 $
317:4	v.	Surrey at Lord's	1965 +
317:5	v.	Scotland at Leeds	1986 #
314:8	v.	Northamptonshire at Scarboough	2016 +
310:5	v.	Leicestershire at Leicester	1997 +
309:5	v.	Minor Counties at Leeds	1997 #
307:3	v.	Essex at Chelmsford	1995 +
307:4	v.	Somerset at Taunton	2002 $
304:7	v.	Wiltshire at Trowbridge	1986 +

AGAINST YORKSHIRE

375:4	for Surrey at Scarborough	1994 $
363	for Lancashire at Manchester	2018 +
350:6	for Worcestershire at Leeds	2018 +
348:9	for Hampshire at West End	2018 +
345:4	for Somerset at Taunton	2005 $
342	for Worcestershire at Worcester	2017 +
339:7	for Northamptonshire at Northampton	2006 +
338:5	for Somerset at Leeds	2013 +
335:5	for Durham at Leeds	2017 +
334:8	for Derbyshire at Leeds	2017 +
329:8	for Surrey at The Oval	2009 +
325:7	for Northamptonshire at Northampton	1992 $
314:4	for Northamptonshire at Leeds	2007 +
313:7	for Surrey at Leeds	2017 +
310:7	for Northamptonshire at Scarborough	2016 +
309:3	for Warwickshire at Birmingham	2005 $
308:6	for Surrey at The Oval	1995 +
306:8	for Somerset at Taunton	2002 $
302:7	for Leicestershire at Leeds	2008 $
298:9	for Leicestershire at Leicester	1997 $
297:3	for Australians at Leeds	1989
294:6	for Gloucestershire at Cheltenham	2010 $
293:9	for Lancashire at Manchester	1996 +
293:9	for Leicestershire at Leicester	2018 +
292	for Sussex at Hove	1963 +

LIST A HIGHEST INDIVIDUAL SCORES

BY YORKSHIRE

191	D S Lehmann	v.	Nottinghamshire at Scarborough	2001 $
175	T M Head	v.	Leicestershire at Leicester	2016 +
174	J M Bairstow	v.	Durham at Leeds	2017 +
164	T Kohler-Cadmore	v.	Durham at Chester-le-Street	2018 +
160	M J Wood	v.	Devon at Exmouth	2004 +
152*	G S Ballance	v.	Northamptonshire at Northampton	2017 +
148	C White	v.	Leicestershire at Leicester	1997 $
148	A McGrath	v.	Somerset at Taunton	2006 $
146	G Boycott	v.	Surrey at Lord's	1965 +
144	A Lyth	v.	Lancashire at Manchester	2018 +
142	G Boycott	v.	Worcestershire at Worcester	1980 #
141*	M D Moxon	v.	Glamorgan at Cardiff	1991 #
140	P S P Handscomb	v.	Derbyshire at Leeds	2017 +
139*	S P Fleming	v.	Warwickshire at Leeds	2003 $
139	G S Ballance	v.	Unicorns at Leeds	2013 $

AGAINST YORKSHIRE

177	S A Newman	for	Surrey at The Oval	2009 +
172	D C Boon	for	Australia at Leeds	1989
171	J M Vince	for	Hampshire at West End	2018 +
161	D J G Sales	for	Northamptonshire at Northampton	2006 +
155*	B A Richards	for	Hampshire at Hull	1970 $
146*	S Young	for	Gloucestershire at Leeds	1997 $
143*	C M Spearman	for	Gloucestershire at Bristol	2004 $
141*	B J Hodge	for	Lancashire at Manchester	2007 +
140*	P D Trego	for	Somerset at Taunton	2013 $
137*	M Klinger	for	Gloucestershire at Leeds	2015 +
137	I R Bell	for	Warwickshire at Birmingham	2005 $
136*	N Hussain	for	Essex at Chelmsford	2002 #
136	M A Lynch	for	Surrey at Bradford	1985 $
135*	D J Bicknell	for	Surrey at The Oval	1989 +
133	A D Brown	for	Surrey at Scarborough	1994 $

MOST RUNS IN LIST A MATCHES

742	v.	Lancashire at Manchester	2018 +	Y 379:7	L 363
696	v.	Worcestershire at Leeds	2018 +	W 350:6	Y 346:9
690	v.	Devon at Exmouth	2004 +	Y 411:6	D 279:8
688	v.	Somerset at Taunton	2005 $	S 345:4	Y 343:9
683	v.	Derbyshire at Leeds	2017 +	Y 349:7	D 334:8
680	v.	Northamptonshire at Northampton	2006 +	Y 342:3	N 339:7
674	v.	Durham at Leeds	2017 +	D 335:5	Y: 339-4
659	v.	Surrey at The Oval	2009 $	S 329:8	Y 330:6
633	v.	Worcestershire at Worcester	2017 +	W 342	Y 291
625	v.	Surrey at The Oval	2005 $	Y 334:5	S 291
624	v.	Northamptonshire at Scarborough	2016 +	N 310:7	Y 314:8
613	v.	Somerset at Taunton	2002 $	Y 307:4	S 306:8
605	v.	Leicestershire at Leeds	2008 $	Y 303:4	L 302:7
604	v.	Surrey at The Oval	1995 $	S 308:6	Y 296:6
602	v.	Surrey at Leeds	2017 +	S 313:7	Y 289:9
601	v.	Lancashire at Manchester	2014 +	Y 324:7	L 277

LIST A BEST BOWLING

BY YORKSHIRE

7-15	R A Hutton	v.	Worcestershire at Leeds	1969 $
7-27	D Gough	v.	Ireland at Leeds	1997 +
6-14	H P Cooper	v.	Worcestershire at Worcester	1975 $
6-15	F S Trueman	v.	Somerset at Taunton	1965 +
6-18	D Wilson	v.	Kent at Canterbury	1969 $
6-27	A G Nicholson	v.	Minor Counties at Middlesbrough	1972 #
6-27	P W Jarvis	v.	Somerset at Taunton	1989 $
6-32	S A Patterson	v.	Derbyshire at Leeds	2010 $
6-36	A G Nicholson	v	Somerset At Sheffield	1972 $
6-40	R J Sidebottom	v.	Glamorgan at Cardiff	1998 $
5-13	D Gough	v.	Sussex at Hove	1994 $
5-16	S Stuchbury	v.	Leicestershire at Leicester	1982 $
5-16	G M Hamilton	v.	Hampshire at Leeds	1998 $
5-17	A G Nicholson	v.	Nottinghamshire at Hull	1972 $
5-18	P W Jarvis	v.	Derbyshire at Leeds	1990 $

AGAINST YORKSHIRE

7-32	R G D Willis	for	Warwickshire at Birmingham	1981 #
7-33	R D Jackman	for	Surrey at Harrogate	1970 +
6-15	A A Donald	for	Warwickshire at Birmingham	1995 $
6-18	R E East	for	Essex at Hull	1969 $
6-25	G Chapple	for	Lancashire at Leeds	1998 $
6-32	M T Coles	for	Kent at Leeds	2012 $
6-48	T I Moore	for	Norfolk at Lakenham	1969 +
5-15	B R Lander	for	Durham M C at Harrogate	1973 +
5-15	Sarfraz Nawaz	for	Northamptonshire at Northampton	1975 $
5-16	B S Crump	for	Northamptonshire at Bradford	1969 $
5-16	G C Holmes	for	Glamorgan at Swansea	1985 $
5-20	R E East	for	Essex at Colchester	1979 $
5-22	R D Jackman	for	Surrey at The Oval	1978 $
5-24	C J Tunnicliffe	for	Derbyshire at Derby	1981 #
5-24	C W Henderson	for	Leicestershire at Leeds	2004 $

LIST A ECONOMICAL BOWLING

BY YORKSHIRE

11-9-3-1	C M Old	v.	Middlesex at Lord's	1979 #
8-5-3-3	A L Robinson	v.	Derbyshire at Scarborough	1973 $

AGAINST YORKSHIRE

8-4-6-2	P J Sainsbury	for	Hampshire at Hull	1970 $
8-5-6-3	M J Procter	for	Gloucestershire at Cheltenham	1979 $

LIST A MOST EXPENSIVE BOWLING

BY YORKSHIRE

9-0-87-1	T T Bresnan	v.	Somerset at Taunton	2005 $

AGAINST YORKSHIRE

12-1-96-0	M E Waugh	for	Essex at Chelmsford	1995 +

LIST A HAT-TRICKS FOR YORKSHIRE (4)

P W Jarvis	v. Derbyshire at Derby	1982 $	D Gough	v. Ireland at Leeds	1997 +
D Gough	v. Lancashire at Leeds	1998 $	C White	v. Kent at Leeds	2000 $

LIST A MAN-OF-THE-MATCH AWARDS (137)

M D Moxon	12	M P Vaughan	5	M J Wood	3
G Boycott	11	A Sidebottom	4	R J Blakey	2
D L Bairstow	8	C E W Silverwood	4	G L Brophy	2
C White	8	D Byas	3	P Carrick	2
A A Metcalfe	7	D Gough	3	R A Hutton	2
J H Hampshire	6	P J Hartley	3	L E Plunkett	2
D S Lehmann	6	J D Love	3	P J Sharpe	2
C W J Athey	5	A McGrath	3	G B Stevenson	2
M G Bevan	5	C M Old	3		

One each: T T Bresnan, D B Close, M T G Elliott, G M Fellows, S D Fletcher, G M Hamilton, S N Hartley, P M Hutchinson, R Illingworth, C Johnson, S A Kellett, B Leadbeater, M J Lumb, A G Nicholson, S Oldham, S A Patterson, R M Pyrah, P E Robinson, R D Stemp, F S Trueman and D Wilson.

ALL LIST A CENTURIES 1963-2018 (115)

C W J ATHEY (2)

118	v.	Leicestershire	at Leicester	1978 $
115	v.	Kent	at Leeds	1980 +

D L BAIRSTOW (1)

103 *	v.	Derbyshire	at Derby	1981 #

J M BAIRSTOW (2)

114	v.	Middlesex	at Lord's	2011 $
174	v.	Durham	at Leeds	2017 +

G S BALLANCE (3)

139	v.	Unicorns	at Leeds	2013 $
103 *	v.	Unicorns	at Scarborough	2012 $
152 *	v.	Northamptonshire	at Northampton	2017 +

M G BEVAN (2)

103 *	v	Gloucestershire	at Middlesbrough	1995 $
101	v	Worcestershire	at Scarborough	1995 $

G BOYCOTT (7)

146	v	Surrey	at Lord's	1965 +
142	v	Worcestershire	at Worcester	1980 #
108 *	v	Northamptonshire	at Huddersfield	1974 $
106	v	Northamptonshire	at Bradford	1984 #
105	v	Australians	at Bradford	1972
104 *	v	Glamorgan	at Colwyn Bay	1973 $
102	v	Northamptonshire	at Middlesbrough	1977 #

R J BLAKEY (3)

130	v	Kent	at Scarborough	1991 $
105 *	v	Warwickshire	at Scarborough	1992 $
100 *	v	Gloucestershire	at Cheltenham	1990 $

D BYAS (5)

116 *	v.	Surrey	at The Oval	1996 #
111 *	v.	Lancashire	at Leeds	1996 $
106 *	v.	Derbyshire	at Chesterfield	1993 $
104 *	v.	Hampshire	at Leeds	1999 #
101 *	v.	Nottinghamshire	at Leeds	1994 $

M T G ELLIOTT (3)

128 *	v.	Somerset	at Lord's	2002 +
115 *	v.	Kent	at Leeds	2002 $
109	v.	Leicestershire	at Leicester	2002 $

S P FLEMING (1)

139 *	v.	Warwickshire	at Leeds	2003 $

M J FOSTER (1)

118	v.	Leicestershire	at Leicester	1993 $

A W GALE (2)

125 *	v.	Essex	at Chelmsford	2010 $
112	v.	Kent	at Canterbury	2011 $

J H HAMPSHIRE (7)

119	v.	Leicestershire	at Hull	1971 $
114 *	v.	Northamptonshire	at Scarborough	1978 $
111 *	v.	Sussex	at Hastings	1973 $
110	v.	Durham M C	at Middlesbrough	1978 +
108	v.	Nottinghamshire	at Sheffield	1970 $
106 *	v.	Lancashire	at Manchester	1972 $
100 *	v.	Warwickshire	at Birmingham	1975 $

T M HEAD (1))

175	v.	Leicestershire	at Leicester	2016 +

P S P HANDSCOMB (1)

140	v.	Derbyshire	at Leeds	2017 +

P A JAQUES (1)

105	v.	Sussex	at Leeds	2004 $

S A KELLETT (2)

118 *	v.	Derbyshire	at Leeds	1992 $
107	v.	Ireland	at Leeds	1995 +

T KOHLER-CADMORE (1)

164	v.	Durham	at Chester-le-Street	2018 +

J A LEANING (2)

131 *	v.	Leicestershire	at Leicester	2016 +
111 *	v.	Essex	at Scarborough	2014 +

A Z LEES (1)

102	v.	Northamptonshire	at Northampton	2014 +

D S LEHMANN (8)

191	v.	Nottinghamshire	at Scarborough	2001 $
119	v.	Durham	at Leeds	1998 #
118 *	v.	Northamptonshire	at Northampton	2006 +
105	v.	Glamorgan	at Cardiff	1995 +
104	v.	Somerset	at Taunton	2002 $

D S LEHMANN *(Continued)*

103	v.	Derbyshire	at Leeds	2001 #
103	v.	Leicestershire	at Scarborough	2001 $
102 *	v.	Derbyshire	ar Derby	1998 #

J D LOVE (4)

118 *	v.	Scotland	at Bradford	1981 #
118 *	v.	Surrey	at Leeds	1987 $
104 *	v.	Nottinghamshire	at Hull	1986 $
100 *	v.	Gloucestershire	at Gloucester	1985 $

R G LUMB (1)

101	v.	Nottinghamshire	at Scarborough	1976 $

A LYTH (5)

144	v.	Lancashire	at Manchester	2018 +
136 §	v.	Lancashire	at Manchester	2016 +
132*	v.	Leicestershire	at Leicester	2018 +
125 §	v.	Northamptonshire	at Scarborough	2016 +
109 *	v.	Sussex	at Scarborough	2009 $

(§ consecutive days)

A McGRATH (7)

148	v.	Somerset	at Taunton	2006 $
135 *	v.	Lancashire	at Manchester	2007 +
109 *	v.	Minor Counties	at Leeds	1997 #
106	v.	West Indies	at Scarborough	1995
105 *	v.	Scotland	at Leeds	2008 +
102	v.	Kent	at Canterbury	2001 $
100	v.	Durham	at Leeds	2007 +

G J MAXWELL (1)

111	v.	Worcestershire	at Worcester	2015 +

A A METCALFE (4)

127 *	v.	Warwickshire	at Leeds	1990 +
116	v.	Middlesex	at Lord's	1991 $
115 *	v.	Gloucestershire	at Scarborough	1984 $
114	v.	Lancashire	at Manchester	1991 #

M D MOXON (7)

141 *	v.	Glamorgan	at Cardiff	1991 #
137	v.	Nottinghamshire	at Leeds	1996+
129 *	v.	Surrey	at The Oval	1991 $
112	v.	Sussex	at Middlesbrough	1991 $
107 *	v.	Warwickshire	at Leeds	1990 +
106 *	v.	Lancashire	at Manchester	1986 #
105	v.	Somerset	at Scarborough	1990 $

C A PUJARA (1)

101	v.	Worcestershire	at Leeds	2018 +

R B RICHARDSON (1)

103	v.	Nottinghamshire	at Nottingham	1993 $

J A RUDOLPH (9)

132 *	v.	Sussex	at Scarborough	2011 $
127	v.	Somerset	at Scarborough	2007 $
124 *	v.	Middlesex	at Scarborough	2010 $
120	v.	Leicestershire	at Leeds	2008 $
118	v.	Gloucestershire	at Leeds	2009 +
106	v.	Warwickshire	at Scarborough	2010 $
105	v.	Derbyshire	at Chesterfield	2010 $
101 *	v.	Essex	at Chelmsford	2010 $
100	v.	Leicestershire	at Leeds	2007 +

K SHARP (3)

114	v.	Essex	at Chelmsford	1985 $
112 *	v.	Worcestershire	at Worcester	1985 $
105 *	v.	Scotland	at Leeds	1984 #

S R TENDULKAR (1)

107	v.	Lancashire	at Leeds	1992 $

M P VAUGHAN (3)

125 *	v.	Somerset	at Taunton	2001 #
116 *	v.	Lancashire	at Manchester	2004 +
116 *	v.	Kent	at Leeds	2005 $

C WHITE (5)

148	v.	Leicestershire	at Leicester	1997 $
113	v.	Ireland	at Leeds	1995 +
112	v.	Northamptonshire	at Northampton	2006 +
101 *	v.	Durham	at Chester-le-Street	2006 +
100 *	v.	Surrey	at Leeds	2002 +

D J WILLEY (1)

131	v.	Lancashire	at Manchester	2018 +

M J WOOD (5)

160	v.	Devon	at Exmouth	2004 +
118 *	v.	Cambridgeshire	at March	2003 +
115 *	v.	Derbyshire	at Derby	2002 #
111	v.	Surrey	at The Oval	2005 $
105 *	v.	Somerset	at Taunton	2002$

YOUNUS KHAN (1)

100	v.	Nottinghamshire	at Nottingham	2007 +

LIST A PARTNERSHIPS OF 150 AND OVER 1963-2018 (49)

274 3rd wkt T M Head (175)   and J A Leaning (131*)   v. Leicestershire at Leicester
                                                                                      2016+
242* 1st wkt M D Moxon (107*)   and A A Metcalfe (127*)   v. Warwickshire at Leeds   1990 +
235 2nd wkt A Lyth (144)   and D J Willey (131)   v. Lancashire at Manchester
                                                                                      2018 +
233* 1st wkt A W Gale (125*)   and J A Rudolph (101*)   v. Essex at Chelmsford   2010 $
213 1st wkt M D Moxon (141*)   and A A Metcalfe (84)   v. Glamorgan at Cardiff   1991 #
211* 1st wkt M D Moxon (93*)   and A A Metcalfe (94*)   v. Warwickshire at Birmingham
                                                                                      1987 #
207 4th wkt S A Kellett (107)   and C White (113)   v. Ireland at Leeds   1995 +
202 2nd wkt G Boycott (87)   and C W J Athey (115)   v. Kent at Leeds   1980 +
201 1st wkt J H Hampshire (86)   and C W J Athey (118)   v. Leicestershire at Leicester
                                                                                      1978 $
198* 4th wkt M T G Elliott (115*) and A McGrath (85*)   v. Kent at Leeds   2002 $
195 1st wkt A Lyth (84)   and A Z Lees (102)   v. Northamptonshire
                                                                       at Northampton 2014 +
192 2nd wkt G Boycott (146)   and D B Close (79)   v. Surrey at Leeds   1965 +
190 1st wkt G Boycott (89*)   and R G Lumb (101)   v. Nottinghamshire
                                                                    at Scarborough 1976 $
190 5th wkt R J Blakey (96)   and M J Foster (118)   v. Leicestershire at Leicester
                                                                                      1993 $
189 2nd wkt J M Bairstow (174)   and J E Root (55)   v. Durham at Leeds   2017 +
186 1st wkt G Boycott (99)   and J H Hampshire (92*)   v. Gloucestershire
                                                                    at Scarborough 1975 $
186 1st wkt G S Blewett (71)   and D Byas (104*)   v. Hampshire at Leeds   1999 #
184 3rd wkt M P Vaughan (70)   and D S Lehmann (119)   v. Durham at Leeds   1998 #
181 5th wkt M T G Elliott (109)   and A McGrath (78)   v. Leicestershire at Leicester
                                                                                      2002 $
176 3rd wkt R J Blakey (86)   and S R Tendulkar (107)   v. Lancashire at Leeds   1992 $
176 2nd wkt T Kohler-Cadmore (164)
                                    and C A Pujara (82)   v. Durham at Chester-le-Street
                                                                                      2018 +
172 2nd wkt D Byas (86)   and D S Lehmann (99)   v. Kent at Maidstone   1998 $
172 3rd wkt A McGrath (38)   and D S Lehmann (191)   v. Nottinghamshire
                                                                    at Scarborough 2001 $
171 1st wkt M D Moxon (112)   and A A Metcalfe (68)   v. Sussex at Middlesbrough 1991 $
170 4th wkt M J Wood (105*)   and D S Lehmann (104)   v. Somerset at Taunton   2002 $
170 1st wkt A W Gale (89)   and J A Rudolph (120)   v. Leicestershire at Leeds   2008 $
167* 6th wkt M G Bevan (95*)   and R J Blakey ((80*)   v. Lancashire at Manchester
                                                                                      1996 #
167* 1st wkt C White (100*)   and M J Wood (57*)   v. Surrey at Leeds   2002 +
167 1st wkt M D Moxon(64)   and A A Metcalfe (116)   v. Middlesex at Lord's   1991 $
167 1st wkt M J Wood (65)   and S P Fleming (139*)   v. Warwickshire at Leeds   2003 $
166 1st wkt M D Moxon (82*)   and A A Metcalfe (70)   v. Northamptonshire at Leeds
                                                                                      1988 #
165 1st wkt M D Moxon (80)   and D Byas (106*)   v. Derbyshire at Chesterfield
                                                                                      1993 $
165 1st wkt M D Moxon (70)   and D Byas (88*)   v. Northamptonshire at Leeds
                                                                                      1993 $
164* 2nd wkt G Boycott (91*)   and C W J Athey (79*)   v. Worcestershire at Worcester
                                                                                      1981 $
164 3rd wkt A McGrath (105*)   and J A Rudolph (82)   v. Scotland at Leeds   2008 +

LIST A PARTNERSHIPS OF 150 AND OVER *(Continued)*

164	3rd wkt	J A Rudolph (84)	and A McGrath (73)	v. Glamorgan at Scarborough	2008 $
161	1st wkt	M D Moxon (74)	and A A Metcalfe (85)	v. Wiltshire at Trowbridge	1987 +
160*	1st wkt	G Boycott (70*)	and M D Moxon (82*)	v. Cheshire at Oxton	1985 +
160*	5th wkt	G M Fellows (80*)	and C White (73*)	v. Surrey at Leeds	2001 +
160*	3rd wkt	A Lyth (60*)	and G S Ballance (103*)	v. Unicorns at Scarborough	2012 $
160	1st wkt	G Boycott (67)	and J H Hampshire (84)	v. Warwickshire at Birmingham	1973 $
159	2nd wkt	G Boycott (92)	and D B Close (96)	v. Surrey at The Oval	1969 +
157	2nd wkt	K Sharp (71)	and R J Blakey (79)	v. Worcestershire at Worcester	1990 $
156	4th wkt	P S P Handscomb (140)	and G S Ballance (63)	v. Derbyshire at Leeds	2017 +
155*	1st wkt	A Lyth (67*)	and A Z Lees (69*)	v. Derbyshire at Scarborough	2014 +
154*	2nd wkt	J H Hampshire (111*)	and B Leadbeater (57*)	v. Sussex at Hove	1973 $
153	4th wkt	Younus Khan (100)	and A W Gale ((69*)	v. Nottinghamshire at Nottingham	2007 +
153	1st wkt	A Lyth (132*)	and T Kohler-Cadmore (74)	v. Leicestershire at Leicester	2018 +
150*	5th wkt	S N Hartley (67*)	and J D Love (82*)	v. Hampshire at Middlesbrough	1983 $

LIST A HIGHEST PARTNERSHIPS FOR EACH WICKET

1st wkt	242*	M D Moxon (107*)	and A A Metcalfe (127*)	v Warwickshire at Leeds	1990 +
2nd wkt	235	A Lyth (144)	and D J Willey (131)	v. Lancashire at Manchester	2018 +
3rd wkt	274	T M Head (175)	and J A Leaning (131*)	v.Leicestershire at Leicester	2016+
4th wkt	207	S A Kellett (107)	and C White (113)	v. Ireland at Leeds	1995 +
5th wkt	190	R J Blakey (96)	and M J Foster (118)	v. Leicestershire at Leicester	1993 $
6th wkt	167*	M G Bevan (95*)	and R J Blakey ((80*)	v. Lancashire at Manchester	1996 #
7th wkt	149*	J D Love (118*)	and C M Old (78*)	v. Scotland at Bradford	1981 #
8th wkt	89	R J Blakey (60)	and R K J Dawson (41)	v. Leicestershire at Scarborough	2002 $
9th wkt	88	S N Hartley (67)	and A Ramage (32*)	v. Middlesex at Lord's	1982 $
10th wkt	80*	D L Bairstow (103*)	and M Johnson (4*)	v. Derbyshire at Derby	1981 #

ALL LIST A 5 WICKETS IN AN INNINGS 1963-2018 (56)

C W J ATHEY (1)

5-35	v	Derbyshire	at Chesterfield	1981 $

AZEEM RAFIQ (1)

5-30	v	Bangladesh A	at Leeds	2013

M G BEVAN (1)

5-29	v	Sussex	at Eastbourne	1996 $

P CARRICK (2)

5-22	v	Glamorgan	at Leeds	1991 $
5-40	v	Sussex	at Middlesbrough	1991 $

H P COOPER (2)

6-14	v	Worcestershire	at Worcester	1975 $
5-30	v	Worcestershire	at Middlesbrough	1978 $

D GOUGH (4)

5-13	v	Sussex	at Hove	1994 $
7-27	v	Ireland	at Leeds	1997 +
5-25	v	Surrey	at Leeds	1998 $
5-30	v	Yorkshire C B	at Harrogate	2000 +

G M HAMILTON (2)

5-16	v	Hampshire	at Leeds	1998 $
5-34	v	Sussex	at Scarborough	2000 $

P J HARTLEY (4)

5-36	v	Sussex	at Scarborough	1993 $
5-38	v	Worcestershire	at Worcester	1990 $
5-43	v	Scotland	at Leeds	1986 #
5-46	v	Hampshire	at Southampton	1990 +

M J HOGGARD (3)

5-28	v	Leicestershire	at Leicester	2000 $
5-30	v	Northamptonshire	at Northampton	2000 $
5-65	v	Somerset	at Lord's	2002 +

R A HUTTON (1)

7-15	v	Worcestershire	at Leeds	1969 $

R ILLINGWORTH (1)

5-29	v	Surrey	at Lord's	1965 +

P W JARVIS (3)

6-27	v	Somerset	at Taunton	1989 $
5-18	v	Derbyshire	at Leeds	1990 $
5-29	v	Northamptonshire	at Northampton	1992 $

J A LEANING (1)

5-22	v	Unicorns	at Leeds	2013 $

A C MORRIS (1)

5-32	v	Young Australia	at Leeds	1995

M D MOXON (1)

5-31	v	Warwickshire	at Leeds	1991 #

A G NICHOLSON (4)

6-27	v	Minor Counties	at Middlesbrough	1972 #
6-36	v	Somerset	at Sheffield	1972 $
5-17	v	Nottinghamshire	at Hull	1972 $
5-24	v	Derbyshire	at Bradford	1975 #

C M OLD (2)

5-33	v	Sussex	at Hove	1971 $
5-38	v	Northamptonshire	at Sheffield	1972 $

S OLDHAM (1)

5-32	v	Minor Counties	at Scunthorpe	1975 #

S A PATTERSON (2)

6-32	v	Derbyshire	at Leeds	2010 $
5-24	v	Worcestershire	at Worcester	2015 +

A U RASHID (1)

5-33	v	Hampshire	at Southampton	2014 +

A SHAHZAD (1)

5-51	v	Sri Lanka A	at Leeds	2007

C SHAW (1)

5-41	v	Hampshire	at Bournemouth	1984 $

A SIDEBOTTOM (2)

5-27	v	Worcestershire	at Bradford	1985 #
5-27	v	Glamorgan	at Leeds	1987 +

R J SIDEBOTTOM (2)

6-40	v	Glamorgan	at Cardiff	2003 $
5-42	v	Leicestershire	at Leicester	2003 $

C E W SILVERWOOD (1)

5-28	v	Scotland	at Leeds	1996 #

G B STEVENSON (4)

5-27	v	Berkshire	at Reading	1983 +
5-28	v	Kent	at Canterbury	1978 #
5-41	v	Leicestershire	at Leicester	1976 $
5-50	v	Worcestershire	at Leeds	1982 #

S STUCHBURY (1)

5-16	v	Leicestershire	at Leicester	1982 $

N D THORNICROFT (1)

5-42	v	Gloucestershire	at Leeds	2003 $

F S TRUEMAN (1)

6-15	v	Somerset	at Taunton	1965 +

C WHITE (2)

5-19	v	Somerset	at Scarborough	2002 $
5-25	v	Lancashire	at Leeds	2000 #

D WILSON (2)

6-18	v	Kent	at Canterbury	1969 $
5-25	v	Lancashire	at Bradford	1972 #

ALL LIST A PLAYERS WHO HAVE TAKEN 4 WICKETS IN AN INNINGS 1963-2018 (166) AND BEST FIGURES

11	C M Old	4-9 v	Durham M C	at Middlesbrough	1978 +
10	C White	4-14 v	Lancashire	at Leeds	2000 $
		4-14 v	Surrey	at The Oval	2005 $
9	A Sidebottom	4-15 v	Worcestershire	at Leeds	1987 #
8	P W Jarvis	4-13 v	Worcestershire	at Leeds	1986 $
8	D Gough	4-17 v	Nottinghamshire	at Nottingham	2000 #
8	G B Stevenson	4-20 v	Essex	at Barnsley	1977 #
7	S D Fletcher	4-11 v	Kent	at Canterbury	1988 $
6	C E W Silverwood	4-11 v	Leicestershire	at Leicester	2000 $
6	H P Cooper	4-18 v	Leicestershire	at Leeds	1975 +
5	S Oldham	4-13 v	Nottinghamshire	at Nottingham	1989 #
5	R M Pyrah	4-24 v	Netherlands	at Rotterdam	2010 $
4	P Carrick	4-13 v	Derbyshire	at Bradford	1983 $
4	R K J Dawson	4-13 v	Derbyshire	at Derby	2002 $
4	T T Bresnan	4-25 v	Somerset	at Leeds	2005 $
4	G M Hamilton	4-27 v	Warwickshire	at Birmingham	1995 $
3	R A Hutton	4-18 v	Surrey	at The Oval	1972 $
3	A G Nicholson	4-15 v	Kent	at Leeds	1974 $
3	P J Hartley	4-21 v	Scotland	at Glasgow	1995 #
3	A L Robinson	4-25 v	Surrey	at The Oval	1974 $
3	R D Stemp	4-25 v	Gloucestershire	at Bristol	1996 $
3	M P Vaughan	4-27 v	Gloucestershire	at Bristol	2000 $
3	A U Rashid	4-38 v	Northamptonshire	at Northampton	2012 $
2	M K Bore	4-21 v	Sussex	at Middlesbrough	1970 $
		4-21 v	Worcestershire	at Worcester	1970 $
2	J D Woodford	4-23 v	Northamptonshire	at Northampton	1970 $
		4-23 v	Warwickshire	at Middlesbrough	1971 $
2	G J Kruis	4-17 v	Derbyshire	at Leeds	2007 $
2	D Wilson	4-22 v	Nottinghamshire	at Bradford	1969 $
2	V J Craven	4-22 v	Kent	at Scarborough	2003 $
2	M A Robinson	4-23 v	Northamptonshire	at Leeds	1993 $
2	S A Patterson	4-28 v	Worcestershire	at Worcester	2011 $
2	S N Hartley	4-32 v	Derbyshire	at Leeds	1989 #
2	A U Rashid	4-38 v	Northamptonshire	at Northampton	2012 $
2	A McGrath	4-41 v	Surrey	at Leeds	2003 $
2	D J Willey	4-47 v	Derbyshire	at Derby	2018 +
1	R Illingworth	4-6 v	Middlesex	at Hull	1983 $
1	M Johnson	4-18 v	Scotland	at Bradford	1981 #
1	G S Blewett	4-18 v	Lancashire	at Manchester	1999 +
1	G M Fellows	4-19 v	Durham	at Leeds	2002 $
1	A P Grayson	4-25 v	Glamorgan	at Cardiff	1994 $
1	C J Elstub	4-25 v	Surrey	at Leeds	2001 $
1	D S Lehmann	4-26 v	Devon	at Exmouth	2002 +
1	C Shaw	4-29 v	Middlesex	at Leeds	1988 +
1	A G Wharf	4-29 v	Nottinghamshire	at Leeds	1996 #
1	F S Trueman	4-30 v	Nottinghamshire	at Middlesbrough	1963 +
1	J D Batty	4-33 v	Kent	at Scarborough	1991 $
1	P M Hutchinson	4-34 v	Gloucestershire	at Gloucester	1998 $
1	A K D Gray	4-34 v	Kent	at Leeds	2002 $

1	A Shahzad	4-34	v	Middlesex	at Lord's	2010 $
1	P M Stringer	4-35	v	Derbyshire	at Sheffield	1969 $
1	C S Pickles	4-36	v	Somerset	at Scarborough	1990 $
1	M J Hoggard	4-39	v	Surrey	at Leeds	2000 #
1	R J Sidebottom	4-39	v	Bedfordshire	at Luton	2001 +
1	K Sharp	4-40	v	Wiltshire	at Trowbridge	1987 +
1	T L Best	4-46	v	Essex	at Chelmsford	2010 $
1	Azeem Rafiq	4-47	v.	Lancashire	at Leeds	2017 +
1	A C Morris	4-49	v	Leicestershire	at Leicester	1997 $
1	L E Plunkett	4-52	v	Kent	Canterbury	2016 +
1	D B Close	4-60	v	Sussex	at Hove	1963 +
1	B O Coad	4-63	v.	Derbyshire	at Leeds	2017 +
1	M J Waite	4-65	v.	Worcestershire	at Worcester	2017 +

CAREER AVERAGES FOR YORKSHIRE

ALL LIST A MATCHES OF 40 TO 65 OVERS 1963-2018

Player	M	Inns	NO	Runs	HS	Av'ge	100s	50s	Runs	Wkts	Av'ge	Ct/St
Ashraf, M A ...	22	6	4	3	3*	1.50	0	0	895	23	38.91	4
Athey, C W J ...	140	129	14	3,662	118	31.84	2	25	431	19	22.68	46
Azeem Rafiq ...	30	21	8	222	52*	17.07	0	1	1,160	41	28.29	12
Bairstow, D L ..	403	317	71	5,180	103*	21.05	1	19	17	0	—	390/31
Bairstow, J M ..	**43**	**39**	**4**	**1,051**	**174**	**30.02**	**2**	**3**	**0**	**0**	**—**	**33/3**
Baker, T M	4	1	0	3	3	3.00	0	0	89	4	22.25	3
Balderstone, J C	13	11	2	173	46	19.22	0	0	38	2	19.00	3
Ballance, G S ..	**60**	**56**	**9**	**2,559**	**152***	**54.44**	**3**	**17**	**0**	**0**	**—**	**21**
Batty, J D	38	16	7	50	13*	5.55	0	0	1,297	42	30.88	18
Berry, P J	1	0	0	0	—	—	0	0	28	0	—	0
Best, T L	5	1	1	8	8*	—	0	0	166	10	16.60	1
Bevan, M G	48	45	12	2,110	103*	63.93	2	19	540	28	19.28	11
Binks, J G	30	21	3	247	34	13.72	0	0	0	0	—	26/8
Blain, J A R	15	8	3	34	11*	6.80	0	0	462	14	33.00	3
Blakey, R J	373	319	84	7,361	130*	31.32	3	35	0	0	—	369/59
Blewett, G S ...	17	17	0	345	77	20.29	0	2	196	11	17.81	7
Booth, P A	5	2	1	7	6*	7.00	0	0	147	3	49.00	1
Bore, M K	55	24	10	90	15	6.42	0	0	1,600	50	32.00	15
Boycott, G	264	255	38	8,699	146	40.08	7	63	1,095	25	43.80	92
Bresnan, T T ..	**175**	**126**	**31**	**2'007**	**95***	**21.12**	**0**	**7**	**6,277**	**190**	**33.03**	**51**
Broadhurst, M ..	1	0	0	0	—	—	0	0	27	0	—	0
Brook, H C	**7**	**5**	**0**	**68**	**24**	**13.60**	**0**	**0**	**0**	**0**	**—**	**3**
Brooks, J A	12	4	1	7	6	2.33	0	0	461	15	30.73	3
Brophy, G L ...	68	57	12	1,240	93*	27.55	0	9	0	0	—	67/14
Byas, D	313	301	35	7,782	116*	29.25	5	44	659	25	26.36	128
Callis, E	1	1	0	0	0	0.00	0	0	0	0	—	0
Carrick, P	304	206	53	2,159	54	14.11	0	2	7,408	236	31.38	70
Carver, K	**17**	**4**	**4**	**52**	**35***	**—**	**0**	**0**	**440**	**14**	**31.42**	**2**
Chapman, C A ..	10	7	4	94	36*	31.33	0	0	0	0	—	7
Claydon, M E ..	7	2	0	15	9	7.50	0	0	293	8	36.62	0
Cleary, M F	4	3	1	50	23*	25.00	0	0	159	2	79.50	0
Close, D B	32	31	2	631	96	21.75	0	3	475	23	20.65	14
Coad, B O	**17**	**6**	**5**	**15**	**9**	**15.00**	**0**	**0**	**748**	**20**	**37.40**	**5**
Cooper, H P ...	142	74	34	483	29*	12.07	0	0	4,184	177	23.63	26
Cope, G A	37	20	13	96	18*	13.71	0	0	1,020	24	42.50	9
Coverdale, S P .	3	3	2	18	17*	18.00	0	0	0	0	—	3
Craven, V J	42	39	5	580	59	17.05	0	2	353	21	16.80	14
Dalton, A J	17	16	1	280	55	18.66	0	1	0	0	—	7
Dawood, I	25	20	4	260	57	16.25	0	1	0	0	—	18/8
Dawson, R K J ..	92	58	12	431	41	9.36	0	0	2,784	91	30.59	31
Dennis, S J	56	24	11	114	16*	8.76	0	0	1,736	42	41.33	7
Elliott, M T G ..	6	6	3	394	128*	131.33	3	0	0	0	—	0
Elstub, C J	10	4	4	6	4*	—	0	0	290	12	24.16	0
Fellows, G M ...	95	79	15	1,342	80*	20.96	0	6	836	22	38.00	27
Fisher, I D	28	12	3	68	20	7.55	0	0	708	29	24.41	6
Fisher, M D ...	**27**	**14**	**9**	**201**	**36***	**40.20**	**0**	**0**	**1,039**	**27**	**38.48**	**7**
Fleming, S P ...	7	7	1	285	139*	47.50	1	1	0	0	—	3
Fletcher, S D ..	129	32	18	109	16*	7.78	0	0	4,686	164	28.57	34
Foster, M J	20	14	1	199	118	15.30	1	0	370	6	61.66	6
Gale, A W	125	116	11	3,256	125*	31.00	2	17	0	0	—	24
Gibson, R	6	4	1	19	9	6.33	0	0	158	5	31.60	1
Gilbert, C R	5	4	0	55	37	13.75	0	0	199	8	24.87	2

Player	M	Inns	NO	Runs	HS	Av'ge	100s	50s	Runs	Wkts	Av'ge	Ct/St
Gillespie, J N	18	4	1	29	15*	9.66	0	0	601	18	33.38	6
Gough, D	214	120	33	1,280	72*	14.71	0	1	6,798	291	23.36	43
Gray, A K D	31	19	7	130	30*	10.83	0	0	843	25	33.72	8
Grayson, A P	66	49	8	587	55	14.31	0	1	1,441	39	36.94	19
Guy, S M	32	23	4	282	40	14.84	0	0	0	0	—	35/11
Hamilton, G M	101	70	18	1,059	57*	20.36	0	2	2,803	121	23.16	15
Hampshire, A W	4	3	0	3	3	1.00	0	0	0	0	—	1
Hampshire, J H	234	223	24	6,296	119	31.63	7	36	26	1	26.00	69
Hannon-Dalby, O J	5	1	1	21	21*	—	0	0	202	5	40.40	3
Handscomb, P S P	9	9	1	504	140	63.00	1	3	0	0	—	5
Harden, R J	19	16	2	230	42	16.42	0	0	0	0	—	1
Hartley, P J	219	145	49	1,609	83	16.76	0	4	7,476	283	26.41	40
Hartley, S N	171	154	31	2,815	83*	22.88	0	13	2,153	67	32.13	52
Harvey, I J	28	27	2	637	74	25.48	0	3	950	30	31.66	8
Head, T M	4	4	0	277	175	69.25	1	1	0	0	—	1
Hodd, A J	32	23	5	368	69*	20.44	0	1	0	0	—	39/8
Hodgson, D M	12	10	1	272	90	30.22	0	3	0	0	—	10/2
Hodgson, L J	6	2	0	9	9	4.50	0	0	161	4	40.25	1
Hoggard, M J	83	28	19	41	7*	4.55	0	0	2,682	118	22.72	7
Hutchison, P M	32	11	8	18	4*	6.00	0	0	844	43	19.62	3
Hutton, R A	107	80	25	1,075	65	19.54	0	4	3,000	128	23.43	27
Illingworth, R	41	15	11	171	45	42.75	0	0	793	40	19.82	14
Ingham, P G	12	10	4	312	87*	52.00	0	2	0	0	—	2
Inzamam ul Haq	3	3	0	69	53	23.00	0	1	0	0	—	0
Jaques, P A	43	42	2	1,588	105	39.70	1	13	0	0	—	16
Jarvis, P W	144	74	28	529	42	11.50	0	0	4,684	213	21.99	33
Johnson, C	129	102	22	1,615	73*	20.18	0	4	28	2	14.00	33
Johnson, M	14	6	3	34	15*	11.33	0	0	455	12	37.91	2
Katich, S M	3	3	2	79	40*	79.00	0	0	0	0	—	2
Kellett, S A	56	51	3	1,207	118*	25.14	2	4	16	0	—	13
Kettleborough, R A	10	6	3	71	28	23.66	0	0	72	3	24.00	4
Kirby, S P	29	12	3	38	15	4.22	0	0	1,061	24	44.20	6
Kohler-Cadmore T	9	9	0	472	164	52.44	1	3	**0**	**0**	**—**	**11**
Kruis, G J	55	22	11	138	31*	12.54	0	0	1,793	62	28.91	9
Lawson, M A	4	4	0	30	20	7.50	0	0	141	3	47.00	1
Leadbeater, B	105	100	19	2,245	90	27.71	0	11	95	5	19.00	26
Leaning, J A	42	37	7	996	131*	33.20	2	5	**154**	**7**	**22.00**	**20**
Lee, J E	4	0	0	0	0	—	0	0	116	7	16.57	0
Lees, A Z	42	39	2	1,109	102	29.97	1	8	0	0	—	15
Lehmann, D S	130	126	20	5,229	191	49.33	8	38	1,990	79	25.18	41
Lester, E I	1	1	0	0	0	0.00	0	0	0	0	—	0
Love, J D	220	203	33	4,298	118*	25.28	4	18	129	5	25.80	44
Lucas, D S	5	2	0	40	32	20.00	0	0	187	3	62.33	1
Lumb, M J	104	98	8	2,606	92	28.95	0	18	28	0	—	31
Lumb, R G	137	123	13	2,784	101	25.30	1	16	0	0	—	21
Lyth, A	114	107	8	3,553	144	35.88	5	16	**346**	**4**	**86.50**	**50**
McGrath, A	275	253	39	7,220	148	33.73	7	44	2,514	79	31.82	91
Maxwell, G J	8	7	1	312	111	52.00	1	2	144	3	48.00	4
Metcalfe, A A	194	189	15	5,584	127*	32.09	4	36	44	2	22.00	44
Middlebrook, J D	18	11	3	61	15*	7.62	0	0	530	13	40.76	5
Milburn, S M	4	2	1	14	13*	14.00	0	0	118	2	59.00	1
Miller, D A	3	3	0	45	44	15.00	0	0	0	0	—	3
Morris, A C	27	17	5	212	48*	17.66	0	0	464	21	22.09	5
Moxon, M D	237	229	21	7,380	141*	35.48	7	49	1,202	34	35.35	77

Player	M	Inns	NO	Runs	HS	Av'ge	100s	50s	Runs	Wkts	Av'ge	Ct/St
Nicholson, A G	120	46	22	155	15*	6.45	0	0	2,951	173	17.05	16
Nicholson, N G	2	2	1	1	1*	1.00	0	0	0	0	—	2
Old, C M	221	169	38	2,572	82*	19.63	0	10	5,841	308	18.96	56
Oldham, S	106	40	21	192	38*	10.10	0	0	3,136	142	22.08	17
Padgett, D E V	57	54	3	1,069	68	20.96	0	2	25	1	25.00	13
Parker, B	73	61	8	965	69	18.20	0	1	18	0	—	12
Patterson, S A	**88**	**36**	**19**	**230**	**25***	**13.52**	**0**	**0**	**3,173**	**110**	**28.84**	**17**
Pickles, C S	71	48	20	375	37*	13.39	0	0	2,403	63	38.14	23
Plunkett, L E	28	21	10	327	53	29.72	0	1	1,060	33	32.12	17
Pyrah, R M	114	75	20	978	69	17.78	0	2	3,572	133	26.85	35
Pujara, C A	8	8	1	370	101	52.85	1	3	0	0	—	4
Ramage, A	34	17	8	134	32*	14.88	0	0	1,178	30	39.26	3
Ramsden, G	1	0	0	0	—	—	0	0	26	2	13.00	0
Rana Naved -ul-Hasan	17	16	1	375	74	25.00	0	3	681	26	26.19	5
Rashid, A U	**104**	**72**	**21**	**1,039**	**71**	**20.37**	**0**	**1**	**3,863**	**135**	**28.61**	**33**
Read, J	1	0	0	0	—	—	0	0	0	0	—	1
Rhodes, S J	2	1	0	6	6	6.00	0	0	0	0	—	3
Rhodes, W M H	21	17	2	252	46	16.80	0	0	364	11	33.09	8
Richardson, R B	28	28	6	993	103	45.13	1	8	0	0	—	5
Richardson, S A	1	1	0	7	7	7.00	0	0	0	0	—	0
Robinson, A L	92	36	19	127	18*	7.47	0	0	2,588	105	24.64	14
Robinson, M A	89	30	16	41	7	2.92	0	0	2,795	91	30.71	7
Robinson, O E	3	2	2	16	12*	—	0	0	66	0	—	4
Robinson, P E	135	123	15	2,738	78*	25.35	0	14	0	0	—	47
Root, J E	**23**	**22**	**3**	**747**	**83**	**39.31**	**0**	**5**	**280**	**7**	**40.00**	**10**
Rudolph, J A	65	62	10	3,090	132*	59.42	9	19	37	0	—	32
Ryan, M	3	2	1	7	6*	7.00	0	0	149	5	29.80	3
Sadler, J L	1	1	0	19	19	19.00	0	0	0	0	—	0
Sanderson, B W	10	2	1	14	12*	14.00	0	0	247	8	30.87	5
Sayers, J J	31	30	2	594	62	21.21	0	5	79	1	79.00	2
Scofield, D	3	1	0	0	0	0.00	0	0	111	2	55.50	1
Shahzad, A	30	22	7	243	59*	16.20	0	1	1,182	34	34.76	7
Sharp, K	206	191	18	4,776	114	27.60	3	28	48	4	12.00	68
Sharpe, P J	91	86	4	1,515	89*	18.47	0	8	11	0	—	53
Shaw, C	48	20	10	127	26	12.70	0	0	1,396	58	24.06	8
Sidebottom, A	236	131	47	1,279	52*	15.22	0	1	6,918	260	26.60	51
Sidebottom, R J	113	51	22	303	30*	10.44	0	0	3,631	124	29.28	24
Silverwood, C E W	166	94	33	892	61	14.62	0	4	5,212	224	23.26	25
Smith, N	7	2	1	5	5	5.00	0	0	0	0	—	2
Smith, R	3	2	0	17	17	8.50	0	0	0	0	—	1
Squires, P J	56	48	5	708	79*	16.46	0	3	4	0	—	10
Starc, M A	4	2	2	5	4*	—	0	0	181	8	22.62	1
Stemp, R D	88	28	10	118	23*	6.55	0	0	2,996	100	29.96	14
Stevenson, G B	217	158	23	1,710	81*	12.66	0	2	6,820	290	23.51	38
Stott, W B	2	2	0	30	30	15.00	0	0	0	0	—	0
Stringer, P M	11	8	6	29	13*	14.50	0	0	256	15	17.06	0
Stuchbury, S	22	8	4	21	9*	5.25	0	0	677	29	23.34	2
Swallow, I G	8	5	3	37	17*	18.50	0	0	198	2	99.00	5
Swanepoel, P J	3	2	2	9	8*	—	0	0	100	3	33.33	0
Tattersall, J A	**8**	**5**	**1**	**143**	**89**	**35.75**	**0**	**0**	**0**	**0**	**—**	**5/1**
Taylor, C R	6	5	0	102	28	20.40	0	0	0	0	—	0
Taylor, K	10	10	0	135	30	13.50	0	0	168	11	15.27	3

Player	M	Inns	NO	Runs	HS	Av'ge	100s	50s	Runs	Wkts	Av'ge	Ct/St
Taylor, N S	1	0	0	0	0	—	0	0	45	1	45.00	1
Tendulkar, S R .	17	17	2	540	107	36.00	1	1	167	6	27.83	3
Thornicroft, N D	14	7	4	52	20	17.33	0	0	591	17	34.76	3
Townsley, R A J	5	4	1	81	34	27.00	0	0	62	0	—	1
Trueman, F S ..	11	9	1	127	28	15.87	0	0	348	21	16.57	5
Vaughan, M P ..	183	178	13	4,966	125*	30.09	3	29	1,860	60	31.00	56
Wainman, J C ..	4	3	1	51	33	25.50	0	0	201	5	40.20	1
Wainwright, D J	48	21	13	150	26	18.75	0	0	1,427	38	37.55	16
Waite, M E	**11**	**9**	**2**	**246**	**71**	**35.14**	**0**	**1**	**424**	**13**	**32.61**	**0**
Wardlaw, I	17	10	4	56	18	9.33	0	0	686	24	28.58	3
Waring, J	1	1	1	1	1*	—	0	0	11	0	—	0
Warren, A C ...	1	1	0	3	3	3.00	0	0	35	1	35.00	0
Wharf, A G	6	1	1	2	2*	—	0	0	176	8	22.00	1
White, C	292	266	39	6,384	148	28.12	5	28	6,120	248	24.67	84
Whiteley, J P ...	6	4	0	19	14	4.75	0	0	195	2	97.50	1
Widdup	4	4	0	49	38	12.25	0	0	0	0	—	2
Wigley, D H ...	1	1	0	0	0	0.00	0	0	38	0	—	0
Willey, D J	**16**	**12**	**1**	**327**	**131**	**29.72**	**1**	**1**	**646**	**28**	**23.07**	**2**
Williamson, K A	13	11	0	279	70	25.36	0	1	42	1	42.00	6
Wilson, D	61	47	8	430	46	11.02	0	0	1,527	76	20.09	22
Wood, G L	1	1	0	26	26	26.00	0	0	0	0	—	0
Wood, M J	145	134	14	3,270	160	27.25	5	14	76	3	25.33	57
Woodford, J D ..	72	57	14	890	69*	20.69	0	2	1,627	77	21.12	25
Younus Khan ...	11	8	0	248	100	31.00	1	0	144	2	72.00	5
Yuvraj Singh ...	9	9	0	196	50	21.77	0	1	197	3	65.66	1

YORKSHIRE T20i CRICKETERS 2003-2018 (Correct to October 29, 2018)

For England

Player	M	I	NO	Runs	HS	Av'ge	100s	50s	Balls	Runs	W	Av'ge	Best	4wI	Ct/St
BAIRSTOW, J M ...2011-18	27	22	6	396	60*	24.75	0	2	—	—	—	—	—	0	23
BRESNAN, T T ...2006-13/14	34	22	9	216	47*	16.61	0	0	663	887	24	36.95	3-10	0	10
PLUNKETT, L E ...2006-18	20	11	4	42	18	6.00	0	0	435	575	23	25.00	3-21	0	6
RASHID, A U ...2009-18	33	14	8	47	9*	7.83	0	0	654	818	31	26.38	3-11	0	9
ROOT, J E ...2012-18	28	26	4	787	90*	35.77	0	4	84	139	6	23.16	2-9	0	15
SHAHZAD, A ...2010-11	3	1	1	0	0*	—	0	0	66	97	3	32.33	2-38	0	1
VAUGHAN, M P ...2005-7	2	2	0	27	27	13.50	0	0	—	—	—	—	—	—	0
WILLEY, D J ...2015-18	24	17	5	152	29*	12.66	0	0	491	691	28	24.67	3-20	0	9

For Scotland

Player	M	I	NO	Runs	HS	Av'ge	100s	50s	Balls	Runs	W	Av'ge	Best	4wI	Ct/St
BLAIN, J A R ...2007-8	6	3	1	4	3*	2.00	0	0	120	108	6	18.00	2-23	0	1
HAMILTON, G M ...2007-10	12	8	0	90	32	11.25	0	0	—	—	—	—	—	0	3
WARDLAW, I ...2012/13-13/14	4	1	0	1	1	1.00	0	0	96	145	9	16.11	4-40	0	0

YORKSHIRE PLAYERS WHO PLAYED ALL THEIR T20i CRICKET AFTER LEAVING YORKSHIRE

For England

Player	M	I	NO	Runs	HS	Av'ge	100s	50s	Balls	Runs	W	Av'ge	Best	4wI	Ct/St
BATTY, G J ...2009	1	1	0	4	4	4.00	0	0	18	17	0	—	—	0	0
GOUGH, D ...2005-06	2	0	0	0	—	—	0	—	41	49	3	16.33	3-16	0	0
LUMB, M J ...2010-13/14	27	27	1	552	63	21.23	0	3	—	—	—	—	—	—	8
SIDEBOTTOM, R J ...2007-10	18	1	1	5	5*	—	0	0	367	437	23	19.00	3-16	0	5

Overseas Players
(Qualification: 20 t20 matches for Yorkshire)

For South Africa

Player	M	I	NO	Runs	HS	Av'ge	100s	50s	Balls	Runs	W	Av'ge	Best	4wI	Ct/St
RUDOLPH, J A ...2006	1	1	1	6	6*	—	0	0	—	—	—	—	—	0	0

T20 RECORDS SECTION
TROPHY WINNERS 2003-2018

		Yorkshire's Position				*Yorkshire's Position*
2003	Surrey	Group N 2 (6)	2011	Leicestershire	Group N 6 (9)
2004	Leicestershire	Group N 5 (6)	2012	Hampshire	Final
2005	Somerset	Group N 4 (6)	2013	Northamptonshire	Group N 6 (6)
2006	Leicestershire	Quarter-Final	2014	Warwickshire	Group N 5 (9)
2007	Kent	Quarter-Final	2015	Lancashire	Group N 8 (9)
2008	Middlesex	Group N 3 (6)	2016	Northamptonshire	Semi-Final
2009	Sussex	Group N 5 (6)	2017	Nottinghamshire	Group N 5 (9)
2010	Hampshire	Group N 6 (9)	2018	Worcestershire	Group N 5 (9)

SEASON-BY-SEASON RECORD OF ALL T20 MATCHES
PLAYED BY YORKSHIRE 2003-2018

Season	Played	Won	Lost	Tie	N R	Abd	Season	Played	Won	Lost	Tie	N R	Abd
2003	5	3	2	0	0	0	2012/13	6	2	3	0	1	0
2004	5	2	3	0	0	0	2013	10	2	7	1	0	0
2005	8	3	5	0	0	0	2014	11	6	5	0	0	3
2006	9	4	4	0	1	0	2015	14	5	8	1	0	0
2007	8	4	4	0	0	1	2016	15	8	6	0	1	1
2008	9	5	3	1	0	1	2017	12	6	5	1	0	2
2009	10	4	6	0	0	0	2018	16	8	8	0	0	0
2010	16	6	9	1	0	0							
2011	15	6	7	0	2	1		181	83	87	5	6	10
2012	12	9	2	0	1	1							

ANALYSIS OF T20 RESULTS V. ALL TEAMS 2003-2018
DOMESTIC MATCHES

		HOME				AWAY				
Opponents	Played	Won	Lost	Tied	N. R	Won	Lost	Tied	N. R	Abd
Derbyshire	27	8	7	0	0	8	3	0	1	0
Durham	31	10	4	1	0	6	9	0	1	0
Essex	1	0	0	0	0	0	1	0	0	0
Glamorgan	1	0	0	0	0	1	0	0	0	0
Hampshire	1	0	0	0	0	0	1	0	0	0
Lancashire	27	8	4	1	0	4	9	1	0	3
Leicestershire	21	5	5	0	0	3	7	1	0	1
Northamptonshire	12	3	3	0	0	4	1	1	0	2
Nottinghamshire	29	6	7	0	1	4	11	0	0	1
Sussex	2	0	0	0	0	1	1	0	0	0
Warwickshire	12	4	3	0	0	0	3	0	2	2
Worcestershire	9	4	1	0	0	1	3	0	0	1
Total	**173**	**48**	**34**	**2**	**1**	**32**	**49**	**3**	**4**	**10**

Abandoned matches are not included in the list of matches played.

OTHER MATCHES

		HOME				AWAY				
Opponents	*Played*	*Won*	*Lost*	*Tied*	*N. R*	*Won*	*Lost*	*Tied*	*N. R*	*Abd*
Uva	1	0	0	0	0	1	0	0	0	0
Trinidad and Tobago	1	0	0	0	0	1	0	0	0	0
Sydney Sixers	1	0	0	0	0	0	1	0	0	0
Mumbai	1	0	0	0	0	0	0	0	1	0
Highveld	1	0	0	0	0	0	1	0	0	0
Chennai	1	0	0	0	0	0	1	0	0	0
Lahore Qalandars	1	0	0	0	0	0	1	0	0	0
Hobart Hurricanes	1	0	0	0	1	0	0	0	0	0
Total	**8**	**0**	**0**	**0**	**0**	**3**	**4**	**0**	**1**	**0**
Grand Total	**181**	**48**	**34**	**2**	**1**	**35**	**53**	**3**	**5**	**10**

ABANDONED T20 MATCHES (10)

2007	v. Lancashire at Leeds
2008	v. Leicestershire at Leeds
2011	v. Northamptonshire at Leeds
2012	v. Lancashire at Manchester
2014	v. Warwickshire at Birmingham
	v. Lancashire at Leeds

v. Worcestershire at Worcester
2016   v. Nottinghamshire at Leeds
2017   v. Northamptonshire at
                Northampton
v. Warwickshire at Birmingham

T20 HIGHEST TEAM TOTALS

BY YORKSHIRE

260-4	v.	Northamptonshire at Leeds	2017
233-6	v.	Worcestershire at Leeds	2017
227-5	v.	Nottinghamshire at Leeds	2017
223-5	v.	Nottinghamshire at Nottingham	2017
226:8	v.	Birmingham Bears at Leeds	2018
223:6	v.	Durham at Leeds	2016
215:6	v.	Northamptonshire at Leeds	2016
213:7	v.	Worcestershire at Leeds	2010
212:5	v.	Worcestershire at Leeds	2012
211:6	v.	Leicestershire at Leeds	2004
210:3	v.	Derbyshire at Derby	2006
209:4	v.	Nottinghamshire at Leeds	2015
207:7	v.	Nottinghamshire at Nottingham	2004
202:8	v.	Lancashire at Manchester	2015
200:3	v.	Durham at Leeds	2018
200:5	v.	Nottinghamshire at Leeds	2014

T20 HIGHEST TEAM TOTALS

AGAINST YORKSHIRE

231:6	for Lancashire at Manchester	2015
225-5	for Nottinghamshire at Nottingham	2017
222:6	for Derbyshire at Leeds	2010
221:3	for Leicestershire at Leeds	2004
215:6	for Nottinghamshire at Nottingham	2011
215:6	for Durham at Chester-le-Street	2013
212:5	for Nottinghamshire at Nottingham	2018
210:7	for Nottinghamshire at Nottingham	2004
208:7	for Worcestershire at Worcester	2010
207:6	for Lancashire at Manchester	2005
201:5	for Nottinghamshire at Leeds	2014
204:7	for Lancashire at Manchester	2016
196-7	for Worcestershire at Leeds	2017
195:8	for Derbyshire at Leeds	2005
195:4	for Nottinghamshire at Nottingham	2006
193:5	for Sussex at Hove	2007

T20 HIGHEST INDIVIDUAL SCORES

BY YORKSHIRE

161	A Lyth	v.	Northamptonshire at Leeds	2017
118	D J Willey	v.	Worcestershire at Leeds	2017
109	I J Harvey	v.	Derbyshire at Leeds	2005
108*	I J Harvey	v.	Lancashire at Leeds	2004
102*	J M Bairstow	v	Durham at Chester-le-Street	2014
101*	H H Gibbs	v.	Northamptonshire at Northampton	2010
96*	M J Wood	v.	Nottinghamshire at Nottingham	2004
92*	G J Maxwell	v.	Nottinghamshire at Leeds	2015
92*	J E Root	v.	Lancashire at Manchester	2016
92*	A Lyth	v.	Durham at Leeds	2018
92	P A Jaques	v.	Leicestershire at Leeds	2004
92	J M Bairstow	v.	Durham at Leeds	2015
91	A W Gale	v.	Nottinghamshire at Leeds	2009
89	A J Finch	v.	Nottinghamshire at Leeds	2014
88	A J Finch	v.	Lancashire at Manchester	2014
87	A Lyth	v.	Durham at Leeds	2017

AGAINST YORKSHIRE

111	D L Maddy	for Leicestershire at Leeds	2004
101	S G Law	for Lancashire at Manchester	2005
101	A D Hales	for Nottinghamshire at Nottingham	2017
100*	G M Smith	for Derbyshire at Leeds	2008
100	Sohail Akhtar	for Lahore Qalandars at Abu Dhabi	2018
97	B J Hodge	for Leicestershire at Leicester	2003
96*	A B McDonald	for Leicestershire at Leeds	2011
94	L E Bosman	for Derbyshire at Leeds	2010
91*	G Clark	for Durham at Leeds	2015
91*	R A Whiteley	for Worcestershire at Leeds	2015
91	M A Ealham	for Nottinghamshire at Nottingham	2004
91	P Mustard	for Durham at Chester-le-Street	2013
90*	S R Patel	for Nottinghamshire at Leeds	2015
90*	B A Stokes	for Durham at Leeds	2018
88*	P D Collingwood	for Durham at Chester-le-Street	2017
85	A Flintoff	for Lancashire at Leeds	2004
83	J Moss	for Derbyshire at Leeds	2005

T20 BEST BOWLING

BY YORKSHIRE

6-19	T T Bresnan	v.	Lancashire at Leeds	2017
5-16	R M Pyrah	v.	Durham at Scarborough	2011
5-19	Azeem Rafiq	v.	Northamptonshire at Leeds	2017
5-22	M D Fisher	v.	Derbyshire at Leeds	2015
5-21	J A Brooks	v.	Leicestershire at Leeds	2013
4-18	M A Ashraf	v.	Derbyshire at Derby	2012
4-19	A U Rashid	v.	Durham at Leeds	2017
4-20	R M Pyrah	v.	Durham at Leeds	2008
4-20	A U Rashid	v.	Leicestershire at Leeds	2010
4-21	R M Pyrah	v.	Worcestershire at Leeds	2011
4-21	B W Sanderson	v.	Derbyshire at Derby	2011
4-21	J A Brooks	v.	Derbyshire at Leeds	2013
4-23	Rana Naved	v.	Nottinghamshire at Leeds	2009
4-24	A U Rashid	v.	Nottinghamshire at Nottingham	2008
4-25	R J Sidebottom	v.	Durham at Chester-le-Street	2012

AGAINST YORKSHIRE

4- 9	C K Langeveldt	for	Derbyshire at Leeds	2008
4-19	K H D Barker	for	Warwickshire at Birmingham	2010
4-19	J S Patel	for	Warwickshire at Leeds	2014
4-19	R Rampaul	for	Derbyshire at Chesterfield	2018
4-21	J Needham	for	Derbyshire at Leeds	2009
4-23	A J Hall	for	Northamptonshire at Northampton	2011
4-23	M W Parkinson	for	Lancashire at Leeds	2017
4-25	J A Morkel	for	Derbyshire at Chesterfield	2013
4-25	I G Butler	for	Northamptonshire at Leeds	2014
4-25	M A Wood	for	Durham at Birmingham	2016
4-31	Shakib al Hasan	for	Worcestershire at Worcester	2011
4-32	C A Ingram	for	Glamorgan at Cardiff	2016
4-37	K K Jennings	for	Durham at Chester-le-Street	2015
4-38	S J Harmison	for	Durham at Leeds	2008
3- 3	J K H Naik	for	Leicestershire at Leeds	2011
3- 6	B J Hodge	for	Leicestershire at Leicester	2003

T20 ECONOMICAL BOWLING

BY YORKSHIRE

4-0-12-2	T T Bresnan	v.	Lancashire at Manchester	2008

AGAINST YORKSHIRE

4-0-9-4	C K Langeveldt	for	Derbyshire at Leeds	2008

T20 MOST EXPENSIVE BOWLING

BY YORKSHIRE

4-0-65-2	M J Hoggard	v.	Lancashire at Leeds	2005

AGAINST YORKSHIRE

4-0-77-0	B W Sanderson	for	Northamptonshire at Leeds	2017

T20 HIGHEST AND LOWEST SCORES BY AND AGAINST YORKSHIRE
PLUS INDIVIDUAL BEST BATTING AND BOWLING

The lowest score is the lowest all-out score or the lowest score at completion of the allotted overs, five-over matches not included.

Yorkshire versus:

		By Yorkshire	Against Yorkshire
Derbyshire			
Highest Score:	In Yorkshire	198:4 at Leeds 2005	222:5 at Leeds 2010
	Away	210:3 at Derby 2006	170:5 at Chesterfield 2018
Lowest Score:	In Yorkshire	102 at Leeds 2018	124 at Chesterfield 2014
	Away	109 at Derby 2012	119:7 at Leeds 2007
Best Batting:	In Yorkshire	I J Harvey 109 at Leeds 2005	G M Smith 100* at Leeds 2008
	Away	A W Gale 79* at Chesterfield 2009	B A Godleman 71* at Chesterfield 2018
Best Bowling:	In Yorkshire	M D Fisher 5-22 at Leeds 2015	C K Langeveldt 4-9 at Leeds 2008
	Away	M A Ashraf 4-18 at Derby 2012	R Rampaul 4-19 at Chesterfield 2018
Durham			
Highest Score:	In Yorkshire	223:6 at Leeds 2016	191:6 at Leeds 2015
	Away	186:8 at Chester-le-Street 2014	215:6 at Chester-le-Street 2013
Lowest Score:	In Yorkshire	95 at Leeds 2014	116:8 at Leeds 2009
	Away	90:9 at Chester-le-Street 2009	98 at Chester-le-Street 2006
Best Batting:	In Yorkshire	J M Bairstow 92 at Leeds 2015	G Clark 91* at Leeds 2015
	Away	J M Bairstow 102* at Chester-le-Street 2014	P Mustard 91 at Chester-le-Street 2013
Best Bowling:	In Yorkshire	R M Pyrah 5-16 at Scarborough 2011	S J Harmison 4-38 at Leeds 2008
	Away	R J Sidebottom 4-25 at Chester-le-Street 2012	M A Wood 4-25 at Birmingham 2016
Essex			
Highest Score:	Away	143:7 at Chelmsford 2006	149:5 at Chelmsford 2006
Best Batting:	Away	G L Brophy 43 at Chelmsford 2006	J S Foster 48* at Chelmsford 2006
Best Bowling:	Away	A Shahzad 2-22 at Chelmsford 2006	T J Phillips 2-11 at Chelmsford 2006
Glamorgan			
Highest Score:	Away	180:8 at Cardiff 2016	90 at Cardiff 2016
Best Batting:	Away	D J Willey 79 at Cardiff 2016	J A Rudolph 26 at Cardiff 2016
Best Bowling:	Away	A U Rashid 4-26 at Cardiff 2016	C A Ingram 4-32 at Cardiff 2016
Hampshire			
Highest Score:	Away	140:6 at Cardiff 2012	150:6 at Cardiff 2012
Best Batting:	Away	D A Miller 72* at Cardiff 2012	J H K Adams 43 at Cardiff 2012
Best Bowling:	Away	R J Sidebottom 2-20 at Cardiff 2012	C P Wood 3-26 at Cardiff 2012

T20 HIGHEST AND LOWEST SCORES BY AND AGAINST YORKSHIRE
PLUS INDIVIDUAL BEST BATTING AND BOWLING (Continued)

The lowest score is the lowest all-out score or the lowest score at completion of the alloted overs, five-over matches not included.

Yorkshire versus:

		By Yorkshire	Against Yorkshire
Lancashire			
Highest Score:	In Yorkshire	185:8 at Leeds 2015	186:6 at Leeds 2015
	Away	202:8 at Manchester 2015	231:4 at Manchester 2015
Lowest Score:	In Yorkshire	111:8 at Leeds 2009	131:9 at Leeds 2004
	Away	97 at Manchester 2005	104:3 at Manchester 2003
Best Batting:	In Yorkshire	108* I J Harvey at Leeds 2004	85 A Flintoff at Leeds 2004
	Away	92* J E Root at Manchester 2016	101 S G Law at Manchester 2005
Best Bowling:	In Yorkshire	6-19 T T Bresnan at Leeds 2017	4-23 M W Parkinson at Leeds 2017
	Away	3-15 Azeem Rafiq at Manchester 2011	3-10 D G Cork at Manchester 2005
Leicestershire			
Highest Score:	In Yorkshire	211:6 at Leeds 2004	221:3 at Leeds 2004
	Away	182:5 at Leicester 2017	183:6 at Leicester 2017
Lowest Score:	In Yorkshire	134 at Leeds 2006	113:9 at Leeds 2013
	Away	105 at Leicester 2013	147:9 at Leicester 2012
Best Batting:	In Yorkshire	92 P A Jaques at Leeds 2004	111 D L Maddy at Leeds 2004
	Away	77 I J Harvey at Leicester 2005	97 B J Hodge at Leicester 2003
Best Bowling:	In Yorkshire	5-21 J A Brooks at Leeds 2013	3-3 J K H Naik at Leeds 2011
	Away	3-42 L E Plunkett at Leicester 2017	3-6 B J Hodge at Leicester 2003
Northamptonshire			
Highest Score:	In Yorkshire	260:4 at Leeds 2017	165:7 at Leeds 2014
	Away	181:3 at Northampton 2014	180:5 at Northampton 2010
Lowest Score:	In Yorkshire	162:7 at Leeds 2014	129:7 at Leeds 2018
	Away	144 at Northampton 2011	132:7 at Northampton 2011
Best Batting:	In Yorkshire	161 A Lyth at Leeds 2017	65 R E Levi at Leeds 2017
	Away	101* H H Gibbs at Northampton 2010	76 R E Levi at Northampton 2014
	In Yorkshire	5-19 Azeem Rafiq at Leeds 2017	4-25 I G Butler at Leeds 2011
	Away	3-15 T T Bresnan at Northampton 2016	4-23 A J Hall at Northampton 2011

399

T20 HIGHEST AND LOWEST SCORES BY AND AGAINST YORKSHIRE PLUS INDIVIDUAL BEST BATTING AND BOWLING (Continued)

The lowest score is the lowest all-out score or the lowest score at completion of the allotted overs, five-over matches not included.

Yorkshire versus:

Nottinghamshire

		By Yorkshire	Against Yorkshire
Highest Score:	In Yorkshire	227-5 at Leeds 2017	201-4 at Leeds 2014
	Away	223-5 at Nottingham 2017	225-5 at Nottingham 2017
Lowest Score:	In Yorkshire	141-8 at Leeds 2008	155-6 at Leeds 2009
	Away	112-7 at Nottingham 2010	136-6 at Nottingham 2008
Best Batting:	In Yorkshire	92* G J Maxwell at Leeds 2015	90* S R Patel at Leeds 2015
	Away	96* M J Wood at Nottingham 2004	101 A D Hales at Nottingham 2017
Best Bowling:	In Yorkshire	4-23 Rana Naved-ul-Hasan at Leeds 2009	3-38 J T Ball at Leeds 2014
	Away	4-24 A U Rashid at Nottingham 2008	3-16 H F Gurney at Nottingham 2016

Sussex

		By Yorkshire	Against Yorkshire
Highest Score:	Away	172-6 at Cardiff 2012	193-5 at Hove 2007
Lowest Score:	Away	155 at Hove 2007	136-8 at Cardiff 2012
Best Batting:	Away	68* J M Bairstow at Cardiff 2012	80* C D Nash at Cardiff 2012
Best Bowling:	Away	2-22 T T Bresnan at Cardiff 2012	3-22 S B Styris at Cardiff 2012

Warwickshire

		By Yorkshire	Against Yorkshire
Highest Score:	In Yorkshire	226-8 at Leeds 2018	176-4 at Leeds 2018
	Away	157-7 at Birmingham 2018	158-2 at Birmingham 2018
Lowest Score:	In Yorkshire	121-9 at Leeds 2010	145 at Leeds 2015
	Away	131 at Birmingham 2010	
Best Batting:	In Yorkshire	73 T Kohler-Cadmore at Leeds 2018	69* L J Evans at Leeds 2014
	Away	79 G S Ballance at Birmingham 2018	51* A J Hose at Birmingham 2018
Best Bowling:	In Yorkshire	3-21 T T Bresnan at Leeds 2017	4-19 J S Patel at Leeds 2014
	Away	3-25 S A Patterson at Birmingham 2010	4-19 K H D Barker at Birmingham 2010

T20 HIGHEST AND LOWEST SCORES BY AND AGAINST YORKSHIRE PLUS INDIVIDUAL BEST BATTING AND BOWLING (Continued)

Yorkshire versus:

		By Yorkshire		Against Yorkshire	
Worcestershire					
Highest Score:	In Yorkshire	233:6	at Leeds 2017	196:7	at Leeds 2017
	Away	187:7	at Worcester 2010	208:7	at Worcester 2010
Lowest Score:	In Yorkshire	117	at Leeds 2015	109	at Leeds 2010
	Away	142	at Worcester 2011	183:7	at Worcester 2011
Best Batting:	In Yorkshire	118 D J Willey	at Leeds 2017	91* R A Whiteley	at Leeds 2017
	Away	40 G S Ballance	at Worcester 2018	56 A N Kervezee	at Worcester 2011
Best Bowling:	In Yorkshire	4-21 R M Pyrah	at Leeds 2011	3-29 B L d'Oliveira	at Leeds 2015
	Away	3-30 A Shahzad	at Worcester 2011	4-31 Shakib al Hasan	at Worcester 2011
Chennai					
Highest Score:	Away	140:6	at Durban 2012	141:6	at Durban 2012
Best Batting:	Away	58 G S Ballance	at Durban 2012	47 S Badrinath	at Durban 2012
Best Bowling:	Away	3-23 I Wardlaw	at Durban 2012	2-12 J A Morkel	at Durban 2012
Highveld					
Highest Score:	Away	131:7	at Johannesburg 2012	134:5	at Johannesburg
Best Batting:	Away	31 P A Jaques	at Johannesburg 2012	32 Q de Kock	at Johannesburg
Best Bowling:	Away	2-21 S A Patterson	at Johannesburg 2012	2-23 A M Phangiso	at Johannesburg
Hobart Hurricanes					
Highest Score:	Away	144:1	at Abu Dhabi 2018	140:7	at Abu Dhabi 2018
Best Batting:	Away	72* T Kohler-Cadmore	at Abu Dhabi 2018	38 C P Jewell	at Abu Dhabi 2018
Best Bowling:	Away	2-29 K Carver	at Abu Dhabi 2018	1-24 J Clark	at Abu Dhabi 2018
Lahore Qalandars					
Highest Score:	Away	184:5	at Abu Dhabi 2018	189:4	at Abu Dhabi 2018
Best Batting:	Away	37 H C Brook	at Abu Dhabi 2018	100 Sohail Akhtar	at Abu Dhabi 2018
Best Bowling:	Away	2-26 J E Poysden	at Abu Dhabi 2018	2-36 Shaheen Shah Afridi	at Abu Dhabi 2018
Mumbai					
Highest Score:	Away		at Cape Town 2012	156: 6	at Cape Town
Best Batting:	Away			37 D R Smith	
Best Bowling:	Away	2-36 Azeem Rafiq	at Cape Town 2012		

T20 HIGHEST AND LOWEST SCORES BY AND AGAINST YORKSHIRE PLUS INDIVIDUAL BEST BATTING AND BOWLING (*Continued*)

Yorkshire versus:

Sydney Sixers

		By Yorkshire			Against Yorkshire		
Highest Score:	Away	96:9		at Cape Town 2012	98:2		at Cape Town 2012
Best Batting:	Away	25	J E Root	at Cape Town 2012	43*	M J Lumb	at Cape Town 2012
Best Bowling:	Away	1-21	Azeem Rafiq	at Cape Town 2012	3-22	M A Starc	at Cape Town 2012

Trinidad and Tobago

		By Yorkshire			Against Yorkshire		
Highest Score:	Away	154:4		at Centurion 2012	148:9		at Centurion 2012
Best Batting:	Away	64*	G S Ballance	at Centurion 2012	59	D Ramdin	at Centurion 2012
Best Bowling:	Away	3-13	R J Sidebottom	at Centurion 2012	1-16	K Y G Ottley	at Centurion 2012

Uva

		By Yorkshire			Against Yorkshire		
Highest Score:	Away	151:5		at Johannesburg 2012	150:7		at Johannesburg 2012
Best Batting:	Away	39*	D A Miller	at Johannesburg 2012	29	S H T Kandamby	at Johannesburg 2012
Best Bowling:	Away	2-29	M A Ashraf	at Johannesburg 2012	3-32	E M D Y Munaweera	at Johannesburg 2012

T20 MAN OF THE MATCH AWARDS (84)

A W Gale	8	J M Bairstow	3	H H Gibbs	2
A Lyth	7	I J Harvey	3	P A Jaques	2
A McGrath	6	J A Leaning	3	T Kohler-Cadmore	2
T T Bresnan	5	D A Miller	3	A Z Lees	2
R M Pyrah	5	A U Rashid	3	M J Lumb	2
D J Willey	5	K S Williamson	3		
Azeem Rafiq	4	A J Finch	2		

One each: G S Ballance, J A Brooks, M E Claydon, M D Fisher, S P Fleming, D S Lehmann, G J Maxwell, J E Root, J A Rudolph, B W Sanderson, J J Sayers, A Shahzad, D J Wainwright and C White

T20 PARTNERSHIPS OF 100 AND OVER 2003-2018 (21)

150	2nd wkt	A Lyth	(66)	and D J Willey	(79)	v. Northamptonshire at Northampton 2018
137*	2nd wkt	A W Gale	(60*)	and H H Gibbs	(76*)	v. Durham at Leeds	2010
131	1st wkt	A Lyth	(78)	and P A Jaques	(64)	v. Derbyshire at Leeds	2012
129	2nd wkt	A W Gale	(91)	and M P Vaughan	(41*)	v. Nottinghamshire at Leeds	2009
129	2nd wkt	T Kohler-Cadmore	(46)	and D J Willey	(80)	v. Lancashire at Leeds	2018
127	1st wkt	A Lyth	(161)	and T Kohler-Cadmore	(41)	v. Northamptonshire at Leeds 2017
124	2nd wkt	I J Harvey	(109)	and P A Jaques	(37)	v. Derbyshire at Leeds	2005
124	2nd wkt	A Lyth	(161)	and D J Willey	(40)	v. Northamptonshire at Leeds 2017
121	3rd wkt	J A Rudolph	(56)	and A McGrath	(59)	v. Leicestershire at Leicester	2008
116	1st wkt	A W Gale	(70)	and P A Jaques	(48)	v. Leicestershire at Leeds	2012
110*	4th wkt	A Lyth	(92*)	and J A Tattersall	(53*)	v. Durham at Leeds	2018
108	2nd wkt	I J Harvey	(108*)	and P A Jaques	(39)	v. Lancashire at Leeds	2004
108	2nd wkt	A Lyth	(59)	and H H Gibbs	(40)	v. Worcestershire at Leeds	2010
106	2nd wkt	D J Willey	(74)	and A Z Lees	(35)	v. Northamptonshire at Leeds 2016
104	1st wkt	A W Gale	(43)	and J A Rudolph	(61)	v. Leicestershire at Leicester	2009
104	2nd wkt	A Z Lees	(63)	and J A Leaning	(60*)	v. Warwickshire at Leeds	2015
103*	5th wkt	G S Ballance	(64*)	and A U Rashid	(33*)	v. Trinidad & Tobago at Centurion 2012/13
103	1st wkt	A W Gale	(65*)	and J A Rudolp	(53)	v. Leicestershire at Leicester	2010
101	2nd wkt	M J Wood	(57)	and M J Lumb	(55)	v. Nottinghamshire at Leeds	2003
101	3rd wkt	A J Hodd	(70)	and G J Maxwell	(92*)	v. Nottinghamshire at Leeds	2015
100	4th wkt	A Z Lees	(59)	and J A Leaning	(64)	v. Northamptonshire at Northampton 2016

T20 HIGHEST PARTNERSHIPS FOR EACH WICKET

1st wkt	131	A Lyth	(78)	and P A Jaques	(64)	v. Derbyshire at Leeds	2012
2nd wkt	150	A Lyth	(66)	and D J Willey	(79)	v. Northamptonshire at Northampton 2018
3rd wkt	121	J A Rudolph	(56)	and A McGrath	(59)	v. Leicestershire at Leicester	2008
4th wkt	100	A Z Lees	(59)	and J A Leaning	(64)	v. Northamptonshire at Northampton 2016
5th wkt	103*	G S Ballance	(64*)	and A U Rashid	(33*)	v. Trinidad & Tobago at Centurion	2012/13
6th wkt	76	J E Root	(92*)	and L E Plunkett	(22)	v. Lancashire at Manchester	2016
7th wkt	68*	T T Bresnan	(45*)	and A U Rashid	(29*)	v. Warwickshire at Leeds	2014
8th wkt	54	T T Bresnan	(51)	and J D Middlebrook	(29*)	v. Lancashire at Manchester	2015
9th wkt	33*	A U Rashid	(5*)	and D Gough	(20*)	v. Lancashire at Leeds	2008
10th wkt	28*	A U Rashid	(28*)	and G J Kruis	(12*)	v. Durham at Chester-le-Street	2009

ALL WHO HAVE TAKEN 4 WICKETS IN AN INNINGS (19)

M A ASHRAF (1)

4-18	v.	Derbyshire	at Derby	2012

AZEEM RAFIQ (1)

5-19	v.	Northamptonshire	at Leeds	2017

T T BRESNAN (1)

6-19	v.	Lancashire	at Leeds	2017

J A BROOKS (2)

5-21	v.	Leicestershire	at Leeds	2013
4-21	v.	Derbyshire	at Leeds	2013

M D FISHER (1)

5-22	v.	Derbyshire	at Leeds	2015

C J MCKAY (1)

4-33	v.	Derbyshire	at Leeds	2010

RANA NAVED-UL-HASAN (1)

4-23	v.	Nottinghamshire	at Leeds	2009

S A PATTERSON (1)

4-30	v.	Lancashire	at Leeds	2010

R M PYRAH (3)

5-16	v.	Durham	at Scarborough	2011
4-20	v.	Durham	at Leeds	2006
4-21	v.	Worcestershire	at Leeds	2011

A U RASHID (5)

4-19	v.	Durham	at Leeds	2017
4-20	v.	Leicestershire	at Leeds	2011
4-24	v.	Nottingham	at Nottingham	2008
4-26	v.	Lancashire	at Leeds	2011
4-26	v.	Glamorgan	at Cardiff	2016

B W SANDERSON (1)

4-21	v.	Derbyshire	at Derby	2011

R J SIDEBOTTOM (1)

4-25	v.	Durham	at Chester-le-Street	2012

CAREER AVERAGES FOR YORKSHIRE

ALL t20 MATCHES 2003-2018

Player	M	Inns	NO	Runs	HS	Av'ge	100s	50s	Runs	Wkts	Av'ge	Ct/St
Ashraf, M A ...	17	1	0	4	4	4.00	0	0	462	17	27.17	1
Azeem Rafiq ...	95	37	24	153	21*	11.76	0	0	2,489	102	24.40	36
Bairstow, J M .	**63**	58	11	**1,231**	**102***	**26.19**	**1**	**4**	**0**	**0**	**—**	**27/8**
Ballance, G S ..	**74**	64	8	**1,366**	79	24.39	0	4	**0**	**0**	**—**	**40**
Best, T L	8	3	2	10	10*	10.00	0	0	243	7	34.71	4
Blakey, R J ..	7	5	1	119	32	29.75	0	0			—	5/1
Bresnan, T T .	**110**	85	33	**1,150**	51	22.11	**0**	**1**	**2,797**	**110**	**25.42**	**41**
Brook, H C	**10**	10	3	**244**	44	34.85	**0**	**0**	**13**	**0**	**—**	**0**
Brooks, J A	23	0	0		—		0	0	582	22	26.45	11
Brophy, G L ..	54	46	9	717	57*	19.37	0	2	0	0	—	25/7
Carver, K	**10**	**2**	**1**	**2**	**2**	**2.00**	**0**	**0**	**208**	**8**	**26.00**	**5**
Claydon, M E ..	7	2	2	14	12*	—	0	0	188	5	37.60	2
Coad, B O	**8**	**2**	**1**	**3**	**2***	**—**	**0**	**0**	**194**	**7**	**27.71**	**5**
Craven, V J	6	6	4	76	44*	38.00	0	0	67	0	—	3
Dawood, I	11	8	3	44	15	8.80	0	0	0	0	—	5/2
Dawson, R K J .	22	8	3	71	22	14.20	0	0	558	24	23.25	7
Finch, A J	16	16	0	332	89	20.75	0	2	24	1	24.00	16
Fisher, M D ...	**22**	**5**	**4**	**24**	**6***	**24.00**	**0**	**0**	**646**	**23**	**28.08**	**7**
Fleming, S P ..	4	4	0	62	58	15.50	0	1	0	0	—	1
Gale, A W	104	97	8	2,260	91	25.39	0	16	0	0	—	30
Gibbs, H H	15	15	3	443	101*	36.91	1	2	0	0	—	8
Gibson, R	3	2	0	32	18	16.00	0	0	30	0	—	1
Gilbert, C R	13	9	2	107	38*	15.28	0	0	0	0	—	7
Gillespie, J N ..	17	4	2	14	8*	7.00	0	0	422	17	24.82	5
Gough, D	17	7	3	42	20*	10.50	0	0	416	16	26.00	2
Gray, A K D ...	8	3	0	17	13	5.66	0	0	211	9	23.44	4
Guy, S M	10	6	1	44	13	8.80	0	0	0	0	—	2
Hamilton, G M .	3	3	1	41	41*	20.50	0	0	0	0	—	1
Handscomb, P S P	7	6	0	97	31	16.16	0	0	0	0	—	3/3
Hannon-Dalby, O J	2	0	0	0	—		0	0	58	3	19.33	0
Harvey, I J	10	10	1	438	109	48.66	2	2	258	10	25.80	4
Head, T M	4	4	0	113	40	28.25	0	0	4	0	—	0
Hodd, A J	17	14	4	147	70	11.30	0	1	0	0	—	9/6
Hodgson, D M ..	16	14	2	213	52*	17.75	0	1	0	0	—	9/1
Hodgson, L J ...	2	1	0	39	39*	—	0	0	59	2	29.50	1
Hoggard, M J ..	15	2	1	19	18	19.00	0	0	472	13	36.30	4
Jaques, P A	34	32	3	907	92	31.27	0	6	15	0	—	5
Kirby, S P	3	0	0	0	—		0	0	119	4	29.75	1
Kohler-Cadmore, T												
	26	26	1	681	75	27.24	**0**	**5**	**0**	**0**	**—**	**14**
Kruis, G J	20	5	3	41	22	20.50	0	0	486	19	25.57	6
Lawson, M A K .	2	1	1	4	4*	—	0	0	87	3	29.00	1
Leaning, J A ...	**47**	41	11	**839**	64	27.96	**0**	**2**	**30**	**0**	**—**	**22**
Lees, A Z	37	36	2	857	67*	25.20	0	4	0	0	—	12
Lehmann, D S ..	9	9	3	252	68	42.00	0	0	180	8	22.50	4
Lumb, M J	26	26	3	442	84*	19.21	0	4	65	3	21.66	8
Lyth, A	**101**	92	3	**2,240**	161	25.16	**1**	**11**	**193**	**6**	**32.16**	**49**
McGrath, A ...	66	61	12	1,403	73*	28.63	0	8	698	23	30.34	26
McKay, C J ...	8	6	3	54	21*	18.00	0	0	258	10	25.80	1
Marsh, S E	11	11	4	289	60*	41.28	0	2	0	0	—	1

Player	M	Inns	NO	Runs	HS	Av'ge	100s	50s	Runs	Wkts	Av'ge	Ct/St
Maxwell, G J ...	12	12	1	229	92*	20.81	0	1	264	12	22.00	6
Middlebrook, J D	4	2	2	33	29*	—	0	0	101	4	25.25	1
Miller, D A	14	13	4	457	74*	50.77	0	4	0	0	—	7
Patterson, S A .	62	9	4	9	3*	1.80	0	0	1,784	61	29.24	9
Plunkett, L E ..	42	31	10	353	36	16.80	0	0	1,146	44	26.04	13
Poysden, J E ..	2	0	0	0	—	—	0	0	48	3	16.00	1
Pyrah, R M	105	71	21	593	42	11.86	0	0	2,315	108	21.43	40
Rana Naved-ul-Hasan	8	8	2	63	20*	10.50	0	0	159	11	14.45	2
Rashid, A U ...	103	63	20	577	36*	13.41	0	0	2,668	110	24.25	34
Rhodes, W M H	18	16	3	128	45	9.84	0	0	283	13	21.76	2
Robinson, O E..	7	3	0	5	3	1.66	0	0	162	6	27.00	3
Root, J E	33	29	7	633	92*	28.77	0	4	269	4	67.25	11
Rudolph, J A ...	39	35	5	710	61	23.66	0	3	145	6	24.16	7
Sanderson, B W	4	0	0	0	0	—	0	0	74	6	12.33	0
Sarfraz Ahmed .	5	4	0	53	42	13.25	0	0	0	0	—	3/1
Sayers, J J	17	14	0	253	44	18.07	0	0	0	0	—	5
Shahzad, A	22	16	4	129	20	10.75	0	0	576	17	33.88	5
Shaw, J	5	2	1	1	1	1.00	0	0	138	2	69.00	1
Sidebottom, R J .	40	16	10	87	16*	14.50	0	0	1,069	42	25.45	9
Silverwood, C E W	9	5	2	32	13*	10.66	0	0	264	7	37.71	4
Starc, M A	10	2	1	0	0*	0.00	0	0	218	21	10.38	1
Swanepoel, P J .	2	1	1	2	2*	—	0	0	60	3	20.00	1
Tattersall, J A .	16	10	2	191	53*	23.87	0	1	0	0	—	10/4
Taylor, C R	2	2	1	10	10*	10.00	0	0	0	0	—	0
Thompson, J A	9	6	3	22	12*	7.33	0	0	208	8	26.00	4
Vaughan, M P ..	16	16	1	292	41*	19.46	0	0	81	1	81.00	2
Wainman, J C ..	2	1	1	12	12*	—	0	0	49	1	49.00	0
Wainwright, D J	26	9	6	23	6*	7.66	0	0	551	21	26.23	9
Waite, M J	6	3	3	34	19*	—	0	0	81	2	40.50	3
Wardlaw, I	10	1	1	1	1	—	0	0	179	5	35.80	5
Warren, A C ...	2	0	0	0		—	0	0	70	4	17.50	0
White, C	33	31	0	570	55	18.38	0	2	132	2	66.00	8
Willey, D J	33	32	1	1,104	118	35.61	1	7	859	29	29.62	14
Williamson, K S	12	11	0	302	65	27.45	0	1	37	3	12.33	3
Wood, M J	15	15	3	328	96*	27.33	0	2	32	2	16.00	11
Younus Khan ...	2	2	0	55	40	27.50	0	0	32	2	16.00	0
Yuvraj Singh ...	5	5	0	154	71	30.80	0	1	51	5	10.20	0

SECOND ELEVEN CHAMPIONSHIP 1959-1961 AND 1975-2018

SUMMARY OF RESULTS BY SEASON

Season	Played	Won	Lost	Drawn	Tied	Abandoned	Position in Championship
1959	10	4	1	5	0	0	7
1960	10	1	3	6	0	0	14
1961	9	2	2	5	0	1	11
1975	14	4	0	10	0	0	4
1976	14	5	5	4	0	0	5
1977	**16**	**9**	**0**	**7**	**0**	**1**	**1**
1978	15	5	2	8	0	1	4
1979	16	5	0	11	0	0	3
1980	14	5	2	7	0	1	5
1981	16	2	3	11	0	0	11
1982	16	2	3	11	0	0	14 =
1983	11	5	1	5	0	3	2
1984	**15**	**9**	**3**	**3**	**0**	**0**	**1**
1985	14	3	3	8	0	1	12
1986	16	5	1	10	0	0	5
1987	**15**	**5**	**2**	**8**	**0**	**1**	**1 =**
1988	16	4	1	11	0	0	9
1989	17	2	3	12	0	0	9 =
1990	16	1	6	9	0	0	17
1991	**16**	**8**	**1**	**7**	**0**	**0**	**1**
1992	17	5	2	10	0	0	5
1993	17	6	1	10	0	0	3
1994	17	6	2	9	0	0	2
1995	17	7	1	9	0	0	5
1996	17	6	3	8	0	0	4
1997	16	8	5	3	0	1	2
1998	15	4	2	9	0	1	9
1999	16	3	8	5	0	1	14
2000	14	5	2	7	0	1	5
2001	12	8	2	2	0	1	2
2002	12	5	1	6	0	0	3
2003	**10**	**7**	**1**	**2**	**0**	**0**	**1**
2004	7	2	0	5	0	1	8
2005	12	2	4	6	0	0	10
2006	14	6	4	4	0	0	3
2007	12	4	5	3	0	0	10
2008	12	4	4	4	0	2	5
2009	9	5	0	4	0	0	(Group A) 2
2010	9	2	4	3	0	0	(Group A) 8
2011	9	0	4	4	1	0	(Group A) 10
2012	7	1	2	4	0	2	(North) 9
2013	9	3	4	2	0	0	(North) 4
2014	9	2	1	6	0	0	(North) 4
2015	9	2	4	3	0	0	(North) 7
2016	9	2	3	4	0	0	(North) 5
2017	8	2	0	6	0	1	(North) 4
2018	9	3	1	5	0	0	(North) 5
Totals	610	196	112	301	1	19	

Matches abandoned without a ball being bowled are not counted as a match played. The Championship was divided into two groups from 2009, each team playng each other once. The two group winners play for the Championship

ANALYSIS OF RESULTS AGAINST EACH OPPONENT

County	Played	Won	Lost	Drawn	Tied	Abandoned	First Played
Derbyshire	59	13	8	38	0	3	1959
Durham	34	11	6	17	0	2	1992
Essex	13	9	2	2	0	0	1990
Glamorgan	40	11	3	26	0	2	1975
Gloucestershire	10	3	3	4	0	0	1990
Hampshire	12	4	1	7	0	0	1990
Kent	26	5	4	17	0	1	1981
Lancashire	71	14	19	38	0	3	1959
Leicestershire	33	15	7	10	1	1	1975
MCC Young Cricketers	8	4	1	3	0	0	2005
MCC Universities	4	1	1	2	0	0	2011
Middlesex	18	7	2	9	0	0	1977
Northamptonshire	51	16	6	29	0	2	1959
Nottinghamshire	60	17	13	30	0	4	1959
Scotland	2	1	0	1	0	0	2007
Somerset	18	9	3	6	0	0	1988
Surrey	36	9	9	18	0	2	1976
Sussex	16	6	5	5	0	0	1990
Warwickshire	64	23	13	28	0	0	1959
Worcestershire	43	20	6	17	0	0	1961
Totals	618	198	112	307	1	20	

Note: Matches abandoned are not included in the total played.

Largest Victory   An innings and 230 runs v. Glamorgan at Headingley, 1986
Largest Defeat   An innings and 124 runs v. Gloucestershire at Bradford, 1994
Narrowest Victory   By 1 run v. Lancashire at Old Trafford, 2003
Narrowest Defeat   By 8 runs v. Derbyshire at Harrogate, 1982

Highest Total

By Yorkshire: 585 for 8 wkts dec v. Lancashire at Scarborough, 2017
Against Yorkshire: 567 for 7 wkts dec by Middlesex at RAF Vine Lane, Uxbridge, 2000

Lowest Total

By Yorkshire   66 v Nottinghamshire at Trent College, 2016
Against Yorkshire: 36 by Lancashire at Elland, 1979

Highest Match Aggregate

1,470 for 39 wkts   v. Gloucestershire at Cheltenham, 2001

Highest Individual Score

For Yorkshire: 273* by R J Blakey v. Northamptonshire at Northampton, 1986
Against Yorkshire: 235 by O A Shah for Middlesex at Leeds, 1999

Century in Each Innings

For Yorkshire:	C White	209* and 115*	v. Worcestershire at Worcester, 1990 (The only instance of two unbeaten centuries in the same match)
	K Sharp	150* and 127	v. Essex at Elland, 1991
	A A Metcalfe	109 and 136*	v. Somerset at North Perrott, 1994
	R A Kettleborough	123 and 192*	v. Nottinghamshire at Todmorden, 1996
	C R Taylor	201* and 129	v. Sussex at Hove, 2005
	A W Gale	131 and 123	v. Somerset at Taunton, 2006
	J J Sayers	157 and 105	v. Lancashire at Leeds, 2007

Century in Each Innings *(Continued)*

Against Yorkshire:

N Nannan	100	and 102*	for Nottinghamshire at Harrogate, 1979
G D Lloyd	134	and 103	for Lancashire at Scarborough, 1989
A J Swann	131	and 100	for Northamptonshire at York, 1998
G J Kennis	114	and 114	for Somerset at Taunton, 1999

Most Career Runs

B Parker   7,450 in 122 matches (average 40.48)

Best Bowling in an Innings

For Yorkshire: 9 for 27 by G A Cope v. Northamptonshire at Northampton, 1979
Against Yorkshire: 8 for 15 by I Folley for Lancashire at Heywood, 1983

Best Bowling in a Match

For Yorkshire: 13 for 92 (6 for 48 and 7 for 44) by M K Bore v. Lancashire
at Harrogate, 1976
Against Yorkshire: 13 for 100 (7 for 45 and 6 for 55) by N J Perry for Glamorgan
at Cardiff, 1978

Most Career Wickets

Paul A Booth   248 in 85 matches, average 29.33

Totals of 450 and over

By Yorkshire (30)

Score	Versus	Ground	Season
585 for 8 wkts dec	Lancashire	Scarborough	2017
538 for 9 wkts dec	Worcestershire	Stamford Bridge	2007
534 for 5 wkts dec	Lancashire	Stamford Bridge	2003
530 for 8 wkts dec	Nottinghamshire	Middlesbrough	2000
526 for 8 wkts dec	MCC Young Cricketers	High Wycombe	2017
514 for 3 wkts dec	Somerset	Taunton	1988
509 for 4 wkts dec	Northamptonshire	Northampton	1986
508	Durham	Riverside	2017
502	Derbyshire	Chesterfield	2003
501 for 5 wkts dec	MCC Young Cricketers	Stamford Bridge	2009
497	Derbyshire	Chesterfield	2005
495 for 5 wkts dec	Somerset	Taunton	2006
488 for 8 wkts dec	Warwickshire	Harrogate	1984
486 for 6 wkts dec	Glamorgan	Leeds	1986
480	Leicestershire	Market Harborough	2013
476 for 3 wkts dec	Glamorgan	Gorseinon	1984
475 for 9 wkts dec	Nottinghamshire	Nottingham	1995
474 for 3 wkts dec	Glamorgan	Todmorden	2003
474	Durham	Stamford Bridge	2003
470	Lancashire	Leeds	2006
469	Warwickshire	Castleford	1999
462	Scotland	Stamford Bridge	2007
461 for 8 wkts dec	Essex	Stamford Bridge	2006
459 for 3 wkts dec	Leicestershire	Oakham	1997
459 for 6 wkts dec	Glamorgan	Bradford	1992
457 for 9 wkts dec	Kent	Canterbury	1983
456 for 5 wkts dec	Gloucestershire	Todmorden	1990
456 for 6 wkts dec	Nottinghamshire	York	1986
454 for 9 wkts dec	Derbyshire	Chesterfield	1959
452 for 9 wkts dec	Glamorgan	Cardiff	2005

Totals of 450 and over

Score	For	Ground	Season
567 for 7 wkts dec	Middlesex	RAF Vine Lane, Uxbridge	2000
555 for 7 wkts dec	Derbyshire	Stamford Bridge	2002
530 for 9 wkts dec	Leicestershire	Hinckley	2015
525 for 5 wkts dec	Sussex	Hove	2005
502 for 4 wkts dec	Warwickshire	Edgbaston Community Foundation Sports Ground	2016
493 for 8 wkts dec	Nottinghamshire	Lady Bay, Nottingham	2002
488 for 8 wkts dec	Warwickshire	Castleford	1999
486	Essex	Chelmsford	2000
485	Gloucestershire	North Park, Cheltenham	2001
477	Lancashire	Headingley	2006
471	Warwickshire	Clifton Park, York	2010
458	Lancashire	Bradford	1997
454 for 7 wkts dec	Lancashire	Todmorden	1993
450 for 7 wkts (inns closed)	Derbyshire	Bradford	1980

Completed Innings under 75

By Yorkshire (6)

Score	Versus	Ground	Season
66	Nottinghamshire	Trent College	2016
67	Worcestershire	Barnt Green (1st inns)	2013
68	Worcestershire	Barnt Green (2nd inns)	2013
69	Lancashire	Heywood	1983
74	Derbyshire	Chesterfield	1960
74	Nottinghamshire	Bradford	1998

Against Yorkshire (10)

Score	By	Ground	Season
36	Lancashire	Elland	1979
49	Leicestershire	Leicester	2008
50	Lancashire	Liverpool	1984
60	Derbyshire	Bradford	1977
60	Surrey	Sunbury-on-Thames	1977
62	MCC YC	High Wycombe	2005
64	Nottinghamshire	Brodsworth	1959
66	Leicestershire	Lutterworth	1977
72	Sussex	Horsham	2003
74	Worcestershire	Barnsley	1978

Individual Scores of 150 and over (68)

Score	Player	Versus	Ground	Season
273*	R J Blakey	Northamptonshire	Northampton	1986
238*	K Sharp	Somerset	Taunton	1988
233	P E Robinson	Kent	Canterbury	1983
230	T Kohler-Cadmore	Derbyshire	York	2017
221*	K Sharp	Gloucestershire	Todmorden	1990
219	G M Hamilton	Derbyshire	Chesterfield	2003
218*	A McGrath	Surrey	Elland	1994
212	G S Ballance	MCC Young Cricketers	Stamford Bridge	2009
209*	C White	Worcestershire	Worcester	1990
205	C R Taylor	Glamorgan	Todmorden	2003
204	B Parker	Gloucestershire	Bristol	1993
203	A McGrath	Durham	Headingley	2005
202*	J M Bairstow	Leicestershire	Oakham	2009
202	A Z Lees	Durham	Riverside	2017
202	M J Wood	Essex	Stamford Bridge	2006
201*	C R Taylor	Sussex	Hove	2005
200*	D Byas	Worcestershire	Worcester	1992
200*	A McGrath	Northamptonshire	Northampton	2012
192*	R A Kettleborough	Nottinghamshire	Todmorden	1996
191	P E Robinson	Warwickshire	Harrogate	1984
191	M J Wood	Derbyshire	Rotherham	2000
191	M J Lumb	Nottinghamshire	Middlesbrough	2000
189*	C S Pickles	Gloucestershire	Bristol	1991
186	A McGrath	MCC Universities	York	2011
184	J D Love	Worcestershire	Headingley	1976
183	A W Gale	Durham	Stamford Bridge	2006
174	G L Brophy	Worcestershire	Stamford Bridge	2007
173	S N Hartley	Warwickshire	Edgbaston	1980
173	A A Metcalfe	Glamorgan	Gorseinon	1984
173	B Parker	Sussex	Hove	1996
173	R A Kettleborough	Leicestershire	Oakham School	1997
173	T Kohler-Cadmore	Northamptonshire	Desborough	2018
172	A C Morris	Lancashire	York	1995
170*	R A J Townsley	Glamorgan	Harrogate	1975
169	J E Root	Warwickshire	York	2010
168	M J Wood	Leicestershire	Oakham School	1997
166	A A Metcalfe	Lancashire	York	1984
166	C A Chapman	Northamptonshire	York	1998
165*	A Lyth	Durham	Stamford Bridge	2006
165	J J Sayers	Sussex	Hove	2006
164*	A W Gale	Leicestershire	Harrogate	2002
164	J C Balderstone	Nottinghamshire	Harrogate	1960
163*	J E Root	Leicestershire	Oakham	2009
163	A A Metcalfe	Derbyshire	Chesterfield	1992
162*	D Byas	Surrey	Scarborough	1987
162*	R Gibson	Leicestershire	York	2016
161	H C Brook	Lancashire	Scarborough	2017
160	A A Metcalfe	Somerset	Bradford	1993
157	J J Sayers	Lancashire	Headingley	2007
155	S M Guy	Derbyshire	Chesterfield	2005
154*	C R Taylor	Surrey	Whitgift School	2005
153*	A A Metcalfe	Warwickshire	Bingley	1995
153	C White	Worcestershire	Marske-by-the-Sea	1991

Individual Scores of 150 and over *(Continued)*

Score	Player	Versus	Ground	Season
153	R A Stead	Surrey	Todmorden	2002
152	A A Metcalfe	Gloucestershire	Bristol	1993
151*	P E Robinson	Nottinghamshire	York	1986
151*	S J Foster	Kent	Elland	1992
151*	J J Sayers	Durham	Stamford Bridge	2004
151	P J Hartley	Somerset	Clevedon	1989
151	A McGrath	Somerset	Elland	1995
151	V J Craven	Glamorgan	Todmorden	2003
150*	K Sharp	Essex	Elland	1991
150*	G M Fellows	Hampshire	Todmorden	1998
150*	S M Guy	Nottinghamshire	Headingley	2005
150*	J A Leaning	Worcestershire	Worcester	2011
150	K Sharp	Glamorgan	Ebbw Vale	1983
150	S N Hartley	Nottinghamshire	Worksop	1988
150	C R Taylor	Derbyshire	Chesterfield	2003

7 Wickets in an Innings (31)

Analysis	Player	Versus	Ground	Season
9 for 27	G A Cope	Northamptonshire	Northampton	1977
9 for 62	M K Bore	Warwickshire	Scarborough	1976
8 for 33	B O Coad	MCC Young Cricketers	York	2018
8 for 53	S J Dennis	Nottinghamshire	Nottingham	1983
8 for 57	M K Bore	Lancashire	Manchester	1977
8 for 79	P J Berry	Derbyshire	Harrogate	1991
7 for 13	P Carrick	Northamptonshire	Marske-by-the-Sea	1977
7 for 21	S Silvester	Surrey	Sunbury-on-Thames	1977
7 for 22	J A R Blain	Surrey	Purley	2004
7 for 32	P W Jarvis	Surrey	The Oval	1984
7 for 34	P Carrick	Glamorgan	Leeds	1986
7 for 37	P M Hutchison	Warwickshire	Coventry	2001
7 for 39	G M Hamilton	Sussex	Leeds	1995
7 for 40	M K Bore	Worcestershire	Old Hill	1976
7 for 44	M K Bore	Lancashire	Harrogate	1976
7 for 44	J P Whiteley	Worcestershire	Leeds	1979
7 for 51	J D Middlebrook	Derbyshire	Rotherham	2000
7 for 53	J P Whiteley	Warwickshire	Birmingham	1980
7 for 55	C White	Leicestershire	Bradford	1990
7 for 58	K Gillhouley	Derbyshire	Chesterfield	1960
7 for 58	P J Hartley	Lancashire	Leeds	1985
7 for 63	M J Hoggard	Worcestershire	Harrogate	1998
7 for 65	M K Bore	Nottinghamshire	Steetley	1976
7 for 70	J D Batty	Leicestershire	Bradford	1992
7 for 71	J D Batty	Hampshire	Harrogate	1994
7 for 81	K Gillhouley	Lancashire	Scarborough	1960
7 for 84	I J Houseman	Kent	Canterbury	1989
7 for 88	I G Swallow	Nottinghamshire	Nottingham	1983
7 for 90	A P Grayson	Kent	Folkestone	1991
7 for 93	D Pickles	Nottinghamshire	Nottingham	1960
7 for 94	K Gillhouley	Northamptonshire	Redcar	1960

12 Wickets in a Match (6)

Analysis		Player	Versus	Ground	Season
13 for 92	(6-48 and 7-44)	M K Bore	Lancashire	Harrogate	1976
13 for 110	(7-70 and 6-40)	J D Batty	Leicestershire	Bradford	1992
13 for 111	(4-49 and 9-62)	M K Bore	Warwickshire	Scarborough	1976
12 for 69	(5-32 and 7-37)	P M Hutchison	Warwickshire	Coventry	2001
12 for 120	(5-39 and 7-81)	K Gillhouley	Lancashire	Scarborough	1960
12 for 162	(5-78 and 7-84)	I J Houseman	Kent	Canterbury	1989

Hat-tricks (4)

Player	Versus	Ground	Season
I G Swallow	Warwickshire	Harrogate	1984
S D Fletcher	Nottinghamshire	Marske-by-the-Sea	1987
I G Swallow	Derbyshire	Chesterfield	1988
M Broadhurst	Essex	Southend-on-Sea	1992

Second Eleven Performance Of The Year Award

The Trophy was instituted in 2013 to reward a Second Eleven performance with either bat or ball that stood out from the ordinary and turned the course of the game.

2013	M D Fisher	6-25	v. Leicestershire (One-Day Trophy)	
				Grace Road, Leicester
2014	J A Leaning	102	v. Nottinghamshire (T20)	Trent College, Nottingham
2015	M J Waite	143	v. Lancashire (Friendly)	Scarborough
2016	W M H Rhodes	137		
		and 114*	v Lancashire (Friendly)	Liverpool
2017	J W Jack Shutt	4-19	v. Middlesex in the Trophy Final	Headingley
		and 4-12	v. Derbyshire in the T20	Alvaston and Boulton
		to secure two victories.		
2018	J Wharton	162	v. Leiestershire (Friendly)	Kibworth CC
		in only his second Second Eleven match.		

ANNUAL REPORT
and
Statement of Account
for the year ended
December 31, 2018

CHAIRMAN'S STATEMENT

ROBIN SMITH

In some ways the past year might be regarded as unsuccessful. The season was mostly spent in the bottom half of the table, the financial picture remained tight, and we underwent an unexpected and potentially disruptive change in the chairmanship at the half-way point.

Indeed, I have assumed the responsibilities of the chairmanship for the second time when an uninformed outsider might consider the Club's fortunes to be waning. This theoretical outsider would be wrong, however, because I take up the reins with great confidence and with firm foundations in place both on and off the field.

On the field, despite a series of unexpected problems — our opening game washed out, last-minute departures to the IPL, injuries, England (including England Lions) call-ups, and five different captains — we ended the season above the half-way point in the table. This was achieved despite having started our last game with the arithmetical risk that we could be relegated. A good win at New Road took us to fourth, disguising the turmoil and tensions of a difficult season. The inherent instability of the First Division was thereby starkly illustrated. The reality is that one quarter of the division is relegated each year, and it is to be welcomed therefore, in my view, that greater stability is to be introduced by increasing the size of the division in 2020 to 10 teams, the transition being achieved by relegating only one county next season while promoting three from the Second Division. For one year only the relegation risk is more than halved, and thereafter it remains materially reduced.

However, because the fixture schedule is too crowded to accommodate more games, only 14 Championship matches will be played, mean-

414

ing that a seeding system will have to be introduced to identify those counties which we will play only once. Far from ideal, members may think, but it is at least in accordance with the County Championship's chequered history of competition formats.

There was, of course, much debate within the ECB about these proposed changes, throughout which members can be assured that the Club maintained its passionate defence of Championship cricket. This will not change, and happily it continues to be acknowledged within the game that financially successful Test cricket is dependent on a thriving Championship. Nevertheless, the pressures created by one-day cricket, including the World Cup, mean that only two home Championship games can be accommodated next season in the mid-summer months of July and August, one at Emerald Headingley and one at Scarborough.

I refer members to the Director of Cricket's report for an assessment of the Club's players and other resources as we approach the coming season. In my own report I simply record that a huge amount of analysis and communication has been undertaken over the closed season by the cricket management, and I am confident that Yorkshire will take the field next April with a competitive squad, ably led by Steven Patterson, and with as much pride, commitment and ambition as ever was displayed by a team wearing the white rose.

Off the field the coming season will see the inauguration of the new Emerald Stand, in which members will be able to enjoy superb viewing positions towards the Carnegie Pavilion. It is a fine building, and one which brings Emerald Headingley into the front rank of Test grounds worldwide, as well as providing year-round income under a new joint venture arrangement with Leeds Rugby.

Notwithstanding a loss last year, we were able to utilise positive *Ashes*-related cash-flow in repaying £1.8m of debt, thereby embarking upon the first step in a debt-reduction programme which will remain a feature of the Club's finances for the next few years. We have been cautious in the assumptions on which our budget projections for next year are based, particularly in the extent of the new business which the Emerald Stand will generate, but we are nonetheless confident that the Club will return to sustainable profitability from 2019 onwards. Various factors will influence this improving trend, further details of which can be found in the reports of the Chief Executive and the Director of Finance. Having been close to the Club's management for the past 20 years, and having been intimately involved in some difficult financial challenges during that time, I hope I can be forgiven for taking much pleasure from this achievement. It has been a long haul, involving a lot of sterling work by management, but I believe the Club has got there!

This report would be incomplete without a reference to the "new competition". I make no apology for stating that the Club's financial interests will be served by the competition's success and that we are therefore fully supportive of the ECB in this endeavour, which is to create a fresh competition attractive to sponsors and new worldwide audiences alike. The Club, along with the MCC and the other 17 first-class counties, is a stakeholder in the new competition, and can look forward to an additional basic payment from the ECB of £1.3m per annum as well as staging fees and food-and-drink returns for each match played at Emerald Headingley. The home team playing at Emerald Headingley in this competition will not be a Yorkshire team, however. The Club's role at matches will simply be that of the ground provider, much in the same way as it is for Test matches and ODIs.

The Club continues to enjoy the closest of relationships with the Yorkshire Cricket Board and the Yorkshire Cricket Foundation under the "Yorkshire Cricket" banner, and I pay a warm tribute here to Andrew Watson, the YCB Chief Executive, and to Will Saville, the YCF Head of Foundation. The YCB's promotion of the amateur game, particularly its running of County Age Group cricket, constitutes the foundation stone on which, ultimately, Yorkshire and England teams are built. The YCB continues to undertake work in promoting cricket with the young (starting with five-year-olds under the ECB's brilliant All Stars project) and the YCF runs a variety of impressive initiatives (for, instance beach cricket during the Scarborough Cricket Festival) designed to give new young audiences an enjoyable introductory experience of the greatest of games. It is from these beginnings that the players and supporters of the future will come. I add in this regard that the Club is deeply appreciative of the financial support which the Emerald Foundation and the Yorkshire Cricket Charitable Youth Trust continue to provide for various youth initiatives.

I have been greatly encouraged, too, to observe the Club's heritage being protected and promoted by the YCF and its Archives Committee. This has involved co-operation with the MCC Museum which last year displayed on loan in the Lord's Long Room the Club's fine portrait by Ernest Moore of Wilfred Rhodes.

I am grateful to all members for their continued support of the Club which never wavers even in the most challenging of times. I pay tribute, too, to my predecessor, Steve Denison, for his unremitting and enthusiastic hard work for the Club throughout his chairmanship, which ensured my trouble-free take-up of the reins in July. Communication with members has continued throughout the year through meetings of the Members' Committee (which are routinely attended by the Chief Executive, the Commercial Director and myself) and through regular members' forums during the season. We are a members' club, and I regard easy communications with members (to which our imaginative website makes a significant contribution) as being at the heart of our affairs. I pay tribute to our loyal and committed staff who have worked tirelessly and always with good humour on our behalf.

If you can, take a closer look next season at our youngsters, the Academy, the Second XI, and at our emerging new business in the Emerald Stand. Attend even more matches, if that were possible, to see our exciting first team compete in all formats. You can have confidence in the Club's future.

> ROBIN SMITH TD DL
> Chairman
> The Yorkshire
> County Cricket Club

CHIEF EXECUTIVE'S REPORT

MARK ARTHUR

The executive team had always viewed 2018 to be a tough year for us both on and off the field. And, it was! On the field, despite a really good pre-season, the players and coaching staff had to contend with many differing challenges, which have been well documented in Martyn Moxon's report. Watching the emergence of some of our younger players, with strong match-winning performances, and dealing with the pressure that the County Championship brought towards the end of the season, gives me confidence that trophies will be attainable over the next five years.

I am in a privileged position in that I know what the cricket department are trying to achieve, how they set out to achieve it, and how they overcome any adversity to give the players the best opportunity of success in the future. It can be frustrating at times, but that is part and parcel of the game we love. I am sure that many Members often wonder, as I do, how good would we be with all our players available for all matches. Once again, Joe Root, Jonny Bairstow, Adil Rashid, Liam Plunkett and David Willey represented our country with distinction. We wish them all the best in 2019 for both the ICC World Cup and, of course, the *Ashes,* which return to Emerald Headingley for the first time in 10 years.

England recorded two notable wins at Emerald Headingley in 2018 with victory against Pakistan in the June Test match and an impressive defeat of India in the ODI. Despite the reduced capacity due to the construction the atmosphere inside the ground was special.

On the home front, there was success for the Club at Under-17 level in the three-day Championship. Richard Damms, with support from all the Pathways coaches, continues to develop players with potential to become professionals. Top-class coaching, tough competition and attaining a winning mentality are vital ingredients for any aspirational cricketer.

There was also success for three of our league clubs. Richmondshire CC won the ECB National Club Championship; Hanging Heaton CC won the Vitality Club T20 competition, and Folkton and Flixton CC won the National Village Cup at a Lord's final. That was a most enjoyable day! So, all three men's national competitions were won by Yorkshire clubs.

We say goodbye to Jack Brooks, Alex Lees, Andrew Hodd, Liam Plunkett, Azeem Rafiq, James Wainman and Jonathan Read from the playing staff this year, and I would like to thank them all for bringing success to the Club, as well as wishing them well in the future.

Off the field we produced another solid performance, and I thank the executive team for their hard work and dedication. With reduced capacities and operating within the difficult conditions of a construction site we still managed to achieve an EBITDA of £515,000. However, for most of 2018, we have been planning for 2019, which will be an exceptional year for the Club. It is not only an opportunity to showcase the new-look Emerald Headingley to the world, but also a one-off chance to make significant inroads into our debt. I am anticipating income to rise by 100 per cent in 2019. With careful cost control the Finance Director should be able to give you some good news this time next year.

And with an India Test in 2021 and the *Ashes* again in 2023 we have much to look forward to.

The Emerald Stand is looking magnificent, and will no doubt be one of the talking points this coming season. It will completely transform our business as well as return the Club to the top table when it comes to the allocation of international cricket beyond 2024. But it is not just the Emerald Stand which changes our fortunes. The Headingley Pavilion has also been revamped and, by marketing these two facilities together with our partners Leeds Rugby we are able to offer first-class conference and banqueting facilities all year round.

The ECB has recently launched their strategy for 2020 to 2024. It is called Inspiring Generations, and it sets out to make cricket a more relevant game to more people while maintaining its core support. The new broadcast deal with Sky and the BBC has given the game an opportunity to invest wisely in its future. Yorkshire Cricket will undoubtedly benefit from the investment in this region and will be tasked by the ECB to deliver on set objectives during this five-year period. It is a wonderful opportunity and a very exciting time for those who are involved in grass-roots cricket.

More detail will emerge this year about the new Hundred Ball Competition, which will be played during the months of July and August from 2020. We will be staging four matches per season at Emerald Headingley, and we will ensure that further details are communicated to Members as and when they are available.

A personal note of thanks from me to Steve Denison, who stood down as Chairman of the Club half way through the season. Steve took over from Colin Graves in 2015. He was heavily involved in the re-structuring of the Club's debt, and the relationship with Leeds City Council, which has given us a solid platform upon which to thrive in the future. His enthusiasm, passion and support for the Club was infectious.

Finally, I would like to thank all Members, 1863 Members, The Emerald Group, Mazars, our Partners, Stakeholders, the many volunteers, and the Members' Committee for their continued support.

Enjoy the season.

MARK ARTHUR
Chief Executive
Yorkshire County Cricket Club

DIRECTOR OF PROFESSIONAL CRICKET'S REPORT

2018 had similarities to the previous season in all competitions. A fourthplace finish in the Specsavers County Championship, a group-stage exit in the Vitality Blast and a semi-final defeat in the 50-over competition, one stage further than last year.

In the Royal London One-Day Cup we played some outstanding matches once again leading up to the semi-final. However, we came up against an incredible individual performance, James Vince scoring 171 meaning that we failed to reach the final. That meant that we were knocked out of the competition for the fifth consecutive **MARTYN MOXON** year at the knock-out stages, which is frustrating, and we need to find a way of going one step further. Being knocked out of the Vitality Blast at the group stages was disappointing. We had some good performances, but ran out of steam at the end, losing three of the last four fixtures. We were badly affected by changes in the plans of Adil Rashid and Billy Stanlake. We had based our strategy around having them for the vast majority of the competition, but a change in policy from Cricket Australia meant no Billy, and Adil's Test selection meant that he missed the final seven games. We certainly missed them.

Going forward, we need to improve both our bowling and batting at the end of an innings in particular.

We had another challenging year in the Specsavers County Championship. However, the way we played under pressure towards the end of the season was very pleasing and encouraging. We batted much better as a team, and consequently got the results we needed, finishing fourth.

Unfortunately, once again there were many challenges to overcome throughout the season. It started as a selection headache heading into the season, but soon turned into a different kind of challenge. Liam Plunkett and David Willey were selected for the India Premier League one week before the start of the season. Adil Rashid had also opted to play just white-ball cricket at that stage. Steven Patterson and Matthew Fisher were sidelined with injuries.

Our preparations going into the season were badly affected by the "Beast from the East". Having come back from a pre-season tour in Potchefstroom in good form and spirits we spent the next two weeks training indoors, and did not bowl a ball against Essex in the first game.

We had to contend with a change in captaincy after Gary Ballance was taken ill and felt it best to relinquish the role. Steven Patterson took over, but suffered two fractured fingers, meaning that he missed large chunks of the season. When Steven was fit he did an outstanding job, both on and off the field, and gave us experience and stability. Once again, our overseas players didn't score the volume of runs you would expect, and some of our own talent continued to struggle to perform.

It was undoubtedly the most difficult year I've experienced with regards to contract negotiations, as there were so many factors involved in the decision-making process. Ultimately, we made decisions on availability and affordability. However, all this has now been resolved, and the signings we have made, Josh Poysden, Mat Pillans and Will Fraine, are all players with potential who, with support, can become important players for us in the future.

There is a lot of work to be done, but we have some exciting talent at the Club. Our challenge is to win now, but at the same time give opportunities to our younger players to determine who has the ability and mentality to perform at a higher level in the future.

We have seen a growing maturity from Tom Kohler-Cadmore, who played beautifully to score two hundreds in the Championship towards the end of the season. The emergence of Jonny Tattersall as a 'keeper and a batsman was great to see. Harry Brook showed what he is capable of in all formats. Jordan Thompson's performances in the T20s were encouraging, along with Matthew Waite's contribution in the Championship towards the end of the season after recovering from a long-term ankle injury. James Logan made his debut in the last game, and equipped himself well.

In the Second XI there were encouraging performances from Tom Loten, Ben Birkhead, James Wharton and George Hill. George and Dominic Leach were rewarded for their efforts with an England Under-19s call-up this winter.

The Under-17s, under Richard Damms and Graham Tippin, won the three-day Championship with outstanding individual and team perform-ances throughout the competition. It was also very pleasing to see how our young Academy team grew in the Premier League and improved throughout the year. They struggled early-season, but by the end of it had become very competitive, and had improved immeasurably, both as individuals and as a team.

Given that several of our seamers have suffered injuries over the last couple of seasons, we must ensure that we nurture our younger lads over the next couple of years. With this in mind, and to ensure that we can manage their workloads, we are planning on recruiting an international bowler to complement this group.

We have to accept that we are in a transitional period, particularly with regards to the Championship. History tells us that it takes some time to build a team ready to win a title. When you look back to us win-ning in 2001 the process started back in 1997. Similarly, with Durham, who won back-to-back Championships in 2008 and 2009, that process started in 2001. Surrey won it three out of four years in the early-2000s, but then not again for another 16 years. Sussex won it three out of five years between 2003 and 2007, but have not featured since. With our 2014-15 successes it started in 2010 when, if we had beaten Kent in the last game, we would have won the Championship.

Everyone at the Club wants to win trophies, but we have to be patient, while challenging ourselves to improve as quickly as possible. With this in mind we have appointed Paul Grayson as our batting coach. Paul will work from age groups, all the way up to the First XI, and will bring vast experience, not only on batting, but also on the game as a whole. He will complement our current support staff very well.

I would like to take this opportunity to thank the ground staff, both at Emerald Headingley and around the county, for all they do. Also, thanks must go to the Board and all of the staff at the Club for their help and support.

There is so much to look forward to this year. We have the World Cup, the *Ashes* and a group of young Yorkshire players aiming to grow into a successful team. I hope everyone enjoys the summer and, as ever, would like to thank you for your continued support.

MARTYN MOXON
Director of Professional Cricket
Yorkshire County Cricket Club

FINANCE DIRECTOR'S REPORT

PAUL HUDSON

From a financial perspective there have been three important milestones during 2018. These involved the reversion of the catering and pouring rights to the Cricket Club, the repayment of debt to our lenders, and the continuing construction of the new stand. These are addressed in the following paragraphs:

Firstly, we are delighted that as of November 1, 2018, the catering and pouring rights have returned to the Club. This had been due to happen on January 1, 2021, but was brought forward as part of our agreement with Leeds Rugby to build the new stand. This will have a significant favourable impact on the financial results of the Club going forward.

Secondly, when the Club's borrowings were restructured in 2015 it was with the two-fold aim of making the interest burden affordable, while aligning the reductions in the capital sum with times when the Club would have an ability to make repayments.

With this in mind, we did not anticipate being able to make any significant capital repayments during 2016 and 2017. We did, however, envisage being able to make some repayments in the years 2018 to 2020. The borrowing facilities were aligned accordingly. To that end I am delighted to be able to report that during 2018 we were able to repay £0.5m to HSBC and £0.5m to the Graves family trusts, in accordance with the respective loan agreements. We also paid a lump sum off the Investec floodlight loan of £600,000. There remain small repayments due on this loan in 2019, at the end of which title in the floodlights reverts to the Club. Together with other small repayments this brings the total debt repayments in the year to £1.8m. Further, our loans, borrowings and overdrafts net of cash balances reduced from a level of £24.6m at the end of 2016 to £20.6m at the end of 2018. That is a reduction over the two years of £4.0m. The ability to be able to report these debt reductions is a result of a number of factors, not least of which is the receipt of advanced ticket sales in respect of the 2019 *Ashes* Test.

These are significant steps, as we are finally in the position of being able to reduce our debt burden. There are further repayments due in 2019 of £3.5m to the Graves family trusts. As we continue to repay our debt facilities we in turn are reducing our interest cost each year.

Thirdly, we are now receiving payments under the Brand Promotion Agreement for the Emerald Headingley Stadium. These are helping to fund the fit-out costs of the new stand, on which together with some works on the Old Pavilion we have spent £574,000 during the 2018 year. These sums are shown within fixed-asset additions.

The construction work on the new stand continues to progress, and at the time of writing is both on schedule and within budget.

The next round of funding of the game from the ECB covers the period 2020 to 2024. As the exact figures and structure of this funding becomes apparent this will be incorporated into our financial planning, and will form the basis of structuring the next period of our borrowing, and repayments. This process will commence later in 2019.

Turning to the Income and Expenditure Account, as anticipated this was a difficult year compared to 2017, which had received the benefit of a one-off distribution from ECB of £1.0m representing a share of television revenues given to all counties for the 2018 India tour. This was received and recognised in 2017. All other areas of income and expenditure were broadly in line with previous years and our expectations. The net result for the year was an earnings before interest, tax, depreciation and amortisation of goodwill of £515,000 (2017 £1,144,000) and an income of £8,853,000 (2017 £9,661,000).

2019 promises to be an exciting year on the field of play. With proper financial care it should also be one where we see further reductions in our debt.

PAUL HUDSON
Director of Finance
Yorkshire County Cricket Club

RECENT FINANCIAL TRENDS

	2018	2017	2016	2015	2014
	£000	£000	£000	£000	£000
Income:					
International ticket and hospitality revenue	2,498	2,686	2,399	2,441	2,181
Domestic ticket and hospitality revenue	999	932	1,005	836	538
Subscriptions	828	742	740	652	564
England and Wales Cricket Board	2,119	3,152	2,638	2,481	2,194
Commercial income	2,291	1,998	1,881	1,905	1,797
Other	118	150	131	50	33
Total Income	**8,853**	**9,660**	**8,794**	**8,365**	**7,307**
Cost of sales	(2,032)	(2,208)	(2,109)	(1,993)	(1,746)
Cricket expenses	(3,386)	(3,326)	(3,055)	(3,168)	(2,765)
Overheads	(2,920)	(2,982)	(2,554)	(2,610)	(2,311)
EBITDA	**515**	**1,144**	**1,076**	**594**	**485**
Interest	(797)	(805)	(794)	(639)	(1,050)
Depreciation	(556)	(513)	(465)	(435)	(439)
Capital grants release	190	188	186	177	178
(Deficit)/surplus before exceptional items	**(648)**	**14**	**3**	**(302)**	**(826)**
Exceptional items	—	(68)	—	781	500
(Deficit)/surplus before taxation	**(648)**	**(54)**	**3**	**479**	**(326)**
Loans, borrowing and overdrafts net of cash	**20,636**	**22,942**	**24,636**	**24,055**	**23,929**

CORPORATE GOVERNANCE

The Board is accountable to the Club's members for good corporate governance, and this statement describes how the principles of governance are applied.

THE BOARD

The Board is responsible for approving Club policy and strategy. It meets bi-monthly, or more frequently if business needs require, and has a schedule of matters specifically reserved to it for decision, including all significant commercial issues and all capital expenditure.

The Executive Management Team supply the Board with appropriate and timely information, and Board Members are free to seek any further information they consider necessary. The Board has formed various committees to assist in the governance of the Club's affairs.

NOMINATIONS AND GOVERNANCE COMMITTEE

The Nominations and Governance Committee is formally constituted with written terms of reference, which are defined in the Club Rules and reviewed regularly. It consists of the President, Secretary and two other Board members, currently Robin Smith and one vacancy to be filled at the April Board Meeting.

AUDIT COMMITTEE

The Audit Committee meets to provide oversight of the financial reporting process, the audit process, systems of internal controls and compliance with laws and regulations. It is chaired by Stephen Willis, and meets with the external auditors as part of this process. The other members of the committee are Katherine Mathew and Hanif Malik.

REMUNERATION COMMITTEE

The Remuneration Committee assists the Board in developing and administering a fair remuneration policy for the Club and determining remuneration of senior employees. It is chaired by Stephen Willis, and the other member of the committee is Robin Smith.

MEMBERS' COMMITTEE

The Club encourages effective communication with its members, and the Members' Committee, as defined in the Club Rules, is appointed for that purpose.

INTERNAL CONTROL

The Board acknowledges its responsibility to maintain a sound system of internal control relating to operational, financial and compliance controls and risk management, to safeguard the members' interests and the Club's assets, and will regularly review its effectiveness. Such a system, however, is designed to manage and meet the Club's particular needs and mitigate the risks to which it is exposed, rather than eliminate the risk of failure to achieve business objectives, and can provide only reasonable and not absolute assurance against material mis-statement or loss. The Club considers the key components to provide effective internal control and improve business efficiency are:

- Regular meetings with senior management to review and assess progress made against objectives, and deal with any problems which arise from such reviews.
- A financial reporting system of annual budgets, periodic forecasts and detailed monthly reporting, which includes cash-flow forecasts. Budgets and forecasts are reviewed and approved by the Board.
- A management and organisation structure exists with defined responsibilities and appropriate authorisation limits and short lines of communication to the Non-Executive Chairman.
- A Senior Independent Director is appointed by the Board, whose role is to serve as a sounding board for the Chairman and act as an intermediary for other directors. The position is currently held by Stephen Willis.

DIRECTORS' RESPONSIBILITIES

The directors are responsible for preparing the Annual Report and the Club's financial statements in accordance with applicable law and regulations. Co-operative and Community Benefit Society law requires the directors to prepare financial statements for each financial year. Under that law the directors have elected to prepare the financial statements in accordance with UK Accounting Standards, including FRS 102 The Financial Reporting Standard applicable in the UK and Republic of Ireland.

The fi nancial statements are required by law to give a true and fair view of the state of affairs of the Club and of the income and expenditure of the Club for that period. In preparing the Club's financial statements, the directors are required to:

- select suitable accounting policies and then apply them consistently;
- make judgements and estimates that are reasonable and prudent;

- state whether applicable UK Accounting Standards have been followed, subject to any material departures disclosed and explained in the financial statements, and
- assess the Club's ability to continue as a going concern, disclosing, as applicable, matters related to going concern; and
- use the going-concern basis of accounting unless they either intend to liquidate the Club or to cease operations, or have no realistic alternative but to do so.

The directors are responsible for keeping proper books of account that disclose with reasonable accuracy at any time the financial position of the Society and enable them to ensure that its financial statements comply with the Co-operative and Community Benefit Societies Act 2014. They are responsible for such internal control as they determine is necessary to enable the preparation of financial statements that are free from material mis-statement, whether due to fraud or error, and have general responsibility for taking such steps as are reasonably open to them to safeguard the assets of the Club and to prevent and detect fraud and other irregularities.

The directors are responsible for the maintenance and integrity of the corporate and financial information included on the Society's website. Legislation in the UK governing the preparation and dissemination of financial statements may differ from legislation in other jurisdictions.

DISCLOSURE OF INFORMATION TO AUDITOR

The members of the Board who held office at the date of approval of the Annual Report and Accounts confirm that, so far as they are aware, there is no relevant information of which the Club's auditor is unaware; or each member has taken all the steps that he ought to have taken as a member to make himself aware of any relevant audit information or to establish that the Club's auditor is aware of that information.

INDEPENDENT AUDITORS' REPORT

TO THE MEMBERS OF THE YORKSHIRE
COUNTY CRICKET CLUB

We have audited the financial statements of The Yorkshire County Cricket Club ("the Club") for the year ended December 31, 2018, which comprise the Income and Expenditure account, Balance Sheet, Cash Flow statement, Statement of Changes in Equity and related notes, including the accounting policies in Note 1.

In our opinion the financial statements:

- give a true and fair view, in accordance with UK accounting standards, including FRS 102 The Financial Reporting Standard applicable in the UK and Republic of Ireland, of the state of the Club's affairs as at December 31, 2018, and of the income and expenditure of the Club for the year then ended; and
- comply with the requirements of the Co-operative and Community Benefit Societies Act 2014.

Basis for opinion

We conducted our audit in accordance with International Standards on Auditing (UK) ("ISAs (UK)") and applicable law. Our responsibilities are described below. We have fulfilled our ethical responsibilities under, and are independent of the Club in accordance with, UK ethical requirements including the FRC Ethical Standard. We believe that the audit evidence we have obtained is a sufficient and appropriate basis for our opinion.

The impact of uncertainties due to the UK exiting the European Union on our audit

Uncertainties related to the effects of Brexit are relevant to understanding our audit of the financial statements. All audits assess and challenge the reasonableness of estimates made by the directors and the appropriateness of the going-concern basis of preparation of the financial statements. All of these depend on assessments of the future economic environment and the Club's future prospects and performance.

Brexit is one of the most signifi cant economic events for the UK, and at the date of this report its effects are subject to unprecedented levels of uncertainty of outcomes, with the full range of possible effects unknown. We applied a standardised firm-wide approach in response to that uncertainty when assessing the Club's future prospects and performance. However, no audit should be expected to predict the unknowable factors or all possible future implications for a company, and this is particularly the case in relation to Brexit.

Going concern

The directors have prepared the financial statements on the going-concern basis as they do not intend to liquidate the Club or to cease its operations, and as they have concluded that the Club's financial position means that this is realistic. They have also concluded that there are no material uncertainties that could have cast significant doubt over its ability to continue as a going concern for at least a year from the date of approval of the financial statements ("the going concern period").

We are required to report to you if we have concluded that the use of the going-concern basis of accounting is inappropriate or there is an undisclosed material uncertainty that may cast significant doubt over the use of that basis for a period of at least a year from the date of approval of the financial statements. In our evaluation of the directors' conclusions we considered the inherent risks to the Club's business model, including the impact of Brexit, and analysed how those risks might affect the Club's financial resources or ability to continue operations over the going-concern period. We have nothing to report in these respects. However, as we cannot predict all future events or conditions, and as subsequent events may result in outcomes that are inconsistent with judgements that were reasonable at the time they were made, the absence of reference to a material uncertainty in this auditor's report is not a guarantee that the Club will continue in operation.

Other information

The directors are responsible for the other information, which comprises the Chairman's Report, Chief Executive Report, Director of Cricket's Report, President, Board Members, Staff and Players, Director of Finance's Report, Corporate Governance Statement, AGM Minutes, Members' Committee Report, Board Attendance and Players Appearances for 2018, Yorkshire Cricket Foundation Manager's Report, Archives Committee Report and Notice of AGM and Agenda. Our opinion on the financial statements does not cover the other information and, accordingly, we do not express an audit opinion or any form of assurance conclusion thereon.

Our responsibility is to read the other information and, in doing so, consider whether, based on our financial-statements audit work, the information therein is materially mis-stated or inconsistent with the financial statements or our audit knowledge. Based solely on that work, we have not identified material mis-statements in the other information.

Matters on which we are required to report by exception

Under the Co-operative and Community Benefit Societies Act 2014 we are required to report to you if, in our opinion:

- the Club has not kept proper books of account; or
- the Club has not maintained a satisfactory system of control over

- its transactions; or
- the financial statements are not in agreement with the Club's books of account; or
- We have not received all the information and explanations we need for our audit.

We have nothing to report in these respects.

Directors' responsibilities

As more fully explained in their statement the Club's directors are responsible for the preparation of financial statements which give a true and fair view; such internal control as they determine is necessary to enable the preparation of financial statements that are free from material mis-statement, whether due to fraud or error; assessing the Club's ability to continue as a going concern, disclosing, as applicable, matters related to going concern; and using the going-concern basis of accounting unless they either intend to liquidate the Club or to cease operations, or have no realistic alternative but to do so.

Auditor's responsibilities

Our objectives are to obtain reasonable assurance about whether the financial statements as a whole are free from material mis-statement, whether due to fraud or error, and to issue our opinion in an auditor's report. Reasonable assurance is a high level of assurance, but does not guarantee that an audit conducted in accordance with ISAs (UK) will always detect a material mis-statement when it exists. Mis-statements can arise from fraud or error and are considered material if, individually or in aggregate, they could reasonably be expected to influence the economic decisions of users taken on the basis of the financial statements.

A fuller description of our responsibilities is provided on the FRC's website at *www.frc.org.uk/auditorsresponsibilities.*

The purpose of our audit work and to whom we owe our responsibilities

This report is made solely to the Club in accordance with Section 87 of the Co-operative and Community Benefit Societies Act 2014. Our audit work has been undertaken so that we might state to the Club those matters we are required to state to it in an auditor's report and for no other purpose. To the fullest extent permitted by law we do not accept or assume responsibility to anyone other than the Club for our audit work, for this report, or for the opinions we have formed.

CHRIS BUTT for and on behalf of KPMG LLP,
Statutory Auditor
Chartered Accountants
1 Sovereign Square, Sovereign Street, Leeds LS1 4DA

FEBRUARY 9, 2018

INCOME AND EXPENDITURE ACCOUNT
for the year ended December 31, 2018

	Note	2018 £	2017 £
Income			
International ticket and hospitality revenue		2,498,366	2,685,777
Domestic ticket and hospitality revenue		999,030	932,095
Subscriptions		828,003	742,389
England and Wales Cricket Board		2,119,265	3,152,158
Commercial income		2,290,617	1,998,447
Other income		117,781	149,785
		8,853,062	9,660,651
Cost of sales			
International match and hospitality expenditure		1,264,002	1,456,773
Domestic match and hospitality costs (home fixtures)		586,517	517,291
Retail		181,977	233,077
Catering		171	1,241
		(2,032,667)	(2,208,382)
Cricket expenses			
Staff remuneration and employment expenses		2,585,810	2,611,654
Match expenses (away fixtures)		225,638	211,204
Development expenses		443,700	400,008
Other cricket expenses		130,433	103,503
		3,385,581)	(3,326,369)
Overheads			
Infrastructure and ground operations		1,191,570	1,130,685
Commercial		799,445	773,413
Administration		729,940	897,901
Ticket and membership office		198,701	179,997
		(2,919,656)	(2,981,996)
Earnings before interest, tax, depreciation and amortisation		15,158	1,143,904
Interest		(797,485)	(804,833)
Depreciation	5	(555,648)	(513,535)
Release of Capital Grants	10	190,315	188,191
		(1,162,818)	(1,130,177)
(Deficit)/Surplus before exceptional item and taxation		(647,660)	13,727
Exceptional item		—	(67,699)
Deficit before taxation		(647,660)	(53,972)
Taxation	4,11	286,804	(971)
Deficit for the year after taxation		(360,856)	(54,943)

BALANCE SHEET

as at December 31, 2018

	Note	2018 £	2018 £	2017 £	2017 £
Assets employed:					
Investments	14		50		50
Fixed Assets	5		28,852,481		28,694,742
Current assets:					
Stocks		104,211		117,158	
Debtors	6	2,509,845		1,230,849	
Cash at bank and in hand		1,817,901		1,345,277	
		4,431,957		2,693,284	
Creditors: amounts falling due within one year	7	(12,997,845)		(6,469,314)	
Net current liabilities			(8,565,888)		(3,776,030)
Total assets less current liabilities			20,286,643		24,918,762
Funded by:					
Creditors: amounts falling due after more than one year	8		18,766,152		22,947,100
Deferred income — capital grants	10		4,887,669		4,977,984
			23,653,821		27,925,084
Capital and Reserves					
Called up share capital	12		228		210
Capital redemption reserve			662		680
Income and expenditure account			(3,368,068)		(3,007,212)
			(3,367,178)		(3,006,322)
			20,286,643		24,918,762

These accounts were approved by the Board on February 8, 2019.

ROBIN SMITH, Chairman
PAUL HUDSON, Club Secretary

CASH FLOW STATEMENT
for the year ended December 31, 2018

	Note	2018 £	2017 £
Cash flows from Operating Activities			
Defi cit for the year		**(360,856)**	(54,943)
Adjustments for:			
Depreciation of tangible assets		**555,648**	513,535
Loan interest payable		**797,485**	804,833
Capital grants released		**(190,315)**	(188,191)
Taxation		**(286,804)**	971
(Increase)/decrease in trade and other debtors		**(992,192)**	235,578
Decrease in stocks		**12,947**	12,368
Increase in creditors		**4,180,098**	1,232,165
Interest paid		**(797,485)**	(804,832)
Net cash inflow from operating activities		**2,918,526**	1,751,483
Cash flows from investing activities			
Purchase of tangible fi xed assets	5	**(713,387)**	(156,589)
Capital grants received		**100,000**	100,000
Acquisition of investment in joint venture company	14	**—**	(50)
Net cash outflow from investing activities		**(613,387)**	(56,639)
Cash flows from financing activities			
Proceeds from new loans		**—**	42,800
Repayment of borrowings		**(1,128,085)**	(100,000)
Repayment of fi nance lease liabilities		**(704,430)**	(98,797)
Net cash outflow from financing activites		**(1,832,515)**	(155,997)
Increase in cash in the period		**472,624**	1,538,847
Cash and cash equivalents at January 1		**1,345,277**	(193,570)
Cash and cash equivalents at December 31		**1,817,901**	1,345,277

STATEMENT OF CHANGES IN EQUITY
for the year ended December 31, 2018

	Called Up Share Capital £	Capital Redemption Reserve £	Income and Expenditure Account £	Total £
Balance at January 1, 2017	210	680	(2,952,269)	(2,951,379)
Deficit for the year after taxation	—	—	(54,943)	(54,943)
Balance at December 31, 2017	210	680	(3,007,212)	(3,006,322)
Balance at January 1, 2018	210	680	(3,007,212)	(3,006,322)
Additional share capital for new members	18	(18)	—	—
Defi cit for the year after taxation	—	—	(360,856)	(360,856)
Balance at December 31, 2018	**228**	**662**	**(3,368,068)**	**(3,367,178)**

433

NOTES TO THE ACCOUNTS

for the year ended December 31, 2018

1. Accounting policies

These financial statements were prepared in accordance with Financial Reporting Standard 102. The Financial Reporting Standard applicable in the UK and Republic of Ireland (FRS 102) as issued in August 2014 and the Co-Operative and Cummunity Benefit Society Act 2014. The amendments to FRS 102 issued in July 2015 have been applied. The presentation currency of these financial statements is sterling.

Under section 100 of the Co-Operative and Community Benefit Society Act 2014 neither the Yorkshire Cricket Foundation nor Headingley North South Stand Limited meet the definition of a subsidiary. The Co-Operative and Community Benefit Society Act 2014 only requires a consolidation to be prepared where investments meet the definition of a subsidiary. In addition, under section 9.3(g) of FRS 102 an entity is exempt from preparing consolidated financial statements if not required by the applicable statutory framework (in this case, Co-Operative and Community Benefit Society Act 2014). As such, no consolidated accounts have been prepared

(a) Income

All income is accounted for on an accruals basis, except for donations which are accounted for in the year of receipt.

Income represents amounts receivable from the Club's principal activities. Income is analysed between international-ticket and hospitality revenue, domestic-ticket and hospitality revenue, subscriptions, England and Wales Cricket Board, commercial and other income:

International-ticket and hospitality revenue

Relate to amounts received from ticket sales and hospitality directly attributable to staging international cricket matches in Yorkshire.

Domestic-ticket and hospitality revenue

Relate to amounts received from ticket sales and hospitality directly attributable to staging domestic cricket matches in Yorkshire.

Subscriptions

Subscription income comprises amounts receivable from members in respect of the current season. Subscriptions received in respect of future seasons is treated as deferred income.

England and Wales Cricket Board (ECB)

ECB income relates to fees receivable, including performance-related elements, in the current season distributed from central funds in accordance with the First Class Memorandum of Understanding. ECB fees received in respect of future seasons are treated as deferred income. ECB distributions receivable to fund capital projects are treated as deferred income and are released to the Income and Expenditure Account by equal instalments over the expected useful lives of the relevant assets in accordance with accounting policy (c) Fixed assets and depreciation, as set out below.

Commercial Income

Commercial income relates to amounts received from stadium-naming rights, ground advertising, retail operations, catering guarantees, indoor cricket-centre facility hire, dinners and other events. Advertising income received in respect of future seasons is treated as deferred income.

Other Income

Other income relates to amounts received from sundry items which mainly consists of donations, car parking and any other income not falling into the above categories.

(b) Investments in jointly controlled entity

Investments in jointly controlled entities are carried at cost less impairment.

(c) Fixed assets and depreciation

All expenditure in connection with the development of Emerald Headingley Cricket Ground and the related facilities has been capitalised. Finance costs relating to and incurred during the period of construction were also capitalised. Depreciation is only charged once a discrete phase of the development is completed.

Depreciation is calculated to write down the cost of fixed assets by equal annual instalments over their expected useful lives.

The periods generally applicable are:

Emerald Headingley Cricket Ground and Cricket Centre

Buildings	Carnegie Pavilion	125 years
	Other buildings	50 years
Fixtures		4 years
Plant & Equipment	Between 4 and 10 years	
Office equipment		2-4 years

Freehold land is not depreciated.

All other expenditure on repairs to Emerald Headingley Cricket Ground and other grounds is written off as and when incurred.

(d) Carnegie Pavilion

The Club's contribution towards the design and build cost of the Carnegie Pavilion is £3m, of which £1.5m is payable over 20 years under a 125-year lease agreement. The £3m, together with the associated legal, professional and capital fit-out costs of the areas within the Pavilion that he Club occupies, have been capitalised and are being depreciated over the 125-year lease term. The £1.5m, payable under the lease agreement, has been treated as a finance lease within the financial statements with the capital element reported within Creditors (Finance leases), and the interest element charged to the Income and Expenditure Account on a straight-line basis over the 20-year term.

(e) Stocks

Stocks represent goods for resale and are stated at the lower of cost and net realisable value.

(f) Grants

Capital grants relating to the development of Emerald Headingley Cricket Ground (including the Yorkshire Cricket Museum) and Cricket Centre are included within the Balance Sheet as deferred income, and are released to the Income and Expenditure Account by equal instalments over the expected useful lives of the relevant assets in accordance with accounting policy (c) Fixed assets and depreciation, as set out above.

Grants of a revenue nature are credited to the Income and Expenditure Account in the same period as their related expenditure.

(g) Trade and other debtors/creditors

Trade and other debtors are recognised initially at transaction price less attributable transaction costs. Trade and other creditors are recognised initially at transaction price plus attributable transaction costs. Subsequent to initial recognition they are measured at amortised cost using the effective interest method, less any impairment losses in the case of trade debtors. Short-term instruments have an amortised cost materially equal to transaction price unless otherwise stated.

(h) Interest-bearing borrowings classified as basic financial instruments

Interest-bearing borrowings are recognised initially at the present value of future payments discounted at a market rate of interest. Subsequent to initial recognition, interest-bearing borrowings are stated at amortised cost using the effective-interest method, less any impairment losses.

(i) Cash and cash equivalents

For the purpose of presentation in the cash-flow statement, cash and cash equivalents include cash in hand, deposits with financial institutions which are subject to an insignificant risk of change in value, and bank overdrafts. Bank overdrafts are presented as current borrowings in the balance sheet.

(j) Taxation

Tax on the surplus or deficit for the year comprises current and deferred tax. Tax is recognised in the Income and Expenditure Account except to the extent that it relates to items recognised directly in equity or other income, in which case it is recognised directly in equity or other income.

Current tax is the expected tax payable or receivable on the taxable income or deficit for the year, using tax rates enacted or substantively enacted at the balance sheet date, and any adjustment to tax payable in respect of previous years.

Deferred tax is provided in full using the balance sheet liability method. A deferred tax asset is recognised where it is probable that future taxable income will be sufficient to utilise the available relief. Tax is charged or credited to the income statement except when it relates to items charged or credited directly to equity, in which case the tax is also dealt with in equity. Deferred tax liabilities and assets are not discounted.

2. Financial Position

Going concern

The financial statements are prepared on a going-concern basis, which the directors believe to be appropriate for the following reasons. The Club meets its day-to-day working-capital requirements through an overdraft facility, which is repayable on demand in addition to loans from the Graves Family Trusts and HSBC. Details of the loans and overdraft maturity analysis which impact on the financial position can be found in Note 8.

The Club is in a net current-liability position of £8.6m (2017: £3.8m) and net liabilities of £3.4m (2017: £3.0m) at December 31, 2018. These positions include current deferred income of £7.6m (2017: £3.0m) which relates primarily to the advance ticket sales of the Ashes test series scheduled for the summer of 2019. These tickets are more expensive and sell earlier and quicker than other Test series.

The Board have prepared cash-flow forecasts which show that the Club will continue to operate within its current facilities and pay creditors as they fall due for at least the next 12 months from the date of approval of the accounts. Summer 2019 brings not only the Ashes Test match and an ODI, but also four ICC World Cup fixtures to Emerald Headingley, all of which attract increased corporate-hospitality sales in addition to the increased cash flow associated with the return of the pouring rights to the Club. These enhanced incomes mean that the Club is expected to be profitable for the financial year 2019 and cash neutral following capital repayments of the debt. The Board have prepared reasonable downside sensitivities to cash-flow forecasts, which show that while certain scenarios would restrict the net cash inflow there are a number of opportunities to mitigate against these downside sensitivities, if requried, to remain within the committed facility arrangements and allow the capital repayments of the debt as they fall due. These cash-flow forecasts also assume the renewal of the Club's current overdraft facility of £0.5m (2017: £0.5m) upon its annual expiry in May 2019 under the normal course of business, which has been the case since the facilities were last restructured in 2015. In the unlikely scenario that the facility is not renewed the above opportunities and mitigating actions would be taken to remain within the new facility arrangements.

Furthermore, during the course of 2019 the Club will also begin the process to restructure the Graves Family Trust debts, and have received positive confirmation from the Trustees that they are both willing and expecting to go through with this planned debt restructure, which is expected to commence in summer 2019. This debt restructure will be coupled with the next round of funding for the game from the ECB for the period 2020 to 2024.

Based on the above indications, the directors are confident that the Club will have sufficient funds to continue to meet its liabilities as they fall due for at least 12 months from the date of approval of the accounts, and therefore have prepared the accounts on a going-concern basis.

3. Staff Numbers and Costs

The average number of persons employed by the Club (including directors) during the year, analysed by category, was as follows:

	2018	2017
Players (including Academy and Yorkshire Diamonds)	43	42
Non Playing Full Time Staff	51	48
Seasonal and Casual Staff	15	15
	109	105

The aggregate payroll costs of these persons were as follows:

	£	£
Wages and salaries	3,549,883	3,781,710
Social security costs	375,773	414,500
Contribution to Pension Plans	263,951	286,977
	4,189,607	4,483,187

	2018	2017
	£	£
4. Taxation		
Deficit for the year after taxation	**(360,856)**	(54,943)
Total tax credit/(expense)	**286,804**	(971)
Deficit for the year before taxation	**(647,660)**	(53,972)
Tax at 19.00% (2017: 19.25%)	**123,056**	10,388
Expenses not deductible for taxation purposes	**(950)**	—
Reduction in tax rate on deferred tax balances	**113,243**	(1,429)
Fixed asset permanent differences	**(73,069)**	(88,687)
Non taxable income	**98,536**	90,538
Adjustments in respect of prior periods	**25,988**	(11,781)
Total tax credit/(expense)	**286,804**	(971)

The tax credit for the year represents deferred tax and as such is a non-cash item which has been fully recognised in the income and expenditure account. No charges have been recognised in other income or directly in equity. A similar situation existed in 2017.

A reduction in the UK corporation tax rate from 21% to 20% (effective from April 1,2015) was substantively enacted on July 2, 2013. Further reductions to 19% (effective from April 1, 2017) and to 18% (effective April 1, 2020) were substantively enacted on October 26, 2015, and an additional reduction to 17% (effective April 1, 2020) was substantively enacted on September 6, 2016. This will reduce the company's future current tax charge accordingly. The deferred tax asset at December 31, 2018, has been calculated based on these rates.

5. Fixed assets (See next page)

6. Debtors

	2018	2017
	£	£
Trade debtors	**1,284,504**	363,888
Deferred tax asset (see Note 11)	**906,832**	620,028
Other debtors	**318,509**	246,933
	2,509,845	1,230,849

7. Creditors: amounts falling due within one year

	2018	2017
ECB fl oodlight loan (see Note 8)	**100,000**	100,000
HSBC Bank Loan (see Note 8)	**—**	500,000
CJ Graves Accumulation and Maintenance Trust Loan (see Note 8)	**1,750,000**	250,000
J Graves Accumulation and Maintenance Trust Loan (see Note 8)	**1,750,000**	250,000
Trade creditors	**1,053,258**	793,457
Finance leases (see Note 13)	**88,124**	704,298
Social security and other taxes	**350,293**	545,369
Other creditors	**65,761**	87,021
Accruals	**236,020**	252,480
Deferred income	**7,604,389**	2,986,689
	12,997,845	6,469,314

| | Cricket Centre | | Emerald Headingley Cricket Ground | | | | | |
	Freehold Land and Buildings £	Plant & Equipment £	Freehold Land and Buildings £	Plant and Equipment £	Improvements to Leasehold Property £	Office Equipment £	Assets in the course of construction £	Total £
Cost								
At January 1, 2018	608,624	780,094	27,112,792	5,211,412	4,453,421	450,263	—	38,616,606
Additions	—	18,797	8,750	69,960	—	42,091	573,789	713,387
At December 31, 2018	608,624	798,891	27,121,542	5,281,372	4,453,421	492,354	573,789	39,329,993
Depreciation								
At January 1, 2018	191,603	770,529	3,412,164	4,797,421	324,697	425,450	—	9,921,864
Charged in the year	17,913	2,998	283,065	180,253	42,522	28,897	—	555,648
At December 31, 2018	209,516	773,527	3,695,229	4,977,674	367,219	454,347	—	10,477,512
Net book value								
At December 31, 2018	399,108	25,364	23,426,313	303,698	4,086,202	38,007	573,789	28,852,481
At December 31, 2017	**417,021**	**9,565**	**23,700,628**	**413,991**	**4,128,724**	**24,813**	**—**	**28,694,742**

During 2017 the construction of the new shared stand with Leeds Rugby commenced, together with the construction of the new Leeds Rugby south stand. Work has continued in 2018 for the two projects combined, which is being financed by Legal and General Pensions Limited. In addition, the two Clubs are funding certain fit-out costs themselves. The costs are being directly incurred and capitalised by Legal and General Pensions Limited. The asset is then leased to Leeds City Council over a 42-year term. The cricket interest in the stand is then leased by Leeds City Council to Headingley North South Stand (Cricket) Limited, company number 10750426, being a wholly owned subsidiary of Headingley North South Stand Limited, company number 10747361. The Club's interest in Headingley North South Stand Limited is disclosed in Note 14. Commencing in August 2019 the Club will pay a licence fee for the use of the stand, as set out in Note 13. The Club's total commitment to the fit out costs, which are included in Assets in the Course of Construction, is up to £1.4 million. At the year end £443,000 had been incurred.

	2018	2017
	£	£
8. Creditors: amounts falling due after more than one year		
HSBC Bank Loan (see below)	**2,569,014**	2,569,014
ECB Floodlight Loan (see below)	**100,000**	200,000
ECB Scarborough Cricket Club Loan (see below)	**40,000**	40,000
CJ Graves Accumulation and Maintenance Trust Loan (see below)	**4,703,500**	6,453,500
J Graves Accumulation and Maintenance Trust Loan (see below)	**4,703,500**	6,453,500
CJ Graves 1999 Settlement Trust Loan (see below)	**5,500,000**	5,500,000
Debentures	**345,315**	373,400
Finance leases (see Note 13)	**804,823**	893,079
Deferred income	**—**	464,607
	18,766,152	22,947,100

Loan, borrowing and overdraft maturity analysis:		
In one year or less or on demand	**3,688,124**	1,804,298
In more than one year but not more than two years	**15,122,000**	3,688,256
In more than two years but not more than five years	**2,794,014**	17,841,014
In more than five years	**850,138**	953,223
	22,454,276	24,286,791

Loan descriptions

During 2017 the HSBC loan was renegoiated to extend the period over which capital payments are made. £500,000 was repaid in 2018 with the balance to be repaid in instalments during 2021. The loan carries an interest rate of 2% above the Bank of England base rate in return for a First Legal Charge over the Cricket Centre and a Third Legal Charge over Emerald Headingley Cricket Ground. HSBC Bank plc also has a fixed and floating charge over all of the assets of the Club, subject to the Legal Charges referred to above.

CJ Graves Accumulation and Maintenance and J Graves Accumulation and Maintenance Trusts loans were last renegotiated during 2017. The loans stand at £6.45m, each bearing an interest rate of 4.625% plus any rise in Bank of England base rate over 0.5%. Capital repayments were made in 2018 (£250,000 each Trust) with further repayments due in 2019 (£1.75m each Trust) and the outstanding balance repaid by December 31, 2020. The two Trusts have been granted by the Club a joint First Legal Charge over Emerald Headingley Cricket Ground and joint Second Legal Charge over the Cricket Centre.

A further loan of £5.5m from the CJ Graves 1999 Settlement Trust bears an interest rate of 0%. Full capital repayment of this loan is due on December 31, 2020. The Club has granted Second Legal Charge over Emerald Headingley Cricket Ground and Third Legal Charge over the Cricket Centre.

An additional loan was made available by the ECB towards the cost of instaling the floodlights at Emerald Headingley Cricket Ground. The total available loan is £700,000, all of which was drawn down in 2015. £500,000 has been repaid to date, with further payments to be made in the coming years at a rate of £100,000 per year until the loan is repaid. The current policy of the ECB is to award a capital grant of the same value as the repayment, resulting in no cash outflow for the Club.

The ECB have also made available a £40,000 loan for capital improvements at Scarborough Cricket Club (SCC) and this will be repaid in 2020 by way of a capital funding payment from the ECB. YCCC has loaned this money to SCC to enable them to carry out the work on the same basis that it has been borrowed from the ECB. The SCC debtor forms part of the Other Debtors balance in Note 6, and the transactions have created no cash inflow or outflow for the Club and have no impact on the Income and Expenditure Account.

9. Financial instruments

	2018 £	2017 £
Assets measured at cost less impairment		
Trade Debtors	1,284,504	363,888
Other Debtors	318,509	246,933
Cash	1,817,901	1,345,277
Liabilities measured at amortised cost		
Term Loans	21,216,014	22,316,014
Debentures	345,315	373,400
Finance Leases	892,947	1,597,377
Loan commitments measured at cost less impairment		
Trade Creditors	1,053,258	793,457
Social security and other taxes	350,293	545,369
Other creditors	65,761	87,021
Accruals	236,020	252,480

10. Deferred income - capital grants

At January 1, 2018	4,977,984	5,066,175
Received in year	100,000	100,000
Released to Income and Expenditure Account	(190,315)	(188,191)
At December 31, 2018	4,887,669	4,977,984

11. Deferred tax asset

At January 1, 2018	(620,028)	(620,999)
(Credit)/Charge to Income and Expenditure Account for the year (see Note 4)	(286,804)	971
At December 31, 2018 (see Note 6)	(906,832)	(620,028)

The elements of recognised deferred tax are as follows:

Difference between accumulated depreciation and capital allowances	317,211	352,954
Tax losses	(1,223,377)	(972,982)
Short-term timing differences	(666)	—
	(906,832)	(620,028)

12. Share capital

Allotted, called up and fully paid Ordinary shares of 5p each	228	210

During the year there was an increase in qualifying members of 364. The total number of qualifying members as at December 31, 2018, was 4,557 (2017: 4,193). Each member of the Club owns one Ordinary share, and the rights attached thereto are contained within the Club's rules, which can be found on the Club's website or from the Secretary on request.

13. Leasing commitments

Finance lease liabilities are payable as follows:

Minimum Lease Payment	2018	2017
In one year or less	88,124	704,298
Between two and five years	300,000	313,256
More than five years	504,823	579,823
	892,947	1,597,377

The Club currently has two finance leases. The first is with Leeds Beckett University relating to the Carnegie Pavilion. This lease is for 125 years, with lease payments being made for 20 years until 2030, after which a peppercorn rent is due. The second lease is with Investec in relation to the floodlights instaled during 2015. This lease will be repaid in 2019 at which point ownership of the floodlights will revert to the Club.

Non-cancellable operating-lease rentals are payable as follows:

Minimum Lease Payment	**2018**	2017
In one year or less	**230,192**	31,010
Between two and five years	**397,708**	620,022
	627,900	651,032

Operating lease payments amounting to £37,199 (2017: £41,704) were recognised as an expense in the Income and Expenditure Account. In August 2019 the Club will begin to pay a license fee for use of the redeveloped North South Stand starting at £579,655 per annum, rising annually in line with RPI. The license is to be renewed annually at the discretion of the Club.

14. Investments

Cost: At January 1	50	—
Addition	—	50
Cost: At December 31	50	50

The Club has invested £50 for 50% of the paid-up share capital of Headingley North South Stand Limited, company number 10,747,361 of Emerald Headingley Stadium St. Michael's Lane, Headingley, Leeds, LS6 3BR. This company has been incorporated to facilitate the re-development of the North South Stand.

15. Related Party Transactions

By way of the Articles of Association of the Yorkshire Cricket Foundation (YCF), the Club has the power to appoint two trustees to the board of the YCF. During the year Mark Arthur and Robin Smith were Board Members of the Club and Trustees of the YCF. During 2018 the YCF awarded non-capital grants of £29,533 (2017: £34,888) to the Club. During the year the Club made no donations to the YCF (2017: £23,320). The balance owed at December 31, 2018 was £9,914 (2017: £3,876).

Mark Arthur was also a Board Member and Director of the Yorkshire Cricket Board (YCB). During 2018 sales to the YCB of £99,526 (2017: £79,036) were made in return for goods or services provided by the Club. All sales have been either settled in cash or form part of the trade debtors' balance at the year end. The balance owed at December 31, 2018, was £8,805 (2017: £6,358 was owed by the Club to the YCB).

The Club is a founding member of Park Avenue Bradford Limited (PABL), along with the YCF and YCB, a private company limited by guarantee, with an investment of £nil. Mark Arthur acted as a board member and director of both the Club and PABL, while Paul Hudson and Andy Dawson acted as board members and directors of PABL and employees of the Club. During 2018 there were no transactions between the Club and PABL. During 2017 the Club made a contribution of £15,000 towards the startup costs incurred by PABL operating the Bradford Park Avenue site.

The Club invested £50 by way of paid-up share capital in Headingley North South Stand Limited (HNSS) in 2017 (see Note 14). Mark Arthur, Paul Hudson and Andy Dawson all acted as directors of this company in addition to their roles with the Club. Costs of £688,547 were recharged to the Club from HNSS in 2018, and were all either settled in cash or form part of the trade-creditors' balance at the year end. At December 31, 2018, £338,413 was owed by the Club to HNSS (2017: £72,670 was owed to the Club by HNSS).

Robin Smith was a Non-Executive Director of Bartlett Group (Holdings) Limited. Costs of £3,006 (2017: £3,006) were incurred by the Club from one of its subsidiaries and were settled in cash during the year.

The total compensation of key management personnel (including directors) as defined in the staff list in the year amounted to £654,025 (2017: £841,771).

16. Pensions

The Club operates defined contribution pension schemes for the benefit of certain employees. The employee and employer contributions during the year were £356,810 (2017: £388,774). The assets of these schemes are administered in funds independent from those of the Club. Of this £3,915 was unpaid at the end of the year (2017: £45,818).

17. Audit Fee

The Club paid its auditor £20,500 (2017: £19,750) in respect of the audit of these Financial Statements.

New deal follows Cap

Ripon-based seamer Ben Coad has signed a two-year contract extension, keeping him at Emerald Headingley until the end of 2021. Coad, whose rise has been quite remarkable, has now taken an impressive 103 wickets in 24 first-class fixtures at an average of 17.70. Capped last September, he became the 182nd player to wear the 11-petalled badge instituted by Lord Hawke. He scooped the 2018 Players' Player of the Year award, and looks central to the Club's plans for years to come.

York re-visited

The City of York this summer sees Championship cricket return after a gap of 129 years with Yorkshire's match against Warwickshire, starting on June 17 at Clifton Park. Yorkshire's only previous visit was in 1890, the first officially recognised season of Championship cricket. The match took place at the now defunct Wigginton Road ground and Yorkshire, captained by Lord Hawke, beat Kent by eight wickets.

MEMBERS' COMMITTEE
CHAIRMAN'S REPORT

The following served on the Members' Committee during the year.

Chairman:	**Graeme Greenfield**
Elected Members:	**Charlotte Evers** **Richard Levin** **Howard Ray**
Appointed Members:	**Graeme Greenfield** **Chris Woodthorpe** **Andrew Kilburn**
In Attendance:	**Robin Smith,** Board Director **Mark Arthur,** Chief Executive **Andy Dawson,** Commercial Director

There were seven full committee meetings during the year. Each meeting is appropriately recorded with the detailed minutes subsequently being submitted to the main Board. The openness and accessibility of the Board continues and, as Chair of the Members' Committee, I continue to attend the full board meetings to ensure that our members' views are represented.

**GRAEME
GREENFIELD**

Three Member Forums were held during the season. For the first time we met before the commencement of play of a one-day game. The Chief Executive and the Commercial Director were in attendance to answer questions and provide insight and further background information.

At the second forum, held at Scarborough, we welcomed Martyn Moxon, the Director of Cricket Development, who was open and honest in his appraisal of the performance of the teams. This was a great success and we hope to repeat this in the future. At the third forum, held in the Long Room, the Chief Executive was challenged by those in attendance on a number of issues and, as always, he answered the questions in an open and honest way. Attendance continues to grow with over 150 members at each forum.

Throughout the forums Mark Arthur has continued to report on the ground development, and I am sure all members will be delighted with the new stand. Members' access to the stand during county games has been a regular topic for discussion at our Committee meetings, and we hope that members will have access to two levels at each county game.

Once again membership continues to grow, but the challenge will be to maintain this growth. The Members' Committee will continue to work alongside the management team to support this continued growth.

The Committee discusses many issues during the season, ranging from umbrellas to pass-outs to the end-of-season presentation and the occasional conversation about cricket.

The next few months promise to be an exciting time at Emerald Headingley, and I hope that all members embrace both international and domestic cricket. The introduction of a fixture at York has been welcomed by everyone I have spoken to, and I look forward to seeing YCCC taking the field in York in June.

All members of the Committee welcome your comments and views. Please do not hesitate to speak to any of us during the season or email us at *ycccmemberscommitee@gmail.com*.

In conclusion, I would like to express my sincere appreciation to all my Committee colleagues this year for their love of the game and particularly Yorkshire County Cricket Club. They continue to give up their free time for the benefit of all members, and all have made a good contribution to Membership Committee meetings this year.

It has been a privilege to be Chairman of the Members' Committee, and I look forward to hearing your views in the coming season, either at forums or during the tea interval in the Long Room at most county games.

GRAEME GREENFIELD
Chairman,
Members' Committee
Yorkshire County Cricket Club

THE HEAD OF YORKSHIRE CRICKET FOUNDATION'S REPORT

Community without Boundaries

2018 has been another fantastic year for The Yorkshire Cricket Foundation. Once again we have been able to engage with more people across Yorkshire's communities than ever before, using the brand of Yorkshire Cricket, to raise participation, improve education attainment, reduce heath inequalities and teach our communities about Yorkshire Cricket's rich history and heritage.

During the last 12 months there have been a number of key achievements and exciting developments which include:

- A new cohort of 25 students on to the first year of the Yorkshire Cricket College, taking total numbers to 46;
- A successful bid to the Lord's Taverners to extend the Wicketz Programme to Hull. This represents our first full-time role in the east of the county;
- Creation, development and delivery of the Cric-Eat programme, a scheme to tackle holiday hunger in young people;
- Begin the process towards museum accreditation;
- Our archives and heritage offering continues to develop, including the England Captains wall outside the museum, and taking the museum around the county. The Women's World Cup was also displayed at various events;
- Creating an innovative programme called *Hits & Missus* designed to engage women and girls in cricket.

In addition to these project specific developments we have made significant strides with our communication and PR, ensuring that we are able to proactively promote and inform everyone of the work of the Foundation.

Once again we have received incredible support from the Emerald Foundation, who have been with us since the beginning. They have been instrumental in getting us to where we are today as a charity, and I would like to take this opportunity to thank them for all they do for The Yorkshire Cricket Foundation.

Yorkshire Cricket is going through an exciting period at the moment as we look ahead to an action-packed 2019 with the World Cup and Ashes. These two major events provide us with a brilliant opportunity to increase our charitable impact. As always we work in close partnership with Yorkshire County Cricket Club, Pro-Coach and The Yorkshire

Cricket Board to ensure that everyone has the opportunity to get involved in cricket. We are very grateful for all three organisations' support over the last 12 months which, as always, was invaluable.

WILL SAVILLE
Head of Foundation
Yorkshire Cricket Foundation